A Concise History of
Indian Literature
in English

New Expanded Edition

A Concise History of Indian Literature in English

New Expanded Edition

Edited by

ARVIND KRISHNA MEHROTRA

Published by

PERMANENT BLACK
'Himalayana', Mall Road, Ranikhet Cantt,
Ranikhet 263645
perblack@gmail.com

Distributed by

ORIENT LONGMAN PRIVATE LTD
Bangalore Bhopal Bhubaneshwar Chandigarh
Chennai Ernakulam Guwahati Hyderabad Jaipur
Kolkata Lucknow Mumbai New Delhi Patna
www.orientlongman.com

ISBN 978-81-7824-484-6

First Published 2008
New Expanded Edition 2017

Indian History Classics

Typeset in Agaramond
by Guru Typograph Technology, Dwarka, New Delhi 110075
Printed and bound by Manipal Technologies Limited, Manipal

Contents

Editor's Preface

There have chiefly been two previous histories of Indian literature in English: *Indian Writing in English* (4th edn. 1984) by K.R. Srinivasa Iyengar, and *A History of Indian Literature in English* (1982) by M.K. Naik. *Indian Literature in English* (1990) by William Walsh limits itself to the twentieth century and is sketchy even then.

No literary history can be expected to cover everything, and I am only too well aware of the omissions in this one. Most saddening is the absence of Ananda Coomaraswamy, the art historian, and a discussion of periodicals, journals, and little magazines in English. Essays on these topics were commissioned along with two others ('The Historian as Author' and 'The Pulp Artists'), but they failed to reach us. We hope to recommission them for inclusion in a future edition.

The other omissions, if omissions they be, arise from the kind of history this is—from the way it has been planned and executed. Though conceived as a comprehensive and wide-ranging whole, so that it takes up not only the canonical poets, novelists, and dramatists of the past two hundred years but also scientists, social reformers, anthropologists, and naturalists who have by broad consensus enriched the body of Indian writing in English, it is made up of separate essays, each by a different contributor. To these essays, which are devoted either to a single author (Rammohan Ray, Kipling, Tagore, Sri Aurobindo, R.K. Narayan) or to a group of authors ('The Dutt Family Album: And Toru Dutt', 'From Sugar to Masala: Writing by the Indian Diaspora') or to a genre ('The Beginnings of the Indian Novel', 'Poetry Since Independence'), the contributors have brought their own points of view and their own writing styles. In these omnibus essays which deal with a group of authors or a genre, the decision to include or leave out a particular author was made by the contributor of that particular essay. The editorial guidelines only asked that authors' dates of birth and (where applicable and available) death be mentioned, and that critical vocabulary be kept to a minimum. As there were going to be no footnotes, references to secondary material have been avoided.

Written by specialists, this is a book for the non-specialist reader. Biographical information on authors who feature in it has been provided, and the account of their work is historically contextualised. The essays themselves can be read selectively, to follow, for instance, the development of a genre—poetry, the novel—over two centuries, or in the order in which they appear, which is chronological. A word of caution, though, is necessary. Since this is not a narrative literary history whose possible plots 'can be reduced to three: rise, decline, and rise and decline' (David Perkins in *Is Literary History Possible?*, 1992), there is not one continuous story but several disjunct ones being told in these pages. Nor is there a unifying voice running through the text; beginning is not tied to conclusion, nor past to present.

Applied to Indian literature in English, which is made up of discrete units and has come about more through a process of accretion, words like 'development' and 'growth' are perhaps inappropriate. Few writers claim an 'Indo-Anglian' descent, indeed most would not miss the opportunity to deny it. Since the literary pasts they have drawn on have invariably been multiple and other than their own, stretching from the earliest English poems to Günter Grass, the sense of belonging has never been very strong. For a literature whose development has been piecemeal and ragged, or like a fresh start each time, an encyclopaedic arrangement which eschews both continuity and closure has seemed appropriate.

Unlike an anthology, a literary history cannot afford to be too partial or too quirky. Whereas the appeal of an anthology is strongly connected with its editorial slant, a literary history expresses a general consensus. However, if the history is of a literature which has not been much historicised, and of which the earlier attempts at a history have been more like acts of enumeration, consensus can be difficult to reach and here looks tentative rather than authoritative. Since the notion of what is authoritative has in any case been shown up as temporary, if not altogether ephemeral, perhaps this is only a blessing in disguise.

A second and related question facing the historian of Indian literature in English is whether the 'India' in 'Indian literature in English' is coterminous with the India of the political map, or is to be used in a wider, imaginative sense. As I discovered, the answer is a bit of both.

An international border is rigorous, but literary borders are porous, ill-defined, and overlapping, especially if the literature is new and has a colonial past. Often its writers, to their discomfiture, fall in two, sometimes more, literary territories. Among this number are Kipling and Bharati Mukherjee, one born in Bombay and the other in Calcutta, one British and the other a naturalised American, one a stoical imperialist and the other emphatically a part of contemporary American literature. Kipling, like nobody else, described Anglo-Indian life in the late nineteenth century; Mukherjee, a hundred years later, writes about Indian immigrants to the New World. To have left out either for reasons of nationality would have meant leaving out a part of the experience of India, of the Indian experience. It would have made the history more cohesive but less complete.

While literary borders are porous, they do not seem porous in the same way to everyone. Seeing it from London, Salman Rushdie and Elizabeth West include Bapsi Sidhwa and Sara Suleri, two Pakistani authors, in the *Vintage Book of Indian Writing 1947–97* (1997). Seeing the same border from New Delhi, I had, in this case, a different perspective from which soft literary borders and hard international boundaries looked much the same. Had I included Pakistani writers who have engaged in certain ways with events and issues unmistakably Indian, I would have had no grounds for excluding writers from Bangladesh and Sri Lanka, and perhaps from Myanmar and Nepal. But this book would then have acquired a quite different literary and political contour, and become a history of the literature in English of the Indian subcontinent.

Literary borders meet also in Wiltshire, where V.S. Naipaul lives. Marked prominently as a feature in three literatures—Caribbean, British, and Indian—Naipaul is at home in none. 'One of the most important voices in the story of modern literature', Rushdie says in the introduction to his anthology, 'is regrettably absent from this book, not by our choice, but by his own.' For those who believe it is possible for a writer to have more than one literary nationality, or perhaps not have any, Naipaul, who has made the wounding pursuit of self-definition his lifelong work-in-progress, is an iconic figure.

In contrast to Naipaul, but of an earlier generation, is Aubrey Menen. In 'How I was Initiated into the Best Tribe', an essay in *Dead Man in the Silver Market* (1954), Menen wrote:

> 'Breathes there a man (it has been said) with soul so dead That never to himself hath said This is my own my native land?' I cannot answer the question but I find it flattering, if the principle behind it is true. I have a soul which so far from being dead is three times livelier than most other people's for I have no less than three native lands which, provided I pay my taxes, I can call my own.

Menen's 'three native lands' are England, where he was born and educated, Italy, where he lived for most of his life, and India, where he spent his last years and where he died. However, there is a downside to the triple claim he makes, which, given his lively soul, he may not have seen. If V.S. Naipaul will foreseeably be remembered by three literatures, Aubrey Menen is in danger of being forgotten by at least two. Like ficus in crevices, writers can flourish between literatures (and between nations); they can, as well, disappear without a trace between them.

Future historians will view and interpret the past differently from us. Authors given several pages here may be dismissed by later historians in a brief paragraph; in much the same way, authors left out of earlier histories or mentioned passingly are covered at some length in this book. To write, or even compile, a literary history is to build on shifting sands. And yet the task cannot be wholly futile. 'Each history', David Perkins says, 'leaves a deposit of accurate information and reasonable interpretation to be synthesised by the next, along with the deposits of other previous histories.' This book has been long in the making and, even as it was being put together, several of its living subjects—V.S. Naipaul, Salman Rushdie, and Amitav Ghosh, among others—were putting out new books. An enterprise such as this, which tries to cover all the important literary ground from Rammohan Ray to Arundhati Roy, cannot endlessly keep pace; fresh material can only be incorporated in repeated revised editions. Meanwhile, it is hoped that the deposit of new information in the present volume is sufficiently accurate and thick, and the interpretations sufficiently reasonable and reasonably expressed.

The present book reprints the full text of *An Illustrated History of Indian Literature in English* (2003), minus the illustrations, and with some minor emendations and corrections of fact. This concise version of that larger work is intended to be of use to students of Indian writing in English, as well as to general readers.

The present new edition (2016) is an expansion of the first edition (2008) and corrects some of the omissions mentioned above. It contains five more chapters (nos. 25 to 29): one each on Shobhaa De and pulp fiction, Ramananda Chatterjee and the *Modern Review*, Jadunath Sarkar, Ananda K. Coomaraswamy, and D.D. Kosambi.

July 2016 ARVIND KRISHNA MEHROTRA

Introduction

Arvind Krishna Mehrotra

Hindoostan, has by the people of modern Europe, been understood to mean the tract situated between the river Ganges and Indus, on the east and west; the Thibetian and Tartarian mountains, on the north; and the sea on the south.

—Major James Rennell, Introduction to *Memoir of a Map of Hindoostan; or, the Mogul's Empire* (1786)

The expression 'India' shall mean British India, together with any territories of any native prince or chief under the suzerainty of Her Majesty, exercized under the Governor-General, or through any Governor or other officer subordinate to the Governor-General of India.

—Interpretation Act of 1889

. . . the State of Chhokrapur, if indeed it ever existed, has dissolved away in the new map of India.

—J.R. Ackerley, Preface to the 2nd edn of *Hindoo Holiday* (1st edn 1932; 2nd edn 1952)

This volume, which covers almost two hundred years of the literature written largely by Indians in English, has for its starting point the year 1800. The date has no literary significance but is chosen for its rough and ready usefulness: by 1800 there was no real challenge left to the British domination of India from either the other

European powers in the region—the Dutch, French, and Portuguese—nor, except for the Marathas, from the native states. British domination eventually covered all aspects of Indian life—political, economic, social, cultural. The introduction of English into the complex, hierarchical language system of India has proved the most enduring aspect of this domination.

By 1800 the battles of Plassey (1757) and Buxar (1764) were fought and lost. Siraj-ud-Daula's defeat at Plassey was less at the hands of Col. Robert Clive than at those of the compradors of Bengal, the Jagat Seths. Seeing their profit margins reduced by Mughal impositions on their commerce, these wealthy Hindu and Jain merchants and bankers, together with powerful members of the nawab's court, plotted his overthrow, a conspiracy in which the East India Company joined. Militarily the battle was not more than a skirmish; according to one estimate there were only seventy-two dead after counting the figures on both sides, but as Joshua Marshman wrote in his influential *Bharatvarsher Itihas* (1831), it 'changed the destinies of sixty million people in a vast kingdom'.

Among those whose destiny it affected was Dean Mahomed (1759–1851), the author of *The Travels of Dean Mahomet* (1794), the first book ever written and published by an Indian in English. Born in Patna into a family that had traditionally served the Mughal empire, he joined, as had his father and brother before him, the East India Company's Bengal Army in 1769 and travelled with it as a camp follower and subaltern officer for the next fifteen years, going as far north as Delhi. His book, in the form of a series of letters to a fictive friend, is in large measure based on his experiences in the colonial army. In 1784 he emigrated to Ireland, settling down in Cork and marrying a young local Anglo-Irish woman. He also converted to the Protestant faith. In later life, after unsuccessfully running the Hindostanee Coffee House near Portman Square, London, he set himself up as a 'Shampooing Surgeon' in Brighton, where his herbal 'Indian Vapour Bath' was immediately popular and attracted the patronage of King George IV who, in 1822, bestowed a Royal Warrant upon him.

Plassey effectively brought Bengal under Company rule and, following Mir Qasim's defeat, Buxar added the contiguous territory of

Avadh to the areas already under British influence. The Company now controlled the eastern Gangetic plain from Benaras to Calcutta. In the following year, 1765, the Mughal emperor appointed the East India Company his diwan (or chief financial manager) of the provinces of Bengal, Bihar, and Orissa, thereby enabling it to collect revenue on his behalf. Known as the Treaty of Allahabad, this arrangement has been called 'the truly inaugural moment of the Raj'. The Company's accession to diwani, Ranajit Guha says in *An Indian Historiography of India* (1988), 'brought together in one single instance all the three fundamental aspects of colonialism in our subcontinent, namely, its origin in an act of force, its exploitation of the primary produce of the land as the very basis of a colonial economy, and its need to give force and exploitation the appearance of legality.'

There is to this inaugural moment of the Raj, as there was sometimes to the Raj itself, a touch of farce. When, thirty years later, the painter Benjamin West depicted the treaty—*Lord Clive receiving from the Moghul the Grant of the Duanney*—he showed the Mughal emperor Shah Alam in an imperial setting, seated under a canopy on a raised throne, from where he hands Clive a rolled document. There are elephants in the background and in the foreground attendants. Clive's party, consisting of six Englishmen, is shown on the left of the canvas. Some of the Englishmen appear to be talking in whispers to each other, as do some of the Indians. The reality was quite different: Clive actually received 'the Duanney' in his tent. Two of the six Englishmen in the picture were not present with him in Allahabad on that day, and the emperor's throne, far from being a canopied, oriental affair, was in fact Clive's dining table surmounted by an armchair.

At about the time Shah Alam was being reduced to a piece of rococo furniture, Captain James Rennell, who had already spent five years in the country and carried out extensive surveys of the coastal areas of southern India, was appointed by Clive as the first Surveyor-General of Bengal. The *Bengal Atlas* that Rennell brought out in 1779, the culmination of more than a decade's effort, was the first modern atlas of the province. As more colonial administrators realised the importance of cartography to empire building, Rennell's pioneering effort was duplicated in other British-controlled Indian territories, notably by Captain Colin Mackenzie in the Deccan, and by him and Major

William Lambton, after the fall of Tipu Sultan in 1799, in Mysore. Corresponding with the labours of these soldier-engineers, the British set about mapping the intellectual, cultural, and historical dimensions of their new territories. Comparative philology, lexicography, and translation were some of the areas opened up by Sir Charles Wilkins, Nathaniel Brassey Halhed, Sir William Jones, John Gilchrist, and Henry Colebrooke, all of whom are now remembered as pioneering 'Orientalists'.

The British interest in Indian languages, as Halhed bluntly said, arose from the necessity of having to cultivate 'a medium of intercourse between the Government and its subjects, between the natives of Europe who are to rule, and the inhabitants of India who are to obey'. But the scholar-administrators who busied themselves with Persian and Sanskrit, 'Moors' and Bengali, were not always patronising in their attitude, nor did they put their newly acquired skills always to imperialist uses. Even Halhed, who wrote and printed one of the earliest Bengali grammars by a European, is remembered also as the first Englishman to be influenced by Oriental mysticism. The best known, Sir William Jones, the Calcutta Supreme Court judge and founder (in 1784) of the Asiatic Society of Bengal, built a formidable reputation as an Oriental scholar even before he made his passage to India. He engaged more comprehensively with Indian civilisation than any Englishman has since: orthography, mythology, literature, chronology, chess, the zodiac, botany, music, and natural history are some of the subjects on which he contributed authoritative articles for the early volumes of *Asiatick Researches*. Described recently as 'one of the greatest polymaths in history', Jones laid the foundation of historical linguistics when, in the 'Third Anniversary Discourse' (1786), he made the assertion that Sanskrit, Greek, and Latin 'have sprung from a common source, which, perhaps, no longer exists'. He went on to posit the notion of a common homeland for mankind, from which it had centuries ago migrated to different parts of the globe. The Hindus, he said,

> had an immemorial affinity with the old *Persians*, *Ethiopians*, and *Egyptians*, the *Phenicians*, *Greeks*, and *Tuscans*, the *Scythians* or *Goths*, and *Celts*, the *Chinese*, *Japanese*, and *Peruvians*; whence, as no reason appears for believing, that they were a colony from any one of those

> nations, or any of those nations from them, we may fairly conclude that they all proceeded from some *central* country, to investigate which will be the object of my future Discourses . . .

The Utilitarian philosopher James Mill, perhaps remembering this and similar passages, was later to exclaim that the years spent by 'Oriental Jones' in India had been a waste.

Between Jones's universalist and surreal ideas of race and Halhed's administrative ruler–ruled paradigm there is a world of difference. Nevertheless, there had appeared by 1800 an assortment of texts in English—grammars, dictionaries, teaching aids, phrase books, and translations of literary works, digests, and compendiums—which, like Rennell's *Bengal Atlas*, were meant to facilitate colonisation and explain the new acquisition both to the Company's servants in India and to an avid literary and scientific community back home in England.

II

'Expanding like the petals of young flowers', wrote Calcutta's Henry Derozio in a sonnet addressed to his students at Hindu College, 'I watch the gentle opening of your minds'. What nourished these young minds, bringing 'unnumbered kinds / Of new perceptions' to them, was colonial education.

For twenty-five years before the founding of Hindu College in 1817, and for nearly twenty years after it, the nature and purpose of colonial education and the Company's role in it had been furiously debated in London and Calcutta by Britishers and Indians. In 1792, in one of the earliest discussions on the subject, a director of the East India Company had stated: 'we [have] just lost America from our folly, in having allowed the establishment of schools and colleges . . . [I]t would not do for us to repeat the same act of folly in regard to India.' All the same, the folly was about to be repeated, though consensus on the kind of folly it would be was not easy to arrive at. In the debates that followed, the 'Committee of the Protestant Society' took issue with the Clapham sect. Rammohan Ray, who said in 1823 that 'the Sanskrit system of education would be best calculated to keep this country in darkness', similarly took up the cudgels on behalf of English education for Indians and against the 'Orientalist' Horace H. Wilson. Matters came to a head during the Anglicist–Orientalist controversy of 1835, to be resolved once and for all by Thomas Babington Macaulay's 'Minute on Education' of the same year. It said in its most cited part:

> We must at present do our best to form a class who may be interpreters between us and millions whom we govern; a class of persons, Indian in blood and colour, but English in taste, in opinions, in morals, and in intellect.

'Bleddy Macaulay's minutemen! . . . English-medium misfits . . . Square-peg freaks' is how a character in Salman Rushdie's *The Moor's Last Sigh* (1995) describes the 'class of persons' it was Macaulay's mission to create. The class had long been in the process of formation and consisted largely of the new urban élite, the rising bhadralok population of Calcutta. Many of them were immigrants with landed property in the interior districts, but were drawn to the city by the promise of office jobs in the expanding British administration, the key to which was a knowledge of English. For 'the sons of respectable Hindoos' there was Hindu College, where they acquired, as the Committee on Public Instruction observed in 1830, 'a command of the English language, and . . . familiarity with its literature and science . . . rarely equalled by any schools in Europe'. Of how English was learned by aspiring natives at the other end of the educational spectrum, in the hamlets and villages of Bengal, Lal Behari Day has left a moving account. In the chapter on 'English Education in Calcutta before 1834' in *Recollections of My School-days*, serialised in *Bengal Magazine* between 1872 and 1876, Day writes:

> When I was a little boy I had a sight of one of these Vocabularies, which used to be studied by a cousin of mine in my native village at Talpur. The English words were written in the Bengali character, and the volume, agreeably to the custom of the Hindus, began with the word 'God.' As a curiosity, I put below the first words of my cousin's Vocabulary, retaining the spelling of the English words as they were represented in the Bengali character:

Gad : Isvara
Lad : Isvara
A'i : A'mi
Lu : Tumi
Akto : Karmma
Bail : Jamin

In the course of time, several East Indian gentlemen of Calcutta lent their services to the cause of Native education. They went to the houses of the wealthy Babus and gave regular instructions to their sons. They received pupils into their own houses, which were turned into schools. Under the auspices of these men, the curriculum of studies was enlarged. To the *Spelling Book* and the *Schoolmaster* were added the *Tootinamah* or the *Tales of a Parrot*, the *Elements of English Grammar* and the *Arabian Nights' Entertainments*. The man who could read and understand the last mentioned book was reckoned, in those days, a prodigy of learning.

One consequence of the changes taking place in Indian society under colonialism was that Indians had mastered the coloniser's language (as the colonisers had mastered theirs) and, going one step further, had by the 1820s begun to adopt it as their chosen medium of expression. These pioneering works of poetry, fiction, drama, travel, and belles-lettres are little read today except by specialists, but when they were published they were, by the mere fact of being in English, audacious acts of mimicry and self-assertion. More than this, the themes they touched on and the kinds of social issues they engaged with would only be explored by other Indian literatures several decades later. Krishna Mohan Banerjea's *The Persecuted* (1831) might not be good theatre, but the subject of Hindu orthodoxies and the individual's loss of faith in his religion had not been taken up by any Indian play before it. Banerjea, who was eighteen years old when he wrote *The Persecuted*, soon afterwards converted to Christianity. He was one of the leading lights of 'Young Bengal', as Derozio's disciples called themselves, and founder-editor of *The Enquirer* (1831–5).

Kylas Chunder Dutt's 'A Journal of Forty-Eight Hours of the Year 1945' (1835) is about an imaginary armed uprising against the British.

Insurrection seems a commonplace idea, until we realise that the idea is being expressed for the first time in Indian literature, and would next find expression only in folk songs inspired by the events of 1857. It is uncanny that the year of the uprising in Dutt's imagination comes within two years of India's actual year of independence; uncanny, too, the coincidence that the work should have been published in the same year that Macaulay delivered his 'Minute'. In a double irony, the insurgents are all urbanised middle-class Indians with the best education colonialism could offer, the very class Macaulay had intended as 'interpreters between us and the millions whom we govern'. A fable like 'A Journal of Forty-Eight Hours', where the 'language of command' is stood on its head and turned into the language of subversion, suggests itself as the imaginative beginnings of a nation.

A second and no less profound consequence of colonial education was the transformation it brought about in the literature of the Indian languages. To begin with, it introduced Indians to the potentialities of prose, a medium relatively unknown to them. Writing about the spread of journalism in the 1840s—the decade which saw the launch of *Digdarsan* and *Prabhakar* in Marathi, *Vartaman Tarangini* in Telugu, *Tattvabodhini Patrika* in Bengali, and *Khair Khwah-e Hind* in Urdu—Sisir Kumar Das in *A History of Indian Literature*, volume VIII (1991), says:

> A majority of the writers associated with the journals either knew English or were exposed to the English language, and this conditioned their world-view and literary style to a great extent. Most of them . . . did not write with literary pretensions; but all of them, consciously or unconsciously, took part in the great experiment which brought about a real breakthrough in Indian literature. An awareness of social problems, a rational view as opposed to a theocentric universe, a spirit of enquiry, a desire to examine one's past heritage—all these appeared in prose rather than in poetry. Here is the historic importance of prose in Indian literature.

This magisterial volume covers the period 1800–1910 and is subtitled 'Western Impact: Indian Response': the metaphor of collision, suggesting destruction and debris with signs of survival in its midst, is well chosen. It is one way of looking at the literature of the nineteenth century. We can also see the period in terms of hybridisation and variety, of mutation and the inevitable divides brought about by colonialism.

Among the earliest poets to take part in 'the great experiment' was Rangalal Banerjee, whose *Padmini Upakhyan* (1858), written at the request of a patron who wanted a poem that was not 'in bad taste' or 'lacking in virtuousness', took its story from Col. James Tod's *Annals and Antiquities of Rajasthan* (1829). It told of Hindu valour and heroism in medieval times, during the reign of Allauddin Khilji. In the course of the poem, making a switch from looking at the past to examining the present, Banerjee inserted a free translation of some lines of Thomas Campbell—'From life without freedom / Oh, who would not fly? /For one day of freedom / Oh, who would not die?'—giving them to a Rajput king to speak. The poem, which appeared a year after the rebellion of 1857, ends abruptly on a pro-British note, but its patriotic message would not have been lost on its readers: for the Muslim Khilji they would simply have read the current dispensation. The equation seems unfortunate with hindsight, but then that is hindsight. Banerjee was in the employ of the British and could not afford to bite the hand that fed him. Bankimchandra Chattopadhyaya was also to cunningly locate his nationalist novel *Ananda Math* (1882) in the past, and for precisely the same reason.

Though *Padmini Upakhyan* was a modest success at the time (a third reprint came out in 1872), it is today remembered chiefly for a long preface in which Banerjee unambiguously states reasons for importing English elements into his Bengali work. He writes:

> Firstly, many Bengalis who do not know the English language think there is no superior poetry in that language, and it is important that they be rid of such delusion. Secondly, the more poems that are composed in the Bengali language along the purer system of English poetic conventions, the more we shall witness the exit of the immodest, mean body of poetry that currently exists . . . [Translation by Rosinka Chaudhuri]

Rangalal Banerjee's contemporary, Michael Madhusudan Dutt, the inventor of blank verse in Bengali, was another who drew on Tod's

Annals—for his play *Krishna Kumari* (1861). However, just how completely the insular world of the Indian writer had been infiltrated by its contact with English is shown by what Dutt wrote in defence of an earlier play, *Sermista* (1858), which was based on a story from the *Mahabharata:* 'I am writing for that portion of my countrymen', Dutt said, 'who think as I think, whose minds have been more or less imbued with Western ideas and *modes of thinking*, and that it is my intention to throw off the fetters forged for us by a servile admiration for every thing Sanskrit.' Both Rangalal Banerjee and Michael Madhusudan Dutt were products of that intellectual and cultural awakening—turmoil would be a better word—known as the Bengal Renaissance. It came in the wake of colonialism, and its beginnings were the writings of Rammohan Ray. Bengal tasted the exotic fruits of the awakening first, but it rapidly spread to other parts of the country, especially in the decades following 1857.

Though made in the context of Empire, Lord Curzon's metaphor that 'We are trying to graft the science of the West on an Eastern stem' could be a description of the work not just of the poets and dramatists but of the early novelists as well. The novels that were abundantly and cheaply available to them, except for the *Vicar of Wakefield* and the novels of Scott, were by Benjamin Disraeli, Bulwer Lytton, Marie Corelli, Wilkie Collins, and G.W.M. Reynolds. It was to these minor figures of the Victorian era that Indians turned when they crafted their first fictions.

Between 1866 and 1889, during the halcyon days of the Raj, Nandshankar Mehta in Gujarati, Bankimchandra Chattopadhyaya ('the Scott of Bengal') in Bengali, Samuel Vedanayakam Pillai in Tamil, M.V. Rohalkar in Marathi, Kandukuri Viresalingam Pantulu in Telugu, and O. Chandu Menon in Malayalam were among several who published novels that, though written in the 'vernaculars', were mediated by English fiction, and sometimes had the support of English officials. 'The former education inspector of our State Mr Russell', wrote Nandshankar Mehta in the Introduction to *Karan Ghelo* (1866), 'has expressed to me his desire to see Gujarati books written along the lines of English novels and romances. I have written this novel according to that plan.' And Samuel Pillai, who was a district munsif, states in the preface (written in English) of *Piratapa Mutaliyar Carittiram, or The Life and Adventures of Prathapa Mudaliar* (1879) that in his book, whose object it was 'to supply the want of prose works in Tamil', he has 'represented the principal personages as perfectly virtuous, in accordance with the opinion of the great English moralist Dr Johnson.'

Mehta's and Pillai's are probably the first novels to have been written in Gujarati and Tamil, as is O. Chandu Menon's *Indulekha* (1889) in Malayalam. In the dedicatory letter to W. Dumergue, who translated *Indulekha* 'into the "lingua franca" of the East', Chandu Menon gives his reasons for writing the novel:

> First my wife's oft-expressed desire to read in her own language a novel written after the English fashion, and secondly a desire on my part to try whether I should be able to create a taste amongst my Malayalee readers, not conversant with English, for that class of literature represented in the English language by novels, of which at present they (accustomed as they are to read and admire works of fiction in Malayalam abounding in events and incidents foreign to nature and often absurd and impossible) have no idea, and . . . to illustrate to my Malayalee brethren the position, power and influence that our Nair women, who are noted for their natural intelligence and beauty, would attain in society, if they were given a good English education; and finally—to contribute my mite towards the improvement of Malayalam literature which I regret to observe is fast dying out by disuse as well as by abuse.

Indulekha came out of Menon's attempt at translating Disraeli's *Henrietta Temple* (1837), which he abandoned after only a few pages, deciding wisely to write his own novel instead. Though thematically a love story with impediments and a happy ending, and on occasion containing stylistic elements of the folk tale, it is in every other respect radically different from previous works in Malayalam. Set 'in our own times', its events occur in an identifiable place ('not far away from Native Cochin'), and it is written, says Menon, 'in the style of Malayalam which I speak at home with such Sanskrit words as I might use in conversation with an educated Malayalee.' Just twenty years earlier the Marathi writer Naro Sadashiv Risbud, who was an admirer of the *Arabian Nights*, had wondered if the reader was ready for a story 'about the things we experience daily'; the success of *Indulekha* shows that at least the Malayalam reader was. The first printing sold out within three months and there were sixty reprints until 1971, a figure which would not have surprised Chandu Menon in the least, who said in the preface:

> Others again asked me, while I was employed on this novel, how I expected to make it a success if I described only the ordinary affairs of modern life without introducing any element of the supernatural. My answer was this: Before the European style of oil-painting began to be known and appreciated in this country, we had—painted in defiance of all possible existence—pictures of Vishnu as half man and half lion, pictures of the deity of the chase, pictures of bruteheaded monsters, pictures of the god Krishna with his legs twisted and twined into postures in which no biped could stand and blowing a cowherd's horn . . . Such productions used to be highly thought of, and those who produced them used to be highly remunerated, but now they are looked upon by many with aversion. A taste has set in for pictures, whether in oil or watercolours, in which shall be delineated men, beasts, and things according to their true appearance, and the closer that a picture is to nature the greater is the honour paid to the artist. Just in the same way, if stories composed of incidents true to natural life, and attractively and gracefully written, are once introduced, then by degrees the old order of books, filled with the impossible and the supernatural, will change, yielding place to the new.

Taken together, Menon's preface and dedicatory letter read like a manifesto of Indian literature, one of several that were written in the nineteenth century. Arising out of a colonial situation, they capture the spirit of a future age. Their key words are 'innovation', 'intelligence', 'style', 'elegance', 'skill', and the key phrase is 'new departure'. Decades later, Ezra Pound would echo them in his dictum 'Make it new'.

Though its poems, plays, and novels appear now to be didactic and purposeful, the colonial avant-garde had done its job: it had brought a new 'English' imagination—new forms, new situations, a new sense of time and a new spatial bustle—to literatures that were 'fast dying out by disuse as well as by abuse'. Rabindranath Tagore articulated the same liberating sentiment in *My Reminiscences* (1914). '[O]ur hearts' he wrote, 'naturally craved the life-bringing shock of the passionate emotions expressed in English literature. Ours was not the aesthetic enjoyment of literary art, but the jubilant welcome of a turbulent wave from a situation of stagnation . . .'

Chandu Menon, who had risen from sixth clerk to munsif to sub-judge in the Madras Presidency, was, in appreciation of his services to the government, conferred the title of Rao Bahadur. But he would have found the second honour that came to him in the shape of a certificate from Queen Victoria, Empress of India, 'in recognition of the services rendered by him in the cause of Malayalam literature', not less glory-giving.

III

The exposure to English that colonialism necessitated led some Indian writers to discover prose and the realist novel, or blank verse and the sonnet, whose grafts they inserted in their tropical languages and where they have since flourished. Other writers with a similar social background and with the same Macaulayan education reversed the procedure, as it were, and sought to tie and wax themselves to an English stem. Though there were no misgivings about this writing initially—nor indeed about English—things started to change in the 1870s.

The misgivings appear to be on several counts, but all of them, in the period before independence, have to do either with some form of nationalism or with the mother-tongue syndrome, which are often the same thing. In the period after independence the mother-tongue syndrome quickly hardened into nativism, of which there can only be one—pernicious—kind.

The good-natured scolding Bankimchandra Chattopadhyaya gave Romesh Chunder Dutt for not writing in Bengali is an example of the proto-nationalist point of view: 'You will never live by your writing in English . . . Look at others. Your uncles Gobindo Chandra and Shoshi Chandra and Madusudhan Dutt were the best educated men in Hindu College in those days. Gobindo Chandra and Shoshi Chandra's English poems will never live, Madhusudan's Bengali poetry will live so long as the Bengali language will live.' Coming from one who had himself abandoned English after writing his first novel in it, the words had their effect. Dutt published his first Bengali novel, *Bangabijeta*, in 1874 and went on to write five others. He also continued to write prolifically in English, his classic work being a two-volume indictment of British economic policy titled *Economic History of India* (1902 and 1904). The book made a deep impression on Gandhi, who refers to it in *Hind Swaraj* (1910). Out of his quarrel with others came Dutt's writings in English, and out of the quarrel with himself those in Bengali. He described himself as a 'literary patriot'.

In the nationalist period the posthumous gains of writing in the mother tongue versus writing in English paled into insignificance before the more immediate need to forge a national language, whose absence was felt by all sections of the Indian intelligentsia. 'If you want to draw a nation together there is no force more powerful than a common language for all,' Bal Gangadhar Tilak said as early as 1905, addressing a meeting of the Nagari Pracharini Sabha at Benaras. What this common language was going to be—Hindi, Urdu, or Hindustani—was still not clear, though Tilak himself meant Hindi by it. Five years later, joining his voice to Tilak's, Gandhi wrote in *Hind Swaraj*: 'To give millions a knowledge of English is to enslave them. The foundation that Macaulay laid of education has enslaved us.' And, 'A universal language for India should be Hindi.' By Hindi Gandhi always meant Hindustani. The term denoted a mongrel language spoken by both Hindus and Muslims across much of northern India which, in 1925, he defined as 'a resultant of Hindi and Urdu, neither highly Sanskritised nor highly Persianised nor Arabianised.' Gandhi left the choice of writing this Hindustani in either 'Persian or Nagari characters' to individual users of it.

Issues of language are seldom resolved overnight, and in fact the Hindi–Hindustani question was being debated, often bitterly, until the 1940s. Eventually, Gandhi's Hindi (or Hindustani), which had Nehru's complete support, lost out to the Hindi of the Hindi Sahitya Sammelan, a literary institution established in 1910 to fight for Hindi's cause, and whose early meetings had been attended by nationalist leaders like Sarojini Naidu and C. Rajagopalachari. It was this Hindi, Sanskrit-blest, purged of Urdu elements, and 'written in Devanagari script', which came to be enshrined in the Constitution as 'The official language of the Union.'

While the battle over language raged, overall it was little more than a sideshow to the freedom movement. If the Indian novel in English had its first birth in 1864, when Bankimchandra Chattopadhyaya's *Rajmohan's Wife* was serialised in *The Indian Field*, and its third in the 1980s, when Salman Rushdie's *Midnight's Children* and I. Allan Sealy's *The Trotter-Nama* were published, its second coming is in the Gandhian nationalist phase which began in the 1920s. The factor which is common to these novels is Gandhi. From K.S. Venkataramani's *Murugan, The Tiller* (1927) to Bhabani Bhattacharya's *So Many Hungers* (1947), Gandhi is present in the fiction of the period both in the flesh and, through his ideas, in the spirit. He is present also in more hidden ways.

After reading Gandhi's description in *Young India* of his encounter with Uka, a sweeper boy, Mulk Raj Anand went back and rewrote *Untouchable* (1935). He felt that his narrative, compared with the simplicity and austerity of Gandhi's, was 'artificially concocted'. Subsequently, when he read out the novel to Gandhi in Sabarmati Ashram, Gandhi advised him 'to cut meretricious literariness' from it. It's a piece of advice Ford Madox Ford might have offered a young writer. When Anand rather mawkishly wanted to know whether he should continue to write exclusively in English, Gandhi's response was characteristically forthright. 'The purpose of writing is to communicate, isn't it?' he said. 'If so, say your say in any language that comes to hand.'

Between Gandhi's many-sided opposition to English and his encouragement of Anand there is no contradiction. His opposition was not to English but to what it symbolised: political slavery and cultural degradation. 'I know husbands who are sorry that their wives cannot talk to them and their friends in English. I know families in which English is being made the mother tongue', he had written in *Young India* in 1921. If English in the nationalist period symbolised everything that was wrong with the country, Hindi and the mother tongues suggested everything that was right. English stood for the colonial past, shortly to be left behind; the 'vernaculars' for the times ahead, soon to unfold at a midnight hour made famous by Nehru's 1947 speech and now done to death by repeated literary invocation.

The Constitution of 1950 that gave Hindi 'official language' status also provided that English 'shall continue to be used for all the official purposes of the Union' for a period of fifteen years, until 1965. It was a provision made at Nehru's insistence and, by the proponents of Hindi, denounced at the time. Speaking before the Constituent Assembly on 8 November 1948, when preparations for drafting the Constitution were getting under way, Nehru, without mentioning Hindi directly (though the audience was left in no doubt what he meant), said:

> Any attempt to impose a particular form of language on an unwilling people has usually met with the strongest opposition and has actually resulted in something the very reverse of what the promoters thought . . . I would beg this House to consider the fact and to realise, if it agrees with me, that the surest way of developing a natural all-India language is not so much to pass resolutions and laws on the subject, but to work to that end in other ways.

Languages, Nehru had written in a letter from Almora Jail to his daughter Indira in Santiniketan, were 'desirable and . . . tricky things'. They had to be learnt willingly, and at an early age; they had to be wooed. To impose a language on others, more so an 'official language', was repugnant to him. Furthermore Nehru was aware, as early as 1948, of the resistance to such an imposition. He always described Hindi as 'a national language' or as 'one of the national languages', yet he was among the first political leaders to realise that the southern half of the country, which spoke Telugu, Kannada, Tamil, and Malayalam, would never accept Hindi. He touched repeatedly on the dangers inherent in legislating on language, on making it the subject of 'resolutions and laws'. In fact he would be preoccupied with these thoughts even in the months preceding his death in 1964.

The 'opposition' to imposing 'a particular form of language on an unwilling people', which Nehru had warned against, arrived as if on cue. In the early 1960s, as the year in which English was to cease 'to be used for all the official purposes of the Union' drew near, the enthusiasts of Hindi—forgetting that Hindi was now a regional language like any other and no longer possessed the pan-Indian aura it did during the freedom movement—renewed their agitation to remove the language of colonial rule. But now a counter-agitation was launched in the non-Hindi-speaking states of the south, thus dividing the country into two camps: an anti-English camp and a pro-English one.

The north was for abolishing English from educational institutions and from the state administration and for switching over to Hindi; in the south people agitated for the opposite reason: for retaining English and against imposing Hindi upon them. Since Hindi was now to be the sole 'official language', the people of South India feared they would be compelled to learn it—their fear was not unfounded. The Hindi poet Dhoomil has called this period in post-Independence Indian history 'The Night of Language':

In the eyes of the true butcher,
Your Tamil misery
And my Bhojpuri grief
Are one and the same.
In the mouth of that beast,
Who is one thing in the street
And another in parliament,
Language is a piece of meat.
So quitting the street's darkness,
Come out into the street
—Not language but man
Has to be put right first—
Come out in the fourteen
Tongues that you speak.

[Translated by Arvind Krishna Mehrotra]

In this extract the 'true butcher' and 'hungry beast' is the politician who raises the emotive issue of language for his own selfish ends, leaving the real issues untouched.

The Official Language Bill was brought before parliament in 1963 and passed the same year, extending the constitutional recognition of English beyond the fifteen-year period. It reassured non-Hindi speakers that English would continue to be used in their states so long as they did not themselves want a change, nor would a knowledge of Hindi be compulsorily required of anyone seeking employment in the central government. Tamil Nadu greeted the news by eliminating the teaching of Hindi from its secondary schools, Uttar Pradesh having already adopted a similar measure against English.

In the debate on the bill, speaking with a passion that came to be expected of him when the subject was language, Nehru explained why he was pressing for retaining English in India. The British invasion, he said, had 'administered a shock' to our people, but the shock had its positive side. Our languages, which like our lives had become 'static', were made 'more dynamic' through their contact with English. English would 'serve as a vitaliser to our languages' in the future, as it had in the past. Succeeding events, both linguistic and literary, have proved Nehru right.

Nehru had succeeded in stopping the clock which was ticking away for English. It is all the more paradoxical, therefore, that just when the threat seemed to lift and the future of English in India looked secure, Indian literature in English came to be seen as a historical aberration and a literary dead-end. The best-known statement of this point of view was, unfortunately, penned by Buddhadeva Bose, who, apart from being one of the finest Bengali poets of the post-Tagore generation, wrote some excellent essays in English and whose translations of modern Bengali poetry (Jibanananda Das, Amiya Chakravarty, Samar Sen, Benoy Majumdar) are unsurpassed even today. Bose's entry in the *Concise Encyclopaedia of English and American Poets and Poetry* (1963), edited by Stephen Spender and Donald Hall, is on Indian poetry in English, but the attitude behind it is not confined to verse alone. It begins:

> It may seem surprising that Indians, who have always had a firm poetic tradition in their own languages, should ever have tried to write verse in English. That they did so, was the outcome of the anglomania which seized some upper-class Indians in the early years of British rule. Sons (and sometimes daughters) were sent to England even before they had reached teen-age, and there they spent all their formative years. Thus it was that English became the poetic vehicle of a number of gifted Indians . . .

And it famously concludes:

> As late as 1937, Yeats reminded Indian writers that 'no man can think or write with music and vigour except in his mother-tongue'; to the great majority of Indians this admonition was unnecessary, but the intrepid few who left it unheeded do not yet realise that 'Indo-Anglian' poetry is a blind alley, lined with curio shops, leading nowhere.

The quote from Yeats is inaccurate, and the date, 1937, is incorrect. Bose was obviously quoting from memory. What is more important, though, is that the statement hit home and a response was delivered six years later in the form of a 600-page compilation, by far the largest work of its kind yet, called *Modern Indian Poetry in English: An Anthology and Credo* (1969), edited by P. Lal and published by Writers Workshop, Calcutta, a small publishing house run by Lal himself.

Lal had decided to speak on behalf of the 'Indo-Anglians', or maybe he was stung by Bose's description of him as a 'publisher and publicist', a 'representative figure' of 'a new group who are assiduously courting the Muse of Albion'. At any rate, he sent cyclostyled copies of Bose's entry to seventy-five poets, along with a questionnaire. Among the questions the recipients had to answer were: 'What are the circumstances that led to your using the English language for the purpose of writing poetry?' 'What are your views on the "Indo-Anglian" background?' and 'Do you think English is one of the Indian languages?' The sixth question—there were seven in all—referred specifically to Sri Aurobindo, whom Bose had praised by saying, 'In authenticity of [English] diction and feeling Sri Aurobindo far out-shines the others . . .' The questionnaire quoted this and added archly: 'Your comments, please.' Some of the replies and comments are given below:

> I thought we have had more than enough of whether or no English should be used in India as a means of communication—creative communication included. Mr. Bose might be irrelevant since English is *there* and a work of erudition or art is acceptable or not acceptable on merit. And there are fairly accurate instruments of assessing merit regardless of a writer's nationality, his ancestry, personal or group stress or history, or his ethnic and cultural credits and debits. (G.V. Desani)

> I . . . agree that Indo-Anglian poetry is lined with curio shops, and I am amused that Mr. Bose professes an admiration for the crassest of them all, Sri Aurobindo. (Nissim Ezekiel)

> I do believe that the tradition back of me is not of Rabindranath Tagore or Aurobindo. I would rather say that my background is Auden and MacNeice, William Carlos Williams and Wallace Stevens. Sarojini Naidu and Toru Dutt never excited me in the sense that *The Waste Land* and *The Glass Menagerie* did. (Srinivas Rayaprol)

> I do not quite know how to reply to your questions because I have really no strong opinions on Indians writing in English. Buddhadeva Bose has strong opinions on why they should not; you are persuaded that they should. I think the real question is whether they can. And if they can, they will. (A.K. Ramanujan)

> The circumstances that led me to write in English are simple—I belong to that unfortunate minority, anglomaniacs all, who even puked in English when three weeks old. My umbilical cord was anglicised. (Lawrence Bantleman)

The replies to the questionnaire, however, take up only a small part of the book's 600 pages. The bulk of it consists of the work of 132 poets, arranged alphabetically from Alford to Yousufzaie. There are also biographical notes and, in most cases, photographs. One poet is disguised as a common North Indian labourer; another, cigarette in hand, strikes the pose of a matinee idol. Both are bearded. Lal provides a long and somewhat urgent introduction.

The language question was a 1960s issue in India and it has largely been forgotten. Since then, English has crept back into the northern states, but, with state governments washing their hands off it, public demand is met by private initiative. 'English-medium' nursery schools with names like Little Angles, Jesus-Marry, and Tinny Tots (the last being the name of one such school in Vikram Seth's *A Suitable Boy*, 1993) are to be found in many parts of Uttar Pradesh and Uttaranchal, Madhya Pradesh and Bihar, and it would be safe to assume that the children who attend them are learning English by methods not too different from those by which Lal Behari Day's cousin learnt his 170 years ago. On the other hand, the South imbibes whatever Hindi it does by watching Bollywood films and television serials.

While there has largely been a lull on the language front, the picket from which Bose fired his blunderbuss has seldom been inactive. In fact it has become the Siachen of Indian literature. In 'Does Language Matter?', a piece which appeared in the *Times of India* of 26 March 1988, Sham Lal, a former editor of the paper, wrote:

> If the nationalists' dream of developing Hindi as the link language has gone sour, so has the westernizers' dream of domesticating English . . . Mr. Raja Rao's brave talk that 'we shall have the English

> language with us and amongst us, and not as guest or friend, but as one of our own, of our caste, our creed, our sect and of our tradition' was a bit of blarney. Curiously, he also said that English 'is the language of our intellectual make-up and not of our emotional make-up'. But can a person reserve the nuances of his thought and feeling for two separate languages without developing a split personality?

Sham Lal ends by saying: 'There was a time when a British writer jeeringly described Indian writing in English as "Matthew Arnold in a *sari*" and an Indian professor hastened to correct him and said it would be more appropriate to compare it to a "Shakuntala in skirts".' Among those who have joined Buddhadeva Bose and Sham Lal behind the sandbag of the mother tongue is Bhalchandra Nemade, Tagore Professor of Comparative Literature at the University of Bombay and well known as a Marathi novelist. Given below are three extracts from his *Indo-Anglian Writings: Two Lectures* (1991):

> What is understood today as 'Indo-Anglian Writing' is one of the latest nomenclatures of a body of books, hyphenisedly christened by university academicians. The writer of this 'Inglish' species of Indian literary production is one who is Indian by birth or association and who, for a variety of reasons best known to himself, writes not in his mother tongue, but in English . . . Since India is a country fabulous in all kinds of idiosyncrasies, it is futile to question the existence of this writing and to be fair to it, let us accept it as an abnormal case of a historical development, even as wryly as Saros Cowasjee, who treats it like a disease: 'this is not a healthy trend, but it is there', she [*sic*] says.

> To be precise, the mode of operation of English as a supra-language in India has been cultural-written-formal rather than social-oral-conversational in the national linguistic context. Such a written variety which has not emerged from the soil is highly detrimental to creative use . . . The English language has become thus a pathetic necessity for post-Independence Indians, the widows of the British Empire, and it is retained in India mainly because it maintains what can be called 'equality of disadvantage' among Indians of different mother-tongues. It survives on the impoverishment resulting from multilingualism encouraged by our tolerant national culture; and by occupying the position of a supra-language, it aggravates this impoverishment further.

> Whereas every word in the mother-tongue presents its own geology, the words in a foreign language offer insipid solidarity to the writer's competence. A foreign language thus suppresses the natural originality of Indian writers in English, enforcing on the whole tribe the fine art of parrotry. It is worth noting in this context that the cases of Indians praising Indians' command over English are more frequent than those of Englishmen making patronising understatements about Indians' use of English. This smacks of the Crusoe–Friday relationship, since an Indian nightingale does not receive even the status of a crow in the history of English literature.

The nightingale reference is to Sarojini Naidu, whom Gandhi called the 'Nightingale of India'.

There is the odd similarity between what Bose said in 1963 and what Nemade said in 1991. There are also profound differences, reflecting the change in the political climate from Nehru's time to nearer our own. Nemade, with passionate intensity, perceives cultures as being either strong, unitary, and male, or weak, diverse, and female. Weak cultures allow for a high degree of tolerance, but the more tolerance they show the more weak and impoverished they become. It is a vicious circle, and one in which 'our tolerant national culture' is now trapped. A weak culture, nevertheless, needs to be held together, howsoever loosely; just as a houseful of widows needs to have a man around, if only to douse the flames when the widows set each other ablaze. In the case of a weak culture like India's, the cause of whose weakness is linguistic diversity, the presence of a dominating 'supra-language' is 'a pathetic necessity'. English performs the 'supra-language' function, but at the same time, because of the position it occupies, it impoverishes the mother tongues further. Nemade's view of language and Indian society is everything that Nehru's was not.

Nemade had expressed similar views earlier, and they were even more immoderate. In a special issue of *New Quest* (May–June 1984) on nativism he wrote:

> A most ridiculous trend . . . is the way some of our writers strive to become 'national' and even 'international' by getting their work translated into English. This has become a spurious means of building literary reputations. It is time we realised the fact that beyond our own

'language group' all that we do smacks of mediocrity. Like the sadhus camping in the Ram Leela ground in Delhi in G.V. Desani's *All About H. Hatterr*, our writers and politicians seem to carry the nameboards: 'All-India Sadhu' and 'International Sadhu' and so on.

Nemade's opinions should have caused an uproar but didn't, and except for Adil Jussawalla and Vilas Sarang (both, like Nemade, being from Bombay), nobody else took any notice of them. Quoting him on nativism, Jussawalla points out that Nemade defines nativism 'in Hindu revivalist terms', a phrase which encapsulates Nemade's cultural and political positions. Jussawalla's concluding sentences, in more ways than one, read like a prophecy:

> I fear the qualities of racist arrogance, self-centredness and isolationism are very much there in Nemade's concept of Nativism. If they don't doom the country to extinction, they may well doom the growth of a vital, imaginative and critical literature. Words are far from dead. In the best of literature, they free imprisoned visions and make us see whole societies and situations afresh. The state of our own society may never have seemed so awful as it does now.
>
> Let it not be said in the future that by failing to find alternatives to the . . . regressive parochialism of our writers, we allowed it to become too awful for words. ('The New India, The New Media and Literature', *The Indian P.E.N.*, Jan.–Feb. 1985)

Compared with Nemade's extreme views, Bose's little sneer ('courting the Muse of Albion') and the caricature Sham Lal alludes to ('Shakuntala in skirts') seem like friendly gestures. Their jibes are a part of the history of colonial humour which goes back to the nineteenth century, when the figure of the Bengali babu was lampooned in any number of poems, songs, and pantomimes, and in the popular art of Battala wood engravings and Kalighat paintings. Here is the babu in Mokshodayani Mukhopadhyaya's wholly unforgiving send-up:

> Alas, there goes our Bengali babu!
> He slaves away from ten till four,
> Carrying his servitude like a pedlar's wares.
> A lawyer or magistrate, or perhaps a schoolmaster,
> A subjudge, clerk, or overseer:

The bigger the job, the greater his pride;
The babu thinks he's walking on air.
Red in the face from the day's hard labour,
He downs pegs of whiskey to relax when he's home.
He's transported with pride at the thought of his rank—
But faced with a sahib he trembles in fear!
Then he's obsequious, he mouths English phrases,
His own tongue disgusts him, he heaps it with curses.
The babu's learned *English*, he swells with conceit
And goes off in haste to deliver a speech.
He flounders while speaking, and stumbles and stutters,
But he's speaking in *English*: you must come and hear.

. . . .

The babu speaks a patter of Bengali and English
But he berates the English with all his heart.
These sports are but nocturnal; wiping his mouth, in the morning
The babu is respectful and sober again.

[Translated by Supriya Chaudhury]

'Bangali Babu' appears in *Women Writing in India*, volume I (1991), edited by Susie Tharu and K. Lalita. It was written around 1880, the decade in which Mokshodayani Mukhopadhyaya's younger contemporary, Rudyard Kipling, who had a masterful ear for such things, was listening to patter of a quite different sort: 'part English, part Portuguese, and part Native', it was the speech of 'the Borderline folk'. The Borderline, says Kipling in 'His Chance in Life', an early story, is

> where the last drop of White blood ends and the full tide of Black sets in. It would be easier to talk to a new-made Duchess on the spur of the moment than to the Borderline folk without violating some of their conventions or hurting their feelings. The Black and the White mix very quaintly in their ways . . . One of these days, this people—understand they are far lower than the class whence Derozio, the man who imitated Byron, sprung—will turn out a writer or a poet; and then we shall know how they live and what they feel. In the meantime, any stories about them cannot be absolutely correct in fact or inference.

What Mukhopadhyaya's conceited babu and Kipling's 'Borderline folk' were to the society of their day, the writer in English is to India's post-Independence literary space. An 'anglomaniac' with a 'split-personality', he is even now looked upon as a half-caste whose mixed literary parentage, 'part English . . . and part Native', is embodied, permanently, in the hyphenated phrase 'Indo-Anglian'.

IV

The animosity towards Indian literature in English stems in large measure from the animosity towards the social class English has come to be identified with: a narrow, well-entrenched, metropolitan-based ruling élite that has dominated Indian life for the past fifty and more years. But literature as a category is inclusive rather than exclusive. It is more complex, less homogeneous, than a social group, and cannot always be made coextensive with it. While it is true that many who write in English in India belong to the metropolitan élite, it is also true that many who write at all, irrespective of language, belong to a privileged stratum. Growing up in small mofussil towns, they have attended local schools and their early education has been in an Indian language. These languages (Oriya, Marathi, Kannada) have, at times, been vehicles of creative expression for them as much as English. The Mysore-born A.K. Ramanujan, whose mother tongue was Tamil, published his first collection of English poems, *The Striders*, in 1966, and three years later followed it with his first collection in Kannada. And Ramanujan's is by no means an isolated case. Arun Kolatkar's poems in Marathi and English started appearing in journals in the 1950s, and he has continued to publish, like Dilip Chitre, in both languages since. Not all Indian writers in English write in two languages of course, but they are nevertheless drawn from a mixed bilingual élite which is far from exclusively metropolitan.

Writing in two languages—an affliction not confined to poets—is one of several ways in which bilingualism expresses itself. Another is translation, especially translation by authors of their own work from an Indian language into English. Though the nature of these translations (with the exception of Tagore's) and the necessity of doing them have rarely been commented on, they have had a long history which goes back to Michael Madhusudan Dutt. In recent decades, among those who have made translations of their work into English are the Malayalam novelist O.V. Vijayan and the Kannada playwright Girish Karnad, and their translations have been widely acclaimed. However, for an insider's view of what negotiating a text in two languages involves, and to know what the pleasures and pitfalls of 'dual citizenship in the world of letters' are, we have to go to Vilas Sarang.

In 'Confessions of a Marathi Writer' (*World Literature Today*, Spring 1994), Sarang says that the first full-length book in English he read was Jim Corbett's *The Man-eating Leopard of Rudraprayag*, at age sixteen. Before this, he read books only in Marathi. Sarang's 'first mature story' was written soon after, in 1963, when he was an MA student at Bombay University. 'As it happens,' he confesses, 'I wrote this story in English.' When the Marathi magazine *Abhiruchi* wanted the story, he offered to make 'a hasty crib, to my mind unsatisfactory and lacking the style of the original'. It was thus published first in Marathi in1965. The English version of the story, 'Flies', had to wait until 1981, when it appeared in *London Magazine*. 'As by then', Sarang writes, 'my other, later stories written in Marathi had appeared in English as translations, I allowed this story to appear in *LM* as "Translated from the Marathi", and that is how it stands in my 1990 collection, *Fair Tree of the Void* (Penguin India). Well, there's a "Marathi" writer for you.'

But even those stories that he first wrote in Marathi 'are often covertly English'. 'As a matter of fact,' he says, 'I regard the English versions of my stories as the definitive text, and the "original" Marathi as only a stage toward the final casting.' Why Sarang has bothered to write in Marathi at all is a question he answers himself:

> For most of my adult life, my stream of consciousness has flowed in English, and it is in a way odd that, when I sit down to write, I switch to thinking in Marathi. My conscious mind may function through English, but my unconscious is rooted in Marathi; and to draw upon the resources of my unconscious, I must go through the initial rites of passage in my native tongue. However, the conscious part of my mind being situated in English, it still remains necessary to recreate the text in English. To write first in Marathi, then re-do the text in English, is thus a means of reconciling the two halves of my divided psyche.

The authors Sarang admires are Kafka, Hemingway, Camus, and Beckett, and he sees himself as belonging, in a modest way, to the 'international modernist tradition'. 'Marathi literature is so hopelessly mired in the stick-in-the-mud middle-class ethos and reflexes', he says, 'that, from the beginning, I refused to have any truck with the sensibility it represented. The narrow, and subtly caste-marked, paths of Marathi literature I saw as something to avoid at any cost; a largely self-invented international tradition offered a liberating route to self-realisation.' Still, there were Marathi writers associated with the *Navakatha* (New Story) movement in the 1950s, like Gangadhar Gadgil, Vyankatesh Madgulkar, and Aravind Gokhale, whom Sarang read avidly when young, and he is quick to acknowledge that if he has been able to 'achieve some distinction as a short-story writer', it's because he 'stand[s] on their shoulders'.

Coming to bilingualism, by which he means having an equally strong allegiance to two languages and laying claim to two literary traditions, Sarang describes the 'tricky situation' bilingualism can put the Indian writer in:

> Marathi readers have frequently complained that my Marathi sounds as though it were translated from English, and I daresay they are not entirely off the mark. At the same time, whenever I have written directly in English, there sometimes came the complaint that it did not sound quite English . . . It can be the unenviable fate of the bilingual writer to be turned away from both houses he considers his own. People everywhere have a very possessive and exclusive attitude to what they consider *their* language.

The early 1960s, according to Sarang, was 'probably one of the best and liveliest periods in Marathi literary history'. The first generation of post-Independence writers, brimming with confidence and possessing 'a new sense of identity' had come to maturity. Short-lived little magazines, often run by the writers themselves, mushroomed everywhere, and when they closed down new ones took their place. 'Avant-gardism, experimentation, and creative crankiness were in vogue. The air was full of excitement.' Sarang's Marathi contemporaries were Bhalchandra Nemade, Arun Kolatkar, and Dilip Chitre, and in 'Confessions' he mentions each of them in turn. He describes Nemade's

Kosla (The Cocoon), a section of which he translated for Adil Jussawalla's pathbreaking anthology *New Writing in India* (1974), as a novel 'that overnight changed the face of Marathi fiction and its style', and calls it 'the finest symbol of the brash and daring creativity of that period'. Equally 'brash and daring' were Kolatkar and Chitre, who wrote 'a poetry informed simultaneously by the work of medieval Marathi poet-saints and the French symbolists and their modernist heirs'. 'I count myself fortunate', says Sarang, 'that I began publishing my work at a time like this.'

But that time is past. When Sarang looks back on it and what it promised, it's as though on a golden age. Those who were once the 'champions of modernism and innovation'—Kolatkar, Chitre, and Sarang himself—'seem like lone rangers in an unconducive, hostile environment.' In place of the 'experimentation and creative crankiness' of the early 1960s, there is at work in Marathi literature '[a] kind of cultural fundamentalism, closely allied to its religious variety'. 'As I remarked in an article published in *Indian Literature* in 1992', he says, ' "The Marathi literary world today resembles a little pond crowded with frogs croaking at each other in self-satisfaction." '

Given this 'regressive mood', Sarang is not too surprised by 'the rise of a phenomenon called nativism (*deshivad*)'. What does surprise him, though, is that 'its leader is Bhalchandra Nemade, the one-time avant-garde, tradition-breaking author of *Kosla*, with the practitioners of "rural literature" as its principal followers. They have accused writers such as Chitre, Kolatkar, and myself of being "slaves of Western culture".' Sarang is not one to pull his punches. He replies to the slavery charge by calling nativism 'a retrograde, hidebound, and perniciously limiting movement. It is a movement by people who are afraid of the world, who want to retreat into their little hole in the dirtheap.'

Sarang's essay reiterates many of the ideas and issues we have met with before, in Derozio and Young Bengal, in Rangalal Banerjee and Michael Madhusudan Dutt, in Chandu Menon, Tagore, and Nehru. Sham Lal asked if one can write in 'two separate languages without developing a split personality', and Sarang shows not only that one can, but that the condition of 'split' is what keeps a literature in good shape, keeps it from becoming a 'little hole in the dirtheap'. Equally important for us, Sarang touches on something which has always been known but is seldom remarked on, much less examined: the presence of the Indian languages in Indian literary works in English, and the corresponding presence in Indian-language texts of English. 'We are all instinctively bilingual', Raja Rao said in the foreword to *Kanthapura* (1938). This instinctive bilingualism is what umbilically ties the writing done in English to the other Indian literatures.

In the resistance to Indian writing in English, however, there has never been any let-up. In each decade new ways are found to marginalise it. If in the 1960s it was likened to 'a blind alley . . . leading nowhere', in the 1990s it was seen as a phenomenon occurring not here, in India, but abroad. 'Writing for export' is how the Kannada novelist U.R. Anantha Murthy, a former chairman of the Sahitya Akademi (the National Academy of Letters), reacted on the Amul India Show to the success of Arundhati Roy's *The God of Small Things* (1997). The feeling that readers of such novels are mainly in the West and that the writing is essentially being done for them is now common, so much so that any attention a work receives is put down to the changed marketplace, to the large advance a novel occasionally fetches, to the publicity it generates in the Indian media. In the words of the historian Sumit Sarkar, '"Indo-Anglian" writing had to wait for postcolonial times to become a significant literary genre, under conditions of intensified globalisation.' If this is an insight into the conditions that have recently made Indian writing something of a commodity to be sold via advertising hype, it needs, all the same, a corollary: unlike Coca-Cola, a piece of writing is savoured best in the place where its secret recipe is from, and more often than not it is only really possible for it to be most satisfyingly consumed in the same place too.

A case in point is I. Allan Sealy's first novel *The Trotter-Nama* (1988). Sealy, who lives in India and New Zealand and is of the generation of 'Indo-Anglians' born after Independence, spent seven years writing the novel, at the end of which he repaired to London where the manuscript made the publishers' rounds. In a short essay he contributed to *Indian Review of Books* (Oct.–Nov. 1993), Sealy recounts his brush with the conditions of globalisation:

> In a way my journey to London was instructive. 'Why London?' I am sometimes asked. I took my script there because I liked the way the British produced books, and I did not like the way books were produced here. (As it happened the Americans [Knopf] produced a handsome

> first edition, and the British [Penguin] a shoddy offprint.) But there would have been a colonial component to my anxiety. If so, I got my deserts. Not one British newspaper reviewed the book when it appeared. Its discovery was an Indian critical undertaking; Indian papers and journals, Indian reviewers made its reputation. I am making a political, but I hope not chauvinistic, point. What my own experience taught me was that an English literary culture was coming of age here—and I had been blind to it.

The marketplace is in any case a fickle thing. In the *TLS* of 8 August 1997, Amit Chaudhuri takes, as a writer should, a long view of the matter and sounds a cautionary note. 'We are, apparently', he says,

> in the midst of some sort of resurgence in Indian writing (in English). Few writers themselves will feel confident, in their hearts, that they are living and working in a creative boom, though they may be forgiven if they take advantage of the probably short-lived monetary benefits of its supposed existence; but journalists and publishers are busy assuring us that there is good cause for excitement . . . How much of the resurgence has to do with what publishers in England consider the marketability of Indian fiction, and how much of it is genuine achievement, will take at least twenty or thirty years, or more, to decide.

There is in *The Trotter-Nama,* which is dedicated to 'The Other Anglo-Indians', a section devoted to Henry Derozio. He appears in the novel as Henry Luis Vivian Fonseca-Trotter. In sharp contrast to the man-who-imitated-Byron figure mentioned derisively in Kipling's story, Fonseca-Trotter is a prospective indigo planter turned revolutionary poet and Hindu College lecturer ('ink, not indigo, he declared loftily, was his medium'), whose 'students flocked to hear his sparkling but closely reasoned lectures, which ranged from speculative philosophy to poetic justice, and afterwards they gathered around him, won over by his charm and springy hair, to broach the issues of the day: the condition of India, the mastery of Europe, the unacknowledged legislators of the world.' At these meetings, which lasted well into the night, the students, in defiance of social norms, would drink wine and eat beef, and once during a particularly convivial evening 'they tossed the bones of their feast into the house of a friend to taunt his orthodox father'. Fonseca-Trotter gets thrown out of his job as a result but dies soon after, aged twenty-three, in a cholera epidemic.

This is a literature whose writers have seldom acknowledged each other's presence. The reason is perhaps that outside a common geography—'the tract situated between the river Ganges and Indus'—and their location in the English language there is little else they felt they could share. Sealy's tribute to Derozio, a tribute from one Anglo-Indian writer to another, from one 'Indo-Anglian' to his literary forebear, is exceptional. It is also among the few times that the literature has encrypted its history in one of its texts. Art, it has been said, is its own historian.

Two other moments stand out, both very different from the above and from each other. The first occurs in Nirad C. Chaudhuri's *The Autobiography of an Unknown Indian* (1951):

> In a Bengali magazine subscribed to by my mother there had appeared in 1901 an illustration showing two Bengali girls in the late Victorian English dress. 'Who are these girls?' we asked in some perplexity, for they, though dressed like English girls, did not look English. My mother explained that the older girl was Toru Dutt, the young poetess who was the only Indian whose English verse was recognised as poetry in England, and the other girl was her sister Aru. They were the daughters of Govinda Dutt of Rambagan and had died young, we were further told. In fact, the picture had been published as an illustration to a Bengali poem mourning their death. When we first saw their picture I could not read the poem or anything at all. But I felt very proud that a Bengali girl had secured a place in English literature. My brother also felt proud. So did our parents.

The second is in V.S. Naipaul's *Letters Between a Father and Son* (1999). On 5 October 1950, Seepersad Naipaul wrote to Vidia, then in his first term at Oxford:

> *Do send me a copy of R.K. Narayan's Mr Sampath.* The book is very favourably spoken of in *The Year's Work in Literature, 1949*—an annual publication of the British Council. Narayan is spoken of as 'the most delightful of Indian novelists writing in English . . . in a way that no

English writer of our time can rival.' It is published by Eyre and Spottiswode, Ltd, 6 Great New St., London, EC4. The price is not given. I shall refund you the money.

Sealy's adoring portrait of Derozio; Chaudhuri's Bengali pride in Toru and Aru Dutt; Seepersad Naipaul making a touching request of his son for an R.K. Narayan novel: in moments like these, almost unknowingly, a literature becomes aware of itself, which is a different thing from others becoming aware of a literature. The former is indigenisation; the latter globalisation.

Whether one looks at the nineteenth century, when the English language was a mould into which the Indian writer tried to cast himself—the poems in *The Dutt Family Album* (1870) are an example of this—or at the twentieth, when the writer has become the moulding agency, a striking feature of Indian literature in English is that there have been no schools, literary movements, or even regional groups within it. Its history is scattered, discontinuous, and transnational. It is made up of individual writers who appear to be *sui generis*. They are explained neither by what went before them nor by what came after. But this is now changing. 'Hard to imagine I. Allan Sealy's *Trotter-Nama* without Desani. My own writing, too, has learnt a thing or two from him', Rushdie has said recently; and Mukul Kesavan, who heard Rushdie read from *Midnight's Children* in Cambridge in 1981, has described it as a 'religious experience'. Kesavan, who was a research student at the time, brought out his own Rushdie-inspired first novel, *Looking Through Glass* (1995), fourteen years later. This literary effort, alongside those by others who were contemporaries at Delhi's St Stephen's College in the 1970s, has been somewhat playfully described as a 'school' in *The Fiction of St. Stephen's* (2000).

Though the literature's past does not reflect its present, maybe its present, which has increasingly become self-perceiving and self-recognising, holds in it the seeds of its future.

V

A more personal word or two in conclusion. If you also have been a part of the literature being mapped, then its contour will somewhere bear a likeness to your own.

As a seventeen-year-old thirty-seven years ago, when I was in the small towns of Uttar Pradesh and Madhya Pradesh hammering out my first poems on a grandfatherly typewriter, Indian literature, whether in English or in the Indian languages, was not something I was even dimly aware of. I cannot say what thoughts filled my adolescent mind then, except that I was in love with the smoothness of the black keys and the long space bar, and with the clattering sound they made when pressed. Nothing, I felt, could be lovelier than the sight of a line forming on a white sheet, letter by letter; no movement more graceful than the carriage's as it slid from right to left; no music sweeter than the bell's which rose warningly from the depths of the machine and which meant that the carriage could proceed no further.

Recently, while emptying out a steel almirah in my house in Dehra Dun, I came across carbon copies of a few of those early poems and read them with embarrassment first, but afterwards in the expectation of learning a little about myself and the kind of literary fledgling I was in 1964. Some of the poems I looked at used capital letters, but others did not. My subjects were the indestructibility of love and the earth's destruction, and I used words like 'adieu' and 'gloam'. The shorter poems, of which there were several, seemed to be written in the belief that anything of haiku length is automatically also profound. In 1964, the year Nehru died, the year V.S. Naipaul's *An Area of Darkness* was published, I was sitting in darkness's heart, in a bungalow in Allahabad, in a railway waiting room in Bilaspur, and as scores of Indian poets—from Henry Derozio to Srinivas Rayaprol—had done before me, I was taking my bearings from distant stars. The two I took mine from were e.e. cummings and Kahlil Gibran.

1
The English Writings of Raja Rammohan Ray

Bruce Carlisle Robertson

Vac, Speech, once upon a time escaped from the gods, and settled in the trees. Her voice still resounds in wooden instruments.

—*Taittiriya Samhita*

Languages are jealous sovereigns and passports are rarely allowed for travellers to cross their strictly guarded boundaries.

—*Rabindranath Tagore*

On a dusty road in Bhagalpur, at about 4 o'clock on the afternoon of 1st January 1809, a Collector, newly arrived in his district, dismounted to inspect a brick kiln. The Collector had been knighted: he was Sir Frederick Hamilton. He had been promoted to serve as the East India Company's senior official within the most important mofussil district of the Bengal diwani. His residence was hard by, and from what followed a little later it is possible to surmise he was working off the effects of the previous evening's revels. Sir Frederick was, on that day, a man of considerable importance and master of all he surveyed.

Down the road on which the Collector had paused came a colourful ornamented palki, a carriage-box with its doors slightly ajar to keep out the dust while permitting its inmate a little circulation. The palki was virtually a procession: it was carried on the shoulders of four smartly attired coolies and preceded by four liveried 'chuprassys', advertising the fact that the traveller they served was a native gentleman of means and significance. This cavalcade passed by the dismounted firangi who seemed engrossed in important matters—too important, at any rate, to sully himself with road-level comings and goings.

Of what happened next, two accounts survive. The first is a letter from Babu Rammohan Ray, the traveller in the palki, to Lord Minto, the Governor-General of India. The second is the official report of Sir Frederick Hamilton, the newly arrived Collector. I quote the first account—Rammohan Ray's narrative of the episode—at some length because it is historic for two interrelated reasons: it captures the moment of the birth of modern Indian national self-consciousness and it marks the decisive appearance, two hundred years ago, of English as a language of modern India. Rammohan Ray begins the story:

> . . . at about 4 o'clock in the afternoon, your Petitioner passed in his palanquin thro' a Road on the left side of which Sir Frederick Hamilton was standing among some Bricks. The Door of the Palanquin being shut to exclude the dust of the Road, your Petitioner did not see that Gentleman nor did the Peon who preceded the palanquin apprise your Petitioner of the circumstance, he not knowing the Gentleman, much less supposing that, that Gentleman (who was standing alone among the Bricks), was the Collector of the district.

Sir Frederick remembered it differently:

> While Standing on the Top of the Kiln, I observed coming towards it, a Palanquin highly decorated, attended by four Chuprassys. I turned to a Servant of mine and enquired who it was coming along; he replied Mr. Digby's Dewan, Baboo Rammohan Roy.

Babu Rammohan Ray:

> As your Petitioner was passing, Sir Frederick Hamilton repeatedly called out to him to get out of his palanquin, and that with an epithet of abuse too gross to admit of being stated here without a departure from the respect due to your Lordship.

Sir Frederick:

> He passed within about 6 feet of where I was standing, elegantly dressed; in Blue Silk, and Silver Fringe, his Palanquin doors wide open; I said not a syllable to him. I took no notice of him nor he of me.

Babu Rammohan Ray:

> One of the servants of your Petitioner who followed in the retinue, explained to Sir Frederick Hamilton, that your Petitioner had not observed him in passing by; nevertheless that Gentleman still continued to use the same offensive language, and when the palanquin had proceeded to the distance about 300 yards, from the spot where Sir Frederick Hamilton had stood, that Gentleman overtook it on Horseback. Your Petitioner then for the first time understood that the Gentleman who was riding alongside of his palanquin, was the Collector of the District, and that he required a form of external respect, which, to whatever extent it might have been enforced under the Mogul Governor, your Petitioner had conceived from daily observation, to have fallen, under the milder, more enlightened and more liberal policy of the British Government, into entire disuse and disesteem.

Babu Rammohan Ray went on:

> Your Petitioner then, far from wishing to withhold any manifestation of the respect due to the public officers of a Government which he held in the highest veneration, and notwithstanding the novelty of the Form in which that respect was required to be testified, alighted from his palanquin and saluted Sir Frederick Hamilton, apologising to him for the omission of that act of public respect on the grounds that, in point of fact, your Petitioner did not see him before, on account of the Doors of his palanquin being nearly closed.

The Babu explained that he would not have recognised the Collector anyway since they had not before met. Sir Frederick did not acknowledge this:

> When he had passed about 600 yards, he sent one of these Outrunners with his salam, that he did not know it was the Collector, or he would have stopped. I immediately rode after him, desiring to know what he

> meant by sending his salam to me, as I have said nothing to him—that if he thought he ought to have made the salam instead of sending, he should have returned as the Distance was so trifling. I reproached him for his want of Civility, and warned him how he did so again to other Gentlemen, lest he might find one who would not keep his temper with him so well as I had done . . .

At this point it was stalemate. The focus immediately shifted from the relative personal status of the adversaries to the face-saving issue of what, if any, discipline the Babu's 'chuprassy' should receive for his insolence in presuming to be Babu Rammohan Ray's spokesman—as though his master's equal; and more egregious yet—the equal of the Collector. Despite courteous and sincere apologies, conveyed according to outdated Mughal protocol, Sir Frederick arrogantly brushed off the Babu's conciliatory gesture, demanding that the insubordinate servant be fired on the spot. It was Sir Frederick's view that Rammohan Ray had refused to play according to the rules. Both accounts agree however that the incident ended abruptly when Sir Frederick beat a strategic retreat. In writing to Lord Minto, Rammohan recorded the limits of the authority of the new foreign *de facto* sarkar as negotiated that day on a road near Bhagalpur.

Rammohan's narrative is significant for many reasons. First, it documents the essential civility of English governance in early-nineteenth-century Bengal. Second, it demonstrates the non-hierarchical nature of the English language in early colonial discourse. An Indian employee of the Company at the remotest fringe of authority successfully cut through the baffles of an alien bureaucracy and reached the seat of power simply by effective use of the 'language of command'—to use Bernard Cohn's phrase. Third, it reveals that the terms of legitimacy of the new *de facto* sarkar were negotiated, not imposed. Rammohan Ray not only cracked the foreigner's code but used it to set the limits of British governance in India. Sir Frederick was censured.

The Bhagalpur incident was a paradigmatic moment in Rammohan Ray's own turbulent life. It persuaded him that the rule of law actually worked. It was his use of the English language that gave him a voice. English was his passport across borders. Unlike the irascible Collector of Bhagalpur, who was slow to catch on, he knew his place in the new order.

This seemingly trivial incident in 1809 symbolically heralds a new era for European and Bengali alike. Modernity was dawning, writes Paul Johnson in *The Birth of the Modern: World Society 1815–30* (1991). Johnson quotes an Englishwoman's lament to a friend: 'The natives no longer get out of their palanquins and bow' when they pass Europeans. Ironically, the incident at Bhagalpur was a birthpang of modernity felt more in Europe than India.

In broadening the arena of discourse Rammohan Ray appropriated what he believed to be one of the greatest benefits conferred on India by the English, namely access to the world outside. English was already the dominant world language. Since Persian had ceased to be the language of exchange, Rammohan Ray adopted English. One foreign language replaced another as the lingua franca of governance in India. With the new language came new fields of reference. Rammohan Ray's career is largely about him negotiating these new minefields of reference and surveying the new territory of the English language in India. This is another chapter in the story of the domestication in India of a foreign language—a story which begins with Vedic Sanskrit. In the English-language writings and communications of Rammohan Ray and his contemporaries—Radhakanta Deb (1784–1867), Henry Louis Vivian Derozio (1809–31), Prasannakumar Thakur (1801–68), Ramgopal Ghose (1815–68), Brajmohan Majumdar (1784–1821), Chandrasekhar Deb (b. 1810), Pyarichand Mitra (1814–83), and Kisorichand Mitra (1822–73)—all of whom knew how to deal with shifting, grinding linguistic faultlines, English became the new Indian coin of exchange.

The images of Rammohan Ray that have survived come almost exclusively from his own writings and from contemporary English-language documents. English speakers, European as well as Bengali, kept the best records, or at any rate the only ones that have survived. Nuances of English vocabulary, grammar, and syntax locate Rammohan and his contemporaries in a specific culture in which they seem the co-ordinates on the surveyor's scope, the very sinew, flesh, and lineament of any account of early English in India. They indicate how hospitably the English language was received in its new home.

Kisorichand Mitra's memoir, 'Rammohan Roy', in the *Calcutta Review* (December 1845), candidly portrays Rammohan Ray from the viewpoint of restless, impatient Young Bengal, as an enigmatic figure in no hurry to make difficult decisions. Chandrasekhar Deb's English-language 'Reminiscences of Rammohan Roy', published in the Bengali-language *Tattvabodhini Patrika* (November–December 1872), records an offhand comment by Rammohan Ray to a fellow Bengali: 'The Hindus seem to have made greater progress in sacred learning than the Jews, at least when the Upanishads were written . . . If religion consists of the blessings of self-knowledge and of improved notions of God and his attributes and a system of morality holds a subordinate place, I certainly prefer the Vedas.' This is perhaps the single most revealing piece of information about Rammohan Ray, the man and his loyalties. More important, in the present context, this confession, spoken in Bengali, was recorded as an English excerpt within a Bengali newspaper. The audience dictated the medium and the message.

The English language caused a new era of communications in early-nineteenth-century Bengal. Rammohan Ray was fundamental to the birth of this era. Through English, he and his contemporaries discovered that they, Bengali Hindus and Muslims, had common cause with Irish Catholics, Scottish Presbyterians, and Spanish patriots—namely, representative government and religious tolerance. Spain's *Constitution Politica de la Monarquia Espanola* of 1812 was dedicated to 'Liberalismo del Noble, Sabio, y Virtuoso Brama Ram-Mohan Roy' in recognition of his world stature as a patron of international anti-monarchism. Jeremy Bentham acknowledged Rammohan Ray's membership in the exclusive nineteenth-century world club of champions of liberty like Jose Del Valle in Guatemala, Simon Bolivar in Colombia, and Maria da Gloria in Portugal.

Rammohan Ray was born in Radhanagar, Bengal, in 1772. His great-grandfather, Krishnachandra Bandyopadhyay, a Rarhi Kulin (noble) brahmin, claimed descent from Narottam Thakur, a follower of the fifteenth-century Bengali Vaishnava reformer Chaitanya. Among Kulin Brahmins—descendants of the six families of brahmins imported from Kanauj by Ballal Sen in the twelfth century—those from the Rarhi district of West Bengal were notorious in the nineteenth century for living off dowries by marrying several women. Kulinism was a synonym for polygamy and the dowry system, both of which Rammohan campaigned against. Krishnachandra received the Mughal title 'Raya Rayan' for service as a revenue official under the Nawab of Bengal during the reign of the Emperor Aurangzeb. The title was contracted into 'Ray' and replaced the family caste name, as was customary among Laukika (worldly) brahmins in Mughal service. Rammohan's grandfather, Brajabinod, a devout Vaishnava, served under two nawabs, and Rammohan's father, Ramakanta, carried on this family tradition. After the defeat of the last Mughal governor by the British in 1757, Ramakanta procured a zamindari under the Burdwan Raj family. Rammohan Ray was proud of his family's Mughal connections.

Tarini Devi, Rammohan's mother, was the second wife of Ramakanta. Very little is known of her family other than that they included distinguished Sakta priests (devotees of the goddess Sakti) from Chatra near the Danish settlement of Serampore. Judging by the title, Rammohan's maternal grandfather, Shyama Bhattacharya, was a Vaidika (scholarly) brahmin. Tarini Devi, being devout and a devoted mother, ensured that her son received instruction from Sakta swamis. One of the earliest and most lasting influences upon Rammohan was in fact a Sakta tantrik. Rammohan's mother was also responsible for his early instruction in Sanskrit. She instilled in her son a deep-rooted sensitivity to suffering, particularly among women.

While his mother pushed him in the direction of the religious scholar's life, Rammohan's father educated him in Arabic and Persian, the languages of commerce, in preparation for public administration. Both his parents, particularly his mother, strongly disapproved of his rejection of image worship. Rammohan attempted to escape a turbulent extended household by taking to the open road as a sanyasin, an itinerant mendicant, but his mother successfully discouraged this. Endless theological disputes with his father finally drove him from home. Only in the end was there an emotional reconciliation, at the bedside of his dying father. There would be no reconciliation with his mother, who attempted unsuccessfully to disinherit him on the grounds of apostasy. All the same, Rammohan resolved the tug-of-war between competing parental ideals by fulfilling both.

Overcoming his aversion to the British, he sought his fortune in Calcutta, the seat of British power, where through moneylending he came into contact with lower East India Company officials. In 1803 he became munshi (private secretary) of John Digby. Rammohan rose rapidly through the ranks to sarristadar (head clerk of court), soon becoming Digby's diwan (head assistant) in the revenue department. Digby became his close friend and confidant, and is an important source of information about Rammohan's early years:

> At the age of twenty-two he commenced the study of the English language, which not pursuing with application, he, five years afterwards, when I became acquainted with him, could merely speak it well enough to be understood upon the most common topics of discourse, but could not write it with any degree of correctness.

Digby continues:

> By pursuing all my public correspondence with diligence and attention, as well as by corresponding and conversing with European gentlemen, he acquired so correct a knowledge of the English language to be enabled to write and speak it with considerable accuracy. He was also in the constant habit of reading the English newspapers, of which the Continental politics chiefly interested him and from thence he formed a high admiration of the talents and prowess of the late ruler of France . . .

How much did Rammohan Ray depend upon English-speaking friends for help in his English compositions? Contemporaries like Kisorichand Mitra observed in the *Calcutta Review* that 'The truth is Rammohan Roy was exceedingly ambitious of literary fame.' The editor of *Gyananeshan* commented:

> We remember a conversation with him in which he mentioned his endeavours at the first commencement of his literary career to become a poet, 'but failing' he said 'to excel Bharut Caunder Roy, the author of *Unnadah Mongul*, in his poetical diction, in which I could

only equal him I turned my attention to prose writings and never ceased practising . . . [until] I effected that polish in my style to which I have arrived, though I had not a single writer before me to be guided by his example.' Emulation and a love of fame were very prominent features in the character of Rammohan Roy, and once moved by them he would never desist from his purpose. (*Bengal Harkaru*, 12 February 1834)

His closest friends were candid in their judgement of his fluency. J.C.C. Sutherland perhaps had the last word in 'Reminiscences of Rammohan Roy': 'Roy's spoken English was fluent though not the best of his Bengali contemporaries, and his composition, at his own urging, was frequently watched over by European friends, because he was very conscious of style and literary refinement' (*Literary Gazette*, February 1834).

Rammohan's training in Persian had gained him entry into the Bengal civil servants pool but the scholarly side nurtured by his mother showed itself with the publication, in 1803, of *Tuhfatu'l-Muwahhidin*. Composed in a curious mixture of Persian and Arabic, which was then the commercial dialect, *Tuhfat* s tirred up a cauldron of controversy by its attack upon religious leadership, particularly Brahmins.

While in Calcutta Rammohan continued his Sanskrit studies under several preceptors, settling down under the tutelage of Mrityunjay Vidyalankar, eminent Supreme Court pandit. From 1815 to 1823 he published Bengali-language subcommentaries on the commentaries of Shankaracharya on the *Kena, Isa, Katha, Mundaka*, and *Mandukya* Upanishads. He published simultaneous English-language versions of the first four. In 1819 he founded the Atmiya Sabha, a debating society, to provide a forum for the discussion of his own doctrines as well as of current political and social events.

This burst of literary activity established Rammohan as an exponent of the Vedanta school. The French Société Asiatique elected him to honorary membership in 1824. His Hindu pandit critics, however, branded him a Buddhist, a dangerous freethinker. In 1820, when Rammohan published *Precepts of Jesus*, the Serampore Baptist missionary Joshua Marshman denounced his rejection of the Doctrine of the Trinity as a new form of Deism. A widely publicised debate ensued in which Rammohan's four *Appeals to the Christian Public* (1820–3) were answered by Marshman's *A Defence of the Deity and Atonement of Jesus*

Christ in Reply to Rammohun Roy (1820). Rammohan Ray was now an international celebrity, praised by British and American Unitarians alike for his courageous agreement with them.

In 1823 controversy erupted once again. As founder and editor of two vernacular weekly newspapers, the Bengali *Sambad Kaumudi* and the Persian *Mir'at'l-Akhbar*, and as founding member of the English-language *Bengal Herald*, he orchestrated a public protest about the Governor-General's censorship of the press. In three memorials, the last an unprecedented open letter to King George IV, Rammohan argued that free speech and freedom of religion were natural rights every just ruler is obliged to protect. This marked a turning point in his life, away from religious polemic to championing social, educational, and political causes.

In 1822 he had founded his English-language medium, Western-curriculum-based Anglo-Hindu School. The next year he publicly protested the British government's proposal to make Sanskrit the medium of instruction in public schools. Rammohan's argument was that Sanskrit had never been the language of the masses and was, furthermore, a useless anachronism in the modern international world. Yet in 1826 he founded his own Vedanta College to train his growing band of followers—non-brahmin and brahmin—to read and teach Vedanta in Sanskrit.

The most controversial of Rammohan's public campaigns was his opposition to sati. His first tract against it had been published in 1818. *Sambad Kaumudi* regularly editorialised against sati, denouncing it as barbaric and un-Hindu. In his *Brief Remarks Regarding Modern Encroachments on the Ancient Rights of Females According to the Hindu Law of Inheritance* (1823) Ray argued that there had been a pattern in Bengal of crimes against women, in clear violation of ancient Hindu law. Governor-General Bentinck, largely (though not exclusively) instigated by Rammohan Ray, responded to the growing public outcry by outlawing sati in 1829.

The majority of the Hindu community of Calcutta was outraged. They viewed this as unconscionable foreign interference in their sacred, personal institutions. Rammohan had, of course, argued that sati was a modern corruption of sacred ancestral regulations. Unintimidated by his powerful personal political clout, the Hindu community, many of whom were ardent champions of reform, prepared to influence the British Parliament against such interference.

On the eve of his departure for England early in 1829, to counter his opponent's pro-sati petition, Rammohan founded the Brahmo Samaj. This was to carry on his work of reform from the defunct Atmiya Sabha, and to teach Vedanta as the purest expression of Vedic religion. He had other reasons for the trip to England, a country whose traditions he greatly admired: Akbar II, the King of Delhi, had appointed him special envoy to negotiate an increase in the royal purse. Rammohan had been granted the title 'Raja'.

Raja Rammohan Ray was the first high-caste brahmin to travel to England. Overseas travel was forbidden to brahmins, so in England he was a novelty. The *Times* wrote:

> We hail his arrival as a harbinger of those fruits which must result from the dissemination of European knowledge and literature, and of those sound principles of rule and government which it is the solemn obligation of Great Britain to extend to her vast and interesting empire in the East. We have in RMR an example of what we may expect from such an enlightened course of policy. (13 June 1831)

In England he successfully countered the pro-sati lobby. But after a brief trip to Paris, where he had a much-publicised audience with King Louis Philippe, he succumbed to what was probably a chronic respiratory ailment. He died on 27 September 1833, in the care of Unitarian friends in Bristol. He was reportedly buried, not cremated, in Arno's Vale Cemetery, where his old friend Dwarkanath Tagore later erected a cenotaph. In its obituary for him on 30 September 1833, the *Times* said: 'He wrote and spoke English with ease and accuracy and even elegance . . . but upon his whole demeanour there was a charm of modesty and reverence that produced the most agreeable effect on all who saw or conversed with him . . . A more remarkable man has not distinguished modern times.'

Rammohan Ray's use of the English language developed in three stages as he experimented with literary styles, grammatical refinements, and vocabulary. His focus changed from petition to polemic and finally exclusively to public instruction. English was for him not only the language of command but also that of documentation, of histories, of narrative, theological disputation, and personal reflection. Each of these genres is represented in his writings.

No one owns a language, Rammohan argued — not the Brahmins, not the English. All the evils of his society, he believed, could be traced to the Brahmin assumption that their interpretation of sacred literature, of the Sanatana Dharma, could be locked away in the Sanskrit language. He was adamant that the Vedic tradition, the only authentic foundation of modern Hindu society, be an open and generally available book. For this reason he tore down the 'dark curtain' of Sanskrit with translations of five Upanishads into Bengali and English.

Belonging to the first stage of Rammohan's English writings is his historic Bhagalpur letter (1809), parts of which are reproduced above. The second stage (1816–23) reflects a period of rancorous controversies. It begins with *Translation of an Abridgment of the Vedant* (1816), includes English versions of his *Kena* (1816), *Isa* (1816), *Katha* (1817), and *Mundaka* (1819) Upanishad expositions, *A Defence of Hindoo Theism* (1817), and *A Second Defence of the Monotheistical System of the Vedas* (1817). This period also includes his famous tracts against sati, *Translation of a Conference between an Advocate for, and an Opponent of the Practice of Widow Burning* (1818), *A Second Conference* (1820), *Brief Remarks regarding Modern Encroachments on the Ancient Rights of Females according to the Hindoo Law of Inheritance* (1822), and ends with the *Precepts* controversy (1820–3).

Rammohan had joined the Baptist missionary Bible translation team of William Adams and William Yates as their guide through the minefields of Bengali reference in the effort to produce an idiomatically and culturally correct version of the Bible. When he published his own edited version of the New Testament Gospels, *The Precepts of Jesus*, the Serampore missionaries parted company from him, denouncing him as a heathen and a Deist. Explaining the purpose of *The Precepts* in *The Second Appeal to the Christian Public*, Rammohan answered his pandit and missionary critics: 'The only reasons assigned by the Compiler . . . for separating the Precepts from abstruse doctrines and miraculous relations of the New Testament, are, that the former are liable to the doubts and disputes of Free-thinkers and Antichristians, and the latter are capable at best of carrying little weight with natives of this part of the globe, the fabricated tales handed down to them being of a more wonderful nature.'

With the exception of the *Translation of an Abridgment of the Vedant*, Rammohan's purpose was polemical. His English reflects growing confidence in his cause, which, in turn, inspired greater freedom to experiment with his expression. In *Second Defence* and even in *Second Appeal to the Christian Public* he formulated his arguments in the Hindu pandit siddhanta/purvapaksha style ('if it is said/then the reply is') of his Bengali versions, but he abandons this in the last two *Appeals* (1821–2). Instead he adopts a more English academic style—with chapter-verse citations and frequent direct quotations—that he learned from the theological writings of John Locke and other Unitarian writers.

In the English *Mundaka* Rammohan's vocabulary changes to reflect current English idiom. In the *Abridgment*, 'akasha' is translated 'void space', in the *Mundaka* it is 'vacuum'; 'anu' is 'small', now it is 'atom'; 'rishi' is 'sages', now it is 'saints'.

While the *Memorial to the Supreme Court* (1823) and the *Appeal to the King in Council* (1824) are petitions against restrictions on the Calcutta press, their hortatory style is similar to that of the *Appeals*, composed at the same time. In fact they share a common topic—religious tolerance. In *Memorial to the Supreme Court*, protesting against censorship of the Calcutta press, Rammohan demonstrated his adroit deployment of the language to touch the sensitive nerve: '. . . nor it is at all wonderful they [natives of India] should in loyalty be not at all inferior to British-born Subjects, since they feel assured of the possession of the same civil and religious liberty, which is enjoyed in England, without being subjected to such heavy taxation as presses upon the people there.'

Some of Rammohan Ray's most memorable lines are in his *Appeal to the King in Council*; for instance—'Divine Providence at last, in its abundant mercy, stirred up the English nation to break the yoke of those tyrants [Muslim kings], and to receive the oppressed Natives of Bengal under its protection.' However, in *Questions and Answers on the Judicial System of India* (1832), he praised Mughal governance for its overall fairness, and muftis (Muslim judges), in contrast to Hindu judges, for their integrity. Nine turbulent years filled with protest against British policies had taken their toll on him. Selective memories of his family's Mughal connection inspired second thoughts about Muslim rule.

After praising George IV in the *Appeal* for granting the natives of Bengal 'the same civil rights as every Briton enjoys in his native country', Rammohan writes, '. . . your Majesty is well aware, that a Free Press has never yet caused a revolution in any part of the world.' Freedom of the press, Rammohan argued, is a universal civil right. Without it there can be no religious tolerance: 'and although they [natives of Bengal] have every reason to hope that the English nation will never abandon that religious toleration which has distinguished their progress in the East, it is impossible to foresee to what purpose of religious oppression such a Law might at some future time be applied.'

Another polemic of the same period, *A Letter to Lord Amherst on Western Education* (1823), persuasively argues against public education in Sanskrit, the so-called private language of brahmins, in favour of a modern Western-style curriculum of study in English, a language that everyone can learn. Rammohan's notoriety grew when he supported the minority Anglicists against the majority, pro-government Orientalists in heated public controversy. Yet in 1826 he founded the Vedanta College to provide Sanskrit training to, among others, non-brahmins. Rammohan was the toast of London and Boston, but he was a scandal in Calcutta, the prophet without honour in his own country.

While public instruction was always Rammohan Ray's mission, only the third group of his writings most clearly serves this object. He was now at home in the English language. He was no longer composing his thoughts in Bengali and then translating them into English—he was, instead, thinking out issues in English. His confident literary style and fluency were now the subject of considerable favourable comment.

Characteristic of this period are writings such as *A Letter to Rev. Henry Ware on the Prospects of Christianity in India* (1824), *Universal Religion: Religious Instructions Founded on Sacred Authorities* (1829), *Exposition of the Practical Operation of the Judicial and Revenue Systems of India* (1832), *Answers of Rammohun Roy to the Queries on the Salt*

Monopoly (1832), *Settlement of India by Europeans* (1832), and of course the famous autobiographical letter published in the *Athenaeum* and the *Gentleman's Magazine* in 1832. The *Trust Deed of the Brahmo Samaj* (1829) was probably drawn up by lawyers.

Rammohan Ray was a voracious reader of the *Times*, the *Edinburgh Review*, missionary journals, and contemporary European literature. He modelled his expression on what he read, including the King James Version of the Bible, and the writings and speech of those he admired—John Digby, his long-time friend and employer; William Adam and William Yates, his Baptist friends; J.C.C. Sutherland and James Silk Buckingham, both newspaper editors in Calcutta; and Jeremy Bentham, John Locke, Horace H. Wilson, Henry T. Colebrooke, and Sir William Jones.

Rammohan Ray's letters to Lord Lansdowne and Prince Talleyrand mark the high point of his epistolary style. The first letter dated 20 June 1832 expresses the moral outrage of an equal, a titled gentleman:

> Rajah Rammohun Roy presents his compliments to the Marquis of Lansdowne, and feels very much obliged by his Lordship's informing him of the day (Saturday next) on which the argument on the Suttee question, is to be heard before the Privy Council.
>
> R.R. will not fail to be present there at 11 o'clock to witness personally the scene in which an English Gentleman (or Gentlemen) of highly liberal education professing Christianity is to pray for the re-establishment, of suicide, and in many instances actual murder.

The economy of language and use of irony show Rammohan's confidence both as campaigner and as writer of English. The Lansdowne letter was the opening statement of his campaign to be the first Member of Parliament for India. Bentham supported him.

The letter to the French Minister of Foreign Affairs, dated 20 December 1831, is more important for what he says than how he says it. Remonstrating in his old polemical style against the regulation requiring a passport for travel to France, Rammohan proposed a Congress of Nations to provide a forum for the airing of international disputes. He rejected the implication that hostility is the natural state of relations between nations. The *Arthasastra* had not yet been discovered: '. . .the ends of constitutional Government might be . . .

better attained by submitting every matter of political difference between two countries to a Congress composed of an equal number from the Parliament of each . . .' The Talleyrand letter reveals how international his outlook had become. In a sense, thus, Rammohan's ease with the idiom of the English language was his passport across all borders. And when the occasion suited him, hc spoke the language of command.

The private debate between Rabindranath Tagore and Mahatma Gandhi over Rammohan Ray's significance to modern India demonstrates that Rammohan continues to polarise Indians. Gandhi's ambivalence towards Rammohan—the reference to him as a pigmy among giants and later his reverence for Rammohan—comes in part from anachronistically superimposing upon Rammohan's various uses of the English language the highly charged linguistic field of twentieth-century Indian-English discourse. Languages, in Gandhi's view, were not only territorial but civilisational markers. Gandhi was not alone in assuming that any early-nineteenth-century Indian who could write English as well as Rammohan did must choose to be one of 'them' or one of 'us'. Rammohan's view, on the other hand, was that language is by its very nature ideologically, even culturally, neutral. This led him to use the language of the new colonial sarkar to define for everyone the new terms of governance. For Raja Rammohan Ray, 'vac' (speech) had indeed escaped the tyrannical gods of party, class, and politics.

Tagore, as the grandson and son of two of Rammohan Ray's closest friends, Dwarkanath and Debendranath, had access to Calcutta's multilingual oral traditions as well as to written family records about this personal family hero—a continuing legacy of nineteenth-century discourse sadly unavailable to Tagore's contemporaries, or us. Even the memoirs that Rammohan mentions keeping in England have disappeared. There are many missing pieces in the puzzle. Tagore dismissed the view held by Gandhi and others that Rammohan's language branded him as a Westerniser. For him, Rammohan was the archetypical poet-rishi, a sage courageously interpreting by precept and personal example the sacred ancestral religion, the Sanatana Dharma, for a bewildering new world which, for many of his contemporaries, gave new meaning to the concept of Kali Yuga (the Dark Age).

Rammohan too was troubled by the thought that he was a victim of his own success. He recognised that many groups would claim him for themselves. Bentham and his less known contemporary Robert Richards viewed him as the crowning glory of the onward march of the British mission to civilise the world. If we keep at it, Richards wrote in *India: or Facts Submitted to Illustrate the Character and Conditions of the Native Inhabitants* (1832), we will have a nation of Rammohan Rays. Bentham, quick to take credit where it was not due, wrote that Rammohan had learned the use of reason from him. Even in America, Rammohan was seen, in the opinion of Ralph Waldo Emerson, as a trophy in the Unitarian cause.

Rammohan Ray's intellectual, social, and literary legacy has, to a considerable extent, been allowed to be hijacked by nineteenth-century British reformers and American Unitarians. This seems regrettable. The incident at Bhagalpur, a defining event of Indian modernity, has been left on the cutting floor within constructions of India's transition from the languages of the old world to that of our own time.

2

The Hindu College

Henry Derozio and Michael Madhusudan Dutt

SAJNI KRIPALANI MUKHERJI

The British agenda for education in India was always very clear. The dissemination of Western education was to establish and perpetuate their own power. As early as 1775 Philip Francis, better known as the antagonist of Warren Hastings, had written in a letter to Lord North:

> If the English language could be introduced into the transaction of business . . . it would be attended with convenience and advantage to Government and no distress or disadvantage to the natives. To qualify themselves for employment, they would be obliged to study English instead of Persian. If schools were established in the districts . . . a few years would produce a set of young men qualified for business, whose example and success would spread, and graft the institution gradually into the manners of the people.

Missionary activity would serve the same end. Prior to the renewal of the East India Company's charter before the Imperial Legislature in 1793, Charles Grant was to define the direction and scope of this species of activity:

> It might be too sanguine to form into a wish an ideal most pleasing and desirable in itself, that our religion and our knowledge might be

diffused over other dark portions of the globe where nature has been more kind than other institutions. This is the noblest species of conquest, and wherever, we may venture to say, our principles and language are introduced, our commerce will follow.

An earlier Orientalist phase, when the British set up a madrassa for Muslims in 1781 in Calcutta and a Sanskrit College in Banaras in 1791, was not inimical to this central design. Overall, the process would help unlock knowledge vital to colonial interests. According to the influential historian Ranajit Guha in *An Indian Historiography of India* (1988), it was knowledge 'concerned with information about the volume and value of agricultural produce, the rules for appropriation of the producer's surplus by landlords and the state, the nature of land tenures and proprietary institutions, the technicalities of estate accounts and above all, the laws and traditions governing the relationship of peasants, landlords and the state.' The disjunction between British administration and the anachronistic continuance of Persian as the language for revenue transactions was brilliantly satirised by Bankimchandra Chattopadhyaya in *Muchiram Gurer Jibancharit* (1880). It seemed expedient for the British to transfer as much as possible of vernacular material into English.

English education was unavailable in Bengal at the start of the nineteenth century except through certain private and missionary establishments. Sherbourne's Academy, where Rammohan Ray had his early initiation into Western education, was one such. Another was Drummond's Academy, where the poet Henry Derozio had his. The Hindu College, which later became Presidency College, was set up in 1817, before the colonial agenda for anglicising education had been fully formalised. It was set up at the request of, and indeed with funding from, a group of Hindus at once élite and orthodox. Rammohan Ray was connected with the talks held in 1816 that led to its formation and would have been on its committee but for the objection from conservative rich Hindus: his views about Hinduism were too heretical and he had close associations with Muslims. Although Rammohan had in a sense initiated the proceedings in a dialogue with Sir Edward Hyde East and David Hare, he voluntarily withdrew so as not to jeopardise the setting up of this institution.

Sir Edward Hyde East was Chief Justice of the Calcutta Supreme Court between 1813 and 1822. His correspondence with the Right Hon'ble Earl of Buckinghamshire, recovered from the records of the Society for the Propagation of the Gospel in Foreign Parts, tells the story with not a little banter. The founders were reluctant even to accept a donation from Rammohan Ray, because they felt 'he has chosen to separate himself from us and to attack our religion' and also because they particularly disliked

> his associating himself with Mussalmen [*sic*] not with this or that Mussalman as his personal friend, but being continually surrounded by them and suspected to join in meals with them. In fact he has I believe nearly withdrawn himself from his brother Hindus whom he looks down upon, which wounds their pride. They would rather be reformed by anybody else than by him, but they are now very generally sensible that they want reformation; and it will be well to do this gradually and quickly under the auspices of government without its sensible interference in details.

The upper-caste group at the helm of affairs in Hindu College in its early years thus attempted to bring Western science, liberal thought, and English language and literature to their sons, but they were at the same time firmly resistant to all threat from cultures alien to their own. In the years to come this initial conflict was to rear its head repeatedly. The colonists and the native Hindu élite had drawn their separate boundary lines.

The growing complicity of the native élite with the colonial project was also very much in evidence. Quoting from the Hindu College records for 1824, Ranajit Guha gives examples of prize essays written in answer to the question: 'Has Europe or Asia benefited most by the discovery of the passage around the Cape of Good Hope to India?'

> Of all the nations of Europe . . . the English have derived the greatest advantage by this passage . . . On the other hand it must be acknowledged, that it has also, in some measure, contributed to the good of Asia, particularly in the countries under the British sway, for in the time of the Mahomedan tyrants, nothing but luxury and oppressions prevailed among the nobles: they had properly speaking,

> no fixed laws for the administration of justice. In fact, the Natives suffered the most mortifying proofs of their cruelties, until Providence, to avert the evil, brought them under the illustrious sway of the English, who not only freed this country from their hands, but have adopted all possible measures for its amelioration, introducing arts, sciences, schools, academies and colleges for the dissemination of knowledge.

Macaulay would formalise this agenda in 1835 and declare with a conqueror's self-confidence that 'a single shelf of a good European library was worth the whole Native literature of India and Arabia.' In 1855 the foreign administration would appropriate this early élitist native venture to turn it into Presidency College, which remains one of Calcutta's premier educational institutions.

A Eurasian of Portuguese origin, Henry Louis Vivian Derozio (1809–31) was educated at Drummond's Academy, where a dour Scotsman, an exile and 'notorious free thinker', initiated him into reading widely in literature and philosophy, the French Revolution and Robert Burns.

Amateur theatricals (for which Derozio wrote the prologues), cricket on the Maidan, and public speaking seem to have been the other preoccupations of this attractive young man, who was to become a symbol of the early phase of the Anglo-Indian educational encounter. When he left Drummond's, after having been its star pupil, he worked for a while for his father and then moved to Bhagalpur to work for an uncle, who was an indigo planter. He had already written some poetry by this time.

The brilliance of his teaching as well as his unorthodox teaching methods have made Derozio something of a legend in the annals of Hindu College. He has also been an enigma of sorts to successive generations of academics, most recently to those in the process of rethinking English studies in postcolonial India. What happened in Hindu College between 1826, when Derozio was appointed to Hindu College, and 1831, when he was compelled to resign? Did his excursions into literature, philosophy, and free thought with his 'tribe of Ben' herald an Indian Renaissance or was it just a flash in the pan?

Which is more important—his identity as one of the earliest writers of Indian literature in English or his identity as an iconoclast? Did he, in any long-term sense, corrupt the many young Hindu students who were drawn into his magnetic field or was the whole episode a storm in a teacup? Why did the missionaries, the orthodox Hindu founders of the college, and the colonial establishment all perceive him as a threat?

Derozio appears to have made his students read a wide variety of texts, from Homer's *Iliad* to Thomas Paine's *The Rights of Man*. Through an Academic Association which he set up, he encouraged free discussion and debate on ideas that had worked—such as dynamite in Europe. From his contemporary Sibnath Sastri's piquant account of those heady days we learn that extra-mural discussions continued long after college hours. Somewhere along the line the students picked up from their mentor the habit of eating what were for them forbidden foods such as pork and beef, and drinking 'tumblers of beer', actions which continue until today to be part of the rites of passage into adulthood. Hindu College boys adopted two precepts. The first: 'He who will not reason is a bigot, he who cannot reason is a fool, and he who does not reason is a slave.' The second: 'Cast off your prejudices, and be free in your thought and actions. Break down everything old and rear in its stead what is new.'

Inevitably, the practices of the Hindu religion came in for some trenchant criticism, some of which may have been from youthful fervour and the desire to bend the stick in the opposite direction. There was great alarm in the orthodox community on account of the actual infringements of the allowable behaviour pattern, and the publicity that these were being given. Derozio was soon identified as 'the root of all evil', especially when 'the junior students caught from the senior students the infection of ridiculing the Hindu religion and where they were required to utter mantras and prayers they repeated lines from the *Iliad*.' A poor brahmin called Brindaban Ghosal, by all accounts an unreliable witness, spread the scandal that the Hindu College lads were all becoming atheists. Having lit the fire, he then stoked it with even wilder allegations. Indeed the terms in which Derozio was asked to 'show cause' are couched by Horace H. Wilson, Visitor to the college, in an uneasy mix of the serious and the frivolous: 'Do you believe in God? Do you think respect and obedience to parents no part of moral duty? Do you think the intermarriage of brothers and sisters innocent and allowable? Have you ever maintained these doctrines in the hearing of your scholars?'

Derozio countered these questions easily enough, but they did not result in his reinstatement. The radical ideas from 'the devil's school of Tom Paine' which he introduced into the minds of his students would have lost much of their potency in the colonial ambience. The Hindu monolith was also in no real danger from a handful of college students. The missionary establishment benefited to some extent from his dismissal as some of his followers, who found themselves outside the pale, converted to Christianity under the influence of Alexander Duff. One wonders if the real reason for Derozio's dismissal was a touch of homophobia in the college's governing body on account of the exclusive male discussion groups over which he presided in his Entally home. A subtext along these lines might be identified from his biographer Elliot Walter Madge's regret that this somewhat flamboyantly dressed young teacher never appeared to show much personal interest in women, though he was vociferous about female emancipation. The women in his poems are a little wooden and lacking in individuality.

In the months that remained to him he continued to edit and write for journals. According to F.B. Bradley-Birt, although he felt deeply 'the manner of his leaving his work in the Hindu College, there was some compensation in the greater freedom his independence gave him.' Members of his 'tribe of Ben' continued to be close to him. There are several moving accounts of their tender care of him in his last days, after he had contracted cholera, though they differ on whether or not he reconverted to Christianity on his deathbed. There are interesting accounts of what happened to some of the representatives of Young Bengal in later years. A more recent analysis demonstrates some of the inherent complexities which prevent them from being viewed by posterity as a homogeneous progressive group. Senior members of the Eurasian community commented approvingly on the talents, the perfect honesty, and the unfettered views of Derozio in his new capacity as editor of *The East Indian*, their daily newspaper, which he edited in his last days. In a report on Doverton College written just before his death, Derozio made a strong appeal to his fellow Eurasians to integrate themselves with native Indians rather than identify with the European colonists: 'They will find after all, that it is in their interest to unite and be cooperative with the other native inhabitants of India. Any other course will subject them to greater opposition than they have at present. Can they afford to make any more enemies?' During the period he also contributed extensively to *The India Gazette, The Calcutta Literary Gazette, The Indian Magazine, The Calcutta Magazine, The Bengal Journal, The Enquirer*, and *The Hesperus.*

In Eng Lit terms Derozio might be said to be on a cusp between the Romantics and the Victorians. He was born the same year as Tennyson and Darwin but died in 1831, only a few years after Byron and several years before the Reform Bill. His poems have a light lyrical touch and the influence of the younger Romantics can be seen everywhere in his work—in its sensuousness, its detailed natural observation, its patriotic fervour. He is everywhere a creative reader in his poems, in which Homer, Tasso, Hafiz, Byron, and Moore are all grist to his mill. Western and Indian mythology mingle easily in his poems but the setting is always determinedly Indian and painted in vivid colours. He is to be seen at his best in his shorter lyrics. In the long title poem of *The Fakeer of Jungheera: A Metrical Tale and Other Poems* (1828), the narrative is swamped by rich description replete with the sights, sounds, and fragrances of the region around Bhagalpur where he spent a short period while working for his uncle before he joined Hindu College. In his own words: 'It struck me as a place where achievements in love and war might well take place and the double character I had heard of the Fakeer together with some acquaintance with the scenery induced me to form a tale upon both these circumstances.'

Like Keats's 'The Eve of St. Agnes', this poem is long on indices and short on narrative function. The central tale of a sati who is rescued by a former lover now turned 'fakeer' is a melancholic one. Nuleeni, in spite of the rescue, is soon to become a widow again when her lover is killed in the battle that ensues.

Indeed a Byronic melancholy appears to be the keynote of many of his poems. One obvious reason for this is the subjugated state of his homeland. Thus 'The Harp of India' mourns this fact in strains very similar to Moore's 'The Harp of Erin'. In 'The Golden Vase' the note of patriotism in fact becomes a little overpowering:

Oh! when our country writhes in galling chains,
When her proud masters scourge her like a dog;
If her wild cry be borne upon the gale,
Our bosoms to the melancholy sound
Should swell, and we should rush to her relief,
Like some, at an unhappy parent's wail!
And when we know the flash of patriot swords
Is unto spirits longing to be free,
Like Hope's returning light; we should not pause
Till every tyrant dread our feet, or till we find
Graves, which may truly say thus much for us—
Here sleep the brave who loved their country well!
The Moslem is come down to spoil the land
Which every god hath blest. For such a soil,
So rich, so clad with beauty, who would not
Unlock his veins, and pour their treasure forth?
The Hindoo hath marched forward to repel
The lawless plunderer of his holy shrines,
The savage rude disturber of his peace . . .

This reads like something of a fundamentalist Hindu manifesto: but perhaps one ought not to deconstruct the words of this youthful bard too closely. Derozio's strength lies in his shorter poems, like the moving sonnet 'To the Students of the Hindu College':

Expanding like the petals of young flowers,
    I watch the gentle opening of your minds,
And the sweet loosening of the spell that binds
    Your intellectual energies and powers,
That stretch (like young birds in soft summer hours)
    Their wings to try their strength. O! how the winds
Of circumstance, and freshening April showers
    Of early knowledge, and unnumbered kinds

Of new perceptions shed their influence;
    And how you worship truth's omnipotence!
What joyance rains upon me, when I see
    Fame in the mirror of futurity,
Weaving the chaplets you have yet to gain,
    And then I feel I have not lived in vain.

Now and then he appears to shed these solemn tones and write a merry playful verse. A little poem to his sister written when she asked him to get married belongs to this category. The 'Don Juanics' modelled on his favourite Byron are in a delightful comic-satiric vein:

    E'en hearing scandal is a cruel way
Of killing time—some ladies think not so—
    With them 'tis 'chit-chat, rumour, trifling play'—
O'er cups of tea they'll tell a tale of woe,
    Defaming others, and then smiling say,
'O dear! indeed 'tis what all people know;'—
    So tea by folks aspersed is called, in wrath,
By a most fitting title—'Scandal broth!'

('Don Juanics', xlviii)

It is not easy to say what kind of poetry Derozio would have written had he not died so young. The extant verses are often derivative, but we glimpse through them a lively and sensitive mind.

Michael Madhusudan Dutt (1824–73) entered Hindu College in 1833 in the junior department and received a prize there for a recitation from Shakespeare. However, he had to leave the college in 1843 when, despite strong opposition from his father, he embraced Christianity. After briefly attending Bishop's College, Calcutta, he moved to Madras, where he studied Greek, Latin, and Hebrew. In marked contrast to Derozio, he seems at first to have been something of an Anglophile. He wrote exclusively in English in his early writing years. *The Captive Ladie* was published in 1849 and like Derozio's 'The Fakeer of Jungheera' this is a long narrative poem in which it is difficult to sustain one's interest. In *The Anglo-Saxon and the Hindu* (1854), an essay in florid, even purple, prose which has references to and quotations from almost the whole of Macaulay's shelf of European books, the belief in the civilising mission of the Anglo-Saxon in India appears to have reached its apotheosis:

> What wonder then that the Hindu should be what he is? The furious waves of fanaticism, of oppression, have swept over his hapless soul for a thousand years! From the day that the blood-thirsty wolf of Ghiznee bounded across the stupendous rocky barriers of the west desolating her homes, flinging to the dust her idol-gods from their glorious temples, leading her sons and daughters captive, ill-fated Hindustan has been the prey of the invader, the sport of the ambitious and the rapacious Zenobia—chained, not to the chariot of a single conqueror but to those of a hundred, to grace their triumphs!

As against this, the Anglo-Saxon and his glorious language are extolled:

> I have heard would-be Quinctilians talk disparagingly of this magnificent language as irregular, as anomalous. I disdain such petty cavilers! It laughs at the limit which the tyrant Grammar would set to it—it nobly spurns the thought of being circumscribed. It flows on like a glorious broad river, and in its royal mood, it does not despise the tribute waters which a thousand streams bring to it. Why should it? There is no one to say to it—thus far shalt thou go and no farther! Give me, I say, the beautiful language of the Anglo-Saxon. It is the glorious mission, I repeat, of the Anglo-Saxon to renovate, to regenerate, or—in one word to Christianise the Hindu.

There are forty-six references at the end of the piece of which perhaps only five are Indian. The rest include Herodotus, Virgil, Homer, the Bible, Shakespeare, Milton, Cowper, Petrarch, Byron, Horace, and sundry other authors that even Macaulay would not have imagined in a single text.

The plays in English such as *Razia, Empress of Inde* (1858), and *Sermista* (1859), which are translations from the Bengali, employ an idiom which belongs to no period in English literature that one can think of. The following is from *Sermista*:

> *Nati*: Ha! ha! Well answered, thou divine sage! Your bee then takes to its wings at the sight of flowering beauty! Ha! ha! Come, let us go and see whither his Majesty is gone to.
>
> *Vidushaka*: Thou, beautiful, art as the magnet and I—a poor bit of doating iron! O, I long to cling to thee! (*Taking her hand*) Lo! the gods have concealed the ruby cup of their most delicious nectar in thy lips. Prithee, make me immortal with a kiss!

His letters in English, written mainly to his old schoolfriend Gour Dass Bysack, make far more interesting reading and are full of a vigour and humour lacking in his other English writings. One notices in them the eagerness with which he devoured the European classics, the rigorous schedule for learning languages which he set himself, and the strongly creative response he brought to these enterprises. The educationist J.E.D. Bethune had suggested to Bysack that Madhusudan

> might employ his time to better advantage than in writing English poetry. As an occasional exercise and proof of his proficiency in the language, such specimens may be allowed. But he could render far greater service to his country and have a better chance of achieving a lasting reputation for himself, if he will employ the taste and talents, which he has cultivated by the study of English, in improving the standard and adding to the stock of the poems of his own language, if poetry, at all events, he must write.

Madhusudan's letter to Bysack shows his response to this advice: 'Here is my routine; 6 to 8 Hebrew, 8 to 12 school, 12 to 2 Greek, 2 to 5 Telegu and Sanskrit, 5 to 7 Latin, 7 to 10 English . . . Am I not preparing for the great object of embellishing the tongue of my fathers?'

The excitement of the new project is reflected in the Bengali sonnet 'Bangabhasa', in which he discovers the many gems and possibilities of his native tongue. This poem is still mandatory reading for every Bengali schoolchild.

In many ways, then, Madhusudan departed from the agenda laid down by the native élite, and by missionaries and administrators. The rootlessness of the early Derozians had given way to an awesome sense of location which is reflected in most of Dutt's subsequent writing. In

Ekei Ki Bole Sabhyata (1860), a farce, he delightfully satirises élite Bengali gentlemen for whom the discussion on female education in their Gyanataringini Sabha is merely an excuse for debauched living. This play, along with *Buro Shaliker Ghare Raon* (1860) and Dinabandhu Mitra's *Sadhabar Ekadashi* (1866), take the debate on education to a new discursive plane. In 1869 Madhusudan also translated into English Mitra's now famous *Niladarpan* (1860), which was about the inhuman exploitation of workers on indigo plantations.

From now on Madhusudan's major literary efforts would all be in Bengali. Experimentation was to find new and varied focus: in verse forms, in re-reading the old myths, in extending the vocabulary by coining new words, by making existing words more elastic. A somewhat static language was forced to accommodate all these changes. His greater work is *Meghanadavadha Kavya* (1861). It is a creative reader's response to the *Ramayana.* Epic devices borrowed from the great European epics, via Milton (whom he loved above all other writers), find their way into this exciting epic poem. The focus of the work has shifted from Rama, the legendary hero, to Meghnad and Ravana in the rival camp. 'I hate Rama and all his rabble!' he had written in a letter to Rajnarayan Bose. The episodes are selectively expanded to read the *Ramayana* against the grain. He subverts the hegemony of Rama in this pioneering effort to write a secondary epic on the models of Milton and Tasso. Does this express the need to hear the voice of the subjugated or the conquered people? The women characters, such as Pramila, the wife of Meghnad, are given much greater space. Madhusudan drops the grand style to accommodate the changing registers of her speech: she addresses her companions in one, Rama in a second, and Meghnad in a third. This is done with an ease that is missing from his plays in English.

The incorporation of English literary studies into the classroom curriculum of colonial Calcutta had not merely resulted in the 'deposition of Western values into the soul of the educated', as Macaulay had decreed, but had released a new understanding of location after these values were internalised and blended with traditional ones.

The earliest writers of Indian literature in English might seem to us quaint and derivative. One need not, however, view them with historical concessions and condescension. They were the products of a renewal and a rethinking, if not quite a rebirth. Agendas were set up. Some were achieved, some modified, others frustrated. This is the important point about the Hindu College experience.

3
The Dutt Family Album:
And Toru Dutt

Rosinka Chaudhuri

In an essay which remains one of the most vivid and extraordinary testaments to the influences on the colonial mind educated in English in nineteenth-century India, Michael Madhusudan Dutt (1824–73) says:

> I acknowledge to you, and I need not blush to do so—that I love the language of the Anglo-Saxon. Yes—I *love* the language—the glorious language of the Anglo-Saxon. My imagination visions forth before me the language of the Anglo-Saxon in all its radiant beauty; and I feel silenced and abashed.
>
> I have heard the pastoral pipe of the Mantuan Swain . . . I have listened to the melodies of gay Flaccus . . . I have heard of bloody Pharsalia, and learned to love Epicurus . . . I am no stranger to the eloquence of fiery Demosthenes . . . of calm Cicero . . . to Livy . . . to sententious Thucydides . . . I have heard the melodious voice of him who sang . . . of Rama like a Kokila; I have wept over the fatal war of the implacable Courava and the heroic Pandava; I have grieved over the suffering of her who wore and lost the fatal ring; I have wandered with Hafiz on the banks of Rocknabad and the rose-bowers of Mosellay; I have moralized with Saddi, and seen Roustom shedding tears . . . but give me the literature, the language of the Anglo-Saxon! Banish Peto, banish Bardolph, banish Poins; but for sweet Jack Falstaff, kind Jack

> Falstaff, banish him not thy Harry's company; banish plump Jack and banish all the world! I say, give me the language, the beautiful language of the Anglo-Saxon! (*The Anglo-Saxon and the Hindu*, 1854)

The passage is a remarkable indication of the type of literary mind—submerged in classical Graeco-Roman, canonical English, and Orientalist-generated Indian classical traditions—that came into existence in Calcutta by the mid-nineteenth century. Its irony is that it was part of the last independent piece Madhusudan composed in the English language. The subsequent historic shift which Madhusudan made from English to Bengali was symbolic of the changes taking place in Bengal. The latter half of the century witnessed the birth of nationalism—in so much as nationalism signified a pride in and awareness of indigenous culture and tradition. The intellectual and well-to-do middle class in Calcutta, which had spoken English in preference to Bengali, and had found its cultural standards and modes of behaviour in the literature and manners of the West, now turned, with Bankimchandra Chattopadhyaya and Ishwarchandra Vidyasagar, towards the Bengali language and a Bengali identity instead.

Literary Bengali was accepted as a vehicle of expression for general subjects by the time the *Dutt Family Album* (1870) was published from London: yet its status was low enough for Bankimchandra to remark in 1872, in the introductory article of the first issue of his magazine *Bangadarshan*: 'There is one outstanding barrier to the writing of Bengali by educated Bengalis. Educated people do not read Bengali; and what educated people will not read educated people do not wish to write.' Bankimchandra himself had written his first novel, *Rajmohan's Wife* (1864), in English. When he suggested that the eminent historian and translator Romesh Chunder Dutt, a nephew of the Dutts who wrote the *Dutt Family Album*, should contribute in Bengali to *Bangadarshan*, Dutt exclaimed: 'Write in Bengali! But I hardly know the Bengali literary style.' 'Style!' rejoined Bankim, 'Whatever a cultured man like you will write will be style. If you have the gift in you, style will come of itself.' His biographer records this as 'a memorable episode in the life of Mr Dutt, for from that day he turned to Bengali literature.' The English poetry produced by the Dutts—Romesh Chunder himself, his cousin Toru, her father Govin, their uncles Hur and Greece [*sic*], and cousin Omesh—has to be examined considering the atmosphere that prevailed in Calcutta. The low status of Bengali might initially have led to the use of English for poetry, but the idealism over the use of the mother tongue that became progressively widespread made the English verse of the Dutts subsequently seem increasingly out of place.

Towards the end of the eighteenth century Nilmoni Dutt, the original patriarch from whom the Dutt poets descended, was a respected and wealthy figure in Rambagan, Calcutta. His eldest son, Rasomoy Dutt—secretary of the managing committees of both the Hindu College and the Sanskrit College, and a judge of the Small Cause Court in Calcutta—was the father of Govin (1828–84), Hur (1831–1901), and Greece (1833–92) Chunder Dutt, who, along with their nephew Omesh Chunder Dutt (1836–1912), brought out this compilation of verse titled the *Dutt Family Album* in 1870.*

Rasomoy's sons, along with their cousin Shoshee Chunder Dutt (1824–86), converted to Christianity after the death of their father. Their wives, in the words of a contemporary observer, W.S. Mackay, while 'willing to remain with their husbands', remained 'still firm idolaters'. Among the consequences of the women remaining Hindu, the most interesting must be the use of Hindu mythology in her poems by Toru Dutt—the source of her inspiration is said to be her mother, who, according to Edmund Gosse, 'fed her imagination with the old songs and legends of their people, stories which it was the last labour of her life to weave into English verse.' The social and political effects of this conversion were not underestimated by Mackay. 'If the whole family are baptised together', he wrote, 'you may suppose what an excitement it will produce; for, take them all in all, they are the most distinguished Hindoo family under British rule.'

The earliest poetical publication by any member of this family of Dutts was Shoshee Chunder Dutt's *Miscellaneous Verses* from Calcutta in 1848. His brother, Ishan Chunder Dutt, lesser known, also published some verse in *Essays and Poems* (1872). Shoshee Chunder's career as

*Their names have been reproduced here as spelt by them, in anglicised versions of their Hindu names, indicative as that was of their position with regard to the conventional Bengali middle class.

a poet included a volume called *Stray Leaves: or Essays, Poems and Tales* (1864) and *A Vision of Sumeru and Other Poems* (1878). These, however, were far outnumbered by various works of prose, mainly published from London. Among them were *Bengaliana: A Dish of Rice and Curry, and Other Indigestible Ingredients* (1877/8), a collection of journalism and fictional pieces, *The Wild Tribes of India* (1882), *Bengal: An Account of the Country from the Earliest Times* (1884), and *The Great Wars of India* (1884). A publication entitled *Realities of Indian Life* (1885) explained its contents in its quasi-anthropological subtitle: 'Or, Stories Collected from the Criminal Reports of India, to Illustrate the Life, Manners, and Customs of its People'. Shoshee Chunder's treatment of subjects like the Indian tribes is best embodied in the lines from *Othello* that he used as an epigraph in *The Wild Tribes of India*: 'Wherein of antres vast and deserts idle, / . . . It was my hint to speak; . . . / And of the Cannibals that each other eat, / The Anthropophagi, and men whose heads / Do grow beneath their shoulders.' Paradoxically, yet fairly typically for a colonial writer who thus seems to identify with the vantage point of the coloniser in relation to the indigenous races, he also uses the coloniser's values to eulogise freedom from subjugation. In his concluding remarks on the character of the tribal people he asserts: 'The hatred of tyranny which drove their ancestors to their present retreats survives yet in them, the one redeeming feature in their character being the utter abhorrence of thraldom and despotism.' Finally, six thick, handsomely bound volumes gathered many of these individual scholarly works together under the title *The Works of Shoshee Chunder Dutt: Historical and Miscellaneous* (1884–5).

An interesting aside to Shoshee Chunder's career as man of letters is his adoption, at different times, of two separate English pseudonyms. In the first instance, the title page of the two-volume *Historical Studies and Recreations* (1879) states that it was 'Originally published by the author under the *nom de plume* of J.A.G. Barton'; in the second, a three-volume novel called *The Young Zemindar* (1883), as well as *The Wild Tribes of India*, under the fantastic pen-name Horatio Bickerstaffe Rowney.

The unique narrative that unfolds in the title poem of Shoshee Chunder Dutt's major poetical work, *A Vision of Sumeru*, shows the defeat of the Hindu gods—Brahma, Vishnu, Saraswati, Kali, Narayan—by the precepts of Jesus; the only true faith on earth is His, and the old gods are powerless. A considerable part of this volume, however, was taken up with individual pieces incorporating historical and legendary themes, and included poems such as 'Sivajee', 'The Requiem of Timour', and 'Jelaludeen Khiliji'. These poems, like the historical poems in the *Dutt Family Album*, retold romantic incidents and battles from the medieval history of India in English metrical forms. Some other poems in this collection exhibited an abstract nationalism, common in English poetry by Indians in the nineteenth century, that contrasted India's 'glorious past' with its present degeneration.

Among the sons of Rasomoy Dutt, Hur Chunder published two volumes of verse, both from Calcutta: *Fugitive Pieces* (1851) and *Lotus Leaves, Or Poems Chiefly on Ancient Indian Subjects* (1871). He was also a regular contributor to the *Bengal Magazine*. His brother, Greece Chunder Dutt, published his first volume of poems, *Cherry Stones* (1881), from Calcutta; and his second book, *Cherry Blossoms* (1887), simultaneously from Calcutta and London. Greece Chunder also produced a commemorative book of verse called *The Loyal Hours: Poems Welcoming the Prince of Wales and the Duke of Edinburgh on their Advent to India in 1869 and 1875* (1876), a volume that gives us a fairly comprehensive idea of the political and social position occupied by this family in nineteenth-century Calcutta. A poem in the *Album*, 'To Lord Canning, During the Mutiny', also pointedly reaffirms the sentiments of the upper classes the Dutts belonged to. In it the poet pays tribute to the 'noble' role played by Lord Canning after the Mutiny:

> Though a thousand pens condemned thee, mine still should write
>   thy praise;
> Though a thousand tongues reviled thee, mine still should paeans raise;
> For factious clamours heeding not, that only call for blood,
> True to thy duty and thy race, Lord Canning, thou hast stood.
>
> It is not for her trampled flag that England bares her sword;
> It is not for a just revenge upon a murderous horde;
> It is to prove to blood-stained men, self-blinded of their sight,
> That evil hath no chance with good or darkness with the light.

Indians, depicted here as a 'murderous horde', are not only 'blood-stained men, self-blinded of their sight', but also incarnations of 'evil' and 'darkness'. It is the British who are, ultimately, the force of 'good' and 'light' against which the 'evil' Indian, sunk in darkness, 'hath no chance.' Lord Canning, Governor-General of India during the Mutiny of 1857, apostrophised here for having acted 'True to thy duty and thy race', played an important part in the work of reconstruction and reconciliation after the reoccupation of rebel strongholds in Delhi, Lucknow, Kanpur, and Peshawar, convincing Indians that his mission was conciliation, not vengeance. This poem embodies the response of élite Bengalis to the Mutiny, underlining allegiances and loyalties that would have been increasingly looked down upon with the rise of nationalism in India.

The *Dutt Family Album* consists of an assortment of poems—lyrics, ballads, translations from French and German poetry, and, most frequently, sonnets, of which there are sixty-eight on varying subjects. The authorship of individual pieces remains a mystery, the poems having been arranged without any acknowledgement, sequence, or order. Of the *Dutt Family Album* Theodore Dunn remarked that it would remain 'as a memorial of a gifted family, and as a testimony to the influence of those English teachers who were the first to encourage the [*sic*] higher learning in the city of Calcutta.' The love of—indeed the dependence upon—reading reflected in these poems came also from a tradition of an enthusiastic study of English literature in the Hindu College established early by teacher-poets such as Derozio and later D.L. Richardson, the latter's students numbering among them Michael Madhusudan and Govin Chunder Dutt, who were classmates. Rajnarain Basu, a fellow student and later a well-known Bengali educationist and man of letters, wrote of his Hindu College days with reference to Govin Chunder: 'While in college we used to read English poetry so avidly that it would be better to say we devoured it, such was our eagerness. He (Govin) was, in this matter, of the same mind as I was. We used to read poetry by the most obscure English poets, both ancient and modern' (*Atmacharit*, 1909, my translation).

This love for both obscure and canonical English poetry was a part not only of Govin Chunder's sensibility but of every contributor to the *Album*. A poem which articulated that love is 'A Farewell to Romance':

The varied melody of Shakespeare's shell—
The Doric flute of Milton, or the reed
Of 'sage and serious' Spenser ever dear,
In breathless silence heard so oft before
By thee and me, (thou did'st confess the spell;)
Or what less deep, of late, thou loved'st to hear
These strains of Scott that stir the soul indeed.

Another poem, 'On an Old Romaunt', uses Tennyson's 'Locksley Hall' metre to contain the combined elements of fantasy and exoticism derived from textual sources:

Moorish forts in far Granada, portals barred and turbans blue,
Gardens green as blissful Eden, crystal fountains fair to view,
Divans in the proud Alhambra, fairy mosques of Parian stone,
Groups of Moors and whiskered Spaniards, tilting round the Soldan's throne.

Here, aptly enough, in a poem about reading, 'curious volumes' that contain a past entirely constituted of European medieval history are described, invoking Normans and Venetians, Spaniards and Moors. It is difficult to fix the identity of the poet here as anything other than European or English, because no detail, either in the description of the act of reading or in the images which that reading evokes in the poet's mind, gives away his Indianness. This characteristic of the Dutts, of writing in a Western persona, preoccupied with 'larks . . . shrilling overhead' or 'meek snowdrops, couriers of auspicious spring', church bells tolling, or 'merry elves in laughing groups', was also evident in their poems on Christian piety.

Frequently, the poems in the *Album* are modelled in the form of Romantic and Victorian poetry, sometimes with lines from an English poet included within quotation marks. Two poems in the *Album*, 'Wordsworth's Poems' and 'Wordsworth', are dedicated to William Wordsworth: the latter poem, perhaps unconsciously, captures acutely the dilemma of the colonial poet:

There are some faces I have never seen
Which haunt my spirit like a music-strain;
There are some places where I've been
Which stand minutely pictured on my brain.

These sentiments are also a reworking of Romantic themes that Wordsworth, for example, had addressed in 'Yarrow Unvisited', while Keatsian echoes might be discerned in lines such as 'I see Rebecca by the fountain's side / Meek Ruth amid the reapers walking slow' ('Sonnet') or 'Who, on the "viewless wings of poesy", / Have poured—ah, not in vain—a mighty tide of song' ('Sonnet').

The tone in which critics have dealt with the poetry produced by the Dutt family has generally been dismissive. The Dutts were writing in an age when the greatest respect was reserved for men like Bankimchandra, who were propagating Bengali. But even earlier, by the time of Madhusudan in the middle of the century, it had become unprofitable to be an Indian writing in English. As late as 1970, John B. Alfonso-Karkala, in *Indo-English Literature in the Nineteenth Century*, described the *Album* as 'typical of the earlier school of Indo-English poetry when poets were not daring enough to experiment with European metrical forms.' Nevertheless he concludes that 'it cannot be denied that they gained a certain fluency in writing verse according to English rhythm and pattern.' Such a summary is merely an amalgamation of the opinions of the two main critics of nineteenth-century Indian poetry in English, Lotika Basu and T.O.D. Dunn. 'The verses', Basu says in *Indian Writers of English Verse* (1933), 'are close imitations of Scott and Byron. . . . They are imitative and superficial and treat the subjects from a Western point of view . . . [They are] typical of the earlier school . . . whilst showing a certain command over the English language and its metrical forms.' Basu treats these poems ahistorically, as if they were accessible to an automatic comparison with lines written by Byron or Walter Scott. Consequently, terms such as 'imitative' and 'superficial' overlook the complexity of the poems in relation to the colonial contexts. These poems, and their aesthetic value or lack of it, exist meaningfully only within their historical context. Theodore Dunn was more accurate, in fact, about the value of the *Dutt Family Album* when he said the book 'must be of abiding interest to the student of literary history in India.'

A significant number of poems in the *Album* are historical. These poems ('The Death of Mohammed Ghori', 'Jehangire's Lament', 'The Flight of Humaoon', 'Tara Baee'), based on subjects taken from medieval Indian history, are narrative verse tales in the style of Scott's ballads. In most instances, the poems borrow their content from

British histories of particular peoples—from, among others, James Grant Duff's *History of the Mahrattas* (1826), James Tod's *Annals and Antiquities of Rajasthan* (1829–32), and William Erskine's *A History of India* (1854). The romantic quality in the historical verse of the Dutts is evident from the manner in which a typical poem of this sort invokes Scott, complete with the poetic idiom so characteristic of poems such as 'Marmion' and 'Lay of the Last Minstrel'. 'Samarsi', for example, echoes the form and style of 'Lochinvar', as can be seen if their opening stanzas are compared. 'Lochinvar' begins:

> O, young Lochinvar is come out of the west,
> Through all the wide Border his steed was the best;
> And save his good broadsword he weapons had none,
> He rode all unarm'd, and he rode all alone.
> So faithful in love, and so dauntless in war
> There never was a knight like the young Lochinvar.

'Samarsi' begins:

> Samarsi the bold is the pride of his clan,
> But he owns not an acre in broad Rajasthan;
> Samarsi the bold is the hope of the true,
> But his sporran is empty, his henchmen are few,
> For the Moors o'er the Jumna in triumph have come,
> And Samarsi the bold is an exile from home.

This similarity apart, the use in 'Samarsi' of the word 'sporran', defined in the *OED* as 'A pouch or large purse made of skin . . . worn in front of the kilt by Scottish Highlanders', shows conclusively the derivation of the Dutts' idiom from Scott. Walter Scott's intense concern for, and his knowledge of, the Scottish people, their history, culture, and tradition, is mutated in the poems by the Dutts to an effect of alienation or distance, created as a result of the conflict between Scottish idiom and Indian themes. This sort of poetry, born largely out of reading, has a textbook air and typifies the colonial dilemma of being stranded between two worlds.

The preoccupation of the Dutts with the history of India is in keeping with much of the writing in Bengal in the latter half of the nineteenth century. One of the contributors to the *Album*, Hur

Chunder Dutt, in the preface to *Lotus Leaves*, explains it thus: 'We have many histories of India from school-histories up to elaborate treatises, but no work embodying Indian historical incidents and characters and older traditions in a poetical form. Yet India is truly the land of romance and poetry. . .'.

The volume was dedicated to his children, who were '[so] fond of reading the history of India.' Indicating the interest cultivated among Indians in their own newly written history, the historical poems in the *Album* suggest the values imparted by colonial education, for historiography had been practically unknown to Hindus at the beginning of the century. In a famous essay, Bankimchandra had at the time allied the concepts of nationalism and history in a most emphatic manner, asking 'Why is India a subject country?' and answering, '[Because] there is no Hindu history. Who will praise our noble qualities if we do not praise them ourselves?'

Such patriotic fervour found an echo in Hur Chunder Dutt's 'Sonnet: India':

O yes! I love thee with a boundless love,
Land of my birth; and while I lisp thy name,
Burns in my soul 'an Aetna of pure flame'
Which none can quench nor aught on earth remove.
Back from the shrouded past, as with a spell,
Thy days of glory memory recalls,
And castles rise, and towers, and flanking walls,
And soldiers live, for thee dear land who fell;
But as from dreams of bliss men wake to mourn,
So mourn I when that vision is no more,
And in poor lays thy widowed fate deplore,
Thy trophies gone, thy beauteous laurels torn,
But Time shall yet be mocked;—though these decay,
I see broad streaks of a still brighter day.

The Romantic trope of dreaming and waking from a vision, as in Keats's 'Ode to a Nightingale', is rewritten here in nationalist terms. Bearing a striking resemblance to Derozio's 'Harp of India', this sonnet forces itself through the *Album*'s aura of anglicisation and succeeds in forcefully presenting the unrecognised nationalism the Dutts had harboured in their historical poetry. While the affinity with 'Harp of India'—where too past glories are evoked and present miseries mourned, and India's rejuvenation desired—might point towards an unbroken line in the tradition of such nationalist poetry, it is worth remembering that the social and historical realities on which such identical sentiments are based had changed beyond recognition. The poems, in fact, appeared in two different periods, one at a time of abstract idealism regarding India's ancient past—this enveloped the educated Indian and Englishman alike—and the other at the time of widening post-Mutiny rift when Bengalis began increasingly to assert their own identity in spheres ranging from literature and culture to politics.

The frequent sense of alienation in the Dutts' historical poetry—present largely because they write in English—hides the relationship their poems share with an entire corpus of similar poetry in the Bengali language. Their historical poetry is situated very firmly in the cultural milieu of Bengal in the latter half of the nineteenth century. Bengali poets like Rangalal Banerjee (*Padmini Upakhyan*, 1858), Michael Madhusudan Dutt (*Meghanadavadha Kavya*, 1861), Hemchandra Mukherjee (*Birabahu Kavya*, 1862–6), and Nabinchandra Sen (*Palasir Yuddha*, 1875) began the 'renaissance' in Bengali literature with writings that borrowed their form and style from the English poets, and their heroic subject matter from some of the same sources the Dutts had used. These beginnings formed the genesis of an entire tradition of Bengali verse which was to culminate in Tagore's frequently anthologised historical poems such as 'Horikhela' and 'Ponrokkha'.

The Dutts produced two generations of writers of English verse, the second generation consisting of Romesh Chunder Dutt (1848–1909), and his cousin Toru Dutt (1856–77), who was the daughter of Govin Chunder. With the first generation there came to an end an era during which poets writing in English were schooled entirely in Calcutta, not having left the country till after the publication of their verse. On the other hand, R.C. Dutt was educated at University College, London, while his cousins Toru and Aru lived extensively in France and in Cambridge, where they were privately educated. The publication of

English poetry written in India had by then shifted its centre from Calcutta to London. Derozio's and Kasiprasad Ghosh's poems, for instance, had been published from Calcutta, while Toru Dutt and her cousin R.C. Dutt published their books from both Calcutta and London.

In the last two decades of the nineteenth century Hinduism had sprung into intellectual prominence amongst the educated classes of Indians, a state of mind that owed a great deal also to the revival of Sanskrit studies, led by F. Max Müller, whose mission it was to resuscitate the attitude towards Indian culture which had been adopted earlier in the century by the Calcutta Orientalists. From his platform of authority at Oxford, Max Müller spoke enthusiastically of 'our Aryan brother', of the debt of the Western world to the East, and of 'the spiritual relationship which now binds India and England together'. It is fitting, therefore, that Max Müller provided the introduction to R.C. Dutt's *The Ramayana and the Mahabharata: The Great Epics of Ancient India* (1900). The epics had earlier been published as separate volumes in the Temple Classics series, Dutt being the first Indian to render them, in condensed form, into English verse. Some of his other translations are to be found in *Lays of Ancient India* (1894) and *Indian Poetry* (1905).

R.C. Dutt explained in an epilogue that in translating the *Ramayana* and the *Mahabharata* he had condensed, in the case of the former, 24,000 shlokas into 2000 English couplets. Selected passages or cantos which told the leading incidents of the epics were linked together by short notes. The greatest difficulty he faced, however, was how to preserve the 'musical movement' of the Sanskrit in English. To that end he experimented with various English metres which could approximate the sixteen-syllable line that constituted the shloka metre, choosing, finally, the familiar English metre of Tennyson's *Locksley Hall*, which most nearly approached 'the rhythm, the majesty, and the long and measured sweep of the Sanskrit verse', as he demonstrates in a comparison:

Esha Kuntisutah sriman/esha madhyama Pandavah
Esha putro Mahendrasya/Kurunam esha rakshita

(*Mahabharata, i. 5357*)

Yet I doubt not through the ages/one increasing purpose runs
And the thoughts of men are widened/with the process of the suns.

(*Locksley Hall*)

This easiest of Sanskrit metres, the shloka afforded the ancient poets 'a fatal facility', R.C. Dutt complained, weakening many passages with endless repetition. Yet Dutt himself, in his translations, often fared no better than the lesser passages he spoke of. As a reviewer in the columns of *India* complained, the translator had used 'common jingling metres, and more often than not has found it difficult to reach the end of his stanza without false accents, awkwardly transposed phrases, or weak, jarring rhymes.'

In presenting these translations of the classical literature of India, R.C. Dutt was conscious of his role and place in Orientalist scholarship. This is evident from the preface to *Epics and Lays of Ancient India* (1903), where he traces the tradition of Orientalist scholars from Sir William Jones and H.H. Wilson to Max Müller and Edwin Arnold, concluding: 'I shall consider my labours amply rewarded if the present volume can take humble place by the side of Wilson's *Theatre of the Hindus.*'

This long tradition of Orientalist verse, from which R.C. Dutt claims descent, did not however manage to contain the other second-generation Dutt poet, Toru. Arguably the first modern Indian poet in English, she brought the personal and cultural dimensions of her experience into her writing. Her fame today rests largely upon a handful of lyric poems that appeared in the posthumously published *Ancient Ballads and Legends of Hindustan* (1882).

Toru's early years were spent in Calcutta in the 'city house' in Rambagan or at the Dutt's country residence at Baugmaree. After the death of her fourteen-year-old brother, Abju, in 1865, Govin Chunder Dutt decided, in 1869, to take his wife and daughters to Europe, where they remained for four years till the end of 1873. Interestingly, they were the first Bengali women to visit Europe. Aru and Toru Dutt, for a while, went to school in Nice, subsequently attending the Higher Lectures for Women at Cambridge. Soon after their arrival in London, Govin Chunder recalls a conversation—one among 'a hundred that come crowding to my memory':

> *Lord L.* 'What book is that you have in hand?' *Aru.* 'One of Miss Mulock's novels, *John Halifax*.' *Lord L.* 'Ah! you should not read novels too much, you should read histories.' No answer from Aru, Toru answering for her sister. 'We like to read novels.' *Lord L.* 'Why?' *Toru* (smiling). 'Because novels are true, and histories are false.'

Worth recounting for what it tells us of the unique quality of Toru Dutt's mind and her gentle subversiveness in the context of polite social interaction, this incident was one among many such that took place during their stay in London, where they met the city's gentry, went to Drury Lane theatres, and conversed about their intellectual pursuits and literary inclinations.

Toru's first publication, *A Sheaf Glean'd in French Fields* (1876), consisting of translations of seventy French poets (including Hugo, Gautier, Baudelaire, Leconte de Lisle, Nerval, Sainte-Beuve), brought her to the attention of Edmund Gosse, who recalled the day in August 1876 when he happened to be at the office of the *Examiner* newspaper:

> At that moment the postman brought in a thin and sallow packet with a wonderful Indian postmark on it, and containing a most unattractive orange pamphlet of verse, printed at Bhowanipore, and entitled 'A Sheaf Gleaned in French Fields', by Toru Dutt. . . . [W]hat was my surprise and almost rapture to open at such verse as this:
>
> Still barred thy doors! The far east glows,
> The morning wind blows fresh and free.
> Should not the hour that wakes the rose
> Awaken also thee?
> All look for thee, Love, Light, and Song,
> Light in the sky deep red above,
> Song, in the lark of pinions strong,
> And in my heart, true Love.
>
> When poetry is as good as this it does not much matter whether Rouveyre prints it upon Whatman paper, or whether it steals to light in blurred type from some press in Bhowanipore.

The verse picked by Gosse had in fact been translated by Aru.

However, it was Toru who translated most of the 173 poems in the book, and her translations are also the more striking:

Ha! There's the sea-gull. See it springs,
Pearls scattering from its tawny wings,
Then plunges in the gulfs once more,
'Tis lost in caverns of the main!
No! No! It upward soars again,
As souls from trials upward soar.

('Lines: Victor Hugo')

The most interesting part of *Sheaf* was the Notes appended at the end of the volume, more 'astonishing than anything in the text', thought E.J. Thompson. These Notes were critical comments on the French poetry translated in the volume, and were largely written by Toru. Gosse found the Notes 'curious' and 'bewildering', as 'nothing could be more naïve than the writer's ignorance at some points, or more startling than her learning at others.' What Thompson admired in them, on the other hand, was the 'independence and masculinity' of her criticism. 'I remember speaking to Dr Brajendranath Seal of these Notes and the way they found me; and he told me they had made the same impression on him when he first read them. If for the Notes alone, the *Sheaf* merits republication.'

Shortly after her return home, when she was eighteen, Toru published her first essays, including one on Derozio in the *Bengal Magazine* (December 1874). In the years that remained to her, she brought out *A Sheaf* and also worked hard at learning Sanskrit, writing at the same time the poems on Hindu mythology that her father would eventually collect and publish after her death. A few months before it, she had read and admired the French writer Clarisse Bader's *La Femme dans l'Inde Antique* (Women in Ancient India), and asked to translate it into English. A correspondence ensued, and it was in the middle of that correspondence, after a last letter to Clarisse on 30 July, that Toru Dutt died on 30 August 1877, in her father's house in Manicktollah Street, Calcutta, at the age of twenty-one years and six months.

After her death Govin Chunder went through her papers with a view to publishing any material there of literary interest. He found a selection of English translations of the sonnets of Comte de Grammont, a sketch for an unfinished romance, *Bianca, or The Young Spanish Maiden*, a complete French novel, *Le Journal de Mademoiselle d'Arvers*, and the poems which would eventually be her 'chief legacy to posterity', *Ancient Ballads*. The fragment, *Bianca*, was eventually published serially in *Bengal Magazine* (January to April 1878), while the French novel, edited with the help of Clarisse Bader, appeared in 1879 to much critical acclaim.

The poems collected in *Ancient Ballads*, despite their Victorian idiom, were not just accomplished; 'Sonnet—Baugmaree' and 'Our Casuarina Tree' were better than anything written up till then by an Indian in the English language. 'Baugmaree', which takes its name from the place where the Dutt country house was located, is a celebration of trees:

A sea of foliage girds our garden round,
    But not a sea of dull unvaried green,
    Sharp contrasts of all colours here are seen;
The light-green graceful tamarinds abound
Amid the mangoe clumps of green profound,
    And palms arise, like pillars gray, between;
    And o'er the quiet pools the seemuls lean,
Red,—red, and startling like a trumpet's sound.
But nothing can be lovelier than the ranges
    Of bamboos to the eastward, when the moon
Looks through their gaps, and the white lotus changes
    Into a cup of silver. One might swoon
        Drunken with beauty then, or gaze and gaze
        On a primeval Eden, in amaze.

In the use of imagery, as in the description of the seemul's colour as 'Red,—red, and startling like a trumpet's sound', an affinity might be traced between Toru and her contemporary Emily Dickinson (whom, of course, she could not have read). The litany of the names of trees to be found in the Bengal landscape—tamarinds, mangoes, palms, seemuls—is prescient, for the modern reader, of similar lists in the 'Rupasi Bangla' series of poems by Bengal's great lyric poet Jibanananda Das.

The bulk of *Ancient Ballads*, however, is formed by poems such as 'Savitri', 'Sindhu', 'Prehlad', and 'Sita', which are based in Indian mythology. Initially, these were conceived in the tradition of 'genuine' translations from the original Sanskrit in the manner of her cousin R.C. Dutt and the Orientalists who preceded him; the first two poems in the series, 'The Legend of Dhruva' and 'The Royal Ascetic and the Hind', were translations from the *Vishnu Purana*, and first published in the *Bengal Magazine* (October 1876) and *Calcutta Review* (January 1877) respectively. A series of nine poems had apparently been planned, but only seven were found, the gap being filled by reprinting the two translations from the *Vishnu Purana*. The poems, however, ultimately took shape in a style different from that of her Orientalist predecessors. 'Sita' draws upon a childhood memory of three siblings listening to a mother's song:

> Three happy children in a darkened room!
> What do they gaze on with wide open eyes?
> A dense, dense forest, where no sunbeam pries,
> And in its centre a cleared spot.—There bloom
> Gigantic flowers on creepers that embrace
> Tall trees; there, in a quiet lucid lake
> The white swans glide . . .
>
> . . . .
>
> But who is this fair lady? Not in vain
> She weeps,—for lo! at every tear she sheds
> Tears from three pairs of young eyes fall amain,
> And bowed in sorrow are the three young heads.
> It is an old, old, story, and the lay
> Which has evoked Sita from the past
> Is by a mother sung. . . .

The poem is lent poignancy by the fact that of the three children, Toru's brother Abju and her sister Aru, were no longer alive at the time it was written. The poem is also one of the earliest instances of the effective use of memory in Indian poetry in English.

A glance at Toru Dutt's use of language is enough to show the difference between her style and that of her predecessors. The poems her father and uncles wrote, and before them Derozio, Kasiprasad

Ghosh, and Michael Madhusudan, all belong to a recognisable school of nineteenth-century poetry. Toru Dutt's poetry transcends that school, evolving a separate identity. The difference lies in the manner in which her language addresses her experience, her vision radiating beyond the boundaries within which most of the nineteenth-century poetry in English was confined. Her awareness of her own 'Indianness' is not restricted to Indian historical themes and the reworking of Indian legends. The mythological content of her poems does not exist extrinsically, but is integrated with her consciousness, her memory. In her poetry we confront for the first time a language that is crafted out of the vicissitudes of an individual life and a sensibility that belongs to modern India.

4
Rudyard Kipling

MARIA COUTO

Controversial yet popular, complex but accessible, the evaluation of Rudyard Kipling eludes consensus. His response to India, which in the early phase of his career was that of an unmitigated coloniser, was later modified into a deeper understanding and appreciation of a country he came to regard as his only home. His childhood, the seedbed of his imagination, was spent in India. It nurtured contradictions in a sensibility which identified with the cause of Empire and led to an artistic response as complex as the complexity of India. Kipling chronicled what has been described by V.S. Naipaul as the brief, serene decade of British India, and was able to penetrate the heart of the Anglo-Indian's dilemma in the vivid cameos of his short stories. These, taken together, create a complete society with accuracy and humour. The stories outrage and enchant the Indian reader who finds his own responses to Kipling as ambiguous and shot through with torn loyalties as were Kipling's to India.

Rudyard Kipling (1865–1936) was born in Bombay where his father, J. Lockwood Kipling, taught at the Jeejeebhoy School of Art. Later the family moved to Lahore where Lockwood Kipling was appointed Principal of the Mayo School of Art and also Curator of the Central Museum. Kipling's parents were temperamentally poles apart: Lockwood, a kind, gentle, and wise artist, the prototype of the sensitive and enlightened curator in *Kim*; the mother independent, well connected, ambitious, and unsentimental.

Kipling's earliest recorded impressions are of Bombay, which he called 'Mother of Cities'. Cossetted by ayahs and indulgent men servants, he thought and dreamed in Hindustani and had to be reminded to talk to his parents in English. In his perceptive study, *The Strange Ride of Rudyard Kipling* (1977), Angus Wilson traces the elusive magic which lies at the heart of Kipling's best work to the intense absorption of the child and his immersion in the hazards and delights of his Indian upbringing. However, in 1871, when not quite six years old, he was cruelly uprooted and flung into what he afterwards described as 'The House of Desolation', experiencing there years of 'calculated torture—religious as well as scientific'.

As was the practice at the time, Kipling and his sister were sent off to be educated in England, and put in the care of Mrs Holloway and her husband, a retired naval officer, who had advertised their willingness to look after children of English families in India. Although his parents appeared cold and remote in the Victorian manner, they were loving and his home was later to be the bedrock and main sustenance for Kipling the young writer. Yet they were curiously insensitive in the matter of the rude disruption of their son's idyllic Indian days. Kipling never came to terms with the manner in which he and his sister were left behind in Southsea without forewarning of the separation, which made the experience acquire the desolation of abandonment. The parents departed without any explanation, not even saying goodbye, turning their backs on the children for five years. The appalling subterfuge with which the whole exercise was conducted left Kipling bereft, his pain assuaged only by the memory of lost freedom and a world of gentleness and affection in Bombay. The early story 'Baa, Baa Black Sheep' memorably expresses the desolation endured and the lingering bitterness.

Unable to afford university education, which would have led to a career in the civil service, Kipling resorted to joining the United Services College which trained boys destined for military service in the Empire. Although these were good years and formed the basis of *Stalky and Co.* (1899), he was something of a misfit, bad at games and debarred from joining the army because of defective eyesight. As a budding writer with literary ambitions among regimental hopefuls, he developed a constant wariness, observant of moods and tempers, with a certain reserve in his conduct, noting discrepancies between speech and action—qualities which would sustain the precocious and youthful journalist, not quite pukka enough to belong to the sahib caste.

Kipling returned to India in 1882 and left in 1889. He was never to visit it again, except once in 1891. The narrative voice in his writing reveals a divided sensibility, nurtured by five years of bliss in Bombay and seven years of grind in Lahore and Allahabad, where he worked for the *Civil and Military Gazette* and the *Pioneer*, producing these papers almost single-handedly, doing much of the writing himself. The experience immeasurably broadened his knowledge of India and Indian life. An enlightened editor encouraged him to write features and the artist emerged. Some of these stories, later included in *Plain Tales from the Hills* (1888), were the product of a tireless curiosity, of nocturnal wanderings in the streets and bazaars of Lahore, and eavesdropping at the Punjab Club where the professionals talked shop. Although underage, he became a Freemason: 'Here I met Muslims, Hindus, Sikhs, members of the Arya and Brahmo Samaj, and a Jew tyler, who was priest and butcher to his little community in the city. So yet another world opened to me which I needed', he wrote in *Something of Myself* (1937).

When Kipling arrived in England, aged twenty-five, with *Plain Tales from the Hills* published, he was already famous. Well known through his journalism, he was now a much-sought-after figure, the toast of literary London, from which, nevertheless, he kept his distance. Afterwards, however, his tremendous creative energy began to be seen as 'a debauch of production', and his verse perceived as too clever and shallow, 'like smart journalism or . . . a business paper'. The Nobel Prize (1907) notwithstanding, he moved less in literary than in establishment circles, yet refused all national honours.

The loss of his beloved daughter Josephine, and later of his only son in the Great War, his disillusionment in South Africa, and in Vermont where he had tried to make a home after India, marked the reclusive peace he found in Bateman's in his later years. His wife, Carrie, whom he married after a youthful unrequited love, was a resourceful and courageous woman who sustained him yet has been described as 'a ferocious old battleaxe', a virulent anti-feminist to whom her husband was entirely subservient. They were married after the death of her brother, Wolcott Balestier, an American publisher's agent, who was Kipling's literary collaborator and the object of his deep love. Kipling's was a troubled sexuality. He died in 1936, his final years plagued by ill health, constant pain, and a loneliness that seems to have haunted him ever since his childhood in India.

T.S. Eliot began the revival of Kipling's reputation with an introduction to *A Choice of Kipling's Verse* (1941), in which he famously makes the distinction between poetry and verse. He analyses Kipling as a great verse writer who achieves the depth and intensity of great poetry in ballads such as 'Danny Deever' and 'Recessional'. Eliot perceived Kipling's deep love for India beneath his paradoxical, imperialist stance, and called him 'the first citizen of India'. Although Kipling has remained an institution in English letters, a little apart from the great central strand, and continues to be read with pleasure by the young, adult readers today approach his work with a sympathy for his insights: these have endured after the passing away, as he predicted, of the imperialism he condoned. The publication of Edward Said's *Orientalism* (1978) created a renewed interest in writers such as Joseph Conrad and Kipling, in whose work the fragility and wreckage of empire were central. It is Kipling's insights, arising from an enduring bond with India, that redeem the tarnished image of the jingoist. Kipling's best work was written after he left India. The distance from a beloved scene created the necessary detachment and space for reflection which produced what is arguably his finest collection of short stories, *Life's Handicap* (1891), and his most successful novel *Kim* (1901), which Angus Wilson has described as the culmination and essence of all the transcendence that Kipling gained from his Indian experience.

In Kipling's early work, *Plain Tales from the Hills* (1888), *In Black and White* (1888), and *Soldiers Three* (1889), the impulse to justify the Empire impinges on the integrity of the artist. The early Kipling, as an observant young reporter, learned quickly the limits of his freedom to outrage, and filled his newspaper columns with amusing accounts of the club to which his readers belonged. The Simla stories in *Plain Tales* illustrate the frivolous side of the Raj in this little England to which the rulers retreated in the summer. Life was made up of garden parties, rifle matches, and dances, with the attendant scandal and intrigue, male ambition being fanned and promoted by feminine wiles. Women in Kipling are perilous companions, often destructive, though useful when socially powerful, such as Mrs Hauksbee, who is the centre of Simla social life. However, recent critical work points to Kipling's sympathy for lonely regimental wives and young widows whose sacrifice is seldom acknowledged. (This sympathy does not extend to Indian women.) Although he writes about life in the hill station with a knowingness which members of the civil service found irritating, the confidence of his tone belies the fact that he was excluded from the club by education and profession.

These early stories justify the Empire, mythicise the ordeals and courage of the rulers, and accord them heroic status. Even 'The Bridge Builders', one of his finest stories—in which a mature Kipling juxtaposes the world of science and the intractable might of nature and destiny—is not free from bravado and jingoism. Kipling's idealisation of an administration burdened by work in India, regardless of the plight of the ruled and their feelings, often fails by its fixed perspective and predictable narrative line and tone, with its overlay of racial and moral superiority. His work has played a defining role in binding racial and cultural identities, in tales which, far from being plain, reinforce the colour line with political overtones which still prevail.

'His Chance in Life' illustrates a startling racism. It is a heartless endorsement of the received view of the native as child, incapable of effort without direction from the white man. Michele D'Cruze, an Eurasian telegraph signaller, finds the opportunity he needs to win the hand of the girl he loves when he has to contain 'a little Mohurrum riot'. The duty, if well handled, would mean a promotion. The story projects Michele as a spineless man who finds the nerve to take responsibility when he is addressed a 'sahib' by the native police inspector, only to revert to stereotypical behaviour when the white sahib returns: '. . . in the presence of this young Englishman, Michele felt himself slipping back and more into the native . . . It was the White drop in Michele's veins dying out, thought he did not know it.' The assertion of racial stereotype is the sting in the tale.

Kipling's distrust of the Bengali, and indeed of the educated Indian, is evident in 'The Head of the District'. Following on the liberal policies of the British Prime Minister Gladstone, and Lord Ripon, the Viceroy, Indians were appointed to the civil service. In 'The Head of the District', Girish Chunder De, due to take charge of a turbulent border district, flees for his life at the sign of trouble, grateful to his gods that 'he had not taken charge of the district and could still—happy resource of a fertile race! fall sick.' Kipling's descriptive prose serves him with equal energy both to evoke the harshness of life and terrain which hardens the cultivators, salt miners, and cattle-breeders of the district, and to express his undiluted scorn for the emerging Indian middle classes.

From his earliest days in school, Kipling admired authority, discipline, fortitude, and self-sacrifice. His writing is a paean to work, but excludes the bureaucrat at his desk from this ideal. Kipling's kinship with peasant and landscape could not countenance the remoteness of the civil service in which is lacking the bond that exists, for instance, between Find-layson, the engineer in 'The Bridge Builders', and Peroo, the works overseer. Indeed Find-layson is the ideal: the man in the field who believes that 'they are the real pivots on which the Administration turns'. He commends their devotion to the cause: 'Sickness does not matter, because it's all in the day's work, and if you die, another man takes over your place and your office in the eight hours between death and burial.' Peroo is a Kharva from Bulsar, who, weary with seafaring, has moved inland. He is a skilled intermediary between Find-layson, who plans the exact specifications of the bridge, and the labourers who toil at the construction site. He is also equal to the work at hand: 'There was no one like Peroo, serang, to lash and guy and hold, to control the donkey-engines, to hoist a fallen locomotive craftily out of the borrow-pit into which it had tumbled; to strip and dive, if need be, to see how the concrete blocks round the piers stood the scouring of Mother Gunga, or to adventure up-stream on a monsoon night and report on the state of the embankment-facings.' The story describes with vivid precision the invincible, overpowering character and energy of the river pitted against the clanging might of steel and iron, the sullen torrents of darkly swirling water, the turmoil of those trapped in this primordial battle: 'Again the big gong beat, and a second time there was a rushing of naked feet on earth and ringing iron; the clatter of tools ceased. In the silence, men heard the dry yawn of water crawling over thirsty sand.'

Kipling was not an ideologue but a product of his time, an imperialist who propagated the myth of 'the white man's burden' and whose work perpetuated racial stereotypes in the popular imagination. Yet in the fable 'The Man Who Would be King' Kipling reveals an honest comprehension of the exploitative realities of Empire: 'avarice, the thirst for personal glory, the satisfactions of feeding on the homage of dependent people.' In 'The Tomb of the Ancestors' the reality of nineteenth-century India is expressed through the story of the Chinn family who, for many generations, served among the Bhils in Central India. The story does not fudge the relationship between the rulers and the ruled. It reveals Kipling's sense of the human connection and the personal dimensions of peasant life, born, abys André Maurois has emphasised, from Kipling's connection 'with the oldest, deepest layers of human consciousness'.

The emotional ties of childhood were deepened by Kipling's undisputed familiarity with the landscape and district administration of the Raj and a feel for the people and their problems. His work as a journalist enabled him to observe the British administrative machinery from close quarters, to sup with the rulers but live on the fringes of the Civil Lines. From this tension was born the creative impulse which Salman Rushdie describes as a conflict between Ruddy baba, the bazaar boy, and Kipling sahib. Indeed it has often been said that the protagonist of his stories is not the administrator, nor the men from the barracks, but India itself. In his best work, such as 'Without Benefit of Clergy', 'The Miracle of Purun Bhagat', and *Kim*, the artist gives free play to his instinctive bond with the country and its people, although early stories such as 'The Story of Muhammad Din', 'On the City Wall', and 'Lispeth' also illustrate the accomplishment of a writer who could with brevity and pictorial clarity evoke the realities of life and death.

The struggle between what Eliot has called 'the two strata of Kipling's appreciation of India, the stratum of the child and that of the young man', is constant. 'On the City Wall' is a fine example of the unsuspecting ways in which India comes out the winner, although the main narrative line extols the benefits of Empire which draw the great Afghan rebel warrior, Wali Dad, voluntarily back to prison. Kipling's descriptions of the courtesan Lalun's room and her conversation and wiles, the religious procession and riots, the scurrying down side-gullies and alleys, illustrate his intimacy with location and people.

'On the City Wall' gives Indians a voice in an idiolect which does not entirely satisfy, though the literal translation of the metaphors, the expression of sentiment, and the construction of sentences have an authentic ring. Kipling's rendering of the speech of men from the ranks in *Soldiers Three* and *Barrack-Room Ballads* (1892) patronises his characters. George Orwell, who condemned Kipling as a mindless imperialist whose writing is 'morally insensitive and aesthetically disgusting', demonstrates how the writing improves with decockneyfication. Yet it must be remembered that Kipling's work reveals a sympathy for the plight of the empire's foot-soldiers whose uniforms are 'starvation cheap' and who 'guard you as you sleep'. His bitter satire of the hypocrisy of those who cling to status and class does not exclude Queen Victoria:

> Walk wide o' the Widow of Windsor,
> For 'alf o' creation she owns:
> We 'ave bought 'er the same with the sword an' the flame,
> An' we've salted it down with our bones.
>
> ('The Widow of Windsor')

Although he sympathises in the main only with white men in uniform, *Ballads* illustrates Kipling's familiarity with the Indian scene, such as his description of beasts of burden in 'Oonts', whose subject is the camel. The best known is 'Gunga Din', about the bhisti or water-carrier, attached to regiments, who silently performs his duty with compassionate devotion to the fighting tommies:

> An' for all 'is dirty 'ide
> 'E was white, clear white inside . . .
>
> Tho' I've belted you an' flayed you,
> By the livin' Gawd that made you, Gunga Din!
> You're a better man than I am, Gunga Din!

Nirad C. Chaudhuri describes *Kim* as 'the finest novel in the English language with an Indian theme, but also one of the greatest English novels in spite of the theme'. Kipling's evocation of Indian people's habits, language, and distinctive ways of thought has led to recent critical debate on *Kim* as the apogee of the kind of Orientalism which suggests that the Englishman could meet the Orient on its own terms and outwit it. The best-realised characters are Indian, with Kim as one of them, a fact which is used to illustrate the point that Kipling not only wrote about India but belonged to India. Yet the novel is not free from stereotypes. The Oriental lack of a sense of time, 'the happy Asiatic disorder', and the Oriental's disregard for noise and his ability to lie, are instances of it.

Kipling has disparagingly dismissed his most accomplished work as 'nakedly plotless and picaresque'. *Kim* is the story of a quest undertaken by Kimball O'Hara, the son of an Irish soldier, now an orphaned street urchin in Lahore, travelling with his companion, Teshoo Lama, a holy man from Tibet. Sunburnt and unrecognisable as white, Kim, who is nicknamed 'Little Friend of all the world', plays with bazaar boys on equal terms, prefers to speak an Indian language, and is not always comprehensible in his mother-tongue. Familiar exclamations, Hindustani words, and Kim's English, which he speaks with a vernacular rhythm, convey Kipling's sensitivity to the nuances of Indian speech, and the sense of lived life. In *Something of Myself* he would write of the need to use language in ways that 'every word should tell, carry, weigh, taste and if need be smell'.

The lama, a follower of the Middle Way, seeks a river that will wash away sins, and Kim is looking for 'a Red Bull on a green field', which is the regimental crest of the Mavericks, his father's regiment. Their quest reveals an important theme of the novel—the superiority of the active life over the contemplative. In their first encounter the lama's unworldliness captivates Kim, and he initiates the guru–chela, master and pupil relationship by begging on behalf of the holy man. Their meandering journey encompasses the religions, cultures, seasons, and landscapes of large sections of the country along the Grand Trunk Road and beyond. The vivid prose and flavour characteristic of Kipling's best short stories flourish in the wider scope of descriptions of the Grand Trunk Road, 'the backbone of all Hind'.

The Grand Trunk Road, teeming with vitality and a life of varied exuberance, entrances Kim. His irrepressible excitement at 'the broad smiling river of life' is far removed from the indifference of the lama, who is impervious to the flow of a world he wishes to renounce. Yet the lama's worldview engages Kim in a relationship of mutual dependence; the spirited, worldly-wise youth defers to the sage who is in turn guided by Kim: 'Child, I have lived on the strength as an old tree lives on the lime of an old wall.' The growth of this bond, and Kim's initiation into a life of action through the mediation of the otherworldly lama, is revealed through a narrative which involves Kim in high adventure, escapades, and espionage, underpinning which is Kipling's search for synthesis.

Kim is a predominantly male novel with women as a distant presence drawn in to serve the purpose of a male world—for example to nurse Kim back to health. The main characters, Indian and English, endear themselves with their human qualities, their adventures, sense of fun and mischief, and zest. The novel's simple storyline belies its complex, layered structure. Though its charming hero is a favourite with schoolboys, it is a mature work in which the perspective of the imperialist is deepened and subverted by several themes—disguise, appearance and reality, magic and illusion, and the search for identity. This quest has matured into the central theme of the great Indian novel from G.V. Desani's *All About H. Hatterr* (1948) to Salman Rushdie's *Midnight's Children* (1981). These are writers whose identity is indissolubly forged by the Indo-British connection and underpinned by a Western intellectual tradition.

It is his recollections of childhood, the gentle child's close relationship with the Indian members of his household, and his sense of belonging that illuminate *Kim*, but not without characteristic contradictions. These spring from a divided self, described by Ashis Nandy in *The Intimate Enemy* (1983): 'The hero loyal to Western civilisation and the Indianised Westerner who hated the West within him . . . the hero who interfaced cultures and the anti-hero who despised cultural hybrids and bemoaned the unclear sense of self in him.'

In *Kim*, the Indianised Westerner recreates his own consciousness of Indian life, in a visual and aural evocation of man and nature amid the 'bustling and shouting, the bucking of belts, and beating of bullocks,' creaking wheels, and bright fires, when 'India was awake, and Kim in the middle of it, more awake and more excited than any one.' He comes upon the Mavericks, and the Christian chaplains, Father Victor and Father Bennet. Kim treats the latter with scorn, and denies the former the reverence reserved for the lama, an example of the contradictory impulses in Kipling's work, in which missionaries are treated with respect and compassion on other occasions. With his Irish ancestry acknowledged, Kim finds himself sent to a military school. Its restrictions and regimentation, the joylessness of duty and work make him rush headlong back to the freedom of life on the road. Rescued by Mahbub Ali, his Indian mentor in a life of action, it is the lama who, with foresight, steers the course for Kim to assume his role as sahib by finding the resources to educate him at St Xavier's School in Lucknow.

The novel was written at a time when Britain's fears of a Russian invasion determined British Secret Service activities. Kim becomes involved in a Secret Service plot to defeat a Russian-inspired conspiracy to stir up an insurrection. The Great Game holds Kim in thrall, energising the narrative with his appetite for life and adventure. The process paves the way for a reflection on the life of action and the life of renunciation and meditation: the Occidental and the Oriental way, with qualities of observation, the acquisition and use of knowledge as the prerogative of white men. In the end, the imperial vision dominates. And though Kim is torn by conflicting loyalties he does not really have any doubt about his future commitment to the Great Game.

Kipling's art creates an enthralling adventure story with lovable and credible Indian characters while endorsing imperial rule. Although the struggle for Independence was under way, Kipling's class at the time thought it was India's best destiny to be ruled by humane leaders. Here, as in Mowgli's adventures (*The Jungle Book*, 1894)—dazzling and entertaining examples of the principle of domination through knowledge, Kipling's sense of being at home in India merges with his imperial theme. Kipling's boy characters live a charmed life, and it is in this remembrance of things past that his art endures—even when the work is read in the light of decolonisation.

5

Two Faces of Prose

Behramji Malabari and Govardhanram Tripathi

SUDHIR CHANDRA

Of the many patriotic Indians in post-1857 India who felt and utilised the power of English prose for nationalist ends, Behramji M. Malabari (1853–1912) and Govardhanram M. Tripathi (1855–1907) deserve attention. They reveal strikingly similar as well as divergent characteristics. Apart from being close contemporaries they had Gujarati in common as their mother tongue. Both had to struggle hard from early in life. Orphaned young, Malabari was on his own from the age of twelve; and Govardhanram, following the failure of his father's business, was burdened at nineteen with the care of a large joint family. These hardships shaped their adulthood very differently. Malabari learnt to laugh even as he crusaded against evil, oppression, and injustice. Govardhanram turned introspective and highly strung, apprehending an early death. He felt inordinately wronged and nursed a generalised, almost irrational rage.

In an autobiographical vignette that appeared as an introduction to his *Gujarat and the Gujaratis* (1881), Malabari recalled his life at Surat, to which town his mother had migrated after his birth in Baroda: 'I began life at twelve, giving private lessons. One scarcely feels at ease in coaching his elders.' Delighting in overstatement—a characteristic of Malabari's humour—the vignette goes on to tell how he became a regular teacher at sixteen and, harassed by his 'migratory instincts', soon began fretting to give up the job. Having by that time 'scribbled English verses by the yard' and become 'favourably known as a versifier', he fancied himself in the role of 'a journalist and public censor'. He believed, 'with the overweening confidence of youth', that he 'had the right and the power, too, to enlighten the public'. Not yet twenty, he became co-editor of an ephemeral local weekly in English, the kind that mushroomed with the incipient patriotism of later-nineteenth-century Indian youth.

This was in the early 1870s, before the issue of social *versus* political reform erupted into a controversy and forced the Indian National Congress, as a political body, to formally dissociate itself from the Indian National Social Conference (founded in 1887). Prefiguring the controversy, Malabari tells us that while he 'was for treatment of social questions chiefly', his co-editor, 'my friend P., affected politics'. The fledgling editors settled 'this difference by confining each to his own *forte*'. However: 'Our ignorance, even in this, was as boundless, as was our arrogance. But was it not glorious to criticise and ridicule leading men in the country? . . . I turned into prose, every week, two of my versified social essays, of which I had a large supply at home. Did poet ever sacrifice his substance as I did, in those days, in public interests?' Malabari's prose can be self-mocking and this hides the passionate anger with which he assailed the two dominant tyrannies of his time: the colonial dispensation and organised socio-religious orthodoxy. Malabari was sustained in the latter by the memory of his widowed mother. She died young, of ailments that came from poverty and a desperation to give her son a decent upbringing. Malabari was forever guilty about having done nothing to allay her anxieties as she lay dying.

Remembered as a social reformer who authored the famous *Notes on Infant Marriage and Enforced Widowhood* (1884) and as the man who compelled a reluctant bureaucracy to come forward with the Age of Consent Act (1892), Malabari has not really received the notice he deserves. Social reform did not, for him, mean abstention from national issues, let alone politics. 'A free India,' he wrote weeks before the Indian National Congress came into being, was the 'goal towards which the eye of the Indian patriot has been straining.' Reflecting on how subjection weighed upon the politically aware among his generation, he continued: 'It is discouraging enough to find the prospects of freedom so remote, restricted and conditional. But nothing could be so disheartening as to see the party of progress (supporting both political change and social reform) imperceptibly receding from, instead of making towards the desired goal' (*Indian Spectator*, 11 October 1885).

The range and quality of coverage in the *Indian Spectator*, the weekly in English that Malabari brought out virtually single-handed, reflect his many-sided concerns as a patriot. A nationalist who believed that imperialism had smothered endogenous development in Indian society, he was at the same time deeply appreciative of benefits to India from imperialism. A social reformer who successfully campaigned for progressive legislation, he also revered tradition. A polemicist who could switch from ridicule and scorn to subtle arguments, emotional appeal, and angry outburst, he was among Gandhi's precursors in stressing the force of personal moral example in public life. Sensitive to the dialectics binding precept and practice, ends and means, he proposed personal sacrifice—martyrdom—as an instrument of socio-political action.

As testified by the writing and speeches of nationalists like Surendranath Banerjee and Pherozeshah Mehta, or the earlier proceedings of the Indian National Congress, humour, wit, and sarcasm were fairly common in the rhetoric of Malabari's time. Where Malabari himself excelled was in using humour to produce sympathy, pain, and anger. In *Gujarat and the Gujaratis* he describes how 'successive failures of crops and the inexorable demand of the *Sirkar*' during the 1879–80 famine reduced substantial farmers to vagrancy. Then he 'forges' a series of four documents which, to create the effect of reality, he claims to have picked up at Broach. It begins with a district collector 'respectfully' proposing the remission—or at least deferment—of revenue arrears in view of 'the widespread misery of the ryots, their distressing past and hopeless future'. It ends with 'His Excellency in Council' resolving:

> Whereas a certain District Revenue Official (name withheld out of consideration for long service) has thought fit to suggest the remission of our just and lawful dues, it is hereby notified for the general information of the service that His Excellency will visit with his displeasure

> any such weakness, which may lead at any time, but for the vigilance of the Police, to crimes, such as riot, burglary, dacoity, and murder, and ultimately tarnish the fair name of our Rule. Times change, and with them must we. Some of the population may die, that is one means of saving the rest. They may starve, languish, sell their children, or eat them. That is no concern of high-minded Christian rulers. We *must look to the remote future*. There we descry hordes of Afghans and Cossacks overrunning the fair fields of Cashmere. And would it be politic of us to rest before we have made a trans-Himalayan tramway, and till we take our formidable future foes home to Afghanistan and Siberia, wash the one and put the other to bed? Officers are requested to think over these complications before they talk of remission and this and that remedy.

This is hilariously damning. Malabari's sarcasm could be devastating also in its directness. In a *cause célèbre* that divided Hindu society as nothing before, Rukhmabai, a young woman who had been married in childhood, was resisting her husband's petition in the Bombay High Court for the restitution of his conjugal rights. The first judgment, in her favour, had shown that the provision of restitution of conjugal rights was alien to Hindu law and a cruel importation from England. That judgment was set aside, and after the young rebel told the court in 1887 that she would rather go to jail for six months (as the law required) than to her husband, she was ordered to join him within a month. Organised Hindu orthodoxy was jubilant. Malabari was scandalised. He hailed the woman's 'martyrdom' for the cause of her sisters and took on the two tyrannies:

> But the High Court of Bombay, working under Letters Patent from Her Majesty the Queen-Empress, hold a tournament of chivalry, and these Christian umpires rule that a mere woman can have no right to consult her heart, or, may be, her honour. Caste enforces on this Hindu girl a marriage to which she (having been married when she was eleven) was as much a party as any of the Judges of the High Court. And the Judges countenance this outrage, in fact offer to serve as constable and jailor. What could they do?—poor men—such is supposed to be the law of the Hindus. And what could the British Government do?—poor Government—their mission is to perpetuate inequalities. So Rukhmabai should either go to jail or live under the protection of her so-called

> husband's protectors. Perhaps the husband who loves her so, may one day bring another 'wife' to keep her company. What then? The High Court will go on grinding the dead-bones of law, and the Government will go on whistling in sympathy with the process which is grinding the womanhood out of the women of Hindustan. (*Indian Spectator*, 6 March 1887)

Cleansed by compassion of fear in his public life, Malabari could be savage in his criticism but never rancorous. Nor did he take as personal even the virulent abuse that he, a Parsi, got for his pains on behalf of Hindu women. 'I am the widow', he said simply. There was something instinctive about his epicene identification with women, revealed for example during the Bhabhutgar case. This case involved a widow and a man who, pretending to be her husband, lived with her. The matter was reported in prurient detail by most journalists. Malabari's response was:

> Cases of this kind are not so rare as people might imagine, and parents and neighbours are generally too humane to make a noise about such mistakes. 'What happens in his house to-day may happen in ours tomorrow'—thus the neighbours argue with themselves. They will do anything to cover their own and their neighbours' sins. The stories that are told of the contrivances to make widows 'happy' without the 'scandal' of a remarriage are passing into proverbs. But so perverse is human nature that men and women will risk their all, life and honour itself, rather than approve of marriage. (*Indian Spectator*, 9 October 1887)

Given the hold of religious/sectarian sentiment in India, it is astonishing that Malabari should have taken up the cause of Hindu women. Even more that among his confederates were eminent Hindus like Raghunath Rao, Dayaram Gidumal, and Baijnath, whose reformism was an affirmation of their conservatism. But then Malabari was a good Zoroastrian who felt moved by the beauty of the Hindu faith even as he condemned its distortions.

His ultimate touchstone was justice for the oppressed, not just women. Malabari had a way of looking at things from the viewpoint of the disprivileged. For that reason, in matters involving a conflict between British and Indian interests, this viewpoint was inevitably nationalist. But it was a non-élitist viewpoint. He worried about the impact of policies, institutions and persons—colonial as much as indigenous—on those who were most vulnerable. The testimony contained in *Gujarat and the Gujaratis* apart, the *Indian Spectator* stands out among Indian newspapers and periodicals for its anxiety over the underclass.

In concrete terms, the Age of Consent Act was Malabari's sole achievement. To the extent that such measures can be attributed to individual efforts, the Act owed itself to his tireless campaigns in India and England. It raised the age of marital consummation for girls from ten years to twelve. The change was marginal, and the Act was unlikely to be an effective instrument. Yet in a society that considered marriage sacrosanct, practised child marriage, mocked the idea of marital rape, and had organised a massive agitation against the measure, it was a pioneering intervention.

A proper assessment of Malabari, however, will move beyond the Age of Consent Act to seek an understanding of the more elusive and lasting aspects of his intervention. That means a critical examination not only of what appeared in the *Indian Spectator*, but also in the *Voice of India* and *East and West*, both of which were edited by him. The former, inspired by Dadabhai Naoroji, sought to project a united public opinion by carrying excerpts from various Indian periodicals on significant issues of the day. The latter, unlike the one-person show which was the *Indian Spectator*, published discursive as well as creative prose by a large number of contributors, including Govardhanram Tripathi.

Govardhanram was born at Nadiad, a small town near Baroda, in a family of well-to-do Nagar Brahmins. He seems to have had a fairly untroubled existence until he was thirteen. Then life became a series of difficulties and he came to look upon himself as a victim of fate:

> . . . from the fourteenth year of my age [the year of his first marriage] I have been struck with blow after blow, from quarters near and remote, live and inanimate, anticipated and unanticipated. Things which to some come like fortune and to most are a protection have wreaked

> havoc to destroy my ordinary comfort and prospects and my peace of mind from a very tender age, and all my surroundings including my body have repaid my care and attention with what the world would call Ungrateful Monstrosities, but I call attacks of frailty. (*Scrap Book: 1894–1904*)

This was elemental fury. But it sustained Govardhanram's sense of his own nobility. His frequent spasms of anger always ended in forgiveness for his numerous 'enemies'. This also provided the existential propulsion for his personal philosophy of consumption—*utsargasiddhi*—that required the individual will to consume itself in the discharge of its duty to the Great Will in such a way that the consumption became its own *raison d'être*. The fury was turned inward. Govardhanram could never take himself or his malevolent surroundings lightly.

However, he was not masochistically self-besotted. A formidable writer and thinker who has never made a proper appearance on the intellectual map of modern India, he had a sense of mission and faith in his ability to fulfil it. He would reshape his people, the 'nation'. Looking beyond the ephemera of events, he confided to his *Scrap Book*:

> I wish to produce, or see produced, not any this or that event—but a people who shall be higher and stronger than they are, who shall be better able to look and manage for themselves than is the present *helpless* generation of my educated and uneducated countrymen. What kind of nation that should be and how the spark should be kindled for that organic flame: these were, and are, the problems before my mind. (*Scrap Book: 1888–94*)

Literature was the spark he chose, and the flame that followed was *Sarasvatichandra*. Published in four volumes over a period of fourteen years (1887–1901), this first classic of Gujarati fiction influenced generations of readers in a way that is difficult to document. Intertexturing the real and the ideal, it worked its way into their consciousness and offered them models for identification and emulation. Narrating the story of love between Sarasvatichandra and Kumud, it was an epic in prose about their own times. The novel, Govardhanram hoped, would interest the reading classes 'in the principal problems of the day', showing them how India was 'undergoing strange transitions in matters domestic, social, religious, political, and what not'. Saving them from being demoralised by 'this bewildering confusion', it would inspire in them faith in India's capacity, 'in the long run', to achieve 'Progress and Harmony'.

To be able to do this, what Govardhanram needed most was clarity. Wary of 'the evil consequences which we may inflict on our country by our well-meaning follies', clarity became an obsession with him. But the more microscopically he examined things, the more exaggeratedly they loomed before him. The *Scrap Book*, where he sought this clarity, remained till the very end an unresolved dialogue with himself and with the confusing world he lived in.

In this book Govardhanram probed himself in a way not many of his contemporaries did. The assurance of privacy induced onto paper thoughts 'unthinkable' and 'unutterable'. The text, though, may have been cunningly modulated in anticipation of a future readership. Having intended it as a private text, Govardhanram was not unresponsive to its publication when the possibility arose towards the end of his life. The *Scrap Book* was eventually published, with some omissions, in three volumes.

Written, significantly, in English, the *Scrap Book* was begun in 1885 when Govardhanram was thirty. Having obtained his law degree after repeated failures, he had recently resigned his job with the Nawab of Junagadh and shifted to Bombay to practise at the High Court. Around this time was also begun *Sarasvatichandra*. His plan, in view of the early death which he expected would be his fate, was to make from his legal practice a modest saving in ten years and retire to Nadiad at the age of forty to devote himself exclusively to writing. For the rest of his life, the *Scrap Book* recorded the conflicting working of his mind with regard to the self, family, and society (and also his thoughts on life after death). Its final entry, dated 3 November 1906, recorded that, 'growing impotent in sustaining the equilibrium of life', his 'vital forces . . . may be shaken into physical ruin at any time'. He died two months later.

Though written in Gujarati, *Sarasvatichandra* exemplifies, along with Govardhanram's writing in English, how completely the English language had come to dominate the lives and minds of its Indian users. Not atypically for the times, three of the novel's four volumes carried prefaces either in English or in both English and Gujarati (the second volume had no preface). Besides, English is used in the epigraphs at the head of many chapters as well as in interludes, which are of varying length, throughout the novel.

These interludes in English do not necessarily occur, as might be expected, in the course of long-drawn-out discussions on socio-political and cultural issues that abound in the novel. Govardhanram's didactic zeal, as he admitted in the preface to the fourth volume, would not mind sacrificing 'well-known canons of modern art'. His characters sometimes speak English in emotionally charged situations as well. Even his animals and birds speak it. If they must use a human language to communicate, or so Govardhanram seems to have reasoned, it might as well be English. This shows a certain audacity, yet to Govardhanram it occurred almost naturally. As the *Scrap Book* records, he himself occasionally dreamt in that language. In a thinly allegorised sequence in the novel, a monkey and a parrot keep switching between Gujarati and English. We pick up the dialogue where the monkey has concluded his discourse on the survival of the fittest. The dialogue is prefaced with a long quotation from the February 1899 issue of *Nineteenth Century*, and the entire passage is in English:

Parrot : My country has no hope from thee.
Monkey : Nor from thee and thy people, either.
Parrot : You wish my extinction, then?
Monkey : It is not a question of my wish but a matter inevitable in the long run unless you strive to benefit by our Society which I am sure you won't.
Parrot : Would you struggle then to hasten my extinction—if you believe in my doom as an inevitable result of an inexorable law? Why waste your strength to achieve what is sure to come to you without that waste?
Monkey : You are a fatalist; I am not.
Parrot : You would commit a sin because it is destined.
Monkey : I do my duty even when I know the result.
Parrot : I am undone.
Monkey : I can't help it. It is your own doing.

Full of analytical possibilities, this excerpt reflects but one facet of an ambivalence that both castigated and celebrated the colonial connection. There was, though, enough castigation in *Sarasvatichandra* to occasion rumours that Govardhanram had been arrested for sedition. His own reaction reveals the other constituent of the ambivalence, an ambivalence he shared with his educated compatriots. 'My book', he wrote, in the *Scrap Book*, 'is not only loyal, but my innermost soul feels that it is written for and must tend to the welfare of both the rulers and the ruled.'

Stylistically, in its crisp run of light but decisive wit, the monkey–parrot dialogue is very different from Govardhanram's language which, both in English and Gujarati, tends to be ponderous, digressive, and tedious. Govardhanram's Sisyphean search for clarity in the *Scrap Book* heightens our awareness of the ambivalence that runs through *Sarasvatichandra* despite its dénouement, which creates the impression of a resolution. It also makes us suspicious of the consistency that marks his *Classical Poets of Gujarat and their Influence on Society and Morals* (first delivered as a lecture in 1892 and published in 1894). Conceived with a passion for the heterodoxy of 'tradition' and faith in the power of literature to promote such heterodoxy, this pioneering essay in the sociology of Gujarati poetry has as its subtext Govardhanram's vision of a new India. Though he is talking about 'classical' poets, his gaze is fixed on the present:

> The poets of this age [the seventeenth century] are in one sense above the society in which they lived. This society does not seem to have much differed from the one which is vanishing during this our generation under the influence of Western ideas. The poems of Akho, Premanand and Samal, all foreshadowed a society higher than this; and probably their ideal would have been reached, had not political vicissitudes blasted the new life that was beginning to dawn on the country.

Govardhanram reserves his warmest appreciation for Samal, whose fictions he finds 'wonderfully in advance of his times'. *Sarasvatichandra*, too, occasionally echoes this appreciation. Indeed, its very conception, like Samal's 'fictions', is intended to construct 'fresh societies for his audience'.

One such moment of reconstruction is when, referring to the death of the wife of a young relative named Shivlal, Govardhanram writes in the *Scrap Book*: 'Of course a new substitute will be sought for the one that is gone. When a husband dies, the widow cannot get similar relief.' From this anguished expression of personal anger he moves on to a generalised sympathy for the social reformer's view of the case: 'Our reformers complain of this injustice to her. The complaint is as right and the sympathy for her as well deserved as the custom against her is successful in keeping her down.' The entry takes an unexpected turn at this point and concludes:

> But this is not a mere question of rights *v.* might. The custom is based upon joint family exigencies, and the castes that have it not [*sic*] admit divorce, too, on easier terms than the law can afford. New circumstances will probably bring about some happier compromise. In the meanwhile, orthodoxy, with nature's gift of instinct of self-preservation, must hold its own as an iron wall, and reformers grow wiser and less sorrowful with their frequent knocking of heads against the wall, until the wall begins to crumble and the heads grow stronger by frequent exercise in knocking and breaking; and a new scheme of reciprocal adaptation between Family, Caste and Justice sparks out of the friction. But I won't lecture here. (*Scrap Book: 1904–6*)

This miniaturises the drama that Govardhanram needed fourteen years to complete as he vacillated, in the four volumes of his novel, between weeping for the widow Kumud and glorying in her life of negation. The rage nestling behind his calm exterior was never, in contradistinction to Malabari, summoned for a cause.

Yet with all their differences the two men felt close enough for Govardhanram, never keen on journalism, to appear rather regularly during the last years of his life in Malabari's *East and West*. The titles of these contributions—two long essays, 'The Hindu Ideal of Poverty' (1903) and 'The Keynote of the Economics of Hinduism' (1905), and a short story called 'Chuni the Suttee: A Story of Hindu Life' (1902)—indicate the nature of convergence between them. Malabari could not, and as editor need not, have agreed with these contributions. But as one who warmed to his cultural heritage—believing, for example, that the story of Damayanti was 'true'—he must have welcomed Govardhanram's attempt to reinterpret and valorise 'tradition'. For the essays were the early manifestations of years of effort by Govardhanram to understand traditional wisdom and knowledge; he was thinking of indigenous, or Hindu, economics, chemistry, psychology, medicine and, of course, philosophy—and translating it 'into the language of modern ideas'.

As for the story, Malabari read it perhaps differently from its author. Given his radical advocacy of the cause of women, he could not have felt altogether happy with Govardhanram's portrayal of Chuni, 'the Suttee'. A 'born housewife' endowed with 'a wonderful genius for management', she perishes in the cheerful service of her husband and his family. The story ends with her 'ascension':

> It was believed for long that Vishnu himself had visited Chuni in the guise of a *sadhu* . . . that Lakshmi had sent a *Viman* to take her to Vaikunth, and that some people actually heard the bells of the angels and saw the Sati borne away in the celestial vehicle into the region where the clouds gather, the stars twinkle, and spirit meets spirit.

Govardhanram had known a Chuni in real life. His favourite daughter, Lilavati, had died young in similar circumstances, and he had mourned her death in a long elegiac poem, *Lilavatijivanakala*. The poem slides over, by means of idealisation, what the *Scrap Book* is unambiguous about: her husband's family's hand in Lilavati's death. The story falls between the poem and the *Scrap Book*. It shows, for example, Chuni's mother lamenting the hardships that earned her daughter the title of an ideal daughter-in-law. The element of glorification, nevertheless, is unmistakable. In fact, it conforms to Govardhanram's tendency to recognise the seamy existential reality of 'tradition'—of life with the joint family in this instance—and ends up by valorising it in larger cultural terms. For Malabari, in contrast, the pathos and details of Chuni's story possessed a more critical potential and effect.

6

The Beginnings of the Indian Novel

MEENAKSHI MUKHERJEE

Although the 1930s is generally seen as the take-off decade for the Indian novel in English, we can trace its genealogy quite far back into the previous century. Given the Indian apathy towards the preservation of documents from the past and the high rate of paper disintegration in the Indian climate, a good proportion of the books that were published then have perished beyond trace. Despite this, what remains in some of the old libraries of the country is far from negligible.

Two facts stand out when one glances at the title pages of the books that remain. The first is the diversity and range of places from where they appeared. They were published not only from the metropolitan centres of book production like London, Calcutta, Bombay, and Madras, but also from small presses with limited distribution systems in Allahabad, Bangalore, Bezwada, Bhagalpur, Calicut, Dinapur, Midnapur, Surat, and Vellore, making it difficult to claim a continuity of tradition. The second is the eagerness in the titles—*A Peep into, Glimpses, Revelations*, etc.—to promise the unveiling of some mystery presumably pertaining to a seemingly homogeneous space called India (or 'The East' or 'The Orient'). This tendency was perhaps linked with the author's choice of language, because, unlike novelists in the Indian languages who were confident about a sizeable readership within their specific region, the writer in English suffered from an uncertainty about his audience. We surmise from clues embedded in the texts that his implicit target must have been the British reader, if not in England, at least the colonial administrator in India.

The authorising presence of this shadowy reader is intermittently perceived in details of ethnographic documentation or through lexical or semantic emphases. For example, Bankimchandra Chattopadhyaya's *Rajmohan's Wife*, his first and only novel in English, describes as 'salad' some common leafy vegetables in a garden in East Bengal, even though Bengali cuisine then had no concept of uncooked greens, and Lal Behari Day gratuitously announces in *Govinda Samanta* that there are no 'taverns' in Bengal villages for peasants to spend their evenings in; or that young men and women in India have no concept of courtship: 'In Bengal . . . and for the matter of that in all India—they do not make love in the honorable sense of that word. Unlike the butterfly, whose courtship, Darwin assures us, is a very long affair, the Bengali does not court at all. Marriage is an affair arranged entirely by the parents and guardians of bachelors and spinsters.'

The early English novels in India appeared at a time when the genre was still in a malleable stage. Literary historians have cited different dates for the first Indian novel, with Bengali and Marathi vying for first prize, but it is by and large agreed that the novel came into existence in India in the second half of the nineteenth century. This was roughly a generation after Macaulay's 'Minute' decreed English as the language of higher education, exposing an entire class of urban Indian men to British narrative models. But before the new paradigms got indigenised, pre-novel forms of fiction existed in most Indian languages. Even in English, which was a recent entrant in India, we find a few texts that prepare the ground for the emergence of the novel, though they may not share the ideological or generic presuppositions of the later texts.

The earliest extant narrative texts in English may well be two tracts of imaginary history written by Kylas Chunder Dutt and Shoshee Chunder Dutt in 1835 and 1845 respectively. These were 'A Journal of Forty-Eight Hours of the Year 1945', published in the *Calcutta*

Literary Gazette, and 'The Republic of Orissa: A Page from the Annals of the Twentieth Century', which appeared in the *Saturday Evening Hurkaru*. Both project into the future, describing battles of liberation against the British, but end with dissimilar resolutions.

In 'A Journal of Forty-Eight Hours' Kylas Chundur Dutt fixes on a year more than a century later as the date of a crucial Indian confrontation with the British. As it happens, he was only two years off the mark. By this time in the future, Indians would have reached the limits of their tolerance. His piece begins thus:

> The people of India and particularly those of the metropolis had been subject for the last fifty years to every species of subaltern oppression. The dagger and the bowl were dealt out with a merciless hand, and neither age, sex, nor condition could repress the rage of the British barbarians. Those events, together with the recollection of the grievances suffered by their ancestors, roused the dormant spirit of the generally considered timid Indians.

A detailed description follows of battles between the British, led by the Governor Lord Fell Butcher and Colonel John Blood-Thirsty, and a large Indian army of patriots who take their orders from Bhoobun Mohan, a charismatic young graduate, who possesses 'all the learning and eloquence which the Anglo-Indian college could furnish'. In the first round the patriots are victorious, but perhaps the compulsions of his own colonised circumstances made the author desist from pushing this euphoric projection too far. In their attempts to capture Fort William in Calcutta the Indians are badly routed and, even as Bhoobun Mohan exhorts his companions to carry on the struggle, his head is 'severed from his body at a single blow'.

Coming ten years later, the text by Shoshee Chunder Dutt (1824–86) is considerably more radical; the resistance against the British here is led not by an English-educated urban youth but by a tribal from Orissa—the intrepid Bheekoo Barik, chief of the Kingaries. The immediate provocation for battle is the passing of a Slavery Act by the British in 1916. The rebelling forces from Bengal, Bihar, and Orissa combine to defeat an army of ten thousand Irish soldiers commanded by Sir J. Proudfoot, and capture the fictitious fort of Radanaugger. Their victory forces the British to offer some concessions, which they 'deceitfully deferred fulfilling' when the immediate danger is over. The military strand of the narrative is woven in and reinforced by a love story, through which the smouldering fire of the Kingaries is rekindled five years later, and they have another confrontation with the British in 1921. 'On the 13th January of the following year, Orissa proclaimed its independence and though the Government of Pillibheet [the fictitious capital of British India] refused to recognise it, their armies completely evacuated that province, after a few vain efforts to disturb its independence.' The concluding paragraphs of the tract dwell on the subsequent decline of the British empire: 'We regret its fallen grandeur, we regret to see an imperial bird, shorn of its wings and plumage of pride, coming down precipitately from its aery height.'

These early tracts belong to a pre-novel narrative era in India and are not structured by any generic expectation. They do not show any overt dependence on canonical literary texts from England, echoes of which permeate many similar texts; nor do they seem weighed down by the abject servility that the English language indirectly conferred on several later writers. The political radicalism—though of a simplistic variety—of Shoshee Chunder Dutt's tract is visibly absent from his own subsequent novels.

Shoshee Chunder was from the Dutt family of Rambagan, Calcutta, which, in addition to Toru Dutt, produced a number of minor poets in English in the nineteenth century. He was a prodigious writer whose Collected Works, published in six volumes, display an impressive knowledge of philosophy and history. In his short novel *Shunkur* (1885), situated against the backdrop of the 1857 Rebellion, Dutt takes special care to distribute sympathy evenly between the British and the Indians. If officers like Bernard and Mackenzie are despicable enough to rape the woman who has given them shelter, Nanasaheb's treachery and promiscuity are foregrounded as if to provide a balance in villainy. There is an implicit anxiety to uphold the ordinary Indian soldier's loyalty to his British master. Occasional insurgency is projected as merely a temporary reaction to the injustice and ill-treatment by individual officers. Shunkur's vendetta against those who raped his wife is made out to be a purely personal matter with no political overtones. Dutt's major novel, *The Young Zemindar* (1883), does describe resistance movements in different parts of India as seen through the eyes of the hero, Manohar, and his mentor, Babajee Bissonath, who travel across the country only to come to the conclusion that lack of discipline and an absence of leadership doom all attempts at resistance. At the end of the novel, the young zamindar, Manohar, accepts the British presence, grudgingly admitting that 'English rule, with all its drawbacks, is still better than what the Mahomedan rule was.'

By the turn of the century, novel after novel in English seems to be paying direct or veiled tribute to British rule. K.K. Sinha's historical novel *Sanjogita or The Princes of Aryavarta* (1930) is centred around the defeat of Prithvi Raj Chauhan by Mohammad Ghori. The defeat is blamed on internal dissension and a lack of vision in the Rajput camp, a situation which could easily have been seen as a parallel to the British takeover of India. Sinha, however, completely elides the present to go into a nostalgic evocation of the greatness of India's Hindu past. Suddenly towards the end of the novel there is an unceremonious switch to a different rhetoric altogether: 'India appeals to her noble foreign masters for kindness and sympathy, she is indebted to them for her rescue from a chaotic anarchy . . . Undoubtedly, the British Government is the sum of our system; if it were taken away, our entire fabric would fall to pieces . . .'

Even at the beginning of the twentieth century, when nationalism had become a conspicuous strand of thought in most creative writers in the Indian languages, novelists in English continued to display obsequiousness towards the ruler at regular intervals. A. Madhavaiah (1872–1925) in *Thillai Govindan* (1908) airs his views on the relation between imperial rulers and Indian subjects thus: 'With kind treatment the Indian will remain a British subject for years to come. For the matter of that, he will remain so probably after any treatment; but he will show pleasure and pride in being so, if treated kindly.'

This flaunting of subjection occasionally coexists with fierce cultural pride and an assertion of the antiquity and superiority of Indian civilisation in relation to Europe. While recounting the saga of the princely state of Barathpur (readable as an allegory of India), Sarath Kumar Ghosh, the author of *Prince of Destiny: The New Krishna*

(1909), writes: 'When Rome was not built, when Tyre and Carthage were yet unbegotten, the house of Barath reigned supreme over India.' Similarly, K.K. Sinha in the preface to *Sanjogita* proudly proclaims: 'Long before Pythagoras was born in Athens, the theory of transmigration of souls was known to the Hindu people.' Concerned at the decline of this ancient culture and saddened by its spirit of surrender, he traces the downward trajectory of India's greatness from medieval times: 'In point of moral or spiritual advancement, the India of twelfth century was not the India of Rama and Yudhistira just as the India of today is not the India of Prithvi Raj and Samar Singh; there has been a gradual falling off.'

In *Prince of Destiny*, the conversation between father and son on the eve of Prince Barath's departure to England for further education is marked by a melancholy acceptance of the inevitable victory of the younger but more dynamic culture:

> 'Father, when I am in England I shall try to avoid the evil, and seek only the good.'
>
> 'Aye, but it is the good that is in England that I fear the most; the evil could never touch thee.'

In Madhavaiah's novel, when the narrator-protagonist traces his progress from being 'an ordinary Brahmin boy performing his daily ablutions faithfully', if unthinkingly ('believing in child marriage, subjection of women, family deities and ghosts'), to becoming his Westernised and profligate uncle's disciple who reads with admiration 'the works of the American atheists Ingersoll and Draper and the English atheists Bradlaugh and Mrs Besant', irony seems evenly distributed between traditional beliefs and new learning. If an ambivalence about Western civilisation—on the one hand as liberating and on the other as a threat to Hindu identity—continued to mark these early English novels written mainly by Hindu, male, upper-caste writers, there was however nothing ambiguous about their attitude to the Muslim ('the hated Mohammedans that take delight in the ruins of our religion', *Sanjogita*) whom the British had displaced as rulers. The repeated, though marginal presence of a spiritual ment or figure, a guru or an ascetic, in many of these novels serves the double function of proclaiming the ancient philosophical wisdom of Hindu civilisation and admitting its ineffectuality in the colonial arena of action and power.

Over the colonial period one of the most obvious markers of power was familiarity with the English tongue and Western culture, something that all these early writers had in common because of the language they chose to write in. In fact, novelists writing in the Indian languages would have read the same English texts—both canonical and popular—as they were products of the same educational system. The novelists in English, however, displayed their acquaintance with the classics of Western literature more obviously than the others, possibly parading their knowledge as a validation of their status in the eyes of putative British readers. They never mentioned the middle- or low-brow writers who were widely read at the time—G.W.M. Reynolds, Wilkie Collins, Marie Corelli, Benjamin Disraeli—whose influence on the Indian-language novels is well known. On the contrary, Indian writers in English took care to align with the best in various ingenious ways. Epigraphs from Byron, Scott, Cowper, Shakespeare, and Coleridge were common practice, and quotations and references were generously woven into the narrative, whether the context called for them or not. For example, A. Madhavaiah, in *Thillai Govindan*, brings in a literary reference to make a fairly self-evident point: 'Carlyle has said somewhere—perhaps in that huge hotch-potch of facts and fancies—'Sartor Resartus'—that religion is the bond of society'; and K.K. Sinha in *The Star of Sikri* (1893) feels the need to solicit Walter Scott and Shakespeare's support to defend the practice of purdah:

> Women are proverbially liable to be deceived and seduced, they are known to have very weak resolutions. Scott thinks them to be as
>
> > variable as the shade
> > by the quivering aspen glade,
>
> and the immortal bard of Avon truly says:
>
> > Frailty! Thy name is woman.
>
> Is it not proper therefore to keep them as much away as possible from tempting influences?

Sinha even casts the spell of this magic language over the frail heroine of *The Star of Sikri*, Rajni. Not only has she read the *Ramayana* of Tulsidas thoroughly, as becomes a good Hindu woman (it was 'her Vedas, Kalidas, Shakespeare and Milton'), she has also begun reading English 'at the time of the commencement of the story'. Such is her devotion to this new knowledge that she recommends it to the wife of the man she loves: 'Why don't you read English? I have recently begun, and have come up to the *Second Book* of Peary Charan Sircar.' Knowing English was largely a gender-specific skill in nineteenth-century India, restricted to urban, upper-caste men, but in the author's construction of an ideal woman this had become a desired attribute.

So much premium was put on an author's facility with the English language that sometimes it became the chief selling point of his novel. The publishers of *The Prince of Destiny* claimed that since readers in Britain 'cannot be persuaded to believe that Sarath Kumar Ghosh is anything but an Englishman in masquerade', they 'deemed it expedient to publish the author's portrait in the British edition in a dress representative of India in order to convince readers that he is truly Indian.'

But more interesting are the indirect influences of English literature that shape this new genre in India. Echoes of canonical English novels are often perceptible in the texts. For example, Fielding's famous bill-of-fare metaphor at the beginning of *Tom Jones* is replicated on the first page of *Govinda Samanta*:

> I therefore propose . . . to tell you at once in all sincerity and good faith, what you are to expect and what not to expect in this hall of refreshment; so that after being acquainted with the bill of fare, you may each begin to partake of the repast or not, just as you please.

The convention of closure as found in the Victorian novel, where all the characters are neatly served with their just deserts and the loose ends tied up, is faithfully repeated in novel after Indian novel. The brief concluding chapter of *Rajmohan's Wife* begins thus:

> And now, good reader I have brought my story to a close. Lest, however, you fall to censuring me for leaving your curiosity unsatisfied, I will tell you what happened to the other persons who figured in this tale.

This first novel of Bankimchandra Chattopadhyaya (1838–94) occupies a curious place in his career, because his only attempt to write fiction in English got overshadowed by the fourteen powerful novels he subsequently wrote in Bengali. An apprentice work in which several contradictory pulls create interesting tensions in the narrative, the novel was serialised in 1864 in a short-lived journal called *The Indian Field* edited by the author's friend Kisorichand Mitra; it was never published as a book until 1935, four decades after the author's death. Possibly the first English novel to be written in India, it appeared at a time when romance was the acceptable narrative mode and there was no precedent as yet of mimetic rendering of contemporary domestic life in fiction. Yet this story of the beautiful and passionate Matangini married to the villainous Rajmohan is astonishingly rich in detail, especially in descriptions of interiors and the quotidian routine of women's lives in an East Bengal village. Its realism however is modified by other narrative conventions: of Sanskrit kavya, for example in the metaphor-laden description of female beauty; of Vaishnava love poetry, as in Matangini's abhisara through a dark and stormy night; and of the English Gothic novel in its evocation of terror, with beautiful women incarcerated in dark dungeons lit by 'a solitary and feeble lamp', or assaulted by sinister men 'while the massive doors creaked on their hinges'.

Unlike *Rajmohan's Wife*, which deals with middle-class life—as most subsequent novels in English are wont to do—*Govinda Samanta, or the History of a Bengali Raiyat* (1874), its later revised and enlarged edition (1908) renamed *Bengal Peasant Life*, attempts a stark presentation of a poor Ugrakshatriya family in the Bardhaman district of West Bengal which is rendered destitute and landless by the end of the story. The derivative nature of the preliminary pages, with its echoes of Fielding, and the obsequious invocation of 'the gentle reader' to explain cultural details, stand in sharp contrast to the core narrative which is charged with an elemental vitality. Though Lal Behari Day (1824–94) wrote it to enter a contest to document rural life, the novel soon transcended the parameters of ethnography. Through the fortunes of the Samanta family from 1820—when the last sati was performed in the region—to 1870, the year of the great famine, the novel documents in vivid detail the rural Bengal of the nineteenth century.

Starting out as the account of a stable and seemingly organic community—describing planting and harvesting, feasts and festivals, illness and healing, games and story-telling and other quotidian activities of the village—its mood gradually darkens. An epidemic is followed by famine, resulting in debt, loss of land, and Govinda Samanta's migration to the city, where he works as a nameless daily-wage labourer and finally dies an ignominious death. There was no precedent for such a novel in Indian fiction. Fakir Mohan Senapati's Oriya novel about rural oppression, *Cha Mana Atha Guntha* (1902), appeared decades later, and *Govinda Samanta* may even be seen as the precursor to Premchand's Hindi classic *Godan* (1936), though Premchand may never have heard of it.

The only woman who wrote more than one novel in English in nineteenth-century India, Krupabai Satthianadhan (1862–94), is not as well known as she deserves to be, partly because her two novels *Kamala, A Story of Hindu Life* (1894) and *Saguna, A Story of Native Christian Life* (posthmously published in 1895) were only reprinted in 1998, having remained virtually inaccessible to the common reader till then. The uninviting titles, which belie the liveliness and intensity of these two *bildungsroman*, may have discouraged even researchers from tracking them down. Apart from the compelling readability of these books, their contemporary reader is also likely to be struck by the author's concern with gender, caste, ethnicity, and cultural identity—issues that seem crucial now but were hardly so when Satthianadhan was writing. Despite the difference in social milieu, the two novels deal with a similar theme: the predicament of women who resist being cast in the standard mould of domesticity. Kamala and Saguna are both attracted to books and face varying degrees of hostility for such an unnatural inclination. *Saguna* is largely autobiographical. As the daughter of a Christian convert, the protagonist manages, despite the odds, not only to receive formal education, but also to get admission to a medical college, and eventually meets a man who could share her life as an equal.

Kamala's life follows a different trajectory altogether. Daughter of a learned sanyasi, she is brought up in a sparsely populated hilly area, innocent of the ways of the narrowly caste-bound and intrigue-ridden community into which she is married. Reminiscent of the eponymous heroine of Bankimchandra's Bengali novel *Kapalkundala* (1866), Kamala does not understand the behavioural norms of her new world and, despite her best efforts, remains a misfit. Her happiest moments are when her father-in-law allows her to handle his books or when her husband briefly gives her lessons in reading and writing. But these joys are short-lived, because the machinations of the joint family succeed in drawing them away from Kamala. By the end of the novel her errant husband has died of cholera; her long-time admirer, a disciple of her father, is willing to give up his asceticism to marry her, but the novel's Christian author, who might have found this marriage to be an acceptable happy ending, desists from granting an easy solution to her Brahmin heroine. Kamala insists on living alone and working for the poor in the village.

Both novels are set in the same geographical locale, the Deccan plateau near Nasik, and the awesome, craggy grandeur of the hills is woven into the structure of the novels, especially the first one, to serve as a counterpoint to the meanness of crowded lives in the plains. Possibly for the first time in Indian fiction, we have 'untouchable' and tribal men and women individualised and named as part of the cast of characters, and the idea of India as a nation is articulated in terms that have to do with cultural, rather than religious, identity. Early in *Saguna* we find the heroine's much admired elder brother, Bhaskar, initiating her into the deeper principles of Christianity as well as exhorting her to help him serve the country. 'He talked of doing great things, and forgetting that I was a mere girl, he poured out the ambition of his life and grew eloquent over the great work that had to be done for India . . . and looking into my eyes said "And you will help me, won't you?" ' Though brought up on English poetry and Victorian fiction, Saguna nevertheless retains a sharp sense of cultural identity and boldly reprimands a Westernised Indian youth who refers to England as 'home'. She is ironic about a girl in a missionary school who, after a diet of English novels, has started referring to her parents as 'Pa' and 'Ma' and speaks knowledgeably of the fashions of long skirts and short skirts in 'society'. Saguna wryly comments:

> Like many a novel-reading girl she lived in a world of her own making and enjoyed it. She knew that the native Christian community was very

> small and there was no society to speak of, neither long skirts nor short skirts. Her mother wrote a saree . . . Nothing is so startling these days as the unconscious imitation of English customs and manners by the people of India.

These two novels by Krupabai Satthianadhan are not of mere archival interest. They offer a good deal of textual pleasure and represent some of the earliest articulations of feminist and cultural concerns in English by Indian women.

The names of Shoshee Chunder Dutt, Lal Behari Day and Krupabai Satthianadhan may be unknown to Indian novelists writing in English today. But in the interests of literary history it is necessary to set the record straight with an attempt to dispel the general amnesia about these predecessors. Examining the sequence of novels that have been written in English for over a century and a half, critics may speculate on the various continuities and ruptures that mark the game in this country. To me, the most radical difference between early novels in English and those being written today lies not in thematic concerns, formal innovations, or in the texture of language—such variations would be inevitable across this span of time in any body of literature—but in the sense of an audience. The tentativeness of nineteenth-century novelists, not only about writing in an acquired colonial language but also about their readership, has been replaced by an overwhelming confidence among post-colonial writers that the English language belongs to them as much as to anyone else; a text written in a global language has potentially a global constituency, and therefore, as a corollary, a national one too. The issues are not merely literary but are informed by cultural politics and market forces. It is worth analysing the complex circumstances that made Bankimchandra shift from English to his Bengali mother tongue before he could gain national recognition as a writer, while at the end of the twentieth century one would expect the process to be reversed.

7

The English Writings of Rabindranath Tagore

Amit Chaudhuri

Rabindranath Tagore (1861–1941) was the last of fourteen brothers and sisters; the grandson of 'Prince' Dwarkanath Tagore, one of the most successful Bengali entrepreneurs of his time; and son of the spiritually inclined Maharshi Debendranath, who inherited his father's debts, and became one of the founders of the Brahmo Samaj. In a sense, he grew up as an only child, allowed to inhabit a secure but solitary space in a household that was busy in more ways than one, given that the Tagore family was probably the most creative and intellectually active at the time in Bengal. In the young Tagore, however, a different, perhaps alternative, sensibility was taking shape, a sensibility that culminated later in a poetry of lyric utterance which was so much at variance with the epic and grand style of his predecessors that, towards the beginning of his career, he was called, by some, the 'lisping poet'.

Several pages in Tagore's autobiography *Jiban Smriti* (1911; translated into English as *My Reminiscences*, 1917) recount the robust dislike Tagore felt, as a boy, for private tutorials, classrooms, rote-learning; several other pages are devoted to perhaps the most thorough descriptions in Indian literature of the boyhood pleasures of daydreaming, of staring out of windows, verandahs, or into little-used rooms, and constructing fantasies about them. The idea of daydreaming and leisure ('leisure' not in the sense of bourgeois recreation, but in the feminine sense of a break from domestic routine, or a schoolboy's holiday from a private tutorial) would run implicitly through his conception of creativity itself as an interruption of, and release from, work: many of his songs and poems begin with exhortations such as 'No more work for today!' and 'It's a holiday today, friend, it's a holiday today.'

If Tagore hated lessons, he hated English lessons intensely. In his memoirs, Tagore writes of his earliest encounters with that language upon being admitted, at a 'tender age', into the Normal School. His memory goes back to a song he had learnt in class, which was there transformed into the childhood pidgin of a Bengali boy. Capturing all the bafflement, agony, and energy of cultural confusion and intermingling, Tagore transcribes the verse that inhabited the boy's consciousness thus:

> *Kallokee pullokee singill mellaling mellaling mellaling.*
>
> After much thought I have been able to guess at the original of a part of it. Of what words *kallokee* is the transformation still baffles me. The rest I think was:
>
> . . . *full of glee, singing merrily, merrily, merrily!*

Tagore goes on to inform the reader, in subsequent pages, of the boredom and terror he felt, as a boy, learning English; describes the trepidation with which he and his cousins waited, in rainy weather, to see if the English tutor Aghore Babu's black umbrella would appear, as it invariably did; and says several hard things about the language itself. A quality not generally associated today with English—risibility—was obvious to Tagore and his fellow pupils:

> How well do I remember the day our tutor tried to impress on us the attractiveness of the English language. With this object he recited to us with great unction some lines—prose or poetry we could not tell—out of an English book. It had a most unlooked for effect on us. We laughed so immoderately that he dismissed us for the evening.

Resistance to the language continued; to McCulloch's *Course of Reading* Tagore recalls the following response: 'Providence, out of pity of mankind, has instilled a soporific charm into all tedious things. No sooner did our English lessons begin than our heads began to nod.'

Tagore's protestations about the English language have, however, a degree of disingenuousness about them, given the extent to which his sensibility was actually shaped by the writings of the Romantics, and his great receptivity, especially as a composer, to Western influences. The first instance of cultural cross-fertilisation in Tagore's career occurs early, in his teens, in the curious form of a literary fraud. When Tagore was twelve or thirteen, he read for the first time the great Vaishnava poets, Chandidas and Vidyapati, whose works were then being collected by scholars. Tagore was moved by these poems, although, as his biographer J. Kripalani points out, the Brahmoism that Tagore had grown up with—and which his father had done much to consolidate—would have had little in common with the world of these devotional songs. Upon reading, not much later, the story of the boy-poet Chatterton (whose poetry too he admired) and of his fraudulent 'medieval' poems, he decided to perpetrate a comparable fraud himself. Using the pseudonym Bhanusingha, Tagore set about writing a sequence of poems called *Bhanusingher Padabali* (no doubt echoing the *Vaishnav Padabali*), in which he attempted to capture, in Brajbhasha, something of the music of those older texts, and also to emulate Chatterton's feat of reimagining tradition. Tagore recalls that they fooled at least one expert: set to music, they are part of the recognised repertoire of Tagore songs today.

By the time Tagore came to translate the *Gitanjali* into English in 1912 (it was published by Macmillan in London in 1913), he had established himself, after a not inconsiderable spell of revilement from his detractors, as the foremost poet in Bengali; he had finally transcended the cliques and frissons of the Bengali literary world. Most of the major personal tragedies in his life had occurred. Kadambari Devi, his sister-in-law, once his playmate and later his intellectual companion, had committed suicide in 1884; later he lost the wife, Mrinalini, to whom he had been joined in an 'arranged' marriage in 1883; his second daughter, Renuka, had died in 1903 of tuberculosis; in 1907 his younger son Shamindranath died of cholera.

Bengal already had a distinguished lineage of stylists in the English language at the time he undertook the 'translations'—the novelist

Bankimchandra Chattopadhyaya, the poet Michael Madhusudan Dutt, and the historian R.C. Dutt among them. Interestingly, for many of these writers, their English writings had been a preliminary to the Bengali works through which they then made their reputations. There was, for instance, Michael Madhusudan Dutt's return, after years of writing verse in English, to his native tongue with *Meghanada-vadha Kavya* (1861), and Bankimchandra's brief flirtation with English in his first novel *Rajmohan's Wife* (1864), before he set about the task of establishing himself as the first major novelist in the Bengali language. Tagore's poems are 'translations' in only a very general sense; many of the poems in the English *Gitanjali* are not to be found in the Bengali one, but are taken from three other sources, *Naivedya, Kheya*, and *Gitimalya*. The translations turned out to be substantial reworkings, many of them different in almost every imaginable sense from the originals. Moreover, they launched Tagore's international career and contributed to the myth in the West, subscribed to by many readers at the time, and perhaps a handful even today, that Tagore was a poet who wrote in English.

Tagore had completed *Jiban Smriti*, in which he had made those cutting and jocular remarks about English and the English lessons of his childhood, in 1911; the following year he translated the *Gitanjali* into the language he had once found tedious and ridiculous; in 1913, amazed by the success of the poems, he wrote a letter to his niece Indira Devi, in which we hear a new note of hesitancy regarding the language. Somewhat misleadingly, and with excessive modesty, he declared the tentativeness he had always felt in relation to the English language:

> You have alluded to the English translation of the *Gitanjali*. I cannot imagine to this day how people came to like it so much. That I cannot write English is such a patent fact that I never had even the vanity to feel ashamed of it. If anybody wrote an English note asking me for tea, I did not feel equal to answering it. Perhaps you think that by now I have got over that delusion. By no means. That I have written in English seems to be the delusion.

He goes on to say: 'But believe me, I did not undertake this task in a spirit of reckless bravado. I simply felt an urge to recapture through the medium of another language the feelings and sentiments which had created such a feast of joy within me in the days gone by.'

That Tagore was attempting to 'recapture' in 'another language' rather than 'translate' is borne out by how little effort he expended on approximating the metre and content, and even the literary temperament—precise, controlled—that produced the original songs (for the Bengali *Gitanjali* is predominantly a book of songs). The language of the English *Gitanjali* is, to say the least, problematic. While the Indian poets who had earlier written in English—Derozio and the members of the Dutt family among others—show the influence of both literary models from the English cannon and British Orientalist poetry, a poetry often inflected with Persian motifs, and sometimes incorporating historical material, Tagore's prose-poems, ahistorical and more fluid in form and intent than any English literary model would allow, seem apparently little indebted to either.

The poems themselves were received, to a large extent, as Eastern wisdom, and Tagore is open to the speculation that he might have deliberately positioned himself, in these poems and in public life, as an Eastern mystic for the eyes of the West. However, there is ample evidence to show that Tagore had arrived at most of his mystical accoutrements well before he would have had any inkling that he was to become, briefly, a magus in Europe. Moreover, a substantial part of Tagore's 'Eastern' mysticism was actually quite Western and Victorian in its thrust, involving a sharp Ruskin-like critique of utilitarian values, and a valorising of the autonomy and sanctity of the work of art. The proper thrust of this critique can only be assessed if one recalls that it would have been formulated, at its onset, primarily as a reaction to a Bengali society obsessed with professional qualifications and scientific knowledge for the sake of career advancement, and which had no definition or space for writing as a full-time occupation.

Looking back on the English prose-poems themselves, it seems puzzling now that they were ever read or enjoyed for their message or philosophy, mystical or otherwise; so reticent and deliberately uncommunicative are they. Firstly, only a few years before the birth of Practical Criticism, with its emphasis on the autonomy of each poem, and in marked contrast to the finished and individual nature of the 'originals', these prose-poems, confusingly, flow into each other, as if the boundaries and frames separating them were blurred; one might easily mistake one poem for another. The propagation of any 'message' is deflected by the creation, within the English *Gitanjali*, of a dreamscape of repeated words and symbols—'flute', 'instrument', 'lamp', 'song', 'singer', 'garland', 'Lord', 'guest', 'leisure'; what remains with the reader afterwards is neither content, message, observation, nor conceit, but this unresolved network, this dreamscape. The biblical overtones of some of the passages are undermined by the repetition of certain words and phrases that point towards a culture that is both unbiblical and un-Western. For instance, exhortations such as 'No work for the day!' and phrases like 'overflowing leisure' evoke heat, indolence, and the space reserved for rest; a celebration of idleness that is rare in English poetry, except when qualified by proper Protestant ambivalence as in 'The Lotos Eaters' and certain stanzas of the *Faerie Queene*. Similarly, the biblical 'Lord' present in many of these poems is also sometimes addressed, unsettlingly, by the quite unbiblical appellations of 'friend' and 'singer'; these are echoes of Vaishnavite and local folk traditions that had entered and shaped Tagore's artistic world, acting in the English *Gitanjali* as counters representing another tradition, serving here not to illuminate, but to disrupt the continuity of any single (biblical or otherwise) tonality. One might conclude by saying that, for a sequence of poems that had gained such popularity, the English *Gitanjali* says alarmingly little and keeps drawing attention to its textuality and its unresolved linguistic tensions. Firstly, to the fact of its being composed in English, without the poet having observed the proprieties or niceties of the English literary tradition; secondly, by constantly referring, through a series of repetitions, to the presence of another language and thereby, to the pressure of another culture and way of life (as a translation, whose aim is to recreate the original impregnably in terms of the target language, would never do). On one level, thus, the English *Gitanjali* is a poor translation; on another, it is a genuine instance, albeit only a partially successful one, of an Indian bilingual sensibility expressing itself in the English language. The force of Tagore's bilingual (indeed, multilingual) sensibility made his Bengali poems polished, subtle, both preternaturally sensitive to the fleeting sensory stimulus and adept at making the generalised observation: it made his English poems loose, wordy, and reticent at once, a site where categories were mixed up and realigned.

Some of the poems themselves, moreover, provide their own commentary; language and its contingent problems are constantly referred to, indicating how Tagore had struggled to arrive at his idiom even in Bengali. In the English version, the narrative of this struggle has its own peculiar resonance. In Poem 3 (22 in the Bengali *Gitanjali*), we find, 'My heart longs to join in thy song, but vainly struggles for a voice. I would speak, but speech breaks not into song, and I cry out baffled.' Poem 37 (55 in the Bengali collection) ends with 'And when old words die out on the tongue, new melodies break forth from the heart; and where the old tracks are lost, new country is revealed with its wonders', which refers to many things, including Tagore's achievement in Bengali, the historical moment of that achievement, the attempt at 'recapturing . . . feelings and sentiments' in 'another language' that was Tagore's present undertaking; it is also prescient of the great leap that both Indian poetry and Tagore's reputation would take, purely in terms of Western attention, with the publication of the poems.

Some of the liberties that Tagore takes with his translations are telling as well. The very first poem, 'Thou hast made me endless, such is thy pleasure' (which, as a matter of interest, is absent from the Bengali collection, and is taken from *Gitimalya*), has the sentence: 'At the immortal touch of thy hands my little heart loses its limits in joy and gives birth to utterance ineffable.' Here, 'ineffable' is Tagore's addition; there is no word corresponding to it in the Bengali version. It might have been added to compound the mystical tenor of the sentence; but it also signals to the reader, especially the reader of both versions, the limits of the new language, and the difficulties of the poet's undertaking in an idiom that leads him towards what cannot be spoken.

Most of the translations were done, according to Tagore, on board a ship that was sailing for England: 'The pages of a small exercise-book came gradually to be filled, and with it in my pocket I boarded the ship. The idea of keeping it in my pocket was that when my mind became restless on the high seas, I could recline on a deck-chair and set myself to translate one or two poems.' (Tagore had been to England before, as a young man, in 1878, ostensibly to become a barrister; but he returned without taking a degree. The two years he had spent in England then had not been entirely happy ones.) Soon after Tagore arrived in London, he lost the attaché case in which he was carrying his manuscripts on the Underground, on his way to his hotel; the case reappeared the next day at the Left Luggage Office. In a way, the destiny of the poems seems to have been involved with the civic life of London, its arterial routes, modes of transport, and places of hospitality; later Yeats would write: 'I have carried the manuscripts of these translations about with me for days, reading it in railway trains, or on the top of omnibuses and in restaurants, and I have often had to close it lest some stranger would see how much it moved me.' But they were read first by the painter William Rothenstein, who happened to be a friend of Tagore's nephew Abanindranath.

Rothenstein had first met Tagore in Jorasanko, in the winter of 1910–11; as Tagore's most recent biographers, Krishna Dutta and Andrew Robinson, tell us, 'he found himself attracted to an uncle of Abanindranath, who would sit listening while others talked', and had wanted to draw him once for his 'inner charm as well as great physical beauty'. Rothenstein recalled twenty years later in his memoirs, 'That this uncle was one of the remarkable men of his time no one gave me a hint.' 'Back in London', Tagore's biographers say, 'his interest was further aroused by reading a Tagore short story in Calcutta's *Modern Review*. Rothenstein wrote to the family asking for more stories; he also offered his hospitality to Rabindranath, should he visit London as was expected.' Now he was stunned by the poems; he arranged to show them to William Butler Yeats. A group of eminences, including Yeats, Pound (who said he felt 'like a painted pict with a stone war-club' before Tagore), and others, gathered to meet the Bengali poet in London: and, before long, Tagore, with the approbation of the two poets mentioned, was a celebrity in London's literary world.

The range of response to the poems, if laudatory, was baffling and diverse, with everyone who mattered bringing to bear upon them the weight and heat of cultural debates they were already enmeshed in. It was, after all, a time of enquiry into all literary standards, only a few years before Modernism would be formally ushered in, and Ezra Pound was already trying to expedite and articulate change. Pound, the great proponent of the 'concrete' and prose-like hardness in poetry, applauded the *Gitanjali*, in a review published in the *Fortnightly Review* in 1913, for, surprisingly, its simplicity and directness. Pound, with his diverse enthusiasms—for European antiquity and 'high' art, for Provençe and Medieval Europe, for Chinese and Anglo-Saxon poetry—seems to find, in his review, something that reminds him of almost all of them in the *Gitanjali*. The Bengali language is likened to the Greek; the *Gitanjali* is compared to the *Paradiso*, and also cited as a 'balance and corrective' to an exhausted strain of European humanism that began with the Renaissance. This is interesting, for Tagore himself was, in many ways, a product of Enlightenment humanism, although he was its independent-minded interpreter. Even more interesting is the fact that Pound compares Tagore, not to the ancient sages, but to a medieval Provençal 'troubador', because he composed and sang his own songs; and his pupils, who sang these songs 'throughout Bengal', he calls Tagore's 'jongleurs'. The comparison is both apt and misdirected; misdirected because the Tagore-song, and its propagation, has been largely synonymous with the existence and evolution of the Bengali middle class; apt because Pound identifies in Tagore a confluence between 'high' and popular culture that was singular at the time.

Yeats, in his introduction to the *Gitanjali*, took the poems to be the utterance of an 'unbroken' Bengali civilisation, the like of which had passed away in the West; not realising just how much of Tagore's achievement—whether in Bengali writing, or in his musical compositions—was hybrid, very much a product of the colonial situation, the result of borrowings, reworkings, and of influence ranging from English literature, Western music, Vaishnavite literature, Baul songs, Kabir *dohas*, Kalidasa, to the Upanishads. Tagore's intellectual background consists of both Western culture, thus, and a new pan-Indian tradition that was being collated, translated, and made material by teachers, Orientalist scholars, and the English and Bengali printing presses. (In 1778, the first book appeared from a printing press in Bengal; it was a Bengali grammar. Tagore's own incipient ambition to be a writer was not unconnected to the existence of these presses: in *My Reminiscences*, he recalls a moment from his boyhood: 'I remember how once I got the types for the letters of my name from some printing press, and what a memorable thing it seemed when I inked and pressed them on paper and found my name imprinted.') The word 'Gitanjali' itself might be interpreted as being symptomatic of a fresh moment in Indian history; it is translated, characteristically, without any of its original import, as 'Song Offerings'. In Tagore's compound word, he combines 'geet' or 'song' with the Hindu 'anjali', or the offering of flowers during prayers to a deity, to produce this third word, whose resonances are not religious, but secular and aesthetic. The word-mutation retells, allegorically, the contradictory energies that went into the creation of that new thing, the secular and humanist thrust of the Indian Renaissance. Yeats seems unaware, too, of the similarities that the political and cultural upheavals in Tagore's culture bore to those in his own. He seems to have instinctively realised, however, that the imagery in the prose-poems was not really transparent or accessible, but hieroglyphic in character, emblems of a foreign language; he compares a particular image to 'one of those figures full of mysterious meaning in a Chinese picture'.

The subsequent fall in Tagore's literary standing in the West is well known. One of the reasons for this was, at least as far as the translations of his short stories were concerned, Tagore's own timidity about Western literary taste. To Edward Thompson he wrote about a planned selection of translated short stories: 'I wonder whether they will be appreciated by English readers. The associations of Indian life are so foreign to them that these are likely to tax their imagination too much for a perfectly comfortable reading.' According to Thompson, 'More and more he toned down or omitted whatever seemed to him characteristically Indian, which very often was what was gripping and powerful.' *The Gardener* and *The Crescent Moon*, collections of poetry, appeared in 1913, 'translations' from the Bengali in the sense that the *Gitanjali* was. People in the West began to wake up to the fact that they had been applauding something very peculiar indeed; and there was a lack, as there still is, of a critical vocabulary with which to estimate the success or failure of Tagore's 'translations'. The fundamental inarticulacy that lay beneath the responses of Tagore's Western readers caused them to move, in what was an absurdly short time in comparison to the more usual duration for shifts in critical opinion to come about, from extremes of praise to extremes of condemnation. In 1917 Pound was to write in a letter: 'Tagore got the Nobel Prize because, after the cleverest boom of our times, after the fiat of the omnipotent literati of distinction, he lapsed into religion and was boomed by the pious non-conformists. Also because he got the Swedish Academy out of the difficulty of deciding between European writers whose claims appeared to conflict.' Much later, in 1935, Yeats would put the problem down to Tagore's English and to the seemingly predetermined, congenital disability that Indians possessed in relation to that language: 'he thought it more important to see and know English than to be a great poet . . . [he] brought out sentimental rubbish and wrecked his reputation. Tagore does not know English, no Indian knows English. Nobody can write with music and style in a language not learned in childhood and ever since the language of his thought.' It is interesting to note that Tagore would have been the first to agree with Yeats's theory, contrary though it was to multilingual traditions in much Indian poetry, and that the views he expressed about the Bengali language in *My Reminiscences* echoes Yeats's final sentence: 'It was because we were taught in our own language that our minds quickened.' His certitude concerning, and his faith in, the mother tongue, were of course the result of the impact of Western thought upon the Bengali mind; paradoxically, his experimentation with creative writing in English, which ran counter to this faith, was an experimentation with possible selves also brought about by colonialism.

While Tagore grew increasingly busy with the ambassadorial duties of a 'world poet', his unofficial side continued to produce, in Bengali, a poetry of the local, and of personal landmarks, recording, often in a new, relaxed, free-verse style, responses to the Bengali landscape and weather, memories of his long-dead sister-in-law Kadambari, a celebration of the river Kopai, which flows close to Santiniketan. These are among his best works, and have been admirably translated into English by Ketaki Kushari Dyson. It would seem (especially as they were written when Tagore's life was dominated by his global tours, lectures, missions, and public attention) that in them Tagore was reaching into what Katherine Mansfield has called the 'secret self' (and Mansfield was a colonial writing, in London, about her childhood in New Zealand) in what was, as far as the West was concerned, his secret language, Bengali.

Tagore's official side continued to deliver his humane, universalist message, in the form of lectures and essays, of which a substantial number are in English. Some of these texts are certainly susceptible to the criticism of being abstract and, in Pound's words in another context regarding Tagore, 'too pious'. On closer reading, the texts, however, are actually revealed to be much more heterogeneous than one might have suspected, informed by personal idiosyncracies, ideas, and enthusiasms. There is no purely 'official' side; close examination reveals that even the most abstract of his texts in prose embody the nuances and contradictions of his private vision, and are responsive to the pressures of time and place. *Nationalism* (1917), for instance, is an example of Tagore conducting, in English prose, what Yeats called one's 'quarrel with others'. Written during the Great War, it is of course also informed by a horror at the sustained aggression that the European nation-state was capable of; but it is mainly the work of a colonial in the midst of change in his own country, uneasy with the concepts of the nation and of nationalism; for nationalism, he makes clear in his chapter on British nationalism, is synonymous, for him, with colonialism. On India he is prescient: 'Races ethnologically different have in this country come into close contact. This fact has been and still continues to be the most important one in our own history. It is our mission to face it and prove our humanity by dealing with it in the fullest truth.' Thus, '[those] of us in India who have come under the delusion that mere political freedom will make us free have accepted their lessons from the West as gospel truth . . .' Tagore, who wrote this in the second decade of the century, must be one of the first Indian writers to raise the question of whether the secular nation-state is an adequate structure to accommodate India's cultural and religious heterogeneity, its various mainstream and marginal peoples. The quarrel is also a private one, and must be understood in the context of Tagore's discomfiture with the politics of Indian nationalism; his strained, if outwardly respectful, relations with Gandhi; and his ambivalence towards the Swadeshi and terrorist movements in Bengal, which he identifies, in his novel *Ghare Baire* (The Home and the World), with purely masculine drives and energies.

Tagore's other notable work in English prose, *The Religion of Man* (1931), is, as a prefatory note says, 'based on lectures delivered by the author in 1930 at Manchester College, Oxford'. The title refers to a famous, and rather strange, conversation Tagore had with Albert Einstein that year, in which Tagore argued that the realisation and perception of truth and beauty depended upon man, while Einstein pointed out that truth had an independent existence. At the end of this conversation, Einstein had said, oddly and intriguingly for a scientist: 'I cannot prove my conception is right, but that is my religion'—odd not because of the invocation of religion, but because of his confession, to a layman in science, that he could not prove a basic scientific hypothesis.

At first glance, the chapters in *The Religion of Man* read like extended prose-poems rather than fully developed arguments once delivered as lectures. Gradually, however, the shape of certain concerns begins to become visible; for one thing, science is a major actor in the book. (Tagore, as educationist, had once written a book in Bengali popularising science.) Both a critique of and an enquiry into science, the book is, first of all, an example of Tagore's incorporation of scientific vocabulary into his English prose style. The first sentence is a cross between the language of the Genesis and that of physics: 'Light, as the radiant energy of creation, started the ring-dance of atoms in the diminutive sky . . .' Scientific metaphors are used to formulate what are fundamentally philosophical ideas (in this Tagore belongs to his time, and joins T.S. Eliot, with his 'platinum' metaphor for literary creation, and D.H. Lawrence, speaking of 'carbon' in a letter on a similar subject):

> Relationship is the fundamental truth of this world of appearance. Take, for instance, a piece of coal. When we pursue the fact of it to its ultimate composition, substance which seemingly is the most stable element in it vanishes in centres of revolving forces. These are the units, called the elements of carbon, which can be further analysed into a certain number of protons and electrons. Yet these electrical facts are what they are, not in their detachment, but in their interrelationship, and though possibly they themselves may be further analysed, nevertheless the pervasive truth of interrelation which is manifested in them will remain.

An aesthetic point is being made. 'Interrelation' is the quality of synthesis in a work of art; it is also a feature of a poet's entire oeuvre, especially Tagore's, the dynamic set of relations that is vital to the creation, and understanding, of his work; and it refers to the inseparability of the various cultural strands that produce a creative tension in authors such as Tagore.

Interestingly, the book reminds us how much popular science might have informed the images and conceits in Tagore's poetry; the quasi-botanical observation in the first chapter, 'A seed carries packed in a minute receptacle a future which is enormous in its contents both in time and space', reminds one of the famous Poem No. 36 in the collection *Balaka* (Wild Ducks), in which the poet-narrator, witnessing the flight of wild birds in the evening, has a vision of, in Ketaki Dyson's translation, 'millions' of potential 'seed-birds'. Similarly, the description, in the poem 'Briksha Bandana' (A Hymn to Trees), of the movement of vegetation and nature across an earth that was once a desert—the movement is not peaceful, but characterised as a 'war'—owes a great deal to the Darwinian thought about which Tagore expresses reservations in *The Religion of Man*.

The most remarkable chapter in the book, however, has not to do with science at all; it is about one of Tagore's literary antecedents, the devotional Baul sect in Bengal. (The title of the chapter, 'The Man of My Heart', is a translation of a phrase, *moner maanush*, that Baul poets used to refer to God, and which Tagore reused in some of his own songs.) The chapter must be the first instance of a major Indian poet mapping the position of a local tradition—what A.K. Ramanujan called the 'little' traditions—in relation, implicitly, to his own evolution as a poet, at a time when all that was supposed to be valuable in Indian culture were the main scriptural, philosophical, and literary texts in Sanskrit. It is an early example of recovery, by an Indian poet, of an unrecognised influence; it hints at the complex 'interrelationships', between local and mainstream, oral and inscribed, devotional and secular, that went into the creation of the literary imagination of the Indian Renaissance.

Tagore's presence in the English language has recently grown. There are the translations by William Radice, Ketaki Kushari Dyson, by his biographers Andrew Robinson and Krishna Dutta, and most recently a series of Tagore translations under the stewardship of Sukanta Chaudhuri. Almost each publication provokes a controversy, or at the very least disagreement, and in some cases a furore. Scholarly work is being done as well; the Sahitya Akademi has brought out *The English Writings of Rabindranath Tagore*, edited by Sisir Kumar Das, in three volumes (Volume One was published in 1994, Volumes Two and Three were published simultaneously in 1996); the size of the enterprise reminds one that there is more to Tagore's writings in English than the works mentioned above, and other fairly well-known texts such as *Creative Unity* (1922). Moreover, the title of the publication makes a necessary critical point, because it draws our attention to the fact that Tagore wrote not in an unnameable universal language; by isolating his English writings, it both historicises and contextualises Tagore. There have been misleading titles in the past, which have consigned Tagore to a sort of ahistorical, contextless vacuum from which he needs to be rescued; probably the most notable among them is Macmillan's *Collected Poems and Plays of Rabindranath Tagore* (1936), which mainly consists of Tagore's creative reworkings in English, a fact not mentioned in the book. For many years this was the main collection, in English, of Tagore's writings; the distortions caused by the title are self-evident.

The issue, finally, is not so much whether Tagore wrote English well or badly; that particular debate risks ignoring the complexity of his engagement with the language. Paradoxically, it is his English, the language of his public and international persona, that is shaped by his cultural confusion, personal drives, inspirations, and limitations, more nakedly than his Bengali, where the formal accomplishment at first conceals these contradictions; and these contradictions at least partly hold the key to an understanding of Tagore's achievement, his marginalisation in the West, and his continuing interest to us today.

8

Sri Aurobindo

PETER HEEHS

Sri Aurobindo (1872–1950) has an international reputation as a mystical philosopher and is known throughout India as a revolutionary politician. Many of his readers, absorbed in the substance of his 'message', have insufficient awareness of his achievement as a writer of English poetry and prose. Others accept uncritically the judgement of his literary champions without themselves putting in the effort needed to appreciate his place in English-language literature. Difficult of approach, detached from twentieth-century developments, Aurobindo's poetry, essays, and other writings require and reward close reading.

Aurobindo was the first writer of Indian blood and birth to produce a major literary corpus almost entirely in English. Born Aurobindo Ghose in Calcutta in 1872, he was not allowed to learn Bengali, but was sent by his anglophile father to a missionary school in Darjeeling, then to St Paul's School, London, and King's College, Cambridge. He learned English as his first language and mastered Latin, Greek, and French at school, but did not begin studying Bengali and Sanskrit till he became an Indian Civil Service probationer at Cambridge. Years later he wrote a volume of capable Bengali prose, and some verse in that language and in Sanskrit; but English remained always, as he said, his 'natural' if not his 'native' language.

Emulating his brother Manmohan, a friend of Laurence Binyon and Oscar Wilde and later a minor literary figure in India, Aurobindo began writing English poetry as a schoolboy. His early verse, some of which was published later in *Songs to Myrtilla* (1898), shows the influence of the Greek and Latin classics and of English Romanticism. At Cambridge he worked on lyrics, a long ballad, a play, and a philosophical dialogue in the manner of Plato by way of Wilde.

Barred from the civil service by his inability to ride, Aurobindo got a job in the administration of the Maharaja of Baroda before leaving England in 1893. He remained in Baroda for fourteen years. Within a few months of his return to India he began a series of newspaper articles criticising the country's moribund political life. Too radical in his opinions and too lacking in reverence for established leaders, he was muzzled after a few instalments. For more than a decade he published nothing on political subjects. Instead, he mastered Bengali and Sanskrit, wrote criticism (*Bankim Chandra Chatterjee*, 1893–4; 'The Age of Kalidasa', 1902) and did translations (Kalidasa's *Vikramorvasie*, published 1911). Basing himself on Sanskrit sources, he produced two long verse narratives, *Urvasie* (published *c.* 1898) and *Love and Death* (written 1899, published 1921). These show a growing mastery of English blank verse, which would remain his preferred metre throughout.

Aurobindo never doubted that a regular rhythmic line was the right medium for poetic utterance; but he was also a believer in the Romantic cult of the inspired poet. True inspiration could be channelled only by one who had mastered a literature's traditions and tools. When the genuine poet opened himself to inspiration, the result was 'an identity of word and sound, of thought and word, of sound and emotion which seems to have been preordained from the beginning of the world and only awaited its destined hour to leap into existence' ('Poetry', written *c.* 1898). Aurobindo had spent more than fifteen years absorbing the spirit of English poetry from Chaucer to Swinburne; his many languages had given him an extensive if sometimes overly classical vocabulary; his study of Shakespeare, Milton, Tennyson, and poets of the hour like Stephen Philips had given him a technical mastery of English metre. All was ready for the touch of inspiration, which came he reports in a 'white heat' during the writing of *Love and Death*. The result bears comparison with the best of nineteenth-century English narrative poetry:

He down the gulf where the loud waves collapsed
Descending, saw with floating hair arise
The daughter of the sea in pale green light,
A million mystic breasts suddenly bare,
And came beneath the flood and stunned beheld
A mute stupendous march of waters race
To reach some viewless pit beneath the world.

Aurobindo had been convinced since his student days that India had to rid itself of foreign rule if it was to survive as a spiritual entity. No imperial power had ever granted freedom on request; a subject nation had the right to take it by force. From around 1900 Aurobindo and his friends began to organise a revolutionary network with centres in Baroda and Bengal. When the movement against the Partition of Bengal created enough popular enthusiasm to sustain aggressive political activity, Aurobindo left his comfortable job in Baroda and in 1906 came to Calcutta to be principal of the newly created Bengal National College (August 1906). Asked by Extremist political leader Bipin Chandra Pal to contribute to a new English daily newspaper, *Bande Mataram*, Aurobindo soon became its chief editorial writer and one of Bengal's leading political strategists. Thinking back on Aurobindo's *Bande Mataram* writings, Jawaharlal Nehru wrote in 1962: 'The great anti-partition movement in Bengal gained much of its philosophy from him and, undoubtedly, prepared the day for the great movements led by Mahatma Gandhi.'

Aurobindo was, however, no believer in Gandhi's gospel of non-violence. When the revolutionary movement he had started turned to terrorism, it had his tacit approval. A botched assassination attempt of 1908 led to the arrests of Aurobindo and many of his colleagues. During a year-long confinement while his case was under trial, he had a series of mystical experiences that changed the orientation of his life. When he returned to politics after his release in 1909, he looked on the struggle against British imperialism as one part of a mission of world transformation he had received from the Divine. In *Karmayogin*, the English weekly newspaper he founded at this time, political journalism shares space with tracts on education and art (*A System of National Education, The National Value of Art*), articles on yogic philosophy (later published in *The Ideal of the Karmayogin*, 1918, and *Man—Slave or Free?*, 1922), translations from Bankimchandra Chattopadhyaya and the Upanishads, and poems like 'Who' and 'Invitation' that show his ability to make deceptively easy rhythm and diction carry the burden of profound thought and experience.

In February 1910, hearing from friends that the British police were about to arrest him, and from his 'inner guide' that he should leave Bengal for French territory, Aurobindo went to Pondicherry, where he remained for the rest of his life. He at first planned to return to Bengal after a year or two, but soon became absorbed in the solitary practice of yoga. Most traditional yogic paths aim at an escape from the rounds of birth and death in a blissful state beyond the phenomenal world. Aurobindo's 'integral yoga' sees freedom from the world as a first step towards the transformation of the world into a vessel of the divine being-consciousness-bliss (*sat-chit-ananda*). For this transformation, work under the divine guidance is as important as dwelling in the divine presence. During the forty years he passed in Pondicherry, Aurobindo never ceased working with his pen, producing a vast body of poetry, philosophical prose, and correspondence.

Between 1910 and 1914 Aurobindo published nothing, but filled notebooks with research on the Vedas, the Upanishads, linguistics, and other subjects. He also wrote some finely crafted essays on spiritual and cultural subjects (published posthumously in *Essays Divine and Human*, 1994), and poems that are transcripts of spiritual experience or aspiration. 'Meditations of Mandavya' (1913) records the moods of bhakti in a way reminiscent of the songs of the Bengali mystic Ramprasad, or the poems of Tagore's *Gitanjali*:

> Lo, I have cursed Thee, lo I have denied
> Thy love, Thy being. Strike me with Thy rod,
> Convince me that Thou art, O leave it not
> To Thy dumb messengers that have no heart,
> No wrath in the attack, no angered love,
> No exultation in the blow that falls . . .
> There is no sign, there comes not any voice.
> And yet, alas! I know he will return
> And He will soothe my wounds and charm my heart;
> I shall again forgive, again shall love . . .

In 1914 Aurobindo joined forces with Paul and Mirra Richard to publish *Arya*, 'a Review of pure philosophy'. The Richards were obliged to live outside India between 1915 and 1920, but Aurobindo continued to bring out the review single-handedly until 1921. Working on as many as six pieces at a time, he produced every month sixty-four printed pages of prose: philosophy (*The Life Divine*), yoga (*The Synthesis of Yoga*), scriptural exegesis (*The Secret of the Veda, Essay on the Gita*), sociology and political science (*The Human Cycle, The Ideal of Human Unity*), literary and cultural criticism (*The Future Poetry, The Foundation of Indian Culture*)—in all around a dozen books in less than seven years.

Most of the works that came out serially in the *Arya* were revised and republished as books during the 1940s. *The Life Divine* (1939–40) was the first to appear. This unquestionably is Aurobindo's most significant work of expository prose, the principal statement of his philosophy of realistic monism. Like Shankara, the ninth-century formaliser of the philosophy of illusionistic monism (advaita), Aurobindo starts with the perception (gained through mystic experience) of the One Reality (brahman). Aurobindo however rejects Shankara's notion that the world is illusion, maya. It is rather 'the manifestation of the Real and therefore is itself real'. Brahman, in its nature-pure existence (sat), consciousness (chit), and delight (ananda), has 'involved' itself in matter. From this apparently inert, unconscious, and unfeeling substance evolve conscious life and mind. Between the higher nature of sat-chit-ananda and the lower nature of matter, life, and mind is an intermediate plane that Aurobindo calls supermind. Human beings feel the influence of this plane indirectly through intuition, inspiration, the workings of genius. When supermind is able to act directly it will transform the world of knowledge and ignorance, pain and pleasure, life and death, into a divine creation, a Life Divine.

The spiritual life and the life of the world are often thought to be incompatible. Most people are involved in the various activities of life and are indifferent to or incredulous of the Divine. A few are absorbed in a life of meditation and self-discipline—of yoga—and are indifferent to or contemptuous of the world and its activities. Aurobindo rejects this dichotomy: 'All life is yoga' is the epigraph of his major work on the subject, *The Synthesis of Yoga* (1955). Unlike most other teachers of yoga, Aurobindo does not present a fixed technique of practice. Rather he sketches the outlines of a free method of inner development based on the three traditional paths of yoga: the path of action, the path of knowledge, the path of love, as well as his own yoga of self-perfection.

The transformation of life Aurobindo speaks of must include, if it is to be complete, a remoulding of human society. In *The Human Cycle* (1949) Aurobindo traces the evolution of human cultures from the 'symbolic' stage to the age of rationalism and individualism. He predicts that a deeper 'subjective' and spiritual age will follow in which the problems posed by our present civilisation will be resolved. In *The Ideal of Human Unity* (1919, revised edition 1950) he examines the evolution of political aggregates, noting the trend to ever larger units, which will lead in the end to some kind of political unification of the human race. He insists on the need to preserve diversity and avoid uniformity even while overcoming the divisions that continue to plague humanity.

During the six years that followed the cessation of *Arya* in 1921, Aurobindo wrote comparatively little. In 1926 he stopped seeing visitors and even the members of the community of seekers that had formed around him. Leaving the ashram to be run by his collaborator Mirra Richard (now known as the Mother), Aurobindo concentrated himself on the practice of yoga. For some time he remained in touch with his followers through letters. By 1933 he was spending as much as ten hours a day reading and replying to their questions. His replies, published in three volumes in 1972, are filled with insight on all aspects of life, spiritual as well as 'ordinary'. Some of them are written in extremely attractive prose, notably those published along with other texts as *The Mother* (1928).

Early critical reactions to *The Life Divine* were positive. The book was favourably reviewed in the *Times Literary Supplement* by the author and explorer Sir Francis Younghusband, and praised by Aldous Huxley as 'a book not merely of the highest importance as regards its contents, but remarkably fine as a piece of philosophic literature'. Like Aurobindo a product of the classical side of an English public school and university, Huxley was able to appreciate the cadences of *The Life Divine*'s 'periodic' sentences. Many contemporary readers find them intolerably long and involved. Aurobindo seems to want to pack in every ramification of his argument, anticipate every possible objection before putting his full stop. The result can be highly satisfying to a retentive intellect, but demands more effort than most readers, bred on our journalists' prose, are willing to give.

Aurobindo's essays are more stylish and accessible, models of clarity and concision that wear their erudition lightly. Some, like 'The Hour of God' (*c.* 1918), and 'The Law of the Way' (*c.* 1927) owe their appeal to cadences and diction reminiscent of the Bible. Aurobindo's aphoristic writings, influenced by Nietzsche and Indian Sutra literature, have lapidary precision and suggestive depths of meaning:

> The whole world yearns after freedom, yet each creature is in love with his chains; this is the first paradox and inextricable knot of our nature. ('Thoughts and Glimpses')

Among the works published in *Arya, The Future Poetry* (1954) might come as a surprise to some. What does this theory of poetics, illustrated by a detailed history of English literature, have to do with the cosmic preoccupations of *The Life Divine?* To most of us, poetry, if we read it at all, is a source of emotional and intellectual pleasure. To the writers of the Vedas and Tantras, inspired rhythmic language, what they called the mantra, was an expression of the creative power of the Divine. According to Aurobindo, all true poetry partakes in some measure of this power. The greatest poetry, that of Valmiki, Shakespeare, and Dante at their best, is no less divinely creative than the rhythms of the Vedic rishis. Building on ideas elaborated by Matthew Arnold in his *Study of Poetry* (1880), Aurobindo graded poetry according to its level of inspiration and its degree of poetic perfection. The highest poetry came from what Aurobindo termed 'overhead' planes, and approaches the absolute perfection of the 'inevitable' word.

In the poems he wrote in Pondicherry, Aurobindo strove to capture the loftiness and inevitability of the inspired rhythmic word, the mantra. Much, though not all, of this poetry was spiritual in inspiration. Like mystics of all lands and ages, Aurobindo found poetry more suitable for the expression of inner experience than prose. Sometimes he made use of well-established forms, as in the sonnet 'Liberation' (1939):

My mind, my soul grow larger than all Space;
    Time founders in that vastness glad and nude:
The body fades, an outline, a dim trace,
    A memory in the spirit's solitude.

This universe is a vanishing circumstance
    In the glory of a white infinity
Beautiful and bare for the Immortal's dance,
    House-room of my immense felicity.

In the thrilled happy giant void within
    Thought lost in light and passion drowned in bliss,
Changing into a stillness hyaline,
    Obey the edict of the Eternal's peace.

Life's now the Ineffable's dominion;
Nature is ended and the spirit alone.

But Aurobindo was also moved to seek new forms and metres to clothe his inspiration, as in the delicate 'Trance' (1933):

A naked and silver-pointed star
    Floating near the halo of the moon;
A storm-rack, the pale sky's fringe and bar,
    Over waters stilling into swoon.

My mind is awake in stirless trance,
    Hushed my heart, a burden of delight;
Dispelled is the senses' flicker-dance,
    Mute the body aureate with light.

Some of his most interesting metrical experiments are recreations of Greek and Latin forms in English. 'Descent' (1942) gains much of its rushing impetuosity from the trochaic-dactylic movement of its sapphics:

All my cells thrill swept by a surge of splendour,
Soul and body stir with a mighty rapture,
Light and still more light like an ocean billows
    Over me, round me.

Aurobindo's most sustained attempt to recapture the spirit of classical metres in English is *Ilion*, an incomplete epic in dactylic hexameters telling the story of the fall of Troy. Parts of this were published in 1942 as an appendix to *On Quantitative Metre*, a work that contains much of interest on English prosody in general.

In 1916, around the time he abandoned *Ilion*, Aurobindo began work on a poem that would occupy him for the next thirty-five years. In early drafts, *Savitri* (published 1950–1) is a narrative closely following the famous episode of the *Mahabharata*. During successive revisions this 'legend' became a 'symbol' of Aurobindo's yoga. Aswapathy is the aspiring soul of humanity ascending to the home of the Divine Mother. The 'kingdoms' he passes through are the inner and higher 'planes' or states of being that Aurobindo explored during his meditations. Aurobindo describes these in prose in the last chapters of *The Life Divine* and in some of his letters; in *Savitri* he evokes them in lines that have great rhythmic and rhetorical beauty, but at the same time the concreteness of things actually seen:

Abandoned on a canvas of torn air,
A picture lost in far and fading streaks,
The earth-nature's summits sank below his feet:
He climbed to meet the infinite more above.
The Immobile's ocean-silence saw him pass,
An arrow leaping through eternity
Suddenly shot from the tense bow of Time,
A ray returning to its parent sun.

At the summit of his ascent, Aswapathy has the vision of the Divine Mother and implores her: 'Incarnate the white passion of thy force, / Mission to earth some living form of thee.' The goddess descends as the woman Savitri, who lives her predestined year of happiness with her husband Satyavan. When he dies, Savitri follows his soul into the inner worlds and engages Death in epic battle. He begins, full of scorn for the ephemerality of love:

A transient painting on a holiday's floor
Traced for a moment's beauty love was made.
Or if a voyager on the eternal trail,
Its objects fluent change in its embrace
Like waves to a swimmer upon infinite seas.

But in the end Savitri's passion proves stronger. Death, defeated, is revealed as a mask of the Godhead, who tempts Savitri with 'solitary bliss'. She refuses, demanding instead boons 'for earth and men'. Then Savitri and Satyavan, 'A dual power of God in an ignorant world', return to earth, there to enjoy a love that having 'looked upon the face of God', had 'learned its heavenly significance':

> Yet nothing is lost of mortal love's delight.
> Heaven's touch fulfills but cancels not our earth.

The first part of *Savitri* was published in 1950; the second and third parts, posthumously, in 1951. The diverse critical reactions to this epic of almost 24,000 lines epitomise the highly polarised critical response to Aurobindo's oeuvre. K.R. Srinivasa Iyengar closes his discussion of the poem by approvingly quoting the opinion: '*Savitri* is perhaps the most powerful artistic work in the world for expanding man's mind towards the Absolute.' But many younger poets and critics stand unimpressed before Aurobindo's 'outsized reputation', wondering whether *Savitri*, however original and ambitious, has any real poetic value. Opinions so disparate evidently are based on differing sets of critical presuppositions. Most of Aurobindo's advocates accept him as a present-day rishi whose writings should be judged, if at all, in accordance with his own literary theorics. His detractors, situating themselves within twentieth-century critical discourse, find him outmoded and irrelevant. Most of his works were published long after being written, five to fifty years after they might have had an immediate effect on English literature. *Love and Death* came out around the time 'Prufrock' and *The Waste Land* were changing the face of English poetry; *The Life Divine* appeared when Logical Positivism was all the rage. This was a misfortune as far as Aurobindo's reception, during his lifetime, was concerned; but it also saved him from the vagaries of literary fashion. His works continue to be reprinted and discovered by new generations of readers. It is now time to reassess his overall contribution to literature. For this his writings must be read first as literary works among literary works, and second as expressions of the particular genius of their creator.

9

Two Early-Twentieth-Century Women Writers

Cornelia Sorabji and Sarojini Naidu

RANJANA SIDHANTA ASH

Cornelia Sorabji and Sarojini Naidu, who were prominent in public life, and associated with women's causes and politics during the last period of British rule, were also acclaimed for their writing in Britain and British India. Sorabji's books about traditional women who lived in purdah, and her reflections on her life in Britain and India, were reviewed enthusiastically by British and Indian newspapers and journals. Her pro-British and anti-nationalist sentiments were well known. Naidu was famous for her poetry and her brilliance as a public orator. She was prominent in the nationalist movement and became one of Gandhi's most important women colleagues. He gave her the title 'Bharata Kokila'—the Nightingale of India. Today, neither woman is remembered for her writing. Sorabji has been almost forgotten and Naidu, notwithstanding recent efforts to revive her poetry, comes to mind merely as a national icon.

Cornelia Sorabji (1866–1954) was one of the many children of Reverend Sorabji Kharsedji Langrana and Franscina Santya. Her father was a Parsi convert to Anglican Christianity and her mother, of Indian Christian parentage, had been semi-adopted by a titled British couple. Cornelia was born in Nasik, Maharashtra, and educated there and in Poona, where her parents organised their missionary and social work. Though very English in their lifestyle and intimate with the British society around them, the parents were determined to give their children a sense of being Indian. Sorabji was taught the languages of the region—Marathi and Gujarati—and later learnt Persian, Urdu and Bengali for her legal work. A brilliant student, she obtained a scholarship to Oxford where she studied Law. Unfortunately, like all other women, she was not allowed to practise at the Bar until 1923. Returning to India in 1894, she virtually created her own job as Legal Adviser to the Government's Court of Wards. Working in Bengal, Bihar, Orissa, and Assam, she helped the wives and widows of the landed aristocracy whose estates had passed into government hands. The plight of these *purdahnashins*, tradition-bound women confined to the zenana, was central to her social work. She founded the Social Service League in Bengal and attempted to improve the health of mothers and infants. She was active in the movement to raise the age of consent and abolish child-marriage. Her pro-British record was appreciated by the government, which sent her in 1929 and 1931 to speak on its behalf in the United States and Canada. She had divided her life between India and Britain and decided to settle in England on the eve of World War II. Her last years were clouded by physical illness and mental decline; her last book came out in 1936. She died in 1954 with tributes to her work appearing in British papers but barely noticed in independent India.

Cornelia Sorabji's first published work, *Love and Life Behind the Purdah* (1901), is a collection of eleven narratives she called her 'Indian stories'. Some were fictional and others drawn from her first encounters with Indian legal life. Most of them were quite melodramatic, revealing women caught between tradition and change. In 'Love and Death', an Indian woman doctor, given the rare opportunity of training abroad, falls in love with another doctor not knowing that they had been married to each other as infants. During the plague epidemic of 1895 both work hard to save patients using modern medicine. However, when she confronts traditional religion and a sacred fire to appease the gods, she jumps into it, followed by other sacrificial victims. Tradition violated seeks redress. The story was popular enough for it to be reprinted years later in a London magazine.

Stylistically, *Love and Life Behind the Purdah* illustrates several of her mannerisms. She loved syntactic inversions such as 'garbed was she' and 'how know we' and archaic words like 'sward', 'beseem', 'bewraying' and 'thrid'. These recur throughout her books. She was also influenced during her university years by Pateresque purple passages and overdrawn figurative prose. A typical simile compares the chatter of pilgrims to 'some mountain torrent . . . glittering light-imprisoned under the brilliant rays of a lingering death'.

Her second book, *Sun-babies: Studies in the Child-life of India* (1904), and its later supplement, *Sun Babies* (1920), are among her best pieces of writing. She loved children, indeed had an instinctive empathy with them. She never married, though it is said she had a close if platonic relationship with a British judge of the Allahabad High Court who died within a few years of their friendship. Sorabji would have loved to adopt a child, as she wryly admits in the preface to *Sun-babies*. These stories of mainly street children in different parts of India—Srinagar, Allahabad, Calcutta—vividly capture details of daily life: domestic interiors, the drudgery of domestic service in upper-class houses, the camaraderie of homeless bazaar urchins. She uses her delicious sense of irony to keep some of the sadder episodes from descending into sentimentality. She also experiments with English patois to capture Indian dialect. An altercation between a six-year-old boy, employed to scare away birds, and a maidservant is illustrative:

> What know you of the Miss Sahib? . . . Does the Miss Sahib listen to the noise of you? What for is your voice, but to *bak-bak-o*, to jabber and quarrel among the womenfolk of your kind? ('The Chota Chaukidar')

Sorabji's seminal work, *Between the Twilights: Being Studies of Indian Women by One of Themselves* (1908), has a title indicative of her sympathy for women in purdah, who were subjected to domestic patriarchy by family estate managers, household priests, and occasionally by government agents.

For her, these women floated 'elusive in the half-light between two civilisations, sad by reason of something lost, and by reason of the move that may come to be rejected hereafter . . .' Some of the fourteen stories, based on actual events or allegorical in intent, use the stylistic manner of her earlier work. There is lush description with humorous asides, and there is the romanticisation of Indian history. The Rajput's chivalry and the Rajput woman's determination to uphold honour and be a sati appealed to her sense of moral uprightness, though she had to admit that 'suttee' did get misused with time. She was perceptive in describing the plight of the Hindu widow, condemned to a life of misery and self-sacrifice, calling it 'suttee by stealth'. The book's literary merit lies in Sorabji's skill in combining wry humour with detailed descriptions, creating an authentic picture of zenana life:

> Sullenly they lived, silently year in and year out, not a single interest coming from the outside world to distract their attention from their hates and resentments . . . Palace walls shut them in securely, shut them in with their broodings and bemoanings, with the intrigues and loyalties of their several waiting-women, and with one gray-white *Sarus* . . . restlessly walking on his high stilts.

Even when she wrote tracts she embellished them with literary touches. *The Purdahnashin* (1917) was written to advance the cause of better hygiene and child care in the zenana and to influence reform. Teachers and nurses would have to know Hinduism as practised and get to love their charges. Only then, recognising genuine bonds of affection, would orthodox women 'thrid' modern ways with their 'eastern calm'. *Shubala: A Child-mother* (1920) was written to combat the practice of child-marriage and the ruination of girls' health through repeated pregnancies. Sorabji leavens the grim story of a lovely child, prematurely old at eighteen with six children, with humorous descriptions of zamindari offspring driving off with their unfortunate child-brides in flashy Rolls-Royces.

Sorabji was a true bi-cultural—not a hyphenated being but one sharing two cultures and two homes. While she was British in many respects, she continued to wear her sari in the Parsi style, continued to respect the many faiths and philosophies of India's religions without any of the usual Christian missionary's sense of moral superiority. She retold Indian myths and legends (*Indian Tales of the Great Ones: Among Men, Women, and Bird-people*, 1916) with only one judgemental comment, directed against Razia, who failed in her queenship because, unlike wise Queen Victoria, Razia 'thought that for success she must put aside her womanhood'.

Fluent in diverse genres, Sorabji also wrote biographies of her parents and her sister, Susie, who was the well-known head of a large educational institution in Poona. *Therefore* (1924) and *Susie Sorabji: Christian-Parsee Educationist of Western India* (1932) are suffused with religious sentiment and semi-Biblical passages; both books contain Sorabji's desire for an India where people could cross religious barriers and be united in their spiritual and moral ideals.

'Yes, it is true that I have been privileged to know two hearth-stones, to be homed in two countries, England and India', Sorabji wrote in the introduction to her best-known work, *India Calling* (1934). It is partly autobiographical, recounting her childhood in Nasik, her youth at Oxford where Benjamin Jowett, the Master of Balliol, befriended her and introduced her to the great and the good. It recalls British friends, including her closest, Elena Rathbone, who later became Lady Richmond (not Eleanor Rathbone MP, according to some erroneous accounts). There are amusing reminiscences of the interesting characters she met during her days as legal adviser, colourful Hindu widows and clever co-wives. What sounds odd, however, fifty years after Independence, is her inability to recognise the failings of the British colonial system. She was critical of all forms of nationalist activity, describing revolutionary nationalists as 'terrorists'. She thought Gandhi almost a fraud for accepting the title of 'Mahatma', and his views on civil disobedience and non-violent resistance she thought 'were built upon deception, his loyalties upon verbiage'. She was also of the opinion that the fondness educated Indian women seemed to have for terrorism required psychological analysis.

Her last book, *India Recalled* (1936), was a return to her legal experiences in the zamindaris. In it she wrote, once again, on the inability of educated Indian women to improve the conditions of the purdahnashins because of their concern with legislation and demands for women's suffrage. She thought only pioneers like her own mother and Pandita Ramabai had been successful because of their selfless devotion to helping others.

Sarojini Naidu (1879–1949) was the eldest daughter of Dr Aghorenath Chattopadhyay, a scientist, and Varadasundari Devi, who wrote poetry in Bengali. They were Bengalis who had discarded their Brahminism for the Brahmo Samaj and made a new home in Hyderabad, then under the suzerainty of the nizams. Sarojini was a precocious and self-willed girl who for three years attended London and Cambridge universities but returned without a degree. In 1898 she married the man she loved, Dr Govindarajulu Naidu, despite parental resistance. He was considerably older than her and from a different linguistic region and caste. She had four children in quick succession and devoted herself to writing poetry and enjoying a happy domestic life. However, she had always been drawn to the nationalist cause. Through Gopal Krishna Gokhale and Mahatma Gandhi she was initiated into the Indian National Congress, becoming its first woman president at the Kanpur session in 1925. She participated in the many phases of Congress resistance to British rule, from the Civil Disobedience movement of the 1920s to the final Quit India movement of 1942.

Agitating, addressing meetings, courting imprisonment and going to jail, meant sacrificing her poetry. A brilliant speaker, she was sent abroad to propagate the nationalist cause, visiting the United States but also countries with large Indian populations, like Kenya and South Africa. After Independence she was made Governor of Uttar Pradesh and died in Lucknow while in office.

While a collection of Naidu's juvenilia had been published privately by her father in 1896—*Poems* by Miss S. Chattopadhyay—her reputation rests on three volumes published subsequently. They are *The Golden Threshold* (1905), *The Bird of Time: Songs of Life, Death and the Spring* (1912), and *The Broken Wing: Songs of Love, Death and Destiny 1915–16* (1917). A fourth, posthumous volume, *The Feather of the Dawn*, consisting of poems written in the late 1920s, was published in 1961. Naidu was untouched by the modernist movement in English poetry ushered in by Ezra Pound and T.S. Eliot. Her four collections do not differ from each other in form or content but present a continuity of poetic imagination. They revel in metrical variations and in highly embellished images and lilting cadences akin to song, all of which are used to put on show a romantic India of myth and legend. There are also fanciful recreations of rural and city life and poems of patriotism.

In 'Sunalini: A Passage from Her Life', an unpublished autobiographical fragment written in Switzerland before she was married,

Naidu spoke of her sudden realisation that she was a poet with 'new irresistible, unutterable longings and sensations'. These longings found expression in celebrations of women and womanhood, as well as in poems in which the love for her country borders on reverence. The claims of race, gender, class, religion, and ethnicity are not contesting ones in her poetry.

Naidu's two British mentors were Arthur Symons and Edmund Gosse. Symons, who wrote an introduction for *The Golden Threshold*, saw in her verse 'the temperament of a women of the East finding expression through a Western language and under partly Western influences'. Edmund Gosse's advice to Naidu was to strive towards a poetry that was not a '*rechauffé* of Anglo-Saxon sentiment in an Anglo-Saxon setting but some revelation of the heart of India.' Naidu heeded his advice and 'Indianised' her verse with delight. Mythic heroines like Sita and Savitri, Damyanti and Draupadi; legendary figures like Padmini of Chittor and Princess Zebunnissa; and images and poetic conceits from the Urdu ghazal and the *Gita Govinda*—champak and rosebud, bulbul and nightingale—began populating her poetry, framed in anapaests, iambs, and trochees in the alliterative and melodic stanzas that were to become her signature:

> Lightly, lightly, we bear her along,
> She sways like a flower in the wind of our song;
> She skims like a bird on the foam of a stream,
> She floats like a laugh from the lips of a dream . . .

These lines from 'Palanquin-bearers', the much-anthologised first poem in *The Golden Threshold*, conjure up the rhythmic movement of the men carrying palanquins in a metre she used frequently—the anapaestic. She described some of her poems as 'folk-songs' and it is easy to see why.

In another popular poem, 'Bangle-sellers', each of the four stanzas describes bangles of different hues that will match the women wearing them: 'rainbow-tinted circles of light' for happy daughters and wives; 'silver and blue as the mountain mist' for a maiden; 'sunlit corn' and 'the flame of her marriage fire' for the bride; 'purple and gold-flecked gray' for the woman who has 'journeyed through life midway'.

In her public life Naidu was one of the founders of the two premier women's organisations of the day—the Women's India Association and the All-India Women's Conference; she advocated, in opposition to Cornelia Sorabji, the extension of voting rights to women. For all her Romanticism, she was aware of the oppression a Hindu woman lived under—the symbols of a woman's married life, the bangles of Naidu's poems, were broken almost at the very instant of her husband's death. In 'Dirge' Naidu presents a defining moment in a Hindu widow's life:

Shatter her shining bracelets, break the string
Threading the mystic marriage-beads that cling
Loth to desert a sobbing throat so sweet,
Unbind the golden anklets on her feet,
Divest her of her azure veils and cloud
Her living beauty in a living shroud.

Each of Naidu's collections has several love poems, some no more than pastoral idylls, others intensely subjective, about the remembrance of separation and final loss, and of impossible choices like those she had to make between her private world of poetry and domestic concerns, and an all-consuming political life which took her away from her home and family. 'To My Children', with its four eight-line stanzas, one for each of her children, and with the images and hopes patterned around their names—'Golden sun of victory' for the eldest, Jaya Surya—is written without a trace of sentimentality. But the love expressed in most of her verse is not a mother's love. It is heterosexual passion which finds its most developed expression in a long sequence of twenty-four poems titled 'The Temple: A Pilgrimage of Love'. The sequence proceeds from poems of the joy of love, through the pains of being rejected, to an interesting climax of defiance. The woman in love is no medieval bhakta sublimating her desire into devotion to her god, but a strong-willed person whose final declaration rings fearless:

My proud soul shall be unforgiven
For a passionate sin it will ne'er repent,
And I shall be doomed, O Love, and driven
And hurled from Heaven's high battlement . . .

. . . .

My outlawed spirit shall crave no pardon.

Naidu breaks the mould of her own fanciful beguiling verse when she undertakes what might be called her 'public' poetry. Very aware of her identity as an Indian, she frequently said she was no different from other Indian poets—Tagore, Iqbal, Nazrul—caught up in the national movement. Like them, she chose political subjects and shifted from the personal to the nationalist with ease. On Gandhi she composed a sonnet, 'The Lotus', using an improbable metaphor to describe the leader's unique magnetism. Perhaps most surprising in the light of subsequent history was her friendship with Mohammad Ali Jinnah. When she knew him their common goal was to win freedom without dividing Hindus and Muslims. Her poem 'Awake' was addressed to him and recited by her at the 1915 Congress session.

As one of India's finest public speakers in English and occasionally in Persianised Urdu, Sarojini Naidu's career as an orator has yet to be reviewed as an aspect of her creative use of English rhetoric. She knew all the techniques of rhetoric, as is revealed by a study of an early selection of her lectures, *Speeches and Writings of Sarojini Naidu* (1918). She made frequent use of parallelisms by synonym, outright antithesis, repetition, alliteration, and crescendo. Skilled in delivery, with a superb sense of timing and abundant humour, she was as resourceful in her public debates as in her poetry; her verbal flow carried her audience along even when she was not clear in her argument:

> Ours has been an epic struggle, covering many years and costing many lives. It has been a struggle of heroes chiefly anonymous in their millions. It has been a struggle of women transformed into strength and power like Kali . . . It has been a struggle of youth suddenly transformed into power itself . . .

Her words to the second All-India Writers Conference held at Varanasi in 1948 summarise her Romantic view of the importance of impulse and spontaneity in poetic practice, as well as her Nehruvian-nationalist opinion of the issue of an Indian literature in English:

> Be masters of whatever language you like, so long as it is the language of the human heart and spirit. Literature is the only way truth can be kept alive.

10

Gandhi and Nehru

The Uses of English

SUNIL KHILNANI

In the long, uneasy, and interminable task of making English an Indian language, Mohandas Karamchand Gandhi and Jawaharlal Nehru are central figures. Each took the alien language of rule and found ways to make it intimate, fluent, and cantankerous. English made the empire, but they showed how it could be used to unmake it—how the language could be a tool of insubordination and, ultimately, freedom. Neither man was a professional writer (although both could have made their living through writing and journalism), nor did they author fiction or works of the imagination. Their prose is usually read as a mere caption to the busy significance of their lives and acts. Ubiquitous as they are in all other areas of India's twentieth-century landscape, what claim if any do they have to a place in its literary history? The erratic rhythms of politics, not writing, defined their lives. Yet no two Indians exemplified so vividly the extent to which politics is words—a way of structuring human relations through the fragile architecture of language.

They shaped the place and form of English in India in three decisive ways. Gandhi was born in 1869; Nehru died in 1964: their lives encompassed a linguistic century that stretched from the English of legal petitions and imperial proclamations, of diwans, pleaders, and officers of the early Raj, to the official bureaucratese of the Five Year

Plans and the ministries of the independent Indian state. The sheer bulk of their spoken and written words (combined, the published work of Gandhi and Nehru exceed 150 volumes), as well as its historical span, ensured for the English language a countrywide currency. Second, though often ambivalent about the function of English in India, they kept a political commitment to English as a language of public communication. English may have been the 'language of the enemy', yet both wished to accommodate it alongside other Indian languages, recognising it as a vital link not just to the wider world but also between Indians themselves. Finally, the forms in which they wrote—autobiographies, public and private letters, journalistic essays and articles, and works of history—helped to define how these genres came to be understood and used in India, by their contemporaries and by those who came after.

Gandhi's entry into English was, like much of his early life, unsteady and uncomfortable. Born in 1869, the youngest child of the Dewan of Porbandar, he was an ungainly, odd-faced child. He grew, as most Indian sons do, in the company of women. The first language he spoke was Gujarati. At school he was a poor student and wrote badly—his words regularly misspelt, his handwriting ill defined (this was to make him, throughout his later life, dependent on secretaries who could decipher his scrawl). He did not begin to learn English until his last three years of high school, in Rajkot. He floundered: 'English became the medium of instruction in most subjects from the fourth standard. I found myself completely at sea', he wrote in his autobiography. But what he was expected to learn was demanding. From the age of sixteen, prescribed reading included 200 pages of Addison's *Spectator*, 750 lines of *Paradise Lost* (200 to be learned by heart), and *Pride and Prejudice*. Learning the language also removed Gandhi from his own family, opening different realms of experience: 'I was fast becoming a stranger in my own home.'

In 1888 Gandhi sailed for London, a departure and journey that left him linguistically traumatised. Farewell ceremonies required him to deliver a speech, and his first experience of public speaking proved disastrous: 'I had written out a few words of thanks. But I could scarcely stammer them out. I remember my head reeled and my whole frame shook as I stood up to read them.' This vertigo at the prospect of speaking was to be a recurring experience during his years in London. The ship passage to England was equally full of terror: 'I was quite unaccustomed to talking in English, and except for Sjt Mazumdar, all the other passengers in the second saloon were English. I could not speak to them. For I could rarely follow their remarks when they came up to speak to me, and even when I understood, I could not reply. I had to frame every sentence in my mind before I could bring it out.' The voyage was spent in anxious silence, with Gandhi turning his energies to pursuing alimentary interests. He took refuge in a diary, which was continued during his time in London, and which he later translated into arch English: 'Amidst thoughts, I came unconsciously in contact with a carriage. I received some injury. Yet I did not take the help of anybody in walking.'

In London, while learning the law, Gandhi set to the task of making himself an English gentleman. For this, a confident grasp of the language was essential. In his early months he felt acutely his weakness in this respect. To master his fear, he decided to take elocution lessons—his teacher 'recommended Bell's *Standard Elocutionist* as the text book, which I purchased. And I began with a speech of Pitt's.' It was through these first, hesitant steps in impersonation that he was ultimately to find his own voice.

In these early years of life in a foreign culture and language, Gandhi was painfully aware of his timidity, and he had repeatedly to urge boldness on himself to speak. In London, he began to read the daily newspapers (something he had never done in India), and was impressed by the functional, informational style of the press. He developed into a voracious, promiscuous reader: Gibbon, Theosophical pamphlets, and vegetarian tracts, all caught his attention. He moved in a demimonde of immigrant radicals, déclassé intellectuals, spiritualists, and vegetarians. His involvement with marginal vegetarian and religious groups and their publications (for which he sometimes wrote) became, along with the law and journalism, another important influence on his sense of the language.

In 1893 he sailed for South Africa. His two decades there were spent in political activism and legal battles, as well as in bold social experiments, all designed to produce what he referred to as 'right

Indians'. Close friendships with English-speaking Europeans gave him a new ease with the language. In the Transvaal, free from the constraints of India, he established the Phoenix Farm settlement—an attempt at communal living based on principles drawn from European critics of industrialism and from Indian ideas. In South Africa he saw also the humiliations that language could inflict: the whites, he repeatedly noted, invariably referred to Indians as ' "collie", "Mr Samy", "Ramysamy", and the painful expression "coolie clerk".' He displayed a tireless ability to write letters to editors of newspapers and became an expert drafter of petitions and memorials on behalf of the Indian community. He also cultivated what he would later call his 'crankisms' (in 1894, he was advertising himself as the 'Agent' for the esoteric Christian Union and London Vegetarian Society, offering their books for sale, and propagating the ideals of the 'No Breakfast Society'). This rich experience led him not only to establish his own voice and style, it was also to form the basis of his two most substantial books, *Hind Swaraj* and *Satyagraha in South Africa.*

Hind Swaraj was his most rhetorically powerful work. Written in Gujarati, while sailing from England to South Africa, Gandhi worked at an enormous pace, completing the manuscript in ten days. So fast was he writing that, in order to rest his flagging right hand, he wrote part of the manuscript left-handed. There is some irony in this frenetic pace, since one of his targets in the book was what he saw as modernity's obsession with speed, and indeed later he was always to write at a much slower and more deliberate rhythm.

Although *Hind Swaraj* was written in the form of a dialogue between an editor and a reader, in fact the spirit of dialogue was absent. It read more like a series of sermons delivered by the editor (speaking for Gandhi). The purpose of these homilies was to alert Gandhi's compatriots to the dangers of modern civilisation, to warn them against the use of violence in their struggle to expel the British, and to give them a set of guiding principles by which to act.

Published in Gujarati in 1909 by Gandhi's own press at the Phoenix settlement in Natal, he translated it into English himself and published it as *Indian Home Rule*, again from his own press in March 1910. The British, on grounds of sedition, immediately banned it. The South African ban on the book lasted almost thirty years, and was finally lifted in December 1938, the same year that a revised edition was published, which became the standard text. (In 1997 a new edition was published by Cambridge University Press, based on the 1910 English text.)

Although it was to become an iconic work of Indian nationalism, in fact few in India noticed it when it was first published, and it took a decade for it to become well known. An Indian edition, with a new foreword and a 'Note' by C. Rajagopalachari, was first published in 1919. In 1921, Gandhi published the English edition under a modified new title: *Hind Swaraj or Indian Home Rule* (an American edition, published in 1924, had yet another title, *Sermon on the Sea*). The decision to incorporate the Gujarati title into the English edition is noteworthy, suggesting as it does a desire to impress Gandhi's own terminology on the English language. It was a strategy used in later years, as Gandhi developed neologisms and words of his own invention, the most famous being satyagraha ('None of us knew what name to give to our movement. . . . I only knew that some new principle had come into being. As the struggle advanced, the phrase "passive resistance" gave rise to confusion and it appeared shameful to permit this great struggle to be known only by an English name'). By incorporating such words (as well as others like khadi, swadeshi, and ahimsa) into his English writing, he suggested the irreducibility of his vocabulary into English.

Hind Swaraj's status as a nationalist classic was achieved during the period of its South African ban, between 1919 and 1938. Much of its power derived from the clarity of its argumentation and the directness of expression. Gandhi somewhat disingenuously said of it that 'in my opinion it is a book which can be put into the hands of a child'; and it is true that its hallmark is a strong pedagogical desire to explain and convince. It made free with examples, similes, metaphors, and parables, some of them startling in their vividness. One such metaphor (which Gandhi was later to regret) was his lurid reference to Westminster: 'That which you consider to be the Mother of Parliaments is like a sterile woman and a prostitute.'

Gandhi described *Hind Swaraj* as 'a severe condemnation of "modern civilization" '. Of all his writings, it is the most sustained and striking treatment of an important Gandhian theme: the critique of history. Running through the various set-piece dialogues—about Gokhale, terrorism, lawyers, railways—is a polemical critique of one of the central maxims of Western historical consciousness: *historia magistra vitae*. This expressed the idea that history—both as event and as the representation of events in historical writing—provided lessons, examples, and even laws, about the future of human action. The querulous interlocutor of *Hind Swaraj* repeatedly tries to refute the arguments unleashed upon him with the objection that 'it has not occurred in history'. The editor, in turn, sternly advises that 'To believe that what has not occurred in history will not occur at all is to argue disbelief in the dignity of man.'

'History', Gandhi insisted, 'is really a record of every interruption of the even working of the force of love or of the soul', and it was only by kicking the English 'habit of writing history' that Indians could find the courage to release themselves from subjection by another civilisation. The spectre of works such as James Mill's ten-volume *History of British India*, with its repetitious assertion of the necessity of Indian subjection to British rule, had to be laid to rest. But where other Indians chose to defy the drone of British histories by writing their own or by disputing facts bandied by British historians, Gandhi simply rejected all attempts to write 'Indian history'.

Over the next fifteen years—between the publication of *Hind Swaraj* and *Satyagraha in South Africa*—most of Gandhi's writing took the form of journalism. He had first gained experience as a journalist in South Africa, filing freelance field reports on the Boer War (1899) and also serving as a correspondent for Dadabhai Naoroji's *India*. In 1903 two of Gandhi's associates launched *Indian Opinion*, a weekly from Durban, initially published in English, Gujarati, Hindi, and Tamil. Gandhi took it over in 1904. This journal, as also later ones which he started like *Young India* and *Navajivan*, acted as he put it as a 'mirror of part of my life . . . week after week I poured out my soul in columns expounding my principles and practice of Satyagraha as I understand it . . . the journal became for me a training in self-restraint, and for friends a medium through which to keep in touch with my thoughts.'

Satyagraha in South Africa was the longest of Gandhi's books, and stands in important relation to the earlier *Hind Swaraj* and the later *Autobiography*. Gandhi dictated the bulk of the text in Yeravada Jail in

1923–4, and it was published serially in *Navajivan* in 1924–5. Valji Desai (who acknowledged the help of Verrier Elwin and C.F. Andrews among others) translated it into English, and after amendments by Gandhi himself it was published in Madras in 1928. It is the most extended account by Gandhi of his own political practice, and its purpose was to show the principles and logic that guided his actions. It was, he wrote, the 'first attempt to apply the principle of Satyagraha to politics on a large scale.' Unlike *Hind Swaraj*, it was not a statement of a doctrinal moral argument; nor was it primarily a historical document, a factual record of his South African life (although Gandhi insisted that the reader must not 'imagine that any single item in this volume is inaccurate or that there is the least exaggeration at any point'). It was written above all to guide the conduct of the political struggle in India that Gandhi had begun to orchestrate in the 1920s: as he directly stated, 'My only object in writing this book is that it may be helpful in our present struggle.'

The book was designed to show that the concept of satyagraha was derived not from moral theory or doctrine, but from experience and practice. The narrative is driven by the conflict between, on the one hand, Gandhi and his satyagrahis, and on the other, the South African government. Mixing military and religious metaphors, Gandhi portrayed himself at once as a general directing a campaign and as leading disciples on a pilgrimage. The narrative shifts swiftly between scenes describing encounters of high politics—such as Gandhi discussing constitutional niceties with General Smuts and Botha—to accounts of Gandhi's imprisonment in Johannesburg Jail, being fed 'mealie pap'. The flow of the narrative is firm, but broken from time to time by passages of moral instruction and glosses on events, such that Gandhi has repeatedly to urge himself 'to return to our narrative'.

Satyagraha in South Africa exemplified the most distinctive formal trait of Gandhi's writing: the recounting of political events in the form of epic, told in the flattest, plainest prose. Throughout, he took great pains to avoid what he saw as the besetting sin of his compatriots' manner of expression: exaggeration and melodrama. He ruthlessly excised this from his own writing, and achieved striking effects. Take for instance the extraordinary economy with which he describes the event that was to acquire a mythic status as the turning point in Gandhi's life, the event that set him on his path (described at greater length in his *Autobiography*):

> I was pushed out of the train by a police constable at Maritzburg, and the trains having left, was sitting in the waiting room, shivering in the bitter cold. I did not know where my luggage was, nor did I dare to inquire of anybody, lest I might be insulted and assaulted once again. Sleep was out of the question. Doubt took possession of my mind. Late at night I came to the conclusion that to run back to India was cowardly. I must accomplish what I had undertaken. I must reach Pretoria, without minding insults or even assaults. Pretoria was my goal.

Thus was Gandhi launched on his Satyagraha campaign, and on his political destiny.

South Africa, Gandhi concluded, was 'where I had realised my vocation in life.' With this now clear, he left South Africa for India in 1914. There he found a flourishing public debate, conducted through an active political press, with leading political figures all in possession of journals that served as their own personal mouthpieces. Gandhi, already a practised journalist, joined the fray. He started his first paper, an unregistered weekly entitled *Satyagraha*, in 1919—its immediate stimulus was the Rowlatt Act agitation. Shortly after, two other papers were placed under his editorship, the English-language *Young India* and *Navajivan*, a Gujarati monthly. The circulation of *Young India* was small (around 1200), but *Navajivan* reached a wider circle (as many as 40,000).

The Indian press, though often sharply critical of the imperial government, was not free; it was strictly controlled by various press acts, which required papers to be registered with the authorities. Gandhi constantly pushed against restrictions on the freedom of the press, and in 1922 he published a series of articles in *Young India* that were held to be seditious. His language was bluntly provocative: 'Sedition', he wrote, 'has become the creed of the Congress.' 'I am aware that I have written strongly about the insolent threat that has come from across the seas, but it is high time that the British people were made to realise that the fight that was commenced in 1920 is a fight to the finish.'

The article led, inevitably, to his arrest and trial. Staged at Ahmedabad in 1922, it was a performance of high drama, replete with literary qualities. It is important to remember that even more significant than the actual trial itself was the renown it achieved through journalistic and literary reports. Immediately dubbed 'The Great Trial', *Young India* published a full report (with commentary—the end of the trial was described thus: 'There was much sobbing on the part of both men and women. But all the while Mr. Gandhi was smiling and cool . . .') and the transcripts were published in book form. The trial passed into nationalist lore: Sarojini Naidu wrote a famous account of it. Gandhi, in his conduct of it (and indeed it was he, the undertrial, rather than the judge, who set the pace), displayed his rhetorical sensitivity and skill in recognising, constituting, and addressing different audiences. The most immediate audience was of course the imperial state in the form of the judge presiding at the trial and 'the court' itself: but beyond that lay what Gandhi referred to as 'the Indian public'; and beyond that in turn was 'the public in England'. His courtroom speech—based upon a written statement—is masterly in its management of meanings. Subverting the law's desire for impersonality, Gandhi showed his capacity to simultaneously personalise a conflict, giving it a human scale, while also universalising it. Gandhi established the situation as one of personal drama ('I had to make my choice'), and he confronted the judge too with a choice: he could either execute the law and convict Gandhi, or act according to his conscience and resign.

Gandhi hoped to show how law and ethics stood some distance apart in the imperial system. He used the language of the law, with all its proprieties, to turn the entire colonial legal process on its head. This he did by indicting himself: 'I am therefore here to submit not to a light penalty but to the highest penalty. I do not ask for mercy. I do not ask for an extenuating act of clemency. I am here to invite and cheerfully submit to the highest penalty that can be inflicted upon me for what in law is a deliberate crime and what appears to me to be the highest duty of the citizen.' By such methods, Gandhi tore an enormous and irreparable hole in the Raj's fabric of public meaning. He used English legal language and etiquette to drive a wedge between the meanings of the state and those other whom it ruled. The sense of language, he demonstrated, was not continuous across both realms, but signified contrarily. The disparity was embodied in the very fabric of the law: supposedly a neutral form of language, objective, non-contextual, Gandhi showed it in fact to be biased in favour of British interests. 'The law itself', he wrote, 'in this country has been used to serve the foreign exploiter'; it was used to condemn Indians whose 'crime consisted in the love of their country', so that 'the administration of the law is thus prostituted consciously or unconsciously for the benefit of the exploiter.' Gandhi made clear that in indicting himself, he did so according to his own ethical principles of non-violence and not the statutes of British law—which in his words were no less than 'a subtle but effective system of terrorism and an organised display of force.'

The dramatisation of his own life, its transformation into a permanent performance, was Gandhi's greatest literary achievement. Indeed, the life itself, as we have come to know and think of it, is the most perfectly shaped of all modern Indian lives: an exquisite narrative parabola, driven by an unfailing internal momentum. A young hero is exiled from his home in western India to London and then to South Africa; through the injustice and humiliation he suffers there at the hands of his rulers, he learns spiritual and physical fortitude; he returns to pursue a quest to free his homeland of alien rule; he inspires his people to superhuman feats, and leads them to liberty—but at the moment of triumph he is consumed, as his people gain their freedom.

With artful artlessness, Gandhi allowed the details of this life to be constantly witnessed and recorded—befitting for a barrister whose language, manners, and theatrical sense of confrontation were all shaped by his encounter with British law. Gandhi extended an open invitation to fellow Indians (both élite and poor), to his British rulers, and to the world at large, to eavesdrop on him at every moment. His every action became newsworthy: sexual habits, dietary routines and abstinences, bowel movements, fevers and depressions, prayers, spinning, the drinking of a glass of lime juice to break a fast, gathering up a handful of salt, even his silences, became the subject of talk, gossip, and legend. His life, in every mundane detail, perpetually disturbed the euphemistic sensibilities and vocabulary of the Raj and challenged its hypocrisy.

What made him, of all the British crown's subjects, uniquely rebellious was his ability continually to insert the incidents of his daily life into a plotted narrative. Reading Gandhi involves more than reading his words; it means reading the life, itself a work of literary artifice. His actions and habits were his propositions. Out of that most basic of materials, his own body and its rhythms, vulnerabilities and strengths, he extracted taut drama. Gandhi imprisoned, struck by British lathis, fasting, silent, walking across dusty plains, felled by three bullets: his tiny physical frame grew to fill an immense imaginative space, becoming the screen on which the misdemeanours of the entire British empire were shamingly projected.

Famously unarmed, his weapon of subversion was his immense capacity to tell stories, an ability that allowed him not merely to turn his life into a story but to live it as a story, as if it was a theatrical performance, each scene staged and choreographed. All lives are, at least in retrospect, a story; but Gandhi knew prospectively from early on that he wanted to organise the inevitable haphazard trivia of daily life into a formal order (the signs are evident even in the diary he kept during his first voyage to London in 1888, at the age of nineteen). The ambition was commandingly explicit by the mid-1920s, when he began writing and publishing (in Gujarati) a series of weekly newspaper columns under the title 'The Story of My Experiments with Truth', later published as *An Autobiography or The Story of My Experiments with Truth* (Vol. I, 1927; Vol. II, 1929). This 'life-by-instalments' was delivered in the form of a sequence of parables, a modern recension of the Buddhist jataka tradition. As he lived it, Gandhi's life constantly anticipated the biographer: it was a biography-in-waiting, and his great skill as his own biographer was to ensure that whatever he did was always susceptible to at least two descriptive registers. It could be read as a historical and political quest for freedom and nationhood, as well as a spiritual mission of personal purification and salvation. Individual drama was masterfully blended with historical epic.

To write autobiography, Gandhi confessed, was to indulge in something of an unnatural practice, one 'peculiar to the West'. 'But', he continued disarmingly, 'it is not my purpose to attempt real autobiography. I want simply to tell the story of my numerous experiments'; nor was he concerned, he declared, with pleasing his critics—'writing is itself one of the experiments with truth'. It is worth dwelling on the account he gives—midway through his story—of his purposes in writing it, and the circumstances in which it was written. 'When I began to write it', Gandhi explained, 'I had no definite plan before me. I have no diary or documents on which to base the story of my experiments'; he had by now, he wrote, come to understand 'the inadequacy of all autobiography as history'. With surprising insouciance for one given to keeping fastidious accounts and records, he insisted that 'I just write as the spirit moves me at the time of writing . . .'

It was not accuracy but truth that he was after; and the standard of that, he implied, was set not by memoirs or history-writing, but by science. Gandhi described himself in the book as a 'scientist', and one of its central tropes—signalled in the title itself—is that of 'experiment'. His life was to be lived by the scientific method: testing, trial and error, constant revision. The 'experimental' theme recurs: Gandhi writes of 'experiments in the political field' and 'experiments in the spiritual field'; 'experiments on my body' and 'experiments in dietetics'; and 'principal' and 'current experiments'. The weekly instalments of his life-story were as laboratory reports, dissections of lived experience. 'I claim for them [my experiments] nothing more than does a scientist who, though he conducts his experiments with the utmost accuracy, forethought and minuteness, never claims any finality about his conclusions, but keeps an open mind regarding them.'

Less than a fortnight before his assassination in January 1948, Gandhi wrote that 'English and Indian scholars of English believe there is something special in my English.' This special quality is not easy to capture. Gandhi could move seamlessly from low to high styles, and he freely mixed filched cliché and new coinages. Passing through the routine banalities of sentences like: 'That relative truth must, meanwhile, be my beacon, my shield, my buckler. Though the path is straight and narrow and sharp as a razor's edge, for me it is the quickest and easiest', the reader might suddenly be arrested by phrases like 'my Himalayan blunders'. His alchemical capacity to transform the ordinary was matched by an unparalleled ability to coin political slogans—think of 'Quit India' (slogans much of whose force lay in their capacity to mean different things to different audiences, sometimes with ironic effects: 'Quit India', when daubed on city walls by Congress activists, provoked British Tommies to respond with their own graffiti: 'We wish we could'). Gandhi's unornamented style diverged entirely from the mauve prose of earlier Indian autobiographies and political writing. He stressed the value of verbal parsimony, a virtue he said he had learned painfully, through his own timidity: '[My] constitutional shyness has been no disadvantage whatever . . . My hesitancy in speech which was once an annoyance, is now a pleasure. Its greatest benefit has been that it taught me the economy of words.' Perhaps the most distinctive trait of his writing, though, was his forensic skill in arguing a case. Rarely did he fall into the customary mode of Indian political writing: rhetorical bluster. Gandhi's own writing often reads like a lawyer's brief, but without the obfuscations of legal language.

The unique poem that Gandhi wrote does not suggest that he ought to have written more ('Rasiklal Harilal Mohandas Karamchand Gandhi / Had a goat in his keeping / The goat would not be milked / And Gandhi would not stop his weeping'). But he was capable of writing that had a certain sparse poetic beauty. Take for instance the last text he wrote as a book, *Key to Health* (1942; written in Gujarati, the English translation by Sushila Nayyar was revised by Gandhi himself). This is for the most part a typical example of that common Indian genre, the self-help health manual (which Gandhi himself did much to popularise); but it had some striking passages. Gandhi saw particular difficulties surrounding the translation in English of the word 'akash': '"ether" would hardly do, and "emptiness" is horribly inexpressive of the original.' So he evoked the transcendent qualities the term connoted for him:

> Akash might be taken for the empty space surrounding the earth and the atmosphere around it. On a clear day, on looking up, one sees a beautiful mauve blue canopy which is known as akash or sky. So far as we are concerned, this sky or the ether is limitless. We are surrounded by it on every side, and there is no nook or corner without it. . . . Therefore the akash is round and everybody is within it. It is an envelope whose outermost surface is measureless. The lower strata of the akash for a number of miles are filled with air . . . sky or ether is the abode of the atmosphere. One can pump out air, say from an empty bottle and create a vacuum, but who can pump out the vacuum itself? That is akash.

It was here, surrounded by akash, that one might find rest: '. . . the starlit blue canopy should form the roof so that whenever one opens one's eyes, one can feast them on the ever-changing panorama of the heavens. One will never tire of the scene and it will not dazzle or hurt one's eyes. On the contrary it will have a soothing effect on one. To watch the different starry constellations floating in their majesty is a feast for the eyes.'

To Nehru, born in 1889 in Allahabad, English came earlier and more easily than it did to Gandhi. His father Motilal, a lawyer of vast ambition and commensurate success, came from a family well attuned to the language of power. The family had been employed in the Mughal administration, and after the collapse of the Mughal empire in 1857, they quickly supplemented their fluency in Persian and Urdu with English. Turn-of-the-century Allahabad, where Motilal made his career, was a busy administrative hub: the capital of the North Western Provinces, it was home to a university and to the high courts, and was a centre of the English-language press. Judging the lay of the land accurately, Motilal ensured that his son's early instruction was in English, and by the time he was transported to England in 1905 to join Harrow School, Nehru's diction was fluent (if a little stiff). He readily picked up Harrovian argot, explaining it to his bemused father in dutiful weekly letters, often in precocious English (he also wrote weekly letters to his mother, in Hindustani).

A student of natural sciences at Cambridge and then the law in London, Nehru read widely (as a young boy he had, by his own account, superior reading tastes: Lewis Carroll, Kipling, Scott, Dickens, Thackeray, H.G. Wells, Mark Twain, Jerome K. Jerome, Lafcadio Hearn, Bertrand Russell). His literary sensibility is perhaps best described as Edwardian, formed before the rise of literary modernism—for the latter, he never acquired any real feel. As writer, he came to maturity during the 1930s. It was a period when earnest intellectuals and writers were striving self-consciously to be 'popular', to reach a wider audience. Politics, history, philosophy, science, all received such popularising treatment, at the hands of men like H.G. Wells, Bertrand Russell, G.D.H. Cole, Leonard Woolf, and John Strachey. And their books were published by a new breed of publishers, like Victor Gollancz and Allen Lane, who pioneered innovative methods by publishing cheap, rapidly produced paperbacks that dealt with topical issues. While this was the broad context in which Nehru wrote, his writing was more specifically located alongside other Indian political writing of the 1920s and 1930s: M.N. Roy's *India in Transition* (1922), Krishna Menon's *Condition of India* (1933), and R. Palme Dutt's *India Today* (1940), as well as Edward J. Thompson's *The Reconstruction of India* (1930). Avowedly to the Left in their sympathies, such writers prided themselves on delivering rational analysis and logical argument in a popular, plain form.

In this vein, Nehru wrote numerous articles, essays, and pamphlets on political, cultural, and literary subjects, the most famous being *Whither India?* (1932). He was also an indefatigable correspondent, the greatest Indian master of letter-writing in English. But his literary reputation rests on the three long books that he wrote: *Glimpses of World History*, *An Autobiography*, and *The Discovery of India*. Narrative histories all, each entwined personal and public history. These books, viewed as classics of Indian nationalism, are usually read mainly for their content: as statements of the ideas—and anticipation of the actions—of India's first prime minister. But to read Nehru's books merely as textual emanations of political power effaces their literary interest. Written over a period of almost two decades, the three books arguably form the elements of a complex triptych. Each was written while in confinement in prison and against the background of a common predicament. The quarter century before 1947 was one of the most eventful and unpredictable in modern Indian history: no one could have anticipated the political sequence or outcome. In such circumstances, Nehru used historical inquiry and evocation as a way to orient the colonised individual and collective selves during a period of high uncertainty. The crucial point about this type of historical writing was that it was not driven primarily by a curiosity about the past, but was impelled by anxieties about the present and future. The traces of present doubts are everywhere palpable in the writing, rendering it hesitant, digressive, and repetitive—features that make these books stylistically quite distant from the more direct and argumentative style of Nehru's journalism and essays.

Glimpses of World History (1934) was written serially, in the form of letters from Nehru to his daughter Indira, as the full title makes clear:

'*Being Further Letters to his Daughter, Written in Prison, and Containing a Rambling Account of History for Young People*'. Apart from its explicit pedagogic intent—of acquainting his daughter with the facts of world history—the book also represented a significant inflation of the standard ambitions of nationalist intellectuals. Instead of trying simply to produce an Indian history of India, Nehru set out to write an Indian history of the world, to produce a universal history from an Indian point of view. There were two related advantages to such a strategy, as Nehru saw it. It avoided the partiality of nationalist histories and, more importantly, it enabled him to relativise European history: by placing European history against that of the continuous civilisations of India and China, the besetting weakness of all world histories—Eurocentrism, as we today call it—might be avoided. And, a history of the world as a whole could reveal a universal progressive movement that otherwise might have remained hidden. If particular countries or civilisations were looked at individually, it was not apparent whether they were progressing or regressing; there were, after all, plenty of individual cases of relapse and regression. But looked at in unison, an overall pattern of advance and progress became apparent.

Unlike the philosophical histories of a Hegel, Marx, or Spengler, which were built around the advance or decay of a single subject (reason, forms of production, culture) Nehru's accounts of historical movement did not identify a single active principle. Nor was his arrangement of historical events synthetic in its approach. Rather, he aimed more simply to show the chronological adjacency and simultaneity of events across the world. If there was an underlying historical moral to Nehru's tale, it was to claim that the centre of gravity of world history was shifting away from Europe and towards Asia and Africa. Reading *Glimpses*, one senses not a philosophical imagination but one like that of a newspaper editor, laying out different stories on the page. 'I have necessarily dealt separately with continents and countries', Nehru wrote, and 'we have considered different aspects and different movements also separately. But of course you will remember that all this was more or less simultaneous, and history marched all over the world with a thousand feet together . . .' The possibilities of any internal connections between the 'different aspects and different movements' was rarely seriously explored. Nehru's subject was the grandest, most impersonal of themes—the history of the world—but his treatment of it was that of an avuncular autodidact, mixing historical excursus with intimate address to his daughter. Nehru himself shrugged off the scientific and scholarly aspect of his book. 'The first volume has resulted in the press conferring the wholly undeserved title of "historian" on me', he wrote ruefully to his daughter; 'I claim no such distinction'. His approach, he insisted, was not that of a scholar, but of one given to reverie ('we shall dream of the past, and find our way to make the future greater than the past'), and his purpose was to infuse drama into past events, to make them live again. As he explained to Padmaja Naidu, 'Usually I describe past events in the present tense . . . I think the present is preferable as it makes history more vital for the reader and writer. As a matter of fact whenever I have written about past events I have tried to think of them as the present and imagined myself witnessing them . . .'

In fact Nehru weaves a number of different narrative strands through the book, playing with the temporality of individual, national, and international events. Throughout, the reader is kept aware of how the rhythms of private time—family birthdays, the death of his father, illness, prison interviews, and the sending and receiving of letters—have been disrupted for Nehru by the public time of contemporary politics. Condemned to doing time in prison ('My third consecutive New Year's day in prison'), Nehru escaped into the imagined time of history, which he was still at liberty to manipulate: 'In a little paragraph, in two or three sentences, I have disposed of China's history for more than 1000 years. Wonderful is it not, what one can do with these expanses of history?' The historical past, even as it served as an imaginative refuge for the incarcerated Nehru, became also—by its active reworking in his hands—a way of discovering a new vista of possibilities for his country.

Long, repetitive, incorrigibly digressive, *Glimpses* is today probably the least read of his three major books. Nehru himself wrote to his daughter that 'Somebody would have to give me a prize if he wanted me to read it again. It was bad enough to revise it. I refused to read the proofs.' The longest of Nehru's books, it was not his most distinguished. In terms purely of the quality of prose, his *Autobiography* (or, to give it its full title, *In and Out of Prison: An Autobiographical Narrative with*

Musings on Recent Events in India) was his most accomplished piece of writing. Written, like *Glimpses*, in prison—in Almora Jail, between June 1934 and February 1935—it was published in 1936 to ecstatic reviews ('The most vital contribution that any Indian has yet made to political literature', declared the *New Statesman*). An instant bestseller, it was reprinted ten times in its first year of publication, and represented an astonishing international literary success for an Indian, in some ways even more striking than the Tagore phenomenon twenty years earlier.

Political autobiography was already, by the time Nehru was writing his own, something of an established form in India. It was generally used as a platform to deliver windy valedictory self-testimonials. Gandhi had already showed its different potentials, writing in mid-career, in unornamented prose, about subjects not usually touched upon. Nehru took the form still further in new directions.

The *Autobiography* displayed the perfection of Nehru's mature style: a self-containment and restraint that never lost its fluency. Throughout its 600 pages, there is rarely a sense of strain in the writing: it is as if Nehru was always operating at a gear lower than his full capacity. In a passage which showed his own easy ability to throttle-up when necessary, Nehru distinguished his type of holding back from what he saw as the more emasculated self-restraint of the Liberals and Moderates in the national movement:

> Nor is moderation enough by itself. Restraint is good and is the measure of our culture, but behind that restraint there must be something to restrain and hold back. It has been, and is, man's destiny to control the elements to ride the thunderbolt, to bring the raging fire and the rushing and tumbling waters to his use, but most difficult of all for him has been to restrain and hold in check the passions that consume him. So long as he will not master them, he cannot enter fully into his human heritage. But are we to restrain the legs that move not and the hands that are palsied?

The *Autobiography* is a product of Nehru's capacity to give historical shape to the slip-stream of events; his ability to make of his life a 'Life'. In concession to the European style of autobiography, Nehru noted that he wrote his in 'a mood of self-questioning'; his opinions are frankly and often strongly expressed. Gandhi is a constant figure in the story, a kind of alter ego to Nehru's own self. It is Nehru's engagement with the enigma of Gandhi—and especially his views on religion—that provoke some of the most memorable writing in the book. Yet Nehru gives little of himself away: as his official biographer, S. Gopal, noted, 'the *Autobiography* is in one sense a tour de force in that, after over 600 close-knit pages, his privacy remains unbroken.' Even at his most self-confessional and self-doubting, Nehru displays an unfailing English reserve and tact, an obliquity of the personal.

The issue of religion—both as existential choice and as social institution—tested most profoundly Nehru's sense of himself. It removed him from his own country: 'I felt lonely and homeless, and India, to whom I had given my love and for whom I had laboured, seemed a strange and bewildering land to me. Was it my fault that I could not enter into the spirit and ways of thinking of my countrymen?' Nehru concentrated his thoughts on religion around a discussion of Gandhi. But the sense of crisis that religious belief induced in Nehru at this point in his life had its origins closer to home—in his wife Kamala's embrace of religion during the last years of her life (she died while the manuscript of the *Autobiography* was in press). This was one example of Nehru's capacity to magnify personal crises through the lens of larger historical ones, and so at once to keep them at a distance and give the events of his own life historical importance.

Though well aware of Freud and of psychoanalysis, in fact nowhere in the *Autobiography* did Nehru probe himself searchingly or succumb to the vogue for self-analysis. He was to try something like this shortly after the publication of his autobiography; but, typically, it was done in the form of a prank. 'The Rashtrapati', published anonymously in 1937 in *The Modern Review* (Nehru signed the article 'Chanakya'), was proffered as an essay on Nehru's psychology. Published, with some bravura, against the background of dictatorships in Europe and of a struggle within the Congress Party over who, after Gandhi, would be the most important figure in the movement, it warned against Nehru's own authoritarian ambitions. Written in the wake of having read T.E. Lawrence, Nehru's disarming public self-critique was an attempt to domesticate his self-conceit: 'What is he aiming at with all his want of aim? What lies behind that mask of his, what desires, what will to power, what insatiate longings? His conceit is already formidable. It must be checked. We want no Caesars.' But to write such a piece was also of course an expression of self-conceit, and for all his professed self-analysis, Nehru was unable to satisfy one of his acutest critics. 'Surely you do not', he wrote defensively to Padmaja Naidu, 'expect me to psychoanalyse myself in an article . . . you are perfectly right in saying that I have little sense of intuitive perception.'

The *Autobiography* possessed many of the distinctive flourishes in Nehru's literary armoury: the rhetorical question, the sweeping assertion followed by concessive qualification (a style that at once rebuffed and included), and the choice image ('Conceit, like fat on the human body, grows imperceptibly, layer upon layer, and the person whom it affects is unconscious of the daily accretion'). It encouraged an Indian prose committed to clarity and humanist principles of a type that can also be found in some of the novels of the 1930s and 1940s, and indeed it shared with them some common tropes. Examples of this include the constant feminisation of India ('India becomes Bharat Mata, Mother India, a beautiful lady, very old but ever youthful in appearance, sad-eyed and forlorn . . .'), and the resort to pathos when writing of the Indian village dweller: 'They [the kisans] showered their affections on us and looked on us with loving and hopeful eyes as if we were the bearers of good tidings, the guides who would lead them to the promised land. Looking at them and their misery . . . I was filled with shame and sorrow . . . A new picture of India seemed to rise before me, naked, starving, crushed and utterly miserable'.

The *Autobiography* established Nehru's reputation in international circles. After the eccentricities of Gandhi's autobiography, Nehru's revealed a reassuringly normal personality. But how ought we to read the book? What was Nehru hoping to do by writing it? He described his purpose as being to 'trace . . . [his] own mental development, and not write a survey of recent Indian history'; his story was, he confessed, 'wholly one-sided . . . Those who want to make a proper study of our recent past will have to go to other sources . . . this "autobiographical narrative" remains a sketchy, personal, and incomplete account of the past, verging on the present, but cautiously avoiding contact with it.' It is ironic, then, that the book has become an inevitable quarry for numberless biographers and writers about Nehru, who treat it as an authentic source of information about his life. But the extraordinary poise of the book should itself alert us to how disarming Nehru can be: far from providing a simple transcript of his life up to that point, throughout the book Nehru, acutely conscious that his self is on public display, seeks to produce and manage effects.

All autobiography is an act of self-promotion, a calling-card solicitously slipped through the letter-box of history. Nehru's own autobiography established a certain mythology of the man. By writing it at a comparatively young age, it helped to endow him with the quality of perennial youth; it displayed him as a man of cerebral refinement, ambivalent about public life and the pursuit of power, and able to survey the world from Olympian heights. Youthfulness, normality, intelligence, sensitivity, and the close links between Nehru's personal life and the historical currents of the national movement—by stressing these traits, the *Autobiography* helped to pull Nehru out of the contingent of Congressmen jostling for position, and to establish his claim as heir to Gandhi.

After these histories of the self and the world Nehru, once more in prison, turned—in the third panel of his historical triptych, *The Discovery of India* (1946)—to the history of his own country. *The Discovery* is the most complex of his books, showing most visibly the traces of intellectual effort; it also contains some of his richest writing, arising out of his preoccupations with history and culture. Although conventionally read as a statement of Indian nationalism on the eve of Independence, in fact it is not at all triumphalist in tone: there is, rather, a gravity, even melancholy, to it. As with all of Nehru's more extended writing, it emerges out of a personal predicament: incarceration, and the enforced inaction and vista of empty time that this presented.

'My friends', Nehru wrote, 'took it for granted that I would write and produce another book as I had done during previous terms of imprisonment. It had almost become a habit.' Altogether, Nehru spent almost a decade in prison, leaving him plenty of time to pursue his interests in his own personal past and future, in memory and fantasy. 'We live, as Auguste Comte said, dead men's lives, encased in our pasts, but this is especially so in prison, where we try to find some sustenance for starved and locked-up emotions in memory of the past or fancies of the future.' Nehru had a fixed concern with how his life (and works) would look from the perspective of the future. He was sharply conscious of how what appeared important to the contemporary eye would be dismissed as insignificant by the sterner tribunal of history. *The Discovery*, he confessed, grew from an (unpublished) autobiographical fragment written in prison: 'Looking at it now, I realise its little worth; how stale and uninteresting much of it seems. The incidents it deals with have lost all importance and have become the debris of a half-forgotten past covered over by the lava of subsequent volcanic eruptions.' In all his writing, Nehru wished to show how, as he once wrote to Gandhi, 'our prosaic existence has developed something of epic greatness in it'.

Nehru's question in *Discovery* was one that could be asked of an individual life as well as of the life of a society or nation: to what extent is the past a burden, and to what degree can one escape it? His answer was direct and audacious—the best way to escape one's past was to make it up anew, to invent or discover a different past for oneself. That was the task of *Discovery*—to cut away from both British histories of India, as well as Indian histories that emphasised one single religion, region, or identity above all others. More precisely, it tried to offer an answer to the enigma posed by the Sphinx-like character of Indian history: how could a past with so many crisscrossing strands, one so full of interruption, be shown to form a single story, a common history? Nehru's answer—intricate, sometimes gloomy, mainly hopeful—remains still for Indians the most compelling one they have contrived.

Aside from their own particular uses of English, Gandhi and, to an even greater extent, Nehru both helped to define the place of English in India. Between the 1920s and 1940s, their views about the social and cultural functions of English changed. In the 1920s and 1930s, both were more critical and negative towards English. Gandhi's reorganisation of the Congress in the 1920s, which made linguistic groups the basic units of the movement, and his amendment of the party constitution in 1925, had relegated English from its primary place. Nehru too seemed to share the view that the future of English, 'a kind of foster language', would be limited in a free India: unless they cast it off Indians would 'remain slaves to British thought'. During the 1940s, though, there was a new understanding of the functions of English. As the prospect of power approached, and discussions turned to more technical matters of state, English once again became the currency of discussion in Congress circles. Gandhi himself acknowledged the importance of English, and in one of his last articles in *Harijan* (25 January 1948) wrote:

> I cannot discontinue the English *Harijan* . . . My contact with the West is also widening. I was never opposed to the British or to any Westerner nor am I today . . . So English will never be excluded from my small store of knowledge. I do not want to forget that language nor give it up. [However], it cannot become our national language or medium of instruction . . . The rule of the English will go because it was corrupt, but the prevalence of English will never go.

The real contests over English came, however, after Independence. In the decade and a half after 1947, the issue of language became politically charged. On the one hand, demands were lodged from the regions for the creation of new states, defined by linguistic contours, while on the other there were increasing pressures from the Hindi speakers of North India to privilege their language over all others, especially English. In each case, appeal was made to the state, to legislate on matters of language. In his responses to these developments, Nehru arrived at a sophisticated, perceptive view of language. He never had occasion to set this out explicitly, but the outline of his view is discernible from his speeches and writings.

Nehru had already, in the late 1940s, given voice to his disagreement with efforts to treat language as if it were an instrument of state policy, and had expressed his belief in the glacial character of linguistic change. Popular and literary usage, not state-sponsored resolutions, determined the vitality and spread of a language. One year before his death in 1964, in a speech to the Lok Sabha, the Lower House of Parliament, during a debate over the extension of the fifteen-year constitutional recognition of English as an official language, Nehru articulated some of the important strands in his thinking on the subject. He noted, first, that Indian languages had become static and unrepresentative of 'modern trends of thought'. The entry of English in the nineteenth century—while hardly driven by benign reasons—nevertheless had positive effects upon Indian languages. English was a conduit for scientific and technological ideas (Nehru never underestimated the significance of English as a door to modern science), and it had introduced new literary forms. The combined impact was to shatter the 'self-centred' and hermetic aspects of Indian culture: 'Our languages became static because our lives were static. The changes that came with the British invasion of India administered a shock and had its effect on our languages also. It made them more dynamic—brought new forms, the novel, short stories, a new kind of drama, science and technology.'

Nehru went on to remind his parliamentary colleagues that 'India is a multilingual country'. No spoken Indian language, not even Hindi, could claim a privileged position. Hindi too was a 'regional' language, the language of a large northern minority. State policy had to recognise this multilingual character, allowing languages to flourish and adapt but not—and this was Nehru's point—by means of positive legislation or policy resolutions. 'No clerks and no government departments have ever made a language grow', and therefore the state should avoid trying to install a hierarchical model of languages in India—by, for example, classifying languages as 'regional' and 'national'. Language should not be invested with the duty of being a marker of national belonging, with all the emotional freight this carried; rather, it ought to have a functional status.

As Nehru saw it, the primary challenge to English came not from Hindi, but rather from the so-called 'regional' languages. And, exactly because the regional languages were becoming reinvigorated, English would if anything become even more necessary as a potential link language. It was this perception that led him to 'think English would be more widely known in India in the future than now; though it will not be known for better quality.' He acknowledged that in the longer run this linking function might be taken on by Hindi (this would not be a result of legislation, but through the spread of popular forms, especially the Hindi cinema). In fact there is striking prescience to his view, as, three and a half decades later, India entered a period when national governments, made of coalitions reflecting the vigorous linguistic diversity of the country, struggled to find a common natural (let alone ideological) language in which to argue or agree.

Finally, Nehru turned to an explanation of why the efforts to propagate Hindi had so far had little success. Drawing a contrast between Hindi on the one hand, and English and especially Urdu on the other, he argued that successful languages were those which were adaptable and responsive, not those which insisted on their purity. He valued Urdu exactly because it 'is an amalgam, a synthesis of various languages', and it showed 'that when two languages come together, they strengthen each other.' This made Urdu 'dynamic' and 'vital', and gave it 'a strange capacity for adaptation and drawing from other languages . . . [an] adaptability that makes a language strong.' Nehru's argument was a rebuttal of the claims of narrow linguistic chauvinists, who wished to purge and purify languages, and to substitute current speech with dead coin. This made for a language without history, not soiled by daily use. Nehru valued linguistic impurity, an unchasteness that he found in English and in Urdu. As he had earlier put it, 'I am not anxious about the purity of the Hindi language, whether it borrows words from other languages or not.' Indeed, for Nehru the greatness of a language like English was 'that it has kept its doors and windows open for all types of words and it easily incorporates a new word from foreign languages. . . . I think there are at least one thousand Hindi words incorporated into the English language.' A century earlier, Ghalib had noted similar capacities in Urdu: 'Urdu was formerly compounded of Arabic, Persian, Hindi, and Turkish—these four languages. Now a fifth language, English, has entered into it. See the capacity of Urdu. How sweetly this fifth language extends its influence over it! It has assimilated these languages so well that none of them seems an excrescence upon it.' It was these traits that Nehru celebrated, and he saw in Urdu a symbol of the necessary promiscuity of any living language.

Nehru's late statements on the relationship of English to other Indian languages made explicit something that both his and Gandhi's uses of that language had exemplified. Each in their own way had shown, by their distinctive uses of English, the infinite adaptability of the language of the colonisers. And as they did so, they shattered the belief that Indians were less 'natural', less skilled users of the language—so undermining yet another foundational pillar of the empire. By devising for their own purposes a language that could be deployed across a variety of arenas—law courts, public meetings, pamphlets and newspapers, autobiographies and histories, private letters and constitutional drafts—they gave Indians a formidable weapon with which to challenge the British. But perhaps even more remarkably, Gandhi and Nehru gave their countrymen the possibility of an equal conversation with their conquerors.

11

Verrier Elwin

RAMACHANDRA GUHA

Verrier Elwin is the J.G. Frazer of Indian anthropology, a man of letters who strayed into a discipline which likes to think it is something of a science. Both men are regarded by their peers as fine writers but mediocre scientists, yet both have an influence and importance quite out of proportion to their scholarly reputations. Frazer is no more than a footnote in some histories of anthropology, yet *The Golden Bough* is one of the best-known books in the English language, continually in print since its first publication more than a hundred years ago. Elwin too is not always taken seriously by academics, but there continues to be a keen general interest in his career and writings.

Unlike Frazer, who rarely left his desk in Trinity College, Cambridge, Verrier Elwin enjoyed an extraordinarily varied life. Born in 1902, the son of the Bishop of Sierra Leone, he had a brilliant career at Oxford, where he took a Double First, in English and in Theology, before being ordained a priest in the Church of England. He came to India in 1927, to join a small sect, the Christa Seva Sangh of Poona, which hoped to 'indigenise' Christianity. But he quickly threw in his lot with the Congress, winning Gandhi's affection and becoming a camp follower and occasional cheerleader to the growing popular movement against British rule. Seeking fuller immersion in 'the toil, the suffering, the poverty of India', he resolved to make his home among the Gonds. In

1932 he moved with his friend Shamrao Hivale to a remote village in the forests of Mandla district. Hivale and he were to spend some twenty years in Central India, living with and fighting for the rights of tribals. In January 1954 Elwin became the first foreigner to be accepted as an Indian citizen. In the same year, he was appointed anthropological adviser to the Indian government, with special reference to the hill tribes of the north-east. Moving to Shillong, he served for a decade as the leading missionary of what he liked to call 'Mr Nehru's gospel for the tribes'. He died in 1964, a greatly esteemed public figure in his adopted land, the recipient of the Padma Bhushan and countless other medals and awards.

This Englishman, missionary, Gandhian social worker, activist, bureaucrat, and Indian was always and pre-eminently a writer, a man whose richness of personal experience illuminates an oeuvre of truly staggering proportions. A reasonably comprehensive bibliography compiled by the Japanese scholar Takeshi Fujii (in *Journal of South Asian Languages and Cultures*, 1988) runs to thirty closely printed pages—it lists forty books and five hundred articles. As impressive as the quantity is the variety, for Elwin worked in a whole range of genres. He wrote and published poetry, religious tracts, polemical pamphlets, novels, anthropological monographs, folklore collections, official reports and manuals, reviews, editorials, and travelogues. His last work was an autobiography, generally regarded as the finest of all his books.

While the trajectory of Elwin's life was marked by a series of departures, the pattern of his writing career was shaped by his time in Oxford. In his college, Merton, he came under the influence of two mentors of quite different persuasions. The first was his English teacher, H.W. Garrod, an authority on Keats and Wordsworth and a bachelor who played chess and drank with undergraduates. The second was his theology teacher, F.W. Green, who had once been a slum priest in London's East End; he was also a radical in politics who deplored the excesses of capitalism and imperialism without going quite so far as to call himself a 'socialist'. Elwin revered both Garrod and Green, and the influence of his teachers is manifest in the creative tension that runs through all his work, the tension between aesthetics and politics, between beauty of expression and the claims of social relevance.

While he published some poetry at Oxford, Elwin's first full-length works were written while he was with the Christa Seva Sangh. At a time when religious traditions tended to talk past each other, he published two precocious studies exploring the parallels between Christian and Hindu mystical traditions. *Christian Dhyana, or Prayer of Loving Regard* (1930) and *Richard Rolle* (1930) both celebrated 'the bhakti movement in fifteenth-century Europe', the example of the European mystics who carried religion to the people much as the Indian bhakti poets had done. In their joyousness and democratic spirit, remarked Elwin, these mystics 'would have been perfectly at home in India. How well Rolle would have understood Tukaram! How entirely Mirabai would have appreciated Mother Julian!'

These books were admired by Indian Christians, who were themselves searching for points of convergence between a foreign faith and spiritual traditions native to India. Elwin's next work, *Christ and Satyagraha* (which also appeared in 1930), presented to the same audience the theological case for joining Gandhi. Christians, it argues, had biblical sanction for offering civil disobedience to the Raj, for 'the campaign initiated by Mahatma Gandhi, both in its method and spirit, is more in accordance with the mind of Christ than any other similar campaign that the world has ever seen.' Two years later Elwin published *The Truth About India: Can We Get It*? of which a reviewer remarked that 'though the author does not belong to the Congress, the case for the Congress could hardly be put with more convincing advocacy.' The book drew attention to the chasm separating British precept from colonial practice, with the 'champions of liberty' having turned the subcontinent 'into a vast prison-house'. Instead of forcing 'our alien, unwarranted, extravagant, irresponsible rule upon India by the sword', wrote Elwin, the British should take heed of Gandhi's 'message of friendliness and hope' and depart before they were thrown out.

After he went to the Gonds, in 1932, Elwin moved away from politics towards social work and, in time, anthropology. The more he lived with tribals the more he came to see the world through their eyes, a process confirmed and consolidated by his marriage, in April 1940, to a Gond girl. (They were divorced in 1949; Elwin later married another tribal.) Going Gond led also to the overthrow of older and, as it now seemed, incompatible allegiances. When his Bishop refused to renew his licence unless he proselytised the tribals, Elwin resigned holy orders and later left the Church itself. But he also became disenchanted with Gandhism, whose credo of puritanical reform (asceticism, vegetarianism, and prohibition) he found too restrictive for communities that liked their liquor, their sex, and their hunting.

These shifts in loyalties are captured in *Leaves from the Jungle* (1936), Elwin's diary of his early years in Mandla. The book provides revelations, through flashes of irony and wit, of his growing rejection of Gandhi and Christ: as in a description of a khadi mosquito net which, 'though utterly patriotic and highly mosquito proof, appears to admit no air whatsoever', or a confession that he spent a day of rest reading Agatha Christie 'though aware it would be more suitable for me to employ my leisure reciting the Penitential Psalms'. The protective instincts of the anthropologist had replaced the improving agenda of the social worker. 'There are many elements in the Gond ethos which should be conserved,' writes Elwin, 'their simplicity and freedom, their love of children, the position of their women, their independence of spirit . . . their freedom from many of the usual oriental inhibitions.' The tribal, indeed, 'has a real message for our sophisticated modern world which is threatened with disintegration as a result of its passion for possessions and its lack of love.'

This comes from the one preachy passage in the book; otherwise, the defence of tribal life is conducted with an easy wit and lightness of touch. *Leaves from the Jungle* is perhaps the most readable of Elwin's works, an illustration of 'rollicking anthropology' which celebrates the irreverent and irrepressible gaiety of the Gond and their chronicler. It received a wonderful reception: the *New Statesman* remarked that through the diary 'we know the Gonds more intimately and more thoroughly than any primitive people that have been shown to us in books'; 'no European since R.L. Stevenson', commented *The Times*, 'has written so well of a life among browns and chocolates'.

Between 1936 and 1939 the London publisher John Murray brought out each year a book of Elwin's. *Leaves* was followed by *Phulmat of the Hills*, a novel about a tribal woman stricken by leprosy and abandoned by her lover. The narrative is replete with poems, riddles, and stories from tribal folklore, interspersed with straight dialogue. This is an early (perhaps even the first) ethnographic novel, its plot held together by the focus on the fate of its central character. H.E. Bates thought the book 'a piece of the best kind of romance, rich in emotion but unsentimental, rich in colour but firmly rooted in fact . . . realistic and as frank, in its portrayal of love, as Maupassant.' In the next year Elwin published another novel, *A Cloud that's Dragonish*, a whodunit about tribal witches and witchcraft that is less convincing. Then in 1939 appeared *The Baiga*, a massive monograph about a small tribe whose economy was being destroyed by the expropriation of their forests by the state.

'The pen is the chief weapon with which I fight for my poor', wrote Elwin to an Italian friend in July 1938, while completing *The Baiga*. That book was the first in a series of ethnographies and essays through which Elwin fought for his poor, the voiceless aboriginal. Anthropologist at large, roaming through the forests of Central India in search of tribes to study and to protect, he accumulated a huge store of facts, poems, legends, and stories that found their way into a series of weighty but always readable monographs. *The Agaria* (1942) told a melancholy tale of the decline of a community of charcoal iron-smelters ruined by taxation, factory iron, and official apathy. *Maria Murder and Suicide* (1943) explored the causes of homicide in a tribe that was the exception to the Indian aboriginal's otherwise deserved reputation for being both kindly and pacific. *The Muria and their Ghotul* (1947) presented an enchanting picture of the amorous life of a tribe tucked away in the deep recesses of Bastar; it focused on the dormitory, or ghotul, where boys and girls first learnt the art of sex. *Bondo Highlander* (1952) studied the personality of a highland Orissa tribe, the tension between individualism and co-operation in their life. *The Religion of an Indian Tribe* (1955), also set in Orissa, covered all aspects of Saora ritual and belief: it was called (by Christoph von Fürer-Haimendorf) 'the most detailed account of an Indian tribal religion that ever flowed from an anthropologist's pen'. All these works were published by Oxford University Press, as was a pioneering study, *Tribal Art in Middle India* (1951), and five folklore collections (a couple in collaboration with Shamrao Hivale) which appeared under the series title, Specimens in the Oral Literature of Middle India.

Of all these books it is those on the Baiga and the Muria that attracted the most attention. Both studies drew on the intimacy which came from long residence with the tribe; both showcased vivid life histories, born of the novelist's interest in character over social structure; both challenged criticism with their bulk, each book running to more than six hundred pages; and both were lightened by literary allusions, the author being as likely to invoke Huxley and Tennyson as Malinowski and Firth. More pertinent than any of these reasons for the books' fame (and notoriety) was their documentation and indeed joyous celebration of sex in the life of the tribes.

Ancient India was 'rich in sexological literature', remarked Elwin, but recent writers 'have generally been too much under the influence of the prevailing puritan conventions to treat the subject freely.' Science called him to break the taboo, for the Baiga, he found, were ruled not so much by the forest guard and the police constable as by the raging fires of sexual desire. In their lives 'celibacy is unheard of, continence is never practised.' Their children were apparently born with a 'complete equipment of phallic knowledge.' Baiga knowledge of each other's bodies was extraordinarily attentive to detail: the men, for instance, could distinguish between twelve kinds of breasts, ranking them (almost) in precise order of attractiveness.

The book on the Muria ghotul, likewise, presented a detailed, candid, evocative account of premarital sex, of the role of touch and smell in arousing a partner, the use of love-charms in winning a reluctant lover. Sex was fun: the 'best of ghotul games . . . the dance of the genitals . . . an ecstatic swinging in the arm of the beloved.' But it was not, among the Muria, disfigured by lust, or degraded by possessiveness, or defiled by jealousy. More strikingly, the sexual freedom of the ghotul was followed by a stable, secure, serenely happy married life. In the process of growing up, the 'life of pre-nuptial freedom' ended in a 'longing [for] security and permanence'. In any married couple, neither was a virgin absolutely: but *both were virgins to each other*. Before and after marriage, concluded the anthropologist, 'Muria domestic life might well be a model and example for the whole world.'

J.H. Hutton, Professor of Social Anthropology at Cambridge, thought *The Baiga* 'the greatest thing of its kind that has been done', showing 'Elwin's complete entry into the primitive point of view'. Another (and since better-known) Cambridge anthropologist, Edmund

Leach, wrote of *The Muria and their Ghotul* that it 'worthily upholds its author's reputation both as a conscientious ethnographer and as a writer of exceptional aesthetic sensibility.' It was 'Elwin's remarkable achievement to describe [ghotul] behaviour with sympathy, intimacy and detachment. If this part of the book were to appear as a supplementary volume to Havelock Ellis's *Studies in the Psychology of Sex* it would be in proper company. In its own way it is masterly.'

Representing the puritan party was a reviewer of *The Baiga* in *The International Review of Missions*, who complained of 'a gusto strangely out of place in a professedly scientific treatise'. In 'circuses and zoos', he remarked, 'the cages of anthropoid apes are screened from curious eyes, at certain intimate moments of their occupants' lives. Mr Elwin's humble friends and confidants have been less fortunate in this respect than captive chimpanzees.'

In fact, Elwin was much more (and perhaps much less) than a specialist on sex. A chapter on the topic, it is true, was the centrepiece of *The Baiga*: but it was both preceded and followed by an elaborate account of how the state had impoverished the tribe by forbidding the practice of swidden cultivation. The material concerns of tribals were always a priority for the anthropologist, whose works pay close attention to the loss of tribal land, the restrictions on their previously untrammelled use of the gifts of the forest, and their exploitation by non-tribal moneylenders and petty officials. His best-selling pamphlet, *The Aboriginals* (1943), emphasised the economic measures required to safeguard the integrity of the tribes: which, in his view, included the restoration of their forest rights, protection of their lands, and a careful regulation of contacts with the outside world. Recalling what A.E. Housman hoped for *The Shropshire Lad*—that it would one day stop a bullet aimed at a soldier's heart—Elwin said his hope, for his books, was that they may help protect the aboriginal 'from some of the deadly shafts of exploitation, interference and repression that civilisation so constantly launches at his heart.'

Complementary to Elwin's ethnographies were his collections of tribal myth and folklore. Many of the myths were collected by three assistants trained by him—Sunderlal Narmada, Gulabdas, and Ram Pratap Baghel—the editor then doing the work of translation and annotation. Some of the stories in *Folk-Tales of Mahakoshal* (1944) and *Myths of Middle India* (1949) dealt with love and adventure, the chase for a beloved conducted on earth and through the underworld, the man in pursuit of his princess, thwarted by ogres and demons but aided by kindly animals. Other stories spoke of sibling rivalry, the jealousy between brothers, or of the rivalry between queens. The tales showed a 'strong sympathy for the underdog', for the youngest brother and the youngest queen generally triumphed over the hurdles placed before them. Also presented were tribal accounts of natural and human creation, stories rich in expressive imagery, with stars flashing and gods appearing and disappearing, tales of magic and wonder impossible to summarise or condense. Elwin modestly said of the second of these collections that it 'attempts nothing more than to present samples and specimens of an oral literature whose variety and extent is still largely unsuspected by scholars.' However, a reviewer in *American Anthropologist* spoke of the book as 'an aboriginal Purana', a 'landmark in the exploration of the intellectual history of mankind'.

Elwin's lingering literary ambitions also found an outlet in his translations of tribal poetry. *Folk-songs of the Maikal Hills* (1944) and *Folk-songs of Chattisgarh* (1946) both presented in verse-form the songs of the Gond and his neighbours. He was helped once more by local assistants, and by his devoted friend and collaborator Shamrao Hivale. Many of the songs were meant to accompany the Gond dances, the karma, the saila, and the dadaria. A large chunk dealt with romance, often with the parrot as a go-between and carrier of messages between lovers. There were songs of the seasons, and poems about the tortured relationship between mother-in-law and daughter-in-law. Other songs were less traditional, being commentaries on the artefacts of modernity entering tribal life. One poem captured the oppressions of civilisation:

In this kingdom of the English how hard it is to live
To pay the cattle-tax we have to sell a cow
To pay the forest-tax we have to sell a bullock
To pay the land-tax we have to sell a buffalo
How are we to get our food?
In this kingdom of the English how hard it is to live
In the village sits the Landlord
In the gate sits the Kotwar

In the garden sits the Patwari
In the field sits the Government
In the kingdom of the English how hard it is to live.

The Gond may have been thwarted at every turn, but there was at least one remaining source of solace:

Liquor, you turn us into kings
What matter if the world ignores us?
The Brahmin lives by his books
The Panka boys run off with Panka girls
The Dhulia is happy with his basket
The Ahir with his cows
But one bottle makes a Gond a Governor
What matter if the Congress ignores us?

A satirical poem about 'The Soldier on Leave' displayed the continuing innovation in folk poetry:

This year he is enjoying his Holi
A topi on his head, a pair of boots, gaiters
Coat, waist-coat, pantaloons
A five-coloured muffler around his neck
Cigarettes in a packet and a box of matches
He cleans himself with a brush
He has done his hair 'English style'
No oil for him—he puts attar
He looks like a Bengali
His dhoti goes down to his ankles
At home he talks English, the house-folk do not understand
He calls for 'Water' and when they bring bread
He abuses them for their ignorance
'Commere, commere' he says to his friend, 'let's go to the istation'
Babu has shown 'Singal down', the train will soon be coming
He talks English *gitpit gitpit* and no one understands
No more 'Salaam' or 'Ram-ram' for him, he bids you 'Guda moraning'.

The presentation of verses was linked through a narrative commentary which drew parallels between tribal images and civilised ones. A motif or image could remind Elwin of Dylan Thomas or D.H.

Lawrence, or Blake or Wordsworth, or Chaucer or Shakespeare. For good measure, comparisons with the Spanish of Garcia Lorca and the Chinese-to-English renditions of Arthur Waley were also thrown in. A British critic was to later remark that Elwin was 'one of those who puts in everything but the kitchen stove—Aphra Behn and Dryden, Matthew Arnold and Dickens, Rousseau and someone else from India.' Some of this was pure showing-off, but it was also, I think, an attempt to elevate the 'primitive' to the level of European poetry, to show him as part of the greater human family, using the same symbols and images for the same feelings and emotions.

There was to Elwin's collections of folk poetry and myth also a polemical purpose. He hoped that the publication of the poems and tales would help banish the 'dark and gloomy shadow over a great part of aboriginal India of the puritan "reformer" and the missionary of whatever faith', and challenge the leaders of the 'abominable movement' to stop tribal recreations on the grounds that they were 'indecent'. To 'steal a song', wrote Elwin, 'is far worse than to steal gold.' The American Baptists in Assam and the Gandhian nationalists in Orissa were both working overtime to abolish the village dormitory and the great feasts, and to introduce the policy of prohibition among the tribes. But as Elwin pointed out in a 1943 essay, 'the romance and gaiety of tribal life is necessary for its preservation'. The new taboos would destroy the dancing and religious life of the tribals, and fall most heavily on one section among them. For 'so long as song and dance is free, village women get a square deal. With the coming of a taboo on their dancing, comes also a restriction of their freedom, the decay of their morals, the loss of rights.'

In one of those paradoxes in which the history of colonialism abounds, it was this former Oxford don who, through his fine and evocative prose writings, most effectively brought to wider attention the culture and condition of a large group of Indians neglected or despised by Hindu society. This self-appointed spokesman and 'protector' of the tribals was, however, accused by some of wishing to isolate them in their mountain fastness, backward and undeveloped, deliberately kept apart from the mainstream of Indian nationalism and from the emerging Indian nation. Through the 1940s and 1950s, Elwin engaged in a series of lively polemics with his critics. One debate was with Indian anthropologists who accused him of artificially separating tribals from Hindu society; he answered that despite a partially shared pantheon, tribals were marked out from Hindus through their community spirit, the absence of caste, their closeness to nature, and the equality among them of the sexes. A second debate was with social reformers who wished to bring in prohibition and forbid tribal dances; Elwin attacked them as insolent killjoys, with a complete lack of appreciation of cultures other than their own. This lapsed priest also quarrelled with Christian missionaries who believed that a change of religion was the swiftest way of bringing tribals into the modern world. Elwin held Christian reformers to be as aggressive as Hindu ones, as intolerant of tribal art and culture, and as likely to maim new converts by making them ashamed of their traditions.

Elwin was always controversial among Indian intellectuals and politicians: his work was generously praised as well as bitterly attacked (most often on the grounds that he wished to keep the tribals 'isolated' from the national mainstream). But among his admirers was the most important Indian of all, Jawaharlal Nehru. At Nehru's recommendation he was appointed, in 1954, an adviser on tribals affairs to the Government of India, his chief sphere of operation the country's north-east.

In his years as an official, Elwin continued to write prodigiously. Much of what he wrote was for restricted circulation, and almost all of it focused on policy, on what the state could and might do to protect the interests of the tribes. Books for public consumption included *A Philosophy for NEFA* [North East Frontier Agency] (1959) and *A New Deal for Tribal India* (1963), both widely read in their day. He had also been working steadily on his autobiography. But so varied had been his life and so versatile his achievements that when Elwin asked him to suggest a title, his publisher came up with twenty-five different alternatives. They finally settled on *The Tribal World of Verrier Elwin*, to make evident his primary loyalty and identification. The book was sent to press in 1963 and appeared in May 1964, too late for the author to see it, Elwin having died in February.

His autobiography is the crown of Elwin's writing life, a book that moves evocatively but unhurriedly through his work as a Christian for the Congress, a defender of the aboriginal, and an Englishman for India. The preface to *Tribal World* freely acknowledges that 'much of it is written from the Indian point of view'; indeed, he almost called it the 'Autobiography of a British-born Indian'. Within this organising principle, the book contains evocative descriptions of Oxford and of his early years in India, crisp accounts of the tribes he worked with in the 1930s and 1940s, and finally, an extended treatment of his 'phil-anthropological' work in the North East Frontier Agency. With travel reports and book summaries taking the place of the intensely personal narrative of its earlier chapters, the work grows ever more bland with the autobiographer's rise to prominence. Elwin also seemed determined to name and acknowledge every official, high or low, whom he came into contact with; the later chapters thus read somewhat like a long thank-you letter to his Indian friends. There are also some striking omissions—no account is provided, for example, of the vigorous controversies that he initiated and so relished taking part in. Some of the most important people in his life and work, notably his two wives and Shamrao Hivale, have almost no place at all in the book.

For all that it leaves out, *The Tribal World of Verrier Elwin* remains a charming and sometimes very moving work. It ranks with the self-testimonies of Jawaharlal Nehru, Nirad C. Chaudhuri, and Sálim Ali as among the finest autobiographies written by an Indian. Published when tributes to his memory were still fresh in the mind, it was warmly received everywhere. In India the book was read as an account of an exemplary Indian; in the United Kingdom (where it overcame the disadvantage of being released on Election Day) as the story of an eccentrically gifted and risk-loving Englishman; in the United States, as the testimony of the brilliant scholar who turned his back on civilisation. Writing of the scholar, S.C. Dube noted that Elwin 'was not a dry-as-dust technician; he was a poet, an artist and a philosopher' who by his 'individual effort produced more and better work than many of the expensively staffed and large research organisations in the country.' Writing of the saint, Naomi Mitchison said Elwin 'was one of the small handful of people whom I, in my spiritual arrogance, genuinely respected . . . If there were a few thousand Verrier Elwins about, one would really begin to feel quite hopeful about the world.'

The Tribal World of Verrier Elwin won the prestigious Sahitya Akademi Award. The citation called it an 'outstanding contribution to contemporary Indian writing in English', a book written 'with sincerity, courage and charm, revealing a mind in which Western and Indian idealism were uniquely blended.' Western and Indian—but also Hindu and Christian, tribal and civilised, poet and scientist, rebel and official. The circumstances of his life made Elwin a privileged interpreter of cultures (more accurately, perhaps, across cultures). In his autobiography, as in everything else he wrote, one can sense the passionate desire to make one adversary see the truth in the other—to show Hindus the mystical side of Christianity, for example, or the British the justice of the Indian demand for freedom, or the 'civilised' world what it might learn from the tribes, or anthropology what it might learn from literature.

12
Novelists of the 1930s and 1940s

LEELA GANDHI

The period spanning the 1930s and 1940s was momentous both in the history of Indian nationalism and in the history of that lesser creature, the Indian novel in English. Invariably, these histories came together. While the incipient Indian nation frequently supplied the content and inspiration for the incipient novel form, the novel of the 1930s and 1940s in turn played a very important part in imagining and embodying the radical vision of anti-colonial nationalism. As it happens the diverse range of authors who tried their hand—with varying degrees of success—at novel writing included many who dabbled, with varying degrees of commitment, in the social and political issues which preoccupied the great age of Indian nationalism. At the same time, the nation-centredness of this new generation of Indian novelists was tempered by a characteristic cosmopolitanism of outlook and experience. Mulk Raj Anand, Bhabani Bhattacharya, Raja Rao, Aubrey Menen, and G.V. Desani, to name a few, each spent a substantial and formative period of their lives in Europe, and their writing is often, albeit subtly, underscored by the sense of cultural schizophrenia which has become the hallmark of recent and more self-consciously post-colonial Indian fiction. So, for instance, Anand attributes his novelistic negotiation of tradition and modernity to 'the double burden on my shoulders, the Alps of the European tradition and the Himalayas of my Indian past'. Writers like Menen and Desani, likewise, endeavoured to make a creative resource of their cultural hybridity. Thus, caught between the sometimes complementary and sometimes opposing claims of home and the world, the novelists of the 1930s and 1940s owed their inspiration and the conditions for their emergence to two contexts: the social and political upheavals of the 'Gandhian whirlwind' and the era of late-modernism in Europe.

At home, this period marked the most visibly triumphant stage of anti-colonial nationalism, culminating in 1947 with the much awaited event of Indian independence. To some extent, the optimistic mood of these two decades emerged in reaction to the long period of political frustration and uncertainty which haunted the preceding phase of the national movement. While the 1920s began in the wake of the Jallianwala Bagh massacre, with Gandhi's retaliatory call for a systematic and non-violent programme of non-cooperation with the British administration, the movement was contentiously suspended in mid flight by Gandhi following the outbreak of violence at Chauri Chaura. The anticlimactic outcome of non-cooperation resulted in a pervasive mood of disenchantment and scepticism about Gandhi's political wisdom. And with his arrest in March 1922 and subsequent withdrawal from politics for the next six years, not to mention the increasing disunity among the Congress ranks, the national movement submitted to a long and recuperative hibernation.

By 1929, however, the mood changed. The various factions within the Congress temporarily resolved their differences and a newly enthused Gandhi commemorated the last day of the preceding decade by moving a resolution in the Congress session, declaring total independence as the single and most pressing goal of Indian nationalism. The Civil Disobedience movement was thus launched in the uncompromising spirit of this resolution, with millions of people throughout India swearing allegiance to the cause of purna swaraj on 26 January 1930, henceforth to be celebrated as Independence day.

There were two significant consequences of the 1930s Civil Disobedience movement: first, in its appeal for the mass performance of illegal acts, it helped to furnish a significantly popular basis for the energies of Indian anti-colonialism. Second, it postulated Gandhi as the icon of such randomly distributed energies. It was at this time that the 'Mahatma theme' was announced within the nationalist agitation as a uniquely imaginative, carefully symbolic, and irresistibly fictionalisable way of doing politics. This theme found its poetic apotheosis in the events of the Dandi March. On 12 March 1930, with characteristic theatrical verve, Gandhi and a band of followers began a 24-day march to break the prevailing salt laws. On 6 April, on the beach at Dandi, the Mahatma walked to the shore to collect a small lump of salt left over by the waves, and the Salt Satyagraha was inaugurated.

Events such as these find their way into the numerous 'Mahatma novels' of this period, those written in English and in a range of other Indian languages. Premchand's *Premashram* (1921) and *Rangabhumi* (1925) in Hindi, Ramanlal Vasantlal Desai's *Gram Lakshmi* (1940) in Gujarati, G.T. Madkholkar's *Muktatma* (1933) in Marathi, and Satinath Bhaduri's *Jagari* (1946) in Bengali, offer some significant narrations of the Gandhian theme. Apart from the work of the major writers in English, a host of lesser known satellite novels also deploy Gandhi as a governing trope or motif in their fictional exploration of contemporary India. An early example is the work of K.S. Venkataramani (1891–1951). His first novel, *Murugan, The Tiller* (1927), promotes the cause of Gandhian economics through its dramatisation of a heavily allegorical relationship between two friends, the materialist Kedari and the public-spirited Ramu. Predictably, the flamboyant Kedari comes to a bad end while the idealistic Ramu implements the vision of Gandhi's village-based economy by setting up a rural commune with his contrite and newly converted friend. Venkataramani's second novel, *Kandan, The Patriot: A Novel of New India in the Making* (1932), is an even more earnest narrative about the 1930s Civil Disobedience movement. Here, the young Oxford-educated Kandan—who reads like a thinly disguised portrait of a young Gandhi— gives up his prestigious Indian Civil Service job to devote himself to the greater cause of nationalism before succumbing, almost prophetically, to a bullet wound. A further collection of short stories, *Jatadharan and*

Other Stories (1937), likewise amplifies the Gandhian creed of ahimsa, on the one hand, and his violent denunciation of modern civilisation, on the other.

A recognisably Gandhian tone also predominates the fiction of K. Nagarajan (1893–1986), whose *Athavar House* (1937) invokes the larger vicissitudes of Gandhian nationalism as the backdrop for its sensitive chronicle of the fortunes and misfortunes of a Maharashtrian family settled in the south of India. However, it is only in his second novel, *Chronicles of Kedaram* (1961), that Nagarajan introduces Gandhi as a character within the narrative, who is called upon to resolve an incident of religious tension in a small town on the Coromandel coast, where the story is set. Notably, R.K. Narayan's comic portrait of Gandhi in *Waiting for the Mahatma* (1955) is also written much after Independence.

In addition to the wide range of south Indian writers who seem to dominate the scene of 'Gandhian fiction', Bhabani Bhattacharya (1906–88) deserves mention for his first novel, *So Many Hungers* (1947), published a few months after Independence. Set in the context of the 1942–3 Bengal famine and Quit India movement, this complicated and didactic novel takes its characters through a rigorously Gandhian education. It is, at one level, the story of Kajoli, a village girl who righteously rejects the prostitution forced on her by the destitution of her family, to sell newspapers and so also to assume the persona of the Gandhian 'new woman'. At another level, it deals with the spiritual and political growing-up of Rahoul, a Cambridge-educated astrophysicist who simultaneously discovers the limits of intellectualism and Western civilisation, and renounces both in favour of nationalism and village-based economy. Much of his instruction comes by way of his grandfather, Devata, a saintly Gandhian figure with a penchant for the hunger strike, who is responsible for bringing satyagraha to the village of Baruni, where he lives like one of the peasants.

In most of these novels the impact of Gandhism is measured not only in terms of its anti-imperial content but also—and perhaps more significantly—for its impetus to the programme of internal national reform. By and large, the social realism of contemporary fiction seeks its materials and gains its inspiration from the nationalist mobilisation and 'upliftment' of women, workers, untouchables, and peasants. At best, these narratives tend to represent the colonial encounter itself as a shadowy subplot to the larger story of socio-economic transformation. And in this regard, although Gandhi continues to be treated as the ethical centre of the purported turning-upside-down of old hierarchies, a distinctly Nehruvian vocabulary gains currency in the novels of this period.

In a sense, the 1930s and 1940s were also Nehru's decades. In particular, it was between 1933 and 1936 that Nehru not only entered into the most radical and 'Marxist' phase of his political career, but also began to come into conflict with Gandhi's idiosyncratic version of nationalism. As early as 1933 he articulated his conviction that 'the true civic idea is the socialist ideal, the communist ideal', and over the next few years he systematically endeavoured to bring this vision to bear upon the methods and organisational structure of the national movement. The consequent rift between Nehru and Gandhi troubles the message of much contemporary fiction. Faced with a choice between Nehruvian modernity and the distinctly non-modern imperatives of Gandhi's *Hind Swaraj* (1910), most novelists attempt an uneasy synthesis of both views. While the bulk of Gandhi novels faithfully narrate the conversion of Westernised 'foreign educated' protagonists to simple rural ideals, in reality these stories are often unable to entirely eschew the cosmopolitanism of the Nehruvian alternative. For Nehru's Marxism—and his critique of the nexus between world capitalism and imperialism—gestured towards the viability of a more expansive and politically motivated internationalism. In Nehru, to put it differently, the choice between home and the world was not as stark, and his personal cultural syncretism directly addressed the experiences of the novelists writing at the time. His characterisation of himself as 'a queer mixture of the East and the West, out of place everywhere, at home nowhere' captured a mood which still influences the fictional texture of Indian writing in English.

Despite its uneven course, the events generated by the Gandhi–Nehru partnership culminated in 1947 with the fulfilment of purna swaraj. And yet, for all the hyperbolic enthusiasm of Nehru's 'Freedom at Midnight' speech, the optimistic moment of Indian Independence was also that of bloodletting on both sides of the India–Pakistan divide. If Independence narrated the triumphant progress of the national movement, its double, Partition, told an altogether different story—of mutual betrayal, failure, the systematic rift between Congress and the Muslim League, and the estrangement between Muslims and Hindus.

In this regard, it is interesting that several 'nationalist novels' by Muslim writers deal almost entirely with Hindu characters. For instance, Aamir Ali's *Conflict* (1947) is exclusively peopled by Hindu characters, and it negotiates the national movement through its Hindu protagonist Shankar, a village boy whose journey to Bombay leads to his accidental involvement in the Quit India agitation. Likewise, K.A. Abbas's *Tomorrow is Ours: A Novel of the India of Today* (1943), explores the issues of nationalism and untouchability through a female protagonist called Parvati. On the other side, the imaginative energies of the major Hindu novelists similarly fail to conceive of a nationalist Muslim protagonist. And, for all its social radicalism, even the work of major writers like Mulk Raj Anand and Raja Rao remains uneasy in its account of the Hindu–Muslim relationship.

Whether positive or negative, the events of the 1930s and 1940s self-evidently furnished the fictional content for the novels of this period. Rather more directly, the national movement and its leaders also exercised a formal and literary influence upon English prose writing in general. Nehru's long spells in prison resulted in a prolific output of imaginative history writing. In particular, his *Glimpses of World History* (1934) and the monumental *Discovery of India* (1946) both set the tone for a stylistic blend of fact and introspection so characteristic of the novels written during this period. So also, contemporary novelists found a massive resource in the enormous journalistic output produced by the national movement. The two journals run by Gandhi, *Young India* (1919–32) and *Harijan* (1933–48), proved especially influential in disseminating not only the intellectual content and concerns of the national movement, but also in recounting stories about lives and contexts hitherto unavailable to the middle-class writerly imagination. Thus, for example, Bharati Sarabhai's play *The Well of the People* (1943) took its plot from a story published in *Harijan*, and Anand began the redrafting of *Untouchable* after reading an article in *Young India* by

Gandhi, describing an encounter with Uka, a sweeper boy. Gandhi's prose, as Anand records, was exemplary for its realism and clarity: 'The narrative was simple, austere and seemed to me more truthful than my artificially concocted novel.' Anand went on to organise a London-based reading group devoted to the regular perusal of *Young India*. And it was in the pages of the same journal that the young Raja Rao first read Gandhi's autobiography, *The Story of My Experiments with Truth* (Vol. I, 1927; Vol. II, 1929) in serialised form.

While Rao's writing implicitly reflects the influence of Gandhi's autobiography, several of his contemporaries directly acknowledge their debt to this text. For instance, Bhabani Bhattacharya's *Gandhi the Writer* (1969) celebrates *My Experiments* as an indispensable model for the novel form. Drawing attention to Gandhi's instructive concern for detail and everyday life, Bhattacharya praises him as a 'writer's writer' and claims that the best writing in the Indian subcontinent 'bears his counter-signature'. Despite his extravagant rhetoric, Bhattacharya is correct in pointing to a more general and productive confluence between the autobiographical and novelistic prose of the 1930s and 1940s. For it was through texts such as *My Experiments*, Nehru's *Autobiography* (1936), General Mohan Singh's *Leaves from My Diary* (1946), and Vijayalakshmi Pandit's *So I Became a Minister* (1935)—not to mention the profusion of prison letter-writing in this period—that practitioners of the novel form acquired a quite specific understanding of the contiguity between personal and political prose, between narratives of subjectivity and those of nationalism.

As for the question of language, most contemporary novelists managed to write creatively both in English and in their regional language: Bhattacharya wrote his earliest pieces in Bengali, Raja Rao in Kannada, Ahmed Ali in Urdu, and Anand in both Punjabi and Urdu. And while the leaders of the national movement were often undecided about the proper status of English in independent India, some like C. Rajagopalachari appropriatively claimed English as 'Saraswati's gift to India'. By and large, most writers guiltlessly persuaded themselves that English was the best medium for the task of national unification. Not entirely convinced by these arguments, however, Anand sought Gandhi's opinion on the propriety of writing exclusively in English, and the latter's encouraging response was characteristically pragmatic and unsentimental: 'The purpose of writing is to communicate, isn't it? If so, say your say in any language that comes to hand.'

If the last two decades of Indian nationalism were conducive for the emergence of the novel form, the travelling novelists of this era found an equally hospitable environment in the Europe of the 1930s and 1940s. Inflected by the events of the two world wars, these decades sounded, on the one hand, the pessimistic note of civilisational crisis, and on the other, of an expansive—although often narrowly élitist—intellectual cosmopolitanism.

Dissatisfied with mainstream Europe and its cultural baggage, many European intellectuals and writers began to seek their creative resources both within popular culture, as also in the wider non-Western world. Invariably, the new and different cultures revealed by colonialism held out a range of possibilities, and it was especially within modernism that native and foreign influences achieved a productive synthesis. Thus, Pound embarked on an investigation of Japanese Noh drama, Yeats and Eliot—among others—undertook a study of the Upanishads, and Forster unearthed an enormous narrative resource in India. In this milieu, then, the expatriate Indian novelist found Europe gazing longingly upon the 'East', often in the hope of gaining an alternative system of truths. Paradoxically, many of these writers were guided by the prevailing European fashion in their own 'return' to Indian culture and scripture. So, for example, Raja Rao combined his fondness for Baudelaire, Valery, and Gide with a self-education in the *Ramayana* and the *Brihatstotraratnakara*, and in the course of his London years Anand professed a desire to 'liberate the unconscious via the Shakti-Shakta Tantric thought'.

These decades were also marked by the pioneering and apposite efforts of Sarvepalli Radhakrishnan (1888–1975) to interpret Indian philosophy for the West. While in texts like *Kalki, or the Future of Civilization* (1929) Radhakrishnan issued a Gandhian warning about the increasing mechanisation and industrialisation of the modern world, other writings, such as *The Hindu View of Life* (1926) and *An Idealist View of Life* (1932), offered a counteractive palliative in Indian philosophy. In particular, it was in those books which attempted to negotiate the intellectual divide between 'occidental' and 'oriental' thought, such as *East and West in Religion* (1933) and *Eastern Philosophy and Western Thought* (1939), that Radhakrishnan's work became especially accessible to the modernist imagination. Notably, Aubrey Menen's autobiography singles out Radhakrishnan's *The Principal Upanishads* (1953) as pre-eminently suitable for the uninitiated Western reader.

Thus, modernism was not only well disposed to the immediate political concerns of the 1930s and 1940s expatriate Indian novelist, but also instrumental—albeit accidentally—in helping this figure to retain his cultural affiliations. Moreover, many of these novelists benefited materially from the atmosphere of literary, and sometimes economic, patronage which characterised the ethos of European modernism. In particular, it was E.M. Forster who facilitated the early careers of many of the writers under discussion. Anand's *Untouchable* bears the authoritative seal of Forster's laudatory preface. Forster's preface to the Everyman's Library edition of *A Passage to India* also lavishes praise upon Ahmed Ali's *Twilight in Delhi*. This novel was first published, under John Lehmann's editorship, by the Hogarth Press. And G.V. Desani's cult novel *All About H. Hatterr* appeared to favourable reviews by, among others, T.S. Eliot, who spoke for many when saying: 'In all my experience, I have not met with anything quite like it.'

Ultimately, however, modernism proved an ambiguous inheritance. Increasingly under attack for its élitism and for its self-serving engagement with other cultures, it met its match in the increasingly Marxist tone of the 1930s and 1940s. Several Marxist critics and writers raised a cry against the abstruse verbosity and solipsism of modernist writing, and began a campaign for a more simple and accessible prose style. In a wider context, Marxism prepared the foundations for a more politically motivated internationalism—a mood which found expression in the mobilisation of intellectuals for the struggle against Fascism, embodied by the Spanish Civil War. Some expatriate Indian novelists pledged their support to this enterprise. Mulk Raj Anand joined the International Brigade and, on a different note, Rahoul, the hero of Bhattacharya's *So Many Hungers*, begins his conversion to Gandhism after voicing regrets about his cowardly non-participation in the Spanish Civil War during his time in England.

Not only did Marxism politicise the Indian writer's experience of Europe, it also evoked the Nehru-inspired socialism of these decades. Faced with this new and curious bridge between East and West, several expatriate Indian writers submitted to a gradual process of disengagement with the modernist creed. Thus, Anand flamboyantly rejected the intellectualism of Bloomsbury writers, and Aubrey Menen, likewise, increasingly found the 'beautiful people of Bloomsbury' sadly lacking in human kindness. The immediate catalyst to Menen's disenchantment, however, was not Marxism or nationalism so much as a particularly scathing rejection note from Virginia Woolf to one of his young writer-aspirant friends. The quasi-fictional preface to Desani's *All About H. Hatterr* tells a similar tale about the ruthless rejection of the manuscript by 'Betty Bloomsbohemia: the Virtuosa with knobs on'. Judging by these accounts, it would appear that there was, in the end, a happy reciprocity to the eventual estrangement between late-modernism and the Indian writers of this period.

The fiction of the 1930s and 1940s is dominated by the voice of Mulk Raj Anand (1905–2004). Born in Peshawar (now in Pakistan) to a Hindu coppersmith family, Anand's life and work exemplifies the curious dialogue between nationalism and cosmopolitanism, modernism and Marxism, and Gandhism and Nehruvian socialism.

Anand's political career began through an early involvement with the non-cooperation movement of 1921, for which he suffered a brief imprisonment. Soon after this event, and upon the completion of his undergraduate education at Punjab University, he set sail for England to study philosophy at the University of London. Gradually drawn into the fringes of the Bloomsbury circle, he simultaneously developed an interest in Indian philosophy and aesthetics. His first unpublished exercise in English was to write a 2000-page Gandhian confession, which furnishes the material for much of his subsequent autobiographical writing.

The genesis of Anand's first novel, *Untouchable* (1935), recounts his decisive shift from Bloomsbury to Sabarmati. As we have seen, Gandhi's eloquent character sketch of the unknown sweeper Uka, in the pages of *Young India,* so convinced Anand of the inauthenticity of his early draft of this novel that he abandoned the project, returning home to study ancient monuments and live with Gandhi at Sabarmati Ashram. In the course of this communal cohabitation the latter allegedly edited Anand's flawed manuscript, advising him 'to cut down a hundred or more pages' on the grounds that his untouchable hero was too much of 'a Bloomsbury intellectual'.

Untouchable narrates one day in the life of Bakha, an introspective young sweeper who lives in the outcastes' colony in a small cantonment town in northern India. A chain of humiliating experiences leaves Bakha searching for some yet unknown release from the degradation of his life. A range of possible solutions magically presents itself: Bakha's father, Lakha, proposes the age-old and ultimately unsatisfactory creed of philosophic resignation; the well-meaning Christian missionary Colonel Hutchinson promises a life of social equality in Christ; and finally, during a surprise visit and address Gandhi himself declares untouchability as 'the greatest blot on Hinduism'. And yet, although Bakha is enthralled by the epiphanic quality of Gandhi's rousing speech, the last word is with the practical and modern Nehruvian figure, a poet, Iqbal Nath Sarashar, also editor of the journal *Nawan Jug,* who argues that sweepers will only be released from the stigma of untouchability upon the large-scale popularisation of the flush-toilet system.

Untouchable is possibly Anand's most accomplished novel. Quite apart from its structural cohesiveness, its prose subtly picks up the dense corporeality and tactility of Bakha's existence. Moreover, Anand's chosen social context offers a unique perspective on British officials, who are invariably more sympathetic than the bulk of Hindu characters that inhabit Bakha's beleaguered world.

Anand continues his study of the oppressed in his two subsequent chronicles of 'coolies'—*Coolie* (1936) and *Two Leaves and a Bud*

(1937). In both these novels, his concern shifts from questions of caste to those of class. *Coolie* is a Dickensian saga about the misfortunes which beset the young Munoo—an orphan from Kangra—upon his progressive travels from the pastoral idyll of the hills to the big smog of Bombay. In his many incarnations as domestic slave, factory worker, pickle maker, coolie, and rickshaw puller, Munoo gains solace in the generosity and familial kindness of poor people like himself. However, these encounters do little to mitigate the many oppressions he suffers at the hands of exploitative employers before dying of consumption.

Despite its unwieldy details, *Coolie* is an important social chronicle, especially for its sketches of early trade union activity in Bombay and of the complex relationship between colonial factory managers and colonised Indian workers. And, much as in *Untouchable*, this novel also proposes a practical solution—the chimney—to ameliorate the deplorable working conditions of labourers in indigenous factories. But in this novel we can also detect the incipient strains of religious discord: Munoo's world is already complicated by villainous Pathans and by outbreaks of intercommunal violence.

A less successful novel, *Two Leaves and a Bud*, recounts the dashed hopes of Gangu, a Punjabi peasant who has been lured under false pretences to work in the appallingly unhygienic conditions of a tea estate in Assam. In this relentless tale of woe, Gangu is systematically starved before being shot dead by a British officer, who also tries to rape his daughter. There are few moments of respite in this sombre novel, and most of its British characters are one-dimensionally villainous. A happier note informs Anand's subsequent trilogy—*The Village* (1939), *Across the Black Waters* (1941), and the *Sword and the Sickle* (1942). Organised around the varied career of Lal Singh, an erstwhile Punjabi peasant, this trilogy moves across a complex range of geographical and ideological locations. *The Village* develops the opposition between city and countryside, explored in *Coolie*, through the ambivalent desires of the young Lal Singh, who is torn between the comforts of home on the one hand, and the progressive modernity of urban India on the other. Finally, oppressed by the superstition, sexual puritanism, and patriarchal ethos of the village, Lal Singh cuts off his hair despite religious prohibitions to the contrary. Unable to negotiate the subsequent scandal and his own public humiliation, he runs away—after a brief flirtation with the Boy Scouts movement—to join the army. *Across the Black Waters* finds him fighting in Flanders in the course of the First World War. Possibly the only 'world war' novel in Indian English literature, this book shows Anand at his best, recovering some of the restraint and cohesion of *Untouchable*. In *The Sword and the Sickle,* however, the plot is, once again, burdened by Anand's unflagging love of detail. The novel's rambling narrative about Lal Singh's return home from a German prison includes episodes about the hero's unsuccessful flirtation with communism. More prison terms follow, and Gandhism appears again as a superior contestant in the debate with communism.

Gandhism does not fare as well in *The Big Heart* (1945), Anand's last novel before Independence. This sensitive and ambitious book tells the story of Ananta, a street-wise coppersmith who is called 'big heart' because of his earthy and uncomplicated generosity of spirit. Here, Ananta single-handedly takes on the task of bringing the lessons of modernity and mechanisation to his suspicious and unchanging community. The novel underscores Ananta's enlightened vision through long renditions of a sporadic debate between the Gandhian Mahashaji and the Nehruvian poet Puran Singh Bhagat—who is very like the poet figure in *Untouchable*—regarding the competing benefits of tradition and modernity. While Mahashaji subscribes to the vision of Gandhi's *Hind Swaraj,* Anand's sympathies are clearly with Puran Singh, who eloquently espouses the benefits of an industrial revolution. Guided by a similar creed, Ananta eventually sacrifices his life in an attempt to prevent a Luddite assault on the local factory. But for its didactic passages, *The Big Heart* is a compelling novel, and Ananta is possibly the most complex and developed of Anand's characters.

After Independence, Anand's career failed to match the achievements of his earlier work. His first post-Independence novel, *Seven Summers* (1951), is a semi-autobiographical work about Anand's childhood, told as the life of a protagonist called Krishan Chander—who becomes the persona for most of Anand's subsequent autobiographical novels. A curious novel, *The Private Life of an Indian Prince* (1953), follows, telling another autobiographically inflected story about a prince who suffers a nervous breakdown. A more expansive fictionality informs the next novel, *The Old Woman and the Cow* (1960), which sees Anand returning to his favoured peasant theme, and focusing—unusually for him—on the misfortunes and revolutionary transformation of a female protagonist called Gauri. The remaining novels tend to repeat old themes with less success: *The Road* (1963) returns for its inspiration to *Untouchable, The Death of a Hero* (1964) is based on the life of a Kashmiri freedom fighter, and *Morning Face* (1970) and *Confession of a Lover* (1976) continue the slow chronological progression of Anand's autobiography through the fictional persona of Krishan Chander.

Despite their many limitations, Anand's novels are instrumental in the history of the Indian novel in English. Their experiments with social realism, and corresponding attention to the surface of life in pre-Independent India, catches within fiction the complex alliances, misalliances, transformations, and failures of the Indian national movement. Moreover, these novels are pioneering in their effort to render into English the exuberant dialects of northern India.

Although awkward, Anand's exposition of 'pidgin-English' prepares the way for the subsequent linguistic and cultural translations of Indian-English writers.

Many of Anand's literary and political preoccupations reappear in the work of Raja Rao. Born to a Brahmin family from Mysore in 1908, Rao's upbringing and education combine, once again, a distinct blend of Indian and European influences. While his work displays a profound commitment to Indian philosophy, acquired through a lasting attachment to the thought of Pandit Taranath of the Tungabhadra Ashram and Sri Atmanand Guru of Trivandrum, Rao was from 1927 an expatriate, when he left for France to undertake a study of Western philosophy and mysticism. Subsequently he lived abroad, mainly in France and the United States. Less prolific than Anand, Rao wrote only one novel in the period before Independence, *Kanthapura*, to be followed—after a long silence—by *The Serpent and the Rope, The Cat and Shakespeare, Comrade Kirillov,* and most recently, *The Chessmaster and his Moves.* He died in 2006.

Kanthapura (1938) is best known for its classic foreword, which reads very much like a manifesto for the practice of Indian writing in

English. The foreword begins by describing the difficulty of bridging the cultural and historical gap between the English language and the Indian tale: 'One has to describe in a language that is not one's own the spirit that is one's own.' This dichotomy, Rao claims, can only be resolved through a systematic indigenisation of English—by infusing it with the breathless and unpunctuated 'tempo of Indian life'. So also, faced with the indisputably Western origins of the novel form, the Indian writer is required to undertake the rather more difficult task of generic appropriation, by relocating his narrative within the epic tradition of the *Ramayana* and *Mahabharata*. Inevitably, this project requires a departure from the necessarily secular content and structure of the European novel to admit, instead, the random magic or 'legendary history' of some 'god or godlike hero'. But Rao does not secure his objective through a formal 'magic realist' blend of the fantastic and the mundane. Rather more interestingly, he takes as his subject the peculiarly 'secular magic' released into the national movement under the aegis of the Mahatma theme. What follows is a story about the gradual coming of Gandhism to a small caste-ridden village called Kanthapura on the Malabar coast. Narrated as the reminiscences of an old woman, its tone is informed by her preliminary invocation to the goddess Kenchamma, who functions as the presiding deity over the events of the ensuing tale.

The first lessons of Gandhism are brought to Kanthapura by the young radical Moorthy who, despite much resistance from the village orthodoxy, systematically works upon the women to spin their own cloth and to liberate themselves from the unwholesome caste prejudices which have, for centuries, dominated the structure of local existence. Moorthy finally wins over the women by casting the Gandhian message in the form of a traditional Harikatha, which introduces Gandhi as an epic hero, born into a Bania family in 'Gujarat' as a boon to Valmiki by none other than 'Brahma the Self-created one'. While Moorthy's Harikatha is, at one level, a clever ploy to insinuate Gandhi into the religious make-up of his constituency, it is also, quite simply, a retelling with embellishments of *The Story of My Experiments with Truth*—a text which circulates throughout the pages of *Kanthapura*. Moorthy is himself shown to always carry a white khadi-bound copy of this text. As events unfold, the women of the village lose their families and property and suffer grievous injuries in their non-violent satyagraha to defend the rights of the 'coolies' working on the nearby Skeffington Coffee Estate. Undaunted by vicious British officers and the evil 'Mohammadan' policeman, Bade Khan, they become local heroes.

Rao's story idealises the village in the manner of Anand, with the difference that his plot fully integrates within itself the Gandhian insistence upon self-sufficient village polity and economy. It also pursues the specifically Gandhian conviction in the revolutionary potential of women through its focus on the experiences of the women of Kanthapura. However, unlike Anand's work, where women are incidental to the random libidinal and political energies of his heroes, Rao's narrative foregrounds its female characters. In addition to its use of a female narrator, it shows how the conclusive leadership of the satyagraha in Kanthapura is undertaken by a young widow called Ratna. Interestingly, the old Gandhi–Nehru debate also finds its way into the concluding pages of this novel. Now under the spell of Nehruvian socialism, Moorthy—the erstwhile Gandhian—urges the villagers to listen more carefully to Nehru's message of 'equal distribution', on the grounds that the Mahatma is far too saintly for the realpolitik of nationalism. But, in this instance, the women are unpersuaded, and fanatical in their conviction that 'He will bring us Swaraj, the Mahatma'.

Several of the themes which occupy Kanthapura are echoed in Rao's subsequent collection of short stories, *The Cow of the Barricades and Other Stories* (1947). Composed between 1933 and 1946, the stories rehearse, variously, Rao's enchantment with Indian village life, and his preoccupation with the formal puzzle of translating Indian modes of feeling and expression into English. Among these stories, 'Javni' and 'Akkhayya' take up the cause— with Gandhian fervour—of Indian widowhood, while another, 'Narsiga', firmly situates the figure of Gandhi within a religious or mythic idiom. Here, it is the orphan Narsiga who speaks in the voice of the women of Kanthapura, imagining Gandhi's nationalist 'liberation' of India as the culmination of a new *Ramayana*.

With his second novel, *The Serpent and the Rope* (1960), Rao abandons the milieu of his beloved South India for a 'cosmopolitan' story spread across Europe and India. Nominated for a Sahitya Akademi Award in 1963, this late-coming work also marks Rao's somewhat self-conscious shift of focus from Gandhism to Vedanta, and from nationalist narrative to metaphysical fiction. Strongly autobiographical in content, the novel is cast as a sort of spiritual travelogue, recounting the story of Ramaswamy, a grievously self-regarding young intellectual immersed, at a French university, in earnest study of the Albigensian heresy. In France, 'Rama' meets and marries—very unsuccessfully—Madeleine Roussellin, a historian and orientalist par excellence. A trip to Benaras occasioned by the death of his father and a rapid increase of female admirers proves devastating for the Rama–Madeleine marriage, the breakdown of which supplies the framework for much of the philosophising which marks the novel.

Interesting for its early exploration of the now familiar East–West schism, and for its honest rendition of the 'ex-expatriate's' crippling idealisation of India, Rao's second novel is, however, somewhat disabled by the self-indulgence of its soulful protagonist. Unable, also, to do justice to the female protagonists of this narrative, Rao's departure from the concerns of Kanthapura is matched by a decreased empathy for women. At best, the women in the novel offer bland existential accompaniment to the hero's inner odyssey. En route to his guru, Rama must learn to mediate between the competing claims of a baffling array of women: the alternatively voracious and Buddhist Madeleine, the promiscuous Lakshmi, the tantalisingly modern-but-Indian Savithri. Yet, for all the ways in which it is different to Rao's earlier fiction, *The Serpent and the Rope* continues his complex experiments with form and cultural translation, successfully blending elements of the European novel with those of the Indian epic.

With *The Cat and Shakespeare* (1965; an earlier version was published as *The Cat* in 1959), Rao moves even further away from the protocols of realism and deeper into the difficult region of philosophical fiction. Written as a sort of conclusion to *The Serpent and the Rope,* this novel purports to elaborate yet another stage in mystical self-understanding. According to Rao, '*The Serpent and the Rope* is a novel of discovery of the Guru. *The Cat and Shakespeare* shows how one functions after one has found the Guru.' The titles of the two companion novels offer a further insight into Rao's fictional design.

The Serpent and the Rope alludes to a Shankaracharya parable which likens the individual ego's mistaken understanding of reality to an inability to comprehend the distinct yet related natures of serpents and ropes. Yet, such comprehension, as Rama learns at the end of his sentimental education, can only be acquired through the pedagogic intervention of the Guru, or, one who knows. More devotional in its content, the metaphoric import of Rao's cat, in *The Cat and Shakespeare*, derives from the thinking of the eleventh-century philosopher Ramanujacharya, for whom personal salvation is more easily approached through the simple gestures of surrender or faith rather than through the complicated gymnastics of the intellect. And of all available forms of surrender, that of the kitten or cat is held as exemplary. Where infant monkeys actively cling to their negligent parents—as some devotees actively pursue the elusive forms of divinity—the little cat is a model of blind faith, trusting that some powerful maternal agent will graciously lift it above the detritus of existence by the scruff of its unprotesting neck.

With *The Cat and Shakespeare,* then, Rao's hero changes from an earnest seeker into a comic devotee. Combining fragments of Upanishadic wisdom with Shakespearean pontification, the novel tells the story of two friends: Ramakrishna Pai, a divisional clerk in Trivandrum and narrator of the fable, ever preoccupied with the dream of building a three-storey house; and his neighbour, the eccentric and voluble Govindan Nair. It is through Nair, and his peculiar and unorthodox brand of cat-love, that Pai succumbs to the pleasures, or 'play', of devotion. The end of the novel finds him content with everyday felicities—happy in his work and in the knowledge that his beloved Shantha does not grumble in the way of most women. However, even as he modifies his worldly desires—by settling for the hope of a two-storey house—Pai stubbornly holds on to the notion of a secular utopia where all dreams might some day be fulfilled. And, as with his fictional predecessors in Rao's oeuvre, Pai's name for this utopia is 'Gandhi-raj'. 'In Gandhi-raj', as he tells us in a throwaway line, 'everybody will have a house'.

Gandhi also appears intermittently in the pages of Rao's next novel, *Comrade Kirillov* (1976). First published in a French translation in 1965, the revised English version of this book offers a tantalising study of Padmanabha Iyer, a young London-based Indian Marxist who calls himself Kirillov, after Dostoevsky's character in *The Possessed.*

While giving a fascinating account of London in the 1930s and 1940s, the novel comprises, in the main, Kirillov's views on contemporary politics. These views are amplified, every now and then, through his wife Irene—a Czech Marxist—whose diary intersperses the narrative. While Irene's opinions are almost entirely in accord with those held by her husband, she is unable to condone his unhealthy preoccupation with Gandhi. 'At heart', she tells him reproachfully, 'Gandhi is your God. You tremble when you speak of him sometimes.' However, this secret passion, as Irene learns, is simply symptomatic of Kirillov's profound, if guilty, patriotism. For all his intellectual detachment, Kirillov is unable to secure immunity against the emotional pull of his homeland. You can take the Marxist out of India, but—the novel insists—you cannot take India out of the Marxist.

Rao's most recent novel—the first part of a planned trilogy—*The Chessmaster and His Moves* (1988) is informed, to a large extent, by the concerns of *The Serpent and the Rope.* Relentlessly philosophical, and over a decade in the writing, this work is, at one level, a tale of doomed love between Sivarama Sastri, an Indian mathematician based in Paris, and a married woman. As with *The Serpent and the Rope,* the unhappy lovers use the obstacles in their way as a means for introspection and spiritual regeneration, but not before Sastri contemplates the love of some other equally impossible and ill-suited women. A study of the productive dichotomy between inner and outer worlds, between Paris and the Himalaya, Rao's idiosyncratic novel confirms, yet again, his authoritative signature over the characteristic and unique cosmopolitanism of the novelists of this era. More than any other writer of his generation, perhaps, Rao stands out for his outrageous generic anarchy, as also for an unusual brand of South Indian–French cultural hybridity, very different from the predominantly North Indian-English fusion of contemporary Indian writing in English.

Rao's other work includes two further collections of short stories. These are *The Policeman and the Rose* (1978), which gathers and reprints—with the exception of three new pieces—choice examples of his shorter fiction; and *On the Ganga Ghat* (1993), which consists of interconnected stories about Benaras.

While Rao and Anand fictionalise a similar ethos and view of the 1930s and 1940s, Ahmed Ali's writing is underscored by very different cultural imperatives. Born in Delhi in 1910 and educated at Aligarh and Lucknow, Ali taught English at the universities of Lucknow and Calcutta before migrating to Pakistan at Partition. He died in 1994. His first collection of short stories, *Angare,* made a significant contribution to the Progressive Movement in Urdu literature, and he subsequently became a founding member of the All-India Progressive Writers' Association launched at Lucknow on 10 April 1936. His essay 'A Progressive View of Art'—included in the Association's first official publication, *Towards a Progressive Literature*—announced a commitment to the cause of social realism, a method which informs his detailed portraits of Indian-Muslim households in a post-imperialist and pre-Independence Delhi.

Ali's first published short story in English, 'Our Lane', sounds some of the themes which inform his novels. Set in the lane 'Chelon ka Koocha' in Delhi, it documents the last agonies of a neglected and dying ethos. Overrun by poverty and decrepit old buildings, the lane is closed off from the outside world. Ali's story foregrounds the painful gap between the Indian Muslim community and the emerging Indian nation. The national movement is, at best, an unwelcome intrusion into Chelon ka Koocha, manifesting itself through the death of Mirza, the milk-seller's young son, who is shot by a British officer while participating in a procession during the non-cooperation movement. The fragmented composition of the anti-colonial nation is also reflected in the story's account of the profound absence of Hindu–Muslim rapprochement—which underscores the incident where Shera, the gram-seller, is imprisoned for his attempt to carry away, in the course of a violent communal riot at Jama Masjid, the body of the martyr Abdul Rashid, who is responsible for killing the Hindu leader Swami Shradhanand.

Ali's only pre-Partition novel, *Twilight in Delhi* (1940), relocates the scene of Chelon ka Koocha into the world within and around the Delhi-based Nihal household. And it is through the gradual undoing of the Nihals over the years 1910–19 that this novel articulates its larger elegy for the historical erosion of a whole culture. Governed by the authority of their unwilling patriarch, Mir Nihal, this family witnesses a succession of misfortunes. Asghar, the romantic younger son, embarks on an unsuccessful marriage which ends with the death of his neglected wife; Mir Nihal loses his companionate mistress Babban Jan to typhoid; an older son, Habibuddin, dies after a long and painful illness; and a broken Mir Nahal slips into a coma where he remains 'more dead than alive'.

Unlike the nationalist fervour which characterises the work of his Hindu contemporaries, Ali's novel offers a culturally unique view of the colonial encounter. Through the eyes of the aristocratic Mir Nihal, it elaborates a specifically Muslim perception of colonial rule as the loss of Mughal hegemony over India. No longer masters and rulers of Delhi, Nihal and his peers lament their estrangement from the city of their birth and progressively lose their bearings in the new geography of the imperial capital. The national movement does little to compensate for the pervasive sense of loss which afflicts the struggling inhabitants of Ali's novel. The events of the non-cooperation movement barely impinge upon the Nihal family—the young Asghar finds that the pressures generated by his impulsive romantic temperament are far more significant than those facing the country: 'He had his own sorrows to think of, his own life to set right. He was unconcerned whether the country lived or died.' For Mir Nihal, the national movement is suspect on account of its capitulation to foreign ways of thinking and being in the world: 'New ways and ideas had come into being. A hybrid culture which had nothing in it of the past was forcing itself upon Hindustan, a hodge-podge of Indian and Western ways which he failed to understand.' As in 'Our Lane', the agitation only enters the lives of these characters in the form of personal tragedy. Once again, it is a milk-seller, called Mirza, whose nationalist son is gunned down while taking part in an anti-government procession.

While the stories told by Anand and Rao consistently project individual protagonists as symbols for the political turmoil of this period, Ahmed Ali's *Twilight in Delhi* captures the claustrophobic and self-destructive inwardness of a particular class within the Indian Muslim community. Although portrayed critically, Ali's characters offer a significant corrective to the historical view that the national movement was entirely representative of, and always responsive to, the needs of

India's communities. In a sense, this novel begs its readers to reconsider, more objectively, the failure of Indian nationalism to extend its appeal adequately to Muslim inhabitants of the country. Ali's only other novel, *Ocean of Night* (1964), is more narrowly conceived. A sad story about unsuccessful love, it deals almost exclusively with the star-crossed passion of a young courtesan called Huma and her suitor Kabir.

Social realism is virtually absent in G.V. Desani's single novel, *All About H. Hatterr* (1948). The eccentric Govindas Vishnoodas Desani (1909–2000) can only be said to count as an Indian writer by virtue of his ancestry. Born in Nairobi, Kenya, he reputedly ran away from home at the age of eighteen and spent the next twenty-five years in England, where he lectured widely, and to much acclaim, as a speaker sponsored by the British Ministry of Information. His brief from the ministry required him to demonstrate, through his rhetorical prowess, the shared English and Indian commitment to the power of the spoken word. His performances won the praise of Edmund Blunden, who said of Desani that 'his personality, as I know it, is exceedingly alive and interesting, and he promises to be an outstanding representative between East and West, not necessarily in the political sense, but that of general interpretation.' While employed as a BBC broadcaster, Desani composed a long prose-poem-play, *Hali* (1950), in the style of Tagore. A complex verbose and allegorical piece about love, death, and illusion, *Hali* won the praise of many critics, including E.M. Forster, who took special note of its personal and passionate style. The play was performed at the Watergate Theatre in London in July 1950, and later in India. Desani returned to India after the Second World War, where for the next fourteen years he practised Raja and Mantra yoga under the guidance of a variety of teachers. His interest in mysticism and the occult also took him to Japan, where he devoted his energies to Buddhist thought and practice. From 1960 to 1968 he contributed regularly to the *Illustrated Weekly of India*, for which he also wrote an irreverent and polemical column called ' "Very High" and "Very

Low" '. Desani finally migrated to the United States to teach religion and philosophy, and upon his retirement was Professor Emeritus at the University of Texas, Austin.

All About H. Hatterr bears the trace of Desani's improbable life. While it seems, on the face of it, to be a simple exercise in modernist word-mongering, *H. Hatterr* is more a sort of Joycean linguistic burlesque where Indian English—much like Joyce's Irish English—relentlessly jostles against all the known rules of grammar and diction. Shakespeare combines with Indian legalese, cockney with babuisms, Anglo-India rubs up against the pompous drone of Colonial Club talk, and grievously unpunctuated sentences find a temporary hiatus in random and arbitrary capitalisations. Structurally, the novel is more or less a growing up story about the education of the eponymous and mad-hatterish hero H. Hatterr, son of a European merchant seaman and a lady from Penang. Set in British India, it is rigorously organised around a set of seven episodes, involving Hatterr's attempt to find a higher truth. Subdivided into an aphoristic 'Digest', an 'Instruction', a 'Presumption', and an illustrative 'Life-encounter', each episode not only evokes the deadliness of the Seven Sins, but also revolves around Hatterr's disastrous encounters with seven false sages from different parts of India. Despite his best intentions, the gullible Hatterr comes up against the material underpinnings of all mystical pretensions, not to mention the duplicity of all women. While one sage literally strips his devotees to keep his second-hand clothes business in operation, another holy man proves to have the sensibility of a 'real estate actuary'. Hatterr's loyal friend Banerrji keeps attempting to ascribe meaning to his experiences (and consistently thanks him on behalf of India), but to no avail. Finally, disenchanted by the hypocritical religious affectations of Indian culture on the one hand, and the social hypocrisies of British culture on the other, a world-weary Hatterr discovers that the only meaning in Life is Life itself: 'I have no opinions, I am beaten, and I just accept all this phenomena, this diamond-cut-diamond game, this human horse-play, all this topsy-turvyism, as *Life*.'

Desani's intensely self-conscious novel prefigures more recent books like Salman Rushdie's *Midnight's Children* (1981) and I. Allan Sealy's *The Trotter-Nama* (1988). Chronologically, its linguistic experimentation and irreverent handling of the Great Books of the European canon are possibly more revolutionary than those in recent Indian fiction. Desani's slightly precious and arrogant posturing is, in context, both startlingly unusual and useful in the history of the incipient Indian novel in English.

As with Desani, the novels of Sudhin N. Ghose (1899–1965) defy neat classification. Born in Burdwan, educated in Calcutta, Paris, and Strasbourg, literate in a range of Indian and European languages, and equally at home in England and India, Sudhin Ghose appears to share the characteristically dispersed cultural coeordinates of his literary contemporaries. Yet, while his fictional world displays some features of the novel of the 1930s and 1940s, it is also strikingly idiosyncratic.

Ghose's varied literary output includes some journalistic writing, an obscure scholarly tract, *Dante Gabriel Rossetti and Contemporary Criticism* (1928), a study entitled *Post-War Europe: 1918–37* (1939), and three volumes of folk tales gleaned from the Indian subcontinent. He is best known, however, for an interconnected tetralogy of novels—*And Gazelles Leaping* (1949), *Cradle of the Clouds* (1951), *The Vermilion Boat* (1953), and *The Flame of the Forest* (1955)—which record, in the style of a bildungsroman, the growing up of a nameless orphan-narrator over a twenty-year period.

Similar to Anand and to Rao's *Kanthapura,* Ghose's novels dramatise the contrasting ethos of the village and the city. *And Gazelles Leaping* and *Cradle of the Clouds* lovingly idealise the narrator's rural childhood and adolescence in a cosmopolitan kindergarten on the outskirts of Calcutta—where the narrator befriends a Japanese child and a little Chinese boy—and, later, in the happy surrounds of a Santal village. In both novels, however, the malignant forces of the metropolis are always threateningly close at hand, and the youthful city-aspirant narrator is warned by an intrusive observer that 'If you want to prosper in Calcutta. . . you must be subtle. And you must settle there before you are twenty. Otherwise it would mean misery.' Despite this sombre advice, 'the young scholar' departs for the big Calcutta smog, and the remaining two novels chronicle his uneven education and career in the city which worships 'corruption and the Bitch-Goddess'.

The national movement does not really encroach upon the world pictured within Ghose's tales, although a Gandhi-mad character called Charles Andrews Anstruther in *The Flame of the Forest* is self-evidently a fictional counterpart to the Gandhian missionary C.F. Andrews. What distinguishes these novels is the self-conscious Indianness of their narrative structure and sources. In each there is a happy coexistence of disparate realms: the worldly merges with the otherworldly, gods and legends stray into secular territory, and strong friendships are forged between human beings and animals. *And Gazelles Leaping*, for example, recounts the deep emotional bond between the narrator and Mohan, a hypersensitive and self-deprecating elephant who cries on encountering an admonitory sign refusing admission to elephant-kind. Likewise, in *Cradle of the Clouds* we are told how Baiju, a Santal messenger, was—to his eternal regret— fed intoxicating mohua juice by the playful and disruptive dwarf-bears.

While Ghose has been effectively forgotten within India, his work was well received in Europe and North America. However, few critics regarded his tetralogy as novels, preferring to praise them as memoirs or autobiographical sketches.

Aubrey Menen (1912–89) is another important though neglected novelist, whose complex cultural background contributes to his strikingly objective view of both Europe and India. Born in London to an Indian father and an Irish mother, Menen first came to India as a young boy in 1924, when India was still recovering from the collapse of the non-cooperation movement. Exposed early to the worst face of the British empire, he became equally attuned to the caste prejudices of the Nair community in Malabar, to which his father belonged. In the course of his varied career, Menen worked as a drama critic, stage director, press officer, scriptwriter, education officer for the Government of India, and head of the Motion Picture department for the J. Walter Thompson Company in London, before devoting himself to writing full time.

Much like Desani, Menen's intellectual outlook is understood by a sense of both the cultural plenitude of his inheritance and the almost universal system of injustice and hypocrisy running through the orthodox institutions of East and West. While Menen uses an eclectic range of fictional and non-fictional genres in his critique of the competing racisms spawned by the colonial encounter, he is possibly at his insightful and ironic best as an essayist. In collections like *Dead Man in the Silver Market* (1954), for instance, he teases out the singular absurdity of his jingoistic British education, which insisted—with a Hegelian twist—that evolution was a slow and steady progression to Englishness, and that his apelike Indian father was a 'congenital liar whose habits I should tolerate and not rebuke'. On the other side, however, Menen is equally amused by the unshakeable cultural arrogance and anglophobia of his Nair grandmother, whose various attempts to wean him from the barbarity of Englishness include the advice to 'Never take a bath in one of those contraptions in which you sit in dirty water like a buffalo.' Notwithstanding their humour, these essays follow the tone of Menen's other work in their measured and humane effort to negotiate a harmonious balance between home and the world, self and other.

While Menen derives some of his clamouring for a just and open society from the combined inheritance of the national movement and the atmosphere of revolt in post-War Europe, the tone of his writing is significantly informed by his refusal to gloss over or apologise for the fact of his homosexuality—about which he writes with humour and detachment in his autobiography, *The Space Within the Heart* (1970; reprinted 1991 with *It is All Right*). Here, as elsewhere, Menen labours to convey the complexity of a homosexual existence in a sexually repressive, sexually obsessive age. Constantly repudiating shallow gender stereotypes, he uses his homosexuality principally to develop an ironic and critical relation to the world around him. As with his cultural hybridity, his sexual 'dissonance', too, translates into an acute sympathy for the eccentric or different individual, and supplies him with exceptional gifts of autobiographical self-consciousness.

In this long essay—which reads as a sort of 'art of living'—and its posthumously published sequel, an 'art of dying' entitled *It is All Right,* Menen watches and diagnoses himself and his era with a physician's candour. We read of his difficult relationship with his mother, his own sexual growing up, and, later in life, his spiritual self-investigations through a disciplined reading of the Upanishads. So also, these texts offer a fascinating chronicle of Europe in the 1930s and 1940s. Menen irreverently describes the Bloomsbury set: 'as well-bred as racehorses; they even spoke in a whinny'—and 'gay' Paris, whose nightclubbing lesbians and homosexuals 'gave off an air of intense respectability, as though they had left behind them at home a bonny family of offspring all sleeping in their little beds.'

Although Menen directly returns to the subject of homosexuality in a brilliant essay on Leonardo da Vinci, included in a collection called *Art and Money* (1980), the rest of his work implicitly draws upon the culture and aesthetic arising from a certain type—and class—of homosexual experience. So, for example, his novels and essays record a passionate, almost predictable, love for the artefacts of Greek and Roman antiquity, and an utopian attachment to Renaissance and contemporary Italy, 'a country which has always admired physical beauty'. The world of Menen's fiction is often ebulliently homosocial and bears the traces of his own outlawed sexuality in its rigorous objection to all forms of sexual hypocrisy. In *The Abode of Love* (1956) he retells the 'true' story of a wonderfully promiscuous curate, Henry James Prince, who defies Victorian respectability by founding a religion where sexual pleasures receive spiritual sanction and habitation in a comfortable country house. In *The Fig Tree* (1957), a similar kind of satire, we are told about a puritanical scientist, Harry Wesley, whose attempt to invent an oral contraceptive results in the production of a devastatingly aphrodisiacal fig tree.

In other novels, Menen draws upon the creative resources of his mixed parentage. His first novel, *The Prevalence of Witches* (1947), explores cultural misunderstandings between 'civilised' and 'primitive' people. Set in Limbo, a remote outpost of the British empire in India, it tells a fabulous story about the Limbodians' enduring belief in witchcraft which the British administration has learned to ignore. Matters take a more serious turn when a Limbodian chief kills his wife's lover and blames a witch for the crime. This episode, then, becomes the pretext for the novel's light-hearted exploration of the dichotomy between 'science' and 'superstition', faith and rationality. In the course of the ensuing debate, as the main characters gradually come to believe in the prevalence of witches, Menen's story evolves into a critique of Western civilisation. The terms of this critique are sounded by two British and very Wildean characters—the eccentric Political Agent Catullus and his visiting Oxford companion, the exuberant Bay. And as the conversations between these two figures progress, Limbo is transformed into a congenial and homosocial undergraduate room, where a happy company of well-meaning young men endeavour to propose a comic corrective to the cultural prejudices of Empire.

The Stumbling Stone (1949), Menen's last novel before the close of the decade, undertakes a critique of the false piety of London socialites. The novel narrates the misadventures which ensue when the saintly Colley Burton, evicted from independent India after living a blameless life of good works, returns to London to find that a heavily fictionalised and sensational play about his life has made him into a celebrity. Fearful that Burton's displeasure will lead to the end of the lucrative show, the streetwise playwright Lucky Prynne, and his camp lead actor Van Billiter, tempt Burton with charitable work, urging him to use his celebrity status to assist in the rehabilitation of the juvenile offender Chaz Hopkins. Rapidly disenchanted by the way in which the rich and privileged conspire to earn a living—and build a reputation—out of other people's misery, Burton dramatically opts out. In a bid to replace the pieties of charity with the simple enthusiasm of friendship, he conspires to send the erring Chaz for a hedonistic holiday in Rome—a project which he finances with a bribe, gained in return for his support to Prynne's objectionable play. Lucidly written, Menen's humane novel is deeply informed by its context. And yet, while its systematic puncturing of European civility and opposition to the institutions of war and empire gains from the prevailing intellectual milieu, Burton's ethic of irreverence and 'fun' is pure Menen.

Menen's other fictional writing includes *The Backward Bride* (1950), *The Duke of Gallodoro* (1952), and *A Conspiracy of Women* (1966). He never completed a controversial play on Oscar Wilde which he was commissioned to write, but he achieved considerable notoriety for another play, *Rama Retold* (1954), which was one of the first books to be banned in post-Independence India. The text earned the particular displeasure of C. Rajagopalachari, also a translator of the

Ramayana, who dismissed Menen's book as 'impossible', while adding that 'It is also nonsense but of the unreadable kind, i.e. pure nonsense, not genius wearing the clothes of nonsense.'

Despite Rajagopalachari's verdict, Menen deserves a more respected place in the annals of the Indian English novel—as do his contemporaries. Although tentative and often awkward, the novels of the 1930s and 1940s chronicle and respond to a remarkable era in world history. And, contrary to harsh judgement, they are the legitimate forerunners of the new postcolonial or diasporic novels produced by the new generation of postnational cosmopolitans.

13

R.K. Narayan

Pankaj Mishra

As a young student at a rather severe missionary school in Madras, R.K. Narayan (1906–2001) first encountered the English language and was immediately bewildered. Narayan was five years old at the time, part of a middle-class Brahmin family of second-generation immigrants from rural Madras. The family was new to the city, and still close to ancestral ways; an almost religious solemnity had attended Narayan's formal introduction at home to Tamil and Sanskrit, when he was asked to shape the first two letters of the alphabet with corn spread out on a tray.

But Tamil and Sanskrit were a badge of inferiority and occasion for jokes at school, along with everything else that belonged to the old Hindu world broken into by British colonialism; Narayan, as the only Brahmin boy in the class, came in for special mockery by the Christian teachers. The 'first' language at school was English, taught from a textbook imported all the way from England and looking much more sturdy and glossy than the textbooks produced in India. Its glamour also came from the mysteries it contained.

Narayan's first English lesson went along these lines: 'A was an Apple Pie. B bit it. C cut it.' Narayan could see what B and C had been up to; but the identity of A eluded him. He had never seen an apple before, not to mention a pie. The teacher, who hadn't seen an apple either, wondered if it wasn't like idli—the South Indian rice-cake. And so Narayan's education in English began, with everyone in the class 'left free to guess, each according to his capacity, the quality, shape and details of the civilisation portrayed in our textbooks.'

The distant centre of that civilisation—London—was then closed for ordinary natives like Narayan; but its periphery extended even further than India, and its products had travelled everywhere, transforming many different parts of the world. The textbook bewildered Narayan initially but it was also the beginning of an imaginative enrichment for him; and the English magazines he came across in India—*Strand, Mercury*, and *The Spectator*—inspired him to be a writer. Western-style education offered by schools and colleges, such as the one in Mysore that Narayan's father was headmaster of, helped create a dynamic new civilisation in what had been, for at least a century, a somnolent world.

The Madras that Narayan was born into had been the first city of British India, and had become, with its opportunities of education and employment, one of the centres of modernising India in the late nineteenth century. Everywhere across the South, Brahmins left centuries-old rural settings and occupations and moved into towns and cities, where they formed the first administrative middle class. The men in Narayan's own family exemplified the various ways in which a once-rural community, now cut off from its roots, responded to the new world.

His maternal grandfather was a petty government official in the provinces who built up the kind of wealth that income-tax authorities in India call 'disproportionate to the possessor's income'. One of Narayan's two uncles became a successful car salesman; the other was an amateur photographer—one of the first in India—before settling down to edit one of the many serious weeklies in Tamil; and Narayan's father, the stern headmaster, offered a picture of colonial Indian respectability and authority as he bicycled to his college and club each day, 'impeccably dressed in a tweed suit and tie and crowned with a snow-white turban', his appearance part of the newfangled ways that had alienated him from his tradition-minded parents and brothers.

In this somewhat oppressive adult world of work and responsibility and economic security, Narayan was expected by his family to find his own place. But the writer has, from an early age, his own relationship with the world; his mind feeds on daydreaming and irresponsibility, the idle contemplation of life that Narayan, made unhappy by the 'unwarranted seriousness' of school, so often indulged in. He grew up in a small-town-like suburb of Madras and the province of Mysore and was always haunted by his memories of childhood— the catching of grasshoppers and the furtive first cigarettes—of what the narrator of his fourth novel, *The English Teacher*, calls a 'grand period' when 'there was a natural state of joy over nothing in particular'.

That child's license to daydream made Narayan naturally attracted to the freelance writer's life; but it was never going to be easy for him. Modern literature, with its preoccupation with the individual and personal freedom, had only just begun to be understood in a society ruled by custom and ritual. Although Narayan has not mentioned them, the hurdles in his way would have been immense: disadvantages unique to writers from limited societies, who work without a received tradition, who are the first of their kind.

These writers have to overcome their intellectual upbringing before they can learn to look directly at their world and find a voice that matches their experience. The disdain for one's own language and literature taught at school and college; the forced initiation into a foreign language; the groping for knowledge through an abstract maze of other cultures and worlds—these are things that can make for a lifetime of confusion and ambivalence.

There are people who try to reject this experience altogether by turning to what they think is an uncontaminated past: the time before foreign rule when the world was whole and everything was in its place. But Narayan, bewildered by the apple pies of another civilisation, was not much closer to Brahmanical tradition and ritual when he set out to be a writer. He had no use for contemporary or classical Tamil literature which his uncle kept urging him to read, although he renewed that link with his ancestral past much later in life when he published English abridgements of the *Ramayana* (1972) and *Mahabharata* (1978). He saw himself—and, given the time, it is a remarkable self-assessment—as a 'realistic fiction writer'.

But this confidence came later, after he had already published three novels and had become the pioneering Indian writer in English. Before that there was the struggle to make a living: odd-jobbing, journalism for an anti-Brahmin newspaper, reviews of books like *Development of Maritime Laws in Seventeenth-century England* for the Madras daily, *The Hindu.* There were also the inevitable false starts of a writer who acquires both ambition and inspiration from other literatures and civilisations and then flounders with derivative literary forms that cannot accommodate his particular experience of the world. Narayan's first writing efforts, like those of many other Indian writers, were poetic prose pieces with titles like 'Divine Music': the kind of pseudo-Romantic thing that, produced too frequently by Indians, had provoked Kipling into stridently mocking the semi-anglicised native.

Other writers, and other modern literatures, have also gone through these false starts: the imitative Russian writers before Pushkin, the Irish writers of the eighteenth and early nineteenth centuries. For all of these writers, who followed foreign models, the problem was one of recognising that their own experience of the world had intrinsic value and could be written about—something that writers in colonised countries still have to deal with. Narayan's uncle expressed many Indian uncertainties about the realist novel when he read a few typed pages of Narayan's first novel, *Swami and Friends,* which follows the adventures of a small-town Brahmin boy quite like the young Narayan, and said, 'What the hell is this?! You write that he got up, picked up a towel, rinsed his teeth, poured water over his head—just a catalogue!'

Narayan had considerable problems finding a personal literary voice and tone. 'Nibbling' his pen and 'wondering what to write', and finding Malgudi swimming into view, 'all ready-made' and then writing on, without any 'notion of what would be coming'.

Narayan always avoided political or social commentary in his writing and so it is almost startling to come across in the memoir of his early life, *My Days* (1975), an acknowledgement, however indirect, of one of the first and most effective anti-Brahmin agitations anywhere in

India (both low- and upper-caste groups were protesting against the near-monopoly of Brahmins, who constituted less than four percent of the population, over government jobs in Mysore state): 'These days are difficult for Brahmins to get jobs in the government,' warns the headmaster of the small town school Narayan has been teaching at.

Narayan had taken up teaching without much success or joy after a resolutely mediocre academic career and farcically aborted attempts at becoming a railway officer and bank official. He gave up, after two attempts, on his unruly students and dingy living quarters and went home where things weren't good: his father's retirement had demoted the family to the lower middle class, had forced them to move from the old large house Narayan had grown up in. Narayan, still trying to write, couldn't be of much use to his elder brother, who worked until midnight to keep the family afloat, while Narayan stayed at home, typing out a bad play on a noisy oversized typewriter, and annoying his father who wasn't alone in his conviction that Narayan was wasting his time trying to make a living as a writer.

Swami and Friends (1935) came in the middle of a stressful time for the young Narayan, and the novel registers all the small confusions and dislocations of the child reaching the end of an idyllic childhood and facing the grave tasks of adulthood. The setting that, one day, swam into Narayan's view—Malgudi, the colonial district town with its post-office and bank and middle-class suburb and small roadside shops and low-caste slums and missionary school and government bungalows—is the new world of urbanising India that Swami is expected, in the way Narayan was, to find his place in. But Swami is essentially anarchic and it is his great restlessness within this restricted world and premonitions of the drabness that awaits him which make for that unique mix of 'sadness and beauty' that Graham Greene—who helped publish the book—spoke of.

He feels oppressed by authority—the severe Christians at school, his admonitory father—but is also attracted by its promise of stability and identity, and his great infatuation is with Rajam, the police officer's son, with his bungalow and toy rail engine: the symbols of the world of colonial progress and modernity that Swami, too, is being asked to enter. That exalted world, once the exclusive preserve of

Brahmins, is changing fast: it is no accident that Swami's greatest source of fear in Malgudi is the low-caste slum-dwelling ball-boy at his father's tennis club.

The game of cricket, with its simultaneously rule-bound and anarchic nature, offers Swami, as it does to millions of Indians, the best kind of emotional release from the strains and pressures of adjusting to their ever-altering circumstances. But the captain of the cricket team is Rajam, before whom Swami tries hard to pose as a modern rational adult, an act in which the presence of his old affectionate grandmother is a shameful embarrassment.

When Swami, giving in to his natural rebelliousness, runs away from home just before an important cricket match, he knows not only fear and uncertainty but also guilt. His feeling that he has been irresponsible and cowardly, that he has failed to act like a man, overshadows the heartbreaking last two pages where Narayan's swift clear prose—so naturally a part of his alertness to physical and emotional actuality, the randomness of events and emotions—describes Rajam's departure for the bigger world outside Malgudi.

The world offers a more inscrutable face in Narayan's second novel, *The Bachelor of Arts* (1937), where the youthful energy and irony of a young graduate, Chandran, only take him so far. Narayan's dislike for the kind of education Swami and Chandran receive had hardened into conviction by now: the system of education churns out 'clerks for business and administrative offices', and reduces India to a 'nation of morons'. But a lot of clerks is what a dependent economy needs; there is really no way out for the intelligent and sensitive Chandran who joins, as reluctantly as Swami once did, other adolescent students in playing at being grown-up and serious. He is not at ease in the role; he feels 'distaste for himself' as the secretary of his college's historical association; he tries to keep his distance from the revolutionary student and the poet student; he scrapes through his final examinations, feeling 'very tender and depressed'.

It is love—a girl sighted on the banks of the local river—that brings relief from the utter dreariness of his preparations for adult life. But when he finally persuades his parents into arranging his marriage with the girl, whom he never gets to speak to, the horoscopes cannot be matched. A distraught Chandran runs away from home and becomes a wandering sadhu for some weeks. But he soon begins to feel himself a fraud in that role—the religious past of his ancestors can no longer be retrieved—and when he returns to Malgudi, to a semi-secure job and arranged marriage with a good dowry, he is quick to denounce romantic love, quick to accept the smallness of his horizons, and settle down to 'a life of quiet and sobriety'.

Chandran is one of the first in Narayan's long gallery of young restless drifters who, hungry for adventure, very quickly reach the limits of their world and then have to find ways of reconciling themselves with it. The reconciliation itself can never be complete. You can see again and again in Narayan's novels how the encounter with the half-baked modernity of colonialism has deracinated Indians like Chandran; has turned them into what Narayan, in an unusually passionate moment in *The English Teacher*, describes as 'strangers to our own culture, and camp-followers of another culture, feeding on leavings and garbage.'

It is this—a part-feudal, part-modern setting of inchoate longing and vague dissatisfactions and intellectual impotence; the confused inner life of a fragmented makeshift society that has yet to figure out its past or future—it is this, more than the economy and simplicity of Narayan's artistic means, that reminds one of Chekhov.

Like Chekhov's, Narayan's realism can seem homely and nuanced at the same time. Narayan never casts sufficient light on the larger social and historical setting of his fiction, the major historical events—British colonialism, Indian independence, the Emergency— through which his characters drift. Even a quite real setting goes under the imaginary name of Malgudi; and only a few, easily missed domestic details hint at the fact that Swami and Chandran, along with many other Narayan protagonists, are Brahmins marginalised by a fast-changing world.

Nevertheless, the lack of direct political comment doesn't prevent one from seeing in Narayan's novels all the anxieties and bewilderments and disappointments of a generation of Indians expelled from the past into a new world. This tortuous initiation into modernity, which Narayan himself underwent, is what gives his work, particularly the early novels—and despite the inevitable comedy of small-town ambition and drift—an unexpected depth of suffering, which is all the greater for not being perceived or acknowledged by the characters in his novels.

Interestingly, where Narayan seeks consciously to acknowledge and dramatise that suffering, his art loses its special tension and resonance. One of his least successful novels is *The Dark Room* (1938), which takes up, in schematic ways, the condition of women in the changing circumstances of modern India. In Narayan's first two novels, women had been exempt from demanding citizenship in a harsh, discouraging world; they existed on the margins, in the kitchens and bedrooms and inner courtyards, where they were often a source of tenderness. In 1933, Narayan's own marriage to a girl he saw drawing water from a roadside tap—the horoscopes didn't match, but Narayan overrode his parents' objections—gave him access to the lives of women, a whole new range of human experience previously denied him by strict segregation.

In *The Dark Room*, Savitri runs away from home—the escape from oppressive convention is by now a familiar theme in Narayan—and attempts to drown herself after her tyrannical husband, an insurance officer, takes up with a new 'modern' girl in his office, and then invokes, in a classic instance of middle-class hypocrisy, Hindu scriptures to justify his tyranny over his wife. Savitri is rescued by a low-caste couple who provide her shelter in an old decaying temple. But she can't bear its querulous priest, and finally returns home to more familiar constraints and suffering. Once again, Narayan, whose realism lies as much in content as in form, offers no neat ending or resolution: in the last pages of the novel, Savitri sees the low-caste man who had helped her passing her house, but she can't bring herself to invite him in. Class, as much as caste and gender, is a prison here, and we leave her in it, desolate, 'haunted' by the man's 'hungry shining face'.

Human connections are not achieved easily in Narayan's fictional world. Indeed, what often strikes one about that world—something well concealed by Narayan's instinct for humour—is its extraordinary lovelessness. A Brahmanical formality circumscribes the relationships within families, the father being especially aloof, often cold, and romantic love, when it occurs, is either a loss of self-control (*The Bachelor of Arts, Mr Sampath, The Guide, Talkative Man*), or so beset by anxiety and fear (*Waiting for the Mahatma*) that its failure comes, as in *The Painter of Signs*, almost as a relief to the protagonists.

It is what makes so remarkable the first part of *The English Teacher* (1945), where the narrator, Krishna, describes the quiet happiness of suddenly falling in love with his wife. The happiness is celebrated here through the many details of domestic life: the little squabbles, the shopping expeditions, the reading of poetry, the fussiness over the first child, the search for a new house. Elizabeth Bowen was one of the many reviewers of the novel who commented on the rapturous state of Krishna's being, which really derived—in this most explicitly autobiographical of Narayan's novels—from the serenity and joy marriage brought to Narayan's own life. Until his marriage, the novels still unpublished, and the future a discouraging blank, Narayan seems to have been like Krishna, who, when the novel begins, is leading a largely unsatisfactory life as a teacher of English literature, trying to explain the poems of Southey to uncomprehending students at a missionary college. The six years of married life with Rajam, his wife, seemed to have returned Narayan, while he was still in the midst of the long ordeal of growing up and finding a vocation for himself, to that 'joy over nothing in particular' of his childhood.

That the marriage should have a special intensity seems natural when you consider the emotional constriction people in Narayan's world lived with at that time. Women suffered, as *The Dark Room* shows, some of the worst consequences of an old world modernising too fast: the hypocrisy and inconstancy of men released from rules, the lack of support in the new world. But women could also be redeemers; as upholders of tradition and ritual within their homes, they brought some of the calm and security of the supplanted world to uprooted, confused men.

In a world where custom and ritual are losing their hold, but where the pursuit of individual happiness is not yet a culturally respectable endeavour, marriage still offers the most bracing kinds of personal fulfilment to many men. It makes possible their first encounter with women outside their families, and it is often, when love is present, overwhelming. So it was in Narayan's case; and it would have made all the more traumatic the sudden illness and death of his wife in 1939: events that Narayan, who never remarried, returns to often in his stories and memoir, and relates with controlled emotions in the second part of *The English Teacher*, where Krishna's attempts to communicate with his wife through seances— an antidote to grief Narayan himself used before moving on with a renewed determination to live, as Chandran hopes to after his stint as an ascetic, without 'distracting illusions and hysterics'.

There was no dearth of distracting illusions in Narayan's own life at the time. The shock and grief of his wife's death undermined him for a while. It was the seances, his readings in Hindu philosophy, and experiments in Theosophy that helped him recover. But his professional life was still marked by drift. The war had severed his connection with British publishers. In any event, the sales of his books in England were negligible; and in India the books hardly moved out of the warehouses. He had little money, and he spent much time and energy on a magazine-publishing venture that always seemed destined to go nowhere.

These setbacks explain the slightly overdetermined quality of *Mr Sampath: A Printer of Malgudi* (1949), Narayan's first novel after India's independence. The main protagonist Srinivas resolves to live only for himself after being pushed around for much of the novel by the confused ambitions of an eccentric filmmaker, an overambitious printer, and a deranged artist. Philosophical or religious convictions, when too explicitly dramatised, don't normally make for good novels, and Narayan's belief, stated towards the end of *The English Teacher*, that a 'profound unmitigated loneliness is the only truth of life', spoils *Mr Sampath*.

It has some good things, such as the first glimpse of independent India in Narayan's novels, where you can see the old colonial world being cracked open, being infused with the vulgar new energies of people with plans for the future: ambitious men who in the end fail to be bigger than their setting. But, on the whole, *Mr Sampath* must be considered an example of the hit-or-miss quality of Narayan's writing after Independence. The last novels, in particular the misconceived *A Tiger for Malgudi* (1980), where the soul of a human being takes up residence inside a tiger, and the lazily repetitive *Talkative Man* (1985) and *The World of Nagaraj* (1990), illustrate the dangers inherent in a style and vision that cease to renew themselves.

It is where the natural novelist, the unprejudiced observer, stays dominant over the philosopher, where Narayan's belief in the oneness of being—the vision of Vedanta philosophy offered on the last page of *The English Teacher*—translates into an openness to experience and a recognition of human diversity, that the novels work best; they then possess human interest and moral complexity; even a kind of mature beauty.

In *Waiting for the Mahatma* (1955), Narayan uses as background the Indian freedom movement, from which he, like so many other Indian writers of the time, had derived the basic nationalism—that sense of place and time and some idea of who you are—so necessary to the writing of realist fiction.

Narayan, as a young man, was forbidden by his family to have anything to do with the agitators for freedom. The benigner aspects of the British presence in India—the educational institutions, the new career opportunities—had brought their own kind of freedom to many Indians, including people in Narayan's family. His father, the headmaster, knew where his future lay when he adopted modern ways and turned his back on his tradition-minded parents and brothers; and then Narayan's own writing came to depend heavily on patronage by British publishers and readers. He, like many members of the new and insecure colonial bourgeoisie, could not but feel a profound ambivalence about the mass movement against the British—an ambivalence never clearly expressed but always present in his writings.

There is a short story he wrote soon after Independence, 'Lawley Road', which portrays some of the confused impulses and blind nationalism of that anti-colonial struggle. The story describes how the statue of a British administrator called Lawley is scornfully dismantled and sold and then reinstated by the municipal authorities after Lawley is discovered to be the founder of Malgudi. But it is in *Waiting for the Mahatma* that you find a franker ambivalence about that movement and its impact on the Indian masses.

The Indian characters in the novel make of the movement whatever suits their own narrow ends: men eager to revere Gandhi as a mahatma, eager to be touched by his aura of holiness while remaining indifferent to, or simply uncomprehending of, his emphasis on developing self-awareness and an individual vision. There is the corrupt chairman of the municipal corporation who has replaced, just before Gandhi's visit to Malgudi, the pictures of English kings in his house with portraits of Congress leaders; he then worries about the low-caste boy Gandhi talks to sullying his 'Kashmir counterpane'. There is the novel's chief protagonist, Sriram, another feckless young man in Malgudi, who joins the 1942 Quit India movement after falling for Bharati, an attractively gentle and idealistic young woman in Gandhi's entourage.

Sriram drifts around the derelict famine-stricken countryside, painting the words 'Quit India' everywhere, arguing with apathetic and hostile villagers about the need to throw out the British. His weak grasp of Gandhi's message is confirmed by the fact that he lets himself be persuaded by an egotistical terrorist into becoming a saboteur. He is arrested and spends years in jail, longing for Bharati. His abandoned grandmother almost dies and then goes off to live her last year in Benaras; and then Gandhi himself, devastated by the massacres and rapes of Partition, is assassinated on the last page of the novel.

Even before his death, as *Waiting for the Mahatma* shows, Gandhi had been absorbed into the ostentatious puritanism of the men who came to rule India, the uniqueness of his life and ideas appropriated into the strident Indian claim to the moral high ground—a claim first advanced through Gandhi's asceticism and emphasis on non-violence, and then, later, through the grand rhetoric of socialism, secularism, and non-alignment. In fact, Gandhi alone emerges as the active self-aware Indian in the novel, struggling and failing to awaken an intellectually and emotionally torpid colonial society, a society made up overwhelmingly of people who have surrendered all individual and conscious choice, and are led instead by decayed custom and the herd impulse, in whose dull marginal lives Gandhi comes as yet another kind of periodic distraction.

The only other person who embodies individual initiative and positive endeavour in the novel—and he makes a fleeting appearance—turns out to be a British tea planter; and Narayan makes him come out very much on top in his encounter with Sriram. He is friendly and hospitable to Sriram—who has painted the words 'Quit India' on his property. Sriram, unsettled by the tea planter's composure, tries to assume a morally superior position. Narayan shows him floundering, resorting fatuously to half-remembered bits and pieces of other people's aggressive anti-British rhetoric.

The tea planter's energy and entrepreneurial initiative, when assumed by a Westernised Indian, turns into a form of self-delusion in *The Vendor of Sweets* (1967), where Mali, the son of a Gandhian sweet vendor, travels to America for a course in creative writing—Malgudi, like India, reaching out to the modern world—and unexpectedly returns with a Korean-American girlfriend, and an outlandish business scheme to manufacture creative writing out of a machine. The point about Mali's confusion is made, but the machine is not a particularly convincing touch. Narayan had finally travelled to the West in the late 1950s; and his simple-minded, occasionally humorous, take on America and Americans had produced a book (*My Dateless Diary*, 1964) which, much like the rest of his non-fiction, has readability and charm but is ultimately disappointing in its lack of intellectual ambition.

Mali bewilders his father, Jagan, one of many emotionally inadequate fathers in Narayan's novel. Jagan, in fact, could be an older Sriram. He is full of the pious certainties and hypocrisies of someone who thinks he has done his bit for his society by participating, however briefly and shallowly, in the freedom movement. He has been hard on his wife; he cheats his customers and the government, invokes the greatness and permanence of Indian civilisation while dismissing the West as morally inferior. But his fragile Gandhian self-regard collapses before his much-loved son's strange new demeanour and actions; and after Mali ends up disastrously in prison having driven drunk around Malgudi, Jagan has no option but a Hindu-style renunciation of the world.

Bewilderment and retreat to a simpler world: modernity produces the same reactions in *The Painter of Signs* (1977), where Daisy, a young woman, comes to Malgudi—the time is Mrs Gandhi's Emergency—with a fanatical mission to control India's population. Raman, another of Narayan's post-Independence young drifters, is both attracted and perplexed by her sense of individuality and high responsibility, and attaches himself to her as she travels around the countryside, impatiently trying to root out what she sees as superstitious prejudices against contraception among illiterate villagers.

Raman keeps anxiously hoping to win her over even as he is alienated by her coldness, her all-excluding focus on family planning, the government-enforced programme whose slogan (*Hum Do, Hamare Do*, literally: 'the two of us, with just two kids') he paints all over the countryside with as little effect as Sriram had once painted 'Quit India'.

But Daisy has grown up in the progress-minded authoritarian India of Five-Year Plans and 20-Point Programmes—an India trying hard to be as strong and rational and efficient as the Western countries whose models of development it has adopted—and Narayan withholds from her the sensitivity and patience he confers upon Bharati in *Waiting for the Mahatma*. She claims to have little time for love, even though she seems to need it as much as Raman, and she eventually drops Raman after agreeing to marry him. The novel ends with Raman trying to feel relieved, trying to recover his old life of idleness in Malgudi.

It is the point—the unfulfilled dream of freedom, the dream of Narayan's own enchanted childhood—at which many of Narayan's novels end: the point at which you see his characters finally turning away from the challenges of self-creation and individuality and seeking reabsorption into the passivity and sterility of old India. Such non-resolutions expose Narayan to the charge of escapism, especially in India, where serious artists are often expected when not to create suitable role models for young people, to add at any rate to the narrative of nation-building and Indian self-assertion.

But the limitations of Narayan's characters are the limitations of the still raw and shapeless society in which they have their being: limitations that are not overcome, but merely avoided by leap into fantasy and myth that such ready-made forms as magic realism facilitate. It is not easy for colonial writers of realist fiction, particularly early ones like Narayan, to transcend these built-in inadequacies of their material.

It is later writers who, building upon their predecessors' initiative and discoveries, are better able to replace the superstructure of myth and religion with a sense of history. James Baldwin once identified the 'crucial point' in his development as the discovery that he was 'a kind of bastard of the West', and that he brought a 'special attitude' to the monuments and culture of Western civilisation. It is an attitude that every important writer from subject communities has had to formulate in his own way. But Baldwin's discovery of the tormented history that bound him to the West was partly made possible by the African-American writers that preceded him. Narayan, as the first writer of his kind, was always far from attaining such an intellectual overview of his circumstances. Early writers like him usually stay within, and share the prejudices of, the particular historical moment they find themselves in; sometimes offering, as Narayan does in his later novels, quasi-religious explanations for the chaotic unformed nature of their world.

This is why Narayan's political ideas, when spelt out in his non-fiction, seem only marginally more sophisticated than those offered by his characters. In his book about his American travels, Narayan rejects, like Jagan in *The Vendor of Sweets* or Srinivas in *Mr Sampath*, any real engagement with the modern world; fear and insecurity seem to lie concealed underneath his complacent humour. The novels he wrote in the 1960s after his first—and for the colonial writer, crucial—encounter with the West hint at a kind of intellectual self-narrowing that is often the result of the colonial's bewilderment and resentful pride before the metropolitan culture that has partly formed him.

But Narayan, by writing from deep within his small and shrinking world, came to acquire an instinctive understanding of it. He developed with it the special intimacy which is sometimes capable of taking the novelist, if not the essayist, to truths deeper and subtler than those yielded by analytical intelligence. It is the unmediated fidelity his novels have to his constricted experience which make them seem so organic in both their conception and execution, and which also make him now, remarkably, a more accurate guide to the inner life of modern India than such later self-conscious makers of historical narratives as Salman Rushdie and Rohinton Mistry.

The early novels with their energetic young men (Swami, Chandran, and Krishna), the middle novels with the restless drifters (Srinivas, Sriram) and the later novels, with the men wounded and exiled by the modern world (Jagan, Raman) map out an emotional and intellectual journey that many middle-class people in formerly colonial societies have made: the faint consciousness of individuality and nationality through colonial education; confused anti-colonial assertion;

post-colonial sense of inadequacy and failure; unfulfilled private lives; distrust of modernity and individual assertion; and, finally, in middle or old age, the search for cultural authenticity and renewal in a neglected, once-great past.

'The silent spirit of collective masses is the source of all great things', Renan wrote at Turgenev's death. The silent spirit is what Narayan, writing in his own untutored way about men and worlds condemned to ambivalence, renders eloquent in his best novels. His characters don't leave the pages of his books without having achieved a kind of nobility, as part of an all-encompassing vision in which everything is accepted and forgiven. The characters, for instance, in *The Financial Expert* (1952)—small-time conmen, greedy landlords, ingrate children, embittered parents, unhappy wives, exploited villagers—are like people locked in a trance, in Maya, the immense illusion of existence. They busily deceive each other and themselves; and everyone seems lost in the end. No liberation of the spirit, you feel, is likely to happen to these characters. Yet Narayan considers them with sympathy, even affection. We see them as the creator of Maya himself, that great ironic illusionist, would see us. It is this religious-seeming acceptingness that gives Narayan's novels their peculiar irony—an irony rooted not in scepticism and disbelief but faith: an irony that belongs less to the European tradition of the novel than to a Hindu view of the world, in which the conflicts and contradictions of individual men and societies, however acute and compelling, are in the end no more than minor disturbances in the life of an old and serene cosmic order.

The last pages of Narayan's best novel, *The Guide* (1958), find Raju, the chief protagonist, at the end of a lifetime of insincerity and pain. As a professional guide to Malgudi's environs, he invented whole new historical pasts for bored tourists; he seduced a married woman, drifted away from his old mother and friends, became a flashy cultural promoter, and then tried, absentmindedly, to steal and was caught and spent years in jail, abandoned by everyone.

His last few months have been spent in relative comfort as a holy man on the banks of a river: a role imposed on him by reverential village folk. But the river dries up after a drought and his devotees start looking to him to intercede with the gods. Raju resentfully starts a fast, but furtively eats whatever little food he has saved. Then abruptly, out of a moment of self-disgust, comes his resolution: for the first time in his life, he will do something with sincerity, and he will do it for others; if fasting can bring rain, he'll fast.

He stops eating, and quickly diminishes. News of his efforts goes around; devotees and sightseers, gathering at the riverside, create a religious occasion out of the fast. On the early morning of the eleventh day of fasting, a small crowd watches him quietly as he attempts to pray standing on the river bed and then staggers and dies, mumbling the enigmatic last words of the novel, 'It's raining in the hills. I can feel it coming up under my feet, up my legs . . .'

Characteristically, Narayan doesn't make it clear whether Raju's penance does actually lead to rain. He also doesn't make much of Raju's decision, the moment of his redemption which a lesser writer would have attempted to turn into a resonant ending, but quickly passes over it in a few lines.

It is a moment of great disturbing beauty—in which we know something larger and more affecting than the working out of an individual destiny in an inhospitable world. As in his best novels, what Narayan leaves us with here is the sense—and the words are of the forgotten English writer, William Gerhardie, on Chekhov but so appropriate for Narayan—'of the temporary nature of our existence . . . It is a sense of temporary possession in a temporary existence that, in the face of the unknown, we dare not overvalue. It is as if his people hastened to express their worthless individualities, since that is all they have, and were aghast that they should have so little in them to express: since the expression of it is all there is.'

14
Nirad C. Chaudhuri

EUNICE DE SOUZA

Writing about Nirad C. Chaudhuri (1897–1999) in *The Overcrowded Barracoon* (1972), V.S. Naipaul comes to the conclusion that *The Autobiography of an Unknown Indian* 'may be the one great book to have come out of the Indo-British encounter . . . No better account of the penetration of the Indian mind by the West . . . will or can now be written. It was an encounter which ended in mutual recoil and futility. For Chaudhuri this futility is an almost personal tragedy.'

This sense of 'recoil and futility' animates a great deal of Chaudhuri's work, and has resulted in his being called anti-Indian, pro-British, a fascist, a man and writer as atavistic as he says India has become. There are certainly troubling elements in his work, but these have tended to overshadow his achievements: his ability to evoke a sense of place, his humour, his independence of judgement in the teeth of opposition, and his phenomenal ability to keep working and publishing. At a hundred he published his last book, *Three Horsemen of the New Apocalypse* (1997).

Chaudhuri has said that *The Autobiography of an Unknown Indian* (1951) is 'more of an exercise in descriptive ethnology than autobiography'. He is concerned with describing 'the conditions in which an Indian grew to manhood in the early decades of the century', and as he feels that the basic principle of his book is that 'environment shall have precedence over its product', he describes in affectionate and sensuous detail the three places that had the greatest influence on him: Kishorganj, the country town in which he lived till he was twelve; Bangram, his ancestral village; and Kalikutch, his mother's village. A fourth chapter is devoted to England, which occupied a large place in his imagination. Later in the book he talks about Calcutta, the Indian Renaissance, the beginnings of the nationalist movement, and his experience of Englishmen in India as opposed to the idyllic pictures of a civilisation he considers perhaps the greatest in the world. These themes remain preoccupations in most of Chaudhuri's work, as does his 'deterministic' view of culture and politics.

Nirad C. Chaudhuri was one of eight surviving children born to a liberal Hindu family. Circumstances prevented his father, a lawyer, from becoming formally a highly educated man, but he educated himself in English by buying dictionaries, books about idiomatic usage, and classics such as Shakespeare and Dostoevsky. At a time when well-to-do families despised education, Chaudhuri's father encouraged his children to familiarise themselves with a wide range of ideas in the arts and sciences, including music, an art then associated with the morally dubious members of society. He was also concerned with the children's diet, sleep, and physical exercise, a concern unusual for the time. Unusual, too, was his insistence on a nuclear family. All this made Chaudhuri's upbringing 'exceptional', possibly even 'unique'. Chaudhuri also talks about his mother's 'fierce' honesty and, surprisingly in an Indian context, gives us a candid if concerned picture of his mother's hysterical seizures.

What one remembers most of all, however, is the attention to detail, rare in Indian autobiographies; the difference in colour between newly cut and dry straw, the deep, soft dust of the roads, the river in changing seasons, the rain:

> But one of the most attractive and engaging sights of the season was to be seen in the inner courtyard of our house, when there was a heavy downpour. The rain came down in what looked like closely packed formations of enormously long pencils of glass and hit the bare ground. At first the pencils only pitted the sandy soil, but as soon as some water had collected all around they began to bounce off the surface of water

> and pop up and down in the form of minuscule puppets. Every square inch of ground seemed to receive one of the little things, and our waterlogged yard was broken up into a pattern which was not only mobile but dizzily in motion.

The other 'intangible and exotic element', both 'absent' and yet 'real', was Chaudhuri's picture of England, drawn from illustrations in textbooks and magazines, poems and plays, and discussions about wars held with his father. Pro-Liberal and anti-Conservative because of the family environment, the young Chaudhuri is astounded to know that the great Edmund Burke was a Conservative. Napoleon more than shared the honours with Raphael, Milton, Shakespeare, and Luther. Chaudhuri writes, 'If any wholehearted Bonapartists were to be found anywhere in the world at the end of the nineteenth century and the beginning of the twentieth they were to be found in Bengal. All educated Bengalis literally adored Napoleon.' Even the Public Library at Kishorganj contained the memoirs of Napoleon's valet, Constant.

It was partly the earnest study of Napoleon's campaigns, and partly the influence of teachers when the family moved to Calcutta that Chaudhuri opted to study history for his BA—he was placed first in his class—and his MA, which he failed. Chaudhuri lived in Calcutta from June 1910 to March 1942, but he does not feel particularly beholden to the city. He says he learnt a great deal in Calcutta but hardly anything from it. He learned to speak Standard Bengali but did not give up the dialect of the East Bengal area in which he grew up. But he was shy, and the loneliness he felt there developed in him 'the habit of abstracted musing in which I often remain unconscious how many miles and by which roads I have walked.' Chaudhuri illustrates his isolation by pointing out that though he belonged to a literary group of Tagorites, he did not see Tagore till 1927, and then held only one brief, formal conversation with him. He was interested in politics but did not attend three important Congress sessions held in 1917, 1920, and 1928. He saw Nehru for the first time only in 1931, and Gandhi as late as 1934 or 1935.

The most acerbic section of *The Autobiography of an Unknown Indian* concerns the 'atavisation' of the nationalist movement, an idea he often discusses in his later works. Chaudhuri feels that despite Gandhi's best efforts to infuse positive values into his mass movement, he was not sufficiently aware that the masses had their 'unregenerate side'. Xenophobic forms of nationalism were quick to use 'Gandhism' for their own purposes, and it was only towards the end of his life that Gandhi saw that what he had tried to create had 'in politics and in practice come to stand for very little but a congealed mass of atavistic aspirations and prejudices.'

Chaudhuri began writing the autobiography in 1947, the year of Independence, when he was fifty. (Before that, his only publication had been a monograph on the organisation of the colonial Indian army, *Defence of India*, published in 1935.) The autobiography ends with his obtaining a job in a military accounts department, and giving it up because he found it soul-destroying. Despite his academic failure, he ends with belief in himself as a 'scholar gipsy'—a role for which he gave up financial security. His ambition is to build up 'a gigantic *corpus* piling itself up in annual volumes throughout a life-time, a single-handed *Monumenta* of Indian history.' Most important of all, he sees himself as a 'free man'. He writes that 'while I was being carried along by the momentum of our history, most of my countrymen were being dragged backwards by its inertia. We had been travelling in opposite directions, and are still doing so. I can now see both the motions as from an independent point in space. I have found liberation from a nightmare.'

In 1955, at the age of fifty-seven, Chaudhuri went abroad for the first time. Out of this trip came *Passage to England* (1959), an impressionistic account of five weeks in England, two in Paris, and one in Rome. The point of giving these figures, Chaudhuri has said, 'lies in the range and intensity of the experiences I went through in these eight weeks. In that short space of time I saw more paintings, statues, and works of art in general, more plays, fine buildings, gardens and beautiful landscape; heard more poetry and music; ate and drank better; and altogether had a more exciting and interesting time than in all the rest of my life. Hardly less important is the fact that among all these things were a great many that I had longed to see since my boyhood.' In high spirits, and anxious to share his experiences with his countrymen at home, Chaudhuri published some articles in the

Indian press. The articles gave offence, and he was called 'pro-British, which is one of the worst terms of abuse in contemporary India.' This led him to the conclusion that 'there is no greater myth than the much-talked about Indo-British friendship since 1947.'

In England, Chaudhuri felt that what he was seeing 'corresponded almost preternaturally to what I had read about in books, and yet was infinitely more solid, tangible, and therefore more overpowering to the senses.' He writes, again with sensitive observation, of the physical and psychological effects of light in England and in India:

> When the architecture is fine the light sets off its proper beauty. In India I have never seen an architectural ensemble taking shape as does the Place Vendôme in Paris, or the courts and quads at Cambridge and Oxford, all of which seemed to convert even the enclosed air into cubes. I cannot remember any historic building in northern India, with the exception of the Taj at dawn, which conveys the feeling of mass. Our temples, big and soaring as they are, get lost in the upper air, and do not stand out as, for instance, I saw Winchester or Chartres doing. The beauty of our monuments is more like that of a clean-cut etching, it lies in their outline.

In *Passage to England* Chaudhuri advances a thesis which he develops in his next book, the notorious *The Continent of Circe* (1965). After observing the differences in the climates of England and India, he has no difficulty, he says, in understanding why Englishmen, so kind and equable at home, became offensive in India. This also gives him a clue to the understanding of 'Hindu character'. Chaudhuri claims that the situation of the Aryan in India was similar to that of transplanted Englishmen: 'Had the Aryan not been originally a man from a temperate land, mere existence in India could not have made him what he became.' This leads to the conclusion that the English and the Hindus, both victims of Circe, should make allowances for the other, 'mutual tolerance based on the conviction of a shared degeneration'.

Chaudhuri's second thesis is a continuation of one begun in his autobiography. He says that Hindus, far from being non-violent, have always been 'warlike and fond of bloodshed'. Ashoka became non-violent only when there was nothing left to conquer. Sanskrit literature is full of battles and conquests. Hindu moralists, alarmed by the violence of their societies, tried to develop a theory of 'wars of righteousness'. The *Mahabharata* is about one such war. Subhas Chandra Bose's Indian National Army roused 'hysterical enthusiasm' among Indians. As soon as Independence came, 'the first object of their new militarism was Pakistan.' The border dispute with China 'was and remains a minor and even trivial affair, with no danger to the real integrity of India.' But Hindu jingoism provoked the conflict.

If Chaudhuri's theories about the degeneration of the Aryans are questionable, his treatment of what he calls the genetic and cultural 'half-castes', Anglo-Indians and Indian Christians, is virtually pathological. According to him, these communities 'have no very great moral stature' and remain a danger to the Hindus with whom they come into contact because they are 'shoddy and counterfeit' in the cultural sphere. Eurasian girls have a 'deceptive beauty, like that of a lime-coloured, but canker-eaten moss rose'. Muslims come off slightly better, though Chaudhuri's conclusion is that 'there is something unnatural in the continued presence of the Muslims in India and of the Hindus in Pakistan, as if both went against a natural cultural ecology'. *The Continent of Circe* ends with the assurance that 'I have rescued my European soul from Circe'. Chaudhuri would also have liked to save his countrymen (the role of prophet and saviour is one to which he is increasingly drawn), but they do not listen to him. 'They honk, neigh, bellow, bleat, or grunt, and scamper away to their scrub, stable, byre, pen and sty.'

The Intellectual in India (1967), the first of Chaudhuri's books to be published in India, is one of a series of 'Tracts for Our Times'. It offers comments on the Muslim, Hindu, and Western intellectual traditions in India, the Indian Renaissance, and the contemporary situation for intellectuals. Essentially, Chaudhuri believes that India is 'an anti-intellectual country if ever there was one'. Conservative and authoritarian traditions are one problem, poor salaries are another. Even during the Indian Renaissance, the Indian intellectual's task of trying to maintain the Western intellectual tradition in India was 'comparable to that of maintaining agriculture on the edge of a desert, against constant invasion by the sand'. A great deal of contemporary thought remains imitative. The only exceptions are mathematicians and physicists who have done 'outstanding original work'.

To Live or Not to Live (1971) is in one sense a continuation of *The Intellectual in India*. It bases itself on Plato's dictum, 'The uncriticised (or un-examined) life is not worth living', but here the enquiry takes on a wider field. It attempts to consider 'how we can have a happy social and family life under the conditions to which we are born in this country.' Chaudhuri offers us some definitions for our consideration. Genuine social life is not a matter of compulsory or unavoidable meetings with relatives, neighbours, and the like. It is 'to be in the company of people for whom we sincerely care'. But it is rare for people in India to value a person regardless of his wealth or position. Another major shortcoming is the virtual segmentation of the sexes in social life. The joint family has outlived its usefulness because it does not allow its members to develop individual personalities. Nevertheless, women should not be allowed to work, as working women are a threat to the family.

Two biographies followed these relatively minor works: *Scholar Extraordinary: The Life of Professor the Rt. Hon. Friedrich Max Müller* (1974), and *Clive of India* (1975). If they are essentially sympathetic biographies, it is perhaps because in both figures Chaudhuri finds aspects of himself. Max Müller idealised the Aryans, as Chaudhuri does, and Clive, frequently compared to Napoleon, is the type of 'self-assertive hero' that Chaudhuri admires. (He often describes his own writing as a form of self-assertion.)

Max Müller believed in 'cultural proselytisation' and felt this was best served by training young Englishmen at the universities for their future role by teaching them Indian languages and culture. But he was not taken seriously in England, where he lived and worked. Chaudhuri feels this was a fatal mistake because an empire can survive only through strenuous proselytisation. However, all that happened was that the encounter produced a few superficial anglicised Indians, many of whom went to Oxford and Cambridge more for the prestige than for an education. Max Müller too expressed impatience with anglicised Indians at British universities because they lost their natural courtesy and acquired airs and manners they thought were English. In addition to these ideas Max Müller and Chaudhuri share some biographical similarities: both rose from obscurity, both had scholarly aspirations, and both finally moved to Oxford to live and write in a language not originally their own.

For Chaudhuri, Clive was 'the nearest approach in British history to a historical figure of the type to which Napoleon belonged . . . The strongest trait of his personality was an irrepressible urge for self-assertion. And by reason of his character he became the main instrument of the political commitment of Britain in India.' If he does not appear to have the same importance as Napoleon, it is because he played a role off-stage, so to speak, and not at the centre of European politics. Nevertheless, 'the results of the process which was set in motion by his wild personality were more permanent.'

In writing about Clive, Chaudhuri feels he is writing objective history because a 'truly historical biography [would exclude] criticism or apology altogether'. He speculates about Clive's state of mind in situations where no documents are available, because 'if history teaches us anything it teaches that all things are not possible in all ages . . . This is, of course, due to the psychological element, which is variable. It is this element that makes economic interpretation of history an inversion of historical logic by putting effect before cause.' Clive was scarcely aware of the decisive implications of his victory at Plassey and saw it mainly as a solution to a commercial problem, even a temporary solution.

Culture in the Vanity Bag (1976) is intended to be an informal but 'ecological study of Indian clothing and adornment'. This interest in clothes and costumes goes back to his early childhood. Chaudhuri says that the evolution of clothing in India 'repeated within [its] limits the whole pattern of the evolution of human life and culture in the country'. In brief, all cultural movements came from outside; they did not coalesce in India but remained separate and ultimately declined. Chaudhuri's descriptions are animated by great attention to detail, anecdotes, extracts from novels and Sanskrit texts, but the prose sometimes reads like a blurb in a fashion magazine. Among the more amusing accounts are those by foreign women allowed into Hindu women's quarters, who felt shocked by the transparent saris which hid nothing. Apparently, in the nineteenth century, aristocratic Bengali women were in the habit of 'painting the behinds [*sic*] with the scarlet dye of lac' in lieu of a petticoat.

Hinduism, A Religion to Live By (1979), a discussion of beliefs, regional variations, taboos, and myths, derives part of its interest from the fact that he attempts such a discussion despite the fact that he has no faith in Hinduism or any other religion. Yet he hopes the book will lead to 'a better understanding of the religious urge in man, which is innate'. Among his contentions are that, contrary to common practice, no history of Hinduism can be based on the chronology of sacred texts because no texts earlier than the twelfth century AD can be assigned definite dates, and texts, in any case, do not necessarily reflect practice. To write on Hinduism one must use the same sources that were used in writing the political history of India: inscriptions, art objects, religious buildings, accounts of foreign travellers. Even so, there is very scanty evidence for anything before the fifth century. The coming of Christianity forced Hindus to become conscious of their beliefs and practices, and, degraded or otherwise, Hinduism has created 'what must be regarded as the true nationalism of the country'.

Thy Hand, Great Anarch! (1987) is a sequel to *The Autobiography of an Unknown Indian.* 'I come forward', Chaudhuri writes, 'as a witness of this double decline'—the decline of empire and the decline of Bengal as a force in Indian politics and culture. He says that he is probably the only Bengali still living at the end of the twentieth century 'who has seen the entire Bengali revolutionary movement from its beginnings in 1907, has followed its course at first hand, clearly remembers all the important events, and is capable of giving a balanced historical view of it.' The book takes up the national and personal story of where the earlier book left off, in the year 1921 when Chaudhuri's student days came to an end. He began *Thy Hand* in 1979 and completed writing it in 1986.

During the years that the book covers, 1921 to 1952, Chaudhuri was for a time (1937–41) secretary to the Congress leader Sarat Chandra Bose, brother of Subhas. He also became actively and polemically involved in journalism in English and Bengali. Chaudhuri's first appearance in Bengali journalism was a 'severe' review of a new collection of poems by Kazi Nazrul Islam, who, according to Chaudhuri, used 'cheap military claptrap in his poems which were accepted then as the expression of a new revolutionary spirit.' All the young, post-Tagore writers were 'cultural vermin' whose work indicated a radical decline in standards. Tagore himself did not recognise 'the falsity of his standing in the West . . . all his real friends in the West regretted it.' Shantiniketan was 'almost a vaudeville' because of the curious assortment of people who collected there, 'eccentrics, adventures . . . feeble-minded enthusiasts.' Chaudhuri's first article in English was the outcome of the encouragement of Mohitlal Majumdar, Chaudhuri's English teacher at school, who 'made a writer of me almost by main force'. He wrote on an eighteenth-century Bengali poet, Bharat Chandra Ray, in the leading Indian magazine of the period, *The Modern Review*, in 1925. His next article in English was a critical review of *The Heart of Aryavarta* by Lord Ronaldshay who was Governor of Bengal from 1917 to 1921. It was published in *The Statesman*, and criticised the book's thesis that political discontent in India was a byproduct of the basic conflict between two civilisations, one spiritual, the other secular.

Thy Hand is full of lively if tendentious accounts of most of the major political and literary figures of the day. The treatment of Gandhi is more acerbic than it had been so far: Gandhi 'deliberately' played on the xenophobia of the masses. Neither he nor Nehru, and certainly not Subhas, had a single positive idea of what was to follow British rule. The much-acclaimed 'synthesis' of East and West turned out to be nothing more than 'imported phrases on the one hand and archaistic models on the other'. British imperialism, unlike the imperialism of Rome, failed because even in Bengal, where British cultural influence revitalised society, it was the Bengalis and not the British who were responsible for the renaissance. The British, especially the local British, displayed only 'unmeasured rancour' against Indians interested in Western culture.

The arrest of Sarat Chandra Bose made it imperative for Chaudhuri to look for a new job. He had done some broadcasting from the Calcutta station of All India Radio (AIR) on international affairs since 1937, and on the war since 1939. Through this station he was offered a similar job in Delhi, and left Calcutta never to return. He retired from AIR in 1952. In 1970 he went to England, settling down in Oxford, and was to live there for the remaining thirty years of his life.

One of Chaudhuri's later books, *East is East and West is West* (1996), edited by his son Dhruva Chaudhuri, has a picture of Chaudhuri on the cover in bowler hat and bow tie. The book is a collection of articles written for *The Times of India, The Statesman*, and other publications between 1926 and 1994. The earlier ones were written in India, the later ones in Oxford. Chaudhuri's son says he felt he had to collect them to 'show how correct his sense of historical perspective has been'. The book includes the review of Lord Ronaldshay's book as well as a jeremiad about contemporary England, 'blue denim jeans being the most typical symbol of decadence'. There is also a piece on the 'sterility' of anglicised Indians, the irresponsibility of the intelligentsia, the foolishness of Indian politicians after Independence in retaining members of the Indian Civil Service in the bureaucracy, the problems of finding a national language. A curious fact that Chaudhuri mentions is that 'I always call myself a Bengali and not an Indian when I am asked what country I belong to'—this despite the fact that 'I have never succumbed to the Bengali shibboleths about our Bengali identity.'

Chaudhuri has said that his personal experiences have a general relevance: 'The problem which I had to face in my personal life', he writes in *Thy Hand*, 'was how to pass through an age of decadence without being touched by it', especially now that decadence is universal, and human beings 'are being sucked in as were dinosaurs of old.' He feels he was forced into exile because of the hostility to his views in India. 'But wherever I am', he says, 'I cannot be indifferent to my people.'

15

Novelists of the 1950s and 1960s

SHYAMALA A. NARAYAN AND
JON MEE

Over the first two decades after Independence many writers felt there was something unpatriotic about writing in the language of the recently departed colonizer. The ruling triumvirate of Mulk Raj Anand, R.K. Narayan, and Raja Rao continued to write, but it was not until 1960, with Narayan's *The Guide* (1958), that a novel in English won the Sahitya Akademi Award.

In many ways these were unpromising times to embark on a career as a novelist in English, and few writers could sustain themselves as professional writers. Khushwant Singh, for instance, produced a few novels as a small part of his wide-ranging career as a man of letters and opinion-maker in the national press. Manohar Malgonkar (b. 1913), the successful author of *The Princes* (1963), started to write only in the mid 1950s after he had retired from the army and was running a tea plantation. P.M. Nityanandan (b. 1928) produced the first campus novel in Indian English with his *Long, Long Days* (1960), but he was one of several who produced only one novel.

Perhaps the dominant concern of the literature of this period is with character development and psychological depth, often combined with a sense of the alienated individual, dissatisfied with modern life. It may be that this sense of alienation reflects the situation of the Indian writer in English in the 1950s and 1960s, possessed of an education and élite status separating him from the masses, although it might just as easily be seen as an attempt to affiliate Indian writing to the dominant forms of Western fiction at the time. The theme of alienation takes on a special edge in the numerous novels published by women in the period. While they form no particular school, it is their emergence which is perhaps the most striking feature of the period. Writers such as Kamala Markandaya, Ruth Prawer Jhabvala, Nayantara Sahgal, and Anita Desai have had an international readership ever since, a quartet of women writers joining the male trio as India's best-known writers in English until the emergence of the Rushdie generation.

In Khushwant Singh (b. 1915) we witness the persona of a hard-drinking womaniser, but Singh is also the author of books such as *Ranjit Singh: Maharajah of the Punjab* (1962) and *A History of the Sikhs* (in two volumes, 1963–6), which many consider the definitive work in the field. He has collaborated in the translation of the Sikh scriptures for a UNESCO collection, *The Sacred Writings of the Sikhs* (1960), and has translated literature from Punjabi, Hindi, and Urdu. Born in Hadali (now in Pakistan), he was educated at Delhi and Lahore and studied for a short time at St Stephen's College, Delhi. Subsequently he studied law at King's College, London, and practised at the Lahore High Court from 1939 to 1947. After Partition, he worked as a press attaché with the Indian Foreign Service in London and Ottawa, and in Paris with UNESCO. As a journalist, his greatest commercial success was probably his stint as the editor of *The Illustrated Weekly of India* (1969–78), when he raised the weekly's circulation from 65,000 to 400,000.

Singh began his career as writer of fiction with a collection of short stories, *The Mark of Vishnu* (1950), which was followed with what remains the most memorable of his three novels, *Train to Pakistan* (1956, published in the United States under the title *Mano Majra*). He describes it as 'a documentary . . . with a sugar-coating of characters and a story', but it remains the best-regarded novel in English on Partition. It is set in the small village of Mano Majra, on the banks of the Sutlej, where the only event of importance is a train crossing the railway bridge. The Partition is represented as an event which the simple villagers—who have lived peaceably together regardless of religious differences—cannot fathom. Problems arise when interlopers seek to stir up the villagers to attack Muslims travelling on the train to Pakistan. The situation is saved, at the cost of his own life, by a generous and impulsive Sikh peasant, Jugga. Corrupt officials responsible for law and order, and a committed communist worker, Iqbal, are shown as ineffectual in this situation. Throughout the novel, in fact, politics and policy are identified as a kind of bad faith, to be contrasted with the earthy simplicity of villagers. In this sense, for all that it describes very directly the brutal events of the Partition, the novel implies a basic confidence in the people, a gruff romantic nationalism which seems wary of the city and the state. In another sense it is the landscape of India itself, to which its villagers are closely tied, which emerges as the hero of this novel, whose strengths include a swift tempo and wonderful descriptions. Like his second, less successful, novel, *I Shall Not Hear the Nightingale* (1959), which chronicles a Sikh joint family of the 1940s, *Train to Pakistan* reflects Singh's opinion that Indian culture ought to express itself more openly about sex. This view combines with the carnivalesque style of his journalism in *Delhi: A Novel* (1989), which uses a broad historical canvas, a chatty and digressive narrative style, an irreverent tone and content. The main narrator of the novel is an ageing writer (teasingly based on Singh's public image) whose relations with the eunuch Bhagmati open up a window to the varied history of India's capital city from 1265 to the anti-Sikh riots of 1984.

The robustness of Singh's writing is in strong contrast to the style of Ruskin Bond (b. 1934), another writer who established a long career in the 1950s. Bond was born in Kasauli, the small Himalayan hill station, of Anglo-Indian parents who separated when he was little. The early death of his father was to affect Bond deeply and much of his writing is pervaded by a tone of melancholy and nostalgia assuaged only, it would seem, by a delight in nature. Bond's first novel, *The Room on the Roof* (1956), won the John Llewellyn-Rhys Memorial Prize. It presents a lonely Eurasian boy's quest for friendship, and his wholehearted enjoyment of the noisy life of the Indian bazaar, from which he has been kept away by narrow-minded guardians. But Bond's forte is not the full-length novel. He has preferred long stories and seems best as a writer for children. His fiction shares with R.K. Narayan a strong sense that small, provincial towns represent the real India, a view he put forward explicitly in the preface to his *Time Stops at Shamli* (1989):

> Some say the real India is to be found in the village; others would like to think that India is best represented by its big cities and industrial centres. . . . I would say that India is really to be found in its small towns. Small town India—that's *my* India. The India of Shamli and Shahganj, Panipat and Pipalkot, Alwar and Ambala and Alleppey, Kalka and Kasauli and Kolar Gold Fields.

The interest in the emotional lives of small-town folk is reflected in the unobtrusive style of most of Bond's writings. Only in their relationship with nature do his characters seem completely fulfilled, and the social world is often a place of awkwardness and disappointment.

A concern to discover some notion of 'authentic being' runs through the five novels produced by Arun Joshi (1939–93). Educated in India and the United States, Joshi was a management consultant by profession, and headed a research institute in New Delhi. His characters' problems, and the alienation which afflicts them, are presented as universal rather than specifically Indian. The hero of his first novel, *The Foreigner* (1968), is orphaned at an early age. Born in Kenya of an Indian father and an English mother, educated in Britain and the United States, he grows up without ties of family or country and considers the first twenty-five years of his life 'largely wasted in search of wrong things in wrong places'. His love for an American girl ends tragically because he fears emotional involvement, a fear which persists even after he returns to India. Only at the end of the novel is he transformed by the trust and affection of the workers of his factory, who believe that only he can save the factory from closing down and rendering them jobless. *The Apprentice* (1974) is the story of Ratan Rathor, a government official whose soul is corroded by the prevailing atmosphere of corruption in post-Independence India. The son of a freedom fighter who is killed by the British while leading a peaceful procession, the idealistic young man soon comes to believe that he will only survive if he begins to be governed by self-interest. He accepts a bribe and allows defective equipment to be supplied to the army during the Sino-Indian war of 1962. One of the victims of this act is his only childhood friend, now a brigadier, who is court-martialled for abandoning his command at the war front. Ratan Rathor can save his friend's honour by confessing to his own role in the affair; but he vacillates, and the brigadier commits suicide.

A striking feature of Joshi's fiction is his experimentation with different narrative techniques. In *The Foreigner*, the narrative freely moves across time and geographical space; *The Apprentice* is a monologue; *The Last Labyrinth* (1981), which won the Sahitya Akademi Award, is dominated by the trope of the labyrinth, which might also describe its structure. Joshi's last novel, *The City and the River* (1990), is very different in technique from the earlier ones; he gives up first-person narration and the realist mode to write a fable about the corruption of power.

The switch to politics and allegory is typical of the fiction of the 1980s and 1990s, but Joshi never seems entirely comfortable with it. *The Strange Case of Billy Biswas* (1971) is perhaps his best novel. It tells the story of Bimal Biswas and his obsession with adivasi culture. His parents send him to the USA to study engineering, but he takes a degree in anthropology instead. He returns to India to take his place in polite society, marries Meena, a girl from a suitable family and settles down to a secure teaching job at Delhi University. But he finds the life of middle-class India unbearably superficial. During an anthropological field trip to a tribal area Billy meets Bilasia, the woman of his deepest longings, and disappears from civilised society. The novel is shaped by the contrast between Billy's passionate commitment to tribal culture and the more conventional perspectives of the novel's narrator, Romi Sahai, an Indian Administrative Service (IAS) officer and friend from Billy's time in the United States. Joshi's novel gives credence to its hero's dissatisfaction with metropolitan Indian culture by allowing it to be refracted through the less romantic perspectives of his friend. The relationship between the narrator and the hero calls to mind Conrad's *Heart of Darkness*, a novel to which *The Strange Case of Billy Biswas* can be paralleled in other ways. Joshi's narrative is dominated by an idea of the mystery of an essential India, deeply antithetical to modern city life.

Dissatisfaction with the metropolis and modernity is a recurrent feature of the novels of this period, but there is only really one novel which consequently turned to experimenting with non-Western narrative forms: M. Anantanarayanan's *The Silver Pilgrimage* (1961). Anantanarayanan (1907–81) was born at Palaghat in South India. His father, A. Madhavaiah, was one of the earliest Indian novelists to write in English. After an education at Madras University and Gonville and Caius College, Cambridge, Anantanarayanan joined the Indian Civil Service and was a judge of the Madras High Court. *The Silver Pilgrimage* was his only foray into fiction. The model for his account of the adventures of Jayasurya, a prince of sixteenth-century Sri Lanka, is Dandin's *Dasa-kumara-charita* rather than the Western picaresque novel, although its resources are by no means only Indian. Excerpts, arranged as a preface to the novel, include lines from Shakespeare, Donne, and Rilke through to Tamil poets such as Avvayar, Pattinathar, and Tiruvalluvar. The most important function of this prolegomena seems to be to warn the reader against stock responses: the key epigraph is from Jalaluddin Rumi: 'Sell your Cleverness and buy Bewilderment.' The young prince at the centre of the narrative is sent on a pilgrimage by his father, who is concerned by his son's lack of feeling for the hardships of the common man. The narrative itself is baldly chronological. There is no overt psychological depth to the characters, and incident follows incident breathlessly. The narration accommodates folk tales and ballads and shifts to a dramatic arrangement of dialogue when necessary. The most important aspect of *The Silver Pilgrimage*, however, is its humour, which places it in a series of Indian novels in English which recognise no demarcation between farce and philosophy.

No other novelist of the period followed Anantanarayanan's deliberate abrogation of the conventions of the European novel. Innovation can however be found in the psychological depth of the experiences of women characters, although that experience is almost restricted, as one would expect, to the English-educated élite and the complexities of their position in relation to traditional and modern roles for women. Not surprisingly, novels with such women are often autobiographical, and a number of women such as Venu Chitale (*In Transit*, 1951), Zeenuth Futehally (*Zohra*, 1951), and Mrinalini Sarabhai (*This Alone is True*, 1952), published single novels of self-discovery. Attia Hosain's *Sunlight on a Broken Column* (1961) has proved among the most popular of these studies of élite women's consciousness, widely admired for the lyricism of its prose style and its vivid recreation of the distinctive Muslim culture of Lucknow before Independence. Hosain (1913–98) was born into an aristocratic Muslim family in Lucknow, and studied at the city's Isabella Thoburn College. In the 1930s she came under the influence of the nationalist movement and the Progressive Writers Group, before migrating to England in 1947, where she worked as a broadcaster and journalist. Her first book, *Phoenix Fled* (1953), was a collection of stories, and *Sunlight on a Broken Column* was to be her only novel. Through a complicated temporal scheme which ranges backwards and forwards across time, the story is told from the perspective of the orphaned Laila, who has grown up in a joint family presided over by an old patriarch, Baba Jan, her grandfather. Baba Jan enjoys all the privileges of feudalism but graciously lives up to the responsibilities this entails. Laila is encouraged towards Western education, but tradition is strictly observed and the uneasy balance between modernity and tradition in the family is broken only when Laila chooses Ameer Husain—a young man her family believe is beneath her socially—to be her husband. By this stage, after the death of Baba Jan, Laila is living in the home of her more Westernised but autocratic Uncle Hamid. Now the family is caught up in the struggle for Independence and arguments over the prospect of Partition, which eventually divides the family and destroys the harmony associated with Baba Jan's time. Although these national developments and the effect they have on the feudal family are richly detailed in the novel, Laila remains relatively aloof from them. The novel is dominated instead by her personal struggle against the claustrophobia of family authority and, paradoxically perhaps, a nostalgia for the lost world of her childhood.

One woman novelist in whose fiction the personal and the political have been less segregated is Nayantara Sahgal, perhaps unsurprisingly, given that she spent much of her childhood at Anand Bhavan in Allahabad, the ancestral home of the Nehrus. Sahgal (b. 1927) is the second of the three daughters of Vijayalakshmi Pandit (Nehru's sister) and R.S. Pandit (a Sanskrit scholar and lawyer). She studied in missionary schools in India, and Wellesley College, Massachusetts, where she received a BA in history. After her return to India in 1947 she stayed for some time with Nehru in Delhi, and her novels reveal a close acquaintance with the political élite. Two years later she married Gautam Sahgal, a businessman, and had three children. The marriage broke up when she met E.N. Mangat Rai, a civil servant: *Relationship* (1994), a selection of their letters, reveals something of the pressures brought to bear on a couple flouting the middle-class conventions of the time.

Sahgal's novels present the life of the richest sections of Indian society, their hypocrisy and shallow values; at the same time, Sahgal is concerned with the Indian heritage and its value for the educated Indian. Her first novel, *A Time to be Happy* (1958), appeared after two books of autobiography. Sanad, the protagonist and narrator, articulates the problem of identity facing the English-educated élite in words that echo Nehru's *Autobiography* (1936): 'I don't belong entirely to India. I can't. My education, my upbringing, and my sense of values have all combined to make me unIndian . . . Of course there can be no question of my belonging to any other country.'

All of Sahgal's novels show an interest in the way this Western-educated élite has borne the responsibility of political power; major national events provide the background for each of her eight novels. *A Time to be Happy* (1958) presents the coming of Independence, for instance, while *Storm in Chandigarh* (1969) deals with the partition of

Punjab along linguistic lines in 1965. This concern with the way power is used in the public sphere is typically combined by Sahgal with an exploration of the fate of women within the domestic sphere. *Rich Like Us* (1985) is set during the Emergency, but it also includes a treatment of sati as a trope for the entrapment of women in conventional marriages. The novel won the Sinclair Prize for fiction and the Sahitya Akademi Award. Sahgal plots the Emergency against a slow erosion of values among both civil servants and people at large after Independence, a process she traces even further back in two more recent novels, *Plans for Departure* (1986) and *Mistaken Identity* (1988), dealing with the Raj and the Independence movement.

Kamala Markandaya (Kamala Taylor, née Purnaiya, b. 1924) is a writer who attempted, not always successfully, to look beyond the élite in her exploration of similar themes. Markandaya was educated at Madras University. She worked as a journalist before becoming a full-time writer. Married to an Englishman, she settled in Britain, where she died in 2004. Her ten novels present a remarkable range of characters—from Rukmini, a poor peasant woman in *Nectar in a Sieve* (1954), through the urban poor of *A Handful of Rice* (1966), to the highest circles of princely life in *The Golden Honeycomb* (1977). The conflict between tradition and modernity, East and West, runs through all her work. *The Coffer Dams* (1969) and *Pleasure City* (1982) are contemporary examinations of the meaning of 'progress'. In the first novel, British firms build a huge dam, in the second, a luxury holiday resort; in both Markandaya shows how the effects of these developments amount to a kind of neo-colonialism, but her strengths as a novelist lie in her depictions of human relationships. In fact, her descriptions of the life of the poor (in *Nectar in a Sieve* or *A Handful of Rice*, for instance) are often inaccurate in minor details. *The Golden Honeycomb*, her most ambitious work, also has the same drawback and lacks the depth and vividness, for instance, of Malgonkar's depiction of princely life in *The Princes*. Markandaya's writing is more confident when she writes about her own class and *The Nowhere Man* (1972), perhaps her best work, deals with a slice of life—racial prejudice against Indian migrants in Britain, of which she has first-hand knowledge.

The same issue was dealt with in *Bye Bye Blackbird* (1969), one of the earliest novels written by Anita Desai (née Mazumdar, b. 1937), the youngest of the women novelists of this period. This interest in social and political matters has, however, proven to be untypical of her work thus far. Born of a German mother and Bengali father, her fiction seems most confident when it deals with the educated upper-middle classes, but while Sahgal and Markandaya concern themselves primarily with the external political and social circumstances of their characters, Desai concentrates on their psychology. Indeed she has often made her priorities in this respect clear: 'Writing is to me a process of discovering the truth—the truth that is nine-tenths of the iceberg that lies submerged beneath the one-tenth visible portion we call Reality. Writing is my way of plunging to the depths and exploring this underlying truth . . . My novels are no reflection of Indian society, politics, or character.'

Desai's Westernised, educated women appear to have the luxury of freedom of choice, but deeper analysis reveals them to be frustrated and emotionally dependent. Except in her most recent novels, her protagonists have all been women, and range from the daughter and young wife (*Cry, the Peacock*, 1963) to the middle-aged wife and mother (*Where Shall We Go This Summer?*, 1975) to a grandmother and grandfather (*Fire on the Mountain*, 1977). All these women tend to be fragile introverts whose emotional traumas sometimes lead to violent death. Maya in *Cry, the Peacock*, Desai's first novel, is obsessed with the astrological prediction that her marriage is going to end in death in the fourth year. She cannot communicate with Gautam, her husband, who is twice her age. The lack of children is a trope for the sterility of every aspect of the marriage. Most of Desai's novels reveal the break-down of relationships, marital or familial. *Fire on the Mountain* has a multi-linear narrative, which analyses the lack of communication between mother and child and grandchild. Nanda Kaul, an old widow living alone in a house in Kasauli, fails to establish bonds with her great-granddaughter Raka, another introvert. Desai suggests that Nanda's sense of superiority is only a mask, and the novel ends in tragedy.

Clear Light of Day is that rare novel: intensely serious yet very readable. It deals with two sisters from a loveless home. Bimla, the elder, stays on in their decaying mansion in Delhi to look after a mentally retarded younger brother. Tara, the younger sister, is married to a diplomat in the Indian Foreign Service, and visits the house every three or four years when her husband comes to India. Moving back and forth in time, Anita Desai presents the complex web of childhood love and guilt. The parents are presented in an unsympathetic light; the rich father and diabetic mother always away at the club, playing cards. When both parents die, it is Bim, hardly out of her teens, who is forced to take charge of the household. Raja, the elder son, has always admired Hyder Ali, their landlord, and follows him to Hyderabad; he later marries his daughter and inherits considerable property from him. Bim subconsciously resents his easy escape from responsibility. The rift is complete when he sends her a letter in the capacity of a landlord assuring her that she can stay on in their old house as long as she wants to. Bim is quite different from Desai's earlier protagonists. She is hard-headed and mature, and sensibly faces whatever life throws in her way, but remains emotionally disturbed, torn apart by bitterness towards her brother. Finally, she achieves some kind of peace by forgiving Raja and the final moments of the novel, presenting a kind of epiphany, are a triumph of technique with Desai integrating past and present at a symbolic level in an appeal to the kind of transcendence which recurs in her fiction.

Desai's later novels seem to be an attempt to move beyond the sometimes suffocating psychological studies of her earlier work. As part of the attempt she seems to have switched, in novels such as *In Custody* (1984) and *Baumgartner's Bombay* (1988), to male-centred plots. *In Custody* (made into a successful film) deals with the growing disillusionment of Deven, a young college teacher, when he realises that Noor, the Urdu poet he idolises, has feet of clay; but, rather like Bim at the end of *Clear Light of Day*, he comes to accept the complications of their relationship in another vision of renewed possibilities in the closing pages of the novel. *Journey to Ithaca* (1995) is completely

Eurocentric in its vision of India as a land of heat and dust, squalor and godmen, and approximates to Ruth Prawer Jhabvala's work. Although these novels seem more engaged with a wider world, they tend to maintain the idea that freedom is to be found in a kind of Romantic transcendence, a product perhaps of the literary tradition illustrated in the quotations from Keats and Shelley in *In Custody*.

Mention of Ruth Prawer Jhabvala (b. 1927), novelist, short-story and screenplay writer, raises an interesting problem for the historian of literature: is she an *Indian* writer at all? Jhabvala was born in Cologne of Polish Jewish parents and moved to England in 1939, where she studied English literature at the University of London. In 1951 she married an Indian architect, C.S.H. Jhabvala, and lived in Delhi for the next twenty-five years. Jhabvala herself has declared (in an interview given in 1974) that she should not be considered an Indian writer but 'as one of those European writers who have written about India'. After moving to New York in 1975 she has devoted more time to scriptwriting, producing more than fifteen screenplays for Merchant–Ivory films.

Jhabvala's short stories and twelve novels fall into three distinct classes, though their themes are not mutually exclusive. The first four novels are comedies of urban middle-class life in India in a Jane Austenish vein. An important theme is the varying reactions of the Westernised protagonists and their conventional Indian families to the subject of arranged marriage and romantic love. *The Householder* (1960; made into a successful film) is written with much sympathy for the protagonist, a young man who slowly learns the privileges and pains of becoming a householder with the slow growth of love in his arranged marriage. The next four novels, which include *A Background Place* (1965) and the Booker Prize-winning *Heat and Dust* (1975), are ironic studies of the interaction between India and Britain. Jhabvala's satire borders on cynicism, and she increasingly turns to stereotypes in her picture of India. Her recent protagonists are Westerners in India, trying (often with disastrous consequences) to adjust to this land of heat and dust; her earlier novels describe the complicated power relationship in an Indian joint family and the cattiness of women, young and old, who use conversation as a weapon.

In the four novels published after she left India, Jhabvala's work has widened to include American and Jewish characters and settings. *In Search of Love and Beauty* (1983) is about a group of German and Austrian refugees in New York; so is *Shards of Memory* (1995). *Three Continents* (1987) shows Harriet, a young American heiress, turning to India in her search for identity. This is an abiding theme in Jhabvala's novels and short stories: Harriet follows in the footsteps of Lee (in *A New Dominion*, 1972), and Katie from the title story of *How I Became a Holy Mother* (1976). Although it is well over twenty-five years since she left India, the figure of the ubiquitous Swamiji (distinguished equally by charisma and lack of principles) continues to dominate her work: *Shards of Memory* revolves around the founder of a new religion, and its promotion by money-grubbing New Yorkers. Over the years there has been no diminution of Jhabvala's wit and verbal felicity; her craftsmanship has been honed, but her vision tends to be extremely Eurocentric.

The 1950s and 1960s were not a period of great innovation for Indian writing in English, although they witnessed the foundation of writing careers that have lasted over several decades and which, especially for women writers, brought international acclaim. Many of the novels seem highly sceptical of the dominant forms of Indian culture and society, choosing to find a more authentic idea of India in the landscape, the provincial town, or traditional village life. The extreme case is Joshi's hero, Billy Biswas, who can only fulfil his deep sense of longing by joining a tribal society in the heart of India. Perhaps there is a strange kind of denial going on here about the situation of these élite writers in English in relation to the uneducated millions. Certainly, few of them show any affection for the élite, metropolitan lives that most of them lead. Where more recent writers have taken up Raja Rao's challenge of developing forms of the novel that draw on Indian literary tradition, none of the books of this period, with the exception of Anantanarayanan's *The Silver Pilgrimage*, are interested in developing the conflict between tradition and modernity—which are a thematic feature of so many of their stories—into any kind of formal exploration of indigenous narrative forms. The women writers, whose emergence provides this period with one of its few distinctive features, phrased the conflict in relation to the condition of women, but emancipation in their novels is often figured in terms of personal release into what seems a very literary realm of transcendence.

What these novelists did demonstrate was a command of the dominant forms of the English novel, and the right of Indian novelists to be taken seriously in terms of the criteria of Western novel writing. Perhaps this represents a building up towards the cultural capital so conspicuously consumed by the Rushdie generation of the 1980s and 1990s.

16

On V.S. Naipaul on India

Suvir Kaul

Vidiadhar Surajprasad Naipaul, winner of the Nobel Prize for Literature in 2001 and well-known 'Indian' writer on India, was born of Hindu stock in Trinidad on 17 August 1932. He grew up there and went as an adult to Britain in 1950, to study at Oxford, where he established a career as a broadcaster and prolific writer. He continues to live in Britain, and has over the past forty years written several travelogues and many novels, becoming arguably one of the most significant writers in English of his generation. None of this makes him Indian, and in fact there are powerful intellectual and cultural reasons to return him to the Caribbean, as various critics have argued. If we choose to think of India as more than the location of some of his work, and as a necessary part of his imagination, it is because three of his major travelogues have been located in India and because his interest in South Asian affairs has been recurring, even obsessive. V.S. Naipaul—the name deracinated, if rendered more cosmopolitan via the condensation into initials—who is a celebrated commentator on India and things Indian is so as part of his career-long effort to grapple with issues of identity and cultural tradition, with his location as a writer and his choice of subjects, and with the evolution of social and religious systems under the aegis of European imperialism. In short, it is because Naipaul is a post-colonial writer that he is an Indian writer, that he is a West Indian writer, that he is a black British writer.

These are of course not terms that Naipaul would identify with. He has in fact strenuously disavowed the 'West Indian' label, and it seems entirely unlikely that he would see himself as 'black British'. But a writer's corpus goes beyond what he or she acknowledges, and different phases of Naipaul's writing are best understood with reference to his complex West Indianness, his Indianness, his Britishness. The names of nations might seem like unwieldy frames of reference for the work of a polymath like Naipaul, but his writing has never shied away from such references. Indeed, one of the reasons Naipaul's writing has been controversial is the ease with which he invokes the nation or the culture or the particular 'civilisation' that he writes about as an essential, and even adequate, explanation of all the social tensions and weaknesses that he so fluently catalogues. The diagnosis of national cultures, or of subnational and supra-national loyalties, and the play between national, ethnic, and individual identities have been staples of Naipaul's travel writing and his fiction. He is at his richest and most nuanced when he writes of such interplay; equally, his habit of equating individual aberrations with cultural or national traits is what renders his writing thin, culturally insensitive, and open to the charge of being the product of a colonised sensibility, of an anglocentric bias about the world.

'India' shows up in Naipaul's earliest fiction in the reshaped memories, dislocated cultural practices, and ossified religious rituals of the Trinidadian communities that are his subjects. In *The Mystic Masseur* (1957), *The Suffrage of Elvira* (1958), *Miguel Street* (1959), and *A House for Mr Biswas* (1961), Naipaul wrote in a satiric vein of the people and places he had known as a child. *A House for Mr Biswas* is more ambitious and finished than the three earlier books, each of which is a collection of comic or ironic vignettes of community life in Trinidad. The community that Naipaul is most concerned with is that of the Indians who were brought to the islands as indentured agricultural labour after the emancipation of slaves in the region. He writes of their lives with some affection, but even where the comedy is heart-warming, as it is so often in *The Mystic Masseur*, Naipaul's condescension rarely fails to surface. His portrait of Ganesh in this novel warms to the character's opportunism, his entrepreneurial instincts, and his ability to convert misremembered Hindu rituals into a vehicle for self-advancement (his *101 Questions and Answers on the Hindu Religion* becomes a bestseller), but the texture of his life, and of the other characters in the novel, is pasteboard thin, often little better than caricature. However, themes recurrent in Naipaul's writing are initiated in this novel; for instance when Pandit Ganesh Ramsumair, through a series of comic misadventures, is translated by colonial systems of governance into G. Ramsay Muir, MBE. Naipaul's satire suggests his own ambivalent relation with those colonial processes that shaped his life as well as those of his characters.

A House for Mr Biswas thickens Naipaul's engagement with the communities of his childhood in a way that confers novelistic dignity and pathos to the cultural and geographical dislocations of individuals and families, and to the story of their difficult transitions away from the near-feudal social and economic relations fostered by colonialism. Naipaul has acknowledged that a great deal of the novel's intensity comes from the fact that its title character is modelled upon his father Seepersad Naipaul (who wished to be a writer, and whose thwarted literary ambitions might be thought to find fulfilment in the work of V.S. Naipaul and his brother Shiva Naipaul). In this novel, Naipaul bases many events and people on childhood memories. As Mr Biswas tries to break from the claustrophobic hold of the extended Tulsi family into which he has married, his life becomes an allegory of the coming of bourgeois modernity and its values. The building of such a new 'home' is a costly and even destructive process, and Mr Biswas is repeatedly scarred by the attempt. His partial way out is his job as a journalist, which provides him some of the professional and personal authority that his early life has lacked, and which encourages him to write, and to share in a world of English books with his own children. Writing and literacy provide a window into a wider realm, and even though Mr Biswas's own life continues to be dogged by failure and disappointment, his children—Anand and Savi—benefit from his efforts and go abroad to study on scholarships. Naipaul's rendering of the shape of Mr Biswas's life—fatherless, living on the margins of extended family networks, beholden to their oppressive charities and demands, then a father himself who struggles, with mixed results, to create a different life for himself and his family—is generous and concerned enough to raise the pitch of the novel to something akin to tragedy, a tone that is confirmed at its close, as Mr Biswas, burdened by debt and his sense that Anand is not going to return home, wastes into an untimely death. Out of such family history Naipaul created his life of writing: over two decades after he published this novel, Naipaul wrote (in his foreword to the 1984 Vintage edition) that it connected him to 'the passions and nerves of [his] early life', and that he remembered 'the time of writing—the ambition, the tenacity, the innocence. My literary ambition had grown out of my early life.'

Confirmed into his literary life, Naipaul wrote his first travelogue on commission from the government of Trinidad and Tobago. Ironically, and perhaps symptomatically, *The Middle Passage* (1962) does not do much more than reaffirm Naipaul's complicated and often perverse relationship with the colonial cultures of the Caribbean. It puts on view his signature style as an observer of cultures and peoples: he authenticates his narrative by including descriptions of himself and his reactions, but also converts his perennial discomfort with most of what he sees into the censure and denigration of entire cultures and histories. He gains further authenticity for his observations by recording his anger at the brutal histories of colonial slavery and exploitation, but goes on to provide extremely unsympathetic analyses of the inefficiency and ugliness of contemporary societies that leave them not far removed from the times of colonial control. *The Middle Passage* also incorporates an analytical mode that is repeated in many of Naipaul's travel writings, where he engages with a culture via the writing of those who came before. His interlocutors are often colonialist commentators, and while he does dissociate himself from some of their more egregious racism, his own vocabulary echoes their idiom. Perhaps a brief quotation, from Naipaul's essay 'Conrad's Darkness', is useful here: 'And I found that Conrad—sixty years before, in a time of great peace—had been everywhere before me.' For Naipaul, Conrad offers 'a vision of the world's half-made societies': the 'half-made', the mimic, the interrupted and shoddy, the world in terminal decay, these are the materials Naipaul discovers anew, not simply in the manner of Conrad the imperialist, but as one who comes after the master.

These are the burdens Naipaul brought to India when he visited it in 1962; added to them was the special weight of his cultural inheritance, his sense that the 'Indian' aspect of his Trinidadian sensibility could be explained, or rediscovered perhaps in some form of originary plenitude, in the land of his maternal grandfather. His record of his 'return' to India, *An Area of Darkness* (1964), is however a testimonial of the loss of illusions; the fading of the sense, however displaced, of home; the confirmation that India (somewhat differently from the Caribbean) can only be a place of social iniquity, arrested development, and post-colonial decay. He begins this book with an account of all that India meant to him as a child and as an adult ('a country never physically described and therefore never real'); 'an area of the imagination', but which faded in its immediacy of reference as he moves away from Trinidad to London. London, however, offers few compensations: 'It had become the centre of my world and I had worked hard to come to it. And I was lost. London was not the centre of my world. I had been misled; but there was nowhere else to go.' Hence, when Naipaul comes to India, he comes, willy-nilly, looking for home, plagued by 'more than the usual fear of arrival. In spite of myself, in spite of lucidity and London and my years, and over and above every other fear . . . some little feeling for India as the mythical land of my childhood was awakened.'

He leaves behind the isolation and professional anonymity of London ('in the big city I was confined to a smaller world than I had ever known. I became my flat, my desk, my name'), but in India encounters another kind of facelessness, another sort of panic:

> And for the first time in my life I was one of the crowd. There was nothing in my appearance or dress to distinguish me from the crowd eternally hurrying into Churchgate Station. In Trinidad to be an Indian was to be distinctive . . . To be an Indian in England was distinctive; in Egypt it was more so. Now in Bombay I entered a shop or a restaurant and awaited a special quality of response. And there was nothing. It was like being denied part of my reality . . . I was faceless. I might sink without a trace into the Indian crowd. I had been made by Trinidad and England; recognition of my difference was necessary to me. I felt the need to impose myself and didn't know how.

Voice and accent differentiate him ('to talk in a voice whose absurdity I felt whenever I opened my mouth'), and experience after experience confirms him in this new alienation of being not-Indian, racially of a culture but separate from it in every other way.

The loss of self is not the only panic Naipaul admits to; there is also his initial 'hysteria' at the overwhelming poverty he sees around him. Interestingly, when he offers a retrospective account of his reactions to the brutalising poverty he encounters, he does so via the ironic quotation of local voices which remind him that his 'anger and contempt' for the degradation he sees about him are not special 'marks of . . . sensitivity', and that it is his questioning gaze and his 'surprise' that deny the 'humanity' of the dispossessed. The opening sections of *An Area of Darkness* are thus often about the loss of voice and self-possession (including his now-famous description of his attempts to rescue two bottles of liquor from the clutches of the customs bureaucracy that then administered liquor licences in a Bombay under prohibition). What follows in the travelogue can be understood, in all its richness of reportage and observation and its failure of spirit and empathy, as Naipaul's attempt to recover his bearings, to 'impose' himself on his surroundings. That Naipaul fails in this attempt, and is fully cognisant of his failure, is one of the abiding lessons of *An Area of Darkness*; but we need first to spend some time paying attention to all that he sees and chooses to record.

Naipaul sees a great many people spitting and pissing on the streets; he sees beggary and destitution, and he sees the combination of all these activities: 'Indians defecate everywhere. They defecate, mostly, beside the railway tracks. But they also defecate on the beaches; they defecate on the hills; they defecate on the river banks; they defecate on the streets; they never look for cover.' What disturbs Naipaul is not only this national drama of defecation, but the fact that it does not show up in the literate conversation of the culture:

> These squatting figures—to the visitor, after a time, as eternal and emblematic as Rodin's Thinker—are never spoken of; they do not appear in feature films or documentaries. This might be regarded as part of a permissible prettifying intention. But the truth is that *Indians do not see these squatters* and might even, with complete sincerity, deny that they exist: a collective blindness arising out of the Indian fear of pollution and the resulting conviction that Indians are the cleanest people in the world.

I quote Naipaul at some length to suggest characteristic patterns of observation and analysis—his eye for grotesque detail (about whose validity there can be little argument), and his explanations of such grotesquerie not in historical or socio-economic terms but in the more atavistic (and less accurate) terms of religious belief or cultural practice. As with so many of Naipaul's more egregious observations, this one too is true; what is problematic is the relevance here of pollution rituals or of a wilful national blindness or hypocrisy. In some ways, Naipaul knows he treads on thin ice here, which is why these observations are surrounded by, and ratified by, similar comments made by Mahatma Gandhi. The difference is simply that Gandhi saw the production and removal of shit as a social problem and addressed it accordingly; he did not see fit to fashion from it a final comment on 'Indianness'.

This is not simply a question of Naipaul's bad faith, or of the sense that the observer of Indian horrors must somehow earn the right to comment on them. For Naipaul's position in India, as he confesses himself, straddles that of outsider and insider: at Rajghat, as he watches blue-shirted, 'well-fed and well-shod' schoolboys approaching American tourists, old ladies who, 'informed of India's poverty', hand out notes and coins, Naipaul is moved to violence: 'I advanced towards the schoolboys, simple murder in my heart. They ran away, nimble in the heat. The Americans looked assessingly at me: the proud young Indian nationalist. Well, it would do. I walked back to the coach, converting exhaustion into anger and shame.' Naipaul as proud Indian nationalist is ironic, but of interest also are the sources of his anger and shame—is it the chicanery of the schoolboys or the gullibility of the Americans that moves him? Does he think, that is, as an Indian (embarrassed by fraud) or as a tourist (angered by harassment), or is he always condemned to the inchoate emotions of the in-between?

Naipaul describes at length the months he spends in Kashmir (though he nowhere mentions writing, while living in Srinagar, *Mr Stone and the Knight's Companion*, published in 1963). His focus is once again on local corruptions and duplicities, and on the naiveté or cynicism of hotel owners and visiting Indian tourists. He travels in Kashmir, to Pahalgam and to Amarnath, but his descriptions are more concerned with human failings and infrastructural inefficiencies than with landscape or cultural forms, or perhaps it is more accurate to say that for Naipaul the former collapse into, and overpower, the latter. When he leaves Kashmir, this collapse becomes his entry into Indian history, into the rise and fall of kingdoms and civilisations. This is Naipaul on the ruins of Vijayanagar:

> The square-pillared lower storeys of the stone buildings still stand; in the doorways are carvings of dancers with raised legs. And inside, the inheritors of this greatness: men and women and children, thin as crickets, like lizards among the stones.
>
> A child was squatting in the mud of the street; the hairless, pink-skinned dog waited for the excrement. The child, big-bellied, rose; the dog ate. Outside the temple there were two wooden juggernauts decorated with erotic carvings: couples engaged in copulation and fellatio; passionless, stylised. They were my first glimpse of Indian erotic carving, which I had been longing to see; but after the first excitement came depression. Sex as pain, creation its own decay: Shiva, god of the phallus, performing the dance of life and the dance of death: what a concept he is, how entirely of India!

Naipaul's prose strings together the death of empires, stunted bodies (humans as insects), malnutrition, excrement, feeding, the dance of sexuality, and his own febrile excitement and disappointment. The psychic drama of this passage, as the banal and the bizarre add up to a stunning revelation of the contours of Naipaul's imagination (the chapter is, appropriately enough, entitled 'Fantasy and Ruins'), reveals nothing as much as it does the limits of his touristic rationality. Why, we may wonder, should this be so? Naipaul, once again, provides a part answer when he says that it is 'well that Indians are unable to look at their country directly, for the distress they would see would drive them mad. And it is well that they have no sense of history, for how then would they be able to continue to squat amid their ruins, and which Indian would be able to read the history of his country for the last thousand years without anger and pain?' Naipaul looks 'directly', and with a 'sense of history', and rearranges disorder and derangement into a commentary on culture and civilisation. And yet, dislocated himself, Naipaul recognises others—those who live, defecate, and die amidst the ruins—whose lives have no place for the value-laden memorials central to nationalist history (the 'India' Naipaul seeks in Vijayanagar). Their poverty sets them outside the pieties of such history, their pauperised lives at odds with its monuments.

And so, after a year in India, Naipaul prepares to leave, and his mood is reflective: 'In a year I had not learned acceptance. I had learned my separateness from India, and was content to be a colonial, without a past, without ancestors.' He writes this even as he is driven to visit the village in eastern Uttar Pradesh which his mother's father had left as an indentured labourer. This provides no connection or catharsis, and Naipaul produces only vignettes of money-grubbing kin and emotional confusion, till he beats a hasty retreat, refusing to give a ride in his jeep to a boy from the village: 'So it ended, in futility and impatience, a gratuitous act of cruelty, self-reproach and flight.' Finally, at the airport, as Naipaul waits many hours 'intermittently experiencing the horrors of an Indian public lavatory' for his flight to leave India, he slips into 'a creeping stupor' and begins to lose his sense of an Indian reality. Slowly, India becomes 'part of the night; a dead world, a long journey', a 'journey that ought not to have been made; it had broken my life in two.' He writes to a friend who had insisted on fresh impressions of India: 'It was violent and incoherent; but like everything I wrote about India, it exorcised nothing.' In fact, Naipaul learns no separation from India; he feels a 'despair [that] lies too deep for formulation', a fear of losing himself in those 'philosophical' values that he sees as characteristic of India: 'It was only now, as my experience of India defined itself more properly against my own homelessness, that I saw how close in the past year I had been to the total Indian negation, how much it had become the basis of thought and feeling.' This is Naipaul's area of darkness, the troubled liminal space that is forged in the unequal match between his talismanic ancestral memories of India and the mundane miseries of its poverty and brutality. The enduring achievement of *An Area of Darkness*, then, might not be so much its account of India in the early 1960s as its display of the anxieties of the diasporic 'Indian', its staging of the derangement that results from a homecoming to a place that is not home.

In the decade that followed Naipaul wrote prolifically and established a major reputation as a novelist and writer of travelogues and cultural commentary. He won major awards for *The Mimic Men* (1967), *In a Free State* (1971), and *Guerrillas* (1975), and all his other books, *A Flag on the Island* (1967), *The Loss of El Dorado* (1969), and *The Overcrowded Barracoon* (1972) were reviewed extensively, particularly in the United

Kingdom and the United States. He wrote occasional pieces and reviews, some of which are on India and things Indian (collected in *The Overcrowded Barracoon*) and many of which are on questions of empire and its aftermath. The same tone and set of questions prevail, be the area of his enquiry the islands of the Caribbean or societies in other parts of the colonised world: these are 'manufactured societies . . . creations of empire; and for long they were dependent on empire for law, language, institutions, culture, even officials. Nothing was generated locally; dependence became a habit. How, without empire, do such societies govern themselves? What is now the source of power?' However, not all reviews of his work were adulatory: in India, in the Caribbean, and even in London and New York, responses began to take note of his jaundiced reportage, his astonishing opacity to the revisionary intellectual and cultural energies of once-colonised nations, his selective and reductive use of anecdotes to understand and categorise places and peoples of which he had little experience. Those who carefully read Naipaul learnt that each of his books was in some way connected to his project of writerly self-discovery and self-definition, and that in each case the mimic man that Naipaul describes and denigrates is a fearfully imagined version of his protean colonial and migrant self. Even those who celebrated his manifold gifts as a writer of prose began to be more circumspect about the vision embodied in his fiction or the value of his cultural and historical commentary—as his reputation grew, so did the criticism of those who wished to call attention to its dubious sources.

Then, in 1975, Naipaul made another trip to India, this time to chart life under the Emergency regime declared by Indira Gandhi. The book that resulted, *India: A Wounded Civilization* (1977), is once again an act of personal discovery and provides little insight into the near-fascist methods employed by the state in order to conduct business and regulate lives during this period. This is largely because Naipaul is never really interested in examining the difference the Emergency made to Indian political life; for him, this is one more hiccup in the terminal decline of Indian society. After all, 'the India to which independence came was a land of far older defeat; [and] the purely Indian past died a long time ago.' This reference to an original Indian authenticity or purity echoes themes submerged in Naipaul's earlier commentary on India, ideas that his writings have since made more prominent. The India Naipaul recognises is Hindu India, and among the few occasions when he identifies with Indianness he does so with what he thinks of as a long history of Hindu defeat: 'Hinduism hasn't been good enough for the millions. It has exposed us to a thousand years of defeat and stagnation . . . again and again Indian history has repeated itself: vulnerability, defeat, withdrawal.' The unexpected 'us' here is only slightly at odds with the other moments when he stages his relationship with India: 'In India I know I am a stranger; but increasingly I understand that my Indian memories, the memories of that India which lived on into my childhood in Trinidad, are like trapdoors into a bottomless past.' That this 'bottomless past' turns out to be a reactionary dream of an ancient Indian plenitude, against which all Indian history necessarily appears as a waking nightmare, might provide us one more clue to Naipaul's recurrent obsessions and disappointments.

Thus, Naipaul's over-reliance on what might be called the 'Hindu cultural and philosophical system' to explain the brutalities of Indian society is not simply an anthropological inadequacy—it is in fact the keystone of the play of self, ancestral memory, and cultural desire that marks all his writings: 'the starting point of this enquiry . . . has been myself. Because in myself, like the split-second images of infancy which some of us carry, there survive, from the family rituals that lasted into my childhood, phantasmal memories of old India which for me outline a whole vanished world.' Naipaul's skewed sense of the explanatory power of Hindu paradigms and images also leads him to the thinnest of the many inaccurate observations in this book. Not surprisingly, this is on a political phenomenon that he is ill equipped to understand—the Naxalite movement. He quotes the playwright Vijay Tendulkar to the effect that 'Naxalism, as it developed in Bengal, became confused with the Kali cult', and Naxalite violence is to be understood as the 'sacrifice' of 'class enemies' by 'initiates'. Thus, what catches Naipaul's fancy is not Naxalite political agendas and activities (however controversial) but the possibility of reducing them to a bit role in the long drama of Hindu rituals and practices. And this from a commentator quite confident of his generalisations on the lack of historical and social enquiry in India: 'History and social inquiry, and the habits of analysis that go with these disciplines, are too far outside the Indian tradition.' For Naipaul these disciplines are too European to 'be applied to Indian civilisation': 'the European approach elucidates little . . . and makes nonsense of the stops and starts of Indian civilisation, the brief flowerings, the long periods of sterility, men forever claimed by the instinctive life, continually turning to barbarism.' These are strange and indefensible intellectual claims, but they are of a piece with Naipaul turning Naxalites into Kali-worshippers, his drowning of political analysis into the bloody 'barbarism' to which all Indians continually return.

Since 1977, Naipaul's prolific output and prize-wining ways have continued apace: *A Bend in the River* (1979), *The Return of Eva Péron, The Killings in Trinidad* (1980), *Among the Believers* (1981), and *Finding the Centre* (1984) have confirmed Naipaul's stature in the contemporary world of English letters, as they have made him much-discussed and controversial. A somewhat different note begins to surface in his writing with *The Enigma of Arrival* (1987), a tone of reassessment, an acknowledgement, via extened meditation, on the writerly life England affords him, of his own place in that tradition. And, faced with the death of siblings, there is the expressed need for forms of psychic and cultural closure. In the concluding chapter, 'The Ceremony of Farewell', he genuflects towards the colonial past and writes: 'There was no ship of antique shape now to take us back. We had come out of the nightmare; and there was nowhere else to go.' He writes movingly of the death of 'sacred worlds', those of his childhood, of his 'fantasy of home', those he had lived in 'imaginatively over many books', and of each generation and family remaking 'the world for ourselves'. It is tempting to trace changes in his travel-writing and approach to India to this reassessment, for both *A Turn in the South* (1989) and *India: A Million Mutinies Now* (1990) are marked by Naipaul's new-found ability to listen to people (in the southern United States and in India) and to find in their lives evidence of energy and hope rather than of despair or dislocation. And now, in India, there is some re-examination of his earlier response. He notes 'the new confidence of people once poor', and the 'freeing of new particularities, new identities, which were as unsettling to Indians as the identities of caste and clan and region had been to me in 1962, when I had gone to India only as an "Indian".' He now identifies his earlier neuroses: following upon his indentured ancestors, he had 'carried in my bones that idea of abjectness and defeat and shame. It was the idea I had taken to India . . . in 1962; it was the source of my nerves.'

Now, as he recognises the new energies loosed in the country, he sees 'a liberation of spirit', which comes to India ('with its layer below layer of distress and cruelty') as 'a disturbance. It had to come as rage and revolt. India was now a country of a million little mutinies.' It is these mutinies and changes he records, whether it be the belief systems of the Shiv Sena or of separatist Khalistanis, the activism of Dalits or of other groups who have suffered from caste and class oppressions, and he reads in these organised assertions of subnational group identities both a productive and a destructive loosening of the construction of Indian society. He reads women's magazines and is alerted to the way in which they play out the tensions between traditional conventions and alternative possibilities and thus call attention to the changing lives of women. But above all he notices the development of a market economy and the participation of those who had little access to it earlier. The hotel he stayed in at Srinagar in 1962 had five rooms; it now has forty-five, and a large staff to service them. He meets entrepreneurs of all stripes as he travels. He speaks to people whose lives are examples of economic and social mobility, and learns that in the past he had simply been blind to the great variegation that exists even within a seemingly rigid social system. The India that Naipaul believed condemned to stasis and decay still exists—he continues to notice great economic and human distress—but he finds many institutions and people who, in many different ways, are addressing those problems. His India now is an India on a roller-coaster ride, lurching from crest to trough, still stomach-turning in its intensity, but also a source of invigoration, and seemingly in continual forward motion.

Is this Naipaul's final, or even most authoritative, version of India? He might write on India again, as he has partially done in *Half a Life* (2001), but even if he does not, the contours of Naipaul's India can only be traced, as here, in a long encounter with all his books on India. His last vision does not supplant his first—it revises and enriches the former, even briefly apologises for it, but can in no way wish it away. Naipaul's India is the product of a complex process of identification, changeable as the writerly self he fashions, worked of the same materials and embodying similar desires and anxieties. Annually mentioned as a candidate for the Nobel, which he has now won, Naipaul's work is immediately even more the subject of much academic analysis. Closer home, even as Salman Rushdie is credited with initiating the boom in subcontinental writing in English, we must remember that it is V.S. Naipaul who first demonstrated, even to those who reacted angrily to his accounts of India, the possibility of a life of writing. That a Caribbean writer of Indian descent living in Britain should be a prime exemplar of the strengths and debilities of cultural cross-over in a post-colonial world is fitting; after all, it is writers like him who teach us to be less sanguine about, and to look once again at, this strange space called 'home'.

17
Poetry Since Independence

Rajeev S. Patke

The English language has proved to be one of the most enduring legacies of colonialism, even though the inheritance has undergone several transformations. Poets choosing to use English in India during the late 1940s were heirs to a post-Romantic legacy which had transposed a received stylistic repertoire to local materials. This occurred for more than a century, without any radical departure from European tradition, to which local poets were glad to attach themselves as diffident, pleased appanages. While most sustained a sanguine hope of an inert continuity with this tradition, some chose to initiate a new beginning: the latter provide more interesting material, even if the new beginnings represent no more than a shift in allegiance from post-Romantic to modern inclinations.

The poets writing in English came from a variety of backgrounds bridged chiefly by their choice of language. Most read, and quite a few taught, English as an academic subject, others worked in journalism or the media; only a handful had other kinds of professional experience, like Gieve Patel, a doctor; Keki N. Daruwalla, a police officer; and Jayanta Mahapatra, a teacher of physics. Their motives were united on two fronts: they had to write in English, and they had to get round the residual notion that no one could, or should, write poems in a language not their own. For some, like Nissim Ezekiel and Dom Moraes, it *was* their only language. For others, English had to become—as it has, in a manner of speaking—an Indian language. Of the many poets bilingual between English and another Indian language, a few have written poems in both, like Arun Kolatkar and Dilip Chitre. More often, their circumstances contrived that no other language was practical. With many, the choice to write in the other language which they did speak was fed through translation, as in the case of P. Lal, Arvind Krishna Mehrotra, and Jayanta Mahapatra. In most cases the likelihood of choosing to write in another Indian language was displaced by the many seductions of English, although these were not succumbed to without ambivalence—as with R. Parthasarathy; or a sense of dispossession, recuperated only through translation, as in the case of A.K. Ramanujan.

Chief among the temptations of embracing English was the range and scope of the language. The fear of linguistic inadequacy never seems to have bothered Indians aspiring to write poetry in English, despite the plethora of evidence that such a fear ought to have restrained them into a beneficial silence. In the supple folds of the English language the Indian poet has always hoped to dress new intentions, or to discover a new self. The English poetic tradition came to India on the path laid down by Macaulay's 'Minute' of 1835, trailing clouds of literary glory. Colonialism enhanced its glow over the course of a long tutelage, and political independence actually refurbished linguistic dependence. It revealed the language of foreign mastery as the only real *lingua franca* amidst a babble of communal and regional isms. English was the chief instrument of modernity for India. It also offered poets the promise of a wider audience: at home, among the urban élite; abroad, among the discerning (or at least the more sought-after) readership from the West. Exceptions like Kolatkar and Mehrotra only emphasise the general case that although Indian poets have looked for alternatives to British models in American poetry, their assimilation of its voices has not always managed to climb over the ledge of the imitative. Most have shown little interest in the other poetries in English. Although English is spoken volubly all over India, it has never quite developed the foundations of a natural rhythm (except of the inadvertent sort) that poets could build on. Keki N. Daruwalla conceded, in 1980, that Indian poetry had not always been able to shrug off the handicap of writing in what an Australian poet called 'a sort of

Blanket English—it comes through like the wrong side of a perfectly good woven carpet.' This history is an account of those who have worked, in their fashion, at turning the carpet right side up.

If we look for an efficient cause to a general tendency, it is the example of Nissim Ezekiel that has prevailed. Others working concurrently, or following after, also helped in fostering a new poetry in the process of finding a voice for themselves. Ezekiel had been publishing poems since 1945; his first two volumes appeared within five years of Independence: *A Time of Change* (1952) and *Sixty Poems* (1953), followed by *The Third* (1960), *The Unfinished Man* (1960), and *The Exact Name* (1965). Other poets who began writing in the late 1940s included the precocious Dom Moraes, Kamala Das, and Ramanujan. Many more began their careers in the 1950s, including Kolatkar and Parthasarathy; while the 1960s and the 1970s would prove to be the high point of Indian poetry in English; followed, more recently, by the emergence of several promising talents.

Before the poets could consolidate a field they had to have publishers. The first two volumes of Indian poetry in English to be published after Independence came from London (Ezekiel and Moraes). While a number of poets have since published in the West, most have found local publishers. From 1950, *The Illustrated Weekly of India* established a long tradition of hospitality to poetry in English, in a format ensuring nationwide circulation. Other periodicals, with smaller lifespans, or local circulations, followed. By 1958, P. Lal had set up the Writers Workshop in Calcutta and the first of what was to become a flood of Indian English poets would be published by this press from 1959 onwards, self-subsidised in more than a monetary sense, the significance of the enterprise greatly in excess of its worth. Small presses like Clearing House, Newground, and Praxis, run at irregular intervals from Bombay, have been selective as publishers, while several larger publishing houses had their own series, including Arnold-Heinemann and Oxford University Press (from the mid 1970s), and Viking, Rupa, and Disha (from the 1980s).

The readership sought by the Indian poet in English has been divided between a large but nebulous potential audience in the West, a potentially large but often unsatisfactory readership at home, and the acceptance of fellow practitioners. The last has proved the most gratifying for poets, giving the current canon a consensual look. From the late 1960s, a vigorous campaign was conducted through anthologies by poets, in which, after some prefatory polemics from anthologists who did not quite practice what they professed (P. Lal, *Modern Indian Poetry in English: An Anthology and Credo*, 1969, and Pritish Nandy, *Indian Poetry in English*, 1972), an anti-Romantic canon was consolidated, chiefly by Saleem Peeradina (*Contemporary Indian Poetry in English: An Assessment and Selection*, 1972), R. Parthasarathy (*Ten Twentieth-Century Indian Poets*, 1976), and Keki N. Daruwalla (*Two Decades of Indian Poetry: 1960–80*, 1980). The current trend contextualises poetry in English within a renewed awareness of the symbiotic relation between creativity in English and the role of translation in a multilingual and multicultural context.

By the late 1940s little had been left untouched in the stylistic realm of Indian poetry by the faded meretriciousness of a borrowed romanticism, which continued to eke out a life of vacuous plushness. In contrast, Ezekiel's first five volumes came armed with a more hard-headed set of assumptions which corresponded to the mood reflected concurrently by poets writing in England, in which the neo-Romanticism of poets like Dylan Thomas was being overtaken by poets like Philip Larkin, whose development exchanged the Yeatsian cloak and swagger of *The North Ship* for the worsted Hardy of *The Less Deceived*. Ezekiel's work is clear of all historical and mythopoeic baggage. Although he also writes free verse, the early preference leans towards simple stanzas shaped to a steady rhythm. The syntax aims, *à la* Pound, at sustaining the virtues of good prose. Rhetoric is eschewed. Emotional indulgence is avoided. A tonal register and a standard of commitment were thus laid down—personal, modest, self-deprecatory, ironic, urban, sceptical—for subsequent poets to emulate or heed.

Born into a family of Bene Israeli descent in 1924, Ezekiel grew up in Bombay speaking mainly English and some Marathi. In 'Background, Casually' Ezekiel projects a personality whose timorous distaste at the rough and crude aspects of his environment changes, under pressure of circumstance, to a self-possession that can cut. In 1948, Ezekiel went bohemian in London, doing odd jobs, studying philosophy, leading a life of poetry and poverty. Three and a half years later, back in Bombay, a varied career ensued, held together by the common thread that most of what he took up—advertising, reviews, art-criticism, writing plays, editorial work on journals, teaching—kept him close to the media and to the print medium. Poster poems, 'found' poems, translations from Marathi, plays, and experiments with 'Very Indian Poems in Indian English' give the later Ezekiel a more gregarious look in contrast to the earnestly introverted young man of the early volumes. Trendy experiments with LSD in the late 1960s and early 1970s reflected a desire for change which had consequences in the looser, more meditative work that engaged spiritual issues from a secular perspective in *Hymns in Darkness* (1976) and *Latter-Day Psalms* (1982). Ezekiel died in 2004.

Ezekiel's career is underpinned by a dogged preoccupation with the pursuit of self-knowledge. The virtues of his work as a whole share in the defects of the parts. The style can be prosy, and prosaic: dry statements are preferred to metaphor or image; imagery doesn't always carry the full weight of feeling; sense overrides emotions; feelings are overshadowed by the need to rationalise. Experience is translated, as it were, into Esperanto. It is the poetry of a reasoning sensibility, abstracting general truths from concrete particulars, struggling with personal misgiving which must be tidied into thoughts before they can be felt as ideas. The poet is often satisfied with an ascetic's relish in laconicism. But what is often tart or sharp is also sometimes only arch, especially in the many poems about sexuality and desire, where the steadfastness of an honest intent is not always enough to keep the confessional from sounding trite, bland, or coy. Ezekiel is master of an enslaving irony in which scepticism punctures humbug; but since such irony is based on a principle of doubt which can extend to self-doubt, it is unable to sponsor anything that is unbridled, untrammelled, or unqualified. Ezekiel's is thus a small flame, unlikely to startle into incandescence, but not easily snuffed out.

Lest we scoff at this as a form of emotional anaemia, it is worth remembering that Ezekiel was medicinal to the history of forms in a way that transcends the desiccation of some of the work. From the 1960s onwards, his poems built on a reliable set of personal strengths:

irony about the self and its many self-evasions; scepticism about the claims people or the world-at-large make for themselves; a desire for the truth which does not succumb to the assuasions of a metaphor or a woman; stamina in the faith that, 'Brought face to face with his own clumsiness', he will grow unwonted strengths; and a search for what is perhaps best described as a loquacious quietude.

Ezekiel is the poet laureate of the ordinary. He seeks to transmute the mundane, in himself and in his surroundings, in such a way as to lead—not to quiescence—but acquiescence. He manages to comprehend ineptitude with humour, and to speak of what is real when it is also unlovely, and inglorious. He is also *the* poet of the Indian city:

Barbaric city sick with slums,
Deprived of seasons, blessed with rains,
Its hawkers, beggars, iron-lunged,
Processions led by frantic drums,
A million purgatorial lanes,
And child-like masses, many-tongued,
Whose wages are in words and crumbs.

('A Morning Walk')

Bombay—its sprawl, squalor, and vitality—becomes a metaphor for the living spaces of urban India to which the poet gives himself in a spirit of resolve. The disengaged outsider makes an insider's declaration of intent:

I have made my commitments now.
This is one: to stay where I am,
As others choose to give themselves
In some remote and backward place.
My backward place is where I am.

('Background, Casually')

Ezekiel's poems in Indian English show him venturing successfully into modes no longer preoccupied with the self, in which he can empathise better with the unsympathetic aspects of his linguistic and cultural milieu. In these poems, *what* is being said is refracted through *how* it is said. The ugly can be taken on its own terms when its self-conceit is treated with derision, while derision is made tolerable when lanced by sympathy. Exaggeration hovers just this side of distortion, imitation never quite slips into full caricature. The humour is benign because the butt of each joke is non-malignant, even if the joke nurses a little malice:

In India also
Gujaraties, Maharashtrians, Hindiwallahs
All brothers—
Though some are having funny habits.
Still, you tolerate me,
I tolerate you,
One day Ram Rajya is surely coming.

You are going?
('Very Indian Poems in Indian English: The Patriot')

What makes these Indian archetypes funny is not merely how they mangle the language, but how they lack self-awareness. What makes them human is the warmth and feeling behind the sentiments they express, which even the disfigured language will not hide. The expressive possibilities exploited in these poems may be limited (in comparison to what poets from Africa or the Caribbean have shown possible in dialect, patois, pidgin, and creole); they may verge on the sentimental; also, they could easily lead to an effect of the ad nauseam. But they also break the stranglehold exercised on poetic style by the notion of a standard language. In them, performance exceeds competence. To have opened this small account with the rag-bag syndicate of the ostensibly substandard forms of linguistic practice, allowing poetry to explore parts of the human structure it had not earlier known it could accommodate or inhabit, is no small part of Ezekiel's contribution to the post-Independence investment in poetry.

For Dom Moraes (1938–2004), the formal poise for which the young Ezekiel had to work hard was always at hand. Preternatural facility, abetted by quick success, spoilt the young poet after the early flush of acclaim: *A Beginning* (1957), published when he was nineteen, was followed by *Poems* (1960), *John Nobody* (1965), and *Beldam &*

Others (1966). England became a kind of home, although his sense of affiliation to its culture was not without discomfort: 'All of you now have homes, Peter, not me' ('For Peter'). Of the young Moraes one might say what William Empson once remarked of an American poet, that one wishes he had more things to say, because he evidently knew how to say them. Moraes had been to all the places one could go to, knew most of the right poets, and seemed to be writing poems that both sides of the Atlantic approved; but the early volumes find no relish in their own accomplishment:

His picture smiled at him: he stared at it.
The style was charming and remote,
Some taste, a manner, and a little wit.

('Landscape Painter')

The poetry everywhere has a sharp eye for the unnerving, the ominous, and the grotesque:

The spraddled turkey waited for the knife.
The scything holly clashed: the pleading peal
Of bells swung Christ back on a horny heel
To clutch the cross like a desired wife.

('Christmas Sonnets')

Rarely does the experience of companionship or love show a calming influence, as in 'A Letter':

The westward haven of the traveller's tale
I have forgotten, making landfall where
Chin in your hand, you sit, and gentle things
Drift on your dream, transparent river where
The swan sleeps with her young under her wings.

After the late 1960s, the Muses appeared to have abandoned Moraes for a while. Meanwhile he continued a busy life, travelling all over the world as correspondent and prolific writer of prose. When poetry returned, seventeen years later, the facility for form, syntax, metre, and rhyme, and the natural propensity for dense textural effects resurfaced, unimpaired. In his note to *Collected Poems 1957–87* (1987), Moraes claims that 'In 1982 something happened to me which I cannot account for. I not only started to write poetry more, but a new style seemed to come to me without my ever trying to master it.' The later work is not mannered, nor is it veiled by a patina of literary affect, and the poetry of travel comes across much more tangibly in *Serendip* (1990). But continuities are not difficult to find. The guilt from the early 'Vivisection', at having killed the unicorn of poetry, recurs in later poems like 'Progressions' and 'Rictus':

> A crablike hand crawled on a file
> As Rictus crouched upon his chair.
> His haggard face hung from its smile.

'Craxton', in which an eerily solicitous manservant is intent on getting an author to write, culminates in 'His huge dry hands' serving the master 'A soupspoon and a bowl of blood'. It belongs to the 1960s, but in style it is of a piece with the poems of the 1980s. For the poet living through the effect of a Rimbaud *manqué*, the resurgence of poetry must have been self-renewing, even if the later work is not self-evidently new. What holds the oeuvre together is a sophisticated texture combined with a passion for paring material down to its essentials. 'Steles' is lapidary: 'The word works. The world doesn't.' A stoic accumulation of 'Winterhoard in dead treebole' is nursed with care, making Moraes an exemplary presence on the poetic scene of his birthplace, Bombay, to which he returned in the 1980s.

From the poets who began publishing in the 1960s, the one who made the deepest impression is Kamala Das (1934–2009). Her poetry spoke with fierce and unsparing honesty about the difficulties of being a woman and a wife in a time and for a culture which had trained women to a long tradition of silence. Born in Malabar, she was educated mainly at home and turned early to poetry, like her mother. She is bilingual and writes fiction in Malayalam. Her books of poems are *Summer in Calcutta* (1965), *The Descendants* (1967), *The Old Playhouse and Other Poems* (1973), and *Collected Poems Vol. 1* (1984). *My Story* (1975) is frank as autobiography, its honesty a compound of the strident and the disingenuous, qualities also found in some of her poems.

Das is gifted with a capacity for the startling image matched by a disconcertingly direct approach to experience:

At 4 a.m. the sea decides to open its windows
And look out with rheumy eyes

('At 4 a.m.')

Her poems struggle to develop a sense of self which is alternatively sustained and thwarted by her own sexuality, defined and disfigured as that is, in its turn, by being trapped in the rut of social institutions. Her poems count the cost suffered by freedom and honesty, in the relation between emotional and sexual needs, in marriage, and outside. A recent poem, 'A Widow's Lament', pins the self in a sharp image:

My man, my sons, forming the axis
while I, wife and mother
insignificant as a fly
climbed the glass panes of their eyes.

Yet it would be a mistake to suppose that she is obsessed with sex and marriage and social roles. What she is intent on is honesty of impulse, and a sense of direction to the flow of her wants and feelings. 'An Introduction' is reasonably accurate as a personal manifesto, notwithstanding, or because of, the disingenuity of some of its assertions:

The language I speak
Becomes mine, its distortions, its queerness
All mine, mine alone. It is half English, half
Indian, funny perhaps, but it is honest,
It is as human as I am human, don't
You see? It voices my joys, my longings, my
Hopes, and it is useful to me as cawing
Is to crows or roaring to the lions . . .

She can speak of the various depredations the human is susceptible to with a poignance which is more stark for being clear-eyed. Her grandmother is remembered in 'Elegy' as

A woman wearied by compromise
Her legs quilted with arthritis
And with only a hard cough
For comfort.

Nani, the pregnant maid who hanged herself in the privy, whose body danced like 'a clumsy puppet' (for the children's delight, as they were told by grandmother), who will later be subject to a 'designed deafness' which erases her existence from grandmother's recollection, provides the occasion for troubled questions:

They are lucky
Who ask questions and move on before
The answers come, those wise ones who reside
In a blue silent zone, unscratched by doubts
For theirs is the clotted peace embedded
In life, like music in the Koel's egg,
Like lust in blood, or like sap in a tree . . .

('Nani')

Das has lived and felt her way through many feminine selves, including

the fat-kneed hag in the long bus queue
The one from whose shopping bag the mean potato must
Roll across the road.

('Gino')

She can be scornful of male desire, as for 'The Latest Toy', which asks that the woman not speak with

A voice, softened as though with tears. He said then, his
Dark brow wrinkling, oh please don't become emotional,
Emotion is the only true enemy of joy.

And there is that side to the poetry which appears to flaunt a flamboyant lust:

Gift him all,
Gift him what makes you woman, the scent of
Long hair, the musk of sweat between the breasts,
The warm shock of menstrual blood, and all your
Endless female hungers.

('The Looking-glass')

Other poems, like the long, thoughtful 'Composition', show her tired at having to 'extrude/autobiography', accepting growth (and not death) as life's tragedy, walking towards the freedom to 'discompose', and preferring tenderness to love, as 'The Old Playhouse' says, 'For love is Narcissus at the water's edge, haunted / By its own lonely face.' Her 'Advice to Fellow-swimmers' is—

do not enter a river that has no ocean
to flow into, one ignorant of destinations
and knowing only the flowing as its destiny . . .

Her poetry may be narrow in focus, careless of decorum, unremitting in its intensity, reckless in its emotional abandon, lacking in irony. But there is no voice more direct in Indian poetry in English. It shatters more careful virtues into debris, offering simply the vulnerability of its own candour. Her iconoclasm has led to her work being misread as sensationalist, just as it has lent itself to the cause of feminism. The confessional aspect of her work has made her seem like an Indian Sylvia Plath. But Das is driven less towards suicide than love, and in its wake all mishaps and misunderstandings are ultimately accepted without regrets.

There have been a number of would-be Modernists on the scene of Indian poetry in English whose work illustrates the uncertain rewards of the experimental and the modish approaches. Shiv K. Kumar (b. 1921), for instance, turns cultural disjunctions between East and West, or within his own life, over the slow spit of his own sardonicism, in a sophisticated but knowing confessional cuisine which can exercise as much appeal as it evinces disrelish:

But the brown of my skin defies
all bleachers.
How long will this eclipse last?

('Days in New York')

The prolific Pritish Nandy (b. 1947), whose output made a certain reputation at about the time Das established herself, has not worn well. He began his career in 1967, with four more volumes following in the 1960s and fourteen in the 1970s. Despite avowed Modernist inclinations, what might once have seemed novel comes across today as overwritten. Poems such as 'Near Deshapriya Park they found him at last' seem animated by a journalese notion of poetry. The rhetoric of protest in 'Calcutta If You Must Exile Me' wears too anguished a heart on its sleeve, lacking the resources discovered by other poets addressing other cities (such as Dilip Chitre: Bombay; and Agha Shahid Ali: Delhi). For many like Nandy, a fertile but unfocused fluency has been the poet's undoing.

Arun Kolatkar and Arvind Krishna Mehrotra are the true Modernists of Indian poetry in English. Both are lean, dry, and spare in outlook, especially Kolatkar. Stray poems appeared from him in magazines and anthologies since 1955; they still remain uncollected. His publications in English include the award-winning *Jejuri* (1976). The same year a collection of his Marathi poems also appeared. Kolatkar has been much admired by fellow poets, who have nursed his work enthusiastically into print. Born in Kolhapur in 1932, he studied art in several places in Maharashtra and has since worked as a graphic artist in Bombay. He translates or adapts his own Marathi poems into English (and sometimes the other way round), and his professional interest in art refracts in either language. A reader familiar with Marathi and English can best appreciate the economy of exchange that flourishes in this two-way process of creation. Kolatkar died in 2004.

Jejuri follows a loose narrative sequence enacting a trip to the pilgrimage shrine of Khandoba, situated in a rugged and barren region near Poona. First, in 'The Bus',

Your own divided face in a pair of glasses
on an old man's nose
is all the countryside you get to see.

You seem to move continually forward
towards a destination
just beyond the caste-mark between his eyebrows.

The destination needs a believer, here you get its reverse image. Meanwhile, the priest, whose livelihood depends on the pilgrims' faith in the phallic shrine of Shiva, waits:

Is the bus a little late?
. . . .
With a quick intake of testicles
at the touch of the rough cut, dew drenched stone
he turns his head in the sun
. . . .
The bit of betel nut
turning over and over on his tongue
is a mantra.

('The Priest')

The shrine is the 'Heart of Ruin'. Kolatkar's noncommittal insouciance notes with whimsical accuracy every visual detail to be encountered in a slow amble in and around the shrine, while carefully maintaining a blind spot for the dereliction of faith at the exact centre of what he will not look at directly. Indirection, however, is not evasion. Wallace Stevens has said, in 'The Course of a Particular', that the poet should see nothing that is not there, and the nothing that is. The gods and the faith that are no longer there do not interest Kolatkar; the nothing that now abides does, and to its minutiae he attends with sardonic wit, as if verbal panache were sufficient to elide all bitterness, even if it left the mouth dry, and lips grinning in a grimace. Stevens has described the condition of modernity as that of a need for belief, in which one chooses to believe in a fiction, knowing that there is nothing else to believe in. Kolatkar's poem is like a screen so fascinating in its effects that it disguises almost adequately that which is screened off, an absence.

The roof has come down on the head of the monkey-god Maruti (who once held aloft a mountain); a conduit pipe which should bring water ends like 'a brass mouse with a broken neck'; the main door hangs like 'A dangling martyr'; stone, painted red and dressed in flowers, sits still as stone, dissembling gods and linking the dissemblance; when the gods (whether eight- or eighteen-armed) sit in such darkness, even cowsheds can be mistaken for shrines; the marks made on statues and hill-side could be human or divine; and when a beggar accosts the casual pilgrim, her eyes are like bullet holes, and that is where the cracks begin:

> And the hills crack.
> And the temples crack.
> And the sky falls
> . . . .
> And you are reduced
> to so much small change
> in her hand.
>
> ('An Old Woman')

The mythopoeic imagination which made gods out of grape-seed and demons out of rock is acknowledged, but the poet is more interested in a passing butterfly, 'Just a pinch of yellow' with 'no story behind it'. God is a bad harvest of rock for the barren region (which made such gods, which made such a barren region). Where the reservoirs house 'a hundred years of silt', all one can do is pile stone carefully upon stone. God is a name which can be played back in reverse.

> I know it as fangs
> inside my flanks.
>
> ('A Song for a Vaghya')

Whoever wishes may go ahead and worship inside at the shrine, the poet prefers to have a smoke in the courtyard, while temple-priest and temple-rat live out their complicitous routine inside, and the animal emblems of bull-calf and tortoise sit frozen in stone outside. A whole litany of gods is rejected:

And although I'm sure they're to be praised,
they're either too symmetrical
or too theatrical for my taste.

('Yeshwant Rao')

The herd of legends has returned to its grazing. The only acceptable god-who-will-do is apt to our diminution:

as he himself has no heads, hands, and feet,
he happens to understand you a little better.

('Yeshwant Rao')

The spirit of the place more truly 'lives inside the mangy body / of the station dog'. The poet has difficulty leaving. The station-master

. . . keeps looking anxiously at the setting sun
as if the sunset were a part of a secret ritual
and he didn't want anything to go wrong with it

('The Railway Station')

But something has gone wrong with all the secret rituals. Only the sunset, at its appointed time, comes true as a prophecy.

Jejuri is an extraordinary poem, original in how funny sad can be. Perhaps it is best read as a glass-poem: what you think you see through the glass is the place, what you really see is your own reflection trying to look through. Sylvia Plath tried to imagine two mirrors looking at each other. What do they see?

Dilip Chitre (1938–2009), like his friend Kolatkar, writes poems in Marathi and English. Born in Baroda, educated there and in Bombay, he taught briefly in Ethiopia, and has since been active from Bombay and, for the past fifteen years, Poona, as critic, anthologist, film-maker, painter, and reviewer. His poems in English were published in *Ambulance Ride* (1972) and *Travelling in a Cage* (1991). Chitre has often declared eclecticism an asset for the contemporary Indian poet. 'Ambulance

Ride' has mimetic vigour. Like some of his American models, the anecdotal-confessional approach of *Travelling in a Cage* makes a hopeful start of inverted narcissism:

By now my pubic hair
Was already greying. And I could see the dirty
Old man under my skin. It was not the
Absolute end but the beginning of it.

('Travelling in a Cage 2')

The poet experiments with the *naïf* approach:

I opened the faucets and watched the rushing miracle
Wondered what water really was and why it had to be wet

('Travelling in a Cage 8')

But unbuttoned excitability is not always easy to bring off:

In the cunt of the unknown
I explode without coming
Pitching and tossing

('Travelling in a Cage 12')

When *Travelling in a Cage* does come alive, it can almost make one forget the hit-or-miss, the flash-in-the-pan aspect of the achievement:

In my memory you are a treatise on light
Written in braille

('Travelling in a Cage 6')

Even blindness has holes one can see through.

('The Painter')

Arvind Krishna Mehrotra was born in Lahore in 1947, and has followed an academic career, largely in Allahabad, where, in his teens, he edited *damn you / a magazine of the arts* (1965–8). In 1966 he founded the Ezra-Fakir Press in Bombay, which published his first experimental work, *Bharatmata: A Prayer* (1966). This was followed by *Woodcuts on Paper* (1967), *Pomes / Poemes / Poemas* (1971), *Nine Enclosures* (1976), *Distance in Statute Miles* (1982), *Middle Earth* (1984), which is a selection from the preceding two volumes along with some later work, and *The Transfiguring Places* (1998). *The Oxford India Anthology of Twelve Modern Indian Poets* (1992) presents a lively account of his canon for Indian poetry in English.

Mehrotra's early work is strident in its enthusiasm for an aggressive modernity; from the 1970s onwards he develops a new style and a more convincing tone. His mature work is disarmingly slight in manner, casual in its resourcefulness; its sophisticated obliquity equally capable of the deceptive and the delightful, like the discovery of watercolour when you had given up oils as dark and heavy:

> Reconsider, first, the oblong of light
> Already there when you open
> The door to a high-ceilinged room;
> Then, halfway up the wall, the alcove
> Filled with painted clay toys;
> Above it, in the skylight, a white
> Moistureless cloud. Yes, the replenished hour
> Illuminates the house; light heals the day.
>
> ('October')

The Indira Gandhi Emergency (1975–7) cannot have received a more droll requiem than 'House by the Mill':

> A woman addresses the nation.
> What big ears she
> Has. The fabulous Red Riding-Hoods
> In gladed wood
> Burn flare-ups, but freedom's too prudent
> To risk its skin.
> O house by the mill we're trapped in.

Accuracy of description is disposed and disarrayed by a subtly restrained wit. Associative free play dissolves the distinction between imagination and a free-floating fancy. The results can touch the reader with a realisation of the unexpectedly true. In 'Engraving of a Bison on Stone', the nondescript land we walk and live on is described in a series of simple declarative sentences:

> The land
> Cannot sign its name, it cannot die
> Because it cannot be buried,
> It understands the language,
> It speaks in dialect

This is the art of an engaging stylist who practices a surreal minimalism, capable of suggesting far beyond what is stated. The risk taken in such practice is that when the unpredictable magic of fortuity deserts the poem, cleverness seems contrived and randomness prevails. When the method works, reading a poem is like walking into a room clear of attitudes and preconceptions, too well-aired and spare even for irony, in which, in the clear light of an abstracted day, the oddest medley of objects, persons, non-events, memories, and fantasies is hospitable to a whole series of odd and inadvertently felicitous collocations:

> Together with Shaporjee,
> The tallow-white Parsi next door, and Roger Dutt,
> The school's aromatic geography teacher, he goes up
> In a hot-air balloon and, on the leeward
> Side of a Stanley Gibbons catalogue, comes down
> Near a turret in Helvetia or Magyar,
> Stamp-sized snowflake-like countries
> Whose names dissolve like jujubes on my tongue.
>
> ('The Roys')

The kind of idiom many contemporary poets in India have come to prefer—sceptic, ironic, rationalist—comes more naturally to an English-speaking West-oriented urbanite, unimpressed by the spiritualism, superstition, mythopoeism, and agrarianism that characterises much of India. It is in this context that the contribution made to

Indian poetry by so many individuals who happen to be Parsi (at least by birth) becomes significant in setting, for contemporary poetry, the tone that Daruwalla (himself a Parsi, though not from Bombay) demanded in the introduction to his 1980 anthology: 'What Indian poetry needed was . . . a modern sensibility in confronting the confusion, bewilderment and disillusion of the times.'

Daruwalla's own work looks long and hard for alternatives to the constrictions of his age and times. The experience he has acquired in a long professional career as a senior police officer, reinforced by a robust temperament, gives his poems a wide access both to the turbulence, and to the stiller pulse that is the life of India in the metropolis, the provinces, and the hinterland. Born in Lahore in 1937, Daruwalla obtained a degree in English before joining the Indian Police Service. Apart from writing short stories and editing a trenchant anthology of poetry, he has published *Under Orion* (1970), *Apparition in April* (1971), *Crossing of Rivers* (1976), *Winter Poems* (1980), *The Keeper of the Dead* (1982), *Landscapes* (1987), and *A Summer of Tigers* (1995).

Daruwalla is candid without being disingenuous when he declares that 'There is little that is urbane or sophisticated about my poetry. I avoid a well-groomed appearance and strive for a sort of earthy poetry . . . I tend to make my verse as condensed and harsh as possible . . . Significant incidents I turn into what I call "incident-poems". However, I try and involve myself with attitudes to things rather than the incident itself.' The force with which a poem provides him reasons for arriving at an attitude is what makes Daruwalla's practice distinctive. A wide spectrum of the variety of contemporary India is subjected to a sharp, unsentimental scrutiny. Many poems dramatise incidents as if reported by an angry, concerned journalist, which, in a sense, they are. Forthright, and impatient with cant, a Daruwalla poem is not content merely to note and observe; it acts like an exhortation to action, even if the action is an act of the mind. *Winter Poems* bears an epigraph from Wallace Stevens which is apposite to Daruwalla's perception of his place and its time:

It is equal to living in a tragic land
To live in a tragic time.

For the unbelieving Daruwalla, while the Parsi carries his hell with him, traditional Hindu pieties can be readily upturned by the experience of a 'Boat-ride along the Ganga':

> And while the *pandas* calculate
> the amount of merit that accrues to you
> at each specific ghat you cross the pyres
>
> bowing your head to the finality of fate.
> Behind the heat-haze rising from the fires,
> objects shimmer, dance, levitate.
> You face reality on a different plane
> where death vibrates behind a veil of fire.
> . . . .
> When we disembark, the waterfront ahead
> is smothered by night, redpeppered with fires
> as *doms* and *mallahs* cook their unleavened bread.
>
> Dante would have been confused here.
> Where would he place this city?
> In Paradise or Purgatory, or lower down
> where fires smoulder beyond the reach of pity?

Of the unbelieving, anti-parochial, castigating, raw, and masculine aspects of Daruwalla, Ezekiel wrote in 1972 that 'He has a desperately independent air, as if he was born fully-grown from the head of some hitherto unrecognised goddess of poetry.' Over the decades, Daruwalla has taught himself to practice control, and to widen his range, most notably in personal poems like 'To My Daughter Rookzain', and in his many dramatic monologues based on historical figures. One such impressively cadenced utterance is 'The King Speaks to the Scribe', in which Ashoka meditates on atonement after slaughter, enslavement, severed relationships, and the ashen taste of pride, with a simple dignity which asks that the scribe engrave with care the lessons learned from the terrible carnage:

> Your words will have to reach across to them
> like a tide of black oxen crossing a ford.

More recent poems, such as 'The Poseidonians' and 'Daeiros', show him grow confidently into the strengths of this reflective manner, with a measured style which traverses a wide range of historical experience with insight.

Another poet with a sceptically questioning sensibility, and a Parsi background, is Gieve Patel (b. 1940), who has lived all his life in Bombay, where he works as a general practitioner. As a painter, he has held several one-man shows in Bombay and Delhi. Apart from *Poems* (1966), *How Do You Withstand, Body* (1976), and *Mirrored, Mirroring* (1991), he has written three plays centred on Parsi life and themes. Patel speaks with a quiet but distinctive voice, ranging across a scale from detached but sharp observation, through tolerant scepticism, to occasional but controlled vehemence. His poems are generally lean of shape, and spare of movement and gesture. They are characterised by quick, unexpected figurative turns, and complex attitudes. His steady-eyed appraisal confronts the disorienting aspects of experience on a middle ground between evasion and involvement. In learning to acknowledge an honest ambivalence, his poems abjure all facile resolutions:

I am friendly, I smile, I am
No snob. Lepers don't disgust me. But also
Tough resistance: I have no money. . .

('Nargol')

To give in to the leper-woman's importunity would be a form of entrapment in the guilt she banks on. But not to give her money is another kind of giving in. As the poet walks away, insouciance is shrugged aside in sober recognition:

I have lost to a power too careless
And sprawling to admit battle,
And meanness no defence.
Walking to the sea I carry
A village, a city, the country,
For the moment
On my back.

In his second volume, many poems still adopt the viewpoint of an onlooker, but a new rhetoric and passion emerge in the engagements forced upon contemplation by the violence of contemporary India. In 'The Ambiguous Fate of Gieve Patel, He being neither Muslim nor Hindu in India', the communalism which has bedevilled an ostensibly secular state is placed in laconic perspective with a neat energy which does not sacrifice any of its balance: 'To be no part of this hate is deprivation.' Patel is good at the non-encounter narrated with wry, sour relish:

The sexual odour of rejected women overpowers me.
I am called grotesquely to account
For ecstasies they may have missed.
I am a chameleon about to swallow a nauseous butterfly.
Look, I'm turning green.

('Just Stretch Your Neck')

His third volume represents an interesting extension of earlier preferences. The free verse relaxes into longer lines, extending its range to expansive anecdotes casually recounted, as if by a voice overheard. Where the poet had once questioned the need for a God, preferring 'to pare / My fingernails and weep profoundly / Before the crescents' ('To Make a Contract'), the need is now acknowledged, in a typically questioning way:

Honest cloud
Concealing nothing but the body of God,
Restore my lost assurance! . . .

. . . .

What's in store now for numskull touch?
What for simpleton sound?

('Simpleton')

The poetry 'Cannot believe there could be / Living without quarry or burden', but everywhere regards the spectacle with an irony leavened by compassion, in a lively watchfulness which is both sober and salutary.

Despite a reflective vein, K.D. Katrak (1938–2007) has not met a wide response, and his thoughtful poems have been in and out of the poets' anthologies. In comparison, Adil Jussawalla (b. 1940) has fared better, in spite of a meagre corpus, confined to two volumes. Educated in Bombay and at Oxford, he lived in England for thirteen years before returning to Bombay in 1970. He has published *Land's End* (1962) and *Missing Person* (1976), and is influential as a critic, reviewer, columnist, and editor. His poems show a sophisticated auditory imagination, and versatile stylistic resources. The title poem of his first volume, published when he was twenty-two, is a *tour de force* of tactile wordplay:

> Atlantic breakers boom, the sea-gulls fall
> Downwind to sheets of spray, the fast
> Seas roll, slump and shower
> Across the thrusted coastland . . .

'Nine Poems on Arrival', in *Missing Person*, show more than mere versatility—the wariness and anxiety of the returned expatriate:

> Contact. We talk a language of beads
> along well-established wires.
> The beads slide, they open, they
> devour each other.
>
> . . . .
>
> Dry clods of earth
> tighten their tiny faces
> in an effort to cry. Back
> where I was born,
> I may yet observe my own birth.

Beyond issues of sophistication, Jussawalla's poetry is preoccupied with the problem of defining for the existential self an identity that will surface when the formative agents of his personal histories and cultural locations (multiple and conflicting) contrive against the enterprise. In 'Missing Person', where these issues come to the fore, 'Exile's a broken axle'. To set the wheel of the self in motion, even if downhill, the poet deploys a whole battery of Modernist and post-Modernist techniques, including cinematic montage, complex puns and allusions, and abrupt switches within a polyphonic repertoire of styles drawn from an impressive range of sources. There is much to admire in how Jussawalla's poetry dramatises, but in terms of what it enacts there is also a lot to worry about (in both senses). The anger is modish, the end-result is a sincere, stylised despair:

> He travels the way of devotion
> but no sky lights
> his street.
>
> A river of pills brings him no raft.
> Death goes awash with wishing.
>
> Cripples his own mouth then, sits
> killing his tongue, sits
> barred up behind his teeth.
>
> Bright sparks
> on the international back-slapping circuit
> are picking up prizes like static.
> He's for the dark.
>
> ('Scenes from the Life 9')

Wallace Stevens, in 'Six Significant Sketches', speaks of how he dislikes the way an ant crawls in and out of his shadow. Many Indian poets like Jussawalla have found English (and Western) cultural traditions fall like the shadow of a structure which the ant of their poetry has struggled to cross. In a 1978 interview, Jussawalla said that 'to completely smash this structure . . . you go through a process of terrible disintegration'; in 1987, in 'Being There: Aspects of a Crisis', he reassured himself that 'while "Missing Person" is about such a disintegration, my own personal disintegration has neither been very fundamental nor terrible.' But if he (and others like him) might apply Stevens's figure as a fable to their predicament, no ant need fear disintegration at the hand or foot of what is only a shadow, especially when it has been willingly sought as umbrage.

Jayanta Mahapatra and R. Parthasarathy are poets whose sensibilities are exceptionally responsive to the interactions between consciousness and silence. Both made their mark in the 1970s. Of the two, Mahapatra is more ready to relinquish the certainties of the self to disembodiment, more enamoured of silence than he is prodigal of metaphor. Born into a middle-class Christian family in Cuttack in 1928, he grew up in a small-town atmosphere. Trained in physics, he lectured in a local college for all his professional life, while turning increasingly to poetry after the late 1960s. Mahapatra thus came late, and intuitively, to poetry; the elective affinities he recognises are with European and Latin American, rather than English or American poets. From 1968 he began publishing in journals all over the English-speaking world, especially the United States, and since then his prolific output has achieved widespread recognition. His books of poems are *Close the Sky, Ten by Ten* (1971), *Svayamvara and Other Poems* (1971), *A Rain of Rites* (1976), *A Father's Hours* (1976), *Waiting* (1979), *The False Start* (1980), *Life Signs* (1983), *Dispossessed Nests: The 1984 Poems* (1986), *Selected Poems* (1987), and *Burden of Waves and Fruit* (1988). *Relationship* (1980) and *Temple* (1989) are two ambitious long poems. He has also translated poetry from Oriya, written stories for children, and edited the journal *Chandrabhaga* (1979–85), recently revived.

If the chief strength of Mahapatra's poetry is the spontaneous fertility of his metaphors, not to have the desire or the mechanism to control their profligacy but to willingly submit to their inclinations is also the principal reason why what is memorable in a Mahapatra poem is as often the individual line, image, or group of lines, as a unified totality of poetic experience. He is predisposed to blurring all manner of boundaries, so that experience is encountered by the reader through the poet's consciousness, as across a low threshold permissive to all that it can register. The syntax remains adequate without being distinctive, as also the free verse he prefers.

Mahapatra's poetic world is distinguished for the unyielding privacy of a resilient but amorphous inwardness. A solitary and introverted temperament broods on

> the gleaming skin of three kingdoms,
> the mineral, vegetable and animal . . .
>
> (*Relationship*, Eight)

He is particularly responsive to fugitive nuances of feeling and evanescent shades of thought; ascribing through a welter of metaphor, a fresh being to every person, object, or phenomenon with which he empathises, dissolving the phenomenal relation between the subject and the object of experience. In 'Rains in Orissa', 'Something like moss wells up in the day's green eyes'. In 'Summer's End':

> The notes on an unseen bird
> drip from my eyes, like dry tears.
> A pariah dog howls at the front gate,
> the instant turns away
> like a practised whore
> from one who loves her.

Memory and desire, sensory experience and symbolic resonance merge seamlessly in a poetry which engages the Indian scene from the specificity of an agrarian-feudal Orissa moving haltingly towards the various forms of modernisation brought about by time and political necessity. The world let in by the poetry retains, in all its varied flora and fauna—temples, ruins, fishermen, daughters, whores, beggars, priests, politicians, and vultures; the susurrus of its rain, the swelter of its summer heat, the breathing of its pyres, and the soughing of its wind—the lineaments of a lived reality as well as a felt historical and mythic past. Each phenomenal inhabitant of this dual existence is allowed its fullest measure of twilight-like in-betweenness. The outer world merges with an inner world of familial presences and memories. The two interact in osmosis as if through a permeable membrane, feeding the energies of one into the other, amplifying or neutralising resonance through incessant conjunctions between outer and inner, making the unconceived appear inevitable through the fortuities of metaphor. 'Grandfather', who 'starving, on the point of death . . . embraced Christianity . . . in 1866', is asked:

> Did you hear the young tamarind leaves rustle
> in the cold mean nights of your belly?

In 'Life Signs', talking of his father,

> In his eyes,

dirty and heavy as rainwater
flowing into earth, is the ridicule

my indifference quietly left behind . . .

Mahapatra, like Daruwalla, is able, without strain or conscious effort, to accommodate a very wide range of experiences into his imaginative world. He comes to these experiences with very little by way of a settled position, or even the desire to arrive at a settled position (in this he differs from Daruwalla, who is more purposive): 'one must try somehow to reach the border between things understandable and ununderstandable in a poem, between life and death, between a straight line and a circle', he says. It is only in the two long poems that his ambition strains at tackling problems of coherence and continuity, although it is to his credit that he has essayed long poems at all; most post-Independence poets confine themselves to the shorter poem or the sequence. In *Relationship*, he is determined to circumvent time by laying siege to myth and history; in *Temple*, he is bent on dissolving the self in a plurality of feminine experience, from puberty and rape, to love, companionship, old age, and beyond death, into the mythic.

If silence, for Jayanta Mahapatra, has been like a threshold which he recrosses every time a poem shuttles a weave of myth, history, memory, and dream across the abyss separating consciousness from the many shades of nothingness, for Parthasarathy silence is like a door with double hinges, and one that can jam. Apart from some early work collected in *The First Steps, Poems 1956–66* (1967), Parthasarathy is the author of a single, slim, periodically revised work, *Rough Passage* (1977, 1980). Born near Tiruchirapally in 1934, he was educated in Bombay and in England. He followed a career in publishing and is currently an academic. The composition of *Rough Passage* was spread over more than two decades and individual poems have been published separately, but a common style and a sensitive use of free verse arranged in triads hold the sequence together in three sections, progressing from the theme of 'Exile' through 'Trial' to 'Homecoming'. The first and the last themes link naturally enough, while the middle section accommodates poems of love, sexuality, and desire ('my limp tongue thickens in your furrow'), leaving one wondering whose trial this might be.

Rough Passage begins by shedding an attachment to an England of the mind: in school, 'spoonfuls of English / brew never quite slaked your thirst' ('Trial 2'). This is later shrivelled by the poet's experience of the real place:

> lanes full of smoke and litter,
> with puddles of unwashed
> English children.
> . . . .
> Standing on Westminster Bridge,
> it seemed the Thames had clogged
> the chariot wheels of Boadicea to a stone.
>
> ('Exile 2')

Parthasarathy has been obsessed by guilt at the deculturation entailed for him in the use of English; he has argued that the only viable alternative to the disenchantment of 'whoring after English gods' is to Indianise or colonise English. In trying to accomplish this, the sequence struggles to avoid a triple bind: to be obliged into a precious or a sullen silence if the language proves recalcitrant to the experience; to find the experience either lost or degraded in having to adapt to the possibilities of the language rather than having the language adapt to the needs of the experience, 'my tongue hunchbacked / with words'; to realise that experience and language relate (or do not relate) without always lending themselves to politicisation on a nationalist or a nativist front. If one *can* write in a language, to declare oneself *enchained* to that language can appear wilful and self-stultifying. To claim to be at the end of one's 'dravidic tether' requires either that one shed the dravidism or that one write at its sole behest. But Parthasarathy is not satisfied with Tamil, and in embracing his corner of the world, he tells himself:

> I have exchanged the world
> for a table and chair. I shouldn't complain.
>
> ('Homecoming 10')

But complain he does. The sequence ends on a self-diminishing note, leaving itself little choice beyond 'the small change of uncertainties' ('Homecoming 14'). Since 1980, Parthasarathy has practised silence more than poetry. The sequence and his career demonstrate the price paid, as well as the value of the commerce transacted, when a poet confronts his post-coloniality with this kind of honest and riddling ambivalence.

Women writing poetry after Kamala Das have had to learn to walk in terrain which, even if adjacent, must be mapped using a wider focus, and greater sophistication. Within her shadow, it has proved difficult to come up with anything really new, as the work of Gauri Deshpande, and several other women poets, illustrates. Deflationary irony and tongue-in-cheek understatement make a clearer impression, as in Charmayne D'Souza's *A Spelling Guide to Woman* (1990):

> Today,
> I was God.
> I let a human
> exercise his free will
> and say NO to me.
> ('God For a Day')

How an antithetical style might achieve results is best exemplified in the very different approaches of Eunice de Souza and Imtiaz Dharker. Eunice de Souza was born in 1940 into the Goan Christian community. The Goans are 'individuals', as Mehrotra remarks in his anthology, 'whose English keeps the flavour of natural idiom without sounding picturesque or "babu".' This the poet captures with uncanny accuracy. She was educated in Bombay and in the United States, and after a brief stint of teaching in England she has lived in Bombay, active as a critic and academic, publishing *Fix* (1979), *Women in Dutch Painting* (1988), *Ways of Belonging: New and Selected Poems* (1990), and *Selected and New Poems* (1994). She has also edited *Nine Indian*

Women Poets (1997). Her tone has the precision of the miniaturist, etching the unsentimentally elegiac in lines of wry sharpness. The manner at its truest rings clear as struck glass, at other times it is brittle and jagged, and can cut many ways, not least the poet. She brings economy and understatement to a practice as unsparingly honest as that of Das, and even less inclined to lie on a quilt of soft options, or use the pelt of kind thoughts for comfort. A poem beginning with 'Forgive me, mother', ends

> In dreams
> I hack you.

'Advice to Women' suggests that women might learn to cope with 'the otherness of lovers' by keeping cats, because:

> That stare of perpetual surprise
> in those great green eyes
> will teach you
> to die alone.

However, all is not woman *agonistes*. 'Women in Dutch Painting' assures us that she knows women who 'are calm, not stupid', 'and not just in painting', like Anna, whose 'voice is oatmeal and honey'.

The poetry of Imtiaz Dharker (b. 1954) develops a more elaborate rendition of those aspects of the feminine which bespeak a divisive and an embattled predicament, for which the veil, and the borderline dividing two zones, become the dominant metaphors in her first volume, *Purdah* (1989). Born in Lahore, she was raised in Britain and lives in Bombay, where she scripts and directs audiovisuals and has edited poetry for *Debonair*. In *Purdah*, Dharker offers deeply felt evocations of the experience of growing up as a woman in an Islamic society. 'Purdah II' elaborates on how the symbolic veil divides and suppresses:

They veiled their eyes
with heavy lids.
They hid their breasts,
but not the fullness of their lips.

. . . .

But woman. Woman,
you have learnt
that when God comes
you hide your head.

In 'The Child Sings',

She is nothing, but a crack
where the light forgot to shine.

'A Woman's Place' rehearses the cathechism that a woman should stifle screams as well as smiles, for

No one must see your serenity cracked
even with delight.

In this condition, for a woman to write is to 'scratch at paper, hoping to draw blood'. In love too there are dividing lines, and these constitute a domestic 'Battle-line' behind which 'distrustful lovers' retreat, only to find 'barbed wire sinking in'. In 'No-man's Land', 'We are countries out of reach':

It is the women who know
you can take in
the invader, time after time,
and still be whole.

Lines of one kind or another dominate the visual field of her work, dividing, enclosing, cutting into separate pieces what could be whole. Dharker is a graphic artist, and has exhibited in India and overseas. Her most recent volume, *Postcards from God* (1994), juxtaposes poems with drawings of two types: first, finely-pencilled faces in close-up, drawn as studies in ramshackle ordinariness, just this side of the grotesque, often with superimposed reticulations, as of bars or grilles;

and second, views, either of old buildings, or their interiors, or views glimpsed out of their windows, again with superimposed grids, like bars. The symbiotic relation between poetry and graphic art is mutually enhancing, as when a basket of eggs dangling from crooked supports is imaged as

fragile curves of white
hung out over the dark edge
of a slanted universe,
gathering the light
into themselves,
as if they were
the bright, thin walls of faith.

('Living Space')

In contrast to the personal quality of the first volume, the early parts of the second draw back a little from their materials, as if to make abstract elbow-room. Towards the end, as poetry re-engages with the grit of contemporary Bombay, the distance is again closed-up. A visual mode, as of a moving camera, controls the eye

rippled with power, pricked with light.
These are the images I will send you.

('Postcards from God II')

Of the poets who begin publishing in the 1980s, the most interesting are Manohar Shetty and Vikram Seth. Shetty was born in Bombay in 1953, and worked in a variety of jobs before settling down in Goa. Apart from stories, he has published *A Guarded Space* (1981), *Borrowed Time* (1988), and *Domestic Creatures* (1994). Shetty, like Seth, discloses formal incantations, but these are expressed in a more guarded manner, in poems whose movement of thought is not readily retrieved from the surface rhythm of the verse, but insinuates itself, like an undertone you have to listen for, before it is heard. The strange scope of his poetic world is defined by containment, and that which escapes containment, by the surreal within the real, and by the amenability of the repulsive. His domestic creatures are lizard, pigeon, spider, and cockroach. He has a connoisseur's eye for the disquieting, which he nurses as one might collect familiars or shells: 'The trapped blank lights' of 'Fireflies' in grass-cram-med bottles; the dregs of ants, 'rust / coloured pinheads', in 'Morning Tea'; and 'Bats' like hung umbrellas, wrapped shut like catatonics or giant bow-ties. Being bewildered, or unhinged, or dazed, or numb with torpor, occurs naturally in his poetry. To inhabit this dark wonderland is to be 'In a Strange Place', a tangled wilderness painted by a Dada-like lunatic with green fingers, 'flowers drooling / And shaking their heads'. In 'Jackfruit',

> Who would have imagined a blister
> to bloat in this ripening heat
> to this pendulous
> softness and hardness.

'Foreshadows' conjures up bored crocodiles, purring wildcats, giant butterflies, and shrill birds; the poem ends with the poet's mouth exposing 'hungry tusks'. Another poem provides a kind of double paralysis in the form of a dramatic monologue from a 'Mannequin', whose wish, that she might be like a mirror in which the creased selves she sees passing around 'this rich ring of light' could be smoothed into self-possession, comes unstuck at the realisation that

> I cannot go beyond
> This fixed fond smile.

It is quite a sea-change from Shetty's world of dark corners to Vikram Seth's energetic and cheerful kitsch. Seth was born in Calcutta in 1952, and educated in Dehra Dun, and at Oxford and Stanford universities. Apart from *Mappings* (1981), *The Humble Administrator's Garden* (1985), *The Golden Gate* (1986), *All You Who Sleep Tonight* (1990), and *Beastly Tales from Here and There* (1991), he has written an award-winning travel-book, *From Heaven Lake* (1983), the enormous novel *A Suitable Boy* (1993), the libretto for an opera, *Arion and the Dolphin* (1994), and a novel set in the world of Western classical string instruments titled *An Equal Music* (1999). The wide success of his narratives makes Seth the most well known among contemporary Indian authors.

Seth's metrical propensities make for a change from the general preference for free verse among Indian poets writing in English. In the event, his facility turns out to be a mixed blessing: the reader can be swept on a flood mixing doggerel, parody, banality, romanticism, and sentimentality with much else that is fascinating. Seth is a gifted *pasticheur* of styles. He can be neat:

> In wreathes of ache and strain
> The bent rheumatic potter
> Constructs his forms with pain.
>
> ('Profiting')

He can be painterly:

> Wistaria twigs, wistaria leaves, mauve petals
> Drift past a goldfish ripple. As it settles
> Another flower drops. Below, redly,
> The fish meander through the wistaria tree.
>
> ('A Hangzou Garden')

Or sharp:

> The plaster statue of a man in red
> With pudgy vehemence and rolled-up sleeves
> Proclaims the oppressive heritage is dead.
> Inside the hall six workmen renovate
> The verveless splendour of a corpse of state.
>
> ('The Great Confucian Temple, Suzhou')

His poetic styles are a curious mix of the modern and the Victorian. His forté is light verse, and his true métier is Victorian narrative. To have restored the drive of narrative to verse is Seth's principal contribution to poetry. *The Golden Gate* incorporates the quirks and turns of a contemporary conversational idiom into tetrameters of Hudibrastic brio and a Byronic or Audenesque bravado:

Now Bjorn the Swedish runner's leering
At Rose with cold, appraising lust.
She shudders and adjusts an earring.
With reassuring spite and trust
The Van Camps battle on, unthinking:
'No, darling, I have *not* been drinking.
Thanks for the sweet thought, anyway.'
'It's nothing, darling. Any day!'
While, bowed down with the gray futility
Of his dank thesis, Kim Tarvesh
Ogles convexities of flesh
And maximizes his utility
By drowning in his chilled Chablis
His economics Ph.D.

(4.12)

Seth's verse is always readable; even if the pleasure does not always find room in which to deepen into reflection, when bustled by rhyme and metre from charming, to cute, to rollicking, to droll, to quaint effects with such deftness.

Fifty years after Independence, with individuals as variedly gifted as those we have surveyed working at the loom, along with expatriate poets like Agha Shahid Ali and Sujata Bhatt, the carpet of Indian poetry in English could be said to be in reasonable flying order, right side up, woven, at its best with the natural ease of a poem like 'Stationery' by Agha Shahid Ali:

The moon did not become the sun.
It just fell on the desert
in great sheets, reams
of silver handmade by you.
The night is your cottage industry now,
the day is your brisk emporium.
The world is full of paper.

Write to me.

18

From Sugar to Masala

Writing by the Indian Diaspora

SUDESH MISHRA

There is a distinction to be made between the old and new Indian diasporas. This distinction is between, on the one hand, the semi-voluntary flight of indentured peasants to non-metropolitan plantation colonies such as Fiji, Trinidad, Mauritius, South Africa, Malaysia, Surinam, and Guyana, roughly between the years 1830 and 1917; and on the other the late capital or postmodern dispersal of new migrants of all classes to thriving metropolitan centres such as Australia, the United States, Canada, and Britain. We must modify this assertion to include, under the category of 'old', for instance, the Shamsi merchants who commenced settling along the coast of East Africa in the nineteenth century and Surat's traders, who followed the *girmityas* (indentured labourers) to Fiji after 1879; and those from privileged or comprador classes who found themselves drawn to imperial London, sometimes as emissaries for nationalists, sometimes as seekers of a 'sound' Oxbridge education, sometimes driven simply by an implanted nostalgia. Although the old diaspora is made up of communities that hail from different provinces, who speak different languages and practise different religions, and who are often inspired to leave 'home' for quite dissimilar reasons, the category is justifiable on the grounds that the earlier or older migration happened in the context of (and was determined by) colonialism in the heyday of capitalism. For, after all, it was CSR, a giant Australian sugar corporation, that initiated the migration of indentured labour to the Fiji Islands. Likewise, under the category of 'new', we have to include those descendants of the old diaspora who, together with the wave of post-Independence emigrants from the subcontinent to sundry metropolitan centres, are the willing subjects of—or unwillingly subjected to—a postcolonial or transnational political economy. The writers I have included in this chapter belong to the old (say, Subramani) or to the new (say, Rohinton Mistry) Indian diasporas, or to both (say, David Dabydeen) simultaneously, and since Seepersad Naipaul (1906–53), a second generation Indo-Trinidadian born in the canefields of Caroni, affords one of the earliest examples of the first sort, we may as well begin with him.

Seepersad Naipaul's collection of short stories, originally appearing in 1943 as *Gurudeva and Other Indian Tales* and revised and republished in 1976 as *The Adventures of Gurudeva and Other Stories*, is a pioneering imaginative work that lays the foundation for subsequent narratives, including those by his sons, Vidiadhar and Shivadhar Naipaul. The stories are concerned with the quotidian lives and quixotic struggles of the girmit or sugar diaspora. Naipaul depicts an estranged community attempting to articulate itself in a landscape it shares with those cultural others (particularly Afro-Trinidadians) who, though caught in a kindred struggle for deliverance from the nightmare of history, rarely figure in the diasporic imagination and then only as adversarial definers of the enclave community. A sometime journalist for *The Trinidad Guardian*, Naipaul writes in a style at once staccato and racy, meshing standard English, Trinidadian creole, and Hindi patois, generating a tonal effect that hovers between light raillery and disturbing, though risible, social satire. In the end, however, the stories retain a barrack realism that guides us beyond the rustic banter into the very midst of a community whose value systems are in a serious state of disarray. Read structurally, 'The Adventures of Gurudeva', the title story of the collection, describes a rogue's progress through the various stages of juvenile husband, wife-beater, *ghatka-wallah*, jailbird, bogus pundit, and jilted adulterer; but read discursively, it becomes an account of a displaced community that mistakes half-knowledges, ritualised gestures, and ersatz beliefs for cultural identity itself. On the one hand the girmit diaspora refuses to admit that mobility and mutability go hand in glove, even as it proves this truth in its hybrid speech-acts, in its sartorial, sexual, and religious departures, and on the other, having lost significant bits of the living cultural body, it can no longer bequeath semantic pattern to its present reality.

The Adventures of Gurudeva and Other Stories foreshadows the longer narratives and verse studies by subsequent writers of the old and old–new diasporas whose personal narratives remain hitched to the dour history of plantation colonies. Shiva Naipaul (1945–85) was one such writer. Born in Port of Spain, Trinidad, Naipaul read Chinese at Oxford, graduating in 1968. A journalist, columnist, and fiction writer, Naipaul chose to live in England but made regular forays abroad, reporting and commenting on places both oddly familiar, such as Trinidad and Surinam, and familiarly odd, such as India and Africa. In his tragicomic novels, *Firelies* (1970) and *The Chip-Chip Gatherers* (1973), keeping one eye dimly on his father and the other sharply on his brother, Naipaul writes about the interfamilial power-plays, the existential hopelessness, the cultural stuffiness, the wealth-based hypocrisy, the panic-stricken mimicry, the jealousies, the poverty, the violence, and the contradictions that hasten the disintegration of the Indo-Trinidadian enclave, which appears, despite its commercial spirit and competitive ethos, incapable of becoming more than an unlikely chimera haunted by subcontinental memories. Naipaul tends to view the girmit diaspora as a sow that devours its struggling farrow. Consequently, in *The Chip-Chip Gatherers,* Ramsaran is defeated in his attempts to rise above his penury by changing his religion, while Mrs Lutchman, the heroic protagonist of *Fireflies* who tries to make something of her life, is crushed by patriarchy and circumstance, losing her husband to a heart attack, her sons to metropolitan havens (the Mahavilayats of America and Britain), and her independence to her extended family.

Education and flight are offered as routes out of the communal despair, although they fail to lessen the sense of panic afflicting the diaspora in its new situation. Naipaul writes of this affliction in a candid account of his time at Oxford, published in *Beyond the Dragon's Mouth* (1984), a brilliant book that juxtaposes stories with journalistic snippets and travel pieces, thereby betraying the generic restlessness of the uprooted writer:

> The summer sky, so benign, so unthreatening, was transformed into a wheeling amphitheatre of undefined menace; a maelstrom of annihilating vacuity. Staring at it, wave upon wave of raw fear swept through me. I imagined myself a body: a nameless corpse to be picked up from the street. It was as if all the secret terrors accumulated from birth had broken loose of their chains and come upon me in one overwhelming, retributive flood.

What this passage captures is a terror of anonymity, of not being able to leave one's mark on the world, experienced here as an overpowering physical malady. It is as if colonial history takes possession of the body of the diasporic individual with the same effacing logic with which it possessed the body of his indentured ancestors. This sense of existential panic, of nomadic terror, which may take the form of an abstract homesickness (in the absence of an actual home) or the nausea of namelessness is not allayed but experienced with redoubled intensity by those who opt for a second displacement. Panic, nausea, schizophrenia, hysteria, time-lag, estrangement, violence, nostalgia, madness: these feature, variously as symbol, malady, or organising principle, in many a text by writers of the girmit diaspora, including Harold Ladoo (Trinidad-Canada), Subramani (Fiji), Cyril Dabydeen (Guyana-Canada), David Dabydeen (Guyana-England), K.S. Maniam (Malaysia), and Neil Bissoondath (Trinidad-Canada).

In his novel *No Pain Like This Body* (1972), Harold Ladoo (1945–73), drawing on his childhood in the farmlands of Trinidad and using a style variously creolised, jejune, rhapsodic, and surreal, tells the story of a rice-growing Indo-Trinidadian family which ekes out a living in a settlement under siege from forces within itself and beyond. While disease and death, tempests and floods, snakes and scorpions take their natural toll on the family, it is finally the patriarch's excessive alcoholism, idleness, and violence that destroy its nervous domesticity. In the end the mother, who embodies the resilient spirit of the girmit diaspora attempting to create a design out of the poverty and chaos, is driven insane when her child is stung to death by a scorpion. The novel ends with her disappearance into the elemental darkness, fleeing from a home that was never homely.

Like Ladoo, Subramani (b. 1943), the son of peasant farmers who went on to become Professor of Pacific Literature at the University of the South Pacific, Fiji, writes of poverty, alienation, and madness but sets his stories among the girmit diaspora in Fiji. In 'Sautu' (*The Fantasy Eaters and Other Stories*, 1988), Dhanpat, one of the girmitya inhabitants of the village of the title, ironised to represent dereliction rather than 'peace, abundance and prosperity', experiences a sense of panic at the tail-end of his life. Sautu is the psychosocial village of the sugar diaspora, built on land leased from the *taukei*, the indigenous Fijian, and tenanted by angst-ridden peasants. After his familial bonds have been snapped with the death (in sinister circumstances) of his wife Ratni, and the marriage or departure of his three children, Dhanpat experiences a profound sense of existential cleavage bordering on mental collapse. His ailment does have an individual dimension, but it cannot be isolated from his relationship with his village. Sautu, the narrator tells us, is 'like its inhabitants . . . an aberration, a contortion of history on that landscape.' Dhanpat eventually recognises that his enclave existence is based on a subconscious refusal to accommodate forces, ideas, cultures, and histories that engirdle it. After such knowledge, there is the inevitable loss of reason, the feeble cathartic gesture and the final entry into madness. Dhanpat is removed to a mental asylum and the land reverts to the taukei, the indigenous landowner.

Often the girmit diaspora responds to its lack of psychological and geographical tenure, echoed variously in Dhanpat's predicament and in Shiva Naipaul's panicky response to the repetition of a historical effacement by buying property or by building a house. Hanuman House, in V.S. Naipaul's *A House for Mr Biswas* (1961), is the original architectural metaphor of this desire. Attempts at psychocultural assertion through house-building usually end badly, as is the case in K.S. Maniam's *The Return* (1981) and in Neil Bissoondath's collection of stories, *Digging Up the Mountains* (1986). An Indo-Malaysian writer of Tamil background, Maniam (b. 1942) grew up in provincial Kedah, Malaysia, and completed his education in England. A professor of

English at the University of Malaya, Maniam sets his work, which includes *The Cord* (1983) and *In a Far Country* (1993), among the descendants of rubber planters indentured in Malaysia. *The Return* is a novel about Ravi, the young narrator born into the Tamil diaspora, who, unlike the enclave community, accepts the inexorability of history and the inevitability of change, preferring the democratic impurities of metropolitan culture (English as opposed to Tamil, London as opposed to Bedong) to the enclave's hierarchised provincialism. His escape from the coolie lines (actual and psychic), which parallels Malaysia's path to independence in 1957, is seen in relation to an ancestral failure to put down roots. In 'Digging Up the Mountains', Bissoondath (b. 1955), author of *On the Eve of Uncertain Tomorrows* (1990), his second collection of stories, and the two novels, *A Casual Brutality* (1989) and *The Innocence of Age* (1992), writes of a similar failure in relation to the life and times of Harry Beharry. Attempting to make a stand in the country of his birth, Beharry buckles under the unpredictability of the post-Independence nation-state. While the country is in the grip of political turmoil, Beharry landscapes the property around his new mansion, intending to call it Middlemarch or Rancho Rico or Golden Bough, thus throwing some doubt on the authenticity of his patriotism. Eventually, when the violence catches up with him (for he is an entrepreneur in the habit of swapping political jerseys), he buys a house in Canada and, in a symbolic rehearsal of his imminent departure, uproots the newly sprouted grass covering his lawn.

A counterpoint to Bissoondath's reductionist account of the postcolonial world is afforded by the two Dabydeens, Cyril and David, who write searingly about the legacy of colonialism but manage to overcome a fashionable despair by seeing possibilities in hybrid encounters between peoples, sexes, and nations. If there is a godfather to their literary endeavours, then it is Sam Selvon (1923–94; Trinidad-England), author of *The Lonely Londoners* (1956) and wayward spirit of Caribbean literature, whose humorous portraits of West Indians in London, dispatched in the tangy creole of the islander, attest to a cultural, sexual, and vocational space-clearing by the subaltern migrant, who will be gregarious, flexible and cosmopolitan—but never at the expense of his or her identity.

Born in Berbice, Guyana, Cyril Dabydeen (b. 1945) emigrated to Canada in 1970. Straddling the old (sugar) and the new (masala) diasporas, he can write acerbically about the unfinished men of the girmit diaspora, exposing their mimicry and chicanery (as indeed he does in his first novel, *The Wizard Swami*, 1985), or cast an empathetic eye on the troubles and travails besetting the new diaspora, as he does in his prolific verse, culminating in *Coastland: New and Selected Poems 1973–87* (1989). In his recent poetry, he offers a transnational or cross-hatched definition of the old diaspora in the process of becoming the new, where Caribbean crabgrass grows on Canada's snowy virginal ground ('Dubious Foreigner'), or, as he says in 'Cogitating', his elegy for Sam Selvon: 'I write my own epitaphs, or hieroglyphs of history; / the creole voice not always an East Indian's— / or African, but constantly shaped by crossings'.

Born in Guyana, educated at Cambridge and based in England, David Dabydeen (b. 1956) makes such 'crossings' his imaginative locus, whether he is writing monographs about black figures haunting the margins of Hogarth's paintings (*Hogarth's Blacks: The Image of Blacks in English Art*, 1985), or about a West Indian engineer exploring the turbulent underworld beneath the decorous veneer of rural England (*The Disappearance*, 1993); or, alternatively, about the ongoing odyssey-cum-ordeal of the coolie diaspora in Guyana (*Coolie Odyssey*, 1988). Crossings, for Dabydeen, are moments of cultural collision, of hybrid encounters that can engender artistic creativity ('Catching Crabs'), linguistic mutation (*Slave Song*, 1984), emotional and physical violence ('London Taxi Driver', 'For Mala'), sexual healing ('Miranda'), or sadomasochistic fantasy ('Nightmare'). For all his angry indictment of colonial arrogance, of racist myopia, Dabydeen sees how history mongrelises every participant, and knows that the collisions of self and other, notwithstanding the resulting hurt and degradation, drives the motor of history, and emancipatory moments are therefore bound up with them.

Whereas the writers of the girmit diaspora, beginning with Seepersad Naipaul, relate the misfortunes of a community displaced, both culturally and physically, by colonial history, constrained by forces from within and beyond into a futile enclavism, only alluding obliquely to India (with the notable exception of the Naipaul brothers), the writers of the old non-girmit diaspora, especially those like Menon Marath (1906–2003), Santha Rama Rau (b. 1923), Balachandra Rajan (b. 1920), and Victor Anant (1927–1999), all born on the subcontinent (Rajan in Burma), tend to engage more intimately with the *matribhumi* or motherland for their narratives, primarily because for them spatial displacement does not translate into generational distance, although the traumas of dislocation, of things falling apart, are no less evident in their work. Sometimes this anxiety is narrativised with reference to some feature of the home country, as is evident in Marath's *The Wound of Spring* (1960) and *An Island for Sale* (1968). In the former novel, written in England where he has lived since 1934, Marath relates the story of a Nair *tharawad* (a stratified joint-family system headed by a matriarch; also a metonym for feudal India) in a state of irreversible decay. Kavamma, the classical matriarch, attributes the decline to British modernity and Gandhian iconoclasm. She fails to see that any system based on a rigid enclavism is bound to have its own rebels and saboteurs, the former wanting to flee from its obduracy and insularity, the latter willing to subvert it for personal empowerment. If the men undermine the tharawad through their passionate wilfulness and murderous recklessness, the women contribute to the breakdown through their ideological inflexibility, their vocational apostasy, their dogged idealism, and their liberal-democratic spirit.

Having left it in his maturity, Marath approaches India with an insider's intimacy, while Santha Rama Rau, who has scarcely spent any time in India (save for two crucial years during World War II), approaches it with an outsider's curiosity, especially in her autobiographical novel *Home to India* (1945). This is an account of her coming to consciousness, both politically and culturally, against the backdrop of nationalistic struggles against the British Raj, resulting in the gradual weakening of her anglophilia, her feelings of bourgeois privilege, and a growing identification with subaltern India:

> For the first time I began to feel that I was ranged, however ineffectively, on the side of the Indians. I was not clear about what our side was against, but now when I saw benches on a station platform marked 'For

> Europeans only', it was a personal insult; when I read in the papers of student demonstrations that were severely punished, I shared something of the student's anger and frustration; when I saw servants curling up to sleep on doormats or in hotel passage-ways, I felt, not embarrassed as before, but resentful of a vague 'They' who had caused all this. Sometimes 'They' were the foreigners who were exploiting the Indians, and sometimes 'They' were Indians who were exploiting each other.

Rama Rau has written many other books, including two novels, *Remember the House* (1956) and *The Adventurer* (1970), three travel books, *East of Home* (1950), *A View to the Southeast* (1957), and *My Russian Journey* (1959), and a playscript of E.M. Forster's novel, *A Passage to India*. She describes herself as a 'poor expatriate' and lives in the United States.

The problems of return after a lengthy expatriatism are more skilfully worked out in the two novels by Balachandra Rajan, *The Dark Dancer* (1958) and *Too Long in the West* (1961). Rajan, better known for his critiques of Yeats, Eliot, and Milton, was educated at Presidency College, Madras, and Trinity College, Cambridge. He was a professor of English at Delhi University (1961–4), but in 1966 left Delhi for Canada. As the title—with its overt allusion to Shiva, who denotes the creation-in-destruction principle—suggests, *The Dark Dancer* deals with individual schizophrenia manifested nationally and national schizophrenia manifested individually. Set in the terrible year of Partition, which was also the happy year of Indian Independence, the novel describes the 'partition' that makes and breaks Krishnan, the Cambridge-returned protagonist, torn between modernity and England, embodied in his lover Cynthia, and tradition and India, embodied in his wife Kamala. The women satisfy conflicting needs in Krishnan, but he loses both in the end—predictably, Kamala dies bravely, attempting to save a Muslim girl in the insanity of Partition, thus signalling the demise of a tolerant India, while Cynthia leaves Krishnan with the parting remark: 'In all our three hundred years of occupation, we haven't done what you've done in three weeks of independence.' The desultory atmosphere of *The Dark Dancer* is conspicuously absent from *Too Long in the West*. Peopled with beaux and belles, wits and butts, it reads like a restoration comedy set in India and played by Indian actors. The novel tells the story of young Nalini, Columbia-educated and

America-returned, put on the marriage market by her orthodox Hindu parents, who have taken the liberty of calling for suitors in a newspaper advertisement. From a line-up of several, Nalini selects the least likely suitor, the malleable barber-cum-revolutionary Raman, thus shrewdly exercising her own choice in a no-choice situation and bringing about a sensible, if uninspired, denouement to the story.

In the novel *The Revolving Man* (1959), Victor Anant (India-Britain), variously a political detainee, a railway clerk, and a newspaper journalist, views homelessness not as the product of a psychological transformation engendered within the migrant by a spatial divide between India and Britain, but as the recognition of the 'other' that colonial modernity enforces. A thinly disguised autobiography, the novel tells the story of John Atma, son of a caste-observing mother and a nondescript father, whose pathological restlessness and recalcitrance spring from the knowledge that the other (modernity, as denoted by the cosmopolitan city, by British Bombay) has split open the unitary self (tradition as denoted by the ancestral village, by feudal Kerala) and that mobility brings about a forgetting, temporary though this may be, of his divided self, of his perpetual Humpty Dumptyness:

> Is it because I was brought up far from my ancestral home, in Bombay, that picaresque port, acquired by England as a queen's dowry, that my instinct is for the homeless life? To take off with precision, to land with sanity, both need a measure of integration beyond my means. I am whole and free only during flight . . . For whichever way you look at it the world and you have meaning for each other only as you honour the bargain you have made in just, mutual recognition, with some loss of dignity but some gain in order on both sides.

Rejecting family, friends, and country, Atma goes to London and weds Queenie, the estranged Christian wife of his friend Tiger, but she rejects him for an Englishman and he returns to Bombay, with their young child Dharma, only to be summarily rejected by his orthodox parents, who observe the dharma of caste, of formalised Hinduism. Thereafter he flees to Kerala, to his ancestral village, to the imaginary womb that would perhaps take care of his son and put together his fragmented self. Anant has recently published a second novel, *Sacred*

Cow (1996), which continues to examine some of the themes of his first novel.

There exists another group of writers from the old diaspora who belong neither to the comprador class nor to the girmit diaspora, but who share some of their preoccupations in relation to its own geopolitical context. Most of these writers come from the professional or trading diasporas who took advantage of the mobility afforded by colonial rule through two centuries, and settled mostly in East or South Africa. They write pre-eminently about the unenviable middle position held by their community, sandwiched between the imperial oppressor on the one hand and the indigenous oppressed on the other, and enamoured of neither.

This middle position is subtly treated in the works of G. Vassanji, born in Kenya in 1950, raised in Tanzania, educated in America, and presently living in Canada. Editor of the *Toronto South Asian Review*, Vassanji is the author of a collection of short stories, *Uhuru Street* (1991), inspired by V.S. Naipaul's *Miguel Street* (1959), and three novels, *The Gunny Sack* (1989), *No New Land* (1991), and *The Book of Secrets* (1995). Vassanji writes mainly of the Shamsi traders of Gujarat who migrated to East Africa in the nineteenth century, and, in tracing this community's sense of familiar temporality, its multiple dispersal across the canvas of history, makes a lasting contribution to diasporic narratives. Vassanji's narrators are one part archival historian, two parts family genealogist, three parts amateur sleuth, and four parts self-conscious theorist, with each adding to the intermeshing web of chronicle and conjecture, coincidence and connotation that drives his stories to their ultimate disclosure. In *The Gunny Sack* this takes the form of a decision made by the narrator, Salim Juma, conveyed in an epistle to his daughter: 'The running must stop now, Amina. The cycle of escape and rebirth, uprooting and generation, must cease in me. Let this be the last runaway, returned, with one last, quixotic dream.' Yet it is the runaway logic of the gunny sack (emblem of dispersal, of sojourn, of infection) that propels, even as it defers, the narrative to its general theoretical statement concerning the absence of pure realms of memory and history. Like the narrator himself, the great-grandson of an African slave and a Shamsi trader, the contents of the gunny sack (language, culture, belief) are inevitably contaminated (or chutneyfied, as Rushdie might say), forgotten only to be remembered, misplaced only to be replaced, transmuted beyond themselves in the course of their many detours and journeys. So that, as is so masterfully expressed in *The Book of Secrets* which won the Giller Prize, it is the questing after the secret rather than its unravelling that provides the teleology of life, both for the historical questor and the sleuth of family secrets.

In the narratives of Ahmed Essop, born in Surat in 1931 and educated in Johannesburg, we enter the segregated world of South Africa, of a nation-state that functions as an aberrant enclave within the global community of nations, and which constructs itself as an aggregation of ethnic enclaves, with the white rulers at the top of the hierarchy, the black majority at the bottom, and the coloured minority wedged somewhere in between. A schoolteacher by profession, Essop has written two collections of short fiction, *The Hajji and Other Stories* (1978) and *Noorjehan* (1990), and two novels, *The Visitation* (1980) and *The Emperor* (1984). While writing morally charged stories about the Indo-African diaspora, and rarely venturing beyond this insulated domain, Essop skilfully captures the momentary fractures within its rigid enclavism, which is both self-espoused and state-enforced, thus disclosing the contradictory logic that sustains the apartheid system, where each group, willingly or under the constraints of the system, defines itself by acknowledging, co-opting, and repelling its others, thereby admitting the adulterations it must negotiate to effect an isolationist self-definition. While we discover aspects of this preoccupation in both his novels, and saliently in *The Emperor*, where Essop writes pungently about an Indian collaborator's attempts to uphold the pedagogical system of his white masters, the most devastating expression of the effects of cultural transgression and of mental enclavism may be found in 'The Hajji', the title story from Essop's first collection. The story revolves around Hajji Hassen, whose fatally ill brother Karim has violated South Africa's sexual, cultural, and topographical apartheid by marrying a white woman, Catherine, and moving to Hillbrow. Hassen rejects his brother's dying wish to return to his own community, justifying his decision by employing a logic that duplicates within the enclave the discourses of the oppressive nation-state:

'He is a white. We live in different worlds.' Hassen's community sees beyond his intransigence and its own fusty enclavism and gives Karim a traditional Muslim funeral. When a penitent Hassen tries to belatedly join the cortége, he is ignored by his fellow Muslims, who no doubt see in the former's inflexibility the inflexibility of the apartheid world around them.

If the old diaspora can be identified through its melancholic withdrawal into zones of exclusivity, the new diaspora can be identified through its conscious occupation of border zones, exemplified by the uneasy interaction between gender, class, ethnicity, nation-states, or, as in the case of Ved Mehta (b. 1934), between the blinded and the sighted. Mehta, who lost his sight through meningitis at the age of four, was born in India and educated at the Arkansas School for the Blind and at Pomona College, California, before completing his studies at the universities of Oxford and Harvard. A staff writer on *The New Yorker* for more than thirty years, Mehta has written hundreds of essays and stories, and published over twenty titles—traversing the genres of fiction, biography, history, theology, philosophy, and travel writing. While he has been duly recognised for the rigour of his scholarship in such socio-historical studies as *Portrait of India* (1970), *Mahatma Gandhi and his Apostles* (1977), *The New India* (1978), and *A Family Affair: India Under Three Prime Ministers* (1982), it is his autobiographical books that have brought him his greatest success. These can be divided into two distinct phases, India-oriented and West-oriented. The India-oriented phase includes *Face to Face: An Autobiography* (1957), which in its first two parts recalls the author's childhood in India before his departure for the United States; *Daddyji* (1972) and *Mamaji* (1979), both filial narratives examining his life in relation to the lives of his Hindu parents; *Vedi* (1982), a powerful exploration of Mehta's time at the Dadar School for the Blind and *The Ledge Between the Streams* (1984), in which Mehta describes his fledging youth during the time of Partition and his family's coerced departure from an ancestral Lahore. The West-oriented phase includes *Sound-Shadows of the New World* (1985), a self-conscious assessment by Mehta of his adolescence and maturity in a deeply segregated America; *The Stolen*

Light (1987), describing his three years at Pomona College, his troubled sexual awakening, and his father's struggles for financial autonomy; and *Up at Oxford* (1992), which gives an engaging portrait, among several others, of the poet Dom Moraes, who was a fellow undergraduate. The last two volumes in Mehta's autobiographical series, 'Continents of Exile', of which *Daddyji* was the first, are *Remembering Mr Shawn's 'New Yorker'* (1998) and *All for Love* (2001). His most endearing book remains *Sound-Shadows of the New World*, which relates his sometimes happy and sometimes frustrating life as a student in the American South. Although he comments perceptively on racial segregation, Mehta reveals that the cause of *his* estrangement had less to do with colour prejudice and more to do with the ignorant paternalism of the sighted towards the blind. Resolving to move through the world of the sighted on equal terms, Mehta jettisons all signifiers of his handicap and uses sound-shadows to traverse the border between blindness and perception, discovering the physical world without calling attention to himself, and learning that mobility itself bequeaths a home-like freedom to the unsighted.

In his ambivalent identification with some aspects of *desh* and *pardesh*, Ved Mehta anticipates the work of many writers of the new or masala diaspora, such as Bharati Mukherjee (India–United States), Farrukh Dhondy (India–Britain), G.S. Sharat Chandra (India–United States), Agha Shahid Ali (India–United States), Saleem Peeradina (India–United States), Rohinton Mistry (India–Canada), Sujata Bhatt (India–Germany), Pico Iyer (Britain), and Meera Syal (Britain). Whereas the writers of the old diaspora tend to concentrate on the chinks within, say, the girmit enclave, the new diasporic writers are inclined to inhabit the liminal or threshold zone of intercutting subjectivities that defines the experience of migrancy.

The narratives of Bharati Mukherjee (b. 1940) provide the best examples of this. Her novels trace the split in the diasporic subject, expressed in that sense of being here and elsewhere, of being at home and abroad. *The Tiger's Daughter* (1972) considers this feeling in relation to Tara, New York-returned and married to an American, as she attempts to reconnect with Calcutta, only to find that everything (Calcutta, her friends, herself) has been affected by an estranging alchemy. *Wife* (1976) examines the darker side of this split when Dimple, unable to cope with the tumult of irreconcilable values and emotions that haunt those in transit between places, roles, and cultures, succumbs to a liberatory madness, culminating in the murder of her husband. In *Jasmine* (1989) the eponymous heroine struggles to cheat the stars by fleeing to America, a country in which personal destiny is connected to individual action rather than, as in India, to the fateful action of the planets. Jasmine describes herself as transitory, as becoming, as rebirthing, and her life becomes a statement on the United States, on the nation-states as a palimpsest marked by successive waves of immigrants (legal and illegal), who in turn are profoundly marked by it.

To mark others and to bear marks on oneself: this is what happens in the liminal zone of nation-states that are always forming, that are defined by the process itself and not its culmination. Almost all the stories in *The Middleman and Other Stories* (1988), which won the National Book Critics Circle Award, inhabit this domain. 'A Wife's Story' captures the rift between an Indian woman in America, who is altered by her new habitat, and her Bombay-based husband, who retains the inviolability of the tourist from the old country; while 'Loose Ends', written from the perspective of an embittered Viet-vet and assassin-for-hire, captures the violence that haunts the diaspora when those identifying exclusively with the nation-state discover that immigrant bodies are redefining *their* country, and making *them* feel excluded: 'They look at me. A bunch of aliens and they stare like I'm the freak.'

> Where did America go? I want to know. Down the rabbit hole, Doc Healy used to say. Alice knows, but she took it with her. Hard to know which one's the Wonderland. Back when me and my buddies were barricading the front door, who left the back door open?

After this the narrator resolves to barricade the back door, raping (and possibly killing) a Gujarati girl whose family owns a wayside motel and who serves as a likely scapegoat for his inadequacies.

Violence in the liminal zone is also a feature of *Bombay Duck* (1990), the effervescent novel by Farrukh Dhondy (b. 1944), mapping the trajectories of sexuality, politics, crime, migrancy, nationalism, zealotry, aesthetics, and ethnicity that connect Delhi and London, upper-class Indians and subaltern West Indians, Jamaican creole and masala English, director David Stream and poet Valmiki, the epic *Ramayana* and the holy Koran. Born in Poona, India, and educated at the universities of Bombay, Cambridge, and Leicester, Dhondy taught English in London schools until 1982, when he gave it up to devote himself to writing. A writer of books for young adults, which include *East End at Your Feet* (1976), *Come to Mecca and Other Stories* (1978), *The Siege of Babylon* (1978), *Poona Company* (1980), and *Trip Trap* (1982), Dhondy's first novel is divided into two discrete though interlinking parts, with each part told in the first person by a different narrator. The first narrator is Gerald Blossom alias Ali Abdul Rahman, a West Indian actor who plays the role of Lord Rama in David Stream's enactment of the epic *Ramayana*, while the second narrator is Xerxes Xavaxa, child smuggler and Parsi historian, who lives his life shuttling between Bombay and London, and who is eventually arrested by the authorities in England. It is in the first part of the novel, however, that Dhondy really hits straps as a storyteller. A sympathetic parody of Peter Brooks's *Mahabharata*, the story revolves around David Stream's stage production of *Ramayana*. Stream aims to dramatise the transglobal, pluralistic character of the world by drawing on various ethnicities for his cast, but personal lives and provincial politics keep interfering with his aesthetic realm. When the production moves to India, it becomes an easy target for the fundamentalists, who see in it one more example of cultural travesty, of foreign denigration of dharma and Hinduism. In a staged riot (as stage fantasy gives way to staged reality), Gerald Blossom (Rama) is wounded and Anjali, the cosmopolitan Indian who plays Sita, is brutally murdered, causing the play to be abandoned. And so the one pure reading is enforced over the many impure readings, because—as Blossom says—'all the world's no fucking stage'.

Like Dhondy, Rohinton Mistry (b. 1952) belongs to the Parsi community that fled to India from Persia to escape Islamic persecution in the seventh century. Mistry himself left Bombay for Toronto in 1975. He studied for a degree at the University of Toronto and worked in a bank until 1985. Presently a full-time writer, Mistry has three books to his name, a short-story collection titled *Tales from Firozsha Baag* (1987) and the novels, *Such a Long Journey* (1991) and *A Fine Balance* (1996). He focuses mainly on the changing fortunes of the Parsi diaspora in India, which he represents both as a self-sufficient enclave community and as an integral part of the nation-state. Above all, Mistry is concerned with encounters in the liminal zone when the Parsi microcosm meets its repressed mirror-self or the macrocosms of India and the West in situations that are variously oppressive, escapist, liberating, discriminatory, hyphenating, violent, and self-defining.

Structurally at least, *Tales from Firozsha Baag* resembles V.S. Naipaul's *Miguel Street.* Like the latter book, it is a collection of stories told from the perspective of the occupants of an enclave community. After charting the slowly fracturing world of the older-generation Parsis in the early stories, Mistry shifts his focus to the already fractured world of the mobile, newer-generation Parsis, who are sometimes twice hyphenated (Parsi-Indian-Canadian) in their itinerancy. Mistry captures both the vanishing certainties of the Parsi community diasporised in India and the ambiguous, ambivalent lives of the Parsi individual diasporised in America and Canada.

Set among suburban Parsis who occupy an apartment block in Bombay and against the backdrop of India's 'secret' war in East Pakistan (Bangladesh), *Such a Long Journey* relates the story of Gustad Noble, bank employee, serenading husband, and responsible father, who attempts to take charge of his modest destiny but discovers that Immodest Destiny has instead taken charge of him. Attempting to make neat ripples of his own, he is betrayed though never vanquished by the greater ripples made by others. Sometimes this betrayal is filial (his son, Sohrab, destroys his parental dreams) and existential (his colleague, Dinshawji, dies tragically); at other times it is fraternal (his friend, Jimmy Billimoria, puts his life in mortal danger) and national (the occupation of the Congress government under Indira Gandhi). Gustad survives his misfortunes with remarkable fortitude, although the narrative of India as a composite whole, depicted by a pavement artist on the wall of Khodadad Building, is finally demolished by the municipal authorities.

In *A Fine Balance*, a complex, magnificent, hurting story told in the best tradition of nineteenth-century realism, Mistry continues to write about how little individual agency counts in a national emergency and how brutally personal initiative is suppressed by caste imperatives. In writing about the defeat of Ishvar and Omprakash, the Chamar tanners turned caste-violating tailors; of Dina Dayal, the Parsi widow in search of economic autonomy; of Maneck Kohlah, the student from the hills hungry for existential answers, Mistry captures the overwhelming forces of history and caste, of politics and patriarchy, of coincidence and destiny that combine to break the human spirit in its quest for value, for betterment, for nobility.

If the border zone is often characterised by things falling apart on the political or ideological levels, it is just as often characterised by things coming together on the imaginative and domestic levels, especially in terms of the mailing back and forth between discourses and countries that is the condition of the diasporic writer. This we observe clearly in the poetry of G.S. Sḥarat Chandra (1935–2000), Saleem Peeradina (b. 1944), Agha Shahid Ali (1949–2001), and Sujata Bhatt (b. 1956). Born in Mysore, India, Sharat Chandra studied law in Canada before settling down in the United States. A professor of English at the University of Missouri-Kansas City, Sharat Chandra has several collections to his name, including *Bharata Natyam Dancer and Other Poems* (1968), *Reasons for Staying* (1970), *April in Nanjangud* (1971), *Once or Twice* (1974), *Heirloom* (1982), and *Family of Mirrors* (1993). He is concerned with 'home' as a sublime point, as the third possibility beyond the topographies of the past and the present. In a poem titled 'In the Third Country' he elects to 'die simultaneously in three countries', rejecting the speeches and rituals associated with the first two deaths, one in India and the other in America, preferring instead the dispassion and anonymity of dying in the country of the Hindu sublime:

In the third country
the wind neither wails
nor stays on your windowsill
your tea cups remain full or empty
it's one season or another
people sleep or people wake

No one wants your whereabouts

But he arrives at this position after persistent and painstaking enquiries into discourses of exile, perhaps best exemplified by poems such as

'Brothers', where fraternal bonding serves as a homing strategy; 'Mount Pleasant, USA', where the persona's lack of roots is expressed in terms of failure and entrapment rather than in the language of responsibility and freedom; 'Once or Twice', where the speaker betrays his perplexity at his countryless status; and 'Borders', where exile causes a splitting and doubling within the persona, so that—as his father observes in 'Letters from My Father'—to recover his sense of wholeness he is obliged to 'look for a third country'.

Unlike Sharat Chandra who posits 'home' as the transcendent, disembodied, and internalised third possibility, Saleem Peeradina, who has published two collections of verse, *First Offence* (1980) and *Group Portrait* (1992), identifies 'home' as his own body discovered, named, and traversed by his children who treat it as a tactile, borderless country, thereby forcing him to acknowledge that equanimity is achieved through a fine balancing of action (body) and contemplation (mind). Born in Bombay and educated at the universities of Bombay and Wake Forest in the United States, Peeradina has increasingly made domesticity and its nuances his dominant concern. In the poem 'Michigan Basement II', he writes:

> I am what I appear
> To them: a country without borders. My space
> Is their turf. I surface, with no place to hide
> Except just below the skin.
> Remaining whole is no longer the point:
> It's staying divided, attaining equipoise.

Peeradina hitches the signifier 'home' not to some national or transcendent signified, but to the body as it moves in the orbit of the family, of relationships.

Unlike Peeradina, Agha Shahid Ali, a Delhi-born poet who lived and taught in the USA, explores the problematic question of home in relation to the translations engendered by memory across spaces and by language across cultures. The author of eight volumes, *Bone-Sculpture* (1972), *In Memory of Begum Akhtar* (1979), *A Walk through the Yellow Pages* (1987), *The Half-Inch Himalayas* (1987), *A Nostalgist's Map of America* (1991), *The Beloved Witness: Selected Poems* (1992),

The Country Without a Post Office (1997), and *Rooms Are Never Finished* (2001), Shahid Ali writes of memory and forgetting in language that is at once circuitous and conceit-enriched, and therefore ghazal-like in its construction, and arbitrary and surprising, and therefore quasi-surrealistic in its visual structuring. Writing about his adaptations of Faiz Ahmed Faiz's ghazals in 'Homage to Faiz Ahmed Faiz', Shahid Ali shows how the process of translating from Urdu into English can be enabling and exiling at the same time: 'In the free verse /of another language I imprisoned / each line—but touched my own exile.' In 'Postcard from Kashmir', a poem of great texture and subtlety, he illustrates the workings of nostalgia as it purifies memory to fit the postcard image of the absent landscape—so that 'home' is no longer a topographical 'there', but an unattainable possibility.

Home is also a nostalgic sublime for Sujata Bhatt, author of *Brunizem* (1988), *Monkey Shadows* (1991), and *The Stinking Rose* (1995), who studied in the United States and lives in Germany, where she works as a translator and freelance writer. If 'home' as the nostalgic sublime is an arrested and idealised photographic moment for Shahid Ali (the 'giant negative' he carries in his memory but which corresponds to nothing but itself), for Bhatt, who likewise views home as an internalised concept, the nostalgic sublime is the ancestral house she takes with her in her travels, but which keeps altering its architecture with every new situation and so 'does not fit / with any geography':

> I am the one who goes away.
>
> Because I must—
> with my home intact
>   but always changing
> so the windows don't match
> the doors anymore—the colours
> clash in the garden—
> And the ocean lives in the bedroom.
>
> ('The One Who Goes Away')

When not flirting with the nostalgic sublime, Bhatt questions the inherent assumptions of language, gender, and culture by interlarding English and Gujarati, thus disrupting both these patriarchal language systems, or praises the erotic and gastronomic uses of the stinking rose, the humble garlic, justly celebrated by lovers and gourmands and unjustly maligned by Anglo-Saxons.

What happens when the subject is foreign-born, whose movement from the wholeness of the national imaginary to the fracturedness of the diasporic symbolic occurs in reverse—say, from Britain to Britain–India? Pico Iyer (b. 1957) and Meera Syal, both born in Britain, provide two answers to this question. In the case of Iyer, an essayist for *Time* magazine and author of *Video Nights in Kathmandu* (1988), *The Lady and the Monk* (1991), *Falling off the Map* (1993), and *Cuba and the Night* (1995), the loneliness of not having a fixed address, of being split between multiple temporalities, instils a desire for lonely places. Like the Naipaul brothers who visit half-formed societies to gain insights into their half-formed selves, Iyer journeys to lonely countries to discover the loneliness that 'is partly in ourselves'.

In her impressive novel *Anita and Me* (1996), Meera Syal, actress and scriptwriter for Gurinder Chadha's acclaimed film *Bhaji on the Beach* (1994), arrives at a less melancholic definition of diasporic selfhood: 'The place in which I belonged was wherever I stood and there was nothing stopping me simply moving forward and claiming each resting place as home.' This process of identity-formation, however, takes a long and convoluted route, littered with false starts and rash detours, over the terrain of the novel. Set in the mining village of Tollington, the story revolves around young Meena, British-born daughter of Punjabi immigrants, whose growth of awareness results in her recognition of the cleft separating Britain and India; in the end Meena concludes that every dwelling place constitutes her as a gypsy.

The movement from Seepersad Naipaul to Meera Syal suggests an important rethinking of the concept of 'home' within the diaspora, especially as this occurs against the backdrop of the global shift from the centring or centripetal logic of monopoly capitalism to the decentring or centrifugal logic of transnational capitalism. Whereas for the sugar diaspora 'home' signifies an end to itinerant wandering, in the putting down of roots, 'home' for the masala diaspora is linked to the strategic espousal of rootlessness, to the constant mantling and dismantling of the self in makeshift landscapes.

19

Looking for A.K. Ramanujan

Arvind Krishna Mehrotra

In looking for ways to describe A.K. Ramanujan and the many disciplines he straddled, one thinks, with reason, of performing men: in his teens Ramanujan had wanted to become a professional magician, and even got a neighbourhood tailor to stitch him a coat with hidden pockets and elastic bands, to which he added a top-hat and wand. Thus outfitted, he appeared before school and club audiences, plucking rabbits and bouquets of flowers out of thin air, just as in later life he enthralled his classes at the University of Chicago with his lectures, and his readers across the globe with a steady flow of poems, translations, and essays. 'Beginning often with a provocative question', Milton Singer has said of his teaching method, 'Raman would proceed to present such a diversity of texts and contexts, oral and written tales, poems, interviews, and conversations, that the answer to the question would become inescapable, not as a dogmatic assertion, but as an invitation to look at the posed question from a fresh perspective.' Another Chicago colleague, Wendy Doniger, has spoken of his contribution to Indological studies as a 'great intellectual trapeze act' performed 'without a net, between two worlds', the Indian and the American. Ramanujan's own view of himself was more down to earth. He called himself the hyphen in Indo-American.

Magician, trapezist, and, especially on first acquaintance, a master of disguise ('I resemble everyone / but myself', as the early 'Self-Portrait' has it), A.K. Ramanujan was born in Mysore in 1929 into a family of Srivaishnava Tamil Brahmins. His father was a professor of mathematics, and Ramanujan grew up in a multilingual environment in which Tamil, Kannada, and English were spoken. He was educated in Mysore and Poona, and in the 1950s taught in various colleges in South India, but mainly in Belgaum. In 1958 he went to the United States to do a Ph.D. in Linguistics at Indiana University, and in 1962 was appointed to the University of Chicago, where he remained for the next thirty years. He died there under anaesthesia, during a botched operation, in 1993.

Ramanujan was thirty-seven when *The Striders* (1966) was published. Thereafter like Philip Larkin's, his books of poems appeared at the rate of one per decade, *Relations* in 1971 and *Second Sight* in 1986. When his *Collected Poems* came out in 1995, its fourth and last section consisted of *The Black Hen*, the collection he was working on and had almost completed at the time of his death. A poem in it, dated 16 March 1992, reads uncannily like a premonition:

Birth takes a long time
though death can be sudden,
and multiple, like pregnant deer
shot down on the run . . .

('Birthdays')

In the United States, however, Ramanujan, the poet, was little known. Perhaps nothing indicates this better than the double-spread illustration called Galaxy of Contemporary Poets in the *Harper Anthology of Poetry* (1981). The galaxy is filled with the starry names of the poets of England and America, and though Ramanujan is one of the stars, his name appears at the very edge, a tiny dot in the bottom right corner. It was not his cunningly made poems, but the five volumes of not less artfully plotted translations from Tamil, Kannada, and Telugu, with their elaborate diagram-filled introductions and afterwords, that made Ramanujan's international reputation. They are *The Interior Landscape* (1967), *Speaking of Siva* (1973), *Hymns for the Drowning*

(1981), *Poems of Love and War* (1985), and, with Velcheru Narayana Rao and David Shulman, *When God is a Customer* (1994).

Ramanujan's other important work was in oral literature and folklore, areas he had pursued since the early 1950s. His very first book, published in 1955, had been a collection of proverbs in Kannada, and during the next forty years he wrote extensively on such subjects as 'The Indian Oedipus', 'On Folk Mythologies and Folk Puranas', and 'Who Needs Folklore? The Relevance of Oral Traditions to South Asian Studies', often drawing on his field notes for examples. Together with his essays on literature and culture, these have been published in *Collected Essays* (1999). It is only appropriate that the last book of his to appear in his lifetime should be *Folklore of India* (1991), many examples within which he had collected himself. Left out of this account are Ramanujan's translation of U.R. Anantha Murthy's novel, *Samskara* (1976), and his writings in Kannada, which include three collections of verse and a novella. Indeed, it has been remarked by a Kannada poet that the only way to do justice to a bilingual writer like Ramanujan is to read his English and Kannada poems together, preferably between the covers of the same book.

If Ramanujan's are some of the most eloquent translations of Indian literature available in English, it's largely because he was a not inconsiderable poet in English himself. In the running battle between the 'literalists' who believe that you can only translate by biting off a good half of your own tongue and those for whom translation is 'to metaphor', to 'carry across', Ramanujan's position is unambiguous. 'The ideal', he wrote in the introduction to *Hymns for the Drowning*, 'is still Dryden's, "a kind of drawing after the life" ', and he says in 'On Translating a Tamil Poem' that 'The only possible translation is a "free" one':

> Translations are transpositions, reenactments, interpretations. Some elements of the original cannot be transposed at all. One can often convey a sense of the original rhythm, but not the language-bound meter, one can mimic levels of diction, but not the actual sound of the original words. Textures are harder (maybe impossible) to translate than structure, linear order more difficult than syntax, lines more difficult than larger

> patterns. Poetry is made at all these levels—and so is translation. That is why nothing less than a poem can translate another.

George Chapman, the translator of Homer and, like Dryden, one of Ramanujan's forebears, put it thus: 'With Poesie to open Poesie'.

Ramanujan separates those elements in a poem that resist translation from those that do not. Levels of diction, syntax, and phrases are the translator's points of entry. Through them he nudges his way into the material, before dyeing it, thread by thread, in the colour of his voice, one that is, like a fingerprint or signature, unique to him. No two translations of the same poem, for this reason, can sound the same. It's a way of translation; there are others. Ramanujan is quick to caution, though, that by free translation is not meant an untethered one. 'Yet "anything goes" will not do', he says, adding immediately afterwards, 'The translation must not only represent, but *re*-present, the original. One walks a tightrope between the To-language and the From-language, in a double loyalty. A translator is "an artist on oath".' Having said this, Ramanujan once again faces in the opposite direction. 'Sometimes', he says, 'one may succeed only in *re*-presenting a poem, not in closely representing it.' Clearly, the tightrope between poetry and Indology, modern English and early Tamil, is not easily walked. Like some of his other essays, 'On Translating a Tamil Poem' ends with a parable:

> A Chinese emperor ordered a tunnel to be bored through a great mountain. The engineers decided that the best and quickest way to do it would be to begin work on both sides of the mountain, after precise measurements. If the measurements are precise enough, the two tunnels will meet in the middle, making a single one. 'But what happens if they don't meet?' asked the emperor. The counselors, in their wisdom, answered, 'If they don't meet, we will have two tunnels instead of one.'

Poet-translators seem to find their chosen material almost serendipitously, and Ramanujan discovered his in a library basement where, in one of his first Saturdays at the University of Chicago, he had gone in search of an elementary grammar of Old Tamil. While looking for it, he stumbled upon the *Kuruntokai*, one of the eight anthologies of classical Tamil ascribed to the first three centuries AD. 'I sat down on the floor between the stacks', he writes, 'and began to browse. To my amazement, I found the prose commentary transparent, it soon unlocked the old poems for me.' Ramanujan's translations of these poems started appearing in American journals as early as 1964, and in 1965 Writers Workshop, Calcutta, published a small selection, *Fifteen Poems from a Classical Tamil Anthology*. This was followed two years later by *The Interior Landscape*, the book which established Ramanujan's reputation as the inventor of Tamil poetry for our time.

Though the influence of Ramanujan's example on the translation of Indian classics into English is yet to be assessed, there is little doubt about the ways in which the translations shaped his own English poems. He was, in the early 1960s, still writing some of the poems that were to appear in *The Striders*, and just as what he knew as a modernist poet reinforced his translations, what he was learning as a translator found its way into his poems. When Ramanujan says of the Tamil poems that often they 'unify their rich and diverse associations by using a single, long, marvellously managed sentence', he could well be describing his own practice. Not only are some of his poems similarly made, but the single syntax-driven sentence can take a page or more to unfold.

Ramanujan also pointed out the correspondence between the ancient Tamil poets and a modern master like Marianne Moore. Explaining why the Tamil poets chose the *kurinci* flower to suggest the mood of first love, he says the choice was partly motivated by a botanical fact: 'a *kurinci* plant comes to flower only from nine to twelve years after it is planted—this identifies it with the tropical virgin heroine who comes to puberty at the same age.' 'Thus is the real world', he says in the afterword to *Poems of Love and War*, 'always kept in sight and included in the symbolic. These poets would have made a poet like Marianne Moore happy: they are "literalists of the imagination", presenting for inspection in poem after poem "imaginary gardens with real toads in them".'

But if the ancient Tamils are among Miss Moore's Borgesian precursors, Ramanujan is among those who learnt from her example: his five-toed lizards, salamanders, quartz clocks, and poem titles that double also as first lines can be traced to her. These and other parallels, resemblances, mediations, and overlaps make his poems and translations of a piece; they seem as two halves of an indivisible whole.

For someone who published only three average-sized collections of verse in his lifetime, Ramanujan's *Collected Poems* surprises by its length. It runs to almost 300 pages. Its other surprise is that there are no other surprises. For instance, the allusions that seem to proliferate in the later work are there from the beginning. They range over many disciplines—literature, philosophy, psychology, anthropology, religion, folklore—and from the *Taittiriya Upanishad* to L.P. Hartley. This is less an indication of his reading, wide as it was, than of the way his kinship-seeking mind worked, the run-on lines wiring up its different parts, or disconnecting them. When the latter happened, as in *Second Sight*, the result could be chilling:

Suddenly, connections severed
    as in a lobotomy, unburdened
of history, I lose

my bearings, a circus zilla spun
    at the end of her rope, dizzy,
terrified,

and happy. And my watchers
    watch, cool as fires
in a mirror.
        ('Looking for the Centre')

Though several poems in *Second Sight* are written in the same two-and-a-half-line stanza, forming a scattered sequence, Ramanujan generally gives a poem a shape that is original to it. His poems, exquisitely crafted, are as much objects to hold between fingers as printed lines to read with the eyes. A good example is 'Poona Train Window'. Its eleven stanzas are conventionally laid out in a column on the page, which is why we do not immediately pick out the underlying design, whose inspiration comes from the very part of the human anatomy Ramanujan contemplates through the train window. The first stanza consists of one line, the second of two, the third of three, and so on till the sixth. Thereafter, in the five remaining stanzas, the number of lines successively decreases, till we come to the last stanza which, like the last first, is of one line. This is how the poem concludes:

> . . . I see a man
>
> between two rocks.
> I think of the symmetry
>
> of human buttocks.

Having once found his style, Ramanujan saw no call to make changes, not even minor ones. His speech is consistently demotic, the stanzas inventive, the tone—in the face of much suffering—wry, bemused, clinical. By comparison, Larkin looks a sentimentalist. The examples below are from *The Black Hen*. The circumstances—a divorce, a medical investigation—belong to a later period ('Pain' in fact was finished weeks before his death), but the droll manner goes back to *The Striders*, where it was first perfected:

> April to June burned
> night and day like
> a temple lamp kept alive
> by a cripple praying
> for her legs
>
> and July was at war,
> bombs overhead,
> napalm fires in the bone,
> children almost drowned
> in a flash flood
> of divorce papers.
> ('August')

> Doctors X-ray the foot, front face and back,
> left profile and right as if for a police
> file, unearth shadow fossils of neanderthals
> buried in this contemporary foot;
> they draw three test tubes of blood as I turn
> my face away, and label my essences
> with a mis-spelled name . . .
> ('Pain')

Full of paradoxes, with also a gift for making them; often autobiographical, but seldom transparently so; tight-lipped, but fantasizing about stripping; deadly serious, but never more so than when being playful; this was Ramanujan. In 'A Poor Man's Riches 1' he refers to the colour of his eyes and, 'classified / in each oblong of visa and passport', the distinguishing 'five moles' on his face. It's a face he hid behind many masks. The changing shapes of the mask and the face behind them are, from different angles, what he probed in poems written over four decades.

Except for *The Black Hen*, which was put together by an eight-member committee after his death, Ramanujan's three previous collections are so arranged that each poem in them illuminates the one following it, and is illuminated by it in return. They are thus doubly lit, throwing unexpected shadows. In *The Striders*, 'No Man Is an Island' and 'Anxiety' appear on facing pages. The former concludes, 'But this man, / I know, buys dental floss.', and the latter, 'But anxiety / can find no metaphor to end it.' Unrelated though the two poems seem to be, they make a joint statement, which is that no amount of flossing will get rid of this thing wedged between the teeth. Ramanujan's word for it here is 'anxiety'; in his other poems it is called 'despair', 'fear', 'anger', 'madness', 'lust'. It is his major theme, even when he is writing in a minor key:

Just comb your hair.
You shouldn't worry about Despair.
Despair is a strange disease.
I think it happens even to trees.

('Excerpts from a Father's Wisdom')

'Snakes', the second poem in *The Striders*, refers to this state of dread metaphorically. Our tormentors are not remote creatures we meet only in woods while taking a walk, but appear where we expect them least: in the cool of libraries, staring out of any 'book that has gold / on its spine', or in the safety of our homes where

Sister ties her braids
with a knot of tassel.
But the weave of her knee-long braid has scales,
their gleaming held by a score of clean new pins.
I look till I see her hair again.

Eventually, the snake is killed—'Now / frogs can hop upon this sausage rope'—only to live another day. It is not long in coming. In 'Breaded Fish', which is only one poem away from 'Snakes', the snake image reappears. This time it is 'a hood / of memory like a coil on a heath', which, when it opens in the speaker's eyes, makes him see not some specially made 'breaded fish'—'a blunt-headed / smell'—that a woman is thrusting into his mouth, but

> . . . a dark half-naked
> length of woman, dead
> on the beach in a yard of cloth,
>
> dry, rolled by the ebb, breaded
> by the grained indifference of sand. I headed
> for the shore, my heart beating in my mouth.

In a poem of twelve lines, the first eleven are one sentence.

'Others see a rush, a carnival, a million, / why does he see nothing, or worse, just one', Ramanujan asks in 'Some People'. When the eye sees one thing and memory apprehends another, an unsuspected crevice opens up between the two, into which there is always a risk of falling. Ramanujan, who knew the risk only too well, often spoke of the mind's terrors in precisely such images. We find them as early as 'The Fall' in *The Striders*, where the poem works out a metaphor taken from parachuting, and as late as the last poem in *The Black Hen*, 'Fear No Fall'. 'Chicago Zen', in *Second Sight*, enacts all the stages of the drama and concludes on a note of mock warning:

> and watch
> for the last
> step that's never there.

Ramanujan, however, is a poet of last steps taken, the plunge made, the descent begun. He is all about being blinded by sight 'in unexpected places': in the middle of 'a whole milling conference / on Delhi milk and China soyabean' in 'Some Place', and in the middle of a street in 'Chicago Zen':

> The traffic light turns orange
> on 57th and Dorchester, and you stumble

you fall, into a vision of forest fires,
enter a frothing Himalayan river,

rapid, silent.

On the 14th floor,
Lake Michigan crawls and crawls
in the window. Your thumbnail
cracks a lobster louse on the windowpane

from your daughter's hair
and you drown, eyes open,

towards the Indies, the antipodes.
And you, always so perfectly sane.

In these episodes of blindness and sight, falling and drowning, self-mockery runs together with the stress of extreme experience, making it a performance by turns delightful and alarming to watch. But Ramanujan does not always pull it off, and there are times in *Second Sight* when he gets carried away, parodying his own act, as in 'Dancers in a Hospital', the first three sections of 'Looking for the Centre', and 'Waterfalls in a Bank'.

To be all one's life both drowning 'towards . . . the antipodes' and standing firmly on dry land; to be held motionless between private grotesqueries and public mask; to exist on two planes at the same time: Ramanujan called this 'living by contraries'. Perfectly sane, though, are the poems' beginnings, giving little hint of the topsyturviness to come. Ironic, chatty, quick-witted, and full of inner rhymes, assonance, and wordplay, their breezy tone, within the space of a line, can turn into a very black storm. They begin as routinely as 'Routine Day Sonnet' ('For me a perfectly ordinary / day at the office'), or as innocently as nursery rhymes ('One two three four five / five fingers to a hand'), and, like routine days and nursery rhymes, end in catastrophe. The same pattern, more or less, is seen in 'Conventions of Despair':

Yes, I know all that. I should be modern.
Marry again. See strippers at the Tease.
Touch Africa. Go to the movies.

Impale a six-inch spider
under a lens. Join the Test-
ban, or become The Outsider.

Or pay to shake my fist
(or-whatever-you-call-it) at the psychoanalyst.
And when I burn

I should smile, dry-eyed,
and nurse martinis like the Marginal Man.
But, sorry, I cannot unlearn

conventions of despair.
They have their pride.
I must seek and will find

my particular hell only in my hindu mind:
must translate and turn
till I blister and roast

for certain lives to come, 'eye-deep',
in those Boiling Crates of Oil . . .

Without breaking the offhand manner, the poem suddenly swings into its subject in the fourth stanza. Ramanujan, who loved paradoxes, conveys hell very differently in the well-known title poem of the same collection in which 'Conventions of Despair' appears:

This bug sits
on a landslide of lights
and drowns eye-
deep
into its tiny strip
of sky.

('The Striders')

Connecting the two depictions, one done in the style of bazaar oleographs and the other a prize-winning piece of nature photography, is the phrase 'eye-deep', which itself is a tag from Ezra Pound. It occurs in *Hugh Selwyn Mauberley*, in a passage lamenting those killed in the Great War:

Died some, pro patria,
non 'dulce' non 'et décor . . .
walked eye-deep in hell
believing in old men's lies . . .

(iv)

'Conventions of Despair' continues for another seven stanzas, but its point has been made, thrice over. Our 'particular hell'—or 'tiny strip / of sky'—in which we burn, blister, and roast, is the one constant we have in 'a landslide of lights'. The rest is a bit of role-playing, a bit of shamming, like taking off and putting on costumes, whether of explorer, scientist, peacenik, or Outsider.

A poet does not bring his unruly 'little demons' under control by shaking his fist at the analyst, but by keeping a meticulous record of their deeds in card-sized stanzas. The following entry, the sixth of eight, is from 'Entries for a Catalogue of Fears':

Like any honest
man, unnerved by the slightest
inquiry into his flawless past,
found spotted all over with horrid fact
by the mere act
of questioning:
or found helplessly handling
my thing
at seventy
on a doorstep
wiping out a whole difficult lifetime
of dignity
and earning only the fascination
of passing
old women.

We catch another glimpse of the man on the doorstep in 'Foundlings in the Yukon'. Written more than twenty years after 'Entries for a Catalogue of Fears', this late poem is based on a newspaper report, the discovery by miners in northwest Canada, near the Arctic Circle, of some seeds that had been 'sealed off by a landslide / in Pleistocene times'. When planted, six of the seeds 'took root / within forty-eight hours / and sprouted / a candelabra of eight small leaves'. These 'upstarts', Ramanujan says,

> drank up sun
> and unfurled early
> with the crocuses in March
> as if long deep
> burial had made them hasty
>
> for birth and season, for names,
> genes, for passing on:
> like the kick
> and shift of an intra-uterine
> memory, like
> this morning's dream of being
> born in an eagle's
> nest with speckled eggs and screech
>
> of nestlings, like a pent-up
> centenarian's sudden burst
> of lust, or maybe
> just elegies in Duino unbound
> from the dark,
> these new aborigines biding
> their time
> for the miner's night-light
>
> to bring them their dawn . . .

As early as 'Towards Simplicity' in *The Striders*, Ramanujan, in what became a favourite strategy of his, had drawn the human body and the natural world into one frame:

> Corpuscle, skin,
> cell, and membrane,
> each has its minute seasons
> clocked within the bones.

The poem projects death as a respite 'From the complexity / of reasons gyring within reasons', a return, if only for a while, to 'simplicity' and 'larger, external seasons'. But whereas 'Towards Simplicity' is Yeatsian and schematic, like a geometrical figure, 'Foundlings in the Yukon' is many-layered, expansive, flowing. No feature of Ramanujan's emotional geography is absent from it, and yet each appears as if newly 'unfurled'. Sexual hunger, lust, the 'horrid fact' which can wipe out 'a whole difficult lifetime / of dignity', are transformed into a metaphor for irrepressible life itself. The Pleistocene rocks in which the 'sealed off' seeds are found, the six seeds that 'took root and 'drank up sun', and the centenarian's 'pent-up' seeds, bind the animal, vegetable, and mineral worlds together to make one of Ramanujan's happiest poems.

Seekers after happiness, though, should turn to Ramanujan's translations. In them, he could be both himself (the skilfull Modernist poet) and somebody else; could inhabit both previous centuries and his own. As he says in a late poem, 'Time moves in and out of me'. Here is an example from *The Interior Landscape*:

WHAT HE SAID

As a little white snake
with lovely stripes on its young body
troubles the jungle elephant
this slip of a girl
her teeth like sprouts of new rice
her wrists stacked with bangles
troubles me.

In the ordering of its lines, the translation from the classical Tamil reminds one of some of his more inventive stanza shapes, but the resemblance ends there. Unlike the interior landscape of his poems, there is no place for razors, kitchen knives, or bandaged heads (the gruesome list could go on) in this one.

But the reader looking for A.K. Ramanujan, where should he turn? To the poems, the translations, or the essays? As befits the magician he set out to be, Ramanujan can be found in the same interconnected work he had, an instant ago, his multiple selves intact, disappeared into.

20
Salman Rushdie

ANURADHA DINGWANEY

To uncover the life and times of Salman Rushdie one need only turn to his fictional works, and then replenish these with details from his interviews and essays. *Midnight's Children, Shame,* and *The Satanic Verses,* each a not-so-neatly bounded fiction about three different nations, parallel the three national identifications of this author from three countries: England, where he lived until very recently; India, where he was born; and Pakistan, where his family lives. Writers often draw upon their own lives and experiences as raw material for their work; Rushdie more so than others. The facts of his life, the incidents and characters that people it, are replayed in his fiction, but with their meaning and significance drawn out, displayed, allegorised. Thus, avid consumers of Rushdie's anecdotes about himself—disseminated in his interviews and essays—are likely to recognise in Saladin Chamcha's life several incidents drawn from his creator's, including the infamous kipper incident in *The Satanic Verses* which Rushdie has pronounced 'absolutely true': 'it's one of the few stories I've used in fiction which needed no embellisment at all.' And if Aadam Aziz in *Midnight's Children* is modelled on his maternal grandfather, also a medical doctor and an enlightened man who encouraged his daughters to get an education, then facets of his father's character and life reappear in Ahmad Sinai, Saleem's father in *Midnight's Children*. Indeed, in the marketing and in reviews of *Midnight's*

Children, readers, with Rushdie's tacit approval, have assumed that Saleem's life corresponds not just with that of his nation, but also with that of his creator: 'Saleem and Salman are after all', notes Rushdie, 'if you look back etymologically, kind of versions of the same name . . . so there are clear affinities made . . . he's the same age as me more or less . . . he grows up in my house, he goes to my school, some of the things that happened to me happen in more interesting form to him.' The conversion of his own life into fiction is evident even more so in *Fury* (2001), which many reviewers have disliked for this precise reason.

Salman Rushdie was born to an affluent Muslim family in Bombay on 19 June 1947, 'only two months', Rushdie is fond of saying, before 'the British left' India. Being the eldest child, and a much-adored only son (Rushdie has three sisters) conferred upon him a sense of his own importance. Bombay, which he calls that 'most cosmopolitan, most hybrid, most hotchpotch of cities', is, to a great extent, India for Rushdie, the major setting as well for *Midnight's Children*, his novel about India's birth; and symbol and embodiment, more recently, in *The Moor's Last Sigh*, of the erosion of the myth of a secular, multilingual, multicultural India.

He was educated, first, at Cathedral School in Bombay, a classic neo-colonial enclave that 'groomed' him, he says, for the exclusive British public school, Rugby, and England, where he was headed next. Rushdie records his shock at discovering that the England of his imagination had little to do with the racist England he encountered when he found one of the boys, who shared his study, scrawling 'wogs go home' on the wall over his chair. From Rugby, Rushdie went to Pakistan, where his parents had moved in 1967, for which move Rushdie never forgave them. After a short stint with Pakistan TV, and frustrated by the censorship he discerned 'everywhere, inescapable, permitting no appeal', Rushdie returned to England, to take a degree in history at King's College, Cambridge. Thereafter, he worked in the fringe theatre in London, and, later, as a copywriter for an advertising agency.

Meanwhile, he was also working at becoming a writer, a vocation he had aspired to from his youth. Rushdie describes how he grew up surrounded by books, 'someone else's—a certain Colonel Arthur

Greenfield['s]', whose library his father had purchased. (Omar Khayyam Shakil, in *Shame*, inherits a library bought by his grandfather from a departing English colonel.) Rushdie's was a family of storytellers: his father, 'a magical parent of young children' because he knew how to tell a story, reappears in *Haroun and the Sea of Stories* as Rashid Khalifa, a well-known storyteller, whose tales 'tall, short, and winding' are 'really lots of tales juggled together'; and his mother was 'the keeper of family stories'. Is it any surprise, then, that storytellers and stories—copious, digressive, enchanting—dominate his fiction?

Rushdie's first published novel, *Grimus*, entered for a science fiction competition, lost the contest, but ended up being published anyway. Critics savaged the book. While Rushdie took the rejection badly, he soon recovered and decided to 'write something much closer to [his] knowledge of the world', an epic novel about India, its past, present, and (possible) future. In preparation for this undertaking, Rushdie and his first wife, Clarissa Luard, embarked on an extended trip to India.

In 'The Indian Writer in England', Rushdie recalls how, on revisiting his house in Bombay, he was 'gripped by the conviction that I, too, had a city and a history to reclaim'; at that moment *Midnight's Children* 'was really born'. Rushdie, who boasts of possessing virtually total recall, set out to assiduously 'recall as much of the Bombay of the 1950s and 1960s [he] could' to serve as material and inspiration for *Midnight's Children*. Published in 1981, it was a runaway success; it won the Booker Prize (in 1993 it was awarded the Booker of Bookers, the best of the twenty-six books to have won the prize from the time it was instituted in 1969), and made him a celebrity lionised by the media the world over.

Shame, his novel set in and about the ruling élite of Pakistan, followed two years later. It was also enthusiastically received, garnering much critical acclaim; it won the Prix du Meilleur Livre Etranger. It was banned in Pakistan, with copies being smuggled in.

Between 1981 and 1985 Rushdie wrote a series of essays reflecting on his location as an expatriate, immigrant writer. Noting how three places, India, Pakistan, and Britain, have more or less equal claim on him, and are thus legitimately subjects of his writing, he denounced those who would restrict him to his subcontinental identity as invoking an 'imperial' notion about what a writer from the third world is expected to write about. At the same time, in a scathing critique of the Raj revival in a spate of films and novels about India—*Gandhi, The Far Pavilions, The Jewel in the Crown, A Passage to India*—Rushdie, in 'Outside the Whale', wrote vociferously against the revival of the imperial mindset in Britain. He also denounced British racism by writing eloquently about the 'new empire in Britain'.

His July 1986 visit to Nicaragua as a guest of the Sandinista Association of Cultural Workers, brought him in contact with 'a government [he] could support' and yielded a travelogue of sorts, *The Jaguar Smile: A Nicaraguan Journey* (1987).

Over the years, from at least 1984, Rushdie was mapping out what was to become his most controversial work, *The Satanic Verses*, in an oeuvre dominated by other controversial works. 'This is the first time', Rushdie is reported to have said after completing it, 'that I have managed to write a book from the whole of myself . . . my entire sense of being in the world.' With the migrant's vision, identities, and concerns as its central preoccupations, *The Satanic Verses* is set in Margaret Thatcher's Britain, with characters who shuttle between Britain and the subcontinent, twentieth-century India and Britain, and seventh-century Asia. *The Satanic Verses* also attempts to embody Rushdie's attitude to Islam, to matters of faith and doubt. Even before it hit the market, the novel caused a stir in the publishing world by garnering a huge advance. When India banned it, a week after its publication in Britain, the stage seemed set for more bannings (Pakistan, Saudi Arabia, Egypt, Indonesia, South Africa, and several other countries with large Muslim populations also banned it) and more controversy, which was assured once Iran's Ayatollah Khomeini pronounced a fatwa against Rushdie. Rushdie went into hiding and remained so for more than a decade.

While in hiding, he wrote a 'children's' book, *Haroun and the Sea of Stories* (1991; promised to his son, Zafar) and put together a collection of essays written between 1981 and 1991, entitled, not inappropriately, *Imaginary Homelands* (1991). He has also brought out a collection of short stories, *East-West* (1994), several of which, Rushdie says, were written for, but did not find place in, *The Satanic Verses*. He has revisited, in *The Moor's Last Sigh*, the narrative and geographical terrain first mined in *Midnight's Children*. His latest novels, *The Ground Beneath Her Feet* (1999) and *Fury* (2001), have not been as well received, the reviews having been more mixed and the reception less spectacularly controversial than for the earlier, political fiction.

Rushdie displays remarkable consistency when it comes to certain ideas, certain literary and philosophical preoccupations, and the formal means through which to achieve them. Fortunately, or perhaps unfortunately, for his readers, he is an enormously self-conscious writer whose novels, comments, and analyses in interviews and essays insistently direct attention to these preoccupations and to his craft. Rushdie is also a very erudite writer; his work is peppered with all sorts of literary echoes, allusions, and puns, each self-consciously deployed with back-patting zeal and pleasure which he invites the savvy reader to share with him.

Predictably, one of the more significant ideas addressed in his non-fictional and fictional work springs from his location as an expatriate and migrant writer. In 'The Indian Writer in England', while defining his and other migrants' identities as plural and partial, at once straddling two cultures and distanced from both, Rushdie speculates about competing values of wholesale assimilation *versus* wholesale rejection of the dominant (or host) culture and values. For Rushdie, neither alternative is acceptable on its own; rather, he recommends that the migrant negotiate the culture and values of both 'native' and 'adopted' homes, strategically drawing upon each to create a new, hybrid identity.

Grimus (1979) represents Rushdie's initial examination of this theme. Its hero, Flapping Eagle, is an American Indian in search of his lost sister, whom he finds on a Mediterranean island under the control of Grimus, an expatriate European magician. (The Mediterranean is midway between the West and the Orient; Rushdie's choice of locale is not accidental.) Through Flapping Eagle, Rushdie explores a figure very like the immigrant, newly arrived in a different country and culture; in this instance, this newly arrived figure tries to uncritically assimilate with the values of the host culture. In 'The Indian Writer in England', Rushdie resolves the problem of assimilation *versus* rejection by highlighting the productive tension, and thus the need for a critically vigilant shuttling between the two opposed positions. In

Grimus, Flapping Eagle seems to have settled for inhabiting only one of the positions:

> Stripped of his past, forsaking the language of his ancestor for the language of the archipelagoes of the world, forsaking the ways of his ancestors for those of the place he drifted to, forsaking any hopes of ideals in the face of the changing and contradictory ideals he encountered, he lived, doing what he was given to do, thinking what he was instructed to think, being what it was most desirable to be.

Flapping Eagle's problems are those of rootlessness, which represents only one element in the dialectic of assimilation and estrangement that Rushdie identifies as making up the hybrid identity of the migrant. More than anything else, perhaps, *Grimus* is valuable because it foregrounds this new writer's attempt to find 'a suitable voice to speak in'.

Unlike Flapping Eagle, Rushdie's is not a problem (if problem it can be called) of rootlessness, but, he says, of a 'kind of multiple rooting', of coming 'from too many places'. While attempting to write something 'closer to [his] knowledge of the world', Rushdie honours this multiple rooting. Residing in London, he next wrote two narratives of the nation, *Midnight's Children* and *Shame*, each focused more or less on India and Pakistan respectively.

Midnight's Children tracks the pre-colonial, colonial, but mostly post-Independence life of India through a narrator and protagonist, Saleem Sinai, whose birth at the moment of India's formal independence from Britain 'handcuffs' him—his life, identity, and destiny—to his nation, much as the life and times of the nation are 'handcuffed' to Saleem's. Jawaharlal Nehru's letter to 'Baby Saleem' predicts: 'your life will be, in a sense, a mirror of our own.' As if to underscore the neat fit between the life of Saleem and that of his nation, Saleem, through his origins and upbringing, is presented as incorporating representative class and other alignments that have gone into the formation of the nation: he is the product of a liaison between a departing British sahib, William Methwold, and a lower-class woman, Vanita, who is married to a Christian street singer; switched at birth with Amina and Ahmad Sinai's real son, he grows up in an affluent Muslim household in cosmopolitan Bombay.

Saleem is a versatile storyteller, writing (or reciting) his own, and his nation's, life and times in a variety of registers and genres, at times rehearsing key moments in the colonial and post-Independence history of the nation, like the Jallianwala Bagh massacre, the two Indo-Pakistan wars, and at other times repeating gossip and 'national scandals' like the Nanavati case. He's also well-versed in the techniques and subject matter of that most ubiquitous icon of the subcontinent's popular culture—Bombay cinema—which he deploys in his own narrative with considerable verve and comic effect.

Saleem's history of India's colonial and post-Independence life also airs some of the salient debates and competing visions for an independent India mapped by nationalist leaders like Gandhi and Nehru. Through Aadam Aziz, Saleem's secular-minded, Germany-returned, progressive grandfather, and Tai, the ancient Kashmiri boatman, the conflict between and the respective values of modernity and tradition are examined. Similarly, the Nehruvian portrait of the modern Indian woman is presented through Aadam Aziz's appeals to his wife, Naseem, to give up purdah and enter the modern world.

Despite Saleem's drive to incorporate as much as he can, despite his effort to render his life as one of epic proportions, he is often brought up short by his recognition of his human frailties—a fallible memory, partial and fragmentary vision. Thus, *Midnight's Children*, paradoxically, insists on its effort to contain all of India and the impossibility of doing so, settling, instead, for, and making much of, the perspective of the person who writes or narrates India: 'There are as many versions of India', says Saleem, 'as Indians'.

The trajectory of Saleem's (and, by extension, India's) life is deeply pessimistic—castrated, prematurely old at thirty-one, his body cracking up into millions of pieces, neither he nor the nation he embodies seeming destined to fulfil the hopes invoked at their births. Nevertheless, Rushdie has always denied this pessimism, pointing to his representation of 'India's talent for non-stop regeneration' as it is exhibited by the sheer plenitude of stories, and stories within stories, that his novel incorporates. *Shame*'s pessimism, however, cannot be argued against.

According to *Shame*'s narrator, an expatriate like Rushdie who has returned to Pakistan for an extended visit, 'Pakistan . . . may best be described as the failure of the dreaming mind . . . perhaps the place was just *insufficiently imagined'*. *Shame*'s narrative focus is narrower: the nation is narrated only through a portrait of its ruling élite, especially this élite's corruption and utter shamelessness. More than anything else, then, *Shame* is an extended, densely metaphoric meditation on the various embodiments of national shame as they exhibit themselves in the public and private spheres.

In the public sphere, which is also the arena of masculinity and male power, the shamelessness, greed, and violence of the ruling élite is presented through the careers and changing fortunes of two politicos, Iskander Harappa and Raza Hyder, and their hangers-on and cohorts. (Iskander and Raza are barely disguised stand-ins for Zulfikar Ali Bhutto and Zia-ul Haq.) If women, like Arjumand Harappa, wish to participate in this sphere, they must 'rise above their gender', literally transform themselves into men. In the private sphere, shame is the cause and product of women's oppression, and of the management of their sexuality. Confined to this sphere, surrounded by the corruption and violence of their male relatives, women either go crazy, or kill themselves, or turn into figures of violent vengefulness. Whatever their ends, their lives as daughters, wives, mistresses of Iskander or Raza are embodiments of what has gone brutally wrong in this insufficiently imagined nation.

Coming from the perspective of a reflective expatriate narrator, who has only occasionally participated in the life of the nation he narrates, *Shame*, unlike *Midnight's Children*, is a vision of Pakistan by an ostensible outsider. Foregrounding the distortions and dislocations his perspective may be heir to (distortions and dislocations, incidentally, that an insider like Saleem is also not exempt from), the narrator also raises questions about the value of an outsider's perspective, the advantage he and by definition the migrant might possess by virtue of their—as Rushdie says in 'The Indian Writer in England'—'long geographical sight'.

Among the interests Rushdie identifies as central to his most controversial work, *The Satanic Verses* (1989), he mentions, first, the desire to 'give voice and fictional flesh to the immigrant culture', which entails an examination of the metamorphoses immigrants undergo, and the divided selves that result from negotiating two or more cultures simultaneously; and second, an attempt to explore the nature of divine revelation from the perspective of a secular person, which entails, in turn, an examination of religious faith *versus* religious doubt.

The book opens with its two heroes, Saladin Chamcha and Gibreel Farishta, hurtling through the sky as they plunge into the English channel—an image that represents, for Rushdie, the 'most spectacular act of immigration [he] could imagine'. *The Satanic Verses* explores immigrant experience in a very specific context, dealing with the lives of immigrants from formerly colonised third world countries in Thatcher's Britain. Migrations, the novel demonstrates, compel radical change: when Gibreel and Saladin land in a Sussex swamp, the former acquires an angel's halo, the latter sprouts horns, grows a goat's hooves, and begins to display an immense erection. In almost all instances, migrants are called upon to adapt, even to remake or reinvent themselves, to which they respond with varying degrees of complexity: the most single-minded either absolutely refuse or agree too willingly, too completely, to their transformation.

Simply transplanting one's native culture on an alien soil is viewed as unrealistic, perverse, politically reactionary, or unworkable. By the same token, remaking oneself completely in the image of the adopted country/culture (which, in this novel, also happens to be that of one's former coloniser's) is also viewed as problematic and politically disabling. Thus, Saladin Chamcha, a deracinated Indian who has striven to be English even before he left Bombay, who feels 'contempt for his kind', and who presumes he's marrying 'bloody Britannia' when he marries Pamela of the aristocratic, plummy English voice, must, in order to become human again, acknowledge the ties that bind him to his people, his family, his Indian past.

As much as several Muslim readers have been offended by Rushdie's portrayal of Islam, critics have remarked on its meticulous religious attentiveness. Rushdie himself notes that the Prophet 'insisted throughout on his simple humanity'. This humanity he sets out to explore via his account of 'Mahound's' career and of 'The Satanic Verses', both of which appear as part of Gibreel's hallucinatory dreams. 'The Satanic Verses' of the title refers to an incident in the life of the Prophet, recorded by early Arab historians, when he accepted that the worship of three female deities, Al-Lat, Al-Uzza, and Al-Manat, was permissible within the bounds of Islamic doctrine; he later repudiated this as an act inspired by the devil. Through this account of 'The Satanic Verses', Rushdie is interested in interrogating the status of religious belief *versus* modern scepticism, the status of religious revelation *versus* human agency.

While identifying the taboos against which his book transgresses, Rushdie mentions his attempt to write about the 'place of women in Islamic society and the Koran'. This attempt is most obvious in the Ayesha episode, which is based on a real-life incident—'The Hawkes Bay case', in which a young woman persuaded a village to make a pilgrimage to the sacred site of Karbala and promised the waters would part. When Rushdie retells what he has described as the 'most extraordinary image of faith that [he had] come across in years', his retelling shuttles between doubt and faith: several pilgrims drown; but those who survive claim that they saw the sea part.

For Rushdie, *The Moor's Last Sigh* (1995), appearing six years after *The Satanic Verses*, and written while in exile, marks the 'completion of a cycle [he] began in *Midnight's Children, Shame* and *The Satanic Verses*—the story of myself, where I came from, a story of origins and memory.' More than anything else, *The Moor's Last Sigh* revisits a particular place, Bombay, and a particular project, the birth and growth of a nation, India, that he first elaborated in *Midnight's Children.* This time, though, it is through the perspective not of a narrator from the Muslim middle class, but from one in whom two other minority communities—Christian and Jewish Indians, settled in Goa—are conjoined. But, like Saleem, Moraes Zogoiby (nicknamed the Moor) is also a magical, extraordinary figure: a physical giant with a deformed hand, he suffers from a rare genetic disease that forces him to grow at twice the rate ordinary humans do.

As in *Midnight's Children* (and through somewhat different means in *The Satanic Verses*), *The Moor's Last Sigh* celebrates mixtures, impurities, hybridity—more than one community and culture, after all, jostle within Saleem Sinai and the Moor. Of these, Bombay, according to the Moor, is the exemplary spatial embodiment: 'Bombay was central, had been so from the moment of its creation: the bastard child of a Portuguese-English wedding, and yet the most Indian of all Indian cities. In Bombay all India met and merged. In Bombay, too, all-India met what-was-not-India.'

In viewing the saga of the da Gama and Zogoiby families, their 'rise, falls . . . tiltoings up and down', we are invited, as in *Midnight's Children* and *Shame*, to compare this saga with that of the nation of which it is a part, and whose rise and fall it parallels. Unlike Saleem, however, the Moor's narrative specifies at some length not only what the nation has become, but what it had promised to be at its birth: reflecting a 'historical generosity of spirit', a 'free' India was supposed to be 'above religion . . . above class . . . above caste . . . above hatred . . . above vengeance . . . above tribe . . . above language . . . above ignorance . . . above stupidity'. It's hard not to discern in this ideal, not only Rushdie's investment in the India that the country's midnight's children were promised, but also a critique of what has come to pass.

The Moor's deep, indeed fundamental, commitment to a tolerant, plural, vibrant intermixture of cultures and communities, is not only central to his portrait of an ideal India, but also an essential tenet of his, and his creator, Rushdie's, artistic creed. Through a description of his mother Aurora Zogoiby's paintings—especially the Moor series for which he serves as model—the Moor articulates it. In these paintings, where Aurora 'reimagin[es] . . . the old Boabdil story . . . in a local setting . . . plac[ing] the Alhambra on Malabar Hill'—a setting which she christens 'Mooristan'—the Moor notes how 'the worlds collide, flow in and out of one another, and washofy away'; 'she was using Arab Spain', he notes, 'to re-imagine India' by overlaying the ugliness of contemporary India, with its religious intolerance and steady erosion of humane, secular values, with those of a tolerant Moorish Spain—'a conjoined Arab, Jewish, and Christian culture' before it broke apart under the pressure of Catholic fundamentalism.

In a 1993 interview in *The Times of India*, Rushdie, 'obviously agonised that India was the first country to ban *The [Satanic] Verses*', remarked that 'the rupture with India is what hurts [him] most . . . to be expelled from India is very painful.' In a September 1995 interview he notes that 'the cycle of novels'—*Midnight's Children, Shame, The Satanic Verses*, and *The Moor's Last Sigh*—that record his 'response to an age in history that began in 1947 . . . is now complete.' He implies he does not expect, therefore, a return to the subcontinent as his primary subject. Between his sense of an enforced exile from India and the measured acceptance, even elegiac embrace, of this exile lies *The Moor's Last Sigh*, which a number of readers have, in fact, read as a novel of leave-taking, 'a last sigh', in the Moor's words, 'for a lost world, a tear for its passing'. The loss, of course, is ours as much as, perhaps more so than, Rushdie's, especially since his work—his critics and admirers alike recognise—put the subcontinent on the map in glorious technicolour.

According to Anita Desai, Rushdie showed English-language novelists in India a way to be 'post-colonial'. There is an entire generation of novelists from India who feel the weight of Rushdie's influence as enabling (or disabling) their own talents. Quite apart from what Rushdie demonstrated via his technique, his vivid descriptions, and his idiosyncratic characters, he showed Indians how the English language could be appropriated, bent in any way one wanted, to achieve sensational effects. To cite but a few examples, all from *The Moor's Last Sigh*, of Rushdie's transforming magic: relentlesly punning his way into his narrative, playing on words, the Moor remarks upon the conundrum of the discovery of India—'how could we be discovered when we were not covered before?'; 'we were not so much subcontinent as sub-condiment . . . [the Portuguese, the French and the English] came for the hot stuff'. Elsewhere, the Moor, a 'Cathjew nut', transcribes his great-grand-mother, Epifania's Indian-English, with hilarious effect: 'In this God-fearing Christian house, British still is best, madder moyselle . . . If you have ambitions in our boy's direction, then please mindofy your mouth . . . Pudding-shudding? Why not? These are Christmas topics frawline.' And, finally, the Moor plays on the similarity between insanity and 'insaaniat' (humanity) to aver: 'Just as I have rejected all supernatural theories, so I will not allow her [Uma, his treacherous lover] to be mad . . . insane persons are excused from moral judgement, and Uma deserves to be judged. *Insaan*, a human being. I insist on Uma's insaanity.'

21

After Midnight

The Novel in the 1980s and 1990s

Jon Mee

The 1980s witnessed a second coming for the Indian novel in English. Its messiah seems to have been Salman Rushdie. The appearance of *Midnight's Children* in 1981 brought about a renaissance in Indian writing in English which has outdone that of the 1930s. Its influence, acknowledged by critics and novelists alike, has been apparent in numerous ways: the appearance of a certain post-modern playfulness, the turn to history, a new exuberance of language, the reinvention of allegory, the sexual frankness, even the prominent references to Bollywood, all seem to owe something to Rushdie's novel. Nevertheless, to attribute everything to a single, personal intervention would be naïve. The pretensions of the messianic critic are irrevocably deflated if he or she reads I. Allan Sealy's account of the origins of his own first novel, *The Trotter-Nama*. Written but not published before *Midnight's Children*, Sealy's novel, like Rushdie's, originally had a narrator born on the midnight hour of Indian Independence. Although Sealy felt that he had to drop this specific idea when he read Rushdie's novel, in the published versions of both stories the fate of the narrator still mirrors the fate of the nation. Sealy's view of the convergence is that it represents 'two writers responding to the same historical moment. They have read the same book, but the book is India. India is dictating, the country is doing the "thinking". We do not write but are written.' The question which follows from Sealy's statement is:

what is the India that is writing these texts? Various economic and social pressures have led to the end of the so-called Nehruvian consensus in India. The idea of unity within—so central to the years of nationalist struggle and the building of the new nation-state—has been displaced by an urgent need to question the nature of that unity. The issue of imagining the nation, the issue of the fate of the children of the midnight hour of Independence, has become a pressing one throughout India. It is an issue which has been debated in all languages. The better novels in English of the past twenty years participate in this larger debate. If Rushdie ushered in a new era of Indian writing in English, it has to be acknowledged that he was more a sign of the times than their creator.

Rushdie's fame may have identified an international audience for Indian writers in English, but commercial developments in English-language publishing within India have played their part in enabling a new crop of novelists to come forward. Many writers who publish abroad now also insist on a separate Indian edition of their work. Ravi Dayal's publishing house has nurtured a group of writers identified with Delhi's élite St. Stephen's College—I. Allan Sealy, Amitav Ghosh, Shashi Tharoor, Upamanyu Chatterjee, Rukun Advani, Mukul Kesavan, and Anurag Mathur were all students at this college in the early 1970s—who self-consciously acknowledge each other's influence in their books. The setting up of Penguin India in 1987 and the emergence of Rupa Paperbacks and IndiaInk provided a marketing network able to deliver more affordable English-language fiction to the expanding urban middle class. It is the world of this middle class which provides the most obvious context for the new Indian writing in English. The ex-schoolteacher Ranga Rao (b. 1936) is no Stephanian and his *Fowl Filcher* (1987) is able to communicate a vivid sense of rural and provincial life, but he still acknowledges that 'the nation itself has moved from the village centrism of the Gandhian era to the city-centrism of the post-Nehru period.' Some critics, however, believe that India's writers in English have taken advantage of this trend to retreat into a metropolitan or cosmopolitan élitism which produces a literature intended only for the English-reading privileged classes within India or the international public outside.

Such views cannot simply be dismissed as reactionary traditionalism: if nothing else they alert the literary critic to the question of the relationship between the novels of the 1980s and the Indian regional languages. One of the legacies of *Midnight's Children* was a vibrant model for rewriting English in dialogue with those languages. Anita Desai has claimed that it was only after 'Salman Rushdie came along that Indian writers finally felt capable of using the spoken language, spoken English, the way it's spoken on Indian streets by ordinary people.' However, Desai's account is not quite accurate. Contemporary novelists rarely attempt streetwise realism. More often they bring different languages into comic collision, testing the limits of communication between them, celebrating India's linguistic diversity, and taking over the English language to meet the requirements of an Indian context, a perspective which receives perhaps its most explicit statement on the often-quoted opening page of Upamanyu Chatterjee's *English, August* (1988): 'Amazing mix . . . Hazaar fucked. Urdu and American . . . I'm sure nowhere else could language be mixed and spoken with such ease.' Nevertheless this kind of reshaping of the language is not entirely without its anxieties. In *English, August*, for instance, the promise of a novel written in a new kind of desi English rather fizzles out in favour of a continual self-conscious questioning of its own linguistic boundaries. The hero, Agastya, like his creator an employee of the Indian Administrative Service, is confronted with a variety of views on the role of English in India when he finds himself a member of the college-educated élite cast adrift on a posting to small-town India. One view he encounters is that India's writers in English are hopelessly alienated from the national culture, 'full with one mixed-up culture and writing about another, what kind of audience are they aiming at'. From this kind of perspective 'there really are no universal stories, because each language is an entire culture . . . great literature has to have its regional tang'.

New novelists of the 1980s such as Chatterjee (b. 1959) have tried to demonstrate that, on the contrary, the Indian 'tang' is not a pure essence but the masala mix of a culture that has always been able to appropriate influences from outside the subcontinent. From this point of view, English is implicated in the polyphony of Indian languages, its colonial authority relativised by entering into the complexity which it describes. Yet translations between the languages that participate in this polyphony are not likely to be an easy process of matching like to like. Hierarchies exist that structure the relationships between India's languages. The English language has a privileged place in Indian culture. It is the language of the former coloniser and remains an élite language, the language of getting on, the language of business, the language identified, above all, with modernity. The best of the novelists, as we shall see below, bring to their writing an awareness of the inequality of access to English and the problems of communication between different classes and cultures within India. Both *English, August* and its less well-received successor, *The Last Burden* (1993), explore the conflict between tradition and modernity in contemporary India without simply privileging one over the other. Indeed it is difficult not to read the troubled relationship between the narrator and his dying mother at the centre of *The Last Burden* as a subtle allegorical account of precisely this conflict.

For some critics the very playfulness of the kinds of language used in recent novels confirms the privileges of a class of Indians without any anxieties attached to their uses of English, and secure enough in their own élitism to experiment with a language they have often spoken from birth. From this kind of perspective the abrogation of standard English is the sign of a certain cultural weightlessness, the deracinated insouciance of élite college boys, or the alienation of those who have lost touch with the national community (if there is such a thing). No doubt social and economic privilege has been important, perhaps even necessary, to the creation of a cultural space in which to rewrite the language of the coloniser. By no means were all of the novelists of the 1980s Stephanians, as Shama Futehally (1952–2004), who was educated in Bombay and Leeds, archly points out in the preface to her *Tara Lane* (1993), but compared to writers in other Indian languages the novelists writing in English do seem to come from a rather uniform and narrow class band: academics, editors, and other inhabitants of the book trade abound. Even so there are problems with assuming the existence of some homogeneous national community from which these writers are distanced by their practice of writing in English. After all, in a country which still has very low levels of literacy, literature in whatever language is not a popular form.

Furthermore, it has been argued that 'the nation has first to be imagined to become real', and these novelists make their own contribution to that process, often in ways that directly raise the issue of the role to be played by the English language in the wider community as part of the broader debate about the identity of the nation as a whole.

It seems to have been the success of *Midnight's Children* which gave these writers the confidence to address such issues. Prior to Rushdie's example the writer in English was more often seeking to demonstrate just how Indian he or she could be while writing in an 'alien' language. In Rushdie's novel the literal cracking up of Saleem represents the end of one cycle of the national imaginary, the fracturing of Nehru's promise 'to build the noble mansion of free India where all her children may dwell'. The figure of the fissuring body politic recurs in *Beethoven Among the Cows* (1994) by Rukun Advani (b. 1955). Advani's narrator fears he is doomed 'to see India crack up like the fragments of my multi-channelled mind'. The death of Nehru in the novel's opening chapter figures as the loss of innocence both for the narrator, who is leaving behind his boyhood, and for the nation for whom the loss of its integrity looms—an idea imaged by the fundamentalist threat to an Indian architectural heritage which includes the Babri Masjid, the Golden Temple, and the Taj Mahal. The allegorical parallel of the growth to maturity of the individual and the growth of an independent India is a recurrent feature in many novels of the period, but not always in Advani's terms of a nostalgia for a lost unity.

There is a suggestion that Nehru's inclusive rhetoric was always a mask for an exclusive reality. In Futehally's *Tara Lane*, for instance, Nehru's promise that 'all of us will stand as one' is haunted by bad faith from the moment it is made. The family of industrialists from which the daughter-narrator comes regards her desire to act on Nehru's speech and collect for famine relief as going 'too far'. As the novel proceeds and the daughter moves out of the cosseted world of the extended family into the city of Bombay, the paternalistic view of society which represents her father's factory as a treasure house which provides both for the family and the workers is revealed as a deception operating in the interests of the middle classes: 'I was protected as if by ear-muffs, and learnt to nod or smile or talk through the metaphorical slits in the muffling.' The family is constantly wrapping and protecting its possessions, drawing boundaries between itself and the crowd outside: 'You had to make sure that the object in question was locked away against thieves, wrapped up against monsoon damp, mothballed against termites, guarded from stains, not paraded before servants'. The unity of the Nehruvian image of India is revealed to be a denial of the nation that lies beyond the family's boundaries.

In Rushdie's fiction, Bombay has served as the place wherein the fractured nation becomes defined by heterogeneity, a place where India's different cultures meet, and where India meets the world, but subsequent representations of India's great commercial city have by no means uniformly endorsed an idea of Bombay as a post-modern utopia. Amit Chaudhuri was born in Calcutta in 1962, but brought up in Bombay before going to university in England, where he lived until recently. In his fiction Bombay figures as the symbol of a disorienting modernity to be contrasted with Calcutta, 'the only city I know that is timeless'. Both *A Strange and Sublime Address* (1991) and *Afternoon Raag* (1993) are permeated by a lyrical sense of the loss of self. What for Rushdie is a supplementarity of identity, the possibility of an idea of Indianness built on the very differences within the culture, is for Chaudhuri more often a lack, a sense of disorienting loss. In Chaudhuri's third book, *Freedom Song* (1998), the child's Calcutta is still present but has been changed by two decades of communist rule and political violence across the country. In his fourth, *A New World* (2000), Chaudhuri writes of a more ambivalent Calcutta, a city no more than a minor place of transit: in fact the focus is not the city but a small family with a divorced son visiting from America.

Much more in tune, perhaps, with Rushdie's comic sense of the lived complexities of Bombay's hybrid culture is *Ravan & Eddie* (1995) by Kiran Nagarkar (b. 1949), one of the few novels which is set totally outside the middle classes. Nagarkar, like Rushdie before him, has worked in the advertising industry, but he has also had a career writing in an Indian language, Marathi, his novel *Saat Sakkam Trechalis* (1974)—subsequently published in translation as *Seven Sixes are Forty-three*—having enjoyed great critical acclaim. Itself originally begun in Marathi, *Ravan & Eddie* is set in a Bombay *chawl* and follows the growth of the two boys of the title whose relationship symbolises the tensions and divisions of India. Ravan is a Marathi-speaking

Hindu. Eddie is a Goan Catholic. The lives of the two communities in the chawl run parallel, but at the same time, in defiance of the logic of geometry, 'here parallel lines which should meet only at the horizon criss-cross each other merrily'. In Nagarkar's Bombay the assertion of difference is constantly being thwarted by strange cultural continuities, none stranger than when the Christian boy joins a right-wing Hindu organisation in order to win the prize of a book of stories from the *Mahabharata*. For all its detailed sense of cultural difference, and for all the farcical comedy of Eddie's mother dragging him from the stage to return him to the bosom of his own community, Nagarkar's novel suggests that this world is also joined by shared stories which are not the special property of any particular group. The chawl, with its different floors given to different communities and different stories, is itself an ironic but not pessimistic restatement of the persistence of Nehru's vision of the nation as a mansion with many rooms.

Perhaps the most sustained response to the opportunities created by Rushdie's precedent has come in Amitav Ghosh's fiction. Originally from Calcutta, Ghosh (b. 1956) was the first of the band of Stephanians to respond with gusto to the challenge of *Midnight's Children*. Having completed postgraduate training at Oxford in social anthropology and currently living in New York, where he teaches, it comes as no surprise to find that Ghosh is a writer concerned with India's place in larger international cultural networks, whose fiction seems directly informed by contemporary academic debates about colonialism and culture. His first novel, *The Circle of Reason* (1986), very much written in Rushdie's magical realist mode, attempts to recover a continuing tradition of cultural exchange for India westwards across the Indian ocean to the Gulf states and Egypt. *In an Antique Land* (1992) returned to this issue, combining travelogue with historical reflection in a text which challenges the privileges of the academic anthropologist's 'scientific' gaze. *The Calcutta Chromosome* (1996) is also concerned with the relationship between science, history, and colonialism in a futuristic detective story. His novel-as-chronicle, *The Glass Palace* (2000), meditates on large historical and nationalist issues such as diaspora, migration, refugees, colonial hegemony, and the economic and cultural subjugation of populous regions by the West.

Ghosh is obviously a novelist given to generic inventiveness and he has been taken by some critics to be a champion of post-modern cultural weightlessness, but his writing is as interested in the ties that bind as in the transitory nature of global culture. The most impressive of Ghosh's novels remains his second book, *The Shadow Lines* (1988), which deals with relations between the different arms of a prospering bhadralok family, the Datta-Chaudhuris, displaced from Dhaka to Calcutta by the Partition. At the centre of the novel is the figure of Tridib who teaches the nameless narrator that all communities, indeed all identities, are imagined or narrated: 'Everyone lives in a story . . . they all lived in stories, because stories are all there are to live in, it was just a question of which story.' Nevertheless, it would be misleading to suggest that Ghosh's novel is uninterested in the particularities of specific cultural locations. If the nation is a fiction, whose boundaries are capable of being reimagined and redrawn, it nevertheless remains a powerful determining presence, as too are the histories of colonialism and racism which haunt the relationships between the Datta-Chaudhuris and the Prices, English friends-of-the-family across two generations. *The Shadow Lines* is a novel filled with the specificities of names, dates, and places, a novel in love with some kinds of cultural difference even while it seeks to imagine a way beyond others. Moreover it shows that different narratives of the self and the nation can collide with devastating effects. Part of its brilliant sense of the complications of cultural identity is its perception that even where cultural difference is radically asserted, when Tridib is killed in a communal riot while visiting his family's old home in Dhaka, it can be shadowed by lines of connection. The riot has been started by the theft of the Prophet's hair in Kashmir, in a city thousands of miles away, in a country from which Dhaka is now partitioned, with the two countries, India and East Pakistan (as it was at the time of the riot) 'locked into an irreversible symmetry by the line that was to set us free—our looking-glass border'. This last metaphor, the figure of the mirror, runs throughout the novel as the sign of those relations which paradoxically connect nations and individuals even as they divide them.

In some respects, *The Shadow Lines* can be thought of as a historical novel. Like *Midnight's Children*, it is interested in recuperating histories squeezed out of the state's homogenising myth of the nation. The riot which kills Tridib in Ghosh's novel has fallen from the pages of history, unrecorded in Calcutta newspapers, Ghosh suggests, because the state and public institutions regard war alone as a 'properly' historical conflict. A series of young novelists has followed Ghosh in trying their hands, with varying degrees of success, at writing historical narratives that display a revisionary scepticism about narrow definitions of the nation. But where *The Shadow Lines* adapts the family romance to this purpose, these writers have more often resorted to a hyperbolic epic mode. Among them is I. Allan Sealy (b. 1951), another Stephanian, who turned from writing a doctoral thesis in Canada on Wilson Harris to produce *The Trotter-Nama* (1988). Sealy has since written several more books: *Hero* (1991); *From Yukon to Yucatan* (1994), a travelogue in which he returns to North America and turns the Western gaze back on itself; and *The Everest Hotel* (1998). But his most striking achievement remains his epic chronicle of a family of Anglo-Indians, a community whose presence troubles the imagining of the nation in terms of the expression of some homogeneous cultural authenticity, an idea which the novel suggests is derived from a colonial mentality. As with Saleem in Rushdie's *Midnight's Children*, the reader is always aware of the struggle of Eugene, the narrator, to include everything in his family chronicle. Indeed Eugene explicitly contrasts his inclusive narrative method, the method of the 'nama' or chronicle, with that of European historiography:

> This foul substance is called what?
> The foul substance is called History.
> And its opposite?
> Is the Chronicle
> Which may be illustrated?
> Profusely.
> Is colourful?
> In the extreme.
> . . . .
> It is the end of Historie.

Sealy's novel implies that historiography as a genre is complicit with the colonising tendencies of the ideas of the European Enlightenment, and with its confidence that all histories can be reduced to a universal narrative modelled after its own. History-writing in the novel is the province of the Anglo-Indian Montagu, whose narrative is 'the best an historian could do', but consequently leaves out not only the fantastic events with which the novel is concerned but also much of what makes up everyday life: 'The bequest of a school occupied him for an entire chapter, while of breakfasts and recipes he made no mention.' Sealy's chronicle form, in contrast, offers to the reader history novelised in the sense that it is open to the diversity of perspectives and languages circulating in the world. Eugene does not speak the privileged language of truth. What he says is continually interrogated, interrupted, and undermined in ways that could be thought of as an attempt to write a kind of newly post-colonial history.

The nama is an old Indianised form and part of Sealy's attempt to unseat historiography is the attempt to displace the genres of the coloniser with those of the colonised. For Sealy this displacement does not take place in the interests of a return to some pre-colonial, essentially Indian identity, an option hardly open to an Indian writer in English, but rather one which involves a distinctively Indian version of modernity. Sealy himself has said that there are countless Indian forms that can be 'revived and intelligently reworked' so that 'Indian modernism need not be a wholesale imitation of foreign objects'.

A similar idea of using traditional Indian literary forms for the purposes of historical narration underpins Shashi Tharoor's *The Great Indian Novel* (1989). Tharoor (b. 1956) is another international Indian who went on from St Stephen's to a career with the United Nations. Perhaps rather too relentlessly, his novel adapts the story of the *Mahabharata* to an allegory of modern Indian history. As the tongue-in-cheek title suggests, *The Great Indian Novel* takes an irreverent view of the development of modern India which is in tune with the scepticism of many recent historical novels. Similarly, he shows few qualms about taking on one of the great epics for such purposes. Rather than simply placing contemporary material in traditional forms, which would be in danger of reproducing the kind of orientalism that has always defined India in terms of the glories of an unchanging past, novelists of this period have been much more willing to rewrite the genres of Indian literary tradition. Nor has Indian tradition simply been understood to be a repertoire of classical literary forms. Hindi film, for instance, has had an important influence on recent fiction, providing a set of symbols, new kinds of narrative technique (as in Ruchir Joshi's *The Last Jet-Engine Laugh*, 2001), and, in novels such as Sealy's *Hero* and Tharoor's *Show Business* (1994), a new subject matter. For these and other novels soaked in the world of popular cinema, definitions of Indian 'tradition' in terms of eternal high-cultural forms are being broken down.

The desire to adapt the European form of the novel to indigenous literary traditions is not new. As early as the 1930s Raja Rao understood the need to tell the history of the nationalist struggle in a form which looked beyond the colonial model of historiography to the 'sthalapurana' or legendary history of the village. In the process, formal history is crowded together with memory, folk-tale, and gossip. If this seems to anticipate novels like *Midnight's Children* and *The Trotter-Nama*, where it differs from them is in the absence of an intrusive narrative voice fracturing the surface of the tale and drawing attention to the process of telling. The 'chutneyfication of history', to use Rushdie's own phrase, is a process of preserving the distinctive tanginess of India, but it is a process which transforms what it preserves. Moreover the chutney metaphor contains within it the idea of a variety of ingredients that go together to make a history which cannot be captured by any one representative part. Rao's novel was able to make use of the single village as a metonym for the nation. The Indian village was often the idealised antithesis of Western industrialism in the literature of the national movement. Recent fiction has been more concerned with the modern metropolis, but it has also importantly been sceptical about any stable relationship between the nation and its symbols. Rushdie's Saleem cracks up under the weight of representing the nation. Sealy's Anglo-Indians are part of the nation but their relation to it is much more problematic than that of Rao's villagers. In contemporary Indian writing in English, the impossibility of using any particular group as a metonym for 'the people' seems to be itself a recurrent trope.

1995 saw two new novelists address the issue of translating Indian history into the novel: Mukul Kesavan (b. 1957) and Vikram Chandra

(b. 1961). For Kesavan, an academic historian by profession, the question of how to write a national history without reproducing the categories of colonialism is an explicitly pressing problem. Drawing on his own research into the relationship between the Muslim population and the nationalist movement, *Looking through Glass* (1995) looks at a community which is often erased from nationalist histories and in the process offers a different, less heroic perspective on the closing years of the struggle for independence. Kesavan's novel begins in the present, with a young photographer taking the ashes of his grandmother to the Ganges. En route he falls from a railway bridge in pursuit of a picturesque shot, but wakes up to find himself in 1942 amid the Quit India agitation. Not only has he travelled across time, but also across cultures: he is taken in by a Muslim family whose Urdu newspaper he cannot even read. In a sense photography is evoked in this framing narrative as the governing metaphor of the whole story. The photograph promises to deliver unmediated reality to its viewer, but the image is framed and focused in ways which always leave something out of the equation. Kesavan's hero becomes mired in history in a way which implies that the historian can provide not a clear window onto the real, but only a lens which frames and refracts what it sees.

If all these novelists share an interest in retrieving suppressed histories, they also foreground, in their different ways, the act of narration. The process of examining exclusions from the national imaginary seems to have brought about a recognition of the nature of history as itself a form of narrative which relies on literary devices, such as emplotment and metaphor, to create its meaning.

In these recent historical novels, the nation tends to be written in terms of its unruly excessiveness. Their form often takes on the shape of what it describes. The Sanskrit aesthetic principle of excessive saying or 'atyukti' is practised to demonstrate that these novels exceed restrictive conceptions of national boundaries. Digressions, repetitions, and fantastic events push the traditional form of the novel to its limits and often at the centre of the textual carnival is the body itself. In Sealy's *The Trotter-Nama* and another rambling mock-epic, Khushwant Singh's *Delhi* (1990), for instance, the body plays an important role as an image for the unruliness of the history not only of Delhi but also of the country of which it is capital. The hijra (eunuch) at the centre of Singh's novel is a sign of the heterogeneity of the nation and Sealy's narrator, Eugene, who begins his story with a dream of 'gulab jamuns in warm syrup', is as enormous as the narrative he produces. The sense of a world filled with endless desire which emerges from some of these novels might be taken to be the literary expression of a new middle-class consumerism which, like the bounteous film-world of the hit *Hum Aapke Hain Kaun* (1994), suggests a world of goods which have only to be imagined to be obtained. It is possible to see in some of these novels a refashioning of the old, orientalist image of India as perpetual change, defined by multiplicity, a kind of endless narrative opportunity, to fit with a new reorientation to the global free market. At the beginning of Vikram Chandra's *Red Earth and Pouring Rain* (1995), another novel replete with epic digressions and fantastic events, not to mention a delight in sex and food, the recently foreign-returned Abhay listens to 'his father's ancient typewriter beat out its eternal thik-thik, creating yet another urgent missive to a national newspaper about the state of Indian democracy.' While what follows is a reworking of history and myth, one wonders whether in this opening rhetorical gesture pressing contemporary political issues are not being put aside to create a space for the idea of India as endless narrative potential. This raises the question of whether Indian politics is trivialised by a novel which returns again and again to the idea of a world constructed of endless narrative.

Chandra is certainly another writer who, like his novel, floats between continents, dividing his time between the United States, where he attended graduate school, and Bombay. The story of *Red Earth and Pouring Rain* revolves around the fate of Sanjay, reincarnated as a monkey that Abhay shoots for stealing his new jeans from the washing line. When Yama, god of death, enters the story to claim the dying monkey, Ganesh intervenes with a deal. If Sanjay can tell his story and keep everyone entertained, he will be saved. His story begins in the period when mercenaries and princes, along with the East India Company, were fighting over the remains of the Mughal empire. Chandra's fictional characters mix not only with gods but also historical figures like Begum Samroo and James Skinner. History in the novel becomes 'The Big Indian Lie', but he warns, 'do not think that this story is untrue, because it is *itihasa*; thus it was.' In the novels of Rushdie, Sealy, Ghosh, and Kesavan, this idea is made the centre of a political inquiry into the ownership of stories, an aspect of the new historical novel which seems absent from Chandra's sense of history as 'Leela, the great cosmic play'. What Chandra does do, like Sealy in *The Trotter-Nama*, is to explicitly differentiate his method from a Western tradition identified in terms of an Aristotelian desire for straight lines and defining essences. In response, Chandra offers the familiar trope of India-as-heterogeneity, but one of the novel's strengths is that it does not simply produce an exoticised spectacle of otherness for a Western readership. Abhay, the foreign-returned student, has to step into the gap created when Sanjay is too exhausted to continue by telling a tale of his scholarship days in America, 'the crucible in which the world's most weightless and alluring myths are perfected'. The crowd that gathers to listen remains as fascinated by this tale drawn from an entirely different mythology, a road movie which takes them across desert skies and into the big city of Houston, as by Sanjay's story of fantastic deeds from India's past. Western modernity is in this way reproduced not as the privileged sphere of truth and reason, but as the site of another mythology which is just as enticing as India's own—a perspective Chandra's novel shares with Sealy's travelogue, *From Yukon to Yucatan*.

In imposing contrast to the ways in which so many of the recent novels draw attention to history as itself a story stands the classic realism of Vikram Seth's mammoth *A Suitable Boy* (1993). This is set in the early 1950s, formative years of the Nehru period, with the passing of the zamindari abolition legislation and the first election of the post-independence era looming. For all its copious realism, it is difficult not to see this novel too as an allegory of nationhood. Where it differs from Rushdie's other literary children is in the confident way that it subscribes to an idea of Indian history as a progress towards the goal of a secular, commercial society in the image of conventional Western models of national development. The novel is based on a romance plot, the choice of a suitable boy for the heroine, Lata Mehra; but although she shows signs of independence, the novel is ultimately one of conformity and what it represents as the inevitability of bourgeois life. The man Lata chooses is neither the son of Calcutta's high society, nor the Muslim boy whose friendship scandalises Lata's mother, but Haresh Khanna of Prahapore, a man who is foreign-returned but from a British technical college rather than the kind of élite institution which Seth himself attended. Moreover it is the shoe trade for which he is being trained, a business profession which brings with it the spectre of the loss of caste. Haresh would seem to represent Seth's idea of properly bourgeois man emerging from religious superstition and social snobbery. Along with its sense of the inevitability of a particular kind of national development—for Haresh's success is surely intended as a parable for the times—comes a nostalgia for a feudal world of Urdu literature and courtly entertainments. *A Suitable Boy* would seem to affirm the idea that the destiny of middle-class India lies in casting aside an obstructive concern with traditional identities in pursuit of secularism in its liberal economic mode. With such confidence about the future of the nation, what is to be left behind can be romanticised in a nostalgia for a world that it views as inevitably lost.

What *A Suitable Boy* shares with some of the more experimental narratives is its size. Male writers, especially, seem to have been drawn to reimagining the nation on an epic scale, a pretension to inclusiveness even where the inevitable failure of that ambition is signalled in the more meta-fictional narratives. Perhaps their assertion of a right to rewrite national history is itself the expression of a certain privilege to which Indian women do not easily gain access. Be that as it may, women writers have recently been having their own say about who constitutes the nation. A series of novels, including *The Dark Holds No Terrors* (1980), *Roots and Shadow* (1983), *That Long Silence* (1988), and *Small Remedies* (2000) have established Shashi Deshpande (b. 1938) as perhaps the leading writer who deals in a direct way with the situation of women in urban middle-class life. Educated in Bombay and Bangalore, where she lives, Deshpande turned to writing relatively late after bringing up her children and training as a journalist in the early 1970s. Her novel *The Binding Vine* (1992) is filtered through the fears, hopes, and uncertainties of an urban middle-class consciousness. The narrator, Urmi, who lives in Bombay, has recently lost her daughter, but she is drawn out of her grief by two experiences, both of which challenge the boundaries of her world. The first is the discovery of a trunk belonging to her dead mother-in-law, packed with poems and diaries, which, to Urmi's surprise, reveals her to have been a woman of great imaginative powers, trapped, violated and eventually killed by a man she did not love. In the process the domestic sphere is revealed to have histories of its own which have gone previously unrecorded. The second experience challenges the limits of Urmi's domesticity, not through confronting it with an image of the history of its repressions but by revealing the contemporary realities of life for women of less privileged classes. Visiting a friend in hospital, Urmi meets the distraught Shakuntala, whose daughter has been brutally beaten and raped. Their developing relationship, haunted by the figure of the daughter who remains unconscious in hospital, is a difficult and uneven one. Although Urmi assumes direction of Shakuntala's life, her modern, reforming gaze has to accept its own limits. Urmi's English-speaking background is a different world from the Marathi culture inhabited by Shakuntala, just as her mother-in-law's poetry, written in Kannada, and which Urmi struggles to translate into English, comes from an unimagined past. Translation becomes a governing metaphor in the novel for the gaps which separate the different cultures that make up the nation, especially as they affect the question of the place of women in the national community.

Gita Hariharan (b. 1954) has not adopted Deshpande's realist mode, though there are thematic similarities in their fiction. Hariharan came to writing after a career as an editor and journalist and shows an interest in literary experimentation in a less epic mode than many of her male counterparts. Whereas nearly all of those novelists who have toyed with the epic tradition have laid some kind of claim to the cultural authority of the *Mahabharata*, Hariharan's *A Thousand Faces of Night* (1992) and *The Ghosts of Vasu Master* (1994) are concerned with rewriting folk tales and children's stories. In the latter, a retired schoolteacher, Vasu Master, succeeds in winning over the problem child Mani by storytelling. The stories are reworkings of the *Panchatantra*. A.W. Ryder's translation of the famous collection of tales, cited in Hariharan's notes, describes the *Panchatantra* as a 'niti-shastra', a textbook of 'niti' or the wise conduct of life. While it is more concerned with the domestic space than the epic canvas of history, the novel explores what it means to be a good citizen and places the problem squarely in relation to the question of what constitutes Indian modernity. Vasu comes to recognise 'the necessity of reconstruction' from the 'dismantled parts of various ideas, beliefs, models' that are his inheritance. His willingness to use whatever lies at hand as material for the stories that eventually seem to heal the boy suggests an attitude to traditional culture which treats it as an open resource for the future, not a closed, epic authority, but something that can be rewritten for present needs. In the mode of Raja Rao's adaptation of the folk form to the story of the nationalist struggle, Hariharan's novels stand as a repudiation of the orientalist view of India as defined by the glorious high culture of antiquity. *A Thousand Faces of Night* focused more specifically on the positioning of Indian women in relation to this orientalist idea of tradition. Hariharan herself returned to India after attending graduate school in the United States and this novel is an account of the foreign-returned Devi's attempt to find a way of living in contemporary India, cunningly interleaved with the tales of heroes and heroines told to her as a child by her grandmother: her use of these tales as part of a fluid tradition of storytelling questions the closed idea of 'tradition'. She anticipates something of Vikram Chandra's sense of Indian culture as an infinite set of perpetually circulating narratives, but her novel has a keener sense of the way these narratives can become ossified into constricting forms, particularly in relation to the way that they are used as containing narratives for women. The achievement of *A Thousand Faces of Night* lies in its sense of the way stories can both liberate and enslave, an insight it shares with Ghosh's *The Shadow Lines*.

A similar struggle to fashion female autonomy in the context of received narratives faces Ammu, the heroine of Arundhati Roy's 1997 Booker-Prize-winning novel, *The God of Small Things*. Roy (b. 1960), who trained as an architect and has also written film scripts, is on her mother's side from a Syrian Christian family and was brought up in South India. Her heroine, who shares Roy's regional and religious background, is a divorcee struggling against the fate laid out for her by convention: 'She was twenty-seven that year, and in the pit of her stomach she carried the cold knowledge that for her, life had been lived. She had had one chance. She made a mistake.' Having already transgressed community boundaries by marrying a Hindu, she compounds the 'mistake' by taking a 'chance' across the boundaries of caste and falls in love with Velutha, a 'paravan'. Like *A Thousand Faces of Night*, Roy's novel places its heroine's story in the context of traditional Hindu narratives. The ferocity of the policemen who beat Velutha to death is foreshadowed by a description of Bhima's beating of Duhshasana; the policemen regard Velutha's relationship with the high-caste Ammu as a parallel to the unrobing of Draupadi by Duhshasana in the *Mahabharata*. Roy shows how such traditional narratives close off possibilities for women, but it is not only against Indian tradition that Ammu and her foreign-returned daughter (the novel's narrator) must struggle to define themselves. *Heart of Darkness* and *The Sound of Music*, to give but two rather incongruous examples, present Ammu and her daughter with alternative identities which they find equally alienating. Narratives of colonialism and Westernisation play their own parts in shaping the choices facing these women. If sometimes this novel seems a little unsubtle in the way it handles such allusions, it does provide a powerful imaginative statement of the way people can find themselves 'trapped outside their own history'. Roy's romance plot, as so often is the case with recent Indian writing in English, stands in a self-consciously uneasy relation to the larger story of the nation. 'Something happened', writes Roy, 'when the personal turmoil dropped by at the wayside shrine of a vast, violent, circling, driving, ridiculous, insane, unfeasible, public turmoil of a nation'. Just as the narrator of *The Shadow Lines* struggles to find a record in the national press of the riot that was a tragedy for his family, so Roy's novel records the dislocations between the 'Small God' of individual lives and the 'Big God' of the nation. In the novels of the 1980s and 1990s, domestic and personal stories never simply mirror an evolutionary course of national development. Both sides of the relationship are more often presented as fractured in themselves and neither simply reflects the other. In Roy's terms, 'the god of small things' remains in an uneasy relationship with its avatar, 'the Big God'. The mirror of history is cracked and distorting.

An overview of contemporary Indian fiction in English reveals an incredible array of talent. Many of the novelists seem to regard India's wealth of literary and mythical tradition as freely available to rewrite in the present. A different perspective might construe this trend as the self-serving attempt by sections of the élite to represent their own modernity in terms of a continuity with India's past, papering over the cracks in the national imaginary, as it were, to affirm their own authenticity. Similarly, the celebration of plurality and openness could be understood as doing the ideological work of economic liberalisation, presenting Indian identity in terms of the shifting surfaces of late capitalism, privileging mobility and cosmopolitanism over local cultures and communities. Such interpretations do fit some of these novels. They offer a useful corrective to those versions of literary criticism which too complacently celebrate post-colonial literature as a subversive rewriting of the authority of the colonial centre. But perspectives which take the more jaundiced view of Indian fiction in English should not be allowed to present an overly simplified picture. It is true that many of these novelists are foreign-returned or divide their lives between India and other places. It is also true that marketers of the Indian novel in English have also shown great canniness. There has developed, over the past few years, a sense that India sells abroad.

Yet any assumption that recent writing is simply doing the ideological work of the globalised middle classes has to concede the complex nature of the relationship between culture and class, especially in the contemporary Indian situation. The idea of India has been subject to reassessment across the whole range of Indian culture in the past two decades, from Bollywood to literary criticism. This broader context, which suggests the need to consider Indian writing in English in relation to the literature of the Indian languages, also suggests that these novels cannot just be dismissed as the treason of an intellectual élite. Originating in conquest and colonialism—still a badge of and means to privilege—the medium by which India communicates with the outside world and often by which the Indian languages communicate with each other, English is perpetually on the internal and external boundaries of Indian culture. By virtue of this position, Indian writing in English is uniquely placed to reimagine the nation. If it has sometimes acted as the instrument of a globalising culture, moving over the surface of Indian culture without acknowledging its privileged position; or, alternatively, re-thematising India as an endless narrative possibility, an infinitely open market, then equally it has been used to situate modernity in relation to India. It has been deployed to call the globalisation of culture to local account, to foreground the difficulties of translation and the possibilities of dialogue. Indian English fiction of the 1980s and 1990s, in short, force us to more fully think through the consequences of regarding English as one of India's languages.

22
The Dramatists

Shanta Gokhale

Modern secular drama came to Bombay and Calcutta with the first decades of the nineteenth century when amateur plays were produced by the British residents of these cities. Later, individuals and troupes on their way to or back from Australia and New Zealand would stop there to perform plays written by the popular English playwrights of the day. Secular playwriting in Bengali and Marathi began after the setting up of universities in Bombay, Calcutta, and Madras in the mid-1850s, acquainting students mainly with two streams of drama—the Shakespearean and the Sanskrit. The new-found pride of Indians, both in themselves and in their culture, spurred them to emulate and translate Shakespeare in their own languages. At the same time translations of the classical Sanskrit plays of Kalidasa, Bhavabhuti, and Narayanabhatta were being done in Marathi, Bengali, Assamese, Oriya, Kannada, Telugu, and other languages.

Though Krishna Mohan Banerjea's *The Persecuted, or Dramatic Scenes Illustrative of the Present State of Hindoo Society in Calcutta* (1831) was the first play in English written by an Indian, it was less a play and more a dramatised debate of the conflict between orthodox Hindu customs and the new ideas introduced by Western education. While anyone interested in English plays preferred to see those written by native English speakers, the majority of Indians preferred those performed in an Indian language. These were often translations or adaptations from Shakespeare, but had been culturally modified to their taste.

The first play in Bengali to emulate Shakespearean tragedy was Jogendrachandra Gupta's *Kritivilas*, produced in 1852. The first original Marathi play, again, took its theme and form from Shakespeare's history plays. It was Vinayak Janardan Keertane's *Thorle Madhavarao Peshwe*, produced in 1851. It is important to note that all professional and serious amateur productions, whether original plays inspired by Shakespeare or translations and adaptations from him or from Sanskrit, were all done in Indian languages. Only college students produced Shakespeare in English.

In two epilogues written in English for their production in Bombay and Poona, we see the double-edged vision with which students looked upon the dramatic culture they had inherited from the British. The first is by B.E. Modie, a student of Elphinstone College, Bombay. It follows a college performance of *The Taming of the Shrew* and was published in *Native Opinion*, 3 March 1867. It suggested, apologetically, that given time Indians too would speak English as well as the English themselves:

Bethink ye that your sweet Avonian swan,
Still flutters strangely over Hindustan.
We know not yet the future of its tone,
The modulations are not yet our own.
We fain would hope that, as it flies along,
'Twill scatter sybil-like its leaves of song,
And o'er parent East new triumphs win,
With but that touch that makes the whole world kin.

The second epilogue followed the production of a Marathi translation by K.P. Gadgil of Narayanabhatta's *Venisamharan*, staged by the students of Poona's Deccan College in 1871. It turned its apologetic gaze upon the dramatic culture of the day. Scornfully rejecting the excesses of the *Ramayana*-based plays replete with song, declamation, and noisy battle scenes which were then popular, Gadgil points to the greater sophistication of the translation where 'No freakish monkeys, no delirious yell, / No Lanka's tyrant fierce with fury fell.'

While the two epilogues are insignificant in themselves, they represent the attitude of the educated, Westernised, urban élite towards the English language and towards 'native' culture, from which it was soon to become culturally distanced.

A playwright who stood apart from others in this socio-linguistic context was Tyagaraja Paramasiva Kailasam (1885–1946). A bilingual writer who was intimately acquainted with Indian literature and who had lived for six years in England, he approached his work in the two languages, English and Kannada, very differently. He believed that 'delineation of ideal characters requires a language which should not be very near to us'. He therefore wrote his English plays, which were often based on stories from the *Mahabharata*, in the style of Shakespeare's history plays but using the bombast and rhetoric of Victorian English. His Kannada plays on the other hand dealt with contemporary themes, and were written in the everyday spoken idiom of the educated Kannadigas, which he called 'Kannadanglo'. A geologist by training, T.P. Kailasam was a sportsman, actor, bohemian, and wit, given to composing and reciting plays to his friends extempore. Five of his plays have been published. His stage directions in these plays clearly show his strong sense of theatre. In this he was unlike most of his contemporaries and immediate successors.

Considering that nowhere except Bombay over the last ten years has English-language theatre been commercially viable, and given that everywhere amateur groups, rather than risk their scarce funds on untried Indian playwrights, have depended heavily on successful plays from the West to attract audiences, an astoundingly large number of plays have been written. More than 200 plays, all written since Independence, are mentioned by S. Krishna Bhatta in the bibliography to his book, *Indian English Drama: A Critical Study* (1987). Most of them have not been performed, many are not even performable, and few are available in print (when they are, it is mostly in periodicals and journals).

In selecting plays for comment below, the following criteria have been used: their availability (with one exception) in published form; their being written for a theatre audience rather than for the reader; and their contribution to theatre art in terms of linguistic or theatrical devices.

The English drama of the two decades immediately after Independence produced very little work of any importance. Most playwrights wrote one or at most two plays, and used the dramatic form more to tell a story through dialogue than to offer a theatrical experience. Like their pre-Independence predecessors—Sri Aurobindo, Harindranath Chattopadhyay, T.P. Kailasam—they wrote chiefly on mythical or religious themes. *Sri Chaitanya* (1950) by Dilip Kumar Roy is a verse play in three acts about Chaitanya's teachings and his conflicts with his wife and mother. The same author, in collaboration with Indira Devi, wrote *The Beggar Princess* (1956), on the life of the saint-poet Mirabai. Others, like V. Srinivas Aiyangar (1871–1954) in *Rama Rajya* (1952), gave a modern interpretation of the epic to reflect the somewhat naïve idealism of the years immediately following Independence. Swami Avyaktananda's *India Through the Ages* (1947) is a collection of ten plays. The theme of the last play, *All Prophets Day*, is national integration and secularism.

The plays of Joseph Mathias Lobo-Prabhu (dates not known) revolved around reformist themes like inter-caste marriage, marital incompatibility, and the education of women. All six of his plays in *Collected Plays* (1954), for instance, deal with these or similar themes. Typically, each play ends in a glib solution to a problem, reducing any effectiveness it may have had as the vehicle of a progressive message. The absence of performance opportunities deprived playwrights of an essential means of learning the craft, and left them without a stake in the development of theatre in the country.

However, four plays written by Asif Currimbhoy (1928–94) during this period deserve serious attention. They are *The Doldrummers* (1960), *The Dumb Dancer* (1961), *Goa* (1964), and *The Hungry Ones* (1965). Born into an illustrious Khoja family of Bombay, Currimbhoy was educated in the United States and for much of his life worked in a multinational oil company. His plays, of which there are twenty-nine in all, are substantial in content and rich in theatrical devices. He uses monologues, choruses, chants, songs, slide projections, sound effects, mime, anything in fact that furthers the dramatic purpose. Despite its importance, his work has yet to be the subject of a full-length study.

The *Doldrummers* revolves around the lives of four young people, Tony, Joe, Rita, and Liza—the Doldrummers of the title—who 'haven't worked in a year of Sundays'. Joe, who is doing his Ph.D., is disillusioned with what the country's freedom has brought him. His life goes on as before, without much purpose. Tony lies in a hammock all day, drinking and playing the guitar, grateful to have a friend who is doing a Ph.D. Rita loves Tony passionately, with an innocence which Joe corrupts by pointing out that if her aim is to ensure that Tony gets everything he wants, and if Tony wants the good life, her only choice is to sell her body. Liza, who is brash, amoral, and gossipy, comes and goes, sometimes as catalyst, sometimes chorus-like. In the end, Joe commits suicide, leaving Rita pregnant, as though leaving in her a hope for the future.

The play moves at a brisk pace. Currimbhoy achieves his social purpose, though not at the expense of his art. He is a deeply compassionate playwright who gives his characters room to reveal themselves. Though he writes from a moral position, he never becomes a moralist. His treatment of a character like Senhora Miranda in *Goa*, an allegory about the liberation of Goa where neither side is to blame and neither really wins, is a case in point.

Senhora Miranda, a woman of mixed parentage who needs to pretend that she is of pure Portuguese stock, yearns to be in Lisbon—about which she has heard so much. This yearning is projected on to a Portuguese do-nothing drunk, Alphonso, for whom she harbours a sexually explicit passion. However much she may lie and pretend, her dark-skinned fourteen-year-old daughter, Rose, is a living reminder of what she really is. Currimbhoy touches upon this aspect of her situation with great sympathy:

> *Senhora Miranda*: Why don't you ask me who her father was?
> *Alphonso*: You've already told me he was Portuguese.
> *Senhora Miranda*: Why don't you ask me who my father was?
> *Alphonso*: You've already told me he was Portuguese.
> *Senhora Miranda*: Ah! . . . it's evident I'm lying somewhere. That girl's either got the blood of her father, in which case he wasn't Portuguese, or she's got the blood of her grandfather, in which case my father was not Portuguese. Why are you silent Alphonso? Wouldn't you like to know where I'm lying? Either my child's a bastard or I am.
> *Alphonso* (*quietly*): I told you before. It makes no difference to me.

Currimbhoy was ignored in India till news of the reputation he enjoyed in the United States reached the country. The Asian theatre scholar Faubion Bowers had declared in New York's *The Village Voice* that Currimbhoy was emerging 'more and more clearly as a playwright of international stature'. *Goa* was produced at the University of Michigan in 1965. In 1968 it was staged at the Martinique Theatre on Broadway and *The Hungry Ones* was performed at the Theatre Company, Boston, and at Café La Mama. *The Doldrummers* was given a tryout at the Actors' Studio. Meanwhile, it had been banned in India. It was only in 1969, after writers like Khushwant Singh and Mulk Raj Anand wrote letters of protest to the *Times of India*, that the ban was lifted and the Little Theatre Group in Delhi staged it.

Another English play to be banned was *A Touch of Brightness* (1968) by Partap Sharma (b. 1939). The play, set in the red light district of Bombay, tells the story of a young street urchin, Pidku, and the attachment he forms for a beggar girl, Prema, who has recently turned up in the neighbourhood. Jealous of the attachment is Benarsi Baba, a pavement-dweller passionate about chess. Pidku is his adopted son. Benarsi Baba sells the girl into a brothel, and Pidku vows to buy her freedom, but by the time he manages to earn enough money to do so, she is dying of venereal disease.

The language of the play is inflected with Hindustani words and expressions like *aiye, bapre baap*, and *kya baat hai*, and these lend authenticity to the speech. *A Touch of Brightness* is in many other respects a flawed work. The characters are not credible, the plot, such as it is, moves jerkily, and there's more sentimentality and melodrama than passion and drama. However, it is the first attempt at showing the seamy side of a country which, in the 1960s, had become the West's spiritual Mecca. The play raised the hackles of India's image-makers, who banned it from going to the first Commonwealth Arts Festival. An editorial in one newspaper asked whether India's image would be enhanced 'by letting drama-lovers in London know the heartening fact of the existence of brothels in this country'. The author filed a writ petition in the Bombay High Court in 1966, challenging the ban. In 1972, the High Court held that the board of censors 'had exceeded its jurisdiction' and the ban was revoked.

The announcement in 1968 by Theatre Group, Bombay, of the Sultan Padmasee Award for Indian plays in English gave much-needed encouragement to a floundering genre. The award was won by Gurcharan Das for *Larins Sahib*, but also in the competition were Gieve Patel's *Princes* and Dina Mehta's *Myth-makers*.

Until 1968, Theatre Group had staged only European and American plays, with the avowed aim of acquainting Indians with Western theatre techniques. Towards the end of the 1960s, however, a strong back-to-the-village movement had started amongst the urban élite, affecting social and cultural attitudes in important ways. The announcement of the award for Indian plays in English could have been Theatre Group's response to this change. The competition was held once again, after a lapse of ten years, but this time the Group was unable to fulfil its promise of staging the award-winning play.

Unlike Currimbhoy, who took up contemporary political and social situations but turned them into passionate dramatic statements, Gurcharan Das (b. 1943) took recourse in history to cull from it a character and a story that had the potential of being turned into a colourful romantic tale. Set in Lahore in 1846–7, *Larins Sahib* (1970) deals with the crisis that overtook the Punjab seven years after the death of Maharaja Ranjit Singh, when the East India Company routed the Sikhs. The legendary Henry Lawrence, a friend of the Indians, is appointed the Company's Agent to the heir to the throne, who was a minor at the time. An intimacy develops between him and Rani Jindan Kaur, Ranjit Singh's widow. She presents him with her late husband's ring. Mysteriously, it seems to crystallise in Lawrence the desire to be the second Ranjit Singh. He begins to like being called the Angrez Maharaja. As this delusion of grandeur takes hold of him, he begins to lose control over events and is finally recalled to Calcutta.

Das colours his language according to the race and class of the speaker. While he gives Hardinge the characteristic idiom of the English upper classes—'Damn these bloody tribes! Damn this bloody country! Damn the whole world . . . This brandy's no good.'—he creates, for some of the exchanges between Lawrence and the Rani, a courtly, allusive idiom:

Lawrence: Fear is only human, said the jackal.
Rani: But the brave are not afraid, said the lion.
Lawrence: Even the bravest are afraid of beautiful women, said the fox.

In the afterword to *Larins Sahib*, Das stated that the characters and events of the play, being based on 'documents and letters exchanged by the principal characters', are historically accurate. Evidently, he did not wish to be seen as interpreting history, but as breathing life into facts. *Larins Sahib* is, as a consequence, a well-crafted piece of colourful dramatic entertainment rather than an attempt to relate the past to the present. Das has written two other plays, *Mira* (acted 1970) and *9, Jakhoo Hill* (acted 1996, though written in 1973–4). These have been collected in *Three Plays* (2001).

Nissim Ezekiel (b. 1924) wrote his plays years after his mentor, Ebrahim Alkazi, had left Bombay for Delhi in 1961 to become the first director of the National School of Drama. Ezekiel had worked closely with Alkazi in Theatre Unit during the latter's years in Bombay, and this stood him in good stead when he came to write his own plays. It would not be wrong to say that Alkazi's was the single most powerful and enduring influence on theatre in Bombay in the 1950s.

Trained in London at the Royal Academy of Dramatic Art, Alkazi conceived theatre as a totality. Set, costume, music, and light design were interwoven with performance and speech to create a language which was new to city audiences used to the melodramatic acting style of star actors who always took centre stage, pushing everybody else into the shadows. During his fourteen years in Bombay, Alkazi directed plays ranging from Greek tragedies to Shakespeare, and from Ibsen to Samuel Beckett and John Osborne.

In Ezekiel's *Three Plays* (1969) are collected *Nalini, Marriage-Poem*, and *Sleepwalkers*. Of the three, *Nalini*, described as a comedy, is generally considered the most successful, as also the more important play, while *Marriage-Poem* shines like a polished gem, but in a very small setting. It explores an upper-middle-class marriage in which the homebound wife craves the attention and love of a husband who, if he ever loved her, is now indifferent. The insecurity of her position drives her to alternate between nagging him and trying to seduce him. He on the other hand is trapped between his dreams of another woman and his feelings of tenderness towards his lonely wife.

Nalini concerns itself with precisely that class of Westernised Indians who were then beginning to express their guilt about being without roots. Both the play's protagonists belong to this class. Significantly, they are advertising executives, dealing in dreams far removed from reality. Bharat speaks for all of them when he says:

> I can't increase India's production of eggs. I can't work for a Family Planning unit. I'm not qualified to be a teacher in a school or college. I have business sense. Can you see me in these clothes, and without a word of any Indian language, helping peasants in a village or organising workers in a trade union? I can't create anything. I can't build anything. I can mix only with people like myself who dress like me. . . . That's why I work in an advertising agency.

This and similar self-revelations come as a result of Bharat being asked by Raj, a friend of his, to help publicise the exhibition of a new painter, Nalini. Bharat imagines Nalini to be a svelte social climber who will allow him to seduce her for his marketing services. But Nalini, with her intelligence, sincerity, and doubts, is, in the end, too complex a person for him to handle. Unlike him, she belongs to the world not of dreams but of real people.

Sleepwalkers is a one-act satire in a minor key on the Indian habit of always looking up to the United States. The opening prayer, intoned by the Indian characters, is 'Give us this day our daily American.' A typical exchange in the play goes like this:

> *Prof. Shah*: In this country Mr Morris, the ideal of many of us is to transcend thought.
>
> *Mr Morris*: We Americans find that too high for us. We prefer to be below thought and not above it.

Like Ezekiel, Gieve Patel (b. 1940) was also inducted into theatre by Ebrahim Alkazi. The apprenticeship began in 1958 while Patel was still an undergraduate, and lasted three years. During this period he helped backstage in Alkazi's Theatre Unit productions, and did a minor role in one of them. The experience of watching Alkazi at work, the frequent conversations with him on theatre, and the sporadic training he received in acting were central to moulding his own vision as playwright.

Patel has written three full-length plays. They are set in south Gujarat, the place where his parents come from, and where some of his own life has centred. His chief protagonists are Parsis, Iranian Zoroastrian refugees who settled in the west coast of India 1200 years ago, fleeing Islamic persecution. This sect, to which he belongs, has carved a cultural niche for itself.

The other presence in the plays is that of the Warlis, tribals who provide labour for the Parsi landlords in south Gujarat. Although they have no speaking lines in the first two plays, they constitute a palpable background. In the last play the Warli presence is brought centre-stage.

The desire to possess and control—people, thought, property—is a leitmotif that runs through the three plays. In the Parsi context, this need to establish control could be ascribed to the chronic insecurities induced by memories of refugee life. But Patel has said that India is a conglomerate of communities that have common aspirations and fears. 'We too are like that!', is an approving remark he hears often enough from his audiences.

Princes (acted 1970) deals with the waning fortunes of Parsi land-owning families shortly after Independence, when the Land Ceiling Act and prohibition began to erode their sources of income. In the play, this sense of loss focuses around a sole male child fiercely claimed by two families as their own. The sickly child cannot withstand the pressures of the tussle. The final act is a predatory dirge, with recriminations exchanged between the families over the boy's deathbed.

Patel believes that language in theatre is a constructed artifice. The English language is uniquely handled in all his plays, and in each play towards a specific end. In *Princes*, syntax and grammar are modified to create rhythms of speech that approximate the heavy, involuted, and sometimes poetic thinking of his rural characters. He says, 'I am not interested in the mistakes that Indians make when they speak English. To reproduce these would be a banal use of speech in theatre. I attempt to create a speech that perhaps does not exist in real life, but which nevertheless appears perfectly natural on the stage when spoken with understanding by actors.'

In *Savaksa*, a play set in a 'large village working its way towards becoming a small town', the provincial characters continue to use this inventive speech, but there are now also characters from the neighbouring metropolis of Bombay, and for these Patel has a language that is more regular.

Savaksa, aged sixty years, is a wealthy provincial landowner and political leader who aspires to marry an eighteen-year-old girl from an impoverished Bombay family. The girl appears interested—Savaksa is an unusual lover to say the least. As part of his wooing he shows her a patch of chronic eczema on his arm, and speaks of it as a pleasurable symbol of power and possession. When the girl's mother refers sympathetically to the continuous discomfort he suffers, and says to him: 'My poor child. You have all my pity', he replies:

> Poor? I am rich! Pity? But why? This house (*gestures to cover his possessions*) and—this skin! Every room is on this skin. This room, feel it here. Ah! Now this room (*tries to locate it on the eczema*)—it is here. (*Scratches a part.*) These are my orchards. (*Caresses.*) These are my servants. (*Chuckles.*)

The growing intimacy between the lovers is interrupted by the girl's elder sister who arrives from Bombay, and hawkishly challenges the assumptions on which Savaksa bases his self-esteem. The relationship is also resented by Savaksa's own brood by a previous marriage—sons, daughter, and daughter-in-law, who on the other hand have always supported his patriarchy. When he is upset by all the conflicts released by his desire to marry a young wife, the daughter-in-law says:

> What is all this! Getting so angry and hurt . . . we don't even know why! We don't even want to know! We leave everything in your hand! That is our benefit. Always!

City and village, poverty and wealth, woman versus man, Patel holds these contradictions in a prism. The only untainted character in the play, the young girl, flees from the grasping dominance of the rest into a none-too-reassuring future. Acted in 1982, the script of *Savaksa* was not published until 1989, when it appeared in the *Bombay Literary Review*.

Mister Behram (1988), Patel's third play, was produced by Stage Two Theatre Society for the Bombay Arts Festival in 1987. Behram, a brilliant lawyer and reformist in nineteenth-century Gujarat, adopts an orphaned tribal boy into his own family, educates him to become a lawyer like himself, and consents to his marriage with his daughter. The play charts the course of Behram's desire to possess and control the young man, Naval, an obsession that destroys all the positive values he has lived by.

Behram's passion makes him increasingly helpless, while Naval's initial bewilderment changes to an understanding of his own heart and mind, and the nature of his relationship with Behram, with Behram's wife Rati, and with his own wife Dolly. The characters Patel now deals with are sophisticated people, and for them speech is a way of keeping pain at bay. Behram says of his foster son:

> I would free him, and free myself. But if I forgot him even for a moment, I hurry to bring him back to mind, as though I feared to wipe away something gentle and lovely that I myself had created. And so I will it all to continue forever—that which most I wish to forget.

The simulated nineteenth-century diction gives classical distance to the intense, searing conflicts in the play. Patel has remarked that Racine is a major influence on him. However, the close conjunction of and interplay between Power and Eros, though it may have its source in Racine, has been put to work to suit the needs of a very different epoch and society.

Cyrus Mistry (b. 1956) entered his first play, *Doongaji House* (1991), for the second Sultan Padamsee Award in 1978. It won the award but was not produced until 1990. In the publisher's note to the book, Adil Jussawalla states that the reasons why the play had to wait for twelve years to be staged 'would provide an accurate picture' of the conditions in which the English-language theatre had been functioning since the mid-1970s.

In 1972, Pesi Khandalawala produced *Ah! Norman*, which turned out to be a commercial hit and is credited with having created a new theatre-going audience in the city. Unfortunately, it was an audience which seemed to want only more slick revues full of *double entendre*.

In such a situation, it is no surprise that a play about the crumbling fortunes of a Parsi family, such as *Doongaji House*, would have problems finding a producer.

Whether on stage or in films, Bombay's Parsis had always been portrayed in a stereotypical way for comic effect. With *Doongaji House* (as also with Mistry's stories, particularly 'Percy' which was made into an award-winning film in 1990), this small community was at last being taken seriously. The production of the play by Stage Two Theatre Society was a huge success, belying the myth that there was no demand for good theatre in the city.

Doongaji House is as much a character in the play as the family occupying it—Hormusji, Piroja, and their daughter Avan. Its decline parallels theirs exactly. Both house and family have known better days:

> *Hormusji*: When Bombay first got electricity—1928 I think—ours was one of the first buildings to install a meter. You know, Avan? It was the tallest building around for miles . . . At night it would glow brightly, like a lighthouse in a sea of dimly-lit fishing boats.

Though only twenty-one when he wrote it, *Doongaji House* shows few of the problems of being the first work of a young writer. Using the conventions of traditional Parsi farce, Mistry brings to his play themes that are universal and existential: the common human desire for happiness, which is often thwarted by forces beyond the individual's comprehension, and the ultimate loneliness and vulnerability of all human beings. A striking feature of the play is its language. The occasional Parsi-Gujarati expression that interlaces the English in which the Pochkhanawalla family conducts business imparts more than just naturalness to their speech:

> *Piroja*: Shall I remind you what happened to your friend Dinsha Kanga? When you went to his bedside in those last days, you came away dripping with sweat. (*Mimics.*) 'Piroja, Piroja, now I have seen too much, now I will never touch a bottle again.' Before his *uthamna* was done, you had started again. (*Pauses for breath.*) As for that great friend of yours downstairs, I wouldn't say any better fate awaits him. Darabshaa. *Salo* loafer!

A year after Mistry won the Sultan Padamsee Award, another Parsi writer, Dina Mehta (b. 1928), won the playwriting competition sponsored by the BBC. Her play *Brides Are Not for Burning* (1993) was broadcast on BBC World Service and its stage version performed in several Indian cities. Unlike Ezekiel, who has said that he writes only about the kinds of people he knows, and unlike Patel and Mistry, who have written about the people they know best, Mehta's play takes its inspiration from a social problem, the killing of brides who do not bring enough dowry. Her characters, though, speak in an idiom that slips from the conversational to the overblown all too suddenly and do not always seem convincing. An example is the following exchange between Malini and Anil about the death of their sister Laxmi:

> *Malini*: Last year three hundred and fifty women died of burns in this city alone, some of them over-insured wives . . .
>
> *Anil*: What are you trying to say?
>
> *Malini*: . . . and when they died—plucked in their bloom by fiery fingers—the husband's family came into a lot of money.

The success of Mehta's play depends less on character and language than on her ability to reveal a social situation in its many-sidedness. Laxmi's death has been declared an accident, but no investigation is made into its causes. It is left to Malini to find out the truth. Mehta's own enquiry into the nature of violence is made through the character of Roy, an anarchist. He is a counterfoil to Anil, who teaches in a school, and is shown to be balanced, thoughtful, and compassionate.

In recent years, Bangalore has also emerged as a centre for Indian plays in English, the most visible playwright there being Mahesh Dattani (b. 1958). Dattani's *Where There's a Will* was first performed by his group, Playpen, in the *Deccan Herald* Theatre Festival in 1988, the same festival at which his *Dance Like a Man* was also performed the following year. The production travelled to Bombay where it was seen by Alyque Padamsee, who offered to direct Dattani's next play, *Tara*

(1990). He also invited Dattani to write a play on communalism, and the result was *Final Solutions*. The play was banned from the Deccan Herald Theatre Festival for dealing with a sensitive issue but was produced by Playpen in Bangalore in July 1993 and by Padamsee in Bombay in December.

Communalism is a difficult theme to handle, not least because the writer should appear to be even-handed. Favouring neither Hindus nor Muslims, he is expected to strike a balance between them. What saves Dattani from the pitfall of equilibrium, from the deadening effect of symmetry, is his historical vision. He shows that communal attitudes have evolved over a period of time and are often based on ignorance.

The other plays in *Final Solutions and Other Plays* (1994) are *Where There's a Will, Dance Like a Man*, and *Bravely Fought the Queen*, each of which bears testimony to Dattani's theatrical imagination. His split sets, hidden rooms, and passages revealed behind lit-up screens and elevated structures create unexpected spaces. They enhance stage movement and quicken the pace of the plays.

At the centre of Dattani's work is the Gujarati joint family settled in Bangalore. *Where There's a Will* is a comment on the role of money in family relationships. The problems faced by a male Bharatnatyam dancer belonging to an illustrious family is the theme of *Dance Like a Man*. Amritlal Parekh is strongly opposed to his son choosing dance as a profession. 'A woman in a man's world may be considered progressive. But a man in a woman's world is—pathetic', he says to his wife, Ratna, who is an ambitious dancer herself. This generational face-off occurs also in *Where There's a Will*, in which Hasmukh says: 'Please let him just drop dead. No, no. What a terrible thing to say about one's own son. I take it back. Dear God, don't let him drop dead. Just turn him into a nice vegetable so he won't be in my way.'

Dattani belongs to a generation of writers who use the English language without either pride or guilt. Asked by a journalist why he didn't write in his own language, he replied 'I do.' While Dattani is the only recent playwright to have produced and published a substantial body of work in English, there have also been writers like Zubin Driver from Bombay and Vijay Padake from Bangalore whose plays have been staged and won critical acclaim but are as yet unpublished. R. Raj Rao

(b. 1955), who teaches at the University of Pune, is yet to write a full-length play, but has brought out a collection of three one-acters and a monologue, *The Wisest Fool on Earth and Other Plays* (1996). The most daring and successful of them is the monologue, 'The Wisest Fool on Earth'. Set in the toilet of a Bombay highrise in which Jay, the protagonist, has been locked by his lover, the play is memorable for its brutal candour and scatological wit.

If Indian drama in English is still in its infancy, the publication of plays is even more so. Publishers will take plays seriously only if they have been produced, but producers will touch plays only if they are commercially viable. And there are not many of these. In short, few plays get published.

23

Five Nature Writers

Jim Corbett, Kenneth Anderson, Sálim Ali, Kailash Sankhala, and M. Krishnan

MAHESH RANGARAJAN

Jim Corbett (1875–1955) is among India's best-known 'Indo-Anglian' authors after Rudyard Kipling and E.M. Forster. The dramatic encounters between the shikari colonel and his elusive, dangerous adversaries are like jungle versions of Sherlock Holmes which continue to enthral new generations of readers long after man-eaters have become a distant memory. *The Man-eaters of Kumaon* (1944), Corbett's first book, remains his most famous. Corbett was a sport hunter long before he took to the pursuit of marauding leopards and tigers. He remained a hunter even after he gave up the trail of such animals. The pride of a sportsman is often evident in his accounts and it is erroneous to suppose, as many people do, that he only shot man-eaters.

One of his finest narratives in *Man-eaters* that does not involve a man-killer is the shooting of a huge male tiger named the Bachelor of Powalgarh. An easy familiarity with individual tigers in the forests of Kumaon is Corbett's hallmark. The Bachelor was far from his usual haunts and, wary of people, had long evaded the bullets of stalkers. Corbett eventually got the better of the tiger and admits to a sense of joy at having bagged such a fine specimen. The animal was duly measured and proclaimed one of the largest tigers taken in the province. To be fair to Corbett, his sense of achievement is mingled with remorse. His sporting ethic, all the same, did not measure up to more recent notions of total preservation. It would be anachronistic to associate such ideas with Corbett. Celebration of life in the outdoors was, in his day, centred around the chase and the hunt, the ability to read pugmarks on a jungle trail, the skill of 'calling up' a tiger in order to be able to shoot it. Fish (especially the great mahseer) were taken with rod and line, deer and peacocks were killed for meat, and leopards were shot for their skins. This was the world Corbett grew up in and never fully transcended. It was the gun, not the camera, that was his chief, though not sole, instrument.

Corbett's was a keen eye and his vivid descriptions of trees and birds and hills reveal another side to his character. His animal biography of the Pipal Pani tiger, first published in *The Hog Hunters Annual* (1931) and included in *Man-eaters*, is a fine sketch of a young tiger's life. There is an attention to detail that takes us to the forest floor in a manner that many have attempted but few succeeded. The animal lived for a time in the huge log of a tree felled for no apparent reason and hollowed by porcupines. In *The Man-eating Leopard of Rudraprayag* (1948) we take a break from the tale of terror spread by the marauder to glimpse, through Jim's eyes, the beauty of the Vale of Kashmir. Corbett was stalking the Kashmir stag, a much-sought-after quarry when—

> I stepped into a fairyland, for the hail that carpeted the ground gave off a million points of light to which every glistening leaf and blade of grass added its quota. Continuing up for another two or three thousand feet, I came upon an outcrop of rock, at the foot of which was a bed of blue mountain poppies. The stalks of these, the most beautiful of all wild flowers in the Himalayas, were broken; even so, these sky blue flowers standing in a bed of spotless white were a never to be forgotten sight.

A few lines later we are back to the Alaknanda river where Corbett spends another long night waiting for the man-eater.

The story of the stag is exceptional in terms of the setting. So attuned are we to his little world that it is easy to overlook how far afield

Corbett had travelled. Born in Naini Tal to domiciled English parents, he was raised there and at Kaladunghi. He first went shooting jungle fowl and deer with his brother Tom, then graduated to leopards and tigers. It was here he learnt how to read tracks on the trail and to tell, from the calls of langurs and peafowl, the movements of big cats along forest paths. He trained soldiers in jungle warfare in Central India, served in Burma, felled trees for railway fuel in Bihar, hunted in the marshlands of the north Indian terai, and later ran a shikar firm in East Africa. Very few episodes from his business and professional life appear in his books. It is the foothills of the Himalayas that occupy centre-stage. One wishes there was more about the lion or cheetah in Africa, or of the dry central Indian jungle, but this is to miss out on the importance of Kumaon and Garhwal in Corbett's eyes. That was his background, his patch of wild grass. His heart was never far from the mountains and his pen rarely takes us to forests outside them.

A sense of terror remains with the reader long after the Corbett classic is put away. *Rudraprayag* is especially fascinating for it is a full-length story of one hunt. All the other books are collections, including the under-rated but gripping *The Temple Tiger and More Man-eaters of Kumaon* (1954). The leopard of the former book was so feared that it 'imposed a night curfew' over a huge swathe of the Garhwal countryside. Roads that bustled with life fell prey to 'an ominous silence' because of its depredations. Similarly, the Thak man-eating tiger held up forestry work in an entire valley. In *The Man-eaters of Kumaon*, we learn of how contractor and labourer both looked to Corbett to rid them of the animal. This paternal attitude of Jim as saviour is often evident in his work but should not detract from his uncanny ability to recreate, some might say embellish, the narrative of the chase. Out on foot, sitting up on a machan, stalking a dangerous killer in thick cover—these are the high points in a Corbett narrative, the moments that readers want to relive time and again. It is not blood lust as much as the cunning of the man-eaters, especially the leopards, that stands out. Caught up in a terrain bustling with human activity and turning to prey on stock or people, they seem to hold sway over an entire population until they run into Corbett. This celebration of victory, so essential to the genre of shikar literature, is evident in all his works. The climax in *The Temple Tiger* provides proof of this sense of achievement:

'Word travelled round the night that the man-eating tiger was dead and when we carried him to the foot of the *ficus* tree next morning to skin him, more than a hundred men and boys crowded round to see him. Among the latter was the ten-year-old brother of the Chuka man-eater's last human victim.'

The killing of man-eaters is always accompanied by a disavowal of any effort to wipe out the tiger as a species. The big cat was a 'large-hearted gentleman of the forest' preying on people due to the force of circumstance. In *My India* (1952) Corbett blames a big hunting party for wounding an innocent beast. The group used several riding elephants and tied up over a dozen baits, something Jim did not like: 'The rifle shot I had heard three days previously had shattered the tiger's lower jaw, the most painful wound that can be inflicted on an animal.' The body of the tiger was found ten days later. In other cases, tigers wounded by gunshot or more natural causes (such as porcupine quills) became a menace. Yet in his books Corbett is mostly silent about the tiger shoots he organised for governors and viceroys alike, or his experiences as a member of the pig-sticking club at Meerut. He takes pains to show himself as a hunter, not a wanton killer.

The reason for this silence is significant. By the time he wrote his first book, Corbett was turning to photography. He managed to create a small jungle 'studio' by damming a small stream and setting up a hide in a tree. Here, he became one of the first persons to shoot on cine film a group of seven wild tigers, including a wild white tigress. Appropriately enough, he entitles this section of his first book 'Just Tigers' and reminds us that most of the striped cats fall into this category, troubling neither people nor stock. This episode is matched by other small telltale signs: the admission in *My India* that he felt guilty about shooting peafowl by moonlight but did so only for food. The camera, which would record nature on film, was preferable to the gun. A photo was of interest to all, the trophy only to its owner. But this transition was never complete. It is true that he sounded the alarm call for conservation but he did not actually lead the struggle to achieve it.

It would be unjust to omit what is perhaps the most distinctive feature of Jim Corbett's India: his picture of village society. He is even sympathetic to the dacoit Sultana, whom he helped track down and capture. Corbett sees the bandit as a local Robin Hood, a victim of social circumstances due to his birth in a so-called Criminal Tribe. Corbett's best tales include an inimitable portrayal of his childhood friend and shooting mentor, Kunwar Singh. 'We had a name', he writes, 'for every outstanding tree, and for every water-hole, game track, and nullah.' These stories in *My India* reveal the desire in Jim, now living in Kenya, to look back to another age in India when he led, and was trusted by, the poor of the country.

His life at the loading yard at Mokameh Ghat includes a chilling account of poverty and death in the time of cholera. This ability to identify with privation in forest or village is what makes Corbett more than a chronicler of the hunt. His narratives carry such a strong emotive charge because their protagonist—usually Corbett himself—sympathises so fully with the underdog, whether the underdog is a mauled tiger or a hounded bandit. There is also here a strong familiarity with superstition and the spirit world of the Indian peasant, specially in *Jungle Lore* (1953), and a facility with homespun, idiomatic English which makes Corbett a rather unique writer of Indian-English prose. His sympathies are so quintessentially with the Indian landscape, its flora and fauna, its inhabitants, while his linguistic skills are derived from the best tradition of British folklore and storytelling for pleasure.

Once he left India in 1947, he had to rely on memories of a world he had lost. It is striking that his last work, *Tree Tops* (1955), finds him comparing the night scenes in the Aberdare forest in Kenya to his own Kumaon. The African forest was, to his trained ear, 'disappointingly silent' except for the laugh of the hyena and the grunt of the rhino. The big cats of Africa hardly appear at all. The pamphlet is a short story about Princess Elizabeth's night at a forest lodge. For once, the writer reveals his ability to interact with the powerful and the famous. For the first time in history, he remarks, a princess ascended a tree to spend the night in a tree-top lodge and came down the next day to become a queen: her father, the king of England, had died even as she slept. Corbett had stood guard that night. But the British empire was dying, and with it the old days of man-eaters and their hunter-storytellers—among whom Corbett reigns supreme.

By this time, southern India threw up a new claimant for the slot of the raconteur of the chase. Kenneth Anderson (1910–74), was a planter of Scottish stock. Unlike Corbett, he chose to stay on in newly independent India. It is unfortunate that his work gets small recognition: this is one of the disadvantages of writing in Corbett's powerful narrative shadow. But Anderson deserves attention on many counts. For one, his terrain is so strikingly different: it is the deep South, varied in its ecology and wildlife. The denizens of the forest are often diverse, ranging from elephants to wild dogs, sloth bears to crocodiles. Anderson's books—beginning with *Man-eaters and Jungle Killers* (1957), down to the last one, *Jungles Long Ago* (1976)—provide rare insights into a changing world.

His descriptions of animal behaviour are excellent, the drama of woodland life being of keen interest to him. We read of a herd of gaur, the great jet-black wild cattle of the southern Indian hill forests, warding off a hungry tiger. In *The Black Panther of Sivanipalli* (1959), he writes with warm sympathy of the sloth bear,

> The sounds he emits can resemble anything from a bagpipe being inflated to the droning of an aeroplane, from the buzzing of an angry wasp to the huffing of a blacksmith's bellows, the latter being a sort of background accompaniment to the buzzing and humming sounds. He will twist and contort his body into all shapes provided he can get at the tasty roots . . . He snores so audibly as to be heard at a distance.

The sporting ethic is deeply inscribed in his worldview, but he has prejudices common to élite hunters of his day: his delight in one animal's antics is matched by a deep bias against certain other species. He is ashamed to shoot dead a pregnant panther by mistake and elephants are killed by him only when they are a danger to humans. But the russet-coloured, terrier-sized wild dog, a pack hunter with a wide range in the South Indian forest, is the subject of his ire. Wild dogs are described as 'merciless hunters' and 'implacable killers' and he is happy to shoot them dead and collect a bounty paid by the government. Competing as they did with sportsmen for deer, wild dogs were seen as rivals for big game. Crocodiles are another species out of favour with Anderson. The destruction of crocodiles in the Cauvery, using fish hooks, was encouraged by fisheries staff and he describes their killing with a rather ghoulish delight. On such counts Anderson's views closely mirror those of his time. Animals that were branded cruel or merciless, or that were seen as plain ugly, had no right to live. His books often celebrate their wholesale elimination.

Not so with the panther and tiger. He is keenly aware of their plight even as he shoots them for trophies or to get rid of cattle lifters or man killers. There is the tiger of Tumkur, a district which 'did not boast of a regular forest but was covered with ordinary scrub jungle', a small island of thickets in a sea of cultivated fields. This account in *Nine Man-eaters and One Rogue* (1961) is not exceptional. We read of panthers who live much more often in the proximity of villages, in small patches of tree cover and bush. The larger tiger, wandering into such grounds, finds life more difficult. The 'mauler' of Rajnagar, which injured and attacked many humans but rarely deigned to feed on their flesh, made its home in rocky terrain broken by grass jungle and boulders, stream beds and bamboo clumps. The tiger took to killing milch cows and mauling herdsmen. In such cases Anderson displays a keen sense of the complexity of the situation. He lived in a period when the conflicts were more acute than in Corbett's day. There are occasions when he seems ambivalent. He celebrates 'progress' even as he bemoans its impact. An engineer, praised for carving out a farm from hill jungles, also turns out to be making money felling huge trees for charcoal.

The diverse landscapes we are taken through are a patchwork quilt of dry scrub jungle and riverine thicket, of teak forests and village grazing grounds, plantations and woodlands. There is not one but many a drama in progress. Lambani tribesmen catch crabs in hill streams, travellers walk down mountain paths. Honey attracts not only a bear with a sweet tooth but also honey collectors out to take some to the nearest market. The jungles Kenneth tramps through are not a pristine wilderness but the habitat of a bustling and vigorous human society. There are people chopping wood, grazing cattle, setting traps for birds, gathering flowers and herbs, and foraging for fuel. Such people assist him in his pursuits or ask his help in ridding them of an animal that has lost its ingrained fear of humans. The cast of actors is large and the sportsman's is only one among many faces. Not being a forest officer, he often winks at the subsistence poacher. In turn, Byra of the Chinar jungle promises him an aphrodisiac guaranteed to win over 'the memsahib you love'. But there is anger at the man who uses a rusty matchlock to slay sambhar at a water-hole. Anderson's deep ambivalence is partly due to his own immersion in the world of shikar. He is proud of his son's bag of seventy panthers but deeply perturbed by city-based hunters who traverse the forest in jeeps, shooting everything on four legs.

In *Jungles Long Ago*, this concern for the future of wildlife takes him to sanctuaries where no shot may be fired. He goes to a different part of the subcontinent, the Gir Forest, the last home of the Asiatic lion. The man whose bullets stopped many a tiger in its tracks now marvels at the relationship of deep trust between forest guards and wild lions. The lions do not react even when a khaki-clad guard pulls at their kill to secure it to a tree (and thereby help the tourists get better pictures)! From looking at animals down the gun-sights of a rifle, Anderson is here coming round to the view of the photographer and the tourist. A striking thing about Anderson's jungle pictures is that the sounds and sights are so well described. There are fig trees near a Muslim shrine heavy with fruit, the dining place of hordes of bats. Drought is a time of spiky dry grasses, when a single match can set a jungle ablaze. He sits in the deep, cool shade of a tamarind tree, listening to the cooing of doves and the cries of peafowl. Dusk leads to a change of cast as the distant hoot of the horned owl takes over. A pall of destruction hangs over the forest. But only in his last book does he venture from his hunting grounds into a sanctuary. This itself is an indicator of how much things had changed from the time of his first book to his last.

Sálim Ali was a different sort of figure. Born in Bombay in 1896, he became a world-renowned ornithologist and was lionised widely by the time of his death in 1987. While his many bird books, starting with *The Book of Indian Birds* (1941) down to the ten-volume *Handbook of the Birds of India and Pakistan* (the latter with S. Dillon Ripley, finally completed in 1976), are very much for the specialist or the bird-watching amateur, his autobiography, *The Fall of a Sparrow* (1985) is a classic of fine prose in its own right. It shows us the multifacetedness of a man whose accounts of people are no less interesting than those of birds. His wit and irreverence towards 'holy cows' is among this book's enduring features.

Sálim Ali grew up in Bombay, a city which still had orchards on its outskirts and forested hills near Vihar lake, where you could meet the occasional panther or boar. In his autobiography he recounts how his romance with birds began. Like his elders in a mercantile Muslim family, he wielded the gun as a small boy, shooting sparrows in the garden. Usually, these birds were cooked in butter and garnished with spices, but one day a strange thing happened: the bird in question turned out to have a yellow throat, and on his elders' urgings he took it across to the Bombay Natural History Society. Sálim walked into a world of trophies, of dead and stuffed animals, to meet the curator of the museum. He was shown drawers full of the carcasses of many different kinds of sparrows. Here he was thunderstruck by the beauty and diversity of India's bird life. Life could never be the same again. By the time he went to Burma in 1914 as a young man in search of a future in wolfram mining, he had already made birdwatching a passion. It was to dominate his life.

But the writer in him is careful to give us glimpses of the narrow ledge on which Indians and Europeans met and worked together. There would be sharp differences on political matters in a climate of growing nationalism: Col. R. Meinertzhagen, his mentor, would exclaim: 'Sálim is the personification of the educated Indian and interests me a great deal. He is excellent at his own theoretical subjects but has no practical ability . . . His views are outstanding. He is prepared to turn the British out of India tomorrow and govern the country himself.' Sálim was one of the early Indians not from a princely or aristocratic lineage to venture into the world of nature studies. His surveys of the countryside and its bird life were only made possible by his contacts with civil officials and many princes. There is much that has a touch of adventure: his wife and he drive through jungle only to find their vehicle stuck in a stream, to be pulled out by bullocks. In Hyderabad state's forests there would be 'the thrill of seeing the forest roads covered with fresh pug-marks of tiger, bear, and other wildlife every morning.' Chenchu tribal trackers and game guides in the South win his admiration for their expert knowledge of the land. The real twists come not in stalking big game but in the unexpected turns in his personal life. As a jobless youth, he began observing baya weaver birds build their nests in Kihim and ended up making new discoveries about bird behaviour. The autobiography shows us how Sálim viewed his subjects—not in a coldly scientific way but with a keen eye for humour. He reveals how male birds all weave nests which their mates inspect before choosing one. Success in love depends on skill at nest-building.

By the 1930s, he was already seen as an authority on India's birds and all doubts were silenced by his continuing stream of books on them. In *Indian Hill Birds* (1949) he talks of how walking on hill tracks in search of birds can be preferable to joining the party circuit of tea and coffee planters. At such a time, he admits, it was still not clear to many of his relatives that his work would ever lead to something of lasting value. One of his uncles believed birdwatching was merely an excuse to justify Sálim's tendency to be a 'shirker and a waster'. Though written when he was a venerable and internationally respected scientist, Ali's autobiography is replete with a mildly self-deprecating humour which, like Corbett's, links his prose to one strand of British non-fictional storytelling—in this case to the tradition of pleasant self-mockery and slightly tongue-in-cheek way of saying things, whether about birds or about his family and other animals.

His dogged defence of sport hunting was, by this time, to lead to strong criticisms from a younger generation of conservationists. But Sálim Ali's views were shaped by his own early life. It was quite normal to shoot antelopes from a car without a licence and sell them to a leading Bombay hotel. On his own camping trips, he often shot animals for food. Ali actually felt the sportsman who adhered to the spirit of fair play was not a danger to wildlife and was also a deterrent to the poacher.

In fact, his dexterity with a shotgun was essential to his work as a student of bird life. Taxonomic studies were only possible if you shot a type specimen of each species. To shoot the bird, then skin the body, record its size, weight, and plumage, preserve it in formalin and catalogue details about its habitat required the scientist to know the crafts of hunting and taxidermy. In a sense, his own background helped enormously. Long before he had set his heart on ornithology, he was acquainted with the outdoors and with stalking. His account of a hunt of the elusive houbara bustard, always a gourmet's delight, in the desert of Sind, shows how difficult shooting could actually be. He also carefully reminds the reader that the bird was not chased towards waiting hunters, as this would be unsporting. Sálim was a guest of his uncle in the civil service, and he commandeered a good riding camel from a willing landlord. On camel back, the sport was challenging: 'You suddenly realise that the bird you have been watching slowly walking away . . . has suddenly vanished, in the twinkling of an eye. It has squatted flat on the foot of a diminutive bush, neck stretched out on the ground. The shikari pulls up your camel and nudges you excitedly to shoot but for you the bird is simply not there.'

Sálim Ali's work as a scientist and conservationist was, however, far more central in his writings than the pleasures of the hunt. This distinguishes him from Corbett and Anderson. There was little point cataloguing the wealth of nature unless something could be done to help save it. He recalls how Bharatpur, once a great hunting ground for mass shoots of ducks and geese, was converted into a reserve for wildlife. Through his works, the joy of discovery takes over from the thrill of the hunt. His life is a journey in quest of the mysteries and marvels of the natural world, where every thicket holds a secret, where the bird in the bush is truly worth two in the hand.

Sálim Ali's concern about conservation was shared by another writer who was never a shikari and very much a preservationist. Kailash Sankhala (1925–94) was unlike the other nature writers in two major respects: he was an administrator and the architect of what, at the time of its launch, was the single largest wildlife preservation effort undertaken anywhere in the world. It is no surprise, therefore, that the challenge of conservation runs like a thread through his books.

The first and last tiger Sankhala shot with a gun was a male in a dry thorn forest of the Aravali hills and it is appropriate that the event is described at the very outset of his autobiography, *Tiger! The Story of the Indian Tiger* (1978). This is the tale of not only the man and his life but of the animal that for him symbolised the spirit of the Indian jungle. As a young forest cadet in the 1950s, he too was required, like all other aspirants to the forest service, to 'bag a tiger'. This rite of passage had the opposite effect and his words are a strange but moving tribute to the victim of his bullet. He saw 'The tiger dead, his legs up and his eyes open. He seemed to look into my eyes and ask the reason for his death. Is this the sport where all rules are in your favour?' The book itself is the story of how his life was now dedicated to another cause: saving the tiger and its forest home. This was the heyday of commercial shikar and he did not find it easy to make headway. His native Rajasthan was ecologically different from Corbett's hunting grounds in the foothills of the Himalaya or Anderson's terrain in the deep south. Half the land was desert, the rest was forest-clad hills dotted with lakes. The latter was where the princes of yore had organised tiger hunts, and which had now become a huge killing field for shikar outfitters. The young Kailash recalled conversations about who had bagged how many tigers and the best way to shoot quarry.

By the 1960s, when he was moving up the ranks of the service, a major shift was taking place in attitudes to wildlife. What Corbett had suggested as a remedy—protecting wildlife—was now looking like a dire necessity. Even the idea of the 'man-eater' came under attack. Sankhala became one of the first to take on Corbett in print, refuting the notion that man-eating was ever as rife as had been suggested. The man-eater was more a victim of increasing human intrusions that denied the predator its living space and natural food. Corbett was now blamed for exaggerating the danger that tigers posed to people and indirectly legitimising the culture of the hunt. The tigers of Corbett Park, Sankhala asserted, would have doubts about the conservationist credentials of the great slayer of man-eaters. In Corbett's place, Sankhala suggested that the less known Fred Champion be seen as the precursor of the conservation movement. This was a forester who, in the 1920s, had abandoned the gun for the camera. This reworking of history had a dual purpose: it gave Sankhala's own efforts greater legitimacy and undermined an ethos of hunting which was still widely prevalent. This effort was critical for it went against the general ethos of his fellow officers—who saw cash in every tree and a trophy in every tiger or leopard. Sankhala talks of how he has shot 'only 43 tigers' and would love to score a century—only in this case you hardly need reminding that these tigers were 'taken' on film, and not with a gun.

As a student of the tiger's life and ecology, Sankhala's works included the lavishly illustrated *Wild Beauty* (1973) and *Tiger Land* (1974). These are the writings of an ecological nationalist for whom the blackbuck and the bird colonies of Bharatpur, the dry Deccan plateau and its wildlife, as also big game animals everywhere, make up the splendour and riches of India. In Sankhala's work we notice that the natural world is less a terrain and more a heritage to be cherished. In this respect it sets the stage for the story of his own endeavours as Director of Project Tiger (1973–7), during which he established a network of reserves to save the great cat and the myriad plants and animals that shared its jungle home. The tiger is now transformed from a potential killer into an emblem of life. It stands at the apex of the food chain, the whole of which is to be saved in select stretches of wild land. Reversing the march of cultivation into forest, the core areas of the reserves become a *sanctum sanctorum* for nature. The religious imagery is far from coincidental. Sankhala wrote in 1978 of how 'No axe falls in the forest, no saw moves on dead and fallen wood.' Here, the cycles of renewal and decay, of death and life, continue uninterrupted by the hunter and the logger. The canvas is broadened to go beyond the destiny of the tiger. Nearly all Sankhala's works contain an account of the ceaseless activity at a water-hole in the Aravalis in summer. Beasts and birds from the smallest to the largest, from the quail to the tiger, arrive to quench their thirst. Kailash Sankhala, perched in a hideout, records their departures and arrivals on film and in his notebook. The very forest tract where he shot a tiger with a gun has become a refuge for wild creatures. From a keeper of captive animals he becomes a protector of the wild. He writes of the men in the field with an enthusiasm that is infectious:

> Panwar is mad about his Minolta camera, capturing the ecological changes in the Kanha meadows, C.B. Singh protests even about angling with a rod and line in the Ramganga river in Corbett park. He is a purist. Deb Roy exchanges fire with poachers even at night in Manas. They know full well that he is a crack shot . . . The commitment is total and the team is perfect.

The later works, written after his retirement from service, return to the same theme. *The Gardens of Eden: The Waterbird Sanctuary at Bharatpur* (1984) is a charming account of the small bird sanctuary where he had served early in his career. In an article he wrote in *Sanctuary* magazine in 1985, even the Thar desert becomes not a barren stretch of land but a place teeming with life. Gazelles scamper in bush country and sand grouse fly in their thousands to the few water-holes. The following sample of his prose indicates the tenor of his writings:

> When I close my eyes I see the nests of half a million flamingoes in the Rann of Kutch, the carpet of a million flowers in the Himalayan meadows, the deciduous forests in late February with their extravagant reds, the lushness of the evergreen forests. I see shaded brooks with fems, with frolicking deer coming down to drink or a tiger sleeping half-submerged in a pool unaware of my presence. Inspite of some inevitable moments of sadness and frustration when I look back over the past half century, I feel I have lived one glorious day after another, watching the splash of colour of the setting sun, hearing the alarm calls of chital and sambar, warning of the presence of a predator prowling in the night.

The revised version of his autobiography, entitled *Return of the Tiger* (1993), has a sense of foreboding and not only in a personal sense. In it, he warns of the inroads of new development projects and admits the need to relate to the people who rely on the forest in a more meaningful way. In the Kachida valley of Ranthambore Wildlife Reserve, he climbs to the top of a hill to tell a fellow conservationist how he has redeemed his pledge. Twenty years ago, he had promised to save the valley, and now he can look back on a job well done.

He died the following year. His accounts survive as a record of a magnificent wildlife heritage, ours to cherish or destroy.

If Sankhala was the man of action, he had a counterpart in a man of ideas. M. Krishnan (1913–96), the most articulate proponent of total preservation, was undoubtedly the most widely read Indian naturalist this century. Armed with a degree in botany, he served briefly as adviser to the ruler of Sandur, a princely state in Mysore. In 1948–9, he began his career as a freelance writer and photographer. Always known as a 'lone wolf' he remains notable for both the outstanding quality of his writings and his black-and-white photographs. His Country Notebook, a column in *The Statesman*, Calcutta, was published once a fortnight for nearly half a century. Some of these early pieces are collected in *Jungle and Backyard* (1961).

Krishnan was scrupulous in his attention to changes in the countryside, and a recurrent theme is the cycle of seasons. March is the time when the Indian roller goes crazy as it begins its courtship rituals; summer is the season of mango blossoms and of the koel song; November, the month when harvesting is done, is the time to stalk the grey partridge. Krishnan was among the first to sound the warning bell about the wildlife of the dry grasslands and the scrub forests. Of the blackbuck antelope he wrote, 'When every acre is held precious . . . I think the beasts and birds of the open country must look to the blackbuck for their salvation, for it is the one claimant for protection among them whose arresting good looks and swift charm might succeed in attracting notice.' Having witnessed the rapid demise of the great herds of the buck in the Deccan, he was already clinically analysing the causes of their decline. The meat-hunters, often servicing the markets in the towns and bazaars, used both traditional and modern techniques against the animals, but the *coup de grâce* was delivered by the extension of cultivation into the areas it inhabited. Krishnan was way ahead of his times, for until very recently Indian conservation efforts have focussed not on grasslands but on forests.

Modesty was never one of Krishnan's traits. Unlike many urban wildlife lovers he had deep roots in Tamil and Sanskrit literature and an intimate knowledge of the southern Indian countryside in particular, which give all his writings a distinctly brahmanical air of knowing precisely what is best and necessary. In 1965, he won a Jawaharlal Nehru fellowship to study the ecology and status of the large mammals of peninsular India. The study, published in 1975 under the title *India's Wildlife: 1959–70*, is a masterpiece. It also reflects his other great strength: his long familiarity with the denizens of the monsoon forest, the gaur and sambhar, the chital and elephant. His view of wildlife never excluded the rich assemblage of India's plants on which its fauna depends. In the book he highlights the destructive forces unleashed in independent India. Hunting menaced not only the survival of species but also radically forced herds of deer to become 'shy and fugitive creatures of the night'. In the past, the forest and sown lands had often been in a tug of war. The boundaries of the jungle had not been fixed; but in his own lifetime the retreat of the woodlands became permanent.

Krishnan's response to these changes was unequivocal. In each of his works, including the superbly illustrated *Nights and Days: My Book of Indian Wildlife* (1985), he argues in favour of a kind of ecological patriotism. India's identity has as much to do with plants and rivers, trees and birds, insects and animals as with the languages and cultures of its people. A sense of national pride required that at least some tracts be preserved in their natural state.

In *Nights and Days*, each anecdote of encounters with animals is accompanied by a photograph. This was what his Country Notebook looked like: in the anthology he put together a selection of his best pieces. The calls of nesting spoonbills draw his attention. 'I can only describe [it] as a strange mixture of a hiss and a growl. It even has an alarm call, a soft sneezing call, very like a man suppressing a sneeze politely in company.' An account of owls large and small reveals how much he likes them, though he reminds us they are 'soft-plumaged, silent-winged, night hunters'.

In the wet grassland of Kaziranga in Assam, he sensed the agony of a mother rhino whose calf had been lifted by a tiger. His sympathy for creatures great and small was not matched by any tolerance for error in human beings. Krishnan's sometimes acerbic remarks are often unforgettable. In *Jungle and Backyard*, turning on Sarojini Naidu's notion that a koel calls 'Lira, Liree', he says devastatingly: 'I have not heard the call. Nor has anyone else.'

Krishnan was very much with Sankhala in his advocacy of a centralised effort to establish inviolate nature reserves. Though familiar with village-based traditions of protecting water birds and sacred groves, he felt that only punitive measures could hold back industrialisation and population growth from nature reserves. The logger and hunter, the gatherer of fruits and flowers and the tourist, all had to be subordinated in protected areas to the interest of the wild. In the *Sunday* magazine annual in 1977 he warned of the need to be vigilant in protection and to resist the temptation to interfere with nature, 'to gild refined gold and paint the lily'.

Krishnan represents the voice of the unrelenting preservationist. In this role his eloquence has not been matched. There is no dearth of zealous wildlife protectors now, but no one now has the same literary flair, that eccentric ability to convey the lived quality of life in the wild and the imperatives of keeping it alive. The wonderful literary connection between wildlife and riveting storytelling, established in India by the work of these five nature-writers, is a curious and quite uniquely remarkable corner of the Indo-Anglian tradition of prose writing. The other interesting fact to remember, in this context, is that Jim Corbett is almost certainly the highest selling Indian writer of imaginative English prose of all time; and Sálim Ali's collected writings on India's birdlife may well come a very close second. No one who cares for the craft of prose, and its importance in delivering an implicit or explicit conservationist message to large audiences, can ever undervalue its achievement.

24
Translations into English

Arshia Sattar

The terrain covered by translations of Indian literature into English is both extensive and thickly sown, making it very difficult to provide even an exhaustive listing of the languages, genres, and texts that have been mapped by translations over the last two hundred years. I will, therefore, restrict myself to trends and examples, citing only those texts and languages that best demonstrate how this territory has been marked and appropriated by Indian and Western scholars and translators.

The history of the translation of Indian literature into English can roughly be divided into three periods: early Orientalism, the Indian awakening, and the post-Independence enterprise. Despite the historical and cultural differences that define each period, we shall see that the translations of Indian literatures exist in a continuum. Persisting ideas, traditions of ideology, and particular agendas form footways and tracks through this terrain.

India existed in the European imagination during the classical period of Greece and Rome primarily through trading contacts. Later, its presence was kept alive through the writings of Islamic historians and philosophers. But it was travellers' tales from the sixteenth and seventeenth centuries that aroused a tremendous curiosity about India in Europe. The country's fabled wealth drew explorers, adventurers, and imperialists, and its heathen population provided an equal incentive for missionaries to come to India. As early as the sixteenth century, European missionaries displayed an interest in Hindu texts: Manuel d'Oliviera translated the *Gyaneshwari* from Marathi into Portuguese, and around the same time Roberto Nobili translated vast tracts of Christian doctrine into Tamil.

A steady trickle of the men of God and the men of the Crown soon because a stream and by the 1750s the British, particularly, had a substantial presence in India. Both missionaries and administrators felt themselves handicapped in their respective enterprises by the lack of access to local languages. Their solution to this problem resulted in a project that would eventually open up India's literary riches both to itself and to the West.

The years 1770 to 1785 have been described as 'the formative period during which the British successfully began the programme of appropriating Indian languages'. The period coincided, more or less, with the administration of Warren Hastings, who was appointed Governor of Bengal in 1772. He strongly encouraged British merchants and administrators to acquire skills in local languages and develop a familiarity with Indian customs. Nathaniel Brassey Halhed's *A Grammar of the Bengal Language* appeared in 1778, and the next fifty years saw a large number of similar works published. In 1785, Charles Wilkins's *The Bhagvet Geeta* became 'the first Sanskrit work made accessible to the scholars of Europe by translation'.

Sir William Jones (1746–94), perhaps the greatest Oriental scholar of all time, arrived in India as a judge in 1783. The following year he founded the Asiatic Society of Bengal, an institution that was to play a critical role in the production and dissemination of cultural information about India. In 1785, Jones embarked on the study of Sanskrit, his twenty-eighth language, and by the end of that decade had translated Kalidasa's *Abhijnanasakuntalam*. Published in 1789, *Sacontala* was arguably the first piece of Indian literature (rather than a religious or legal text) to receive a wide and appreciative European audience.

Jones's initial motivation to study Sanskrit was in order to read and understand Indian laws better, to establish, as he said, 'a standard of Justice'. 'I have left orders at Benaras and Gaya, both holy cities, for the oldest books on the *Hindu* laws to be translated from the *Shanscrit*;

which I am most tempted to learn, that I may be a check on the Pundits of the court', Jones wrote in a letter of 1785. The work begun by him but left unfinished at his death was completed by Henry T. Colebrooke. It was published as *The Digest of Hindu Law on Contracts and Successions* in 1798.

An event of far-reaching consequences for the translation and transmission of Indian texts was, however, the setting up in 1880 of the Serampore Mission Press by three Baptist missionaries, William Carey, Joshua Marshman, and William Ward. Started with the intention of translating the Bible into the languages of India, the Press was within a decade the largest such establishment in Asia, bringing out dictionaries, grammars, textbooks, literary journals, and newspapers, in addition to translations of the Bible.

Also in 1800 was started, by Lord Wellesley, the College at Fort William, Calcutta, for British civil servants. The charter of the College declared that 'before any Civilian could obtain a degree, he was required to demonstrate his knowledge of the native languages'. Not surprisingly, William Carey was among Wellesley's first appointments. Once the College was set up, Indian texts came to be translated into English in ever greater numbers.

Religious texts were initially translated via Persian-language versions that already existed. Using an intermediate language was a common translation practice at the time. Whilst most of the translators and compilers were British, it is more than likely that they worked with Indian assistants and intermediaries. History records the name of at least one Indian involved in this early enterprise: Mohan Prasad Thakur, assistant librarian at the College, compiled an *English–Bengali Vocabulary* in 1810. Later, in 1831, a certain Maharaja Kalee Krishen Bahadur translated the *Mohamudgara*, a short collection of gnomic verses wrongly attributed to Sankara:

> Do not boast of youth, wealth, or relatives for they are perishable, and that too within a short time; curb the illusions with which we are surrounded and seriously contemplate Him by Whom all is upheld.

The Maharaja also translated bits of the *Navaratna*, which is part of another anthology of didactic verses:

> Beggars are ever treated with contempt; the licentious are constantly subject to reproach; the ungenerous incessantly defeated; vicious individuals rejoice in the vices of others; the poor ever meet with disappointment; the fickle-minded are ever uneasy; mournful people are most suspicious; obscene talk dishonours a man; and those who are subject to misers, are involved in more distress.

By the 1830s, a number of religious as well as literary texts had been translated into English, among which were Rammohan Ray's translations of the *Kena, Isa, Katha*, and *Mundaka* Upanishads. In 1813, Horace Hyman Wilson, Assistant Surgeon to the Honourable East India Company and Secretary to the Asiatic Society, published his translation of Kalidasa's *Meghaduta* and dedicated it to the Earl of Minto, Governor-General of India. In the Preface, he says:

> The efforts of *Sanscrit* scholars have hitherto however been directed rather to the useful, than the pleasing, rather to the works of science than imagination. The complicated grammar of the *Hindu* has been most successfully investigated, their myths amply illustrated, and much of their philosophy satisfactorily explained; their astronomical works have been exhibited to the philosophers whose modern attainments have rendered ancient science an object rather of curiosity than information, and their laws are no longer concealed behind the veil of an unknown tongue. . . . It only remains to explore the field of their lighter literature, and transfer some of its most elegant flowers to a European soil.
>
> The drama of *Sacontala* and the songs of Jayadeva have prepared the readers of the West, for the character of *Sanscrit* Poetry . . . the profane Poetry of the *Hindus* affords better specimens of style and taste, than are to be found in the poems which are considered by them as sacred: such as the *Puranas*, the *Mahabharata* and the *Ramayana*: the portions of these works therefore, which on various occasions have appeared before the public, cannot be allowed to detract from the general merits of *Sanscrit* composition, even though it should appear that they have more charms in the eye of literary curiosity, than of public taste. . . .

Wilson's Preface indicates not only the general attitude towards Indian texts that the English translators had, but also gives us a fairly good idea of works that had been partially or completely translated by 1813. It is already clear that though the translators differentiated between religious and 'profane' texts, religious texts were treated and translated as 'literature' as much as they were regarded as spiritual curiosities.

The efforts of men like William Jones, Charles Wilkins, and Henry Colebrooke led to the establishment and institutionalisation of a research tradition that continues, largely unbroken, into modern Indology. The establishment of Oriental studies at the College at Fort William was replicated several times in the next two centuries. Prestigious universities in England, Europe, and the United States set up departments that studied the texts and languages of the East. Like the College, they became, and still are, the producers of translations on a large scale. These universities also continued and ratified the equation that had been set up between Indian religious and literary texts. This continuum can be demonstrated by following the translations of the Sanskrit *Ramayana* that have been published over the last hundred years.

The first extract is from Ralph T.H. Griffith's translation of the *Ramayana* (1870–5). The passage describes the abduction of Sita. Ravana, the king of the rakshasas, appears disguised as a Brahmin and tries to woo the princess. When she turns him down, Ravana throws off the disguise:

> This Ravana urged the lady meet
> For love, whose words were soft and sweet.
> Near and more near the giant pressed
> As love's hot fire inflamed his breast.
> The leader of the giant crew
> His arm around the lady threw:
> Thus Budha with ill-omened might
> Steals Rohini's delicious light.
> One hand her glorious tresses grasped,
> One with his ruthless pressure clasped
> The body of his lovely prize,
> The Maithili dame with lotus eyes.
> The silvan Gods in wild alarm
> Marked his huge teeth and ponderous arm,
> And from that Death-like presence fled,
> Of mountain size and towering head.

Along with Manmatha Nath Dutt (who had completed a seven-volume English translation of the *Mahabharata* by 1895), Romesh Chunder Dutt (1840–1909) was among the few Indians to translate Indian classical texts into English. Dutt's purpose in translating the Indian epics is stated in the Epilogue to his translation of the *Ramayana* (1899):

> Ancient India, like ancient Greece, boasts of two great epics. The *Mahabharata*, based on the legends and tradition of a historical war, is the Iliad of India. The *Ramayana*, describing the wanderings and adventures of a prince banished from his country, has so far something in common with the Odyssey. Having placed before English readers a condensed translation of the Indian Iliad, I have thought it necessary to prepare the present condensed translation of the Indian Odyssey to complete the work.

Dutt is very conscious of the fact that he is one in a long line of *Ramayana* translators. In the Epilogue, he talks in some detail about the translations and editions of the Sanskrit *Ramayana* that preceded his own, making particular mention of the 'talented and indefatigable Mr Ralph Griffith, C.I.E., who has devoted a lifetime to translating Indian poetry into English.' In Dutt's translation, Sita's abduction is described thus:

> Vain her threat and soft entreaty, Ravana held her in his wrath,
> As the planet Budha captures fair Rohini in his path.
> By his left hand tremor-shaken, Ravana held her streaming hair,
>   By his right the ruthless Rakshasa lifted up the fainting fair!
> Unseen dwellers of the woodlands watched the dismal deed of shame,
> Marked the mighty-armed Rakshasa lift the poor and helpless dame.

Griffith's and Dutt's renditions of the *Ramayana* reflect the aesthetic and poetic values of their time. Though more than two decades separated them, they seem to agree on how the *Ramayana* should be represented. The general atmosphere of a romantic ballad transforms the *Ramayana* from Wilson's 'literary curiosity' into a noble poem of love and valour, suitable for the Victorian reading public. These early works also set the tone and marked the territory of translations of Indian literature for the next hundred years. Valmiki's *Ramayana* has had an English translation for practically every generation, though more recent translations appear to prefer prose renderings of the Sanskrit epic metre.

India's fabled oral literary tradition with its unbroken line of tellers now has another line of transmission, another 'parampara': a line of literary translators. Translations of the major Indian texts like the Sanskrit epics, the *Bhagvad Gita*, the works of Kalidasa, and the Upanishads continue to appear with metronomic regularity. The primary thrust for these translations has come from Western universities, which still produce the most prestigious and scholarly versions of the Indian classics. Currently, Princeton University Press is engaged in bringing out the *Ramayana of Valmiki* (1984–) in seven volumes, translated by a consortium of Western scholars. Adding weight to the enterprise is the fact that it is based on the Baroda critical edition and is heavily annotated. The following is a translation of the same passage, describing Sita's abduction, from Volume III: *Aranyakanda* (1991) of the Princeton *Ramayana*. The translator is Sheldon I. Pollock:

> . . . Ravana seized her as the planet Buddha might seize the star Rohini in the sky.
>
> With his left hand, he seized the lotus-eyed Sita by her hair and with his right hand by her thighs.
>
> With his long arms and sharp fangs he resembled a mountain peak; seeing him advancing like Death himself, the spirits of the forest fled everywhere, overpowered by fear.

The Princeton *Ramayana* is determinedly scholarly, with annotations, footnotes, and extensive critical material. The notes take into account multiple readings of the text, multiple manuscript traditions, as well as a wealth of commentaries and glossaries that the *Ramayana* has acquired over the centuries. The changes wrought by modern scholarship and translation practice are obvious. It is the claim of the syndicate of translators that not only has every Sanskrit word been represented in the translation but also that, each time it appears, a Sanskrit word is translated with the same word in English.

Around the same time that Griffith's *Ramayana* was presented to the English reader, Mohini Chatterjee's translation of the *Bhagvad Gita* was published in London. Chatterjee's translation, published in 1887, claimed to have 'a commentary and notes as well as references to the Christian scriptures.' The end of the nineteenth century was a time when Indians publicly redefined themselves and represented their past to themselves. The stated and unstated aims of Oriental policy and British education in India had come to fruition. Under British influence and guidance, Indians had begun to feel the need to reform their society and contemporary cultural practices. Many of them, like Rammohan Ray, for example, believed that Hindu society had existed in a refined cultural state which had to be reclaimed. Soon after that, Max Müller declared that Sanskrit was a language at least as old as Latin and Greek and that Indians were racially and culturally related to Europeans. Thus, many Indians returned to their classical heritage (defined by Sanskrit culture) with a sense of pride. Europe, too, looked to India with new eyes: her cultural artefacts now seemed less alien and her myths and epics were considered to be recastings of Europe's familiar classical texts.

While classical literature and religious texts continued to dominate the translator's landscape in the nineteenth and early twentieth centuries, a beginning had been made in the translation of folk literature also. As early as 1793, W. Franklin's translation of *The Loves of Camarupa and Camalata*, a Braj text from the eighteenth century, was published in London. Franklin, however, had used a Persian version of the tale as the basis of his translation. C.A. Elliot's *Chronicles of Oonao*, a collection of Urdu-Hindi ballads from the early eighteenth century describing Rajput resistance to their Muslim overlords, was published in Allahabad in 1863. F.S. Growse's text and translation of the Punjabi poet Prannath appeared in the *Journal of the Royal Asiatic Society of Bengal* in 1879. By 1888, G.A. Grierson had written *The Modern Vernacular Literature of Hindustan*, a book which distinguishes branches and periods of the literature that came to be known as Hindi. This is an indication that whereas the focus all along was on the classical languages and texts, some attention was being paid to the vernaculars as well as to secular literatures.

In the 1880s and 1890s, journals like *Indian Antiquary* regularly carried 'translations' (which should more correctly have been called retellings) of folk tales from Punjab and various parts of Central India. These were collected by people as diverse as the novelist Flora Annie Steele and Putlibai Wadia, and civil servants like Richard Temple and

G.H. Damant. At the same time, the publications of the many research societies and institutes carried whole or partial translations of regional texts. Buddhist literatures, from Pali and from Sanskrit, were also being explored. T.W. Rhys David's translations of the Pali *Jatakas* in six volumes was published in London between 1877 and 1896 and was shortly followed by E.B. Cowell's version of the same text.

Given the early Orientalists' emphasis on the classics (which were defined as much by language as by time) and the growing popularity of the connection between India and Europe based on linguistic theories, Western translations of Indian literature had focused on ancient Sanskrit texts for more than a century. This preoccupation has continued until fairly recently, one consequence of which has been that the other Indian literatures, by and large, have not been given the attention that is their due. But this is changing; if anything, the tables have been turned on Sanskrit.

There are several reasons for this, and they have as much to do with state intervention as with the growing presence of Indian scholars in the Western academy. Independent India decided to emphasise its rich and continuous cultural heritage as a means to develop national pride and international stature. At the same time, the newly-born Indian state worked hard to promote the Nehruvian idea of 'unity in diversity', suggesting that all regional traditions are but manifestations of a larger, pan-Indian spirit. By the early 1950s, the government-funded Sahitya Akademi (the National Academy of Letters) was entrusted with the task of commissioning and publishing translations of India's regional literatures into other Indian languages as well as into English. Soon, English-language trade publishers stepped in and made translations available, sometimes quite cheaply.

Also in the 1950s, the U.S. State Department started to take an interest in India as an important South Asian nation. Consequently, private funding agencies like the Ford Foundation and Fulbright increasingly gave grants to Indians to pursue higher studies in the United States, some of whom went there to research Indian languages. One such Indian scholar was A.K. Ramanujan (1929–93), whose presence at the University of Chicago for thirty years was central to the new academic interest in Indian languages other than Sanskrit. A distinguished poet and formidable translator, Ramanujan is perhaps the only Indian to have presented a body of work in translation, from

Tamil and Kannada, to an English-reading audience. His translations include *The Interior Landscape* (1967), *Speaking of Siva* (1972), *Hymns for the Drowning* (1981), and *Poems of Love and War* (1985). Before his death in 1993, Ramanujan had been translating Telugu poetry from the seventeenth and eighteenth centuries. *When God is a Customer* (1994), a volume co-edited with Velcheru Narayana Rao and David Shulman, is a collection of courtesan songs.

Together with his essays, which appeared in a collected volume in 1999, Ramanujan's translations have done more to shape perceptions of and attitudes towards Indian literature than anyone since William Jones and Max Müller. More importantly, Ramanujan trained an entire generation of Indian and Western translators to approach texts and contexts in the manner that he had made so successful. Recently, though, Ramanujan's style and approach to translation has come in for severe criticism. In *Siting Translation* (1993), Tejaswini Niranjana examines Ramanujan's translations of Kannada *vacanas* from *Speaking of Siva* and suggests that he perpetuates Oriental stereotypes about the nature of Indian religion and poetry.

To Ramanujan must also go the credit for another major shift in the translation of Indian literature: the acknowledgement of its profoundly oral nature. His insistence on multiple narratives and multiple sources militated against the emphasis on critical editions and 'standard' texts for the epics and story traditions. Ramanujan's interest in folk literature—an interest that culminated in *Folktales from India* (1993)—ranged from folk tales to proverbs, riddles, and jokes. Because of his stature as a poet, scholar, and translator, his personal interests influenced the kinds of material that were deemed worthy of translation. This did much to reduce the overbearing attention paid to classical literatures and languages and it dovetailed nicely with a similar trend in translation in India at around the same time.

In the 1950s and 1960s, the Navya movement swept through Indian regional literatures. This was a consciously modernist movement, one that broke from the classical predilections of the past and redefined the concerns of literature. Navya was heavily influenced by European writing and Existentialism, and the short story was the primary vehicle of its expression. From Hindi to Kannada, Tamil to Bengali, younger writers 'killed their fathers' with a vigorous new prose. There was, at the same time, the heady idealism of a nation newly-born, one in which its intellectuals and artists would talk to each other and exchange ideas. Translation, often into English, was the medium through which this exchange took place.

As we have seen, the translation of non-classical and secular Indian literature is not an entirely recent phenomenon, nor must we be led to believe that the translations were done exclusively by Western translators. Michael Madhusudan Dutt (1824–73), one of the most intriguing figures of the Bengal Renaissance, was translating his own plays from Bengali into English as early as the mid-nineteenth century. Dutt also translated Ramanarayan Tarkaratna's *Ratnavali* (1858) and Dinabandhu Mitra's *Niladarpan* ('The Mirror of Indigo Planting', 1860), the latter being one of the earliest plays of protest in Bengali literature. As late as 1908, performance of the play, which was about the exploitation of Bengali peasants by British indigo planters, continued to be banned in Bengal.

The tradition that Michael Madhusudan Dutt had begun, of Indian writers translating their own work, was continued by Romesh Chunder Dutt, who translated his novel, *The Lake of Palms* (1902), from Bengali into English, but its most famous practitioner yet has been Rabindranath Tagore (1861–1942), who, between 1912 and 1921, brought out no less than six collections of his Bengali poems in English translations. It has recently been argued that the notion we have of Tagore being a bad translator of his own poems ought to be looked at afresh. In *Translation and Understanding* (1999), Sukanta Chaudhuri asks that we acknowledge Tagore's conscious rewriting of his poems and suggests that we read his English renderings as commentaries on his Bengali originals. Tagore's 'English poems', he says, 'incorporate a large corpus of rewritings and recastings, rearrangements and cross-matchings, exegesis and fresh interventions, making up a concurrent and counterpoising creative process, a commentary on the dominant Bengali line, uniquely valuable as being from the poet's own pen.' Chaudhuri's monograph raises compelling questions about the nature and intentions of Tagore's 'translation' enterprise, circumscribed as it was by the colonial period and the poet's awareness of his poetic stature and public persona.

In the period since Independence, the best known among those who have translated their work into English are O.V. Vijayan from Malayalam, Arun Kolatkar and Vilas Sarang from Marathi, Agyeya and Krishna Baldev Vaid from Hindi, Qurratulain Hyder from Urdu, and Girish Karnad from Kannada. Girish Karnad (b. 1938) has talked about the critical choice a writer makes when he opts to write in one language rather than in another. The choice determines the primary audience for the work; more importantly, it determines the literature the work will belong to. Karnad's *Hayavadana* (1973), for example, will always be a Kannada play translated into many languages, and into English by the playwright himself. On the question of translating his own plays, of moving from Kannada to English, Karnad has brought up the notion of 'rewriting'. But though he would prefer to capture the spirit rather than the letter of the original, his translations, unlike Tagore's, remain translations.

Since the 1970s, with publishers playing a bigger role in presenting the literature being written in the Indian languages, translation activity has become somewhat more professionalised. Apart from novels, translated anthologies of short stories and, occasionally, poetry have appeared on the market. Sadly, the translations, by and large, have been of mediocre quality. The 1970s and 1980s saw, too, the birth of small—and short-lived—literary journals like *Vagartha, Setu*, and *Bombay Literary Review*, which encouraged translations. Another journal to publish translations, but of plays, was Rajinder Paul's *Enact*. Its pages enabled playwrights as well as theatre groups to stay abreast of contemporary developments, specially those within the country. The Sahitya Akademi's *Indian Literature* (1957–) has been publishing translations for the past five decades, though of short fiction and poetry mainly. The Sahitya Akademi has also instituted translation awards in the languages recognised by it. However, these awards carry more prestige than monetary value. A series that is well funded and has been widely noticed, perhaps more than any other translation venture of recent times, is the one published by Katha, an organisation which since 1991 has brought out an annual anthology of prize-winning stories in translation.

The mid-1980s boom in English-language publishing has resulted in more translations than ever before. New publishers like Penguin India, Permanent Black, Ravi Dayal, Manas, Stree, Seagull, and Kali for Women, and older ones like Macmillan and Orient Longman, have made translations part of their lists and introduced special imprints for translated writings. There have, at the same time, appeared from the United States heavily packaged translations of Indian texts, chief among which are Gayatri Chakravorty Spivak's translations of Mahasweta Devi.

There now appears to be a conscious effort on the part of publishers to find Indian translators and native speakers of the source language to present texts in English. There also seems to be a shift towards translating primarily for Indian audiences, which is their main market. What this means is that common Indian words are left untranslated, partly because it is assumed that Indian readers will understand them and partly because the attempt is to carry a little of the flavour and rhythm of the original.

This new agenda is a reflection of certain politically compelling post-colonial ideologies that demand that we represent ourselves to ourselves as well as to others. Translations must now emphasise linguistic and cultural difference instead of smoothing them over in an attempt to approximate Western literary modes and rhetoric. It is only fitting that translations, like so much else, should reflect the times in which they are made.

25

Shobhaa De and Indian Pulp Fiction

PADMINI MONGIA

Anybody who followed the flurry of books issued by Penguin India during the late 1980s and early 1990s must have heard the tale—oft told—that it was Shobhaa De's popular novels which indirectly funded the publication of other literary works. While a new novel seemed to be coming out every week, apparently nobody bought these novels, or, at any rate, sufficient numbers did not buy them to sustain their costs of publication. In fact, one writer complained that authors had to fund their own novels by promising to buy an agreed number of copies, enabling Penguin to at least recover the costs of producing them. While bookshops stocked some worthy titles, such as Indrani Aikath Gyaltsen's *Daughters of the House* and Gita Hariharan's *The Thousand Faces of Night*, which sold at the time for a modest Rs 75 in paperback, it was apparently Shobhaa De's sexy novels that sold in the thousands. (In or around the year 2000, Shobha De attached an extra 'a' to her first name and became Shobhaa.) Her fiction—everyone knew this even if they had not read it—was easily digested, slightly off-colour, and full of the passionate loves and lives of pretty, sexually active young men and women.

In 2003 the novelist Amit Chaudhuri wrote a story called 'Prelude to an Autobiography' in which an aspiring writer decides she must surely be worthy of writing her autobiography if Shobhaa De was.

De's memoir, *Selective Memories*, was published in 1998, the year she turned fifty. I mention Chaudhuri's story because De's 'worth' is an issue that shadows much of the work written on and about her. De's many novels (seventeen as I write this) are seen as the opposite of literary fiction, i.e. just the sort that writers like Amit Chaudhuri would not produce and probably not read.

De's novels may not be read by the literary set, or read only in the spirit of sociological inquiry, but her life and career remain of continuing interest to Indians writing in English, not least because of her bestseller status. By now, academic books have been written on De (I know of one edited volume dedicated solely to her), and some university courses have included her writing. Fully aware of her shaky status in the multi-starred universe of Indian writing in English, De enjoys being its bad girl and its most popular one. But exactly where in this universe does she fit, if at all?

Born Shobha Rajadhyaksha in 1948 in Satara, a small town in Maharashtra, De was ten when her family moved to Bombay from Delhi. The fourth child of a home-maker mother and civil servant father, she graduated from St Xavier's College with a degree in psychology and went on to become a fashion model, a copy-editor with an advertising firm, and the founder editor of three successful magazines—*Stardust, Society,* and *Celebrity.* Along the way she married into a wealthy family, divorced her first husband, and then married Dilip De, a shipping magnate. Together they raised the six children they had between them, and De takes great pleasure in pointing out that her daily life is prosaic and stolidly domestic.

What makes Shobhaa De such a popular writer? In the 1990s, when the print run for a work of fiction was ordinarily 2000 copies, Penguin published 5000 copies of De's first novel, *Socialite Evenings* (1988), and 12,500 of the next one, *Starry Nights* (1990). *Socialite Evenings* has since sold 50,000+ copies and *Starry Nights* 55,000+. De's novels—the titles of all but one begin with S, presumably because in time-honoured Indian fashion it is a letter that has been lucky for her—broke a barrier by introducing female protagonists who knew what they wanted and set about getting it, women who expressed and fulfilled their sexual desires openly, women in urban settings who knew or quickly learned how to negotiate difficult terrain to make their own small niches within it. De came to be known as the Jackie Collins of India.

De calls herself an obsessive-compulsive writer; her columns have been published in *MidDay*, *The Times of India*, *The Week*, and various other mass media. Focusing fearlessly on a wide range of issues (restaurant reviews, food, Bombay films, politics), a selection of her commentaries have been collected and published as *Shooting from the Hip* (1994). Her weekly column in *The Times of India* is called 'Politically Incorrect' and reveals the keen, critical mind of a writer interested in examining a host of topics that concern contemporary India. Well respected and feared for her forthrightness, these columns have the masala quality that characterized *Stardust*. Yet though De may be blunt, she is careful to comment only on the public utterances of public figures.

In *Stardust* De oversaw the insightful, sometimes graceless, but always wickedly enjoyable column on film gossip, 'Neeta's Natter'. Using an English liberally peppered with Hindi and exclamation marks, she fashioned an idiom that captured the linguistic fluidity of urban Mumbaikars. More important than the sexual taboos De supposedly broke, it may be this easy prose which is her major contribution to the world of letters. Widely credited with launching and popularizing Hinglish, it is her effortless, colourful, and entirely apt way with words that have brought her a loyal following. Sample the following lines from her blog: 'We are not knowing when rain is coming or going *jor jor se* . . . how it is our fault? We are not *bhagwan*. You peoples are unnecessarily blaming. . . take umbrella and go. Don't trouble again with all this *faltu* talk.' Beyond her lively language, part of her appeal lies in her regular reminders of her *desi*-ness. An unabashed Mumbai lover, De is always a Mumbaikar first and last, no matter where she is in the world. Without being jingoistic, she also always identifies herself and her insights as Indian. Critical she may be of the Indian government, Indian policies, and many things Indian, but De's reference points are repeatedly and flamboyantly home-based. Like her columns, her novels are essentially made for the domestic market. Only De's first two novels have been published in the US, and these two alongside *Superstar India* in the UK. Some of her novels have, however, been translated into European languages, and into some Indian languages (Marathi, Malayalam, Hindi).

Without David Davidar, who established the Indian branch of Penguin and was the force behind the publishing boom associated with the mid 1980s, it is hard to imagine the successes of Shobhaa De. Davidar suggested she try her hand at writing a novel, and what was to be a work of non-fiction on Mumbai became De's first novel, *Socialite Evenings.* This became a bestseller and was reprinted in 1989 and 1990. She then wrote a string of other bestsellers. *Starry Nights* was followed by *Sisters* and *Strange Obsession* in 1992, *Sultry Days* (1994), and, in the same year *Shooting From the Hip. Snapshots,* about six women friends who meet after many years, and *Small Betrayals,* a collection of short stories, came out in 1995. After *Second Thoughts* (1996) came *Surviving Men* (1997), the first in a series of non-fiction works that are part advice column and part critical cultural commentary. The others are *Speedpost* (1999), where De examines her relationship to her children in a series of imaginary letters to them; *Spouse: The Truth About Marriage* (2005); and *Superstar India* (2008). *Shobhaa at Sixty* appeared in 2010, the year which also saw De's first novel for young adults, *S's Secret,* as well as the launch by Penguin India of a new imprint to be headed by De and focused on celebrity memoirs, commercial fiction, and whatever else De considers cutting edge and 'muscular'.

After forty years of work in advertising, journalism, magazine publishing, and novel writing, De had by 2010 become a best-selling brand. According to her publisher, her books now sell upwards of 60,000 copies in hardback. Seeing her own life paralleling that of the nation, De, in *Superstar India,* shows herself as uniquely positioned to comment on India's successes and failures. With its publication in 2008, she was given a digital profile, a first for an Indian writer. This non-fiction work, containing De's reflections on sixty years of Indian Independence, deployed Facebook and a personal blog to reach a wider audience. The target of acquiring 1500 friends within the first six months was achieved in the first two and a half. Within seven months De had a Facebook fan following of 5000, the maximum allowed. An active blogger since 2008, she posts comments regularly, often daily. Interspersed with photographs of herself and the places she visits, De's blog has had countless visitors and almost as many profile views.

De's professional lives—as model, editor, and magazine publisher—

recollected in *Selective Memory* give an insight into the changes that were taking place as India moved into a very different relationship with the media in the early 1970s. Reading De's recollections well after the media revolution and the privatization of television, it is startling to be reminded of how small the advertising and magazine publishing worlds were when she first entered them. The origins of *Stardust*, even now after more than forty years of India's bestselling film magazine, are so shockingly modest that the then naïve Shobhaa needs to be given even more credit for sensing a hunger for irreverence, humour, and gossip that brought the stars down from where established magazines like *Filmfare* had enshrined them.

Socialite Evenings, De's first novel, was loosely autobiographical. Following the fortunes of a young girl, Karuna, who moves from the provinces to the big bad world of Bombay, the novel shows Karuna coming into her own as a member of Bombay's elite and rather empty world. Karuna and her friends Anjali and Ritu move between marriages and affairs, picking up successful business ventures here and there. Rich one day and poor the next, they chug along but show a lot of resilience. Even as Karuna grows into her own, she learns about champagne and wine, perfume and designer labels. So does De's reader. Not the least useful parts of De's novels are the embedded lessons she offers. As her provincial heroine adjusts to Bombay high life, readers learn with the heroines about consumer luxury goods. When *Socialite Evenings* first appeared, imported perfumes and Scotch whisky were the ultimate status symbols and difficult to procure. De's novel offered readers lessons in classy consumption, which her heroine embraced with a weary sense of inevitability.

In other novels as well, De's characters offered a sort of crude road map to many women moving to urban centres or negotiating uncharted terrain in corporate working environments. In *Starry Nights* (also published as *Bollywood Nights*) De follows the fortunes of a young woman from Madras who is brought by her scheming mother to Bombay in order to be made a film star. Asha Rani is exploited by her mother, who sees in her young daughter being physically well endowed the potential for assets even more desirable. Repeatedly reminding the reader of the value of Asha Rani's bra size, *Starry Nights* offers an insider's glimpse into the world of Bollywood stars, directors, producers, and actors, a universe in which everyone is for sale and everything available. Sold first by her ambitious mother, Asha Rani's life unfolds along a series of exploitative affairs through which she learns how to manage her own ambition of becoming a star. She does become one, but she also falls in love with an actor, after which her life begins to spiral out of control. Eventually she moves back to Madras and settles into a comfortable middle class life, running her father's old photo studio. Her distraught heart, however, never prevented Asha Rani from enjoying varied sexual encounters, all rendered in blandly untitillating prose.

This novel, like many others by De, takes the reader into supposedly forbidden territory. So-called sexual taboos—threesomes, lesbian sex—are broken and explored. Men lust after women and vice versa, and little by way of erotic charge and its development is required to get them into bed. Plenty of sexual romping later, though, a reader can be left quite unmoved by the apparently wicked fun men and women have with each other. De may offer readers numerous women protagonists with flutters in their underwear, but her erotic range is unsubtle and often awkwardly simple. All the same, her sexual explorations have struck a chord with a vast readership that has remained faithful to her books and bought them with gusto. The vastness of her readership is what makes De a writer difficult to ignore.

One way to understand De's considerable success is by focusing on reading communities and what they tell us about the place of books in a given culture and at a particular time, in the manner of Janice Radway's path-breaking *Reading the Romance* (1991). Who buys De's novels? Why do they sell in the numbers they do? While no sustained research has been done, one may speculate that the success of De's novels, and increasingly her blog, lie in her work being what is generally termed pulp fiction, written to be mass marketed and consumed in transitional spaces: airport lounges, railway and bus stations, and on journeys. The time covered by the journey, a time of transience, has been viewed by theorists of the novel as one conducive to pulp, namely fiction which thrives on the aspirational promise contained in transience. It is not contradictory to speak of pulp fiction in the context of English language publishing in India, because though only a small percentage of the population speaks English, even this number is around fifty million, India being the third largest producer of books in English after the US and the UK. De's novels, full of naïve young women thrown into Mumbai's business or film worlds, show her heroines blunder and pay for their mistakes as they move towards a stable sense of self and family. *Socialite Evenings, Bollywood Nights*, and *Sisters* (1988, 1990, and 1992 respectively) all rely on the outsider girl who finds her feet.

Offering lessons in upward mobility and the aspirations towards it, her heroines (as in *Sisters*) learn about business and real estate, as does the reader. This aspect of De's novels has been enhanced in some of her non-fiction. Books such as *Spouse: The Truth About Marriage* and *Surviving Men* are just a step away from self-help books. While De has plenty of irreverence peppering whatever she writes about, she takes her role as learned commentator seriously. A fierce supporter of marriage, for instance, she is happy to address her own to share what she has learned about battles worth fighting for and those it was better to let go. Her sensible starting premise is that a marriage can be made to work if the parties involved believe in marriage. De does. Just as her own photograph graces each of her publications, her byline almost always mentions marriage and her role as mother to six children. It may well be this solid domestic base that allows De to write her raunchy novels and still be regarded as a role model. Readers of her blog routinely write in to thank her for showing them a path they, as new Indian women, are trying to demarcate for themselves.

Some critics, though, regard De's works as soft porn, books in which women remove their underwear, have numerous relationships within and without marriage, and generally claw their way to the places they want to reach. Others regard her novels as vacuous and argue that a writer whose characters use their sexual wiles to climb to the top can hardly be called a feminist. Yet De's novels, stories, and non-fiction are replete with intelligent, assertive women who quickly learn the system they operate within and negotiate for their own ends. While their methods are often suspect, there is a no-nonsense quality to many of them. They quickly recognize that they have to live by their wits in a money-grabbing world that is largely immoral, or at best amoral. Having to participate in it means that they may, and do, fall off the deep end, but the energy and ambition they display show a refreshing lack of respect for traditional, ascribed roles. They learn how to swim against the tide and more often than not end up on dry land, safe and sound.

The space opened up by Shobhaa De has since been filled by a variety of pulp forms. Now, fifteen years into the twenty-first century, the novels of Chetan Bhagat and Amish Tripathi are being sold at street corners and convenience stores, chick-lit has been an immense success, and graphic novels are increasingly popular. While the success of Bridget Jones and the American television serial (and film) *Sex and the City* has spawned 'chick lit' phenomena the world over, in India its literary foremother has to be De. As in De's world, the protagonists of chick lit novels are single women in the city. These women have independent incomes, are uncomfortable with older notions and assigned roles, and are certain that they do not have to embrace those roles. Comfortable with drinking, smoking, pre-marital sex, and the consumerist pleasures of purchasing designer clothes and shoes, these women negotiate their way in urban centres towards Mr Right.

The confessional tone of much of this literature is reminiscent of the revelatory method, which De relishes. Her writings use confession to reveal intimate details of the erotic and sexual lives of her protagonists, as do chick lit novels generally. The novels of Anuja Chauhan, a highly successful chick lit writer, have smart, spunky heroines, women more rounded than those we see in De. But like De's heroines, Chauhan's offer both a reflection and a model of possible lives for young, earning women placed outside the context of family. The story of chick lit in India is that of a woman supposedly 'bold, wicked and cheeky'—as various reviewers have described her. These epithets suggest the non-normativeness of the experiences available in such fiction. Often, reviewers in India, when confronted by the tensions between traditional roles and a new world of modern sexual and experiential variety now available to women, have expressed alarm or feelings of threat at the runaway nature of social change, the sudden provision of hedonistic freedoms that have until recently been the monopoly of men. Turning to high-end consumerism, for example, the heroines in these new novels purchase designer clothes to make themselves feel better and more attractive in the dating game. And this is the least of it.

The biggest publishing success of the past fifteen years is Chetan Bhagat (b. 1974). In 2004 he published *Five Point Someone*, now a film, *3 Idiots* (2009). In 2005 his *One Night @ the Call Center* was issued at the affordable price of Rs 95, almost the same price at which novels were sold by Penguin India in the mid 1980s. And 2010 saw the publication of *2 States: The Story of My Marriage*, about the love affair and marriage of two IIM (Indian Institute of Management) graduates, one from Delhi and the other from Madras. Bhagat is an IIT (Indian Institute of Technology) graduate himself who married a Tamilian. Written in simple prose that makes them widely accessible to an audience accustomed to the vocabulary of functional and everyday English, his novels are well paced and can be finished in a couple of hours. Almost no paragraph is longer than a few sentences. Relying heavily on dialogue, Bhagat's novels seem written for film. He manages to reach out to that vast population of Indians who speak English without being completely at home in the language, rather like his characters in *One Night @ the Call Center*. Bhagat's readers are not daunted by his novels, and are in this sense quite different from readers of literary fiction. Instead of writing off non-elite segments of the available readership, Bhagat has shown resourcefulness in recognizing its desire to read novels in English, its need for a novel that speaks to mundane concerns. Other writers, less well known than Bhagat but considerable sellers nevertheless, are even more unashamedly anti-literary. Published by small houses such as Shristi and Expressions, their books are cheaply produced, sell in the thousands, and proclaim, even celebrate, their difference from canonical literary fiction. Western pulp fiction has now a commercially secure counterpart in India.

The 3 Mistakes of My Life (2008), the Bhagat novel which takes on serious social issues, is still able to simplify, with remarkable ease, the growing strength of the Hindu right and the terrible events in Godhra in Gujarat in 2004. In a manner reminiscent of De, Bhagat deftly covers a lot of ground. The works of these two highly successful novelists are not merely light and vaporous. In fact, both are down-to-earth writers dealing with the day-to-day problems that face middle class men and women in urban India. Competition is stiff; people are ruthless; if someone can exploit you they will. Both novelists give us confident, ambitious protagonists, entrepreneurs in the making who manage, despite some losses, to stand on their own feet and move ahead in the new consumer-driven India.

Unlike De's novels, which periodically show interest in the psychological inner lives of protagonists, Bhagat's are peopled by reasonably flat characters. His protagonists are young, just finishing IIT (*Five Point Someone*), getting their first jobs, getting married (*Two States*), working in demanding low-paying jobs (*One Night*), attempting to establish a new business (*The 3 Mistakes*). They aspire to more money than they have but are not driven by consumerism. What does drive them is entrepreneurship, the desire to set themselves up independently and not work for a boss. In De's many novels, some women are rich and some are not; some have a good business mind and others are uninterested in it. The financial independence to which they aspire comes for them inseparable from the imported goods they afford. Fine wines and perfumes, imported cars and clothes, travel to Europe and other places is important for her characters, even as they struggle to find meaning in their inevitably bad marital and relationship decisions. In both De's and Bhagat's successes we can see the growing acceptance of a consumerist India in which the goods money can buy are a given feature of contemporary life.

The publishing process in relation to Bhagat's novels also reveals the new and increasing sophistication in marketing pulp fiction. Deliberately choosing to place his novels in the convenience stores of gas stations, Bhagat's publishers, Rupa & Co., were the first to sense that there now existed a new environment different from the earlier one in which *Midnight's Children* and *The God of Small Things* had appeared. With greater numbers of young earners willing to spend Rs 95 on a book (about the price of a bottle of Coke and a slice of pizza), Rupa & Co. astounded those who follow books in India with staggering sales figures: 2.5 million copies of *One Night*; *2 States*, it is claimed, sells a copy every twenty seconds, and *The 3 Mistakes of My Life* one every seventeen.

At the same time, we should be wary of only marvelling at the new techniques for marketing books and the high sales figures. Rumours abound suggesting both De and Bhagat have invested in their own best-seller status. De was already a celebrity when she was launched; it is said that her shipping magnate husband's wealth was not inconsequential in massaging the sales figures of her books. Bhagat was a successful marketing professional when he became a writer, with money to invest in the marketing of his books. He reportedly spent Rs 5 lakhs ($10,000) of his own money targeting IIT aspirants. Amish Tripathi, who goes only by his first name, launched his very commercially successful Shiva Trilogy also using his own funds. A YouTube trailer was just part of the event; fans appeared carrying trishuls and wearing period costumes. To complicate matters further, there is no reliable system generating the figures used to describe writers as best-sellers. Yet the label is used often and freely, and presumably enhances the sales and success of select works.

Over this period, and gathering speed in the past two decades, new genres of the novel in English have burgeoned in India, which we may call Indian pulp fiction. The variants include chick lit, techie novels, and the Hindu mythological. In the main these are written entirely for consumption in the domestic market—their *desi* idiom and limited vocabulary rule out a readership outside South Asia—and many, carrying a low price, sell in numbers associated until recently only with the popular magazines that proliferated both in English and spectacularly so in the regional languages (in particular Bengali, Tamil, Hindi, and Malayalam). Indian pulp fiction thus seems a logical expansion and natural extension of popular household magazines of the 1970s and 1980s which, providing ordinary readers with a mix of morality, scandal, and social vignette, were great commercial hits. More than the career of any other writer, Shobhaa De's suggests the obviousness of the connection between the cheap magazine and the affordable paperback.

Like her, writers such as Chetan Bhagat, Ravinder Singh, and Amish Tripathi dramatize local issues for a local audience. Instead of being concerned with literariness and revisioning empire in the manner of the writers of the 1980s and 1990s, these new novelists focus on contemporary urban issues which they render in earthy, easy to read, home-grown English. They are often assertively and vocally anti-literary, happy to state how little they themselves have read. If their fiction has no international caché, if their ideas are deemed insular and unreadable by the literary set, if they are never in line to win the big prizes abroad that elite Indian novels have sometimes won, it makes no difference to them: their sales figures within the country speak louder than their words.

That space, opened by Shobhaa De in a small advertising firm in the mid 1970s, has come a long way in the fifty-odd years that have passed since.

26
Ramananda Chatterjee and the *Modern Review*

Margery Sabin

Ramananda Chatterjee, sole founder and editor of the *Modern Review* from 1907 to his death in 1943, has been called the 'Father of Indian Journalism', a tribute soon followed by lament for the paucity of heirs to this legacy. The historian Ramachandra Guha has called fullest attention to the independent humanistic vision that the *Modern Review* fostered. In his essay, 'The Independent Journal of Opinion', Guha mentions *Seminar* and the *Economic and Political Weekly* as current publications comparably independent of parties and ideologies. These analogies, however, give little sense of the way in which Ramananda's monthly became nothing less than a public institution for English-language readers in India during the Indian nationalist movement, as well as an emblem worldwide of the emerging modern nation. The 72-volume run of *Modern Review* now moulders in a few university libraries, while the name Ramananda Chatterjee is largely forgotten.

In a belated Birth Centenary Commemoration (1973)—Ramananda was born in 1865—regret already mingles with reverence as former colleagues and younger admirers measure the condition of journalism in post-Independence India against Ramananda's standards and idealistic vision. Contributors to the *Modern Review* constitute 'an almost complete dictionary of the leaders of the intelligentsia of India during 37 years', according to Jadunath Sarkar, the historian of Mughal India who himself ranks high on the list of the journal's regulars. Yet the journalist Chanchal Sarkar pronounces him an 'extinct giant', 'a mastodon'. The writer Nirad Chaudhuri recalls his own youth, when the *Modern Review* and *Prabasi* (its Bengali counterpart, which Ramananda also edited, from 1901 until his death) constituted 'a fair portion of my literary fare', even as he relegates Ramananda's thoughts and achievements to 'history': 'time-barred for an epoch which is completely different from that in which he lived.' And, in fact, the *Modern Review* has faded from Indian political and historical consciousness.

Yet many of the issues, attitudes, and controversies explored in that journal may have more immediate claims of pertinence now than in 1973. In his commitment to promoting India's potential as a modern, self-governing nation of cultural and economic as well as political strength, Ramananda sustained in his own voice and sponsored in the voices of his contributors fundamental and continuing questions about India's past, present, and future: What constitutes the authentic Indian past? What foreign influences in the present should India welcome or shun? What directions for the future would allow India to become 'modern' without betraying its own identity? Because Ramananda kept his own mind open to shifting events, threats, and opportunities over such a long and tumultuous period, the *Modern Review* can still be appreciated as a reminder of India's intellectual ferment in the decades before Independence as well as a testimonial to Ramananda's own accomplishment.

Ramananda's individual stamp was manifest not only in the journal's ambitious agenda and high quality of editorial production (handled largely by himself), but also in the skilful boldness of Ramananda's arrangement of divergent opinions in each issue and in his extensive Notes on political, historical, artistic, and educational topics—usually running to more than twenty pages at the back. These Notes, more than any of his essays or editorials, show the hallmarks of Ramananda's elusive literary identity: bold but self-effacing, plain speaking but sly, often ironic in a deadpan way calculated to keep at bay the ever-present threat of prosecution.

Born in Bankura to a pious family of pandits, Ramananda was only ten when he came under the reformist influence of the Brahmo

Samaj through a local high school teacher. At eighteen he proceeded to Presidency College in Calcutta, where student political ferment vied with academic obligations for his attention. By 1887 he had already attended the second session of the Indian National Congress in Calcutta, but a serious illness interfered with the successful completion of his degree. Upon transferring from Presidency to the City College, he received First Class Honours in English, went on to an MA (also in English) and began teaching at the City College, while also writing book reviews and topical essays for the Bengali monthly *Dharmabandhu* and the English weekly *Indian Messenger* (organ of the Sadharan Brahmo Samaj).

This arduous combination of teaching, journalism, Brahmo reformism, and political activism continued to be Ramananda's programme for the following fifteen years. In the 1890s he also threw himself into a broad self-education in economics, political science, and history; he extended his political activism as a delegate to Congress meetings and undertook social welfare work, including the design of a Braille system in Bengali. By the age of thirty (1895), he had become prominent enough as educator and public reformer to be offered the principalship of a college, the Kayastha Pathshala, in Allahabad, a position he held while simultaneously expanding his former activities. When he eventually resigned his principalship in 1907, the desire for more time devoted to journalism coincided with his determined protest against the defeat of his proposed educational reforms for Kayastha Pathshala. In 1907 he conceived and launched a new English monthly, *Modern Review*, as 'proprietor-cum-editor-manager', without salary and with mounting debt.

Ramananda's journalistic freedom was almost immediately challenged when in his first year as editor his quietly defiant rejoinder to British stated opinion—that Indian nationalism was breaking down—caught the attention of British authorities in the United Provinces. 'Never in the history of the world has there been committed any aggression that did not end in raising up a greater force of resistance to overwhelm it', he had written. The sentence shows that by 1907 he had already mastered his characteristic style of pithy assertion, backed by confident historical generalization. Surely it was the authority of this style as well as its content that led to the order that he must either close down *Modern Review* or leave Allahabad. Thus his move in 1908 back to Calcutta, where his connection to the Brahmo movement remained close; the location of his dwelling and editorial offices for his first decade in Calcutta bordered the Sadharan Brahmo Samaj prayer hall, whose small printing press he was able to use.

The Brahmo movement further pervaded *Prabasi* and *Modern Review* through Ramananda's intimate involvement with Rabindranath Tagore. During the early struggles of Santiniketan, Tagore consulted Ramananda on everything—from the finances of the school to the textbooks and the school's publicity; during his travels abroad Tagore entrusted him with direct administrative responsibilities for Santiniketan. Many of Tagore's essays, poems, and stories first appeared in *MR*. At the same time, Ramananda retained the independence to include in the journal a variety of subjects and points of view conspicuously at odds with Tagore's increasing aversion to what he saw as the destructive force of Western materialism. Articles featuring industrial progress in India provide dissenting perspectives in the same issues of the journal that also feature Tagore's critiques of these same developments. Although rooted in Bengali culture, *MR* energetically sought to reach and, indeed create, a 'national' readership with diverse interests. The journal not only tolerated but welcomed divergent perspectives as a feature of its cultural modernity.

Ramananda's skilful steering of *MR* through the shoals of British press censorship and anti-sedition laws must count as an equally important accomplishment. One early incident he liked to recall occurred when he and the journal were brought to trial for 'disloyal agitation' during the Punjab Treasonable Conspiracy case in 1909. As Jadunath Sarkar recounts the incident, Ramananda took the occasion to display in the courtroom the frontispiece colour-block prints of the new Calcutta school of Indian art, one of the most striking technical innovations of *MR* (credited to the efforts of U.K. Ray). So charmed and distracted was the prosecuting counsel by these art prints that, instead of pursuing his case against the journal, he recommended that Ramananda publish the prints in an album (which the latter did). The story pleasantly illustrates an alternative mode of Gandhian non-violent demonstration, with Ramananda's appeal based on intellectual and aesthetic as well as moral persuasion.

After 1919, Ramananda's Notes increasingly paid homage to Gandhi as the necessary leader of the Indian national movement, even while arguments and Notes against certain of Gandhi's positions continued to appear, especially in relation to Ramananda's insistence on education as a higher priority than the non-cooperation that Gandhi was advocating among students. The tension between political activism and educational and intellectual development remained a dynamic feature of Ramananda's response to Gandhism throughout the 1920s.

A conspicuous hardening of radicalism nevertheless accompanied Ramananda's greater prominence as a public figure in the later 1920s. His selection for the Indian delegation to the seventh Annual Assembly of the League of Nations in Geneva initiated his first extended European travel, a journey that ended in the intense disillusionment conveyed through his sequence of 'Letters from the Editor' in *MR* during and after the trip in 1926. In Geneva he concluded that the League of Nations was fundamentally committed to preserving the pre-war imperial status quo of the European Allied victors, without any intention of ruffling British feathers in relation to India. He perceived a demeaning subordination of the so-called 'Indian' delegation to its British rulers at the League. Yet he does not advocate India's withdrawal from the League; however disillusioning, he insisted, it was important for Indians 'to gain experience of world affairs'. Yet a sharper cynicism becomes noticeable in subsequent years: for example, in the larger space he gives in the Notes to Gandhi's increasingly militant speeches, in his mounting impatience with Muslim demands, and in his more aggressive solidarity with anti-colonial struggles in China and elsewhere.

Greater toughness also marks Ramananda's open clash with the authorities under the revived and extended anti-sedition Press Ordinance of 1930. Among the books that Ramananda published under the imprint of *MR* was J.T. Sunderland's *India in Bondage*, the individual chapters of which had initially appeared serially in *MR*. When this strongly polemical book went into a second edition, the government suppressed it, seized remaining copies from Ramananda's house, and arrested and fined him. A certain inefficiency (or ambivalence) in the government's zeal for suppression, however, marks the entire event, since Ramananda was able to publish in subsequent issues of *MR* taunting critiques of the Press Ordinance, as well as further polemical articles by Sunderland, including a notice that his suppressed book had now been reissued by an American publisher.

Although stories, photographs, historical essays, and the customary variety of reviews and short notices continued in *MR* through the 1930s, the harder political edge of the journal's final decade made its offering less original and distinctive than before. The tone darkens, especially after the death in 1935 of Ramananda's wife, who had long worked as his helpmate. There remained, however, a familial cast to this ambitious undertaking: his son-in-law, Kalidas Nag, had become an important contributor to *MR* from France (where he had initiated Ramananda's friendship with Romain Rolland); his son, Asoke, already an editor of another journal in his own right, became a more prominent contributor, eventually taking over the editorship of *MR* upon Ramananda's death in 1943. The quality of family intimacy had characterized the core group of contributors throughout: it was an international family, including not only Tagore, Jadunath Sarkar, and Ananda K. Coomaraswamy, but also the Indianized Britishers, Sister Nivedita (Margaret Noble), the Rev. C.F. Andrews, and the American J.T. Sunderland.

The question of what version of the Indian past should guide the development of a modern Indian national consciousness became the preoccupation of this intimate group in the decade before and just after World War I, the years which provide choice examples of the journal's vitality. Was modern India to trace its lineage back through Hinduism to its ancient origins? What place then for the centuries of Mughal rule? And, of course, there was the ongoing question of how to respond to the ongoing influence of the West. The rejection of foreign imports under the slogan of swadeshi was strong in Bengal after the tumultuous British partition of the territory in 1905. The visual arts offered *MR* one of the principal fields for the discussion of cultural swadeshi in the early years for several reasons: nationalist pride in the technical prowess of *MR*'s high quality colour reproductions came together with proximity to Calcutta's School of Art, where under the tutelage of Coomaraswamy a generation of artists was being taught the 'essentials' of Indian art.

The promotion of 'art-culture' as a crucial component of 'national regeneration' depended on a conception of 'the true spirit of orientalism in art', set against European derivatives. Connections between the Calcutta school and the pre-Raphaelites and William Morris' Arts and Crafts revival were made explicit in *MR* by the school's principal at this time, E.B. Havell, and by the writings of Coomaraswamy and Sister Nivedita. The new orientalism was vulnerable to the charge that it corresponded to changes in British taste rather than enacting independence of foreign influence altogether. One chauvinistic response was to insist on the unbroken continuity of the orientalist spirit in India from ancient past to present. Thus Arun Sen, in April 1913, separates the 'new Indian art' from the Pre-Raphaelites on the ground that Indian art is not a 'revival' of something lost but the expression of a living indigenous spirit in India continuous since ancient times. Coomaraswamy earlier led the way in his famous essay, 'On Mughal and Rajput Painting', first published in *MR*, January 1911, identifying a Hindu tradition 'almost entirely free from foreign influence'. In the same year, a review of Coomaraswamy's *The Aims of Indian Art*, signed 'N.' (probably for Sister Nivedita) repeats Coomaraswamy's differentiation between the idealism of Hindu art and both Mughal and European realism. Although Coomaraswamy acknowledged that by the end of the seventeenth century Indian art had become a mixture of Hindu and Mughal features, he reserved his highest praise for the style of what survived from pre-Mughal periods: in the Ajanta wall paintings, in Rajputana, and in the paintings from the remote Himalayan Kangra Valley. These, he argued 'speak a language which is the mother tongue of all those who adore the Bhagavata.' Coomaraswamy and his followers extrapolated freely from the qualities of Hindu painting to the essential features of Indian culture more generally.

Although Ramananda published celebrations of an essential Hindu culture, he was also opening *MR* to opposing arguments. *MR* never aligned itself wholly with what the art historian Tapati Guha-Thakurta calls the 'aesthetic propaganda' of the Calcutta art culture. Juxtaposed against Coomaraswamy and Sister Nivedita were the Mughal histories of Jadunath Sarkar, who presented in *MR* a contrary narrative of Indian history that emphasized a syncretic view of its culture, including its art.

Sarkar countered the art school advocates with voluminous evidence of India's deeply and irrevocably mixed artistic heritage. His long essay of October 1919, 'Art in Muslim India', insists on cross-currents of influence starting early in the Mughal period.

Ramananda in many ways stood more firmly allied with Sarkar in looking forward to a united India emerging from the intermingling of Hindu and Mughal elements. His Notes consistently blame Anglo-Indian troublemaking for the divisions between Hindu and Muslim, and the tracing of identities to the medieval past: 'The sooner the people of India leave medievalism behind and bring themselves in a line with the rest of humanity the better', he asserts in his Notes for February 1913. The admonition is for Hindus and Muslims alike and later informed his impatience with Muslim separatist demands.

Ramananda tried to steer readers toward a nationalism in line with the rest of humanity through his attention to the British and European past, the area of history that he took on as his own responsibility in *MR.* The long extracts from diverse, often obscure historical documents that he became famous for using as the basis of his Notes, together with assorted prints and photographs, may at first glance seem a hodgepodge. Closer attention shows a quite consistent argument in this mixture of materials. Episodes from Roman, Dutch, Islamic and other histories exemplify his universalist maxim about the ultimate triumph of resistance to aggression that got him into trouble with the Allahabad authorities in 1907: 'Never in the history of the world has there been committed any aggression that did not end in raising up a greater force of resistance to overwhelm it.'

Historical extracts became for Ramananda an effective strategy to ward off further charges of 'disloyal agitation' throughout the 1910s and 1920s; the authors who voice his subversive ideas belong to an international community of scholars with little direct engagement in current politics. The Notes for June 1919, the period of violence and severe repression after Jallianwala Bagh, feature long extracts from John Motley's mid-nineteenth-century book, *The Rise of the Dutch Republic*, focusing on the eventual defeat by a resistant population of the tyrannical Duke of Alba in the sixteenth century. Ramananda did not need to risk sedition in his own voice in order to connect the line of humanity from the Dutch to the Indian situation. Although

General Dyer was hardly comparable in power to the Duke of Alba, it is the logic of tyranny that mattered for the connection.

In relation to British history, Ramananda drew on the stash of documents that he had acquired at the beginning of his editorship through association with one Major Vaman Das Basu, I.M.S. (retired), who had bought at scrap rate a huge collection of English publications (dating back to before the 1857 Rebellion). After arduous sorting, the collection provided a precious armoury against late imperial censorship; a plenitude of English voices from the past could be summoned to indict British rule without the editor risking a sentence of his own. Although Ramananda continued to expand this initial stock with contemporary books, newspapers, and official reports, the historical materials offered the best evidence of broken promises, abandoned ideals, and dire predictions of imperial failure announced by British voices themselves.

A fine sense of irony comes through Ramananda's skilful rummages through historical documents, but his reliance on textual extracts also reflects modesty about his own role as writer and editor. He willingly relegated the role of Author in *MR* to others: writers from the past whom he quotes, and among his contemporaries, most admiringly Tagore. Significant differences from Tagore emerge too, mainly through *MR*'s acceptance of modernity's advance. Tagore's reluctance in this area is dramatically audible, even as early as his two-part meditative essay of May and June,1911, 'The Impact of Europe on India'. In Part I, Tagore dramatizes through a dense succession of metaphors the aggressive intrusion of modernity forced by the West upon India, which is personified in turn as an old age pensioner, an ancient walled city, and a boat without sails forced into 'the swift current of Time'. Tagore invents an Indian persona who is resistant but passive in the face of the bullying foreign intruder, somewhat humorously personified as a pitiless taskmaster: 'So . . . Europe suddenly arrived, we know not whence, vigorously nudged our worn ribs once or twice and shouted, "Get up! We want to set up an office in this your bedroom. Don't imagine that the world was sleeping because you were sleeping . . . There goes the bell! It is the world's noonday, it is work time."' Part I ends rather weakly: the voice of Indian old age first defensively calls up memories of past vigour, then shifts to a lyrical embrace of coming darkness, 'such as comes . . . when the hot day, clothing itself in the fulness of its beauty, dips in the darkness of sunset.' The Western call to awakening is finally dismissed as immature and reckless, possibly heading toward an apocalyptic end, 'as when a machine is suddenly thrown out of work, a boiler bursts after accumulating excessive steam and heat.' But Part II of the essay revives the dilemma by reconfiguring the 'fatigue' of India as a self-induced trance that cannot forever suspend natural law. By the end of Part II, the call of progress seems inseparable from survival itself. Yet Tagore reaches acceptance only by limiting its meaning to reforms within Brahmanism—really only a restatement of the nineteenth-century Brahmo reform ethos. The more intrusive energies of modernity evoked in Part I simply disappear from consideration.

Tagore's dramatic and metaphoric style enlivens his presentation of ambivalence, even though his line of argument in these essays lacks Ramananda's rational clarity. By the early 1920s, Tagore's self-identification as Poet alienated him even further from a modern materialism that he linked to aggressive tendencies within nationalism itself. Tagore's 'Letters from the Atlantic' in *MR*, like the lectures he delivered in America at this time, identify the alien spirit of the age with America, where he seems driven to costume himself ever more elaborately in Eastern spirituality. As Poet, he pictures himself turning in spirit to 'the poet's East', now not a place of weary old age but of eternal childhood: 'It is the East of the magnanimous sky and exuberant sun-light, where once upon a time a boy found himself straying in the dim twilight of child-consciousness peopled with dreams.'

For alternative responses to the wake-up call of modernity in areas such as education, the economy, and the management of everyday life, Ramananda turned from Tagore to other Indian voices, many of which also came through letters from America. A steady stream of reports came from Sudhindra Bose, a Bengali who had succeeded in obtaining a PhD and a faculty position in political science at the State University of Iowa—the first Hindu to obtain such a post in an American university. Bose describes in detail a number of American civic institutions that Indians might well emulate to promote social democracy: the circulating public library, the system of the kindergarten, the American farm, and especially the land-grant university, with its combination of liberal arts and practical studies in agriculture, engineering, and forestry. In 'Why Must We Emigrate to the United States of America?' another young Indian, Sarangadhar Das, testifies to the strengthening that comes from the experience of America, with support cited from letters by several other Indian students. This small band of pioneers—Sarangadhar counts sixty matriculating Indian students on the Pacific coast between 1904 and 1911—travelled abroad mainly to pursue degrees in a variety of technical and practical subjects, but it is the extracurricular education in self-reliance that their reports mainly celebrate—a consequence in part of their need to earn their own way in the absence of institutional or familial support for American study. In their criticisms, as in their admiration, Indian students in America continue to refer their observations back to India's situation and the practical need for reform, comparing, for example, the plight of America's 'Negroes' to that of 'Untouchables at home'. The reforms envisioned by radicalized Indian students went far beyond the limited Brahmo agenda repeated by Tagore in these years.

The value of material progress entered *MR* in a lighter spirit through the regular photo-feature called 'Gleanings', several pages in each issue of futuristic announcements of ingenious gadgets and inventions for the practical improvement of private and public life, 'gleaned' mainly from the foreign press: from Chicago, a fire extinguisher which automatically releases a wall of water on the outside of public buildings; from Germany, a suspended railroad run by airplane engines and propellers; from Michigan, a moving platform that goes by itself in an Eat-as-you-go cafeteria. 'Gleanings' also featured more personal contraptions: a new form of artificial leg; a flashlight razor that permits shaving in the dark; an unsinkable bathing suit. An element of the fabulous and the freakish makes for the humour of these inventions, but also speaks for the modern idea of solving rather than submitting fatalistically to the practical problems of everyday life.

Ramananda's interest in modern technology was not limited to gimmicks. One of the most impressive articles in the prewar period of *MR* is a long photo-essay in March 1913, 'The Tata Iron and Steel Works at Sakchee' by Kshirod Kumar Ray. Based on an extensive tour of the steel works, the essay describes the environment, working conditions, and technical operations of smelting, giving the same attention to industrial detail as Coomaraswamy and others were giving in this same year to the Ajanta caves. The parallel deepens from the aesthetic quality that Ray's language gives to the industrial scene, especially as seen at night, when 'the series of electric lights of various colours . . . beautifully illuminate the nocturnal depths of the tangled woods.' Seven remarkable photographs illustrate the essay to create a kind of industrial sublime that had not yet become a fashion even in Western photography. Passages of strangely lyrical prose correspond to the photographs, making the mysterious beauty and vitality of the steel works auditory as well as visual.

Ramananda's repeated juxtaposition of sharply different subjects and viewpoints do not finally signify either contradiction or ambivalence. For him, opposing possibilities do not create pressure for exclusive choices, nor does he strain to synthesize disparate alternatives. The distinctiveness of vision he brought to *MR* was tolerance for variety; he allows multiple versions of the good in the journal's representation of what an invigorated modern India can include. Modern Indian nationalism thus emerges in *MR* as pluralistic and cosmopolitan. The swadeshi that Ramananda sponsors throughout his career—whether in art, politics, or industrial productivity—is cosmopolitan in that it thrives on openness to the worldwide commerce of ideas as well as goods, with Indians venturing out to acquire whatever can be added to the strengths of the emerging modern nation. Ramananda most fully states this credo in one of his longest and most eloquent Notes—in this same year of 1913. Under the heading 'Great Britain's "Mission in India"', the Note opens by posing alternative views: 'One is that the British people are here merely as exploiters, to suck India dry as a spider does a fly. The other is that Britain's work here is to help India in rising in the scale of humanity to the level occupied by the most progressive among nations.' With characteristic tongue in cheek, the Note rejects the exploitative view as too simply 'sordid'. He therefore proposes to argue only in relation to the 'noble' view of empire professed so eloquently by the British themselves from Edmund Burke onward. Whether the British have forgotten or knowingly abandoned the high view of their mission does not matter. The plain reality is that for Indians, playing 'the underdog to the British race for ever, is not a glorious destiny.' Nor, he adds, is the role of cow. Ramananda's tropes here are deliberately lowly, practical, with ironic indifference to the controversial stereotypes of the Hindu sacred cow: 'If a man has to manage a cattle-farm, he has simply to see that the cattle are properly fed and housed and are not cruelly beaten or overworked . . . It may be a foolish fancy but we believe that we are not cattle in the disguise of human beings, but really belong to the human species.' Quickly leaving behind this acerbic tone, the Note then reaches for its own noble humanist vision: first by rejecting all essentialist epithets, such as 'British methods', 'Hindu spirituality', 'Western materialism', 'faithful Islam'. To belong fully to the 'human species' involves accomplishment in every area of human endeavour, he asserts, and towards that goal India must rely on its own resolve, with the British contribution being mainly to cease from blockage.

Ramananda's utterance can upon occasion be lofty, but he is mostly remembered for his avoidance of high rhetoric; many former colleagues recall him explaining that he wanted to write for 'the common man, not the literary person', and so sought 'to convey his ideas in as unornamental a garb as possible, in the plainest Anglo-Saxon words.' Nirad Chaudhuri, known for his own considerable pleasure in ornamental language, somewhat dismissively remarks that Ramananda's style was not 'hotstuff' by Bengali standards. Chanchal Sarkar makes a more respectful version of the same point: 'In English at the time, and even more in Bengali . . . people wrote a heavy, twiddly language . . . Ramananda Babu trained himself to write a simple, terse, muscular English and Bengali.' When Ramananda reaches for 'noble' English words, he does so in the context of accusing the English of having betrayed their own lofty rhetoric, even as they passed it down to Indian writers. For the most part, Ramananda avoided rhetorical flourishes. It was by his lifelong work as an editor rather than by any particular piece of writing that he infused high English phrases such as 'strenuous endeavour and sacrifice' with a new and specifically Indian meaning.

27

History and Literature

Sir Jadunath Sarkar and Oliver Goldsmith

Dipesh Chakrabarty

At the centre of this brief essay is Sir Jadunath Sarkar, who lived between 1870 and 1958. Usually regarded as the doyen of modern history in India, he is also seen as someone superseded by later research. Most of his working life he remained a professor of literature at undergraduate institutions such as Ripon College, Calcutta, Patna College in Bihar, and Ravenshaw College in Cuttack, Orissa. He taught history only in the last few years of his career at the Banaras Hindu University. He retired in 1926 when he was appointed vice chancellor of the University of Calcutta for two years.

Sarkar became a self-taught historian with a strong interest in the last phase of the the Mughal empire. He wrote a five-volume history of Aurangzeb, published between 1912 and 1924. Between 1932 and 1950 he published four volumes of *Fall of the Mughal Empire.* He wrote numerous other books and essays besides these. Sarkar would remain an independent scholar from 1929 on, productive and prolific until the very end of his life. He was knighted in 1929 and is, until now, the only Indian historian to have ever been elected—as he was in 1952—an Honorary Fellow of the American Historical Association.

History shaped by a powerful literary sensibility is what Sir Jadunath Sarkar aspired to write. But which literature and whose literary sensibility? Sarkar's prose is sprinkled with quotations from literary sources—Burns, Tennyson, Shakespeare, Coleridge, and others—who remain mostly unnamed. Himself a professor of English literature, he perhaps expected his reader to be familiar with the literary canon of the Empire, for his relationship to this canon was deep; he was steeped in the imperial lore of the British and their canonical literature, which so many Indian intellectuals fell in love with.

Most telling in this respect—that is, with regard to the question of how the imperial literary canon influenced Sarkar's imagination—are his comments on Rajputana in the eighteenth century when, as he wrote in the first volume of *Fall*, 'the Emperor in Delhi became a lifeless shadow confined within the harem' and all 'unifying bond and common controlling authority was dissolved.' In the absence of a 'superior power to enforce lawful rights', 'Rajputana became a zoological garden with the barriers of the cages thrown down and the keepers removed.' 'The fiercest animal passions raged throughout the land, redeemed only now and then by individual instances of devotion and chivalry which had not yet totally disappeared from human bosom.' 'The wounds' of these 'long suffering' people, the Rajputs, were not healed until 'British peace' was established and 'British suzerainty' accepted, creating conditions, as Sarkar would argue, for the creation an Indian nation. Until then, 'the martial manhood of Rajputana ha[d] sunk into the placid sleep of opium', wrote Sarkar, and went on to quote a couple of unattributed lines from Oliver Goldsmith's long poem, *The Traveller, or A Prospect of Society* (1764), to describe the condition of Rajputs in the eighteenth century:

> Unknown to them, when sensual pleasures cloy,
> To fill the languid pause with finer joy.

This little nugget of English poetry, left anonymous in Sarkar's narrative and serving as a small monument to his colonial education and as a reminder that he was, after all, a teacher of literature, is also a clue to the larger political imagination that influenced Sarkar. While steeped in Persian sources and even sharing in their moods on occasion, Sarkar's sense of drama about eighteenth-century Indian history owed little, it seems, to the narrative spirit of historians or writers of the Mughal period. His reflexes were trained more by the literature of Victorian and imperial Britain than, say, by the Persian literature on Mughal decline. That the 'tragic drama', for instance, of 'murder, suicide and the untimely death of the young' that unfolded in Maratha history after the death of Peshwa Balaji Rao in 1761 should remind him of 'Theban horrors' was symptomatic of the Victorian nature of his literary disposition. Or think of his response to the 'Maratha debacle' at Panipat, which 'was a nation-wide disaster . . . there was not a home in Maharashtra that had not to mourn the loss of a member, and several houses their very heads.' 'It was, in short,' he suddenly said, 'like Flodden Field' – an appeal to the memory of the Scottish–English battle of 1513. But this memory, again, was strongly mediated through imperial literature; immortalized by Sir Walter Scott's ballad on Flodden Field, *Marmion.*

The use of Goldsmith in describing Rajputs also reveals a very nineteenth-century and imperial reading of this eighteenth-century poet. Oliver Goldsmith (of Irish origins) was a hardy perennial of the canon of English literature in the colony. His works were included in the syllabi of Indian universities for a very long time and read continuously from at least the 1880s to the mid-1960s when I was in high school and probably even later. Arthur Barrett, Professor of English Literature at the Elphinstone College in Bombay, published an edition of 'The Traveller' and 'The Deserted Village' as a single book, with an Introduction and Notes, in 1888. The book was reprinted in 1891, 1899, 1904, 1906, 1920, 1926, and 1931 (the last edition I could consult) without a single word replaced. Every year, from at least the 1890s on (when Sarkar went to college), university examinations in Calcutta would contain questions about Goldsmith's writings, with particular reference to the two poems, 'The Traveller' and 'The Deserted Village'. The questions and the expected answers did not change very much either, as one can tell from reading the editor's notes to an Indian edition of both that was put together in Calcutta in the early part of the twentieth century to help university students prepare for their examinations.

Goldsmith's lines quoted by Sarkar in his description of the fallen, opium-induced slumberous state of the once-valorous Rajputs were actually meant to describe the Swiss, the 'bleak Swiss' who, from the fifteenth century onward, had often supplied mercenaries to the fighting armies of Europe—in France, Italy, and elsewhere. And Goldsmith's words, as we shall soon see, did not necessarily represent a wholesale condemnation of the Swiss. The lines cited by Sarkar belonged to a section where Goldsmith discussed the virtues and vices of the rugged Swiss. And his words, while mindful of the miseries of the lives of the Swiss, also spoke of their simple but passionate patriotism:

No product here the barren hills afford
But man and steel, the soldier and his sword;
No vernal blooms their torpid rocks array,
But winter lingering chills the lap of May:
No zephyr fondly sues the mountain's breast,
But meteors glare, and stormy glooms invest.
. . .
And e'en those hills that round his mansion rise
Enhance the bliss his scanty fund supplies.
Dear is that shed to which his soul conforms,
And dear that hill which lifts him to the storms;
And as a child, when scaring sounds molest,
Clings close and closer to the mother's breast,
So the loud torrent and the whirlwind's roar
But bind him to his native mountains more.
Such are the charms to barren states assign'd;
Their wants but few, their wishes all confin'd.

So what made it possible for Sarkar to use Goldsmith's half-admiring description of the Swiss to portray the Rajput as simply subject to 'animal passion'? There is hidden in this apparent misreading of Goldsmith a history of how *The Traveller* was received and read in the nineteenth-century as the British Empire consolidated itself as a world phenomenon. Sarkar's use of the poem was, I want to argue, an instance of a complex imperial-nationalist reading of *The Traveller.* Let me briefly explain this point, however, for that will help to unravel some of the complicated strands of Sarkar's own nationalism.

At the centre of Goldsmith's poem, composed in the 1760s, was a very eighteenth-century political question: If different climes and histories produced different forms of government with the British being, of course, at the top as 'lords of the humankind', did this result in different nations enjoying different degrees of happiness? Goldsmith's answer was unambiguous: 'I have endeavoured to show,' he said in dedicating the poem to his brother, the Rev. Henry Goldsmith, 'that there may be equal happiness in states that are differently governed from our own; that every state has a particular principle of happiness, and that this principle in each may be carried to a mischievous excess.' The poem, discussing the Dutch, the Swiss, the Italians, the French, and the British, was intended to 'illustrate' 'these positions'. Each of these peoples had their own principle of happiness that, paradoxically, was often the cause of the peculiar miseries that each suffered. Thus the 'independence' that the Britons 'prize[d] so high' could also keep 'man from man' and break 'the social tie'. As several commentators have pointed out, Goldsmith was also very mid-eighteenth-century in 'abhorring mountains' when it came to describing the Swiss. As William J. Rolphe observed in his commentary of 1894, Goldsmith's description of Switzerland displayed 'no appreciation of the wild beauty and the grandeur of the scenery which attracts the throngs of tourists in our day.' Rolphe also pointed out that this was remarked on by Macaulay in his *History of England* (Ch.13): 'He [Goldsmith] was disgusted by the hideous wilderness, and declared that he greatly preferred the charming country round Leyden, the vast expanse of verdant meadow, and the villas with their statues and grottoes, trim flower beds and rectilinear avenues.' Such 'indifference to, indeed shrinking from, wild nature . . . [was] characteristic of Goldsmith's time,' observed Frederick Tupper, Jr., in his commentary on *The Traveller* and *The Deserted Village.* 'As Ruskin points out, even Shakespeare abhorred mountains; and to Thomas Gray is usually assigned the distinction of being the first Englishman to appreciate their beauties.' Rolphe's notes on Goldsmith further clarify, referring again to Ruskin's *Modern Painters,* that this attitude was part of the Homeric tradition, where to possess natural beauty was to be composed of 'a fountain, a meadow, a shady grove.' It marked the 'mediaeval mind' and showed up in

Dante's *Divina Commedia.* In a recent and insightful reading of this poem in *ELH* (Fall 2010), Ingrid Horrocks has suggested that the poem both uses and departs from the tradition of 'prospect poems' in developing 'the figure of the wanderer or the traveler'—'Rather than standing and surveying from on high [as was customary in prospect poems], this new observer is imagined as moving through the world, assembling a view of society from multiple fragmentary sights and interactions.' It represents the 'viewpoint of a wanderer who moves through the landscape as the only basis on which sympathy, and so a new community, can be developed.' Horrocks goes on to show how this move could be critical and subversive of imperial ideals.

Goldsmith's lines that Sarkar quoted thus belonged to a very particular eighteenth-century combination of aesthetics and politics that had allowed the poet not to condemn the Swiss in any out-of-hand fashion for their rugged climes and temperament but to use them only as examples of his considered position that, as Macaulay put it in his biography of Goldsmith: 'Our happiness depends little on political institutions, and much depends on the temper and regulation of our own minds.' What, then, allowed Sarkar to misread Goldsmith, as it were, and to use him to convey his own sense of the unmitigated 'tragedy' that he saw as unfolding in eighteenth-century India?

Even a thumbnail sketch of the history of the reception of Goldsmith shows that his position did not go unchallenged in the eighteenth century; but as the British Empire developed a strong faith in its civilizing mission, readers of *The Traveller*—not so much of his other works such as *The Deserted Village*—began to find fault with Goldsmith's politics and increasingly separated his aesthetic from his politics until such separation became routine in the early part of the twentieth century. Eighteenth-century critics sometimes quibbled with Goldsmith's political positions, finding them logically confused. A review published in January 1765 argued: 'it is certain that every individual has a peculiar principle of happiness; but does it therefore follow, that a state composed of these individuals should have the same? Rather the contrary . . .' Dr John Aikin (1747–1822), a naturalist and chemist of 'considerable distinction', found Goldsmith's 'political opinions' marred by 'confused notions and a heated imagination.' Writing in 1796, he said: 'Though it is probable that few of Goldsmith's readers will be convinced . . . that happiness of mankind is every where equal,' there was more philosophical force to the argument that 'man's chief bliss is ever seated in his mind . . . and that a small part of real felicity consists in what human government can bestow or withhold.' An 1803 German edition of *The Vicar of Wakefield, The Traveller,* and *The Deserted Village,* in English with German footnotes, reproduced Robert Anderson's (Goldsmith's physician) memoirs of the poet containing some disagreements with Goldsmith's political opinions as expressed in *The Traveller.* Readers will see that the disagreements did not have much to do with the civilizing mission of the Empire:

> The description of the people of Italy are not less just than that of their country is picturesque and harmonious; but the moralist may object to the conclusion as unfavourable to the interests of virtue . . . The characteristics of the different nations are just and ingenuous but the descriptions are neither full nor perfect. He has contented himself with exhibiting them in those points of view in which they are generally beheld; but the lights are much strengthened by the powers of poetic genius.

Leigh Hunt (1784–1859), the critic and poet, writing in critical appreciation of *The Traveller* in 1846, faulted Goldsmith's logic: 'The fact is that GOLDSMITH thought he was reasoning finely, when he was writing fine poetry only. It is the fault of the poetical argument that the reasoner is apt to forget his logic in his fancy . . . If *The Traveller* had been written in prose . . . it would allure no readers at all.'

Such formal or logical criticism of *The Traveller* gave way to a mode of criticism that was decidedly political in substance as the nineteenth century progressed and liberalism came to supply—for all its contradictions—the ruling doctrines of the British Empire. An 1879 edition by J.W. Hales of *The Traveller* and *The Deserted Village* published from London had this to say by way of editorial comment:

> [I]t is assuredly not true that there is no relation whatever between the government of a country and the happiness of its inhabitants. A government can, as it pleases, or according to its enlightenment, make

> circumstances favourable or unfavourable to individual development and happiness. So *a priori* one would assume; so *a posteriori* one sees that it is. The political indifferentism set forth in *The Traveller* is in fact merely paradoxical. Fortunately, one's enjoyment of the poem does not depend upon the accuracy of the creed it professes.

This challenge to Goldsmith's or Samuel Johnson's (Goldsmith's mentor and promoter) cosmopolitanism fell on sympathetic years in the age of John Stuart Mill, and *The Traveller* found its place in literary canon in the colony only on the condition that students were taught to separate Goldsmith's aesthetics from his politics so that the poem could be enjoyed for its literary qualities alone. A 'model' examination question in N. Mookerji's notes meant to help students at the University of Calcutta read *The Traveller*, quoted two lines from the poem—'How small, of that human hearts endure/ That part which laws or kings can cause or cure'—and asked: 'Whose dictum is this and what is its precise meaning? How far is it right? Does the poem depend for its success on the correctness of this theory?' And this is how the model answer read in part (notice its similarity to the 1879 argument cited above):

> These are among the lines contributed by Dr Johnson to the poem . . . This theory is of course wrong. Forms of government cannot but influence the happiness of society . . . [Dr Johnson] was forgetting that the opportunities for individual freedom and development are in too great a degree under the control of government to make such a generalization valid . . . Happily the poetry of the *Tr.* [sic] does not depend for its success on the correctness of the political theory.

Sarkar's Goldsmith was thus a poet whose eighteenth-century 'political indifferentism'—the thesis that happiness was indifferent to forms of government—had been filtered out by readings that came after the rise of liberalism and the simultaneous consolidation of the British Empire whereby the question of human happiness was connected to particular political choices: an oppressive government could not be conducive to happiness. It was the rise of this milieu that enabled Sarkar to read Goldsmith's description of the Swiss as a negative judgement on their character and apply it to the Rajputs.

Nineteenth-century European history and literature, refracted through the ideological realities of the British Empire in India, constituted a general background for the political ideas and assumptions through which Sarkar read the eighteenth century in India.

28

Ananda K. Coomaraswamy

Michael W. Meister

Ananda Kentish Coomaraswamy (1877–1947) was born in Colombo of an English mother, Elizabeth Beeby, who came from a Kent family experienced in India trade, and a Ceylonese father, Sir Mutu Coomarasawamy, a distinguished jurist, married two years before by the Archbishop of Canterbury. Subsequent to Elizabeth's return to England in 1879 and Sir Mutu's untimely death before he could run for Parliament, Ananda lived in England with his mother from the age of two to twenty-two. He was educated at home, then at Wycliffe College, a public school, and at University College, London, from which he received a First in Geology and Botany in 1900 and a D.Sc. in 1906. He returned to Ceylon in 1902 with his first wife—a photographer and weaver, Ethel Mairet (the name she took as author)—to establish the Mineralogical Survey of Ceylon, of which he became the first director. When both returned to England in 1907, with a significant collection of Ceylonese artifacts, Coomaraswamy purchased a house known as Norman Chapel in Broad Campden, to which the presses of Essex House Press, the successor to William Morris's Kelmscott Press, were soon shifted. On these Coomaraswamy had his first major literary and scientific study—*Mediaeval Sinhalese Art, Being a Monograph on Mediaeval Sinhalese Arts and Crafts, Mainly as Surviving from the Eighteenth Century, with an Account of the Structure of Society and the Status of*

the Craftsman—illustrated with his wife's photographs, hand-printed over a fourteen-month period.

In his introduction to *Mediaeval Sinhalese Art* (1908) Coomaraswamy wrote, in cadences and concepts largely learned from Morris and Ruskin:

> If we would understand the significance and the history of the arts and crafts in India, it will be needful to begin with such survivals of them as we can study readily, and work back from these to earlier times. Hence, even from a wider point of view, I make no apology for writing a large book about a time when the traditions of fine art were stereotyped, and even the traditions of the crafts intensely formalized and rigid. Such an art is, as it were, an outlier, left by long continued denudation, in extent severely limited, yet evidence unmistakable of a former continuity which it helps us to understand.

Coomaraswamy's statement of his intentions as author of this work is informative:

> This book is not primarily intended as a work of scholarship, but is written first of all for the Ceylonese people [although only 425 copies were printed] . . . Secondly, it is meant for those in East and West who are interested in the reorganization of life, and especially of the arts and crafts under modern conditions. Thirdly, an endeavour has been made to render it as far as possible of value to the anthropologist, and to students of sociology and folk-lore.

He did wish his study to be scientific, but also to contribute to arts and crafts agendas in England 'under modern conditions' and rhetorically to lobby for the re-transformation of contemporaneous South Asia, in this case Ceylon. From England's Arts and Crafts movement he had absorbed an abiding respect for guilds, the importance of makers, and the conventions of tradition that he would translate into eastern and then universal terms over the course of his career as writer.

In a letter to Richard Ettinghausen, Director of the Freer Gallery of Art in Washington D.C., Coomaraswamy wrote in 1942:

> I have never tried to have a 'style' but only to state things effectively—so that I was very pleased, too, when [the artist] Eric Gill wrote to

me: 'You hit bloody straight, bloody hard, and bloody often.' I think our valuation of 'literature' (and of art generally) is now fetishistic, the symbol being more important to us than its reference.

To the Indian art historian H. Goetz he wrote in 1939:

> my change of interest from Art History to metaphysics . . . was also a natural and necessary development arising from my former work in which the iconographic interest prevails. I was no longer satisfied with a merely descriptive iconography and had to be able to explain the *reasons* of the forms . . . I could not, of course, be satisfied with merely 'sociological' explanations since the forms of the traditional societies themselves can only be explained metaphysically.

To the protean Indian scholar V.S. Agrawala he wrote the same year:

> An interpretation of the Vedas is not really an interpretation of *Indian* metaphysics but of *metaphysics* . . . My interest is in doctrines that are *true*, rather than because they are *Indian*. The *philosophia perennis* . . . is not a private property of any time, or place, or people, but the birth-right of humanity.

Yet in addressing friends on his retirement at the Harvard Club on 22 August 1947—the same day his web of thoughts on *Time and Eternity* woven from a multitude of religious sources was published in Switzerland—he demurred:

> I am grateful . . . to the American Oriental Society, whose editors, however much they differed from me 'by temperament and training', as Professor Norman Brown [senior Sanskritist at the University of Pennsylvania] once said, have always felt that I had 'a right to be heard', and have allowed me to be heard. And all this despite the fact that such studies as I have made necessarily lead me back to the enunciation of relatively unpopular sociological doctrines.

In these farewell remarks he characterized himself as 'a student of human manufactures', in tune with Ruskin's manifesto that 'industry without art is brutality', 'that men can never be really happy unless they bear an individual responsibility not only for what they do but for the kind and quality of what they *make*', ruminations that returned him near the end of his life to agendas that had absorbed him from his career's beginning.

Following his monumental *Mediaeval Sinhalese Art*, Coomaraswamy's next two books in quick succession, *The Indian Craftsman* (1909) and *Essays in National Idealism* (1909), returned to the second two of his themes, 'reorganization of life, and especially of the arts and crafts under modern conditions' and 'an endeavour . . . to render [my work] as far as possible of value to the anthropologist, and to students of sociology and folk-lore.' *The Indian Craftsman* laid out a traditional view of craft practices, in his biographer Roger Lipsey's estimate, 'primarily a documentation, not a polemic.' And yet his agendas in both books were certainly polemical, made even clearer in the concurrent *Essays in National Idealism* (1909):

> I believe that not only the world at large, but a large part even of the English people, would extend to India a true sympathy in her life and death struggle with an alien bureaucracy. For this struggle is much more than a political conflict. It is a struggle for spiritual and mental freedom from the domination of an alien ideal. In such a conflict, political and economic victory are but half the battle; for an India 'free in name, but subdued by Europe in her innermost soul' would ill justify the price of freedom. It is not so much the material, as the moral and spiritual subjugation of Indian civilization that in the end impoverishes humanity.

That Coomaraswamy struggled to address such issues with a series of assembled essays ending with an attack on the gramophone—'"Ah, you have never heard a good gramophone", I am often told. This mythical instrument I never expect to hear [and is not possible]'—does not distract from the power and passion of his writing. Remarkable is the contemporaneity to Coomaraswamy of his engagement with the more distant past. He hoped to find in *present* evidence 'evidence unmistakable of a former continuity which it helps us to understand', and to apply this to 'the reorganization of life' in his contemporary world. The series of pamphlets, portfolios, essays, collections, and volumes he produced in this period all have this feel of immediate application—as ethnography, social politics, and polemic.

Coomaraswamy left England to travel extensively, now in India, between 1909 and 1912, collecting art and exploring what it might mean to 'become Indian', as would the English novelist E.M. Forster in a later era. Artist Nandalal Bose's arch drawing of Coomaraswamy, *ca.* 1910, lounging at the centre of Abanindranath Tagore's studio in Jorasanko, Calcutta, giving 'craftsman' Nandalal (who was his assistant in cataloguing the family's art collection) artistic instruction, surrounded by three Tagore brothers, captures well Coomaraswamy's temporary co-option in this period of the dress and manners, and issues past and present, of intellectual Bengal. He was but one part of a cosmopolitan circle of like-minded visitors that included the Japanese scholar Okakura Kakuzo and the principal of the Government School of Art, Calcutta, E.B. Havell. A collection of Coomaraswamy's essays that grew out of his experiences in India, *Art and Swadeshi*, came out in 1912; an appointment to establish an Indian national museum did not.

Following his return from India, his publication of the commissioned 'World of Art Series' handbook, *The Arts and Crafts of India and Ceylon* (1913) and particularly of the two-volume *Rajput Painting* (1916), showed Coomaraswamy drawing widely on materials he had collected in India, preparing to take on the mantle of leading historian of India's arts. His scholarly acumen had begun to provide an antidote to the challenge James Fergusson—the pioneering architectural historian on whose comprehensive *A History of Indian and Eastern Architecture* (1876) Coomaraswamy drew—had posed for British readers in the nineteenth century: 'Few among us are aware how much education has had to do with their [*sic*] admiration of classical or medieval art, and few, consequently, perceive how much their condemnation of Indian forms arises from the very want of gradual and appropriate education.' It was precisely this education Coomaraswamy had provided himself through his travels in South Asia, and he was now prepared to instruct. (In 1918 he published a somewhat miscellaneous collection on a variety of Indian subjects—'human welfare' and 'status of women' among them—to which he gave the title *The Dance Of Shiva: Fourteen Indian Essays*, perhaps his most enduring and well-known book.)

In my own teaching of India's art over the years, I have sometimes asked students to compare Coomaraswamy's chapter on 'Indian Sculpture' in *The Arts and Crafts of India and Ceylon* (1913) with Roger Fry's on 'Indian Art' in his *Last Lectures* (1939). Kenneth Clark, in his introduction to Fry's posthumous volume, paraphrased Fry's objective, 'To survey the whole world from the standpoint of a consistent aesthetic theory', and judged him 'the best living English writer on art', but then qualified that, adding: 'Fry was a greater critic when praising than when condemning.' Most students were quick to suspect Fry's penchant for negative rhetoric: 'The general aspect of almost all Indian works of art is intensely and acutely distasteful to me. It is excessive and redundant, it shows an extravagant and exuberant fancy which seems uncontrolled by any principle of co-ordination and, above all perhaps, the quality of its rhythms displeases me by its nerveless unctuous sinuosity.' Yet students intuitively trusted Coomaraswamy's empirical methods 'to take up certain leading types and to endeavour to investigate their psychology and to describe their main stylistic peculiarities', and especially his desire to provide cultural settings for art; they could be less critical of Coomaraswamy's own rhetorical excesses: 'There are tests more universal than those of particular canons or personal likes or dislikes. A great art expresses a clear and impassioned vision of life.'

What students could less easily perceive—rhetoric having so great a literary power—was Fry's greater practice at observing art. Of first-century BC female bracket figures from Sanchi, for example, Coomaraswamy wrote only: 'Another instance of sculpture in the round is afforded by the beautiful bracket figures of the Sānchī gates—dryads, leaning outwards from the trees of their habitation, with fearless and unaffected grace.'

Fry's judgments were of a different critical order:

> In the figures from one of these gates distinctively Indian qualities are already apparent. We note the extraordinary power of imitative realism . . . But what this figure shows also is the extraordinary capacity of these Indian artists to seize and express the most complicated plastic systems. They have perfect freedom of plastic direction . . . [This artist]

> can twist his torso at any angle, can relate his limbs to the trunk in any possible pose. In short, his imagination evolves directly and freely in three-dimensional space . . . This is a very remarkable gift and is one of the chief characteristics of Indian art.

It is not that Coomaraswamy was not thinking or writing aesthetically. He was already working toward defining an 'Oriental aesthetic theory based mainly on Indian and partly on Chinese sources'—freed largely from the sites and objects filling his Indian notebooks and art-historical studies—that flowed into essays he collected over a decade later for Harvard University Press as *The Transformation of Nature in Art* (1934). That volume, without any illustrations, tracked his thinking toward defining a traditional aesthetic. In the first chapter, 'The Theory of Art in Asia', Coomaraswamy wrote without compromise:

> It will be evident . . . that there was a time when Europe and Asia could and did actually understand each other very well. Asia has remained herself; but subsequent to the extroversion of the European consciousness and its preoccupation with surfaces, it has become more difficult to understand the Asiatic point of view . . . Our purpose in the present volume is to place the Asiatic and the valid European views side by side, not as curiosities, but as representing actual and indispensable truth; not endeavouring to prove by any argumentation what should be apparent to the consciousness of the intelligent.

Coomaraswamy characterized his view of artistic production in Asia and medieval Europe in specific ways:

> The procedure on the part of the imager . . . implies a real understanding of the psychology of aesthetic intuition. To generalize, whatever object may be the artist's chosen or appointed theme becomes for the time being the single object of his attention and devotion; and only when the theme has thus become for him an immediate experience can it be stated authoritatively from knowledge.

For comparison he gave a quotation from Dante, 'Who paints a figure, if he cannot be it, cannot draw it.' Historian and theorist Joseph Rykwert presciently characterized Coomaraswamy's intellectual position: 'Rhetoric is an extremely important notion to him. Since all his writings about art, for which as he constantly insists aesthetics is really a misnomer, are attempts to construct a theory of the valuation of art based not on the spectator's function, but the maker's.'

In 1916 Coomaraswamy published two articles on Indian art in the style-conscious *Vanity Fair.* In England he was now liable for conscription and persecuted by the police (he seems to have declared himself a conscientious objector, and was outspoken about independence from empire); in India a possibility of a professorship at Benares Hindu University had not come through. By 1917 he and his collection of Indian miniature paintings had shifted with his second wife, an Englishwoman who under the name Ratan Devi performed on tabla and as a singer, to the Museum of Fine Arts, Boston, where he remained as Keeper and then Research Fellow until the end of his life, never returning to England. The full title of *Rajput Painting: Being an Account of the Hindu Paintings of Rajasthan and the Panjab Himalayas from the Sixteenth to the Nineteenth Century Described in Their Relationship to Contemporary Thought With Texts and Translations* (1916), volumes based on the art-historical research and collection of paintings that helped procure his position in Boston, showed Coomaraswamy operating still within methodologies and intentions honed by his work in Ceylon. It is the 'sociology' of Rajput painting, the social contexts of the art he identified and described, which make the volumes still of value today—'To reconstruct the vernacular culture history of Hindustān is not easy. It is, however, a matter of moment for our study to determine its main outlines; and in doing this we shall find our best guide in the history of literature.' Separating the 'sensuous-spiritual' art of the Hindu Rajputs ('a religious art, and so a popular art' as he had written of Ceylon) from the 'secularizing' paintings of the Mughals' court was his chief intuition.

Lipsey, Coomaraswamy's biographer, contrasted the writer of *Rajput Painting* (1916) with that of his landmark survey, *History of Indian and Indonesian Art* (1927), remarking 'Coomaraswamy's first ten years at the museum were a time of acquisition of that level of knowledge rightly called erudition . . . he acquired a literally encyclopedic knowledge . . .' Coomaraswamy produced remarkable compilations of scholarly observation in this period, more 'inter-factual' than literary in their composition, which remain monuments to art-historical scholarship—a defining series of catalogues of the Museum of Fine Arts' Indian collections (1923–32); *Yakṣas* (1928, 1932), a startling exposition of India's nature spirits; revelatory essays on 'Early Indian Architecture' (1930–1), difficult to read because of their compacted references; *La Sculpture de Bodhgayā* (1935), a documentation of remains from the site of Buddha's Enlightenment. Lipsey characterized this erudition as 'a cold knowledge; he rarely used it tendentiously to argue a point, as so often in younger days. It was a professorial knowledge.' Yet Coomaraswamy's obsessions, audience, as well as style were shifting.

During this extended introduction to professional life in America—and the worlds of *Vanity Fair* and New York, which introduced him to his third wife, Stella Bloch, a talented dancer—Coomaraswamy's scholarly work became more scholastic, embedded in a *philosophia perennis* rooted in pan-medievalism, not in modern thought. When Meyer Schapiro of Columbia University—an historian of both medieval and contemporary art—challenged him on his lack of interest in modern artists shortly before Coomaraswamy's *Transformation of Nature in Art* (1934) was published (in which he pointedly was 'not endeavouring to prove by any argumentation what should be apparent to the consciousness of the intelligent'), Coomaraswamy replied only 'If I should lean over too far on one side [toward the medieval], as you think, it is perhaps after all salutary for the quality of Western art to be challenged, it should lead to a searching for what is sound and fundamental in it [Western art].' Coomaraswamy, who had married a series of artists and moved freely in the artistic circle of the Stieglitz gallery in New York, himself drew, became a photographer, and defended 'photography as art'; yet, from his early involvement with the Tagores, and the nationalist art movement in Bengal, until his death he seems to have valued living art only as he had the surviving crafts in Ceylon: 'Such an art is, as it were, an outlier, left by long continued denudation, in extent severely limited, yet evidence . . . of a former continuity'. All else he discarded.

Lipsey, in his biography of Coomaraswamy, documents his intertwining with currents of intellectual thought from William Morris,

C.R. Ashbee, the Tagores, Okakura Kakuzo, Eric Gill, to René Guénon and Walter Andrae and 'Boston Brahmins', but also the hermetic discourse into which his late work fell. To each successive fascination—the British Arts and Crafts movement, *swadeshi* (Indianness), becoming an 'Orientalist', contributing to the 'Traditionalist' movement of Guénon and others—Coomaraswamy lent a strong scientific methodology and his power of rhetoric (as Joseph Rykwert put it, 'because he was himself a preacher'). The 'inter-factual' nature of a geologist's notebooks, those of an ethnographer, crafts scholar, art historian, philologist, coloured Coomaraswamy's methods as he moved toward texts, filling his notebooks with intercultural cross references and annotations. Reading many of Coomaraswamy's late writings is less a literary pleasure than a fascination with the cut and fit of his ideas. An ambitious essay, 'Some Pāli Words' (1939), published in the *Harvard Journal of Asiatic Studies*, begins:

> In the following article certain Pāli words are discussed, with particular reference to their treatment in the PTS [Pāli Text Society] Dictionary and to their translation in the now completed volumes of the Nikāya volumes of the PTS. References are to the corresponding editions, by volume and page. The discussions of *Atha* (*artha*), *Rasa*, *Vjañjana*, and *Sahājanetta* amount to a first essay in the study of Buddhist rhetoric, and should be read together.

On this long essay, Rykwert commented: 'The construction of a Buddhist rhetoric out of fragments of a dictionary is a remarkable task, and of course the [entries] are so short that he only manages to suggest its outline. But if you turn back [to Coomaraswamy's writings on art], you will find many more elements of such a rhetoric, passim.'

Near the end of his life, Coomaraswamy published two collections of essays, with 'no rights reserved', that in Lipsey's view helped fulfil Coomaraswamy's 'need for something like a manual of study that would permit others to recapitulate his progress': *Why Exhibit Works of Art?* (1943; reprinted as *Christian and Oriental Philosophy of Art*, 1956) and *Figures of Speech or Figures of Thought: Collected Essays on the Traditional or 'Normal' View of Art* (1946). From the latter, a striking essay, '*Saṃvega*: Aesthetic Shock', can demonstrate the 'passionate intensity' with which Coomaraswamy could still argue his subject:

> The Pāli term *saṃvega* is often used to denote the shock or wonder that may be felt when the perception of a work of art becomes a serious experience . . . On the other hand, the 'shock' or 'thrill' need not involve a recoil, but may be one of supersensual delight . . . *Saṃvega*, then, refers to the feeling that may be felt in the presence of a work of art, when we are struck by it, as a horse may be struck by a whip. It is, however, assumed that, like the good horse, we are more or less trained, and hence that more than a merely physical shock is involved; the blow has a *meaning* for us, and the realization of that meaning, in which nothing of the physical sensation survives, is still a part of the shock.

Of Coomaraswamy as writer Lipsey concluded: 'From the beginning, he was a literary artist; putting his thoughts on paper was not a burden but an occasion.' He summed up his personal estimate of Coomaraswamy's long output, and of his own role as a biographer:

> what the early writings lack in intrinsic interest is made up for by the interest of the latter . . . Biography is necessary . . . But to the extent that Coomaraswamy achieved that 'other' and more essential form of himself . . . his portrait in later years will naturally, without forcing, become a more 'ideal' likeness.

Lipsey, in spite of his admiration and his focus on Coomaraswamy's later works, by the end had trouble convincing either himself or us that there was really a difference between the early and late Coomaraswamy, which means not merely that roots were there early and the man developed, as Lipsey implies, but that the roots included nineteenth-century English romanticism, and his works can never be seen separate from that. His late works are products of the same mind, cleansed of youth but not of his young ideas. The development of a style of research and writing, dense, close to sources, meant not to be read easily—what one friendly critic, Lucien Schermann, compared to 'what we call in German "Spitzfindigkeiten"'—Lipsey traces well, nor does he ignore the easier, elegant, continuing polemic style Coomaraswamy still could cultivate. The Coomaraswamy of *Essays in National Idealism* was no less or more the passionate advocate than the author of essays on Vedic terms. However much he retired into his study, Coomaraswamy still was leading, in his terms, the 'active life'—engaged and an advocate. What Lipsey called 'cold knowledge' in his middle art-historical years was a method for passion. His metaphysics were as romantic as his youthful concern for handicrafts. As a writer, however—always stately in his passion and polemics—Coomaraswamy had by the end moved through several audiences, hoping always to find another as he continued to look for 'a former continuity'.

29
The Historian as Writer
The Polished Prose of D.D. Kosambi

Nayanjot Lahiri

Damodar Dharmanand Kosambi is usually remembered as a scholar whose passion for the history of ancient India was matched by his admiration for Marxism. Yet his admirers are not limited to those who are either Marxists or scholars of antiquity. Kosambi is quoted approvingly by medievalists writing on Indian feudalism and by historians of modern India on themes that range from forms of popular expression in the 1857 revolt to the advent of colonialism. That he was by profession and training a mathematician rather than a historian makes his work and its influence all the more remarkable.

Here, though, my focus is not on the man's multi-faceted intellect. Instead I see him as a historian steeped in things literary, and the ways in which his literary sensibility influenced the subjects, the structure, and the character of his history writing. Why should a reader who is interested in Indian writing in English read Kosambi? What would he find in his writings that he is unlikely to find in the historical writings of his contemporaries? How do his narratives reveal his interests, whose range extended far beyond narrow specializations in the study of ancient India'? How did Marxism develop and hinder his insights and writings? These are some questions I tackle while examining

Kosambi's work and life together. Many elements of his life figure in his historical works and give substance to his writings.

Kosambi was born on 31 July 1907 in Goa. Because of the itinerant inclinations of his father (the Buddhist scholar Dharmanand Kosambi), he spent most of his childhood there with his maternal grandfather. The juxtaposition of the old with the new in India, an element that runs through Kosambi's Indological work, was probably first imbued within him over his childhood. His paternal grandfather's farm was situated where the service settlement and the dancing girls' houses of Sancoale's Narasimha temple once stood, while an aunt lived in a house built upon the site where a temple had been and whose bell survived as an object of worship among passers-by.

In 1912, when his father began teaching at Fergusson College in Pune, Kosambi was institutionally exposed to English at the New English School there. An autobiographical account of his intellectual evolution, 'Steps in Science', however, traces his uncommon unfamiliarity with English to the USA, specifically to Harvard College in 1918, where he was taken when Dharmanand Kosambi was invited to complete a critical edition of the *Visuddhimagga* (a book on Buddhist philosophy). It was at schools in Cambridge, Mass., and later at Harvard College in 1926, following a two-year sojourn in India, that the younger Kosambi learnt several European languages as well and began speaking English with an American accent. While the accent remained with him for the rest of his life, his felicity with languages allowed him to dip into the European classics in the original, and later to publish in European-language journals. His relationship with the English language, though, was an ambiguous one. Although his writings are largely in English, towards the end of his life English became for him one more instance of the alien and oppressive world of colonial rule. Writing in 1965, he strongly regretted that 'fourteen years after independence English still remains the official language of administration, big business, and higher education in India. No significant attempts have been made to change over, beyond pious resolutions in shiftless committees.'

Kosambi studied mathematics at Harvard, graduating with distinction in 1929. It was a subject that he would teach and research for the rest of his life. Harvard also made accessible to him an astonishing range of ideas and books. He mentions several authors whose work combines matters scientific and literary, including von Humboldt, Einstein, Freud, and H.G. Wells. This literary appetite would later stamp Kosambi's historical writings. He mentions no Indian litterateur; in fact, only one Indian, Mahatma Gandhi, figures in the reminiscences of a college friend of his Harvard years. Apparently Gandhi's portrait graced Kosambi's room in Cambridge, Mass. Not surprisingly, it was anti-colonial thought which left its mark on Kosambi's first piece of writing in his Harvard freshman year—a short story entitled 'The Kanpur Road'.

'The Kanpur Road' is historical fiction, deploying the 1857 rebellion as backdrop. Its Sikh protagonist, Govind Singh, had assisted the British, cutting down a rebel—his own brother—who had killed a British brigadier under whom Govind Singh had served. What is most striking is not this act of 'fratricidal loyalty' but the lifelong trauma that it unleashes within the old soldier, whose face, slashed in combat by the brother he has overcome, bears a 'great livid scar'; and the star pinned on his chest is 'not to show others my glory, but to remind myself of my grief.' Kosambi parallels this with an ancient encounter, that of the invading Alexander and the indigenous King Porus: Govind Singh 'was worthy to have stood with King Pauravas on that fateful day when the tricky manoeuvres of Yavana invaders prevailed against simple bravery.' Also woven into this tale of ancient and modern tragic heroes are the hunger and disease of the Indian countryside. The narrator of 'The Kanpur Road' had heard this story of Alexander and Porus from his 'village school teacher, now dead of starvation and cholera.' The story prefigures the key intellectual features of Kosambi's later work: finely phrased historical themes with a bearing on the present, all encompassed within a progressive worldview.

When did Kosambi begin writing on ancient India and its history? Not before 1940 and 1941 it seems, when he published a statistical analysis of Taxila and an essay on the poetry of the ancient philosopher-poet Bhartrhari. Having returned to India in 1929, he had spent the next few years teaching mathematics, first at Banaras Hindu University (1929–31), then at Aligarh Muslim University (1931–2), finally settling in Pune where he taught at Fergusson College for the next twelve or so years. Now he ranged beyond his competence in mathematics and began to write about numismatics, ancient texts, classics, and contemporary affairs. By 1939, in an article on 'The Function of Leadership in a Mass Movement' for the *Fergusson & Willingdon College Magazine*, he was describing himself as a Marxist.

Marxian dialectics figures in fact in both pieces that he wrote in this magazine in 1939. In the first, he examines various types of leadership. Good leadership, he says, explains why the communist revolution was successful in Russia but failed in Germany. In the same breath he describes part of Mahatma Gandhi's leadership as belonging to a 'restoration of law and order' genre which devised methods for dissipating excess energy in the lower classes. Evidently, by the time Kosambi became a Marxist he had moved beyond and against Gandhian ideas—unlike his father, who remained devoted to Gandhi. Incidentally, Kosambi's essay was written in the aftermath of the failure of Gandhi's satyagraha at Rajkot, and it was probably this as well as the 1930 satyagraha that Kosambi had in mind when he wrote about Gandhi's leadership. This approach would remain typical of a large part of Kosambi's work. While he would devote asides and paragraphs to a class analysis of social structures ancient and modern, a full critique, as in the case of Gandhi, would frequently fall short of being presented. Yet the ability to be critical of those whom he admired, without fear or favour, later marks his critique of the other powerful Indian leader of his time, Jawaharlal Nehru. Being a 'humble admirer' of Nehru does not prevent Kosambi from pointing out flaws in Nehru's *The Discovery of India* (1946), especially the absence within it of class analysis.

Class analysis features also in the second essay of 1939, which introduces Marxian dialectics into ancient Greece. Writing 'On the Trial of Sokrates', he thinks it would be of 'interest to Marxists' that the method of Sokrates 'was the dialectic one, questioning and cross-questioning, showing up the contradictions in a plausible and even

Note on Contributors

RANJANA SIDHANTA ASH was Editor of the Heinemann Asian Writers Series and reviewed South Asian literature for several British newspapers and magazines. She died in 2015.

DIPESH CHAKRABARTY is the Lawrence A. Kimpton Distinguished Service Professor of History and South Asian Languages and Civilizations at the University of Chicago. He is the recipient of the 2014 Toynbee Prize, which is given to a distinguished practitioner of global history. His most recent book is *The Calling of History: Sir Jadunath Sarkar and His Empire of Truth* (2016).

SUDHIR CHANDRA was Senior Fellow at the Centre for Social Studies, Surat. He is the author of *Dependence and Disillusionment:Emergence of National Consciousness in Later Nineteenth Century India* (1975), *The Oppressive Present: Literature and Social Consciousness in Colonial India* (1992), and *Enslaved Daughters: Colonialism, Law, and Women's Rights* (1998).

AMIT CHAUDHURI is the author of six novels, and editor of the *Picador Book of Modern Indian Literature* (2001). He writes regularly for the *London Review of Books*, the *Times Literary Supplement*, and *Granta*, and has won several prizes, including the Sahitya Akademi Award. He is Professor of Contemporary Literature at the University of East Anglia.

ROSINKA CHAUDHURI is the author of *Gentlemen Poets in Colonial Bengal: Orientalist Texts and Indian Identity* (2002); *Freedom and Beefsteaks: Colonial Calcutta Culture* (2012), and *The Literary Thing* (2014). She has edited *Derozio, Poet of India* (2008) and *A History* poets: 'if for nothing else, Bhartrhari would deserve a place in the front rank of world literature for his consummate handling of so difficult a language as Sanskrit . . . Few could exceed the force of his epigrams, the finality with which the sentiment is rounded out in many of his concluding half-lines.' Through the prism of his poetry and the figures of speech that he employed Bhartrhari is shown to be a Brahmin, but one of a comparatively late period. Much of the essay also problematizes the 'greatness' of Bhartrhari, demonstrating that his concept of renunciation simply did not match up to either that of Western poets like Goethe or those from the East like Sa'di. The comparisons may seem far-fetched, but they reveal Kosambi's wide reading, his immersion in world literature, and a literary sensibility that he would make evident in his later work.

Kosambi approved of Bhartrhari's sentiments as long as these engaged with the dread of poverty, even while frowning upon the poet's idea of renunciation. This may have been because the court poet, through the expression of his fear of poverty, gave away his class status, a status that Kosambi believed tended to be masked in what he describes as a literature of escape. That poetry should largely be valued for its class resonances, and not for its style or multi-layered meanings, is an argument with which not everyone can agree. But one does not have to agree with Kosambi in order to admire the dialectic that structures his work: a great poet's warts are strongly foregrounded, and, just as the reader begins to doubt the artist's greatness, a little-known aspect of his work—the courage to voice fears of not being employed and the attendant poverty that this would bring—is highlighted. The verse that he quotes most approvingly is one which reveals the poet visualizing 'his wife as sad-faced, unfed, miserable, with her worn raiment constantly tugged at by pitiful, hungry, crying children.' So, finally, there is an appreciation of Bhartrhari, but not for reasons of either the style or the expression with which Kosambi had begun. Bhartrhari continued to figure in Kosambi's horizon: he eventually examined some 400 Bhartrhari manuscripts, culminating in a critical edition of the *Satakatrayam* in 1945 and a further critical edition of a Bhartrhari recension in 1946.

By this time, 1945, Kosambi had been invited by the scientist Homi Bhabha to join the Tata Institute of Fundamental Research (TIFR) in Bombay as Professor of Mathematics; he remained there till 1962. The TIFR years were marked by a spate of writings on texts and coins, aspects of ancient India, and books that synthesized his view of ancient India. Naturally, Kosambi's mathematical research continued; in 1949 he delivered lectures on tensor analysis at the University of Chicago and spent time at the Institute of Advanced Study at Princeton, where he met Einstein. The US would figure on his Indological horizon as well. In 1951 he was invited to produce a critical edition of the *Subhasitaratnakosa*, which was eventually published in the Harvard Oriental Series in 1957.

The *Subhasitaratnakosa* was an anthology of Sanskrit poetry compiled by Vidyakara in the twelfth century. Kosambi's study of it followed that of his exposition of Bhartrhari. Vidyakara was shown, on the basis of internal textual evidence, to have compiled his anthology at the Jagaddala Vihara in Malda in the time of the Pala dynasty. In a memorable deduction, Kosambi tells us that the poet was unmistakably Bengali, for he 'brags of the large number of pond fish, highly spiced and fried in oil, that he had gulped down without even troubling to wash up first.' As before, he finds Vidyakara's text wanting in comparison with Western poets. Kosambi cannot recall a single epigram comparable to one in Blake's *Jerusalem:*

Bring me my bow of burning gold;
Bring me my arrow of desire;
Bring me my spear: O clouds, unfold!
Bring me my chariot of fire!
I will not cease from mental flight,
Nor shall my sword sleep in my hand
Till we have built Jerusalem
In England's green and pleasant land.

That England's most popular patriotic song should be compared with verses composed several hundred years earlier by a poet in east India tells us rather more about Kosambi's literary interests and the extraordinary ideas that he sought in Vidyakara than anything much about the *Subhasitaratnakosa*. Unusual literary analogies are in fact an intrinsic part of Kosambi's writings. An Introduction he wrote to *Myth and Reality* (1962) quotes long stanzas from Robert Graves' *White Goddess* and Homer's *Iliad.* While the comparisons are not entirely successful as explanatory devices, they reveal the extraordinary range of Kosambi's reading and the ways in which he could use thoughts on ancient India to show his deep appreciation of Western literature.

Similarly, Kosambi's assessment of Vidyakara's exploration of love reveals perhaps more about his own sensibility than Vidyakara's ideas. It seems that, at least on one count, he believed medieval Indian poetry was better than modern Western verse. In medieval Indian poetry, there was little of prostitution and nothing of 'homosexuality or other abnormalities that now seem proper literary material in the West.' Instead, 'this is love in the direct Indian tradition, sensuous erotic experience that left visible marks (of teeth and nails) upon both participants.' The distinction he highlights is surprising, for even in the 1950s it was well known that in early India same-sex love was as common as in the West, certainly acceptable enough to be depicted on temple carvings and ordinary terracottas. In any case, as with Bhartrhari, after offering samplers of ancient erotica Kosambi reveals that he is more impressed with the poet's allusions to mundane elements, as when a 'dog chases a cat, quail pick up seed at the edge of a muddy field, sparrows scratch in plowed furrows'; or when 'a bull startles the peasant woman butting his way into the hut.' Again, class figures centrally. How it limited the writings of poets of that time is to Kosambi a matter of great interest. Their work, he says, was steeped in an atmosphere of luxury, parasitism, and decay because of the class that patronized it. Its fundamental limitation was that it was a literature 'of and for a class, not a people.' Kosambi's interest in class analysis is criticized by two of his eminent academic friends, Daniell Ingalls and A.L. Basham, the latter arguing that 'many of Professor Kosambi's most valuable insights into his country's history are derived from his Marxism. A certain lack of sympathy for many aspects of the ancient culture of India, and a tendency to judge the past from the point of view of the present, may also stem from the same Marxism.'

The recognition of Kosambi as foundational historian of ancient India really rests on the book that he wrote at the TIFR: *An Introduction to the Study of Indian History* (1956). His definition of history as 'the presentation, in chronological order, of successive developments in the means and relations of production' sets the tone. The past and present are viewed as a continuum, and this way of looking at history is for Kosambi rooted in the nature of the land itself. 'India is a country of long survivals' where 'people of the atomic age rub elbows with those of the chalcolithic.' The element of continuity is highlighted by photographs that juxtapose into proximity an Indus seal depicting a humped bull, a Gandharan Buddhist sculpture depicting a plough, a bull in modern Banaras, and a buffalo relaxing in Pune. If Kosambi had had his way, he would in fact have made the buffalo India's national animal; his explanation for this is delightful: 'Heavy, dark, sluggish, hardy, fertile, productive with little care, far cleaner than it looks, docile enough to be led by a child, but suspicious of innovations and perfectly capable when roused, of charging a tiger or a locomotive, the buffalo would be a fitting national symbol for India.'

To what extent did Kosambi's *Introduction* succeed in sketching a scheme of evolution in which the Indian past is the development of basic changes in the means and relations of production? Kosambi's exploration of prehistory does not succeed in making visible a pre-class tribal society, partly because of the thin evidence he provides. He says less about the remnants of those who peopled the prehistoric past than on tribal survival in modern India. Thick detail is largely limited to his observations around Poona. His descriptions are the accounts of an engaged fieldworker who imbibes many different realities first-hand. He returns again and again to heterogeneous ancient and modern juxtapositions, to the lowland track 'behind the cricket field of the Fergusson College' where microliths pertaining to ancient trade routes had been found. Interestingly, Poona had a similar effect on another of Kosambi's contemporaries, the archaeologist H.D. Sankalia. He apparently found so many stone tools near his residence in Deccan College that his colleagues used to tell him that he was actually occupying the site of his prehistoric residence! However, unlike Kosambi, when Sankalia wrote about prehistory, Maharashtra only figured as one element in the larger archaeological mosaic of the Indian subcontinent.

Class figures prominently also in Kosambi's analysis of the Indus civilization. For him, the main question was how this civilization's class structure was maintained. Since the 'tools of violence' in the form of weapons are flimsy, what 'helped the trader maintain his unequal sharing of profit?' The explanation lay in religion. The centrality of religion in understanding India is developed at length in his analysis of the historical period, a reflection of which he saw at Harappa and Mohenjodaro. Indus religion, he believed, had much in common with Hinduism. The human figures on stamp seals 'showed a bearded three-faced deity which has some of the attributes of the later Hindu god Siva. For that matter, iconotropic seals from the Indus may explain many legends of later Hinduism, as say that of Trisanku.'

Overall, in Kosambi's *Introduction* we find a picture of India after the 'Aryan invasions' which is largely, though not exclusively, confined to north India. Settlements in the Deccan plateau do not figure until more than half his book is done, over most of which he depicts virile Aryans triumphantly sweeping across India, from the north-west where the Aryan hordes destroy the Indus civilization to the 'wilderness of the east' which they settle. It is not that Kosambi lacks a sense of different kinds of cultures coexisting in north India, but the main story is of colonizing Aryans. Today, the archaeological landscape of the vast Gangetic plains, unlike the 1950s when Kosambi wrote, is very different. Prosperous regional cultures can be visualized across ancient north India, and it is impossible to seamlessly integrate these with the Vedic texts. These discoveries were made after Kosambi's time, so one can hardly fault him for being unaware of them. Still, it seems odd that a scholar with such an acute sense of the coexistence in modern India of groups at different social and economic levels wrote a history of ancient India which, instead of suggesting a multihued human mosaic, was a saga of foreign invasions, subjugation, and incorporation.

Prehistory and the transitions that marked its long passage continued their strong hold on Kosambi through the rest of his life. Perhaps his last piece of writing before he died in 1966 was centred on prehistory. Like his first foray into history, and unlike most of his later writings, this too was a short story. 'The Hump on Nandi's Back' sought to communicate the prehistoric past to children.

The story unfolds as a conversation between a human being (Rama, the son of the village headman), a tree (the old Bo tree), and certain fauna (a cobra, a tiger, Rama's dog, and the great bull Nandi). The setting, a pond on the edge of a forest 'beneath the Bo tree of the village god', is used by Kosambi to explain to young readers how humans evolved from hunter-gatherers to agriculturalists. Thousands of years ago, humans lived as animals do today, gathering food: 'They climbed trees for fruits and nuts. They plucked berries and mushrooms. Yams came out of the ground. Like Bhalu they would gather honey. They caught fish just as Bhalu does with his paw.' Over time, they domesticated animals. Rama wants to know how humans made dogs like his Moti. The Bo tree tells him about wolf cubs in the company of man growing tame over time. 'Man made himself what he is' is what the story constantly says, reminding us of the title of a famous work by the Australian Marxist prehistorian V. Gordon Childe, *Man Makes Himself* (1951).

Like the prehistoric humans described in 'The Hump on Nandi's Back', Kosambi too had made himself. A mathematician by profession, he trained himself to be a historian. That he was born and grew up in Goa, with prolific literary interests honed at Harvard, and spent much of his working life asking questions about India's past through the prism of what he observed in the present—all this provides us the picture of the sort of Indian historian that is all too rare. One might add, in the end, that the defining tag of Marxist historian that came to be attached to Kosambi is perhaps what has also diminished an appreciation of this unusual mixture of literary qualities in his writings.

Note on Contributors

RANJANA SIDHANTA ASH was Editor of the Heinemann Asian Writers Series and reviewed South Asian literature for several British newspapers and magazines. She died in 2015.

DIPESH CHAKRABARTY is the Lawrence A. Kimpton Distinguished Service Professor of History and South Asian Languages and Civilizations at the University of Chicago. He is the recipient of the 2014 Toynbee Prize, which is given to a distinguished practitioner of global history. His most recent book is *The Calling of History: Sir Jadunath Sarkar and His Empire of Truth* (2016).

SUDHIR CHANDRA was Senior Fellow at the Centre for Social Studies, Surat. He is the author of *Dependence and Disillusionment:Emergence of National Consciousness in Later Nineteenth Century India* (1975), *The Oppressive Present: Literature and Social Consciousness in Colonial India* (1992), and *Enslaved Daughters: Colonialism, Law, and Women's Rights* (1998).

AMIT CHAUDHURI is the author of six novels, and editor of the *Picador Book of Modern Indian Literature* (2001). He writes regularly for the *London Review of Books*, the *Times Literary Supplement*, and *Granta*, and has won several prizes, including the Sahitya Akademi Award. He is Professor of Contemporary Literature at the University of East Anglia.

ROSINKA CHAUDHURI is the author of *Gentlemen Poets in Colonial Bengal: Orientalist Texts and Indian Identity* (2002); *Freedom and Beefsteaks: Colonial Calcutta Culture* (2012), and *The Literary Thing* (2014). She has edited *Derozio, Poet of India* (2008) and *A History of Indian Poetry in English* (2016). She is Professor in Cultural Studies at the Centre for Studies in Social Sciences, Calcutta.

MARIA COUTO is the author *of Graham Greene: On the Frontier, Politics and Religion in the Novels* (1988) and has published a socio-cultural study of Goa.

EUNICE DE SOUZA retired as Head of the English Department, St Xavier's College, Bombay, in 2000. She is the author of four collections of poems and editor of *Nine Indian Women Poets* (1997) and *Talking Poems: Conversations with Poets* (1999). Her first novel, *Dangerlok*, was published in 2001.

ANURADHA DINGWANEY is Professor of English at Oberlin College, Oberlin, Ohio. She is the author of *Using the Master's Tools: Resistance and the Literature of the African and South Asian Diasporas* (2000), and co-editor of a volume on translation and cross-cultural texts, *Between Languages and Cultures* (1995).

PETER HEEHS is associated with the Sri Aurobindo Ashram Archives and Research Library, Pondicherry. He is the author, most recently, of *Nationalism, Terrorism, Communalism* (1998), and editor of *The Essential Writings of Sri Aurobindo* (1998) and *Indian Religions: The Spiritual Traditions of South Asia* (2002).

LEELA GANDHI is John Hawkes Professor of Humanities and English at Brown University. She is the author of *Postcolonial Theory: A Critical Introduction* (1998), *Measures of Home: Poems* (2000), *Affective Communities* (2005), and *The Common Cause: Postcolonial Ethics and the Practice of Democracy, 1900–1955* (2014).

SHANTA GOKHALE has been Arts Editor of the *Times of India*, Bombay. She is the author of *Rita Welinkar* (1995), a novel, and *Playwright at the Centre: Marathi Drama from 1943 to the Present* (2000). She has also translated from Marathi the plays of G.P. Deshpande, Satish Alekar, and Mahesh Elkunchwar.

RAMACHANDRA GUHA is a historian, biographer, and cricket writer. His recent books are *Savaging the Civilized: Verrier Elwin, His Tribals, and India* (1999), *An Anthropologist among the Marxists and Other*

Essays (2001), and, as editor, *The Picador Book of Cricket* (2001). *India after Gandhi: The World's Largest Democracy* (2007), and *Gandhi Before India* (2013) are his latest books.

SUVIR KAUL is the A.M. Rosenthal Professor of English at the University of Pensylvania at Philadelphia, USA. He is the author of *Thomas Gray and Literary Authority* (1992) and *Poems of Nation, Anthems of Empire: English Verse in the Long Eighteenth Century* (2000), and the editor of *Partitions of Memory: The Afterlife of the Division of India* (2001).

SUNIL KHILNANI is Avantha Professor and Director of the India Institute at King's College, London. He is the author of *Arguing Revolution: The Intellectual Left in Postwar France* (1993), *The Idea of India* (1997), and *Incarnations: India in 50 Lives* (2016).

NAYANJOT LAHIRI was for many years a professor at the History department of the University of Delhi, and is now one at Ashoka University. Her several books include *Finding Forgotten Cities: How the Indus Civilization was Discovered* (2005) and *Ashoka in Ancient India* (2015).

JON MEE is Professor of Romanticism Studies at the University of Warwick. He is the author of *Dangerous Enthusiasm: William Blake and the Culture of Radicalism in the 1790s* (1992), and co-editor of the *Oxford Companion to the Romantic Age* (1999).

ARVIND KRISHNA MEHROTRA the author of five books of poetry, most recently *Collected Poems 1969–2014* (2014), and editor of the *Oxford India Anthology of Twelve Modern Indian Poets* (1992) and Collected Poems in English by Arun Kolatkar (2010). He has translated *The Absent Traveller: Prakrit Love Poetry from the Gathasaptasati* (1991) and *Songs of Kabir* (2011). His essays are collected in *Partial Recall* (2011).

MICHAEL MEISTER is W. Norman Brown Professor of South Asia Studies at the University of Pennsylvania in Philadelphia. He studied with Benjamin Rowland and John Rosenfield at Harvard, and has edited multiple volumes of the *Encyclopaedia of Indian Temple Architecture* (1983–1991); *Discourses on Siva* (1984); *Coomaraswamy:*

Essays in Early Indian Architecture (1992) and *Essays in Architectural History* (1995); *Ethnography and Personhood* (2000); coedited *Multiple Histories* (2002) and *Desert Temples* (2008); and authored *Temples of the Indus* (2010).

PANKAJ MISHRA is the author of *Butter Chicken in Ludhiana: Travels in Small Town India* (1995) and *The Romantics* (2000), for which he won the *Los Angeles Times* Art Seidenbaum Award for First Fiction. He is a regular contributor to the *New York Review of Books* and *New Statesman*, among other journals.

SUDESH MISHRA has taught at universities in Fiji, Australia, and Scotland. He is the author of *Preparing Faces: Modernism and Indian Poetry in English* (1995) and *Diaspora and the Difficult Art of Dying* (2001). He is also a poet (*Tandava*, 1992) and playwright (*Ferringhi*, 2001).

PADMINI MONGIA is Professor of English at Franklin and Marshall College, Pennsylvania. She has edited *Contemporary Postcolonial Theory* (1996) and published numerous articles on Conrad and on contemporary Indian Writing in English, and is currently researching pulp fiction: a version of her essay here appeared as 'What About Shobhaa De? Indian Pulp Fiction meets Indian Writing in English', in *Vernacular Worlds, Cosmopolitan Imaginations*, ed. Stephanos Stephanides, *et al.*, Amsterdam: Brill, 2015.

MEENAKSHI MUKHERJEE retired as Professor of English, Jawaharlal Nehru University, New Delhi. She is the author of *Realism and Reality: The Novel and Society in India* (1985), *Re-reading Jane Austen* (1991), and *The Perishable Empire* (2000), and editor of, among other books, *Rushdie's* Midnight's Children: *A Book of Readings* (1999). She died in 2009.

SAJNI KRIPALANI MUKHERJI is Professor of English at Jadavpur University, Calcutta. Her specialist areas are the literature of the European Middle Ages and Victorian Literature. She has co-edited a festschrift for Jashodhara Bagchi, entitled *Literature and Gender* (2002).

SHYAMALA A. NARAYAN has been Reader in English at Jamia Millia Islamia, New Delhi. With M.K. Naik, she is the co-author of *Indian*

English Literature 1980–2000: A Critical Survey (2001). Since 1972, she has compiled the Indian section of the Annual Bibliography of Commonwealth Literature for *The Journal of Commonwealth Literature* (U.K.).

RAJEEV S. PATKE is Associate Professor of English at the National University of Singapore. He is the author of *The Long Poems of Wallace Stevens: An Interpretative Study* (1985) and co-editor of *Institutions in Cultures: Theory and Practice* (1996).

MAHESH RANGARAJAN is a professor of history at Ashoka University, with a special interest in ecological history. He is the author of *India's Wildlife History: An Introduction* (2001), and editor of *The Oxford Anthology of Indian Wildlife* (1999). He has co-edited *Battles over Nature: Science and the Politics of Conservation* (2006).

BRUCE CARLISLE ROBERTSON has been Lecturer in the School of Arts and Sciences, Johns Hopkins University, Baltimore. He is the author of *Raja Rammohan Ray, The Father of Modern India* (1995), and editor of *The Essential Writings of Raja Rammohan Ray* (1999).

MARGERY SABIN is Lorraine Chiu Wang Professor of English at Wellesley College, Massachusetts. Among her publications related to Indian subjects are her book *Dissenters and Mavericks: Writing about India in English: 1765–2000* (2002), and essays and articles, including: 'Colonial India and Victorian Storytelling' in *Oxford Handbook of Victorian Fiction* (2013), 'In Search of Subaltern Consciousness', *Prose Studies: History, Theory, Criticism* (August 2008), and 'The Sounds of America to Sudhindra Bose', *Raritan* (Spring 2005).

ARSHIA SATTAR has translated *Tales from the Kathasaritsagara* (1994) and the *Ramayana* of Valmiki (1996). A frequent contributor to various magazines where she writes on books and literature, she also teaches courses in classical Indian literatures in India and abroad and runs the Sangam House international writer's residency program outside Bangalore.

Further Reading

It is no secret that Indian literature in English, if not Indian literature as a whole, has been poorly served by its critics. Nineteenth-century Indian literature in English, for instance, has attracted only one brief history so far. It appeared from a small press and has long been out of print. Another area that has suffered neglect is biography, and a third is a study of individual authors. Writers like Cornelia Sorabji, Aubrey Menen, and A.K. Ramanujan ought to have attracted at least one full-length study and at least one serviceable biography: neither is on the horizon. Critical editions (with the exception of Tagore's) are all but unthinkable. That a modern literature could last almost two centuries despite this accumulation of neglect is a small miracle.

Nevertheless, a large body of secondary material, like congress grass, has proliferated around this literature. Much of it is worthless and I have done my best to weed it. The suggestions for further reading which follow are thus preliminary and were largely supplied by the contributors of the individual essays, to which I have added a few of my own. Primary sources have not been given, except in cases where the texts are difficult to come by and are available in new editions or selections.

Introduction

A. Anjaria (ed.), *A History of the Indian Novel in English* (New York, 2015), fills certain gaps in the history of the novel (Suvir Kaul on 'Three Novels of Muslim Life') but the book is essentially for those who don't mind being sullied by the bilge-water of academic writing.

J.B. Alfonso-Karkala, *Indo-English Literature in the Nineteenth Century* (Mysore, 1970).

J.B. Alfonso-Karkala and Leena Karkala, *Bibliography of Indo-English Literature: A Check-list of Works by Indian Authors in English, 1800–1966* (Bombay, 1974).

R. Chaudhuri (ed.), *A History of India Poetry in English* (New York, 2016), has extensive coverage of the 19th century in particular; separate sections on 'Publishers, Publishing Houses, and the Periodical Press' and 'The New Millennium Poets on Themselves'.

S.K. Das, *A History of Indian Literature*, vols VIII and IX (New Delhi, 1991–5), the only history to take as its canvas Indian literature as a whole, including Indian literature in English. Together, the two volumes cover the period 1800–1956; they are invaluable.

M.E. Gibson, *Indian Angles: English Verse in Colonial India from Jones to Tagore* (Athens, Ohio, 2011), 'a tale of arranged marriage among cultures' is how Gibson describes her book, the first to deal with 19th century Anglophone poetry written by both Indians and the British, especially British women; in the literary networks they created through a variety of colonial publications, that include newspapers, annuals, and miscellanies, lie the beginnings of Indian literature in English.

M.E. Gibson, *Anglophone Poetry in Colonial India, 1780–1913* (Athens, Ohio, 2011), a companion volume to the above, with excellent headnotes to the poets in the anthology.

S.K. Jain, *Indian Literature in English: A Bibliography* (Windsor, Ont., 1972).

B.S. Kesavan and V.Y. Kulkarni, *The National Bibliography of Indian Literature, 1900–1953*, 4 vols (New Delhi, 1962–74); vol. 1 includes primary and secondary titles pertaining to Indian literature in English.

M.K. Naik, *A History of Indian Literature in English* (New Delhi, 1982), often reprinted.

M.K. Naik and S.A. Narayan, *Indian English Literature, 1980–2000: A Critical Survey* (New Delhi, 2001). This is a sequel to M.K. Naik's *A History of Indian Literature in English* and contains an extensive bibliography, which is to be used with circumspection.

K.R. Srinivasa Iyengar, *Indian Writing in English* (4th edn., New Delhi, 1984), useful for facts but not much else.

W. Walsh, *Indian Literature in English* (London, 1990).

R.J. Warwick, *Indian Literature in English: A Checklist* (London, 1981).

H.M. Williams, *Indo-Anglian Literature, 1800–1970: A Survey* (New Delhi, 1976).

The English Writings of Raja Rammohan Ray

D.K. Biswas (ed.), *The Corrrespondence of Raja Rammohun Roy*, vol. 1 (Calcutta,1992).

S.D. Collet, *The Life and Letters of Raja Rammohun Roy*, eds D.K. Biswas and P.C. Ganguli (Calcutta, 1962).

Bruce Robertson, *Raja Rammohan Ray, The Father of Modern India* (New Delhi, 1995).

——— (ed.), *The Essential Writings of Raja Rammohan Ray* (New Delhi, 1999).

S. Sarkar, *On the Bengal Renaissance* (Calcutta, 1979), also contains essays on Henry Derozio and Nirad C. Chaudhuri.

S. Tagore, *Raja Rammohun Roy* (New Delhi, 1966).

D.E. White, *From Little London to Little Bengal: Religion, Print and Modernity in Early British India, 1793 –1835* (Baltimore, Maryland, 2013), a major contribution to the circulation of ideas between Calcutta and London during the Romantic period.

The Hindu College: Henry Derozio and Michael Madhusudan Dutt

A. Bose, *Michael Madhusudan Dutt* (New Delhi, 1981).

R. Chaudhuri, *Derozio, The Poet of India: The Definitive Edition* (Delhi, 2008).

R.K. Das Gupta (ed.), *Poems of H.L.V. Derozio, A Forgotten Anglo-Indian Poet* (Calcutta, 1980).

T. Edwards, *Henry Derozio, The Eurasian Poet, Teacher and Journalist* (Calcutta, 1884).

E.W. Madge, *Henry Derozio, The Eurasian Poet and Reformer*, ed. S. Ray Chaudhuri (Calcutta, 1967), first published in 1905, this is an important source for biographical information on Derozio.

G. Murshid, *Lured by Hope: A Biography of Michael Madhusadan Dutt* (New Delhi, 2005).

K.R. Ramachandran Nair, *Three Indo-Anglian Poets: Henry Derozio, Toru Dutt, and Sarojini Naidu* New Delhi, 1987).

A. Riddiford, *Madly after the Muses: Bengali Poet Michael Madhusudan Datta and his Reception of the Graeco-Roman Classics* (Oxford, 2013).

The Dutt Family Album: And Toru Dutt

L. Basu, *Indian Writers of English Verse* (Oxford, 1933).

R. Chaudhuri, *Gentlemen Poets in Colonial Bengal: Orientalist Texts and Indian Identity* (Kolkata, 2002).

H. Das, *Life and Letters of Toru Dutt* (London, 1921).

J.N. Gupta (ed.), *The Life and Work of Romesh Chunder Dutt* (London, 1911)

G.A. Natesan, *Toru Dutt, A Sketch of her Life and Appreciation* (Madras, 1917).

P. Sen Gupta, *Toru Dutt* (New Delhi, 1968).

A. Tickell (ed.), *Selections from Bengaliana*, by Shoshee Chunder Dutt (Nottingham, 2005).

Rudyard Kipling

S.S. Azfar Husain, *The Indianness of Rudyard Kipling: A Study in Stylistics* (1983).

Lord Carrington, *Rudyard Kipling: His Life and Work*, 3rd rev. edn. (London, 1978).

L. Cornell, *Kipling in India* (New York, 1966).

P. Mallett (ed.), *Kipling Considered* (Basingstoke, 1989).

P. Mason, *Kipling: The Glass, the Shadow and the Fire* (London, 1975).

J. Moore-Gilbert, *Kipling and Orientalism* (London, 1986).

A. Nandy, *The Intimate Enemy: Loss and Recovery of Self under Colonialism* (New Delhi, 1983), an influential book, with a section on Kipling.

B. Parry, *Delusions and Discoveries: Studies on India in the British Imagination, 1880–1930* (London, 1972).

H. Ricketts, *The Unforgiving Minute: A Life of Rudyard Kipling* (London, 1998).

A. Wilson, *The Strange Ride of Rudyard Kipling, His Life and Works* (London, 1977).

Two Faces of Prose: Behramji Malabari and Govardhanram Tripathi

S. Chandra, *The Oppressive Present: Literature and Social Consciousness in Colonial India* (New Delhi, 1992), has several pages on Govardhanram Tripathi.

Govardhanram Madhavram Tripathi's Scrap Book, eds K.C. Pandya, R.P. Bakshi, and S.L. Pandya, 3 vols (Bombay, 1958–9).

D. Gidumal, *The Life and Life-work of Behramji M. Malabari* (Bombay, 1888).

——— *Behramji M. Malabari: A Biographical Sketch* (London, 1892).

R.P. Karkaria, *India: Forty Years of Progress and Reform, Being a Sketch of the Life and Times of Behramji M. Malabari* (London, 1896).

The Beginnings of the Indian Novel

B. Chatterjee, *Rajmohan's Wife*, ed. Meenakshi Mukherjee (New Delhi, 1994).

M. Mukherjee, *Realism and Reality: The Novel and Society in India* (New Delhi, 1985), a pioneering work, though it does not specifically take up novels written in English.

———, *The Perishable Empire: Essays on Indian Writing in English* (New Delhi, 2000).

S.K. Mund, *The Indian Novel in English: Its Birth and Development* (New Delhi and Bhubaneswar, 1997).

K.S. Ramamurti, *Rise of the Indian Novel in English* (New Delhi, 1987).

K. Satthianadhan, *Kamala, A Story of Hindu Life*, ed. Chandani Lokuge (New Delhi, 1998).

——— *Saguna, The First Autobiographical Novel in English by an Indian Woman*, ed. Chandani Lokuge (New Delhi, 1998).

The English Writings of Rabindranath Tagore

M. Chakrabarti, *Rabindranath Tagore, Diverse Dimensions* (New Delhi, 1990).

A. Chaudhuri, *On Tagore: Reading the Poet Today* (Delhi, 2012).

K. Dutta and A. Robinson, *The Myriad-minded Man* (London, 1995).

K. Kushari Dyson, *In Your Blossoming Flower-Garden: Rabindranath Tagore and Victoria Ocampo* (New Delhi, 1998).

S. Ghose, *Rabindranath Tagore* (New Delhi, 1986).
M. Lago and R. Warwick, *Rabindranath Tagore: Perspectives in Time* (Basingstoke, 1989).
K. Kripalani, *Rabindranath Tagore: A Biography* (London, 1962).
A. Nandy, *The Illegitimacy of Nationalism: Rabindranath Tagore and Politics of the Self* (New Delhi, 1994).
S. Ray, *Rabindranath Tagore: Three Essays* (Calcutta, 1987).
E. Thompson, *Rabindranath Tagore: Poet and Dramatist* (New Delhi, rpt.1991).
E.P. Thompson, *'Alien Homage': Edward Thompson and Rabindranath Tagore* (New Delhi, 1993).

Sri Aurobindo

G. Ghosal, *Sri Aurobindo's Prose Style* (Pondicherry, 1990).
P. Heehs, *Sri Aurobindo: A Brief Biography* (New Delhi, 1989).
K.D. Sethna, *Sri Aurobindo, The Poet* (Pondicherry, 1970).
———, *The Poetic Genius of Sri Aurobindo* (2nd edn., Pondicherry, 1974).
P. Tyagi, *Sri Aurobindo: His Poetry and Poetic Theory* (Saharanpur, 1988).

Two Early-Twentieth-Century Women Writers: Cornelia Sorabji and Sarojini Naidu

V.S. Narvane, *Sarojini Naidu: An Introduction to Her Life, Work and Poetry* (Hyderabad, 1981).
Sarojini Naidu: Selected Letters 1890s to 1940s, ed. Makarand Paranjape (New Delhi, 1997).
P. Sen Gupta, *Sarojini Naidu: A Biography* (Bombay, 1966).
———, *Sarojini Naidu* (New Delhi, 1974).
C. Sorabji, *India Calling*, ed. Chandani Lokuge (New Delhi, 2000).
S. Tharu and K. Lalita (eds), *Women Writing in India*, vol. 1, 600 BC to the Early 20th Century (New Delhi, 1993).

Gandhi and Nehru: The Uses of English

J.B. Alfonso-Karkala, *Jawaharlal Nehru* (New York, 1975).
S.N. Bhattacharya, *Mahatma Gandhi, the Journalist* (Bombay, 1965).

K. Damodaran, *Jawaharlal Nehru, A Communicator and a Democratic Leader* (New Delhi, 1997).

R. Gandhi, *The Good Boatman: A Portrait of Gandhi* (New Delhi, 1995).

S. Gopal, *Jawaharlal Nehru, A Biography*, 3 vols (New Delhi, 1975–84).

R.D. King, *Nehru and the Language Politics of India* (New Delhi, 1997).

D.G. Tendulkar, *Mahatma: A Life of Mohandas Karamchand Gandhi*, 8 vols, 2nd rev. edn (New Delhi, 1960–3).

Verrier Elwin

R. Guha, *Savaging the Civilized: Verrier Elwin, His Tribals, and India* (New Delhi, 1999).

S. Hivale, *Scholar Gypsy: A Study of Verrier Elwin* (Bombay, 1946).

D. O'Connor (ed.), *Din-sevak: Verrier Elwin's Life of Service in India* (New Delhi, 1993).

Novelists of the 1930s and 1940s

M. Berry, *Mulk Raj Anand: The Man and the Novelist* (Amsterdam, 1971).

K.R. Chandrasekharan, *Bhabani Bhattacharya* (New Delhi, 1974).

S. Cowasjee, *So Many Freedoms: A Study of the Major Fiction of Mulk Raj Anand* (New Delhi, 1977).

M.E. Drewett, *The Modern Indian Novel in English: A Comparative Approach* (Brussels, 1966).

R.M. George, *Indian English and the Fiction of National Literature* (New York, 2013), takes a fresh look at Mulk Raj Anand and R.K. Narayan and how a few writers came to be canonized at the cost of others.

R.L. Hardgrave (ed.), *Word as Mantra: The Art of Raja Rao* (New Delhi, 1998).

S.C. Harrex, *The Fire and the Offering: The English-Language Novel of India 1935–1970*, 2 vols (Calcutta, 1977–8).

T. Khair, *Babu Fictions: Alienation in Contemporary Indian English Novels* (New Delhi, 2000), also covers later novelists like V.S. Naipaul and Salman Rushdie.

M. Mukherjee, *The Twice-born Fiction: Themes and Techniques of the Indian Novel in English* (New Delhi, 1971, with a new introduction, 2001), also covers novelists of the 1950s and 1960s.

M.K. Naik, *Raja Rao*, 2nd rev. edn. (Madras, 1982).

S.A. Narayan, *Sudhin N. Ghose* (New Delhi, 1989).

A. Niven, *The Yoke of Pity: A Study in the Fictional Writing of Mulk Raj Anand* (New Delhi, 1978).

M. Ramanujan, *G.V. Desani* (New Delhi, 1984).

P. Russell and K. Singh (eds), *G.V. Desani: A Consideration of his* All About H. Hatterr *and* Hali (London and Amsterdam, 1952).

G.P. Sarma, *Nationalism in Indo-Anglian Fiction* (New Delhi, 1978), has useful chapters on the pre-1930s novel.

R. Sethi, *Myths of the Nation: National Identity and Literary Representation* (Oxford, 1999).

D.B. Shimer, *Bhabani Bhattacharya* (Boston, 1975).

R.K. Narayan

F. Afzal-Khan, *Cultural Imperialism and the Indo-English Novel: Genre and Ideology in R.K. Narayan, Anita Desai, Kamala Markandaya, and Salman Rushdie* (University Park, PA, 1993).

A.L. McLeod (ed.), *R.K. Narayan: Critical Perspectives* (New Delhi, 1994).

M.K. Naik, *The Ironic Vision: A Study of the Fiction of R.K. Narayan* (New Delhi, 1983).

S. Ram and N. Ram, *R.K. Narayan, The Early Years: 1906–45* (New Delhi, 1996), the authorized biography.

W. Walsh, *R.K. Narayan: A Critical Appreciation* (London, 1982).

Nirad C. Chaudhuri

C. Karnani, *Nirad C. Chaudhuri* (New York, 1980).

S. Dasgupta (ed.), *Nirad C. Chaudhuri: The First Hundred Years, A Celebration* (New Delhi, 1997).

C. Paul Verghese, *Nirad C. Chaudhuri* (New Delhi, 1973).

S. Philip, *Perceiving India through the Works of Nirad C. Chaudhuri, R.K. Narayan, and Ved Mehta* (New Delhi, 1986).

Novelists of the 1950s and 1960s

G.S. Amur, *Manohar Malgonkar* (New Delhi, 1973).

J.Y. Dayananda, *Manohar Malgonkar* (New York, 1974).

Y. Gooneratne, *Silence, Exile and Cunning: The Fiction of Ruth Prawer Jhabvala* (Hyderabad, 1983).

J. Jain, *Nayantara Sahgal* (Jaipur, 1994).

M.P. Joseph, *Kamala Markandaya* (New Delhi, 1980).

V. Krishna Rao, *Nayantara Sahgal: A Study of her Fiction and Non-fiction, 1954–74* (Madras, 1976).

H.M. Prasad, *Arun Joshi* (New Delhi, 1986).

R. Singh (ed.), *A Man Called Khushwant Singh* (New Delhi, 1996), a collection of twelve tributes.

L. Sucher, *The Fiction of Ruth Prawer Jhabvala: The Politics of Passion* (London, 1989).

On V.S. Naipaul on India

S. Cudjoe, *V.S. Naipaul: A Materialist Reading* (Amherst, Mass., 1988).

W. Dissanayake and C. Wickramagamage, *Self and Colonial Desire: Travel Writings of V.S. Naipaul* (New York, 1993).

P. French, *The World Is What It Is: The Authorised Biograhy of V.S. Naipaul* (London, 2008).

R. Hamner (ed.), *Critical Perspectives on V.S. Naipaul* (London, 1979).

P. Hughes, *V.S. Naipaul* (London, 1988).

R.M. Kelly, *V.S. Naipaul* (New York, 1989).

B. King, *V.S. Naipaul* (New York, 1993).

J. Levy, *V.S. Naipaul: Displacement and Autobiography* (New York, 1995).

R. Nixon, *London Calling: V.S. Naipaul, Postcolonial Mandarin* (Oxford, 1992).

S. Rai, *V.S. Naipaul: A Study in Expatriate Sensibility* (Atlantic Highlands, N.J., 1982).

T. Weiss, *On the Margins: The Art of Exile in V.S. Naipaul* (Amherst, Mass., 1992).

Poetry Since Independence

E. de Souza, *Talking Poems: Conversations with Poets* (New Delhi, 1999).

B. King, *Modern Indian Poetry in English* (New Delhi, 1987, rev. 2001), the standard work on the subject and unlikely to be surpassed.

——— *Three Indian Poets: Nissim Ezekiel, A.K. Ramanujan, Dom Moraes* (New Delhi, 1991).

S. Mishra, *Preparing Faces: Modernism and Indian Poetry in English* (Suva and Adelaide, 1995).

V. Nabar, *Endless Female Hungers: A Study of Kamala Das* (New Delhi, 1993).

A. Nerlekar, *Bombay Modern: Arun Kolatkar and Bilingual Literary Culture* (Evanston, Illinois, 2016), explores Bombay's bilingual literary culture of the *sathottari* period (1955–1980) with the focus on Arun Kolatkar; the book is available for free download at http://escholarship.org/uc/item/2pk8z0z9.

G.J.V. Prasad, *Continuities in Indian English Poetry: Nation, Language, Form* (New Delhi, 1999).

M. Prasad (ed.), *Living Indian-English Poets: An Anthology of Critical Essays* (New Delhi, 1989).

——— (ed.), *The Poetry of Jayanta Mahapatra: Some Critical Considerations* (New Delhi, 2000).

R. Raj Rao, *Nissim Ezekiel, The Authorized Biography* (New Delhi, 2000).

L. Zecchini, *Moving Lines: Arun Kolatkar and Literary Modernism in India* (Delhi, 2014), the first full-length study of this major poet and the figures around him; contains archival material not seen before.

Writing by the Indian Diaspora

F. Alam, *Bharati Mukherjee* (New York, 1996).

M. Elias, *S. Menon Marath* (Madras, 1984).

K.L. Gillion, *Fiji's Indian Migrants* (Melbourne,1962).

E.S. Nelson (ed.), *Reworlding: The Literature of the Indian Diaspora* (New York, 1992).

——— (ed.), *Writers of the Indian Diaspora: A Bio-Bibliographical Critical Sourcebook* (Westport, Conn., 1993).

——— (ed.), *Bharati Mukherjee: Critical Perspectives* (New York, 1993).

S.C. Wong, *Reading Asian American Literature: From Necessity to Extravagance* (Princeton, 1993).

Looking for A.K. Ramanujan

The best discussions of Ramanujan are to be found in books by B. King and S. Mishra; *see* readings for 'Poetry Since Independence' above.

Salman Rushdie

L. Appignanesi and S. Maitland, *The Rushdie File* (Syracuse, N.Y., 1991).

T. Brennan, *Salman Rushdie and the Third World: Myths of the Nation* (London, 1990).

C. Cundy, *Salman Rushdie* (Manchester, 1997).

M.D. Fletcher (ed.), *Reading Rushdie: Perspectives on the Fiction of Salman Rushdie* (Amsterdam and Atlanta, 1994).

M. Mukherjee (ed.), *Rushdie's* Midnight's Children: *A Book of Readings* (New Delhi, 1999).

After Midnight: The Novel in the 1980s and 1990s

A. Bhattacharjea and L. Chatterjee (eds), *The Fiction of St. Stephen's* (New Delhi, 2000).

N.E. Bharucha and V. Sarang (eds), *Indian English Fiction 1980–1990: An Assessment* (New Delhi, 1994).

A. Ghosh, *The Shadow Lines* with four critical essays (New Delhi, 1995).

The Dramatists

S. Krishna Bhatta, *Indian English Drama: A Critical Study* (New Delhi, 1987).

M.K. Naik and S. Mokashi-Punekar (eds), *Perspectives on Indian Drama in English* (Madras, 1977).

Five Nature Writers: Jim Corbett, Kenneth Anderson, Sálim Ali, Kailash Sankhala, and M. Krishnan

M. Booth, *Carpet Sahib, A Life of Jim Corbett* (New Delhi, 1987).

D.C. Kala, *Jim Corbett of Kumaon*, 2nd rev. edn. (New Delhi, 1999).

M. Rangarajan (ed.), *The Oxford Anthology of Indian Wildlife*, 2 vols (New Delhi, 1999).

———, *India's Wildlife History: An Introduction* (New Delhi, 2001).

V. Thapar (ed.), *Saving Wild Tigers 1900–2000* (New Delhi, 2001).

Translations into English

S. Chaudhuri, *Translation and Understanding* (New Delhi, 1999).

P. France (ed.), *The Oxford Guide to Literature in English Translation* (Oxford, 2000), has a wide-ranging section, with a good bibliography, on translations from the Indian languages.

S. Mukherjee, *Translation as Discovery and Other Essays on Indian Literature in English Translation* (New Delhi, 1981, rev. 1994).

T. Niranjana, *Siting Translation: History, Post-Structuralism, and the Colonial Context* (Berkeley, 1992).

Shobhaa De and Indian Pulp Fiction

J. Dodiya (ed.), *The Fiction of Shobha De* (New Delhi, 2000).

Ramananda Chatterjee and the Modern Review

'Ramananda Centenary Number', *The Modern Review*, May 1965.

Ramananda Chatterjee: Selected Writings and Tributes, Birth Centenary Commemoration Volume, Benson's Calcutta on behalf of Press Institute of India (New Delhi, 1979).

History and Literature: Sir Jadunath Sarkar and Oliver Goldsmith

Dipesh Chakrabarty, *The Calling of History: Sir Jadunath Sarkar and His Empire of Truth* (Ranikhet, 2016)

Ananda K. Coomaraswamy

The Indira Gandhi National Centre for the Arts, New Delhi, has begun a series of the Collected Works of Coomaraswamy.

J.S. Crouch, *A Bibliography of Ananda Kentish Coomaraswamy* (New Delhi, 2002).

R. Lipsey, *Coomaraswamy: I. Selected Papers, Traditional Art and Symbolism; II. Selected Papers, Metaphysics; III. His Life and Work*, 3 vols (Princeton, NJ, 1977).

A. Moore, Jr., and R.P. Coomaraswamy, ed., *Selected Letters of Ananda Coomaraswamy* (Delhi, 1988).

Mark Sedgwick, *Against the Modern World: Traditionalism and the Secret Intellectual History of the Twentieth Century* (New York, 2004).

The Historian as Writer: The Polished Prose of D.D. Kosambi

D.D. Kosambi, *Unsettling the Past: Unknown Aspects and Scholarly Assessments of D.D. Kosambi*, ed. Meera Kosambi (Ranikhet 2012).

Index